Migration and Remittances during the Global Financial Crisis and Beyond

Migration and Remittances during the Global Financial Crisis and Beyond

Edited by

Ibrahim Sirkeci

Jeffrey H. Cohen

Dilip Ratha

THE WORLD BANK
Washington, D.C.

1 2 3 4 15 14 13 12

This volume is a product of the staff of The World Bank with external contributions. The findings, interpretations, and conclusions expressed in this volume do not necessarily reflect the views of The World Bank, its Board of Executive Directors, or the governments they represent.

The World Bank does not guarantee the accuracy of the data included in this work. The boundaries, colors, denominations, and other information shown on any map in this work do not imply any judgment on the part of The World Bank concerning the legal status of any territory or the endorsement or acceptance of such boundaries.

ISBN (paper): 978-0-8213-8826-6
ISBN (electronic): 978-0-8213-8827-3
DOI: 10.1596/978-0-8213-8826-6

Library of Congress Cataloging-in-Publication Data

Migration and remittances during the global financial crisis and beyond / edited by Ibrahim Sirkeci, Jeffrey H. Cohen and Dilip Ratha.
    p. cm.
 Includes bibliographical references and index.
  ISBN 978-0-8213-8826-6 — ISBN 978-0-8213-8827-3 (electronic)
1. Emigration and immigration—Economic aspects. 2. Global Financial Crisis, 2008-2009. 3. Immigrants—Economic aspects. 4. Emigrant remittances—Cross-cultural studies. I. Sirkeci, Ibrahim. II. Cohen, Jeffrey H. (Jeffrey Harris) III. Ratha, Dilip.
 JV6217.M545 2011
 332.04246090511—dc23

2011032374

Cover image: Diana Ong/Superstock by Getty Images
Cover design: Critical Stages

Contents

Tables

Foreword

THE GLOBAL FINANCIAL CRISIS IN 2008–09 served a harsh blow to 215 million migrants and their families around the world. Migrants faced worsening employment prospects in destination countries, often coupled with tightening entry regulations and vicious anti-immigration rhetoric. Meanwhile, migrants' support to families back home in the form of remittances was ever more important in the face of the rising cost of living.

Remittances are the most tangible link between migration and development. At more than $325 billion per year, remittances sent by migrants to developing countries are larger than official development assistance as well as private debt and portfolio equity flows. Remittances help families all over the world to pay for food, housing, education, and health expenses and even invest in small businesses. At the national level, remittances help offset current account deficits and shore up international reserves.

The 49 authors of this volume analyze remittance patterns and practices across the globe during the recent financial crisis. Some of these studies provide insights into individual and household practices, whereas others focus on national and international flows. Evidence shows that remittances flows were resilient during this crisis. However, the cost of money transfers is still very high, and we need to reduce transaction costs to facilitate remittance flows. Studies in this volume also show that remittances are more than the transfer of money. Gifts, values, skills, and ideas transferred are potentially crucial for long-term socioeconomic development of developing countries.

Despite the breadth of these studies, readers should be warned of the pitfalls of migration and remittances data, which are often incomplete. Official figures of remittances often underestimate actual flows because of the prevalence of informal transfer channels. Considerably more effort is needed to improve the quality of data, reduce transaction costs, and simplify the process of sending remittances.

This book is perhaps the first comprehensive study of remittances during the financial crisis and is a timely addition to the literature. It comes at a time when countries are grappling with the global financial crisis and its aftereffects. The resilience of remittances is good news for developing countries, but leveraging remittances for socioeconomic development remains a key challenge. The studies in this book identify and discuss key patterns observed in remittance practices across the world and possibilities for the future. We hope this book serves students, researchers, practitioners, and policy makers around the world as a useful source of reference.

Otaviano Canuto

Vice President, Poverty Reduction and
  Economic Management

The World Bank

Hans Timmer

Director, Development Economics
  Prospects Group

The World Bank

Acknowledgments

We would like to acknowledge the support provided by the World Bank. We also thank Dr. Pinar Yazgan and Dr. Meghan Craig, who assisted in the copyediting and in the preparation of the bibliography. We are also thankful to our many colleagues who have contributed to this volume as authors or reviewers. We would like to acknowledge the permission given by *Migration Letters* to reprint the following papers, which were first published in a special issue of the journal in October 2010: Mohapatra and Ratha, "Forecasting Migrant Remittances during the Global Financial Crisis"; Acosta, Baez, Beazley, and Murrugarra, "The Case of El Salvador"; Lacalle, "The Impact of the Global Economic Downturn on Remittances from the European Union"; Singh, "From Shock Absorber to Shock Transmitter: Sub-Saharan Africa"; and Naufal and Vargas-Silva, "Migrant Transfers in the MENA Region: A Two-Way Street in Which Traffic Is Changing." We also acknowledge the permission to reprint the paper by Green and Winters, an earlier version of which was published in *The World Economy* (Vol. 33, No. 9, pp. 1053–72). We would also like to thank Otaviano Canuto, Sonia Plaza, Hans Timmer, and Ani Rudra Silwal of the World Bank for encouragement and support at various stages of the book.

Book design, editing, and production were coordinated by Aziz Gökdemir, Stephen McGroarty, Stephen Pazdan, and Nora Ridolfi of the World Bank Office of the Publisher. Nita Congress typeset the book and provided editing, proofreading, and project management assistance. Bill Pragluski of Critical Stages designed the cover.

Contributors

DON ABEL joined the Reserve Bank of New Zealand in 2004 after a 26-year career in a large New Zealand–based commercial bank. As Assistant Governor and Head of Operations, he has a general management function across the Reserve Bank, with particular responsibility in financial, corporate, commercial, and other internal functions. He has a liaison role with other central banks in the Pacific area. He is a member of the Bank's monetary policy and financial stability committees. He has a Ph.D. in geography from the Victoria University of Wellington.

PABLO ACOSTA works as an Economist in the Social Protection Unit, Latin America and the Caribbean region, at the World Bank. Before that, he worked as a research economist in the Andean Development Corporation, at the Ministry of Economy of Argentina, and as a consultant for the World Bank and the Inter-American Development Bank. He holds a Ph.D. in economics from the University of Illinois at Urbana-Champaign.

ŞULE AKKOYUNLU obtained a B.A. in economics and econometrics from the University of Istanbul, an M.Sc. in economics from the University of London, and a Ph.D. in economics from Oxford University. She has held teaching and research positions at the Universities of Oxford, Kent, Bonn, Tel Aviv, California at San Diego, Zurich, and Neuchatel; and the Swiss Federal Institute of Technology Zurich, OTA, and DIW. Her research interests include macroeconomics, international economics, economic history, development economics, econometrics, public economics, political economy, labor economics, demography, and international migration.

JAVIER BAEZ works as an Economist in the Independent Evaluation Group at the World Bank. He is also a Research Fellow at the Institute for the Study of Labor and a Fellow of the Research Network on Population, Reproductive Health, and Economic Development. He holds a Ph.D. in economics from the Maxwell School of Public Affairs at Syracuse University and a master's in public administration and international development from Harvard University.

ALEJANDRO BARAJAS DEL PINO is in charge of the Office of Capital Movements at the Direction for Economic Measurement in Banco de México. He teaches in the Economics and Business Faculty of Universidad Anahuac Norte. His undergraduate studies were at Benemérita Universidad Autónoma de Puebla; his graduate studies were done at El Colegio de México in México City and at the University of California, Los Angeles.

RODOLFO BEAZLEY is an economist, currently pursuing a master's degree at the London School of Economics. Previously, he worked for the Social Protection Unit, Latin America and the Caribbean region, at the World Bank, and as a researcher for the Argentine government. He also did consultancies for the International Labour Organization (ILO) and was a lecturer at the Universidad de Buenos Aires.

DANIÈLE BÉLANGER is Professor of Sociology and Demography at the University of Western Ontario, London, Canada. She holds the Canada Research Chair in Population Gender and Development. She has been conducting research on Asia for 20 years. Her research interests include gender and migration, marriage migration, labor migration, and the migration industry. A specialist on Vietnam, she has been involved in migration-related projects on Bangladesh, Canada, China, India, Japan, the Republic of Korea, the Philippines, and Taiwan, China.

HENRI BEZUIDENHOUT is Senior Lecturer in International Trade at the North-West University of South Africa. In 1997, he received a master's degree in econometrics from the University of Pretoria and proceeded into development economic consultancy. In 2007, he earned a Ph.D. in economics from North-West University, after which he joined the university. Current areas of research include international capital flows, foreign direct investment risk, investment promotion, and regional integration in Africa.

JEFFREY H. COHEN is Professor of Anthropology at The Ohio State University. He received his Ph.D. from Indiana University. He is coeditor of the *Migration Letters* journal and is an officer for the Society of Anthropological Sciences. His research focuses on migration, economic development, and food safety/nutrition. His research has been supported by the National Science Foundation, National Geographic Society, the Fulbright program, and the Russell Sage Foundation. His books include *Cooperation and Community: Economy and Society in Oaxaca* (1999), *Economic Development: An Anthropological Approach* (2002, Alta Mira Press), *The Culture of Migration in Southern Mexico* (2004), and *The Cultures of Migration: The Global Nature of Contemporary Movement* (2011, University of Texas Press).

NICOLAAS DE ZWAGER is Founder and Director of the International Agency for Source Country Information (IASCI), in Vienna. IASCI's competencies lie in field-based research/information systems and migration management and development. Previously, he was the Director for the International Centre for Migration Policy Development and served as Chief of Mission for the International Organization for Migration in Ukraine. He holds a *Doctorandus* from the University of Amsterdam in the Netherlands and a B.A. from the University of Victoria, Canada.

OĞUZHAN ÖMER DEMIR holds M.A. and Ph.D. degrees from Rutgers University. He is a faculty member at the Turkish National Police Academy, where he also works for the International Center for Terrorism and Transnational Crime. He is the coeditor of two books on transnational crime. His academic interests include regular and irregular migration, transnational crime, and border security.

ILIR GEDESHI is Founder and Director of the Center for Economic and Social Studies (CESS), an independent think tank specializing in studying economic, social, and demographic changes, based in Tirana, Albania. CESS has become the main resource center of Albanian migration issues since its foundation in 1995. Previously, he was the Director of the Department of Economy at the University of Tirana. He holds a Ph.D. in economics from the University of Tirana.

NASSIB GHOBRIL is the Chief Economist and Head of the Economic Research and Analysis Department at the Byblos Bank Group, one of the largest banking and financial services groups in Lebanon. He is a recipient of the World Lebanese League's award for Best Economist in Lebanon and the Diaspora for 2009, and Data Invest and Consult's award for Best Sovereign Risk Analyst of 2010. He is a board member of the Lebanese Transparency Association.

JESÚS A. CERVANTES GONZÁLEZ is Coordinator of Statistical Training and of the Program for the Application of the General Principles for International Remittances Services at the Center for Latin American Monetary Studies. Previously, he was Director for Economic Measurement at Banco de México. He holds a master of arts degree and is a Ph.D. candidate at the University of Chicago. He teaches in the Economics and Business Faculty of Universidad Anahuac Norte.

TIM GREEN is an Economic Advisor at the Department for International Development (DFID) in the United Kingdom. After working for the U.K. Financial Services Authority and as an ODI Fellow in the Ministry of Tourism, Industry, and Commerce of the government of Guyana, he joined DFID in 2005 and has worked, among other things, on migration policy in DFID's Policy Division.

GREGORY S. GULLETTE received his Ph.D. from the University of Georgia in environmental anthropology. He has conducted ethnographic fieldwork in Mexico, New Zealand, Thailand, and the United States. He is primarily interested in issues of political ecology, political economy, development, migration, and transnationalism. His most recent research in Thailand centers on the relationships between migration and urban environmentalism in Bangkok.

POONAM GUPTA is a Professor at ICRIER. She has previously worked at the International Monetary Fund and has taught at the Delhi School of Economics. She has also consulted for the World Bank, the International Monetary Fund, and the Asian Development Bank. She holds a Ph.D. in economics from the University of Maryland. Her work has been published in leading academic journals and in collective volumes.

KIM HAILWOOD is the Manager of MoneyPACIFIC, a multiagency project jointly supported by the Reserve Bank of New Zealand, the New Zealand Ministry of Foreign Affairs, and the Ministry of Pacific Island Affairs, in cooperation with the World Bank, to improve Pacific peoples' financial knowledge and awareness. She completed her M.A. (1st class honors) in education (financial literacy) in 2007 and is currently working on a Ph.D. investigating the nature and delivery of financial education in New Zealand.

SHIKHA JHA is a Principal Economist in the Economics and Research Department of the Asian Development Bank. She holds a Ph.D. in economics from the Indian Statistical Institute, New Delhi. Her areas of specialization are development economics, public economics, and agricultural economics. She has published extensively in international peer-reviewed economics journals and in edited books. Her research and operational experience covers several countries in South Asia, Southeast Asia, East Asia, and Central Asia.

RONALD R. KUMAR is affiliated with the School of Government, Development and International Affairs, Faculty of Business and Economics, at the University of the South Pacific, and is a recipient of the Sasakawa Young Leaders Fellowship. His areas of research include macrolevel studies on factors of economic growth with a particular focus on developing countries.

OSCAR GÓMEZ LACALLE has worked in the Directorate-General for Economic and Financial Affairs of the European Commission since 1998. He is currently a member of a unit dealing with globalization, trade, and development, including the economic aspects of migration and financial inclusion. Previously, for the European Commission, he worked on the Spanish economy. He has a degree in economics from the University Complutense of Madrid, Spain, and a degree in international and development economics from the University of Namur, Belgium.

TY MATEJOWSKY is an Associate Professor with the Department of Anthropology at the University of Central Florida. He received his Ph.D. in anthropology from Texas A&M University in 2001. His ongoing research in the Philippines examines numerous issues related to globalization, including fast food, urban development, disaster responses, and international migration.

SANKET MOHAPATRA is an economist with the Development Prospects Group at the World Bank. His research interests include international capital flows, sovereign and subsovereign ratings, poverty, inequality and growth, and the development impact of remittances and migration. He also worked as an economist with the Africa Region of the International Monetary Fund. He holds a Ph.D. from Columbia University and a master's degree from the Delhi School of Economics.

GABRIELA MUNDACA is a faculty member of the Applied Economics Department at Johns Hopkins University. She has worked in the Economics Department of the University of Oslo, Norway; at the World Bank; and in the Research Department of the Central Bank of Norway (CBN). She has also advised the policy departments of the CBN for many years. Her main areas of expertise are financial economics, econometrics, and international macroeconomics. She has published articles in refereed international journals. She holds a Ph.D. in economics from the State University of New York at Stony Brook.

EDMUNDO MURRUGARRA is Senior Economist with the Human Development Department, Latin America and the Caribbean region, World Bank. His areas of interest are human development in health and education, labor economics, and poverty. He led a cross-sectoral team involved in streamlining migration issues in analytical and operational products at the Bank. He has taught at the Pontificia Universidad Católica del Perú and the Central Reserve Bank of Peru, Lima. He is a graduate of the Pontificia Universidad Católica del Perú and holds a Ph.D. from the University of California, Los Angeles.

D. NARAYANA is Professor at the Centre for Development Studies in Kerala, India. He holds a Ph.D. from the Indian Statistical Institute, Calcutta. He has published extensively in international journals, and was a Fulbright Fellow at Harvard and a Visiting

Professor at the University of Montreal. His latest book, *Safeguarding the Health Sector in Times of Macroeconomic Instability: Policy Lessons for Low- and Middle-Income Countries*, coedited with Slim Haddad and Enis Bariş, was published by the Africa World Press (2008).

WIM NAUDÉ is Professor of Development Economics and Entrepreneurship and Director of Research at the Maastricht School of Management. A graduate of the University of Warwick, United Kingdom, he has been a member of international networks and advisory bodies including the International Council for Small Business, the Club de Madrid, and the Households in Conflict Network. He was a Senior Associate Member of St. Antony's College, Oxford, and served on the Faculty of Brown University's International Advanced Research Institutes.

GEORGE NAUFAL is an Assistant Professor of Economics at the American University of Sharjah and a research fellow at the Institute for the Study of Labor. His primary research includes migration and its consequences, mainly the impact of remittances on the remitting countries. His research has focused mostly on the Middle East and North Africa region, with an emphasis on the Gulf countries.

SIMON PEMBERTON is a Senior Lecturer in Urban Geography and Planning at the University of Birmingham. His research interests include community planning and livability, urban resilience and regeneration, the neighborhood impacts of "new" immigration, and outcomes of state rescaling on urban and rural communities. He has published widely in all of these areas, including in the *Journal of Rural Studies, Urban Studies*, and *Regional Studies*. He was Director of the Merseyside Social Inclusion Observatory between 2004 and 2010.

MD MIZANUR RAHMAN is a Research Fellow at the Institute of South Asian Studies, National University of Singapore. His research interests include gender and migration, migration and development, remittances, and migrant businesses. He has written research reports on international migration in Asia for the International Organization for Migration and the United Nations Development Fund for Women. His work has appeared in leading migration journals, including *International Migration, Population, Space and Place, Journal of Ethnic and Migration Studies*, and *Journal of International Migration and Integration*.

SELIM RAIHAN is Associate Professor at the Department of Economics, University of Dhaka, Bangladesh. He is also the Executive Director, South Asian Network on Economic Modelling. His research focuses on international trade and trade policy, poverty analysis using micro- and macroeconometrics, and applied economics such as linking trade policies and poverty using computable general equilibrium of single country and global models. He teaches international trade, economic modeling, quantitative economics, econometrics, development economics, and poverty dynamics.

S. IRUDAYA RAJAN is a Chair Professor at the Ministry of Overseas Indian Affairs (MOIA), Research Unit on International Migration at the Centre for Development Studies, Kerala, India. He has extensive research experience in Kerala. He coordinated five major migration surveys from 1998 to 2009, and has published books and articles on social, economic, and demographic implications on international migration. He is a member of the National Migration Policy drafting group appointed by the MOIA. He edits the annual series *India Migration Report* published by Routledge.

DILIP RATHA is the Lead Economist and Manager of the Migration and Remittances Unit at the World Bank. He is the chair of the advisory group of the Migrating out of Poverty research consortium and a visiting professor at the University of Sussex. His expertise includes migration, remittances, and innovative financing. Previously, he worked at Credit Agricole Indosuez, Singapore; Indian Institute of Management; and Policy Group, New Delhi. He holds a Ph.D. in economics from the Indian Statistical Institute, New Delhi.

JOAQUÍN RECAÑO-VALVERDE has been a Professor at Universitat Autònoma of Barcelona since 2003 and a researcher at the Center for Demographic Studies since 1995. From 1989 to 1995, he worked at the Demographic Institute of the Spanish National Research Council. He has published articles and book chapters on internal and international migration and on demographic methods of analysis.

ANDREA RIESTER holds a Ph.D. from the Martin Luther University of Halle-Wittenberg and is associated with the Max Planck Institute for Social Anthropology. She specializes in development, transnationalism, migration, and remittances and works at the Department for Economic Development and Employment at the German Agency for International Cooperation (GIZ), based in Eschborn, Germany.

MARTA ROIG is Social Affairs Officer at the Department of Economic and Social Affairs of the United Nations. She worked in the Population Division of the United Nations from 1998 to 2010 and at the United Nations Population Fund from 1996 to 1998. She has authored reports and articles on international and internal migration and their linkages with development.

LISA SCULLION is a Research Fellow within the Salford Housing and Urban Studies Unit at the University of Salford, United Kingdom. She has particular research interests in the needs and experiences of Central and Eastern European migrant workers, female asylum seekers and refugees, and Gypsy and Traveller communities. She has published on these issues in journals such as *Social Policy and Society* and the *Community Development Journal*.

MARNIE SHAFFER worked with Somalis in refugee resettlement before pursuing a Ph.D. in anthropology at The Ohio State University. She is writing her dissertation on Somali women's economic lives and gender relations in the Johannesburg community. She also conducted research in Columbus, Ohio, where she explored the economic roles of employed Somali women.

JEEVAN RAJ SHARMA is a Senior Researcher at Feinstein International Center and teaches graduate courses at Friedman School of Nutrition Science and Policy and Fletcher School of Law and Diplomacy at Tufts University. His current areas of research include armed conflict and social transformation, labor mobility and transnationalism, livelihoods adaptation, international aid policy and practice, research collaboration, and governance in South Asia. He has a Ph.D. in sociology of South Asia from the University of Edinburgh.

ANI SILWAL has worked at the Washington, D.C., office of the World Bank since April 2008, most recently with the Migration and Remittances Unit. He holds a master's degree from the University of Maryland, College Park, and a bachelor's from Swarthmore College. He previously worked as a risk analyst for an energy trading firm in Philadelphia.

BHUPAL SINGH is an assistant adviser in the Department of Economic and Policy Research of the Reserve Bank of India, Mumbai. He has also worked as an economist in the Bank of England. His research interests include macroeconomics, international economics, monetary economics, and the financial dimensions of cross-border workers' remittances. He has been a member of the Luxembourg Group on remittances, jointly hosted by the IMF and the World Bank with a mandate to improve the recording of cross-border remittances. He has been the member secretary of the Sub-Group on Foreign Savings for the Eleventh Five Year Plan (2007–12) set up by the Planning Commission, government of India, in 2006.

KARAN SINGH is an economic specialist with eight years of experience in research and analytics. For his research on global public bads, he was invited to the Global Governance School, German Development Institute, Bonn. He has been a lecturer of applied econometrics for postgraduates at Delhi University, South Campus. He has authored several research papers in global governance, development economics, macroeconomics, market integration, and applied econometrics. Currently he is a consultant at ICRIER.

RAJU JAN SINGH is the Lead Economist for Central Africa, based in Yaoundé, Cameroon. Prior to joining the World Bank, he held positions at the International Monetary Fund in Washington, D.C.; at the Swiss Ministry of Finance in Bern; and at Lombard Odier & Cie (private banking) in Geneva. He was also a consultant for the Swiss Agency for Development and Cooperation, working with the central banks of Rwanda and Tanzania, and taught at the Graduate Institute of International Studies in Geneva. He holds a Ph.D. from the Graduate Institute of International Studies.

IBRAHIM SIRKECI is Professor of Transnational Studies and Marketing at Regent's College, London, U.K. He is also the Director of the Regent's Centre for Transnational Studies. Previously, he worked at the University of Bristol. His recent research focuses on human mobility, conflict, human insecurity, remittances, segregation, segmentation, marketing of business schools, and transnational mobile consumers. Most recently, with Jeffrey Cohen, he coauthored *Cultures of Migration* (University of Texas Press, 2011). He is the editor of *Migration Letters* and *Transnational Marketing Journal*.

MEHMET ALPER SOZER received his Ph.D. from Indiana University of Pennsylvania. He is the author and editor of several books. He is currently working at the International Center for Terrorism and Transnational Crime in Turkey. His research interests are terrorism, crime prevention, transnational crime, and community policing.

GUNTUR SUGIYARTO is a Senior Economist, Economics and Research Department, Asian Development Bank. He received his M.Sc. and Ph.D. from the School of Economics, University of Warwick and Nottingham, United Kingdom. His publications include books, journal articles, and papers on key development issues, including competitiveness, tourism economics and impacts, the labor market, underemployment, the minimum wage, poverty mapping, poverty impact analysis, trade liberalization, optimum taxation, oil and commodity prices, and migration and remittances.

CARLOS VARGAS-SILVA is a senior researcher at the University of Oxford, where he is part of the team establishing the new Migration Observatory. His research interests include the economic impact of immigration on receiving countries and the link between migration and economic development in sending countries, with a special focus on the role of migrants' remittances. He has been a consultant for the Asian Development Bank, the Inter-American Development Bank, the World Bank, and the United Nations.

L. ALAN WINTERS is a Professor of Economics at the University of Sussex. He is a Research Fellow at the Centre for Economic Policy Research in London and a Fellow of the Institute for the Study of Labor in Munich. He previously worked at the Universities of Cambridge, Bristol, Wales, and Birmingham. He has been editor of the *World Bank Economic Review* and associate editor of the *Economic Journal,* and he serves on several editorial boards.

PINAR YAZGAN is an Assistant Professor of Sociology at Sakarya University, Turkey. Her recent research focused on the sense of identity and belonging among migrants from Turkey in Denmark. She is a research grant recipient from the Scientific and Technological Research Council of Turkey. Between 2007 and 2009, she conducted fieldwork in Denmark while serving as a visiting researcher at the Danish National Research Center for Social Sciences.

Abbreviations

A8	Accession 8 (countries)
ADB	Asian Development Bank
AML	anti–money laundering
BOP	balance of payments
BOPSY	Balance of Payments Statistics Yearbook
CAGR	compound annual growth rate
CEE	Central and Eastern European
CFT	countering the financing of terrorism
CIGEM	Centre for Migration Information and Management
CPI	consumer price index
CSO	Central Statistical Office
EEA	European Economic Area
EU	European Union
FDI	foreign direct investment
GCC	Gulf Cooperation Council
GDP	gross domestic product
GMM	generalized method of moments
GNI	gross national income
GTZ	German Development Cooperation (Deutsche Gesellschaft für Internationale Zusammenarbeit)
ICRG	International Country Risk Guide
ID	identification
IEC	international education consultancy
IFAD	International Fund for Aid and Development
IFS	Indian Foreign Service
IMF	International Monetary Fund
LCU	local currency unit
LIBOR	London Interbank Offered Rate
M2	money and quasi-money

MENA	Middle East and North Africa
MTO	money transfer operator
NRI	nonresident Indian
ODA	official development assistance
ODI	overseas direct investment
OFW	overseas Filipino worker
OLS	ordinary least squares
ONS	Office for National Statistics
PATI	Programa de Ayuda Temporal al Ingreso
PBS	points-based system
PGA	Programa General Anti-Crisis
PIC	Pacific island country
RBI	Reserve Bank of India
SSA	Sub-Saharan Africa
WDI	World Development Indicators
WEO	World Economic Outlook
WRS	Worker Registration Scheme

All dollar amounts are U.S. dollars unless otherwise indicated.

Introduction: Remittance Flows and Practices during the Crisis

IBRAHIM SIRKECI, JEFFREY H. COHEN, AND DILIP RATHA

IMMIGRANTS TEND TO BE MORE negatively affected by economic crisis than natives, particularly when governments apply strict immigration controls. With the onset of the financial crisis in the latter half of 2008, there were widespread concerns: would migrants return to sending countries and communities in large numbers, adding further economic woes to countries already facing difficulties? Would remittance flows slow and potentially cease? The literature offers little guidance on these questions. It is always a challenge to collect data, analyze, interpret, and make recommendations as the phenomenon under study is still unfolding to reveal new turns and twists. The most recent financial crisis and its repercussions are yet to be completed, and scholars have only begun processing the event. This volume is an effort to bring together in one place fresh thinking and evidence from around the world on the outcomes of mobility in the context of global financial crisis.

Crises are a part and parcel of the global economic system. In the crisis-affected developed countries, migrants were challenged in their new homes as jobs began to disappear. Also there was a rapid growth in anti-immigrant sentiment and rhetoric: where they formerly were often left alone, they now faced discrimination and intimidation and perhaps jail and deportation. In fact, it became easier to scapegoat immigrants during crises.

Although the latest crisis originated in the United States and around financial systems in high-income countries, it has had an important and in some places catastrophic impact on developing nations and migrants. Like political or environmental catastrophes, the global financial crisis contributed to an environment of human insecurity, and migration was one strategic response. To avoid the crisis and to survive its impacts, those who could afford to cross borders became international movers; others moved to domestic destinations; while many simply stayed put and turned to remittances to help weather the storm. In such situations, remittances are critical to the overall survival of the sending nation that struggles with ecological disasters disrupting lives, economic collapse, job market declines, and rising inflation rates (see, for example, the earthquake in Haiti in 2010, the Asian crisis of the 1990s, or the crises that plagued Latin America through the 1980s and 1990s).

Migrant remittances provide a measurable benefit—a lifeline—for sending communities, and they contribute directly and indirectly to the income of sending households (Ratha and Sirkeci 2010: 125). Overall, cash flows, increasing expenditures, and (limited) investments caused by remittances have a substantial impact on the social action and economic health of movers and nonmovers alike.[1] In many parts of the world, particularly in developing countries, the volume of remittances has increased at a tremendous rate over the last decades and proved to be resilient during crises (figure I.1) and in comparison with other international financial flows such as foreign direct investment, overseas aid, and private loans. Remittance flows to developing countries totaled about $75 billion in 1989, $125 billion by the mid-2000s, and more than $350 billion by 2011 despite about a 5 percent decline in 2009 (Mohapatra and Ratha 2011).[2]

In addition to the cash flow, the indirect effects of remittances can be significant for households in migrant-sending areas, including those that may not participate in

FIGURE I.1 Resilience of Remittances Compared to Other Financial Flows to Developing Countries

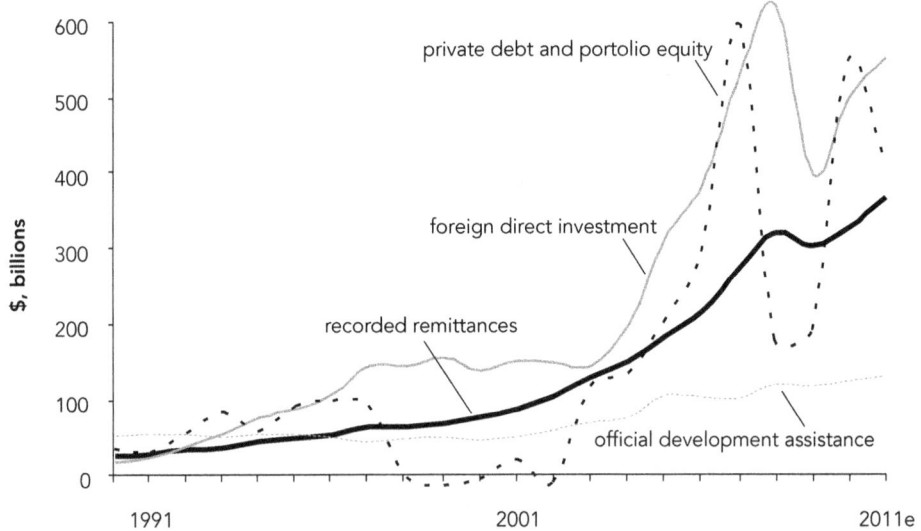

Sources: World Bank Migration and Development Brief 17; Ratha and Sirkeci 2010: 126.

international migration. Massey and Taylor (2004: 157) argue that "the vast majority of research on migrant remittances and savings ignores their indirect effects on migrant-sending economies. As a result, many studies paint a negative picture of remittances and savings for development." According to their assessment, the problem lies in the fact that many studies fail to recognize the effects of nonremittance income and the link between migrants and nonmigrants.

Remittances remain one of the less volatile sources of foreign exchange earnings for developing countries. The literature has indicated for some time that migrant remittances tend to be stable or even countercyclical in response to economic hardship—be it a financial crisis, natural disaster, or political conflict—in a remittance-recipient country (Ratha 2003; World Bank 2006a). This time the crisis began in the United States and Europe, remittance-source countries. Some early literature (for example, Swamy 1981) argued that source country factors are a major determinant of remittance flows.

The economic crisis in a major migrant destination country was expected to adversely affect migrants' income and employment opportunities and hence the willingness and ability of migrants to stay in their host countries and continue to remit funds. To an extent, this expectation was realized as remittance flows registered a decline in 2009 for the first time in recent memory. Nevertheless, it was also remarkable that remittance flows to developing countries fell only 5.2 percent in 2009, proving to be significantly more resilient than private capital flows, which declined precipitously (Ratha and Sirkeci 2010: 126).

Remittance receipts at the global level significantly exceed the aid from advanced economies to developing countries. The debate over the impact of remittances on social and economic inequalities is ongoing. Although some observers argue that remittance patterns are dependent on the motivations that drive migration (these are not economic in all cases), others argue that remittances reduce poverty.

Seddon, Adhikari, and Gurung (2002) argue that redressing inequalities is beyond the concern of migrant remittances. An abundance of evidence is provided by a multitude of studies that confidently argue that remittances are often used for household maintenance and for purchase of consumer goods. Remittances are particularly important for dependent members of households left behind. Orozco (2006), for example, argues that remittances are means to ensure social protection as well as capital accumulation (see also Cohen and Rodriguez 2005). Eckstein (2010) argues that remittances are linked to transnational family social capital and are building blocks for the reproduction of social networks and connections. Evidence is also found that migrant remittances are used to support local community projects and events (Cohen 2004). A separate literature focusing on the role of remittances in relation to conflicts and disasters has also grown in recent years (Fagen and Bump 2006; Justino and Shemyakina 2010; Mohapatra, Joseph, and Ratha forthcoming). Many of these studies focus on natural disasters such as the earthquake in Pakistan or tsunamis in the Pacific; others look at the implications of conflicts in African countries. In these examples, remittances appear as insurance for households as they cope with the shocks of conflict (Davies 2007). Fagen and

Bump (2006) argue that migrant remittances also help prevent displacement in conflict regions while underlining the fact that all forms of migration (including forced migration) generate remittances.

In many countries, remittances play a central economic role, often accounting for up to a third of the value of export revenues in countries such as Bangladesh or the Republic of Yemen. This is why we have paid particular attention to South Asian countries. Remittances are an important source of revenue for many South Asian countries. Generally speaking, the average gross domestic product (GDP) per capita in the region stands at about $1,000. The migrant population from the region also includes a large number of highly skilled people with high incomes. For example, more than 10 percent of physicians trained in the South Asia region have emigrated. These relatively high-earner emigrants send significant remittances. However speculative the relationship of movers to remittances can be, the volume of total remittance flows to South Asia increased more than eight times over the last 15 years (elsewhere, this increase was less than six times). A steady growth in remittances is evident in the cases of Bangladesh and Pakistan, where remittances grew from about $2 billion each in 1990 to about $10 billion each in 2009. Remittances to the four South Asian countries (Bangladesh, India, Maldives, and Pakistan) continued to grow during the financial crisis, while only a slight drop in remittances to India is reported.

Despite the figures one can find in statistical depositories, the estimation of the size of international migrant remittances is complicated by a simple fact: An unknown but probably large share of the flows is sent through informal channels (including pocket transfers). Another problem is the difficulty of assessing the value of in-kind remittances—if we can capture them in our flow statistics.

Understanding the Resilience of Remittances

Remittances tend to be relatively resilient to the crisis. Among other explanations, there are six broader patterns that are key to producing such resilience. First, the more diversified the destinations and the labor markets for migrants, the more resilient the remittances sent by migrants. Thus, countries in South Asia and East Asia that have a large number of migrants in the United States, Europe, and the Gulf Cooperation Council (GCC) countries continued to register increases in remittance inflows despite the crisis; whereas countries in Latin America and the Caribbean that have most of their migrants in the United States suffered a decline (Ratha and Mohapatra 2009).

Second, remittances are sent by the stock (cumulative flows) of migrants, not only by the recent arrivals (in fact, recent arrivals often do not remit as regularly because they must establish themselves in their new homes). Although it is true that in some countries new migration flows declined by 40–60 percent in 2009 compared with 2008, the flow did not become negative. There is also historical evidence indicating migration resilience in this regard (see chapter 3). Thus the size of the stock of migrants either was maintained or continued to grow (at only a slightly slower rate) in destination countries, lending persistence to remittance flows affected in some countries.

Third, contrary to expectations, return migration did not take place as expected, even as the financial crisis reduced employment opportunities in the United States and Europe. Indeed, many countries (such as Spain) offered financial incentives to encourage return, but migrants stayed. Anecdotal evidence suggests that migrants moved from the construction sector to retail trade and agriculture, and in some cases stayed on despite losing their legal status. In fact, many were unwilling to return to their sending communities for fear that future migration would be difficult and they would not be able to come back to their new communities and jobs when the economy recovered. The problem was intensified by the imposition of immigration controls in many destination countries that affected new migration and inadvertently discouraged return.

Fourth, in addition to the persistence of migrant stocks that lent persistence to remittance flows, existing migrants often absorbed income shocks and continued to send money home. They were able to do so because remittances are typically only one expense among many. In many instances (especially in the Gulf countries), unskilled migrant workers reduced consumption and shared accommodations to save money that was later sent home.

Fifth, if some migrants did return or had the intention to return, they tended to take their savings back to their country of origin. Such funds would show up as inward remittances because these are personal transfers from a nonresident to a resident. These individuals also brought new skills and abilities with them, and in some cases the experiences were the foundation for local development. This behavior is similar to the "home bias" in the literature on capital flows.

Finally, exchange rate movements during the crisis caused unexpected changes in remittance behavior. As local currencies of many remittance-recipient countries (India, Mexico, and the Philippines, for example) depreciated sharply against the dollar, they produced a "sale" effect on remittance behavior of migrants in the United States and other destination countries. Goods, services, and assets back home became significantly cheaper and affordable to migrants earning foreign currency. As a result, there was a surge in investment-oriented remittances to many countries in South Asia and East Asia.

The current financial crisis has reduced employment opportunities throughout the world and in both developed and developing countries. Thus, for the first time since the 1980s, remittances to developing countries are estimated to have declined in 2009. The remittance flows represent a much larger slice of foreign currency inflow than does foreign aid to developing countries. For some smaller nations, remittances represent at least a third of their GDP (for example, Haiti, Lesotho, Moldova, Tajikistan, and Tonga). In the last two years, remittance flows to South Asia (for example, Bangladesh, Pakistan, and the Philippines) grew while the flows were weaker in Latin America (for example, El Salvador and Mexico) and the Middle East, North Africa, and Europe. An adverse lagged effect is still a possibility.

The factors affecting remittance flows include the economic opportunities in the destination countries, development and growth trends in both sending and destination countries, influence of the crisis on migrants and their well-being, migrants' attitudes toward consumption, cultural characteristics, migration experiences, currency fluctuations, and so on. Macroapproaches are largely interested in variation in national outcomes (Adams 2003; Glytsos 2002; Taylor and others 1996b), whereas microapproaches are interested in local effects (Binford 2003; Durand and others 1996; Massey and others 1994; Reichert 1981; Taylor and others 1996a).

It is argued that microlevel interdisciplinary approaches with a household focus can offer an alternative view of remittance outcomes (Cohen 2005). In this introduction we tend to stick with macroapproaches and leave the examples to our contributors. However, it is important to understand that microprocesses shape the geography and outcomes of remittances at different levels (individual, household, community, regional, national, and global). Remittances, like migration, do not occur in a vacuum. They link migrants and nonmigrants as well as the destination and the origin in many ways that go beyond dependency or development.

Remittance flows are expected to respond to changes in migration practices. Some relatively recent scholarship argues that transnational migration can facilitate long-term remittance flows (Levitt 2000), whereas other scholars argue that remittances decline as migration matures (Stark 1978). Our question here is how crises—the recent financial crisis in particular—influence remittance flows. Although many studies focus on the influence of remittances on overall accounts, as Massey and others (1998, 2006) have argued, the direct effects of remittances on sending communities are important (also see Cohen 2010).

Finally, cash-strapped governments in remittance-receiving countries may have fiscal stimulus packages to ensure the maintenance of remittance flows (World Bank 2009f). While the effects of remittances on outcomes can be direct for the sending household, wider indirect effects are seen for the sending communities, regions, and countries. This effect is felt through increasing consumption and household spending, but also via investments—albeit the small portions of remittances that are used for this purpose. It is equally important to see that remittances stimulate nonremittance income increases as well as investments. The impact of remittances on nonmigrant households via expenditure linkages indicates that during crises, sending households become more reliant on remittances (for Mexican examples, see Massey and Taylor 2004). These indirect effects alleviate or at least mediate the impact of the financial crisis even as that crisis reaches well beyond the migrant-sending household.

Remittances also proved to be relatively resilient in comparison to private capital flows, and so many remittance-dependent countries became even more dependent on remittance inflows for meeting external financing needs. Indeed, many countries (such as Bangladesh and the Philippines) that obtained new sovereign ratings (with a view to raising bond financing from international markets) benefited from the fact that they had access to a large and relatively stable flow of remittances.

About This Book

This volume presents experiences and patterns of migrant remittances around the globe. Part I begins with key conceptual and methodological issues. Cohen and Sirkeci frame the conceptual discussion. Mohapatra and Ratha argue that the financial crisis has highlighted the need to better forecast remittance flows in many developing countries where they have proved to be a lifeline for poor people and national economies. They describe a simple methodology for forecasting country-level remittance flows that can be consistently linked to medium-term forecasts of global economic growth. Green and Winters give a round analysis of migration, crisis, and remittances from the mid-nineteenth century until today. They particularly highlight the impact of government policies, which first became a driver of migration practices in the nineteenth century, and will likely continue to be so, affecting migrant inflows, returns, and impacts on development. Mundaca demonstrates that economic growth is possible if remittances are not used for immediate consumption of final goods, but rather invested in the formation of working capital, both physical and human. She illustrates how remittances can decrease the probability of prematurely liquidating long-term productive investment.

Part II focuses on Asian experiences covering a vast geography from the Gulf to Thailand. Rajan and Narayana point to the lagged effects of the crisis in the Gulf countries. They maintain that expected severe effects such as massive wage and salary cuts and declines in remittances did not occur because of the quick recovery of oil prices and increased government spending, which moderated adverse impacts. Rahman and Bélanger draw attention to gender differences in remittance-receiving households in Bangladesh. They find that gender differences as well as poverty levels, migration costs, networks, and expectations moderate the use of remittances. Gupta and Singh document trends in remittances to India, which they believe have been quite resilient during the global economic downturn. They argue that only a prolonged slowdown, if it significantly reverses the migration of Indians, will cause a decline in remittance flows.

Singh looks at the shocks affecting the inflows and stability of migrant remittances to India. Using alternative vector error correction models applied to quarterly data, Singh notes that the residual shocks indicating economic or job market uncertainties in the host country and associated precautionary savings could lead to significant fluctuations in remittance inflows in the short run. Mohapatra, Ratha, and Silwal examine remittance patterns in Nepal; the country had an estimated volume of about $3.5 billion remitted in 2010. Supplementing the previous chapter is a brief overview by Sharma that summarizes the history of migration in Nepal. This is followed by a comparison of three small countries with high out-migration—Mali, Nepal, and Tajikistan—by Riester, who argues that stability of remittances is a function of a particular migration pattern citizens of a country have come to adopt.

Gullette relates internal migration in Thailand to development plans and policies and their repercussions for labor mobility, which has been considered as a means to mitigate high poverty rates and unstable employment structures within the predominately agrarian Isaan (northeast) region of the country. Sugiyarto and colleagues provide two chapters, the second of which is a case study, and the first of which focuses on remittance flows in the key corridors of South Asia: United States–Bangladesh, United States–Pakistan, United Kingdom–Bangladesh, and United Kingdom–Pakistan. They suggest that during the crisis, remittances related strongly with better labor market conditions for Bangladeshi and Pakistani migrants in the United States, with less evidence of migrant labor market conditions in the United Kingdom having an impact on remittance flows to Bangladesh and Pakistan. The case study presents results from a Bangladeshi household survey exploring the impact of the global financial crisis on migrants and their families at home.

In part III, two chapters contrast the cases of El Salvador and Mexico, countries that receive substantial volumes of remittances from the United States. Acosta and colleagues show how dramatically the financial crisis hit El Salvador, which saw a sharp decline in remittance flows. They argue that the crisis mostly affected urban youth who faced more difficult labor market prospects and diminishing opportunities to migrate. González and del Pino examine the case of Mexico, the world's third-highest receiver of remittances. They observe that remittance flows from the United States have significantly weakened throughout the financial crisis.

Part IV looks at the effect of the crisis in the European Union on remittance-receiving countries. Lacalle discusses the macroeconomic determinants of remittances, arguing that migrants' income would be the main short-term determinant of European Union remittances. Pemberton and Scullion examine the migration and remittance flows between Central and Eastern Europe and the United Kingdom. Gedeshi and de Zwager claim that mass migration is at the core of the political, economic, and social changes occurring in Albania while pointing out the indirect adverse effects of the crisis for Albania. Roig and Recaño-Valverde present an analysis of Spain, one of the world's fastest-growing immigration destinations for the last decade. They note that 6.6 million immigrants and about €8.5 billion remitted to their home countries made Spain the fifth-largest remittance-sending country in the world in absolute terms, after the United States, Saudi Arabia, the Russian Federation, and Switzerland.

Four articles in part V focus on Turkish migration and remittances. Akkoyunlu forecasts the effects of the 2008 financial crisis on Turkish workers' remittances from Germany based on the medium-term outlook for the German and Turkish economies. The forecasting exercise is based on a previously estimated, tested, and accepted model for Turkish workers' remittances from Germany. The following chapter by Sirkeci looks at the differences in remittance behavior of ethnic segments in the Turkish international migration regime with reference to Kurdish migration to Germany. Yazgan and Sirkeci examine a minor destination for Turkish migrants: Turkish immigrants in Denmark display strong transnational characteristics connecting small towns and villages in Anatolia to Danish towns. These ties are crucial in maintaining remittance flows; qualitative accounts support the remittances' resilience argument. The final chapter in this part describes irregular immigrants in Turkey and their remittance-sending behavior. Demir and Sozer present results from their recent field research, outlining the remittance patterns of permanent, transit, and semitransit irregular immigrants caught by authorities in Turkey.

Part VI moves to the Far East. Matejowsky presents an outline of labor migration from the Philippines, where nationals abroad are an indispensible source of hard foreign currency that, since the 1970s, has done much to keep the national economy afloat. Abel and Hailwood then look at New Zealand and Pacific island countries, for which remittances represent 12 percent of GDP on average. They visit the issue of remittance fees, which are very high in the Pacific region, to determine what works and what does not regarding the region's fee policies. Kumar focuses on another Pacific island nation, analyzing data for the period 1981–2008 to estimate the short- and long-run effects of trade openness, remittances with other capital flows, and the impact of financial development on income in Vanuatu.

Part VII begins with an analysis of remittances as a source of resilience and vulnerability in Sub-Saharan Africa. Naudé and Bezuidenhout discuss the concept of exposure to remittances, noting that level of exposure depends on a country's social and cultural milieu. In this regard, they highlight some gender aspects of the issue and argue that, although females remit a higher proportion of their income than men, they enjoy less exposure to remittances than men. Singh next revisits the argument that remittances are shock absorbers and examines the determinants of remittances in Sub-Saharan Africa. Shaffer's short case study provides a qualitative comparative account of women's remittance practices in two Somali communities in Johannesburg, South Africa, and Columbus, Ohio.

Part VIII contains two chapters on the Middle East and North Africa. Ghobril argues that the region's increasing integration in the global economy and capital markets is making the downturn's impact very visible in terms of declining capital inflows in general, and equity and credit flows in particular. Naufal and Vargas-Silva note that, despite the fact that remittances from the GCC countries to Asia slowed during the crisis, there is no evidence of large decreases. They also argue that evidence for 2010 suggests that remittances to the region will increase.

Next Steps

As can be seen, this volume includes a wide variety of analyses that range from quantitative modeling to qualitative interpretations, and all contribute to our understanding of human mobility in relation to the global financial crisis. One thing that became clear during the recent crisis is that the development community does not have adequate tools and resources for rapid monitoring of migration and remittance flows and their impacts on sending and receiving countries during times of crisis. A key practical next step, therefore, is to devise such rapid monitoring tools.

The crisis likely has not affected migrants and their sending households or nations as badly as once feared. In fact, migrants may have mitigated some of the pain the global crisis might have caused as they tend to work for less, take fewer benefits, and rely relatively little on the state. Additionally, much of their earnings stayed in their destination country and often supplemented social security and payroll taxes. And, during the crisis, remittances sent worldwide continued to provide a steady source of foreign currency to national economies at a time when foreign aid and foreign direct investment fluctuated significantly. These facts lead to the conclusion that removing restrictions on human mobility may thus contribute to enhancing financial flows among nations and to alleviating some of the adverse effects of the global crisis.

On the other hand, at both the household and macrolevels, adverse effects are evident in all countries examined in this book. There are many lessons to be learned, but more importantly many more questions to be asked.

Following are a list of findings we have generated in an attempt to understand and explain remittance practices in relation to the global financial crisis. Each of these has been tested in certain contexts, some at a regional level, some at an individual country level, and some at a subgroup (e.g., ethnic, religious or regional population) level. While all surely need further empirical testing, we believe they point out a few important avenues for future research and analysis:

1. The link between remittances and growth is moderated by financial market conditions. Growth should be understood in terms of not only physical investments but also investments in human capital. Such investments in long-term assets can be vital in crisis situations.

2. Return migration is not a typical outcome of the crisis, yet where it did occur, it may facilitate growth and development in less-developed sending countries (such as Albania) because it can facilitate the flow of financial and human capital to home countries. Generally return was not an issue, and it was moderated by the economic conditions in both sending and receiving countries. Vulnerabilities in destination countries, whether economic (a decline in currency value) or political (as in Lebanon), can encourage remittance flows.

3. The more varied the portfolio of destinations and more jobs available to migrants reduce the adverse effects of the crisis.

4. Tightening admission regimes and immigration restrictions will have adverse effects on remittance flows in the long run.

5. Overall findings suggest that the crisis did cause some decline in remittances (for example, in Mexico), but these were not as large as was feared previously. For instance, despite an evident stagnation of remittances in 2009, remittances from the Gulf to South Asia did not decline overall.

6. Because remittances are used mainly for household expenses and maintenance, the crisis is likely to have affected consumption adversely.

7. Noncitizens and irregular migrants are more vulnerable to crises compared with naturalized and/or regularized immigrants in the United States and the European Union.

8. Ethnic segments within national populations (such as Kurdish Turks in Germany or Latin Americans in Spain) display different remittance-sending and spending patterns than majority ethnic groups.

9. Regional dynamics and country-specific characteristics (of economy, migration histories, and the like) influence remittance flows and remittance usage patterns, suggesting that analyzing remittances at the single-country level has advantages.

10. Culture, society, gender, status, and the strengths and weaknesses of movers mean that remittance flow and usage patterns can differ within populations. For example, unlike men, women do not use remittances for building houses but instead to support relatives (see the Somali case) or to repay loans. Thus it appears that women are more interested in savings, whereas men are more likely to buy land (for example, the Bangladesh case).

11. Remittances vary countercyclically and thus can mitigate the effects of crisis, but they are moderated by the size, location, and income levels of the particular diaspora.

12. When the sending country economy is unable to create employment, emigration continues irrespective of a crisis (as in the Thailand case). However, remittance patterns are not solely determined by macroeconomic factors. Remittance-sending patterns are complex and not always dependent on global economic changes.

13. Cost of remittances is a key driver in the volume of registered remittance flows in Australia and New Zealand.

The studies presented in this volume also recommend policy changes aimed at making remitting an easier and inexpensive practice, while enabling and encouraging individuals and households to invest in long-term assets. Our recommendation is that nations develop policies that facilitate more fluid, less restrictive mobility for humans and the resources (remittances) they generate. The availability of microfinance and small loan facilities is one such mechanism to meet this objective. At both the national and supranational levels, policies and programs could be developed facilitating the use of remittances for long-term investments—including in human capital—promoting entrepreneurship, and creating small loan schemes that can contribute to the alleviation of short-term liquidity needs. Such changes, tailored to both host and recipient country needs, can strengthen remittances' contribution to development.

There are also some practical, relatively straightforward steps that can be taken. For example, eliminating the complexity of transactions and reducing transaction costs would help increase registered remittances. Many small nations, including several of those discussed in this volume, will benefit from systems and policies that enable cheaper and faster remittance transfers. Similarly, improvements in financial literacy and in simplifying transfer facilities as well as expanding their availability (such as ease in opening bank accounts in host countries) will facilitate regular flows.

Notes

1. For the concepts of movers and nonmovers, see Cohen and Sirkeci (2011).

2. Remittance flows to developing countries quadrupled between 2002 and 2008 as a result of (1) increased scrutiny of flows since the terrorist attacks of September 2001, (2) reduction in remittance costs and expanding networks in the remittance industry, (3) the depreciation of the dollar (which raises the value of remittances denominated in other currencies), and (4) growth in migrant numbers and incomes (Ratha 2003).

PART I

Chapter 1
Theoretical Appraisal:
Understanding Remittances

JEFFREY H. COHEN AND IBRAHIM SIRKECI

THE ECONOMIC ROLE OF REMITTANCES in the lives of immigrant workers, their sending communities, and the developing nations they hail from is well documented (World Bank 2006a). The Council of Europe estimated that $72 billion flowed from workers to their homes in developing countries in 2002. This total was well in excess of the total official aid directed to developing nations that year (COE 2006: 7). Through the end of the decade and even during the global financial crisis of 2008 and 2009 remittance rates remained consistently strong and did not drop as did other forms of aid (see figure I.1 in the introduction). Similarly, the Organisation for Economic Co-operation and Development found that at least $126 billion followed the networks that immigrant workers maintained with their sending households and communities in 2005 (OECD 2005). The formal, legal transfers noted by these studies represent large and largely stable amounts of money (Maimbo and Ratha 2005; Ratha, Mohapatra, and Xu 2008; World Bank 2006a), yet they do not include informal, unofficial, and illegal transfers (Christiansen 2008; Lozano Ascencio 1998; Mohan 2002; Shehu 2004). Furthermore, although these are large amounts of money, the studies of remittances often do not acknowledge the anticyclical nature of remittances practices, the role remittances continue to play for movers and their families, and the measurable benefits that go directly and indirectly to developing nations' economies and coffers even in moments of economic crisis (Lianos and Cavounidis 2010). Remittances can cushion the impact of financial crisis and support communities that might otherwise share in the misery of the moment.

Remittances follow their own unique paths and are often critical when sending households struggle to survive and developing nations struggle to create opportunities, improve infrastructure, and grow jobs for young populations. This is particularly true in periods of financial crisis as foreign aid declines, national labor markets collapse, and inflation rates rise. When economic crises face migrants who have relocated to new destination countries, remittance practices often remain central and critical. Finally, we must understand remittances as raw numbers, but we must also recognize that this perspective does little to illuminate the practices of individuals who are working to keep their families together and economically healthy. To understand remittance outcomes we divide our discussion into three sections. First, we define remittances. Second, we explore the value (economic and cultural) of remittance practices for movers and non-movers, nations and families. Finally, in our third section, we explore the impacts of the crisis on remittance outcomes.

Remittances, Migration, and Economics

Remittances are generally defined as economic transfers that follow unidirectional paths from an immigrant worker to his or her sending country and households (Maimbo and Ratha 2005). The amount of money returned by immigrant workers is large and often far more valuable to most countries than direct aid; yet remittances are about more than the formal unidirectional flow of money (Carling 2008). Social scientists understand that formal remittances are important to sending countries. Remittances can influence the balance of trade and support national investments (Adams 1991; de Haas 2005; Skeldon 2008), and remittances also drive investments and sometimes development (Massey and others 1998/2006; Taylor and others 1996a).

Remittance practices and outcomes are also rooted in the migration process itself and reflect the needs of movers and their sending households. Although remittance practices reflect the needs of movers and their sending households, they often do not reflect national economic policies. In fact, it is best to think of migration and remittance practices as the outcomes of the failures of national economic policy to address public needs. As such, it should not be a surprise that often remittances do not follow national economic trends. In fact, remittance practices are often anticyclical and an important response to economic crises (Buch and Kuckulenz 2010). In other words, while economies slow and labor markets contract, remittance rates tend to remain steady or decline more slowly. Furthermore, as labor markets collapse in destination countries (as has happened in the United States and Europe), migrants tend to refocus their efforts and find work in new sectors of the economy, and even though incomes may decline, remittance rates will often remain healthy. Migrants, in fact, take great care to preserve remittance rates, moving together and limiting expenses to save funds that can be sent home.

Remittances are proof of the connections migrants share with their sending households and communities (Guarnizo 2003) and evidence of the importance they hold for movers and nonmovers, who may have few local opportunities to earn money (Mazzucato and others 2008; Yang and Martínez 2006). Remittances are strategic as is migration itself. Migration moves people to labor markets rather than bringing labor markets to new locales, and remittances funnel earnings home. In this sense remittances are an economic hedge, a way to support a household, cover expenses, and perhaps invest even as there is economic decline at the national level. Finally, although the majority of research is focused on remittances as they flow from immigrant worker to their sending households, evidence is growing for a return flow (though often not monetary) from sending households to settled immigrants (Gamburd 2008; Rose and Shaw 2008).

Remittance outcomes are defined by migration practices as we noted above. But the *habitus*, or "the socially and culturally conditioned set of durable dispositions or propensities for certain kinds of social actions" of the sender, his or her household, community, and nation, also defines outcomes (Vertovec 2009: 66; see also Bourdieu 1977) as do the economic and political realities of the movers' world (and these include not only the sending nation, but the destination nation as well). In other words, remittance outcomes are rooted in migration decisions. Migration decisions and outcomes are in large part, as we noted in the introduction, a reaction to violence, whether that violence is physical, economic, political, or otherwise. Migration is also influenced by the strengths and weaknesses that define the mover's life; the advantages and disadvantages that define him or her and his or her household and community; and finally the pulls, pushes, opportunities, and costs that create global economic patterns in sending countries and countries of destination (see Åkesson 2009; Eversole 2005; Lubkemann 2005; Parreñas 2005; Schmalzbauer 2008; Stodolska and Santos 2006).

A migrant's status influences his or her remittance practices. It is important to remember that a majority of movers globally are traveling in the open, often with papers, along well-planned routes and with well-organized plans. This does not mean that migrants are free of harassment; rather, even in the best of situations, migrants face choices that can undermine outcomes. We noted that a migrant's status influences remittance outcomes. So too does the way a migrant is described by his or her destination country. Migrants are recruited to jobs, some to highly skilled positions. The highly skilled migrant is likely to be welcomed into his or her destination country (Cornelius, Espenshade, and Salehyan 2001), earn well, receive benefits, and potentially support higher remittances. The unskilled migrant may find that he or she must sneak across a border, move about without documentation or with questionable documentation, and take lower-wage work with potentially far less to send home.

Deciding on an internal or international destination will influence remittance practices (Trager 2005). The internal mover in a small developing nation can usually find a cohort of individuals from his or her sending region or community. Language is usually not a major problem, and differences that divide nations are not present (although see China for a very different situation). In these internal settings remittances are likely much lower, yet they are not invisible and can be critical to the strategic organization of a household's labor. Nevertheless, it is important to remember that although the international migrant likely faces legal barriers, the internal mover does not; for some movers the sojourn to an internal destination can be destabilizing and lead to far smaller remittances.

For many migrants (whether moving internally or internationally and whether they have papers or not) remittances regardless of their size are a sign of their successful moves. This is true for migrants who are bound for destinations where they can find work that will support those who cannot or will not migrate (Moran-Taylor 2008) and for migrants who leave families searching for opportunities but with little hope of enhancing their household (Lubkemann 2005; Newell 2005; Trager 2005). Remittances are not the same for everyone. Limits on earning may be beyond the control of the mover, but different statuses, destinations, and the like also all influence remittance outcomes. Key factors are the fees involved in transfers as well as who charges the fees (state, private company, bank) and whether money flows through formal or informal means. Furthermore, some sending households are never satisfied with the efforts made by their mobile members, just as some migrant workers cannot or will not remit (Ramirez, Skrbis, and Emmison 2007; Sanchez 2007; Tatla 2002). Of course, a household's response to remittances is largely outside the realm of this discussion, but it is important to remember that factors beyond those noted above and that range from the personal to the psychological can and often do affect remittance outcomes.

Remittance practices are not always predictable—and they shift over time (Massey and others 1998/2006). Early movers have expenses to cover in their moves that can reduce remittance rates. Long-term and settled migrants (the migrant stock in a destination country) have different expenses. Early movers tend to remit to cover immediate expenses as remittances flow to sending households. New movers, younger movers, and movers with young children who cannot contribute to their family's financial well-being also tend to see their remittances channeled to immediate and daily expenses (Stark 1992; Trager 1984).

Older migrants, and immigrants who are settled in their destination communities and hold reasonably steady jobs, often earn more money and earn that money more consistently. As their time in a new destination increases and their work matures, their remittances can become both more regular and larger. The money they return, in part because it may increase over time reflecting higher wages, can be used to cover the costs of daily life and the purchase of consumer goods and potential investments for development (Cohen and Rodriguez 2005; Newell 2005). The migrant stock also does not spend as much money as do new immigrants. Settled migrants typically are not paying off the costs of their moves, have stocked their homes, and are situated to save rather than spend extra income. Although leisure costs may rise, funds are likely still available to remit.

Migrants with older children and migrants from larger families also have opportunities to use their remittances not only to purchase consumer and luxury goods but also to begin to make investments and purchases that can translate into investments (Adams 2006; Brown and Connell 1994; Conway 2007; Lopez and Seligson 1991; Ratha 2007; Remple and Lobdell 1978; Stahl and Arnold 1986; van Doorn 2004).

The experiences of repeat and long-term sojourns tend to translate into better wages and greater success and generate more consistent remittances. This pattern of success also attracts new migrants to join the pool of movers as the entire migration process becomes self-reinforcing (Massey 1990). In a similar fashion, remittance practices can be self-reinforcing. New movers tend to follow and emulate the migrant stock in an area, and like settled migrants, new movers remit.

Finally, a household's overall economic health will influence outcomes. There is a difference in the outcomes for remittances when a household is large, growing, and wealthy (at least by local standards). Larger households do not by definition do better than smaller households; however, where the household includes more working-age adults, the diversity of workers can enhance outcomes. Wealthier households also tend to have opportunities that poor households lack. This can include the opportunity to migrate to an international destination where strong wages can be found. The migrants from wealthier households may also hold better educations that will allow them to access better jobs. Again, the most successful of households are able to build on the diversity of work possibilities (migration, local wage labor, farm work, and the like) to create opportunities to save money and invest in new ways (Sørensen, van Hear, and Engberg-Pedersen 2002); yet the majority of remittances are directed toward the challenges of daily life (Suro and others 2002).

The timing of remittances also has an effect on amounts returned by immigrant workers. It is often difficult for newly settled immigrant workers to remit, and many movers are forced to spend the first portions of their sojourns covering the costs of movement and expenses of establishing new homes. Settled migrants earn over the long term and, in contrast to popular images of their lives, images that focus on the disruptive nature of their arrival and existence, typically follow a fairly stable lifestyle that is rooted in a long-term home, regular job, and shared community of like-minded people. These are the migrants we are most concerned with, and these are the migrants who remit the greatest percentage of funds to their sending households and communities.

A migrant's job at his or her point of destination can also influence remittance practices. Incomes and wages vary from job to job and situation to situation, and in response to age, gender, and legal status (Cohen, Rodriguez, and Fox 2008; Miera 2008; Ryan and others 2009; Semyonov and Gorodzeisky 2005; Shauman and Noonan 2007; Wong 2006). We also know that diversity in the labor market enhances opportunities and allows migrants to remit through economic slowdowns and financial crises. Migrants know this as well; they use their moves to escape violence and settle strategically, combining work, changing jobs when necessary, and balancing immediate needs against long-term goals.

Although the migrant stock of a country is dependable and remits over the long term, remittances can decline over time. In fact, many observers feared that remittance decline or decay might be exacerbated by the global financial crisis and the loss of labor opportunities in the West. We can expect that remittances from migrants will tend to grow over the short term and for an average of about five years, increasing as the migrant worker's income rises, lifestyle stabilizes, and experiences and knowledge of his or her new setting expands. Remittances can also decline (often described as remittance decay) over time. Decline or decay can happen in at least two ways (Gammage 2006; Lowell and de la Garza 2002). First, although remittances are central to the support and improvement of a sending household's overall economic health, as local incomes increase, remittances tend to decline following a fairly standard rate (Hunte 2004). Second, remittances also decline as migrants' stays in destination countries increase and as families are established or reunited (Orozco 2002). Nevertheless, remittances generally prove resilient, and in many situations remittance rates remain largely unchanged over time as new migrants replace old, as migrant stock reinvests in sending households and communities, and as second- and third-generation children of migrants continue the practices of their parents and grandparents. Altruism on the part of the mover, support of a community's traditions, and family pressures can mediate some decline. More importantly, the opportunities to invest and save in the sending community, what is sometimes described as saving for return, keep remittances flowing (Brown 1998).

The variation in remittance practices over time and in relation to the sojourner's situation makes it difficult to define the impact that remittances have on sending households, communities, and sending countries (Brettell 2007). Many developing countries now celebrate their migrants and the money they return to their sending households. In several countries (including El Salvador, for example) remittances are one of the top sources of available investment capital (Landolt 2001), but we find more than investment taking place. In El Salvador, not only do remittances spur the creation of small businesses and investments, they also encourage changes in the way nationals think about their place in the state, the meaning of violence, what is economic well-being, and access to resources and opportunities. Remittances provide nonmovers with the opportunity to demand higher wages and reject the status quo, to push for political and economic reforms, and to organize (Landolt 2001). A similar pattern persists in Tonga, where migrant remittances tend to follow informal paths and are often invested by households in the informal economy and in goods that can be sold at area flea markets (Brown and Connell 1994). The flea markets and the informal channels that most remittances follow help migrants and their sending households avoid the excessive fees charged on remittances but also support organizing and protesting of the status quo. In a more recent paper, Brown (1997) notes that remittances to the Pacific region lead to increased human capital as nonmigrants use the returns made by immigrant workers to support families and generate investments.

We should not assume that all remittances work to improve the situation and mediate violence for sending households. Vertovec (2009) notes that remittances can displace local incomes and increase inequalities, drive consumptive spending, and inflate prices, among other things. Researchers go so far as to describe the resulting situation as a "syndrome" that leaves nonmigrants dependent on remittances and caught in a net of consumerism with few opportunities to escape as traditions are rejected for life in increasingly capitalized market systems (Binford 2003; Reichert 1981).

It is easy to focus on larger remittances and their obvious importance for movers and nonmovers, communities, and nations, yet many migrants cannot afford to return large sums to their homes. Some of these migrants are internal movers who earn relatively little as part of national workforces in countries with low wages and restricted job markets. In a weak labor market where low wages are paid, the migrant may remit, but only at a rate far lower than compatriots who cross international lines and find higher wages in foreign countries.

Other migrants may cross national lines yet find low wages as they move from one developing nation to another developing nation, as is often the case in South-South migration and clear in the outcomes of Sub-Saharan African migration (Cliggett 2005). Gender also complicates remittance rates. Migrant women often find service jobs that pay less than what their male comigrants can earn (particularly if they work as nannies or maids), and they often juggle a job against maintaining a home for other migrants, thus robbing them of time for additional work (Al-Sharmani 2006; Brumer 2008; Curran and others 2005; Gilbertson 1995; Livingston 2006; Moran-Taylor 2008; Pantoja 2005). Remittances for these movers may amount to little more than a few dollars sent every now and again or perhaps a gift of clothing or a toy, yet the remittances are critical to survival and connections (Cliggett 2005). Finally, even as we focus on the important role remittances play in the economic life of sending communities, it is critical to remember that mobility is not always due to economic need but may reflect other kinds of violence, insecurities, and needs.

The value of remittances has increased dramatically even as dollars for direct aid and other forms of support (including national support) has declined (Buch and Kuckulenz 2010). Nevertheless, limits exist to the power of remittances. First, evidence is at hand that even as remittance rates increase, the totals do not replace the decline in state investment. This is especially evident around economic crisis, including the global financial crisis of 2008–09. Remittances did not replace other forms of investment; rather, they were critical as one of the only sources of capital available to developing nations and their people as they coped with the outcomes of the economic collapse in the West. Second, although remittance rates increase, the increase grows as able citizens engage in migration. This "brain drain" risks alienating young, working-age individuals from their sending nation even as their remittances grow all the more important to the continued economic survival of their sending households and communities (Tanner 2005). In a financial crisis, conflicting pressure mounts on migrants. They are expected to remit and support their sending households, yet the very act of migrating can rob a household and nation of its best and best trained members. Yet the flow of remittances is perhaps more critical during crises then at any other time for developing nations threatened with their own financial collapse. Third, concern has been expressed about remittance decay, which (as we noted above) may lead to the long-term decline of investment capital over time (Singh 2010). The global crisis seems to encourage, not discourage, investment and remittances, and this is one area of hope as we continue to explore the data on the impacts of the most recent financial crisis on developing nations.

A second area of interest lies in the value of nonmonetary remittances. Nonmonetary remittances can include gifts in kind, education, investments outside of the economic realm, and the like (King, Dalipaj, and Mai 2006). These remittances can be critical to the survival and health of sending communities and countries and include the growth of "fixed" capital improvements to communities (ranging from investment in infrastructure to investment in building projects) to "flexible" investments that accrue around goods and services that are portable and transferable between populations or that are a foundation for future growth. Lest we be too positive, such remittances can also become a problem, as receiving communities incur new expenses to maintain and build on the fixed and flexible investments that migrants make.

Remittances and the Crisis

Many observers anticipate that remittance rates decline in times of crises, and in fact, during the recent global financial crisis of 2008–09, some evidence suggested that remittances flowed from sending households to migrants struggling in their destination communities. Nevertheless, the reality is that although remittances may decline, they remain critical and quite stable for the survival of sending households and communities. This was clear in disaster-ridden situations, including Haiti in 2010, as in other less fraught examples where remittance rates declined but did not disappear (Orozco 2002). In these situations, households that received remittances often changed their behavior, directing smaller overall remittances to necessities and forgoing luxury purchases but still relying on the money returned to make ends meet. Again, we must be clear: Remittances have proven resilient. They have declined at a far slower pace than foreign direct investment, private debt, or portfolio equity flows and are recovering rapidly in 2010.

Conclusions

Remittances follow set rules, but not simple rules. Remittance outcomes can be counterintuitive and even a bit unexpected. Remittances are not simply indicators of national labor patterns and economic outcomes. To most citizens of sending countries remittances are the most important resource available in the struggle to survive. Yet, at the same time, their very presence often means that nation-states ignore some responsibilities. It is to the contradictory nature of remittance practices that we devote this volume. We hope this collection captures not only the dynamic nature of remittance practices, but also the dynamic and sometimes unanticipated outcome of remittances used by sending households and communities.

Chapter 2

Forecasting Migrant Remittances during the Global Financial Crisis

SANKET MOHAPATRA AND DILIP RATHA

The global financial crisis that started in August 2008 with the collapse of Lehman Brothers led to concerns among policy makers that it would result in precipitous declines in external resource flows to developing countries, which could adversely affect the sustained economic growth and reduction in poverty seen during the previous decade (World Bank 2009b).[1] Given the size and increasing importance of migrant remittances for developing countries, which had reached more than $330 billion in 2008 (see the next section), similar concerns were expressed that a decline in remittances would affect the poorest countries and households that were heavily dependent on remittances. Policy makers needed forward-looking analysis of the impact of the global economic crisis on remittance flows to developing countries.

Migrant remittances have usually been countercyclical with respect to downturns and crises in origin countries (see discussion below). However, unlike past emerging market crises that had started in emerging markets, such as Mexico in 1994–95 or East Asia in 1997–98, the current crisis started in the rich countries and spread to developing countries (Ratha and others 2008). Although numerous studies have documented the importance of both host and home country factors in determining remittance flows (see below), it was not clear a priori how remittances would behave in response to a deep economic downturn in the host countries. To our knowledge, no previous models had been developed for forecasting remittances, a necessary tool for analyzing the impact of the global financial crisis on remittance flows.

This chapter describes a first attempt to develop a methodology to forecast remittances. It exploits an existing bilateral remittance matrix for more than 200 economies developed by Ratha and Shaw (2007) to generate country-level forecasts. The framework allows the forecasts of remittances to be consistently linked to the forecasts of global economic growth.

The next section provides a brief discussion about the rising importance of remittances for developing countries and the need for forecasting remittances. We then discuss the available evidence on the determinants of remittance flows and the extent to which these explanatory variables can be used for forecasting future remittances, followed by a description of the World Bank's methodology for forecasting remittances. The chapter then discusses the results of the forecasts, outlines some of the caveats that need to be considered when using this methodology, and concludes with recommendations for improving the quality of forecasts.

The Rising Importance of Migrant Remittances for Developing Countries and the Need for Forecasting Remittances

Recorded migrant remittances to developing countries are estimated to have reached $316 billion in 2009. These constitute 2 percent of gross domestic product (GDP) for developing countries and nearly 6 percent of GDP for the group of low-income countries; in several countries, these flows are more than a quarter of GDP (Ratha, Mohapatra, and Silwal 2010a). In many countries these flows exceed foreign direct investment, portfolio equity, and debt flows and in some countries official aid. Remittances have been remarkably stable compared with other types of flows, contribute to stabilizing the current account position, and reduce the volatility of capital flows and output volatility of recipient countries (Bugamelli and Paterno 2009; Chami, Hakura, and Montiel 2009; Gupta, Pattillo, and Wagh 2009; Ratha 2005, 2007; World Bank 2006a). Their size and stable and countercyclical nature have implications for improving debt sustainability and creditworthiness of developing countries and these countries' access to international capital markets (Avendano, Gaillard, and Parra 2009, Ratha 2007; Ratha, De, and Mohapatra 2010). Remittance receipts are associated with reduction in poverty, increased household resources devoted to investment, improved health and education outcomes, and higher levels of entrepreneurship (see, for example, Adams and Page 2005; Amuedo-Dorantes and Pozo 2010; Fajnzylber and Lopez 2007; Hildebrandt and McKenzie 2005; Valero-Gil 2009). Remittances can also improve recipient households' access to formal financial services (Giuliano and Ruiz-Arranz 2009; Gupta, Pattillo, and Wagh 2009). The growing importance of remittances for developing countries implies that a need exists to evaluate the sustainability of remittances (whether remittance flows would continue at their current or higher levels) in the short and medium terms.

Determinants of Remittances

Remittance flows are broadly affected by three factors: the migrant stocks in different destination countries, incomes of migrants in the different migrant-destination countries, and to some extent incomes in the migrant-sending country. The size of emigrant stocks is arguably the most important determinant of remittances (Freund and Spatafora 2008; Lueth and Ruiz-Arranz 2007; Ratha and Shaw 2007; Singh, Haacker, and Lee 2009).

The income level of the migrant and the needs of the family at home play an equally important role in influencing both the level and changes in remittances. Several studies have documented that remittances respond positively to an increase in the host country's GDP (Frankel 2009; Glytsos 1997; Ruiz and Vargas-Silva 2010; Vargas-Silva and Huang 2006) and in a negative or countercyclical manner during economic downturns, financial crises, and natural disasters in the migrant-sending country (Clarke and Wallsten 2004; Frankel 2009; Mohapatra and others 2009; Ratha 2010b; World Bank 2006a; Yang 2008b; Yang and Choi 2007). Lueth and Ruiz-Arranz (2008), however, report that bilateral remittances respond positively to increases in both host and home countries' GDP. Some other studies have found that remittances are strongly countercyclical in poorer countries such as Bangladesh and India, but procyclical in middle-income countries such as Jordan and Morocco (Sayan 2006; World Bank 2006a). In terms of the relative importance of home and host country factors, several studies have found that the host country's economic conditions appear to be more important compared with home country factors (Barajas and others 2010; Glytsos 1997; Swamy 1981; Vargas-Silva and Huang 2006).

Other factors such as remittance costs and migrants' vintage also play a role in influencing remittance flows. In a survey of Tongan migrants in New Zealand, Gibson, McKenzie, and Rohorua (2006) find that remittances sent would rise by 0.22 percent if costs fell by 1 percent. Other studies have found that remittances are influenced by interest rate differentials, exchange rate premia (the difference between the official and black market exchange rates), and the duration of migration (El-Sakka and McNabb 1999; Glytsos 1997). Freund and Spatafora (2008) report that recorded remittances depend negatively on transfer costs and the parallel market premium because migrants may prefer to send money through informal channels when transfer costs are high or when the official exchange rate is unattractive. Some authors argue that the skill composition of migrants matters for remittances, but the evidence of this phenomenon is mixed. Whereas Adams (2009), Faini (2007), and Niimi and Ozden (2006) using cross-country data find that countries that have a larger proportion of high-skilled migrants receive less remittances—perhaps because these migrants are also more likely to settle in the host countries and reunite with their families—studies based on microlevel survey data find the opposite result. Bollard and colleagues (2009) using survey data in 11 OECD destination countries find a positive relationship between education levels of migrants and the amounts remitted. Clemens (2009) finds that Nigerian migrant doctors in the United States sent more than $5,000 a year in remittances.

A Simple Model for Forecasting Remittances

Although remittances are influenced by all the above factors, their use in a forecasting exercise is constrained by the lack of reliable forecasts of the future evolution of these explanatory variables. The data on remittance costs are not easy to model, although we know that remittance costs are falling and causing remittance flows to increase. The migrants' vintage, or the number of years lived in the destination country, is also a plausible determinant of remittance flows to the origin countries (Glytsos 1997; Merkle and Zimmermann 1992). New migrants may send more remittances as a percentage of their income because they have better ties back home. However, anecdotal evidence exists that new migrants often have financial obligations (such as repaying loans incurred while migrating) and therefore are unlikely to send remittances immediately after arrival in the host country.[2] Modeling the evolution of variables such as interest rate differentials and official and parallel market exchange rates over the medium term is fraught with similar difficulties.

The model-based remittances therefore rely primarily on the latest available information on bilateral migrant stocks (Ratha and Shaw 2007; World Bank 2011b) and the World Bank and International Monetary Fund's (IMF's) medium-term projections of nominal incomes in the host countries and in the home country.[3] Changes in exchange rates are captured to some extent because projections of nominal GDP factor in plausible assumptions about the evolution of nominal exchange rates.

The forecasts for remittance flows are based on stocks of migrants in different destination countries, incomes in the host country that can influence remittances sent by these migrants, and to some extent incomes in the origin country. Therefore, remittances received by country i from country j can be expressed as

$$R_{ij} = f(M_{ij}, y_i, y_j), \qquad (2.1)$$

where M_{ij} is the stock of migrants from country i in country j, y_j is the nominal per capita income of the migrant-destination country, and y_i is the per capita income of the remittance-receiving country. The bilateral remittance estimates are calculated using the methodology described in Ratha and Shaw (2007) based on migrant stocks in different destination countries, incomes of migrants in the different destination countries, and incomes in the source country (see annex). We assume that migrant stocks will remain unchanged, which is not an unreasonable assumption in the short term. We prepare the forecasts for remittance flows by examining the effects of income changes in destination countries worldwide.

Remittance intensities (I_{ij}) were calculated as the ratio of remittance outflow from country j to migrant-origin country i (R_{ij}) to the nominal GDP of remittance-source country j (Y_j):

$$I_{ij} = R_{ij} / Y_j = \left(R_{ij} / R_j\right) \times \left(R_j / Y_j\right) = r_{ij} I_j, \qquad (2.2)$$

where I_j is the share of remittance outflows R_j to the GDP Y_j of country j. Here r_{ij}, the share of country j's remittance outflows received by country i, was calculated using the bilateral remittance matrix of Ratha and Shaw (2007).

Two approaches were followed to forecast remittances for country i. The first assumes that remittances from remittance source country j to a migrant-origin country i grow at the same rate as migrant incomes in the host country. The second approach recognizes that remittances may grow faster (or slower) than the incomes in the destination country.

Remittance Matrix-Based Approach

The first approach assumes that remittances grow (or decline) at the same rate as migrant incomes in the host country. Remittance outflows from country j were forecast using estimated remittance intensities (I_{ij}) and the projections of nominal gross domestic product for each source country j (Y_j) from the World Bank's global macroeconomic forecasts:

$$\hat{R}_j^{t+1} = I_j \hat{Y}_j^{t+1}. \tag{2.3}$$

The forecasts for remittance inflows for country i were calculated by adding up the share of remittances to country i in the remittance outflows from country j (r_{ij}) for all remittance-source countries:

$$\hat{R}_i^{t+1} = \sum_j r_{ij} R_j^{t+1}. \tag{2.4}$$

Elasticity-Based Approach

An elasticity-based approach recognizes that the remittances may grow faster than incomes in the host country; that is, the elasticity of remittances with respect to the host country may be greater than 1 (Ratha, Mohapatra, and Silwal 2010a). For example, during the precrisis period, remittances grew faster than the GDP of remittance-source countries because of various factors, including improvements in remittance technologies, falling costs, and a steady increase in migrant stocks. The World Bank has used elasticity-based estimates in its most recent projections. Some recent studies have used similar elasticity-based estimates for estimating remittance flows to specific regions that have gaps in official data on remittances.[4]

Consistent with the view that remittances would grow at a lower, more "sustainable" rate in the postcrisis period (2010 and beyond), the elasticity of remittances (R_j) with respect to migrant incomes (MY_j) is assumed to be half that of the precrisis period (2003–08), with an upper bound of 3 and lower bound of 1. These remittance elasticities are used to forecast remittance outflows from each remittance-source country in 2010 and beyond using the latest available forecasts of GDP from the World Bank, using the following formula:

$$\hat{R}_j^{t+1} = R_j^t \left(1 + \eta_j (I_j) \log\left(MY_j^{t+1} / MY_j^t \right)\right).$$ (2.5)

The forecasts for remittance inflows for country i were calculated by adding up the share of remittances to country i in the remittance outflows from country j (r_{ij}) for all remittance-source countries:

$$\hat{R}_i^{t+1} = \sum_j r_{ij} R_j^{t+1}.$$ (2.6)

In later versions, the bilateral migration matrix developed by Ratha and Shaw (2007) was updated with immigrant stock data from various sources to provide the most comprehensive estimates of bilateral immigrant stocks worldwide in 2010 (World Bank 2011b).

Discussion of Results

The model has performed well during the global financial crisis. Despite initial concerns of a sharp decline, the actual decline in remittances in 2009 has been similar to our forecasts. The model predicted correctly that remittance flows to developing countries would decline only modestly, unlike foreign direct investment and portfolio debt and equity flows. The initial forecasting exercise prepared in November 2008 (Ratha, Mohapatra, and Xu 2008) predicted that remittance flows to developing countries would fall by 1 percent in 2009 in the base-case scenario and no more than 6 percent in a low-case scenario (where the last year's flow of migrants was forced to return). Remittance flows were forecast to decline in five of the six developing regions (other than the East Asia and Pacific region) in the base-case scenario. As the financial crisis deepened and the World Bank and the International Monetary Fund revised downward their growth forecasts, the model-generated forecasts of remittances were also revised downward, to a 5–8 percent decline in March 2009 and a 7–10 percent decline in July 2009 (Ratha and Mohapatra 2009; Ratha, Mohapatra, and Silwal 2009a).

The actual outcome in 2009 was a 6 percent decline in remittance flows to developing countries (Ratha, Mohapatra, and Silwal 2009a). In terms of regional distribution, remittance flows declined in five of the six developing regions, but the extent of declines in some regions were larger and in others smaller than initially predicted—East Asia and Pacific, the Middle East and North Africa, and South Asia and Sub-Saharan Africa did better, but Europe and Central Asia and Latin America and the Caribbean performed worse. However, as initially predicted, remittances remained more resilient compared against other types of private resource flows to developing countries.

Several limitations can be identified in the forecasting methodology outlined above. First, the model does not explicitly feature return migration, a key risk factor. We do not have data on return migration for most migrant-destination countries. To account for the additional vulnerabilities that migrants might face during a downturn, we developed a low-case scenario where we assumed that the stock of migrants in high-income countries would decline by the last two years of migrant inflows. (Annual inflows were about 2 percent of migrant stocks for the United States, 4 percent for Europe, and 5 percent for the Gulf Cooperation Council countries; see Ratha, Mohapatra, and Xu 2008). Such a scenario could also be a result of some return migration and a disproportionately larger impact of the crisis on migrants' employment and incomes. The actual returns during the crisis have turned out to be smaller (Ratha, Mohapatra, and Silwal 2009a). This suggests a need for high-frequency data on new migration flows and return.

Second, the model does not fully capture effects of movement of exchange rates. Exchange rate movements such as between the euro and the U.S. dollar, and the dollar and relevant local currency, can affect the value of remittances in dollar terms, as well as the consumption versus investment motive for sending remittances. Even though remittance flows from the Russian Federation to Central Asian countries such as Armenia, the Kyrgyz Republic, and Tajikistan declined by between 15 and 34 percent in dollar terms in the first half of 2009, the decline in terms of the Russian ruble was much smaller because the ruble lost a quarter of its value against the dollar (Ratha, Mohapatra, and Silwal 2009a). Similarly, the depreciation of the Indian rupee and the Philippine peso produced a "sale effect" on housing, bank deposits, stocks, and other assets back home, which made these assets cheaper in foreign currency terms and increased remittances sent for investment motives.

Third, immigration controls and quotas imposed during a crisis are a political decision and therefore difficult to capture in a mathematical model. The forecasting exercise described above attempts to address this risk by developing a low-case scenario that assumes there might be no new flows or that existing migrants might need to return.

Fourth, the model does not capture the response of remittance flows to falling costs. Remittance costs have fallen rapidly during the last decade (Ratha 2005; World Bank 2010c). As discussed in a previous section, the elasticity of remittance flows to remittance costs can be high (Gibson, McKenzie, and Rohorua 2006; World Bank 2006a). Structural equations that estimate remittances as a function of remittance costs are needed, but it would be difficult to undertake this estimation until the quality of data on flows and costs improve.

Fifth, the model does not capture shifts in remittance flows between formal and informal channels. In the precrisis period, remittance flows shifted from informal to formal channels in response to falling remittance costs and intensification of monitoring of informal channels after September 11, 2001. There appears to be a reversal of this trend after the crisis as a weak job market and tightening of immigration controls have resulted in many documented migrants staying on without proper documents and who are probably relying on informal channels.

In conclusion, the financial crisis has highlighted the need for forecasts of remittance flows in many developing countries where these flows have proved to be a lifeline to the poor and the policy makers. Yet much remains to be done to improve the forecast methodology, data on bilateral flows, and high-frequency monitoring of migration and remittance flows.

Notes

1. The World Bank's Global Development Finance 2009 report estimated that net private capital inflows to developing countries fell to $707 billion in 2008 (from a peak of $1.2 trillion in 2007) and were expected to fall further by 50 percent by the end of 2009 (World Bank 2009b).

2. In some of the simulations, we try to capture the vintage effect by examining a low-case scenario where recent migrant inflows of the last one or two years are forced to go back as the economic crisis deepens in the major destination countries, an unlikely but high-impact scenario.

3. The World Bank's projections up until April 2010 have used the bilateral migration matrix of Ratha and Shaw (2007). This is an updated version of the bilateral migration matrix developed by Parsons and colleagues (2007).

4. In the absence of timely and reliable official data on remittances for most Sub-Saharan African countries, Barajas and colleagues (2010) use the elasticity of remittances to income computed by Singh, Haacker, and Lee (2009) and the IMF's GDP estimates to estimate the extent of decline in remittance flows to Sub-Saharan Africa in 2009.

5. This section draws on Ratha and Shaw (2007).

Annex: Estimating Bilateral Remittances

Credible national data on bilateral remittances are not available.[5] Even when such data are reported, they may not be accurate, because funds channeled through international banks may be attributed to a country other than the actual source country. For example, funds flowing from the Gulf region through international banks may be attributed to New York or London (Ratha 2005). Market players and researchers, therefore, have attempted to derive bilateral remittance flows indirectly using bilateral migrant stock data and estimates and assumptions about the remittance behavior of migrants. Harrison, Britton, and Swanson (2004), for example, assume that each migrant sends a fixed average amount.

We have calculated bilateral remittances by allocating remittances received by each developing country among the countries of destination of its migrant nationals. We use three different allocation rules: (1) weights based on migrant stocks abroad; (2) weights based on migrant incomes, proxied by migrant stocks multiplied by per capita income in the destination countries; and (3) weights that take into account migrants' incomes abroad as well as source-country incomes. Each of the three methods is discussed in more detail below.

Using the Share of Migrants in Different Destination Countries as Weights

The first method of estimating bilateral remittances assumes that remittances R_i received by country i are proportional to migrant stocks in the different destination countries. Hence, the weight attached to destination country j is

$$w_{ij} = \frac{M_{ij}}{\sum_j M_{ij}}, \qquad (2A.1)$$

where M_{ij} is the number of migrants from country i in destination country j. Bilateral remittances received by country i from destination country j are therefore $w_{ij}R_i$.

A shortcoming of this method is that it assumes that each migrant sends the same amount of remittances regardless of where he or she lives and no matter what the migrant's income in the host country. The large variance of incomes across migrant-receiving countries (and even across countries within each income group) limits the usefulness of this method. This method yields an upper bound estimate of South-South remittances, however, because it attributes the same amount of remittances to a developing country as to a high-income country.

Using Both Migrants Abroad and Income Level in the Host Country

The second method of estimating bilateral remittances uses migrant stocks in different destination countries and host-country incomes to construct weights. The weight attached to destination country j is

$$w_{ij} = \frac{M_{ij}Y_j}{\sum\limits_j M_{ij}Y_j},$$
(2A.2)

where M_{ij} is the number of migrants from country i in destination country j and Y_j is the average per capita gross national income (GNI) of migrant-receiving country j. Bilateral remittances received by country i from destination country j are therefore $w_{ij}R_i$.

Although this method is superior to the first one, because it takes into account both migrant stocks and the average income of the country where the migrant resides, it assumes that each migrant sends a fixed share of his or her income, regardless of the level of that income or the needs of the family back home. This method yields a lower-bound for South-South remittances.

Using Weights Based on Migrant Stocks, Per Capita Income in the Destination Countries, and Per Capita Income in the Source Countries

The third method tries to correct for the shortcomings of the first two methods. The average remittance sent by a migrant in destination country j (r_{ij}) is modeled as a function of the per capita income of the migrant-sending country and the host country:

$$r_{ij} = f(\bar{Y}_i, Y_j) = \begin{cases} \bar{Y}_i & \text{if } Y_j < \bar{Y}_i \\ \bar{Y}_i + (Y_j - \bar{Y}_i)^\beta & \text{if } Y_j \geq \bar{Y}_i \end{cases},$$
(2A.3)

where Y_j is the average per capita GNI of migrant-receiving country j, $\bar{Y}_i$ is the per capita GNI of the migrant's home country, and β is a parameter between 0 and 1. The amount sent by an average migrant is assumed to be at least as much as the per capita income of the home country, even when the individual migrates to a lower-income country. The rationale is that the migration occurs in the expectation of earning a higher level of income for the dependent household than what the migrant would earn in his or her home country. Ideally, the migrants' income should be taken from household survey data, but in the absence of such data, we use per capita GNI in the host country as a proxy for the migrant's income abroad and per capita GNI in the sending country as a proxy for the dependent household's income (assuming that the migrant's remittances compensate for at least the counterfactual loss of income due to migration).

The level of remittances is assumed to increase with the level of host country income, but at a decreasing rate: $f\beta > 0$ and $f\beta < 0$. The total amount of remittances received by country i is therefore

$$R_i = \sum_j r_{ij} M_{ij}.$$

(2A.4)

The parameter β in equation (2A.3) is estimated for each country such that the total of remittances received is equal to R_i in equation (2A.4). The parameter β is found to be remarkably stable across developing countries (0.74 for Bangladesh and China, 0.78 for India, 0.77 for the Philippines, and 0.67 for Vietnam). To estimate bilateral remittances for all countries, we use the average β (equal to 0.75) for the top 20 remittance-receiving countries. Equation (2A.3) is then used to create weights so that individual remittances from equations (2A.3) and (2A.4) add up to the total remittances received.

A comparison of these estimates for South-South and North-South remittances calculated using the three different methods is provided in the main text. It is usually impossible to verify the accuracy of these bilateral estimates because most countries in the South as well as in the North do not report sources or destinations of remittance flows. A handful of countries (such as Bangladesh and the Philippines) do report sources of remittance inflows, but in these data more flows are likely to be attributed to the United States and Europe, where international banks have headquarters (Ratha 2005). Remittances from South countries may also be underestimated because of restrictions on outward remittance flows and irregular status of migrants (as an example, Bangladesh does not report any remittance inflows from India even though it has a large migrant population in India).

Chapter 3

Economic Crises and Migration: Learning from the Past and the Present

TIM GREEN AND L. ALAN WINTERS

THIS CHAPTER DEALS WITH CRISES and migration and, in particular, with the recent economic and financial crisis and migration:

- How will it affect migration

- Perhaps more important, how should it affect migration, for migration is nothing if not deeply affected by the policy decisions of government

- In the long run, perhaps even more important, how will the crisis help us to understand the most complex and deeply felt of all aspects of globalization—the decision to move to a different country.

At first glance one might think that most migration was due to crises of one sort or another and thus that crises were the *key* issue for us to study. In one sense we can make that true by defining "crises" appropriately, but once one starts reading and thinking through the subject more carefully, that no longer seems true. Surely, crises affect the timing of migration and occasionally mark an identifiable watershed between regimes, but in the end the evidence suggests that migration is a long-run phenomenon responding to long-run determinants. Another thing we did not know at the time was that Tim

This chapter is the basis of the Keynote Address given by Winters at the World Bank's Second "Migration and Development" Conference, September 10–11, 2009, in Washington, DC. We are grateful to participants for comments on the first draft. It was originally published in *The World Economy* 33(9): 1053–72. It is reprinted with permission. The analysis and the views expressed in this chapter are those of the authors and do not necessarily reflect those of the Department for International Development.

Hatton and Jeff Williamson were about to publish a well-put-together little note on the subject on VoxEU.org (Hatton and Williamson 2009), which goes over much of the same ground, and the good sense and wisdom of which we heartily commend.

The chapter comprises four substantive sections. The first offers the briefest of descriptions of the current economic crisis. It is followed by a discussion of migration and crises in the nineteenth century. This is an attractive period to study because it not only saw massive flows of people, but these were largely unencumbered by government policies, and so they offer us a reasonable chance of inferring the real economic and social incentives to migration. In fact, one might better say that the nineteenth century illustrates migration and economic *cycles* rather than migration and economic *crises*, for the sort of fluctuations we just experienced were fairly common then and were more or less accepted as a law of nature.

The third section looks briefly at twentieth-century experience. By that time policy had become more active, and so it is more difficult to back the determinants out from observation, but nonetheless the patterns of crises and migration offer some insight— even if only confirming what had previously been seen. The final substantive section advances hypotheses about what we might expect to see in the twenty-first century and asks whether the preliminary evidence is lending them any credence.

The Economic Crisis, 2008–09

There are many accounts of the financial crisis of 2007–08 and the resulting economic crisis of 2008 to—who knows when.[1] We shall not rehearse them here save to argue that by modern standards we are witnessing a major shock. Not only are incomes and output sharply lower than expected, but we are experiencing a fairly much unexpected decline in global economic intercourse. Thus it may seem particularly pertinent to ask whether the currently poor relation of globalization—migration—will be heavily affected.

Almost uniquely in postwar history, 2009 has seen a decline in the volume and value of international trade. Trade volumes contracted by 0.6 and 2.2 percent in 1981 and 1982 (World Trade Organization, Statistics Database, http://stat.wto.org/StatisticalProgram/ WSDBStatProgramHome.aspx?Language=E), whereas for 2009, the International Monetary Fund (IMF) is reporting a year-on-year decline of 11 percent, which represents a drop of about 16 percent relative to what was predicted for 2009 even as late as mid-2008. In value terms, 1982 and 1983 saw declines of 6.3 and 2.0 percent, respectively, compared with a decline over the 12-month period to October 2009 of nearly $3 trillion or 23 percent. (November 2009 is the latest month for which data are available.) Likewise international capital flows have collapsed, with the Institute for International Finance estimating net private flows to developing and emerging markets of about $435 billion in 2009 compared with nearly $1 trillion in 2007 and $667 billion in 2008.

In terms of real gross domestic product (GDP), the IMF's World Economic Outlook of April 2010 estimates world growth of –0.6 percent for 2009, more than 4 percent below the growth rates expected for that year a year earlier. The losses relative to expected levels were more than 7 percent in Eastern and Central Europe, where the financial collapse had direct effects, and about 1.5 percent in developing countries in Asia, which were dynamic and robust going into the crisis. Allowing a few years for economies to return to previous growth rates, we can expect real GDP (and hence real GDP per head) to be about 8 or 9 percent below the levels we had expected going forward from 2011. Figure 3.1 illustrates.

FIGURE 3.1 Real GDP per Capita with and without the Current Crisis, 1980–2013

a. Advanced countries   b. Emerging and developing economies

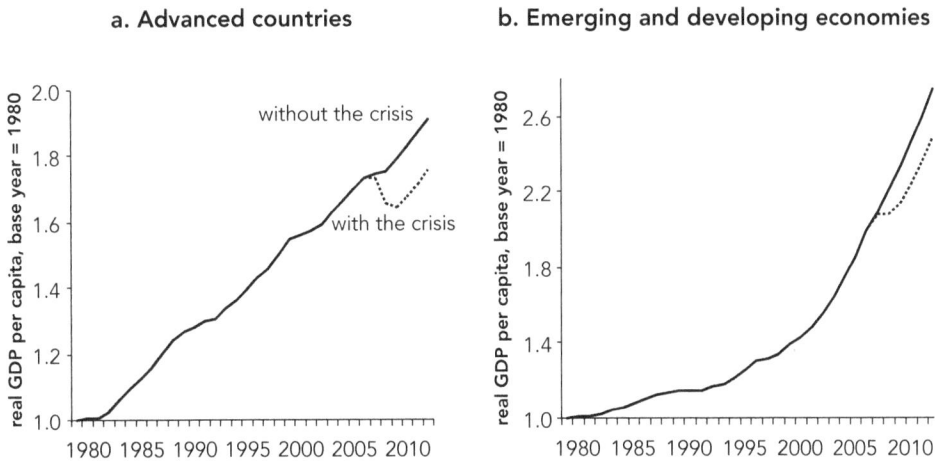

Source: IMF, World Economic Outlook, April 2009, http://www.imf.org/external/pubs/ft/weo/2011/01/weodata/download.aspx.

The Nineteenth Century

Perhaps the best-known example of crisis-led migration among Anglo-Saxon scholars is the Irish Famine of the 1840s. Data are not very reliable for this period, but O'Rourke (1995) has patched together the story. From 1800 the Irish population was increasing steadily. In 1845 half of the potato crop failed, in 1846 nearly the entire crop did, little was planted in 1847, and in 1848 the crop failed again. It is difficult to translate this into changes in GDP of the sort we are used to, but the potato was the staple food of agricultural workers in an agricultural land, so it must have been very large. Moreover, poverty was very extreme in Ireland at the time, so the losses were almost certainly critical for many people.

O'Rourke reports excess mortality of about 1 million over the famine, averted births of around 400,000, and emigration of about 1 million. The numbers do not quite add up, but figure 3.2 shows the fantastic reversal of population trends in the late 1840s. Hatton and Williamson (2005: 47) report from various sources that Irish emigration accounted for 71 percent of total European emigration and 50 percent of immigration over 1846–51, and that between the mid-1840s and early 1850s nearly 1.5 million people left. Obviously these departures are not all due to the famine (many would have left anyway), but it is reasonable to conclude that a good part is.

FIGURE 3.2 Population of Ireland during the Nineteenth Century

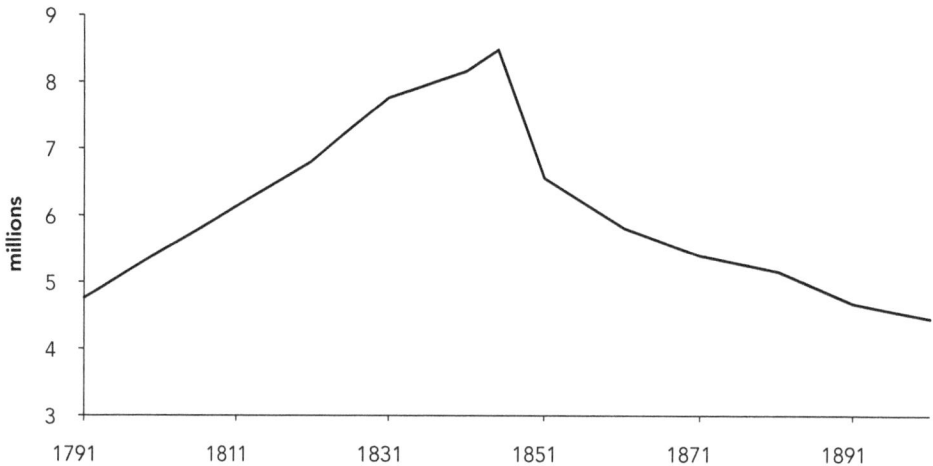

Source: O'Rourke 1995.

One of the most widely accepted ideas in migration work is the importance of networks—"friends and families"—in reducing migration costs. Thus, the Irish famine increased net emigration and emigrant stocks over some counterfactual; the positive feedback loop will lead to greater flows for, probably, many decades.[2] Hatton and Williamson have several times estimated the size of "family and friends effects" and found them large and positive in all cases. In their book (2005) they suggest that, generally, for every 1,000 emigrants abroad, 20 more per year are pulled abroad, and that for Ireland the effect was twice that (41 per year). Thus, if the famine caused 1 million to leave and establish themselves abroad, the future outflow would be 41,000 higher each year, pushing the rate up from 7 per thousand per year pre-famine to 13 post-famine (O'Rourke 1995). On this reading the famine explains perhaps half of Irish emigration from 1850 to, say, 1910—a huge amount.

The Irish famine was a classic economic crisis—exactly the sort of shock that real business cyclists dream about. It was also massive. Other "economic crises" are typically smaller and/or noneconomic in magnitude. "Noneconomic" is a difficult term to get to grips with—see, for example, Winters (1989) on so-called noneconomic arguments for agricultural protections—but loosely speaking, we include conflict, such as in the Democratic Republic of Congo or Rwanda, political repression, including the pogroms, the Iron Curtain, or Idi Amin in Uganda, and natural disasters, such as the Dust Bowl or the island-volcano Montserrat. These surely matter and can have strong effects on population movements, but we save them for another occasion. In economic crises the important events are the ups and downs of the business cycle. The nineteenth century saw relatively large fluctuations in output and income in most countries and very large short-term fluctuations in migration. A natural question is whether they were related, and they offer a good opportunity to study the effects of crises on migration because the period was largely free of policy impediments to mobility. Policy is clearly an important dimension of the response to crises, and we will come to it, but it is useful to keep it separate.

Asking about crises and migration is a bit like the pull versus push debate in migration empirics; see, for example, Thomas (1954). Quite obviously, both matter, but if crises were generally influential, we would expect to see some sign of it in the GDP growth and gross emigration data. Figures 3.3 and 3.4 plot emigration from the British Isles (including Ireland), based on passenger records.[3] Figure 3.3, which refers to the United States, includes non-U.K. citizens, probably in increasing numbers through the century, but for figure 3.4, which looks at total emigration, it is possible to break out citizens after 1853, which we also do. The GDP data come from Maddison (2003) and the emigration data from Ferenczi and Wilcox (1929). We focus on North America so that we can also relate the flows to the U.S. business cycle below. Both series have been standardized for ease of presentation. The correlation between emigration and growth are small, and a regression of emigration on time and growth finds the latter quite insignificant.

One might argue that an interest in crises mandates a focus mainly on periods of contraction or very weak growth, but this, too, yields little signs of connection. Figure 3.5 shows that the years of least growth show only a slight tendency toward higher migration, even allowing for lags.

We have conducted a similar review of the nineteenth-century data for France, Germany, the Netherlands, and Sweden and have similarly found no plausible evidence that downturns in home countries systematically induce higher emigration.

The alternative role for crises is on the "pull" side, with income dynamics in the recipient country influencing migrant inflows. Figure 3.6 explores this for flows from our five example countries to the United States plotted along with the U.S. growth rate of GDP since 1871 (the start of Maddison's GDP series). There are clearly signs of a positive relationship here, with the depressions of 1874–77, 1883–86, 1893–94, and 1907–08 all reflecting declines in emigration to the United States and similar sharp increases in the corresponding upturns.

Even clearer is Hatton and Williamson's (2005) figure reporting detrended (total) emigration rates per thousand for six European source countries—reproduced with modifications in figure 3.7. The striking thing is the similarity of the patterns, which suggests that all may be at least partly caused by a common factor. Sketching in the depressions in the United States (which was the dominant, but far from the only, destination) suggests that, indeed, host country fortunes are a pretty strong determinant of voluntary migration. The shaded areas correspond to periods of U.S. economic downturn.

FIGURE 3.3 Emigration from the British Isles to the United States and British GDP Growth, 1831–1913

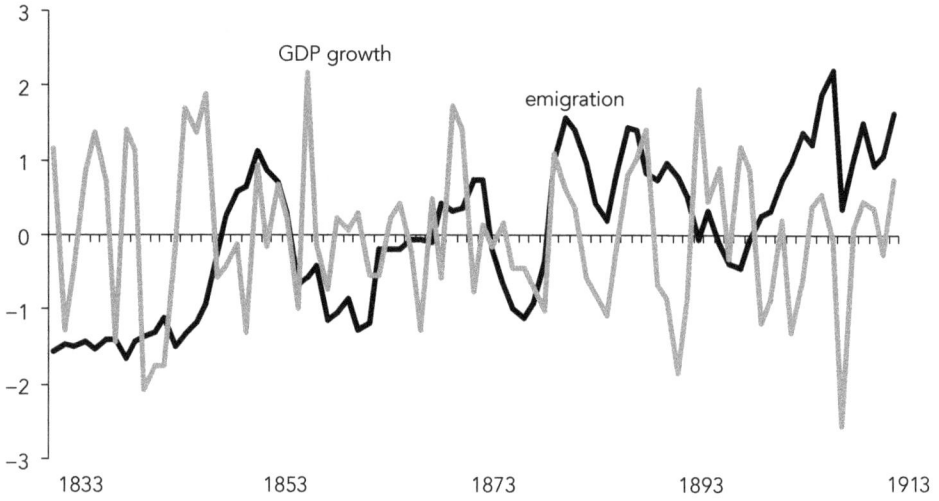

Sources: Maddison 2003 and Ferenczi and Wilcox 1929.

FIGURE 3.4 Emigration of British Citizens from the British Isles to the United States and British GDP Growth, 1853–1913

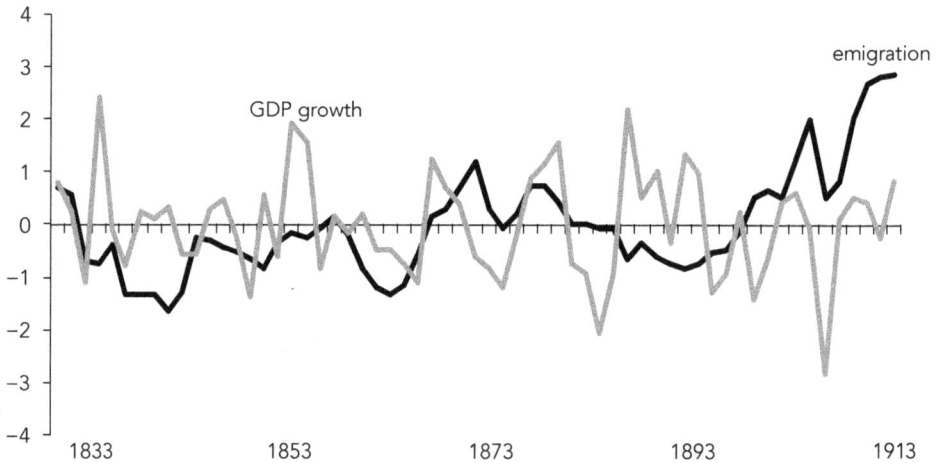

Sources: Maddison 2003 and Ferenczi and Wilcox 1929.

FIGURE 3.5 (Lagged) Emigration of British Citizens from the British Isles to the United States and British GDP Growth, 1853–1913

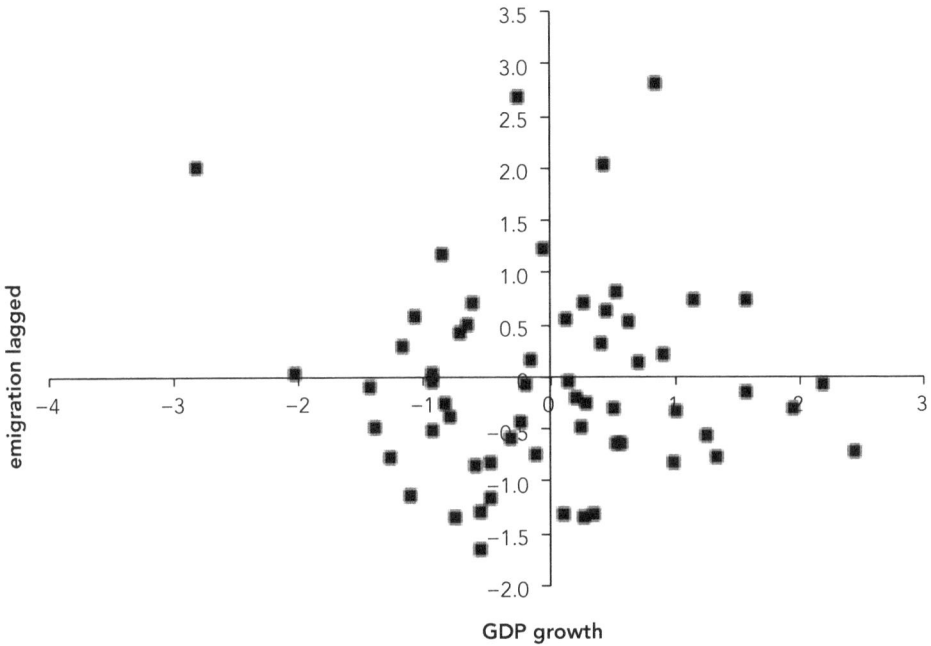

GDP growth

Sources: Maddison 2003 and Ferenczi and Wilcox 1929.

FIGURE 3.6 Emigration to the United States from Five European Countries and U.S. GDP Growth, 1870–1913

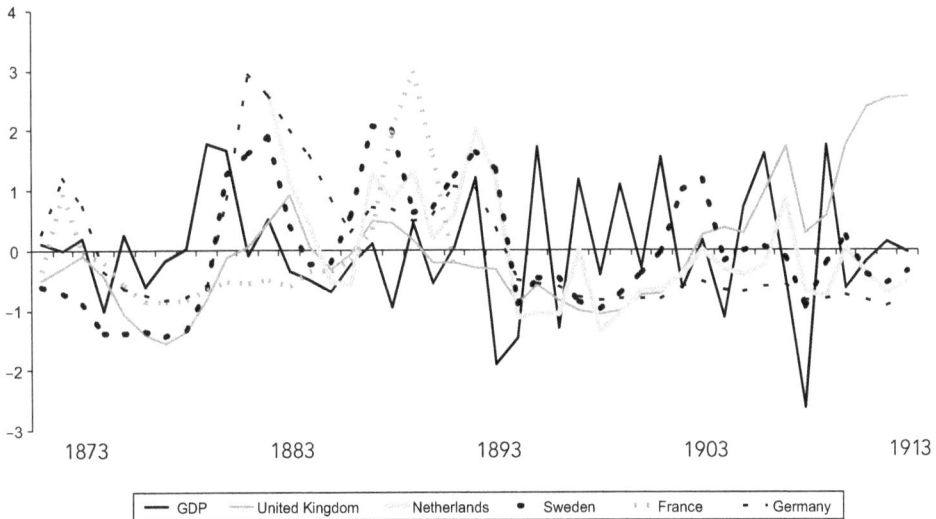

Sources: Maddison 2003 and Ferenczi and Wilcox 1929.

FIGURE 3.7 Emigration Rates to the United States, 1860–1913

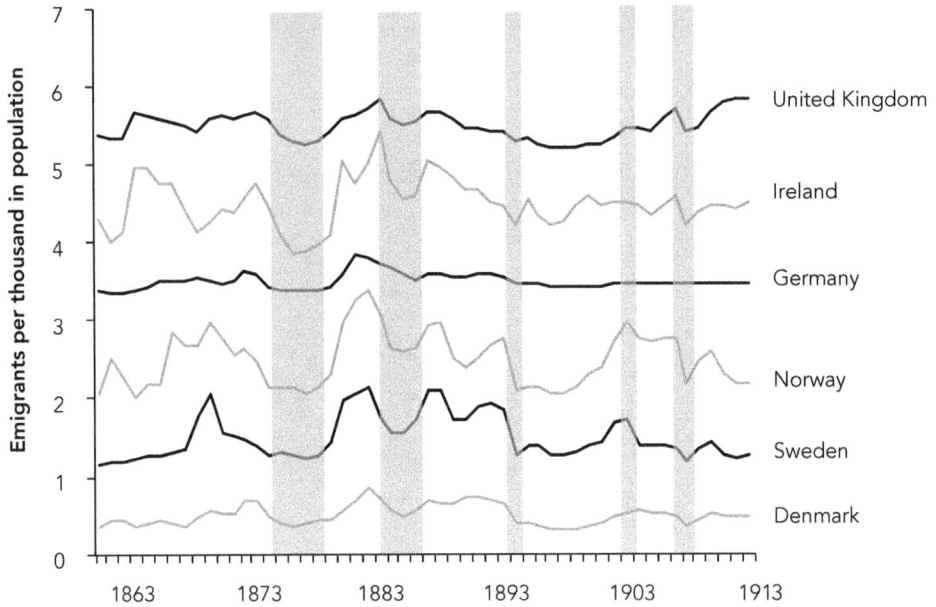

Source: Hatton and Williamson 2005, modified.

The nineteenth century ended with a gradual rise in barriers to immigration into the United States. Hatton and Williamson (2005) explore several explanations for this and find that it is primarily a long-run phenomenon, responding to long-run pressures rather than an immediate response to crises. The latter may impact timing a little, but the attitudes of both the public and of the factor of production-based pressure groups build gradually. Thus their econometric evidence suggests that the principal explanatory variable for the tightening of restrictions is the relative wages of unskilled to skilled workers, and that save through this mechanism, the absolute numbers of migrants have little independent effect.

Taking a longer time horizon, Hatton and Williamson (2009) note that anti-immigrant feeling tends to increase during economic downturns. Here they warn that such attitudes can trigger policy backlashes, especially if the downturn follows extended periods of high immigration, and if there are large cultural and socioeconomic differences between immigrants and natives.

The Evidence of the Twentieth Century

The Great Depression: 1930s

The Great Depression in the United States provides another interesting case study of the impact of an economic downturn on immigration. Inflows to the United States had fallen significantly in the years before the Depression because of a series of restrictive immigration laws, including national quotas and outright prohibitions on immigration from some Asian countries. This caused immigration to fall from an annual average of 800,000 between 1900 and 1914 to about 400,000 per year between 1919 and 1929 (OECD 2009b). Immigration from countries such as Canada and Mexico that were unconstrained by such barriers remained high, however, rising from 13 percent of total inflows in 1921 to 45 percent of the total in 1925–28. Despite these preexisting constraints, the Depression severely curtailed immigration. Between 1923 and 1929 an average of 93 percent of national immigration quotas were filled (with many countries regularly filling their quotas). By 1933 this had fallen to 5 percent. Outflows also increased, with significant returns to Mexico—so much so that net migration was negative between 1932 and 1935 (OECD 2009b).

The 1970s to 1990s

The sharp increases in oil prices in 1973, and the economic slowdown that this triggered in many of the destination countries of the developed world, also had a significant impact on migration. Some countries saw large falls in inflows; total immigration to West Germany fell from 869,000 in 1973 to 423,000 in 1977. Immigration to Switzerland fell from 90,000 to 61,000 over the same period (Salt, Dobson, and Latham 2009). Inflows did not decline evenly across origin countries, however, with migration from more developed origin countries slowing more than migration from the less developed origin countries. Declines in immigration were due at least in part to tighter immigration policies (OECD 2009b). Recruitment from Turkey to Germany fell from 118,000 in 1973 to 6,000 in 1974, and labor immigration was suspended by Belgium and France in 1974.

Outflows from Europe rose slightly over this period, but then fell back again. In West Germany they rose from 527,000 in 1973 to 600,000 in 1975, but back down to 452,000 in 1977. Outflows from Sweden for the same years were 32,000, 21,000, and 15,000, respectively (Salt, Dobson, and Latham 2009), despite large increases in unemployment among non-European migrants in many European countries, as the recession hit the construction and manufacturing sectors that employed large numbers of migrant laborers. Again, returns were more likely among migrants from higher income countries.

In general, therefore, inflows often fell sharply over the period, but typically remained positive. This, combined with limited increases in returns, meant that stocks of migrants in Western Europe did not fall significantly. Indeed, by 1980, stocks were higher in many countries (including France and Germany) than they had been in 1973. Although aggregate numbers recovered, however, the recession did trigger significant structural changes in migratory flows. The guestworker programs were effectively ended through a combination of falling labor demand, negative public opinion, and resulting policy change. Many migrants settled rather than return home, however, and migration for family reunification increased as families settled in many

European countries. In the Gulf countries meanwhile, economic growth triggered the rise in migration to the region from South Asia that continues to this day: Immigration boomed after the early 1970s, with the foreign population in Saudi Arabia increasing fivefold between 1974 and 1990 (Lucas 2005) as inflows from South Asia grew.

Analysis of migration to the United Kingdom during the recessions of 1974–77, 1980–84, and 1991–93 shows a similar pattern of aggregate flows. Inflows slowed temporarily, but there is no evidence of a significant increase in outflows (Salt, Dobson, and Latham 2009). Work by the OECD (2000) found a close correlation between net immigration and economic cycles since the 1960s for a number of OECD countries. There were only a few cases, however, when net migration actually became negative during a downturn. The OECD also found that not only does the relationship vary by country, but also that in some countries it has weakened with time. They attribute this to tightened labor immigration regimes—family and humanitarian flows are much less sensitive to the business cycle than labor migrants.

The Asian Crisis of 1997–2008

In most cases the 1997 Asian crisis had a relatively modest impact on regional migration. As table 3.1 shows, although the number of migrants dipped in some countries, in others it increased throughout the crisis. This was despite attempts by numerous countries to tighten their migration regimes to protect the jobs of domestic workers. In some cases, such as the rice and fisheries sectors in Malaysia and Thailand, employers lobbied against these restrictions because of their reliance on migrant labor and the reluctance of natives to do some of the tasks that they performed (Skeldon 2004).

One exception to the muted response was Malaysia. Table 3.1 shows a large increase and then a decrease in its number of migrants. This probably reflected a boom in 1997 followed by strong efforts to curb numbers, all superimposed on a rising trend of reported migration due to policy efforts to improve data collection.

Hypotheses for the Twenty-first Century

Based on this history and our understanding of the drivers of migration, we can construct a number of hypotheses about what we might expect to see in the current global downturn.

1. Inflows of migrants tend to fall when destination countries go through recessions. Although the expected income differentials that drive most economic migration are clearly affected by conditions in both origin and destination countries, historical evidence suggests that destination country conditions are more influential during downturns.

TABLE 3.1 Official Estimates of the Total Number of Foreign Workers in Asian Economies, 1996–2000

Economy	1996	1997	1998	1999	2000
China[a]	80,000	82,000	83,000	85,000	—
Hong Kong SAR, China[b]	164,300	171,000	180,600	193,700	216,790
Indonesia[a]	24,868	24,359	21,207	14,863	16,836
Japan[c]	610,000	630,000	660,000	670,000	710,000
Korea, Rep.[c]	210,494	245,399	157,689	217,384	285,506
Malaysia[c]	745,239	1,471,645	1,127,652	818,677	799,685
Philippines[a]	4,333	6,055	5,335	5,956	—
Singapore	—	—	—	530,000	612,233
Taiwan, China	—	245,697	255,606	278,000	326,515
Thailand[c]	1,033,863	1,125,780	1,103,546	1,089,656	1,102,612

Source: Skeldon 2004. Original data from "Country Papers Presented at the Workshop on International Migration and Labour Market in Asia," Tokyo, OECD and Japan Institute of Labour, February 4–5, 2002, as submitted by the respective country governments.

Note: — = not available.

a. Estimate of foreign experts only, primarily professionals, the highly skilled, and teachers.

b. Indicates an estimate of foreign domestic workers only, not highly skilled workers.

c. Includes estimate of undocumented workers.

2. Returns may increase somewhat, but these increases tend to be significantly smaller than changes in inflows.

3. Although migration trends are largely driven by long-term determinants, crises could perhaps have longer-term effects if they trigger changes in government policies, structural economic change, or short-run migrations that become long term because of network effects.

4. Some of the commentaries on the impact of the current crisis suggest that migrants are likely to be affected more severely by the recession than native workers, given the kind of work they do, and the risk of discrimination.

5. Economic crises can trigger tighter immigration policies in destination countries, although this is more likely if public pressure for such changes had previously built up.

We need to ask whether past experience is enough to go on. By and large, we would say yes. For example, figure 3.8 plots the fluctuations in GDP growth among likely migration source countries now (1980–2013) alongside those of Britain for the nineteenth century. Average growth is higher, but the current shock is pretty similar to several nineteenth-century ones.

The hypotheses focus on destination countries, and a brief consideration of the relative sizes of incomes across rich and poor countries shows why. An implication of the growth patterns shown in figure 3.1 is that the income differential between rich and

FIGURE 3.8 GDP Growth, Then and Now

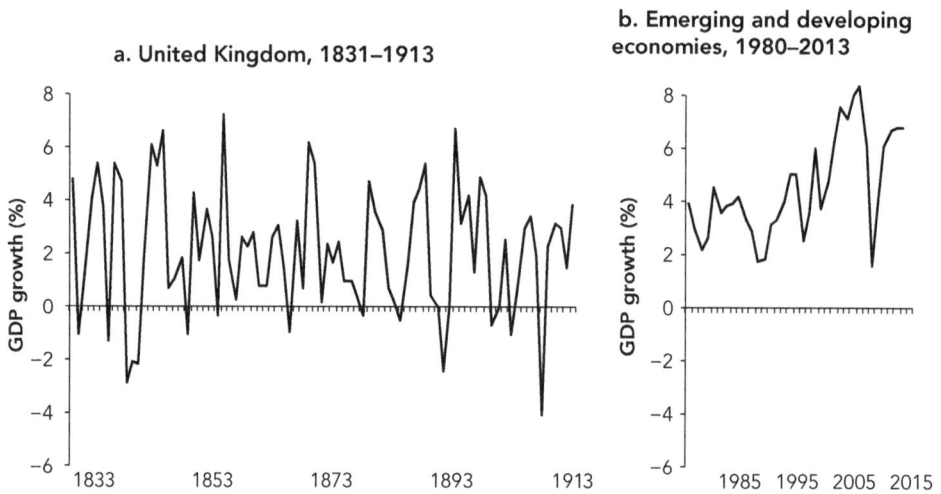

Sources: Maddison 2003 and IMF World Economic Outlook Database.

poor countries—the driver of migration in the simplest of economic models—will be lower over the next five years than the last five. As noted above, advanced and developing economies will suffer approximately the same decline in their incomes relative to expected, so the ratio of their GDPs per head is roughly unchanged. But the same proportionate decline (about 9–10 percent) also applies to the absolute difference between them, and it is generally held that migration responds more strongly to the absolute than to the relative difference. (After all, the costs of migration are absolute: transportation, the psychological costs from being away from home, the costs of re-equipping and learning how to live in a new society, and so on.)

If we apply the real GDP growth rates projected above to the absolute differences in gross national income per head between advanced and developing countries measured in purchasing power parity terms for 2000, the difference peaks in 2007 at about $29,400 and falls to about $27,200 in 2010 before gradually increasing again. The "loss" of differential over the crisis is sufficiently small relative to the absolute gain from migrating that it seems unlikely to make much difference to the incentives to migrate per se.

On the other hand, Martin (2009a) has suggested various reasons why the effects of this recession may be different from that of previous recessions. This recession has hit much of the world (at least high- and middle-income countries) broadly simultaneously, unlike, say, the Asian Crisis. There is an increased understanding of the value of remittances, so origin countries may make stronger efforts to ensure that emigrant populations stay abroad, and the flows of remittances continue. Migration to some countries such as the United States is increasingly based on family reunification, which we might expect to be less sensitive to short-term economic downturns.

Even without these reservations, the degree of confirmation or refutation that we should expect from this exercise is limited. Although the hypotheses are necessarily general, impacts tend to be highly country specific given the range of factors that can affect flows. Thus a good deal of heterogeneity must be expected. The severity of the recession is also likely to be important in determining the magnitude and possibly nature of the impacts, and this is not yet entirely clear. Moreover, the data on migration are poor and slow to emerge. With all these caveats in mind, let us proceed to the evidence about the twenty-first century economic crisis, some of which now is starting to appear.

Inflows of Migrants

We would expect there to be a lag between an economic slowdown and falling immigration, not least because of the delays involved in processing immigration applications. The U.S. Employment-Based Permanent Migration program, for example, has lags of four to eight years (OECD 2009b). Also, countries with quota systems may not see declines in inflows at all if those quotas (such as the H1-B program in the United States) were previously oversubscribed.

Despite this, however, there is evidence that inflows to at least some of the main destination countries are already beginning to slow. Data from the American Community Survey show that net immigration to the United States has slowed, from an annual average of about 1 million between 2000 and 2006 to about 500,000 between 2006 and 2007. Mexican data (from INEGI) support this. International emigration from Mexico fell from 1 million between February 2006 and February 2007 to just over 800,000 for the same period one year later, and from 369,000 in the second quarter of 2006 to 144,000 in the second quarter of 2009 (MPI 2010). The United Kingdom has also seen significant falls in inward migration. Registrations to the Workers Registration Scheme (by migrants to the United Kingdom from the "Accession 8" countries of Eastern Europe) fell by 54 percent between the first quarter of 2008 and the same period a year later, from 46,000 to 21,300, although registrations appear to have stabilized since then. Ireland saw a 57 percent decline in immigration from these "A8" states over the same period (IPPR 2009a). In Spain new entries to their employer-nominated immigration system fell from more than 200,000 in 2007 to 137,000 in 2008. Applications for temporary skilled migration to Australia were 11 percent lower in February 2009 than in the same period the year before.

Although it is possible that some of this slowdown is due to tighter immigration policies, at least some of it is not, such as the A8 migration to the United Kingdom, which is essentially unconstrained by official barriers. Similarly, applications for H-1B visas for the United States have slowed. In 2007 and 2008 all of the 65,000 quota for such visas had been oversubscribed within days of applications being accepted at the start of April. In 2009 only 45,000 applications had been received by August.

There is some evidence that irregular migration flows may also have slowed. Interceptions along the United States–Mexico border fell from more than 1 million in 2006 to 860,000 in 2007 and 700,000 in 2008 (OECD 2009b). These figures should clearly be treated with caution, however. Illegal border crossing is only one form of irregular migration, and varying levels of interdiction will be affected by a range of factors besides changing flows.

In the United States meanwhile, remittances sent home by Mexicans during the first half of 2009 fell by 11 percent compared with the same period the year before. Again, this could easily be because of declining remittances per migrant rather than declining migrant numbers, so it does not offer much independent evidence.

Equally, outflows from some countries do not seem to have been significantly affected by the downturn. Again this may be linked to the sectors in which migrants are working. The number of Indonesian care workers working abroad rose slightly in the first quarter of 2009. Government statistics from the Philippines show no slowing in labor exports by spring 2009, and the Overseas Employment Administration reports that in 2008, 200,000 Filipino workers were recruited to the Gulf, only 4.9 percent less than in 2006 (IPPR 2009b). Questions have been raised about the data here, however, with reports that Filipino labor agencies have been reporting a 30 percent drop in labor exports (BMZ 2009).

Returns

Evidence on returns is more difficult to come by than evidence on inflows, as governments tend to be less concerned with counting people on their way out of the country than they are with counting those on their way in. What information we do have seems to support the idea that there have not been large returns from most destination countries. There seems to be little evidence of large-scale return migration from the United States to Latin America. Suggested explanations for this include the poor employment situation in origin countries and the increasing difficulty of reentering the United States once migrants have left (Ratha and Mohapatra 2009). Even when destination governments have tried positively to encourage return, this has not always been successful. In late 2008 the government of Spain introduced a program offering significant cash inducements if unemployed immigrants agreed to return home and not come back to Spain for three years. The Spanish government offered 80,000 places through this scheme, but by August 2009 only 6,600 immigrants had applied.

Exceptions may be found to this general rule of limited returns. There is anecdotal evidence of significant returns from Russia to some Central Asian countries such as Tajikistan and Uzbekistan, though reliable data for this do not seem to be available, and there have been widespread reports of returns of Poles from the United Kingdom (IPPR 2009b). Suggested explanations for this apparent exception have included the falling value of the pound against the zloty, the low cost of transport, the relative strength of the Polish economy, and the lack of barriers preventing Poles from returning to the

United Kingdom in the future if they wished. Again, though, no hard data are at hand on these returns, so it is difficult to be sure.

Having said this, an expectation appears to exist among numerous origin country governments that there either are, or will be, significant numbers of returnees. Various governments have instituted schemes to assist those who may return home. Uzbekistan has set up "crisis centers" to help returnees or those who have fallen victim to traffickers, and Nepal has established a welfare fund to provide returnees with compensation if their contracts were prematurely terminated and retraining programs for returnees (BMZ 2009). In October 2008 Malaysia's Human Resources Ministry announced that it was prepared to provide repatriation assistance for all Malaysian workers in Singapore who lost their jobs there (MPI 2008), and the Keralan government in India has announced a scheme for providing low-cost loans to migrants returning from the Gulf. The Philippine government has introduced a range of measures to assist returnees, including help in finding new jobs. Between December 2008 and April 2009 this scheme helped 6,500 returning migrants.

Long-Term Structural Effects

It is difficult to draw conclusions at this point about possible long-term changes. There have been reports of large-scale movements of internal migrants in China (and other Southeast Asian countries such as Indonesia) because of declining employment in export-oriented industries, but data are limited, and this could simply be a temporary effect. Until more time has elapsed for changes to have occurred and data to emerge, it is difficult to say anything more, except to note that if changes to immigration policies of destination countries triggered by the crisis become permanent, then this could be a potential source of long-term change.

Impacts on Migrants Relative to Native Workers

There has been considerable concern among those writing about the likely impact of the downturn on migration that migrants are likely to be hit harder by the recession than native workers. Immigrants (especially irregular migrants) often have less secure job contracts, they are more likely to be temporary or part time, they are overrepresented in less-skilled occupations, and immigrant-owned businesses are more likely to go bankrupt. (Gibb 2009; IOM 2009; OECD 2009a, b). They may also face discrimination. A study from Sweden (Arai and Vilhelmsson 2004) found that after controlling for other factors such as education, non-European immigrants faced unemployment risk twice as high as that faced by natives during the economic crisis of the early 1990s.

Evidence that migrants have been more negatively affected by the recession than natives is beginning to emerge. There have been anecdotal reports of migrants being moved from permanent contracts to ad hoc piece work in Thailand (IPPR 2009b), and there have been big increases in numbers of part-time workers in the United States, especially in the retail, food, and construction sectors, which account for 30 percent of immigrant employment (OECD 2009b). As noted above, there are also countries such as Norway and Spain where unemployment has gone up significantly faster among migrants (or at least some groups of migrants) than the population as a whole.

At least some of these differences may simply be due to migrants being concentrated in hard-hit sectors such as construction; this seems to be the case in the Norwegian and Spanish examples mentioned above. Analysis by the OECD suggests that this is not always the case, however (OECD 2009b). They find that, after allowing for the different sectoral distribution of migrants and natives in the United States, if migrants had become unemployed at the same rate as natives, then migrant employment would have fallen by 1.7 percent in the year to November 2008, whereas in fact it fell by 3.6 percent. Although there may be other reasons for this besides discrimination (such as experience and language skills), this suggests that, for the United States at least, differences cannot be fully explained by sectoral distribution. Another study from the United States (Orrenius and Zavodny 2009) suggests that lower education levels among migrants may also be partly responsible for immigrants in the United States being more sensitive to the current downturn than natives.

Evidence from OECD unemployment rates points in the same direction. Figure 3.9 reports the changes in the rate of unemployment between the third quarter of 2008 (before any crisis effects occurred) and the third quarter of 2009 (the latest available) for native- and foreign-born workers. With one minor exception (Norway) all the points lie above the 45 degree line, indicating that the increase for foreign workers exceeds that for native workers. In three cases the difference is very large: Spain (4 percentage points difference, with increases of 5.8 and 9.8 percentage points, respectively, in native- and foreign-born unemployment), Greece (difference is 2.8, 1.8 versus 4.6 points), and Ireland (difference is 2.6, 5.5 versus 8.1 points).

Tightened Immigration Policies

Given the depth of the downturn, the rising levels of migration to the OECD countries over the last 30 years, and the preexisting balance of public opinion in favor of tighter restrictions on immigration (Hatton and Williamson 2009), we would expected many destination countries to tighten immigration policies.

There is indeed considerable evidence to suggest that this is happening in some countries. Russia announced in December 2008 that it would reduce work permits for 2009 by half from 4 million to 2 million (Ratha, Mohapatra, and Silwal 2009b). The United Kingdom has tightened its Points-Based System, increasing skill and wage thresholds. In September 2009 it increased the period for which jobs must be advertised nationally before being opened to non–European Union residents, it raised the minimum salary for a job to be classed as skilled by 17.5 percent, and it required employees to

FIGURE 3.9 Change in Unemployment Rates for Native- and Foreign-Born Workers, Selected OECD Countries, Third Quarter 2008 to Third Quarter 2009

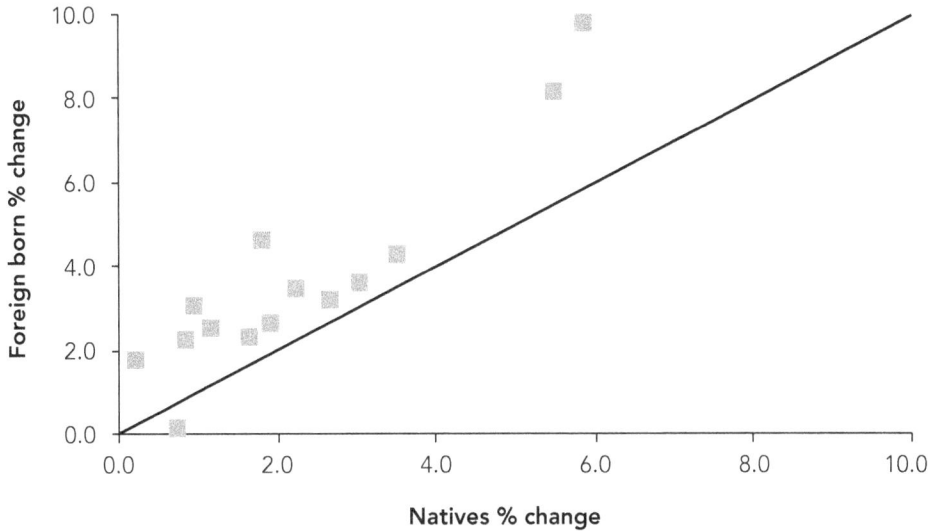

Source: OECD 2010.

have longer tenure in multinational companies before they could be transferred into the United Kingdom as key workers. The U.S. fiscal stimulus package makes it more difficult for beneficiary firms to hire high-skilled foreign workers, although this may make little practical difference given how oversubscribed quotas for such visas are. Australia cut its skilled permanent migrants quota for 2009 by 14 percent against the target initially announced. Italy announced that it will cut its quota for nonseasonal workers from 150,000 in 2008 to zero for 2009 and has made it illegal to provide housing to illegal immigrants. Spain cut its quota for nonseasonal *contingente* workers from 15,000 in 2008 to 900 in 2009 (OECD 2009a).

Policies have not only been tightened in developed countries. Malaysia has canceled work visas for 55,000 Bangladeshi workers and told employers to lay off foreigners before native workers; the Malaysian government has been discussing ways to reduce the number of migrant workers for some time (Martin 2009a). In February 2009 the Republic of Korea announced that it would stop admitting migrants through its Employment Permit System. Thailand, which has an estimated 2 million migrant workers (mostly in construction, agriculture, and fisheries), announced in January 2009 that it would not reregister migrants in 2009, in the hope that they would leave when their permits expired. In Kazakhstan, the authorities imposed a moratorium on the admission of less-skilled workers from April 2009 (IOM 2009).

Although these examples are worrying, they are not universal. Other destination countries such as Canada and some European countries have broadly maintained their immigration stances, despite some tightening at the margins. Indeed, in January 2009 Japan announced programs to offer retraining and Japanese lessons to unemployed Nikkeijin (descendants of Japanese who emigrated to Latin America a century ago, who have since migrated to Japan).

Summary

Broadly speaking, the emerging evidence is in line with what we would expect given the experience of past crises. We see evidence of some slowing of inflows to the major destination countries. Little evidence is at hand of significant returns, except possibly in a few specific cases. There are numerous examples of countries announcing tightened immigration regimes, although this is not true in all cases, and it remains to be seen what the real impact will be. In addition the evidence seems to suggest that migrants are being affected more adversely than equivalent natives.

One theme that runs through much of this study is the impact of government immigration policies. This was much less of a factor in the nineteenth century but does appear to have affected the impact of twentieth-century crises on migration and may do so again this time around. Their structure and operation can affect how much and how quickly inflows respond to changing circumstances, and how likely migrants are to leave. Changes in such policies therefore also affect flows in the short term, and potentially in the longer term if changes become permanent. How governments act over the coming months can therefore be expected to have a significant impact on how this recession affects migration and its associated impact on development.

Notes

1. The various papers and World Economic Outlooks produced by the IMF offer a good overview.
2. O'Rourke argues that in the late 1840s emigration was partly built on previous emigration flows, although most scholars appear to agree that the very poorest did not manage a high rate of emigration during the crisis, which suggests that the friends and family effect had not overcome all the frictions by then.
3. We could have continued the figure to 1913, often taken as the natural break point for nineteenth-century study, but it would have been dominated by a huge upward shift in trend from 1901 onward.

Chapter 4

Remittance Flow, Working Capital Formation, and Economic Growth

GABRIELA MUNDACA

ACCORDING TO RATHA AND COLLEAGUES (2010a), official recorded remittance flows to developing countries reached $307 billion in 2009, down 5.5 percent from $325 billion in 2008. They estimate, however, that remittance flows to developing countries have increased 6 percent in 2010, and they predict that the years 2011 and 2012 will see an increase in those flows by 6.2 and 8.1 percent, respectively. On this basis, it may seem that remittances have not been seriously affected by the global crisis of 2007–08. This is certainly encouraging. However, in addition to the level of remittance flows, it is crucial to analyze how long-run investment decisions made by remittance recipients are affected by their uncertainty about future remittances. This is important because it is well known that developing countries face limited access to credit markets, and prospective small entrepreneurs are more likely to depend not only on current remittances but also on expected future remittances.

In this chapter, I present a theoretical model that aims to explain how uncertainty about future flows of remittances can affect investment decisions and consequently economic growth in the recipient's country. I attempt to show the interlinkages between remittances, economic growth, and the role that financial intermediaries play in the allocation of resources across generations and across time. I thus consider both inter-temporal and cross-sectional risk allocation among recipients of remittances. I also examine how uncertainty about future remittances can create financial distress, especially when recipients of remittances need to withdraw prematurely their initially saved remittances to cope with unexpected adverse income shocks. This could become even more crucial if the financial sector cannot provide greater access to credit markets to long-term investors and entrepreneurs to alleviate them from temporary shocks to their future flows of remittances. Such a state of affairs will necessarily affect long-term capital accumulation and economic growth.

This study extends earlier work (Mundaca 2009) that presents a theoretical model to show how remittances and financial intermediaries can contribute to the growth process. Financial intermediaries (such as banks) effectively channel remittances that are saved by their recipients into sectors in the economy that are potentially productive. The analysis here focuses on how intermediaries can promote capital investment when remittances are invested in productive long-run technologies, as well as how uncertainty about future remittances can erode potential productive investment and then economic growth, and even jeopardize the stability of the financial sector in the country of recipients of remittances. I believe this approach is novel because such problems have never been studied within a context of a theoretical model.

From the literature on financial intermediation we know that one main role of financial intermediaries is to provide liquidity insurance to depositors (Diamond and Dybvig 1983) and to transform deposits by making them available for lending to agents with investment needs. In our setup, deposits will come from both labor income and remittances. This (1) allows risk-averse savers to hold bank deposits rather than liquid and unproductive assets and (2) eliminates (or reduces) certain agents' need for self-financing of investments. Without intermediation, each individual must self-insure against unpredictable liquidity needs, and for this reason he or she will invest (most likely excessively) in liquid and unproductive assets. Also, when agents self-finance their investment projects, they will always face the risk of having to prematurely liquidate their projects if an adverse liquidity shock occurs, to fulfill their liquidity needs. The larger the number of self-financed projects, the more detrimental such premature liquidation would be to the economy. This problem can be avoided with intermediaries.

With intermediation, banks set aside a proportion of the deposits as reserves to meet possible early withdrawals of deposits and use the rest of the available resources for investment in productive capital. This model contains, however, another and less favorable equilibrium in which bank runs can occur because depositors are uncertain not only about the ability of the intermediary to provide the necessary liquidity in a timely manner but also about the future flow of remittances. Expectations of bad economic fundamentals in the country of residence of the migrant that make him or her unable to send remittances can precipitate a bank run because of liquidity constraints that are not alleviated by remittances. I investigate how such financial crises and distress might cause a fall in economic growth.

The theoretical model proposed here indicates that the poorer the country receiving remittances, and the larger the credit constraints that the recipient of remittances faces during his or her life cycle, the more important remittances become for generating productive working capital and economic growth in this country. Importantly, I also establish the conditions under which excess remittances relative to working capital of the remittance recipient can also result in a resource curse in the receiving country. An important lesson to be stressed is that remittances will spur growth if and only if remittances are invested in productive assets.

Review of the Related Literature

Many theoretical papers emphasize the importance of financial intermediation in an economy and as a determinant of its growth rate (Bencivenga and Smith 1991; Bencivenga, Smith, and Starr 1995; Cameron 1967; Goldsmith 1969; Greenwood and Jovanovic 1989; Hicks 1969; McKinnon 1973; Shaw 1973).

A large array of studies, both theoretical and empirical, have considered effects of remittances on the economy. A large part of the theoretical work has focused on the motives for remittances in conjunction with migration. Remittances are now well recognized as part of an informal familiar arrangement that goes well beyond altruism, driven by a variety of motives that may even vary across individuals, with benefits in the realms of mutual insurance, consumption smoothing, and alleviation of liquidity constraints (Andreoni 1989; Cox, Eser, and Jimenez 1998; Rapoport and Docquier 2000; Feinerman and Seiler 2002; Foster and Rosenzweig 2001; Funkhouser 1995; Lucas and Stark 1985; Stark 1991b).

At the macrolevel, the short-run effects of remittances have been analyzed mainly within the framework of trade-theoretical models by considering a small open economy that produces traded and nontraded goods (examples are given in Djajić 1986 and McCormick and Wahba 2000). These studies find that remittances increase the welfare of the remaining residents and not only those receiving the remittances, because all the remaining residents will have new trading opportunities and higher buying power, especially if there is a cost-of-living difference between the country that receives remittances and the country that hosts the migrants sending remittances.

Despite the different considerations and the number of studies generated, consensus is still lacking about the general or typical effect of remittances. Moreover, few theoretical studies analyze how economic downturns in the country of the migrants that send remittances affect economic growth and even cause financial distress in the country of individuals receiving remittances. We find this very important, especially if the country is poor and individuals face credit constraints.

How Can Remittances Contribute to Capital Formation and Economic Growth?

Remittances can promote capital investment and raise rates of growth in the presence of financial intermediaries. The analysis here draws heavily on the contributions of the "endogenous growth" literature of Aghion and others (2005); Bencivenga and Smith (1991); Bencivenga, Smith, and Starr (1995); Lucas (1988); Prescott and Boyd (1987); and Romer (1986) and on the intermediation literature of Diamond and Dybvig (1983) and Mundaca (2009).

Assume that agents have resources derived from labor income and remittances that can potentially be deposited in the banking system. We have in this economy intermediaries (banks) that accept these deposits and transform them into lending resources for many agents with investment needs and hold liquid reserves against predictable withdrawal demand (that is, the law of large numbers operates to make withdrawal demand fairly predictable). Here, as in Diamond and Dybvig (1983), banks are expected to be ready to provide the demanded liquidity, unless expectations shift or economic fundamentals change drastically.

A three-period-lived overlapping-generations model is considered where all agents (including banks) have access to a "liquid" investment that is not directly productive and an "illiquid" investment that yields physical productive capital. Production takes place with the use of working capital owned by the old generation and labor provided by the young generation.

We make the following assumptions:

- The economy consists of a sequence of three-period-lived, overlapping generations. Each generation contains a continuum of agents.

- Time is indexed by $t = 0, 1, 2,...$

- At $t = 0$ there is an initial old generation, endowed with an initial per firm working capital of k_0, and an initial "middle-aged" generation, which is endowed with per firm consumption-good units at $t = 1$. At each t, there is an equal number of young and old agents.

- All young generations are identical. Each young agent is endowed with a single unit of labor supplied inelastically. There are no labor endowments at ages 2 and 3.

- Two goods are found in the economy: a single consumption good and a working capital good. The consumption good is produced using labor and working capital. This working capital comprehends both physical and human capital, and it is owned by the subset of old agents who become entrepreneurs. There are no rental markets for capital.

- When agents are young they receive a certain amount of remittances, rem_t, that need to be invested in their totality in the long-term productive assets. When individuals are middle aged and they decide to become entrepreneurs, they will receive additional remittances, rem_{t+1}. These additional remittances can be deposited in the bank to obtain after one year a rate of return equal to $r>1$, but only if individuals invest in their own human capital at certain costs. In view of these possibilities, middle-aged individuals who have decided to be entrepreneurs could either invest in human capital or use these remittances to alleviate liquidity needs that they might have before or after they decide to be entrepreneurs.[1] By acquiring additional human capital, entrepreneurs will be able to increase their working capital. The costs of investing in human capital need to be paid only when individuals become entrepreneurs (they become old). The return of investing in human capital is assumed to be

$\rho > 1$. Consequently, entrepreneurs will find it worthwhile to acquire human capital if $1 < r \leq \rho$. Such a condition means only that the bank should provide the entrepreneurs with enough resources to pay back their investment costs in human capital by the time they are entrepreneurs. If the remittances are used to alleviate liquidity needs instead of investing in human capital, then $\rho = r = 1$.

- Allocating one unit of the consumption good in the "liquid investment" at t gives one unit of the consumption good at $t+1$ (this technology can be thought of as a storage technology). On the other side, allocating one unit of the consumption good in the "illiquid and long-run investment" (this technology can be thought of as a capital investment) at t gives a return of R units of the physical capital good at $t+2$. If this physical capital investment is liquidated at $t+1$, its "scrap value" is zero units of the consumption good.

- Because remittances are allocated only in the "illiquid" investment, if young agents decide to withdraw their deposits prematurely when facing liquidity needs at $t+1$, they can withdraw *only* the labor income initially saved and its corresponding returns. The purpose of such conditionality is to avoid moral hazard problems. In such a case they will neither own capital nor become entrepreneurs at age 3 (when they are old). As in Mundaca (2009), if remittances are allowed to be invested in the liquid asset to meet early withdrawals, their effect on growth will be much more limited.

- k_t denotes the working capital held by an individual entrepreneur at t and $\bar{k}_t$ the "average" working capital per entrepreneur at t. An entrepreneur who employs L_t units of labor at t produces the consumption good according to the following production function:

$$y_t = \bar{k}_t^{d} k_t^{q} L_t^{1-q}, \tag{4.1}$$

where $\theta \in (0,1)$ and $\delta = 1-\theta$, where δ is just notational difference to emphasize the external effect of $\bar{k}_t$. We assume that capital depreciates completely in one period.

- Defining c_i as age i consumption, the utility function of all young agents will be

$$u(c_1, c_2, c_3; \phi) = -\frac{(c_2 + \phi c_3)^{-\gamma}}{\gamma}, \tag{4.2}$$

where $\gamma > -1$ and ϕ is an individual-specific random variable that is realized at the beginning of age 2 and determines a saver's liquidity needs according to the following probability distribution:

$$\phi = \begin{cases} 0 \text{ with probability } 1-\pi \\ 1 \text{ with probability } \pi \end{cases} \tag{4.3}$$

Equations (4.2) and (4.3) indicate that young agents will save all their young period incomes (wages and remittances) because they do not care to consume when they are young, at age 1. Only a fraction π of the individuals will care about age-3 consumption ($\phi = 1$) and will become entrepreneurs also at age 3. This is possible because by not withdrawing prematurely they will be able to receive, at age 3, the returns on their investment capital funded by both their labor incomes and remittances.

Entrepreneurs' Decisions

Assuming the production function (1) and taking as given the real wage rate, the demand for labor that maximizes the representative entrepreneur's profits will be

$$L_t = k_t \left[\frac{(1-\theta)\overline{k}_t^{\delta}}{w_t} \right]^{1/\theta}. \tag{4.4}$$

If we note that the condition for labor market equilibrium is one in which $L_t = 1/\pi$, after averaging equation (4.4) over firms and equating the result to $1/\pi$, we find that the equilibrium real wage at t is

$$w_t = \overline{k}_t (1-\theta)\pi^{\theta}. \tag{4.5}$$

Given that the marginal value of the working capital is $\theta \overline{k}_t k\, \theta - 1 L\, 1 - \theta$, the level of profits Φ per entrepreneur will be

$$\Phi_t = \theta \overline{k}_t^{\delta} k_t^{\theta} L_t^{1-\theta}. \tag{4.6}$$

By using equations (4.4), (4.5), and (4.6), we can find the reduced form for profits per entrepreneur at t:

$$\Phi_t = \theta \psi k_t, \tag{4.7}$$

The Financial Intermediaries' Decisions

Intermediaries receive deposits from young savers, and although all remittances received at $t = 0$ are invested in the illiquid asset, for each unit of deposit coming from labor income, banks invest a proportion $s_t \in [0,1]$ units of it in the liquid investment and a proportion $n_t \in [0,1]$ units of it in the illiquid investment (capital investment). Thus, each saved unit of labor income is allocated as follows:

$$s_t + n_t = 1. \tag{4.8}$$

If individuals withdraw their deposits made from labor income at $t+1$, they receive r_{1t} units of the consumption good for each unit deposited in the intermediary at t. Withdrawing the deposits made from labor income and remittances *after two periods* will return r_{2t} units of the capital good for each unit deposited again at t. The following constraints should then be satisfied:

$$(1-\pi)r_{1t}\,w_t = s_t\,w_t,\qquad(4.9)$$

$$\pi\,r_{2t}\,(w_t + rem_t) = R(n_t w_t + rem_t).\qquad(4.10)$$

Constraint (4.9) says that the amount of resources that the intermediary invests in the liquid assets, $s_t w_t$, should be enough to satisfy the total demand for liquidity from middle-aged individuals. Thus, middle-aged individuals can withdraw their savings made at their young age to satisfy liquidity needs. Such demand for liquidity should be equal to the pledged returns on the saved labor income $(1-\pi)\,r_{1t}\,w_t$ and it is measured in terms of *units of consumption goods*. Constraint (4.10) indicates that the returns that the bank will obtain at $t+2$ from its investment in the illiquid asset that are equal to $R(n_t w_t + rem_t)$ should be enough to satisfy the entrepreneurs' returns on their deposits made at t that were pledged by the bank. The latter returns equal $\pi r_{2t}(w_t + rem_t)$ and are measured in terms of capital goods.

The problem of the representative intermediary is to maximize the expected utility of the representative young depositor at time t, while anticipating that these young depositors will save their labor income, w_t, plus remittances, rem_t, and that the latter will be allocated only in the illiquid investment. The additional remittances received by middle-aged prospective entrepreneurs are also expected to be deposited. I do not model here the senders of the remittances, but I simply assume that they will get back from the banks their remittances plus returns in the event that the corresponding receiver of such remittances at home does not become an entrepreneur.

Taking into account the law of large numbers, the representative bank will maximize the following expected utility of the representative depositor, evaluated at t:

$$EU = -\left(\frac{1-\pi}{\gamma}\right)\left[r_{1t}w_t\right]^{-\gamma} - \left(\frac{\pi}{\gamma}\right)\left[\theta\psi(r_{2t}\{w_t + rem_t\} + r\{rem_{t+1}\})\right]^{-\gamma}.\qquad(4.11)$$

This expression follows from the fact that at t, all young agents deposit their labor income and remittances, rem_t. At $t+1$, a fraction $1-\pi$ of these agents are expected to experience liquidity needs and withdraw their deposits prematurely, in which case they will not consume at age 3 so that $\phi = 0$. That would imply that each of these early consumers will not be able to make additional deposits because they will not be qualified to receive remittances at $t+1$, rem_{t+1} (at age 2). A fraction π are not expected to withdraw early, implying that they will consume when they become age 3 so that $\phi = 1$. Each of these late consumers will receive r_{2t} units of the physical capital good for every unit deposited when they were young (age 1), which allows them to become entre-preneurs at age 3 and realize profits equal to $\theta \psi k_{t+2}$, where $k_{t+2} = r_{2t}(w_t + rem_t) + r(rem_{t+1})$. There, $r > 1$ is again the return to the additional deposits made out of remit-tances received in the middle age. As mentioned, these remittances received at $t+1$ can be used to alleviate immediate liquidity needs that individuals may have, in which case $r = 1$. Notice, then, that remittances received in the interim can be very useful because they will allow entrepreneurs to continue with their long-term projects even when there are unexpected liquidity needs.

The bank maximizes equation (4.11) with respect to n_t at t while taking into account the constraints (3.8), (3 9), and (3.10), and that $r \leq \rho$; that is:

$$\text{Max}\{EU\} = \text{Max}\left\{ -\left(\frac{1-\pi}{\gamma}\right)\left(\frac{w_t(1-n_t)}{1-\pi}\right)^{-\gamma} \right.$$
$$\left. -\left(\frac{\pi}{\gamma}\right)\left(\theta\psi\left\{\left(\frac{R}{\pi}\right)(n_t w_t + rem_t) + \rho rem_{t+1}\right\}\right)^{-\gamma} \right\}. \tag{4.12}$$

The solution to equation (4.12) is

$$n_t = \frac{w_t - \dfrac{(1-\pi)}{\pi}\Gamma_1\Gamma_2^\gamma rem_t - (1-\pi)\Gamma_1\Gamma_2\rho rem_{t+1}}{w_t\left(1 + \dfrac{(1-\pi)}{\pi}\Gamma_1\Gamma_2^\gamma\right)}, \tag{4.13}$$

where

$$\Gamma_1 \equiv \left(\frac{1}{\theta\psi}\right)^{\gamma/1+\gamma} \tag{4.14}$$

and

$$\Gamma_2 = \left(\frac{1}{R}\right)^{\frac{1}{1+\gamma}}. \tag{4.15}$$

Taking into account equation (4.5), we rewrite equation (4.13) to define what the optimal level of long-run and illiquid investment that should be made by the bank should be:

$$n_t = \frac{\overline{k}_t(1-\theta)\pi^\theta - \dfrac{(1-\pi)}{\pi}\Gamma_1\Gamma_2^\gamma rem_t - (1-\pi)\Gamma_1\Gamma_2\rho rem_{t+1}}{\overline{k}_t(1-\theta)\pi^\theta\left(1 + \dfrac{(1-\pi)}{\pi}\Gamma_1\Gamma_2^\gamma\right)}. \tag{4.16}$$

Equation (4.16) indicates that larger amount remittances, received at both the young and middle ages (at t and $t+1$), should not necessarily lead to more investment in the long-run and illiquid assets, unless the economy is able to accumulate relatively more of the "average" working capital per entrepreneur. Note also that if the probability of becoming entrepreneurs is significantly low—for example, $(1-\pi)$ tends to zero—banks' decisions to invest in long-run assets will become independent of the level of remittances. This is reasonable because if fewer individuals become entrepreneurs, banks are not able to count on the remittances to make long-run investments because such remittances will be sent back to the migrant senders of remittances. On the other hand, an increase in R (Γ_2 is a function of R) would give more incentives to the banks to invest in the illiquid assets. Finally, investment in the risky assets will be larger the larger the remittances received are at t and $t+1$.

It is now necessary and suitable to establish the conditions that give agents the incentives to consume at age 3 or at $t+2$ ($\phi = 1$) and become entrepreneurs:

$$\frac{w_t(1_t - n_t)}{1-\pi} \le \theta\psi\left[\left(\frac{R}{\pi}\right)(n_t w_t + rem_t) + \rho rem_{t+1}\right] \qquad (4.17)$$

Agents who withdraw at $t+1$ will consume $w_t(1-n_t)/(1-\pi)$, while agents who become entrepreneurs will consume $\theta\psi\{[R/\pi][(n_t w_t + rem_t)] + \rho rem_{t+1}\}$. Thus, agents will have more incentives to become entrepreneurs if they receive more remittances not only at their young age (at age 1) that allow them to make long-run investment, but also in their middle age (age 2) that permit them to invest in human capital or alleviate unexpected liquidity needs. If such needs are not satisfied, the probabilities of experiencing a distress or crisis might increase because banks may have difficulties to liquidate at the very short run the long-run and illiquid assets.

Note that it is crucial that the return on the illiquid investment, R, is sufficiently large to avoid a bank run or financial crisis. If intermediaries invest optimally in the risky or illiquid asset (high n_t), and the returns to such investment are high (high R), the possibilities for financial crisis will decrease. This result is a standard result in the literature of financial crisis (Allen and Gale 1998; Diamond and Dybvig 1983). The contribution here is the role that remittances may play in the stability of the financial sector in two different ways. First, remittances may avoid bank runs as remittances may alleviate entrepreneurs' unexpected liquidity needs. Second, intermediaries should never increase their investments in long-run and risky assets only in response to increases in remittances to avoid the formation of bubbles. A larger investment in these assets should respond to not only increases in present and future expected remittances but also how the economy absorbs remittances and translates them into productive working capital.

In summary, equation (4.16) indicates that the allocation of savings into illiquid assets should increase with the amount of remittances received when individuals are young if the average working capital per entrepreneur increases proportionally more than remittances. Otherwise the economy might experience formation of asset bubbles and excessive consumption of final goods.

Equilibrium Conditions

In equilibrium,

$$\bar{k}_{t+2} = k_{t+2} = \left[\left(\frac{R}{\pi} \right) (n_t w_t + rem_t) + \rho rem_{t+1} \right]. \tag{4.18}$$

Equation (4.18) indicates that working capital at $t+2$ depends on the returns (R) on the long-run investments made using wages (w_t) and remittances received at time t (rem_t), the returns on the remittances received at time $t+1$ (rem_{t+1}), whether they are invested in human capital ($\rho > 1$) or simply to alleviate liquidity needs ($\rho = 1$), and the probability that individuals will become late consumers. This should be so because capital formation takes two periods.

Inserting equations (4.5) and (4.16) into equation (4.18) and dividing it b$\bar{k}_t$ yields

$$\frac{\bar{k}_{t+2}}{\bar{k}_t} = \frac{R(1-\theta)\pi^\theta}{\pi\left(1+\dfrac{(1-\pi)}{\pi}\Gamma_1\Gamma_2^\gamma\right)} + \frac{(1-\pi)\Gamma_1\Gamma_2^\gamma(R-1)+R}{\pi\left(1+\dfrac{(1-\pi)}{\pi}\Gamma_1\Gamma_2^\gamma\right)} \times \frac{rem_t}{\bar{k}_t}$$

$$+ \frac{\Gamma_1\Gamma_2\rho(1-\pi)\left(\dfrac{\Gamma_2^{\gamma-1}}{\pi}-1\right)+\rho}{\left(1+\dfrac{(1-\pi)}{\pi}\Gamma_1\Gamma_2^\gamma\right)} \times \frac{rem_{t+1}}{\bar{k}_t} \tag{4.19}$$

or

$$\frac{\bar{k}_{t+2}}{\bar{k}_t} = \alpha + \beta_1\left[\frac{rem_t}{\bar{k}_t}\right] + \beta_2\left[\frac{rem_{t+1}}{\bar{k}_t}\right], \tag{3.20}$$

where

$$\alpha = \frac{R(1-\theta)\pi^\theta}{\pi\left(1+\dfrac{(1-\pi)}{\pi}\Gamma_1\Gamma_2^\gamma\right)},$$

$$\beta_1 = \frac{(1-\pi)\Gamma_1\Gamma_2^\gamma(R-1)+R}{\pi\left(1+\dfrac{(1-\pi)}{\pi}\Gamma_1\Gamma_2^\gamma\right)},$$

and

$$\beta_2 = \frac{\Gamma_1 \Gamma_2 \rho (1 - \pi) \left(\dfrac{\Gamma_2^{\gamma-1}}{\pi} - 1 \right) + \rho}{\left(1 + \dfrac{(1-\pi)}{\pi} \Gamma_1 \Gamma_2^{\gamma} \right)}.$$

Now, under our assumed production function, *output per firm* at time t at equilibrium *equals to* $\bar{k}_t^{\delta} k_t^{\theta} \psi$ or $\bar{k}_t \psi$. Because the number of firms is constant over time, *equation (4.20) also gives the equilibrium rate of growth of output.* We obtain the following results. *First,* equilibrium growth converges to α as $\bar{k}_t \rightarrow \infty$, as long as rem_t and rem_{t+2} do not increase equally much. Moreover, α increases if the return on the long-run investment, R, increases, in which case one should expect a greater fraction of savings to be invested in the accumulation of productive physical capital, and finally a higher level of average working capital and higher growth. *Second,* for a sufficiently low level of $\bar{k}_t$, this economy will experience growth if remittances, both rem_t and rem_{t+2}, are relative larger than the average "per entrepreneur" capital stock, $\bar{k}_t$. In other words, the poorer the economy (such as very low $\bar{k}_t$), the larger will be the effect of remittances on growth.

Conclusions

The purpose of this study has been to determine the mechanism under which remittances can spur growth. It demonstrates that economic growth is possible if remittances are not used for immediate consumption of final goods, but rather invested in the formation of working capital, both physical capital and human capital. It also shows how important financial markets are in generating economic growth.

An overlapping generation model in which young agents derive resources from labor income was considered. These young agents also receive a certain amount of remittances, but they are required to invest them in their totality in long-term productive assets in order to experience economic growth. The results then indicate that if remittances are not invested in these long-term assets, they will not generate growth because they will go directly to consumption of final goods. In our setup, all agents are equal ex ante, and when they are young they can deposit their labor income and remittances in the banking system. Financial intermediaries will then play a crucial role to stimulate economic growth by accepting these deposits and transform them to make them available for lending to a large number of agents with investment needs, and they will hold liquid reserves *only from wages* against predictable withdrawal demand.

When individuals are in their middle age and they decide to become entrepreneurs (and not early consumers), they will receive additional remittances that they can use to invest in human capital, which will add to the formation of working capital. Such an opportunity will allow entrepreneurs (who reach their old age) to obtain higher profits and consequently higher consumption. Alternatively, such remittances can be used to alleviate liquidity needs of only those who become entrepreneurs.

The second important result is that agents will have more incentives to become entrepreneurs if they receive more remittances both at their young age (at age 1) that allow them to make long-run investments as well as at their middle age (age 2) that permit them to invest in human capital and/or alleviate unexpected liquidity needs. If such needs are not satisfied, the probabilities of experiencing a distress or crisis might increase because banks may need to liquidate certain assets to satisfy these liquidity needs. Then it is shown that remittances can decrease the probability of having to liquidate prematurely long-term productive investments or even bank runs in the country of the recipient of remittances during a state of the world in which individuals have unexpected liquidity needs. Therefore not just the return on the illiquid investment alone matters to avoid a bank run or financial crisis, as stated in the standard literature. I illustrate here the role that remittances may play in the stability of the financial sector in the recipient country.

The final result I can infer is that the intermediaries' decisions to invest in the long run with illiquid and risky assets should respond to not only increases in present and future expected remittances but also how the economy absorbs remittances and translates them into productive working capital capacity. This can be used as a guideline by the financial sector for why they should balance their investment in the long run and illiquid assets with the capacity of the economy to grow in real terms. This is essential to avoid financial distress and the creation of bubbles.

Note

1. rem_{t+1} can then be placed in a savings fund for education, which renders $\bar{r}_t$.

PART II

Chapter 5

The Financial Crisis in the Gulf and Its Impact on South Asian Migration and Remittances

S. IRUDAYA RAJAN AND D. NARAYANA

THE EFFECT OF THE CRISIS has been slow to manifest in the six Gulf Cooperation Council (GCC) countries (Bahrain, Kuwait, Oman, Qatar, Saudi Arabia, and the United Arab Emirates). Their basic strengths—a public-funded banking sector and huge trade surplus due to exports of oil, the price of which saw an unprecedented increase in a span of six months in 2008—shielded the GCC economies from adverse impacts during the initial days of the crisis. This, coupled with significant inward foreign direct investments to all GCC countries except Kuwait, also had a beneficial impact (ESCWA 2009).

The GCC economies, however, have begun to feel the impact of the global crisis since the last quarter of 2008. The most significant indicator was the slowdown in the gross domestic product (GDP) growth rate in 2008 and the negative growth rate in 2009 in some of these economies. In the financial sector, the stock markets in all GCC countries recorded a decline, owing to the withdrawal of foreign institutional investors. A number of private-funded domestic and international projects in the Gulf region reportedly were canceled or abandoned, leading to a large number of layoffs or retrenchment of the workforce. Countries such as Saudi Arabia with only 25 percent foreign workers in its workforce compared with much higher shares in the other GCC economies might

This study is funded by the Asian Development Bank, Ministry of Overseas Indian Affairs, government of India, and the Department of Non-Resident Keralite Affairs, government of Kerala.

be much less affected than others (Zachariah and Rajan 2009). The slowdown in the growth rates of GCC economies has particular significance for the South Asian expatriates who are the main migrant labor in the GCC countries. This would, it was expected, affect the flow of migration and cause unexpected large-scale return emigration and falling remittances (Kapiszewski 2006).

In this context, we attempt to tackle the following questions: How has the crisis affected the demand for South Asian migrant workers in the Gulf countries? What strategies did the emigrants adopt to cope with the situation at their place of work (countries of destination) and what is the likely impact of the crisis on the home country in terms of decline in remittances, if any? Did countries in South Asia see large-scale return emigration? Did they find a decline in the outflow of emigrant labor to Gulf countries and inward remittances from them?

Data and Methods

Following an assessment of the trends in expatriate workers and employment structure in the GCC countries based on published data, mapping the trends and patterns of international migration, preferred countries of destination, and trends in remittances over a long period is attempted in this chapter. In addition to the macro-assessment of the situation, the study is based on two surveys: (a) return emigrants in the countries of origin who lost their jobs in the countries of destination due to the financial crisis and (b) return migrants who came back as per the terms of contract migration.

Return Migrant Survey

This survey was conducted in 2009, among emigrants who lost their jobs and were forced to return home because of the financial crisis in the Gulf.[1] It was also aimed at examining their coping mechanisms after their return to their home country. The survey included 50 return emigrants in each of four countries constituting South Asia: Bangladesh, Nepal, Pakistan, and Sri Lanka. In India, the survey was canvassed among 250 return emigrants in five states, selecting 50 each in Andhra Pradesh, Kerala, Maharashtra, Punjab, and Tamil Nadu. Thus the total number of return emigrants surveyed was 450. However, we confess that it was difficult to locate emigrants who lost their jobs in the countries of destination and returned to the countries of origin. The return emigrant survey collected information on household details, the profile of return emigrants, household economic assets, employment, remittances and their utilization, household expenditure patterns, reasons for return, and adaptation and coping mechanisms.

Second Return Migrant Survey, 2009

Return migration from the Gulf is an expected outcome of contract migration. Migrants from South Asia go on contract work to the destination countries, and once the contract ends, they, in the normal course of events, return to the countries of their origin. As of now, we have no estimate of return emigration numbers from the Gulf to South Asia. However, the Centre for Development Studies has completed four large-scale migration surveys (1998, 2003, 2007, and 2008) over the last decade. One of the research objectives of this project is to assess the flow of forced return emigration, that is, return emigrants before the expiration of their work contract from the Gulf region to South Asia. To assess both regular return migrants and the crisis-instigated return emigrants from the Gulf, we revisited emigrant households from the 15,000 contacted for the 2008 Kerala migration survey. We estimated the extent of crisis-instigated return emigrants to Kerala after the revisits. In a later section we apply the same methodology and project the figures to estimate the number of return emigrants from the Gulf to South Asia. In addition, the return migration resurvey of 2009 also estimated the number of emigrants who lost their jobs in the Gulf but had chosen to remain there without returning to their countries of origin. This is new information ("lost job but have not returned"), which will also be generated for South Asia.

Financial Crisis and Growth in the Gulf

The global crisis originating in the United States, and spreading to Europe and Japan, has affected the Middle East through a large fall in the price of oil, reversal of capital inflows, depression of property and equity markets, and losses in sovereign wealth funds.[2] The effect of the crisis varied across the countries depending on country characteristics, such as a high share of oil exports in total exports, large numbers of reexports, and a sizeable share of services in GDP, especially transportation, trade, hotels, and restaurants. In the region as a whole, growth declined from 5.1 percent in 2008 to 2.4 percent in 2009. Among the oil-producing countries, the sharpest slowdown was in the United Arab Emirates, where the exit of external funds contributed to a large contraction in liquidity, a sizeable fall in property and equity prices, and substantial pressure on the banking system. At the other end of the spectrum is Qatar, which grew by about 9 percent in 2009 (table 5.1).

Interestingly, the comparison for the countries shown in table 5.1 of the growth forecast for 2009 and the realized growth shows important patterns. For the developed countries, the contraction forecast and realized hardly shows much of a difference, but the recovery is expected to be quicker. For the South Asian countries as a whole the realized growth is much better than the forecasts, and the recovery is also rapid. The GCC countries show a mixed pattern: Both Kuwait and the United Arab Emirates witnessed contractions greater than the forecasts, whereas the other countries except

Qatar reported growth rates higher than the forecasts. The growth recovery in 2010 and 2011 is on the expected lines (table 5.1).

TABLE 5.1 Real GDP Growth Rates in Selected Countries

annual percentage change

Country	2001	2002	2003	2004	2005	2006	2007	2008	2009	2010	2011
Country of destination											
Bahrain	4.62	5.19	7.25	5.64	7.85	6.65	8.07 (8.38)	6.12 (6.31)	2.64 (3.11)	3.47 (3.96)	3.94 (4.50)
Kuwait	0.22	3.01	17.33	10.24	10.62	5.14	2.51 (4.46)	6.33 (5.53)	−1.14 (−4.82)	2.39 (2.33)	4.34 (4.44)
Oman	7.51	2.57	2.01	5.33	6.02	6.79	6.38 (6.81)	6.18 (12.84)	3.02 (3.59)	3.80 (4.72)	6.00 (4.68)
Qatar	6.32	3.20	6.32	17.72	9.24	15.03	15.35 (26.76)	16.40 (25.42)	17.99 (8.65)	16.37 (15.96)	8.90 (18.58)
Saudi Arabia	0.55	0.13	7.66	5.27	5.55	3.03	3.52 (2.02)	4.63 (4.23)	−0.91 (0.60)	2.90 (3.42)	4.40 (4.51)
United Arab Emirates	1.70	2.65	11.89	9.69	8.19	9.39	6.34 (6.06)	7.41 (5.14)	−0.60 (−2.47)	1.55 (2.43)	3.29 (3.18)
Country of origin											
Bangla-desh	4.83	4.85	5.78	6.11	6.30	6.53	6.32 (6.31)	5.59 (5.96)	5.00 (5.64)	5.38 (5.78)	6.01 (6.26)
India	3.89	4.56	6.85	7.90	9.21	9.82	9.30 (9.89)	7.29 (6.40)	4.52 (5.68)	5.61 (9.67)	6.89 (8.37)
Nepal	5.63	0.12	3.95	4.68	3.12	3.72	3.19 (3.41)	4.70 (6.10)	3.60 (4.86)	3.25 (2.98)	4.81 (4.01)
Pakistan	1.98	3.22	4.85	7.37	7.67	6.18	6.02 (5.64)	5.95 (1.64)	2.50 (3.37)	3.50 (4.79)	4.50 (2.75)
Sri Lanka	−1.55	3.96	5.94	5.45	6.24	7.67	6.80 (6.80)	5.95 (5.95)	2.20 (3.54)	3.59 (7.00)	4.98 (7.00)
More developed countries											
Japan	0.18	0.26	1.41	2.74	1.93	2.04	2.39 (2.36)	−0.64 (−1.20)	−6.19 (−5.22)	0.52 (2.82)	2.17 (1.50)
United Kingdom	2.46	2.10	2.82	2.76	2.06	2.84	3.02 (2.69)	0.71 (−0.07)	−4.09 (−4.89)	−0.40 (1.70)	2.12 (2.02)
United States	0.75	1.60	2.51	3.64	2.94	2.78	2.03 (1.95)	1.11 (0.00)	−2.75 (−2.63)	−0.05 (2.64)	3.53 (2.31)

Sources: International Monetary Fund, World Economic Outlook (WEO) Database, April 2009c; International Monetary Fund, World Economic Outlook Database, October 2010.

Note: Figures in parentheses are from WEO 2010. Data for 2009–11 and 2010–11 are forecasts in the WEO 2009 and WEO 2010, respectively.

Employment Structure in the GCC Countries

In the GCC countries, over 50 percent of the workforce is employed in manufacturing, trade, and construction. Kuwait and Saudi Arabia are the exceptions, where the share of public administration and defense is rather high (table 5.2). The share of construction in total employment increased rapidly during 2001–08 in some of the GCC countries. For instance, in the United Arab Emirates the share of construction-sector employment increased by 5 percent during the period. In Saudi Arabia, the increase in employment in the construction sector during the period was on the order of 300,000.

Construction is one of the major sectors attracting expatriate labor, and so it is important to analyze the effect of the crisis on that sector. Project finance and utilities

TABLE 5.2 Share of Employment across Economic Activities in GCC Countries, 2007

percent

Activity	Bahrain	Oman	Kuwait	Qatar	Saudi Arabia	United Arab Emirates
Agriculture, hunting, and forestry	0.47	9.09	2.60	1.92	4.69	5.00
Fishing	0.01	0.44	0.08	0.43	[a]	[a]
Mining and quarrying	0.49	1.96	1.90	5.27	1.32	1.30
Manufacturing	17.54	10.77	4.43	8.69	7.28	13.00
Electricity, gas, and water supply	0.13	0.33	0.01	0.66	0.96	1.20
Construction	29.86	34.68	14.23	37.14	10.22	20.60
Wholesale, retail trade, and car repairs	24.62	16.18	14.03	12.28	16.10	20.00
Hotels and restaurants	6.55	5.97	2.89	1.96	3.20	4.20
Transport, storage, and communication	4.20	1.30	3.85	4.33	4.42	6.20
Financial intermediaries	3.46	0.29	1.21	1.09	1.08	1.40
Real estate and renting services	7.54	1.77	5.59	3.43	3.22	3.30
Public administration and defense	0.01	—	14.75	6.35	18.03	10.80
Education	1.24	0.76	5.23	3.16	11.96	[b]
Health and social work	0.24	1.91	2.40	2.55	4.33	[b]
Community and personal services	2.11	1.08	4.18	1.54	2.26	4.50
Domestic services	0.06	9.96	21.86	8.79	10.79	8.40
Extraterritorial organizations and bodies	0.21	2.59	0.11	0.21	0.13	—
Not classified by economic activity	0.30	0.90	0.66	0.18	0.01	0.01
Total	100.00	100.00	100.00	100.00	100.00	100.00

Sources: ILO 2008, Ministry of National Economy Oman. For Saudi Arabia and the United Arab Emirates the figures are taken from the country reports.

Note: For Bahrain and the United Arab Emirates figures show the paid employment by economic activity. For Oman figures show expatriate workers in the private sector. Kuwait figures are for 2005. — = not available.

a. Fishing is included in agriculture, hunting, and forestry.

b. Education and health are included in public administration and defense.

have taken a severe beating along with financial institutions in the current crisis. A survey of projects (worth at least $10 million) in mid-2009 reported 10–30 percent cancellations or orders put on hold in the GCC countries (table 5.3). Dubai, which has about 60 percent of all construction projects in the GCC, has taken the largest hit, which in turn has affected the GCC as a whole. Interestingly, the crisis has affected all subsectors—from commercial projects to residential properties.

TABLE 5.3 Projects Affected by the Crisis in the GCC

	Number of projects under construction	Number of projects canceled/ on hold	Total project value ($, billions)[a]	% of projects canceled
Bahrain	148	54	36	27
Kuwait	90	18	114	17
Oman	95	8	38	8
Qatar	124	7	42	—
Saudi Arabia	442	106	387	19
United Arab Emirates	1,372	566	900	29

Source: Proleads, http://www.projectsandleads.com.

Note: — = not available.

a. All projects including those canceled/on hold.

Although new project starts have declined in the United Arab Emirates, high-level activity is continuing in ongoing projects that would be "the envy of many" elsewhere in the world. Evidence indicates increased construction activity in Abu Dhabi, Ajman, and Sharjah. Thus, although new starts have declined and those about to be started have been put on hold, much activity is continuing in ongoing projects.

Gulf Crisis and South Asian Labor: The Links

The link between economic growth and labor flow is through the growth in manufacturing, trade, and construction. Construction, in particular, attracts large numbers of expatriate laborers from South Asia. Any of the factors adversely affecting construction would affect the labor. The quick rebound of oil prices by mid-2009 and the not too unfavorable current account and budget balances have made the governments of the GCC countries bolder and induced them to continue major infrastructure investments. The increase in government expenditures (as a percentage of GDP) was close to 10 points in most of the countries (table 5.4), except Bahrain and Qatar. Fiscal policy has played a crucial role in cushioning the impact of the global crisis in the GCC countries.

TABLE 5.4 Government Expenditure in the GCC Countries, 2006–11

percentage of GDP

Country	2006	2007	2008	2009	2010	2011
Bahrain	28.48	28.70	28.00	31.42	30.83	29.53
Kuwait	31.83	29.94	40.15	47.36	43.22	44.28
Oman	34.44	35.33	29.42	38.73	37.38	37.02
Qatar	26.42	25.37	24.52	26.66	23.22	22.47
Saudi Arabia	31.96	34.36	30.81	44.54	42.80	40.75
United Arab Emirates	18.39	18.98	21.22	32.11	28.34	23.07

Source: World Economic Outlook Database, October 2010.

The interventions in the banking sectors have also been decisive. A further boost has been the, albeit lower but healthy, GDP growth in the whole of South Asia in 2009 and the forecast of higher growth rates in 2010. South Asia and China have emerged as the major trading partners of GCC economies, and the trade outlook does not look very dispiriting.

However, the continuing adverse factors have been the depressed real estate and equity prices in the GCC countries, in particular in Dubai. The recovery will remain fragile as long as private investment does not stimulate growth. Foreign direct investment, which had played a major role in the rapid growth of the precrisis days, fell drastically in 2009 in almost all GCC countries, except Oman, Qatar, and Saudi Arabia. The fall in the United Arab Emirates is from $13.7 billion in 2008 to $4 billion in 2009 (UNCTAD 2010). It is unlikely that the situation will improve until the Dubai World crisis is resolved.[3]

Impact of the Crisis on South Asian Migrant Workers

This section is devoted to an assessment of the impact of the crisis: on the South Asian migrant workers in terms of return emigration, flows of labor emigration from Asia to the Gulf, and inward remittances to South Asia. The assessment is based on the summary results of the emigrant household surveys and a survey of return emigrants carried out to understand the coping mechanisms of individuals and families in times of crisis.

Return Migration to South Asia from the Gulf, 2009

All agencies working on migration and remittances in the South Asian countries and the Gulf region predicted an exodus of return emigrants from the Gulf to their countries of origin following the crisis. The Centre for Development Studies, Kerala, which has undertaken four large-scale migration surveys in Kerala over the last 10 years to estimate the number of emigrants, return emigrants, and remittances, revisited the households of the 2008 survey in 2009 to arrive at reliable estimates of return emigrants.[4] All those in the original sample who had returned were asked to cite the reasons for returning to Kerala. The questionnaire provided 10 possible reasons for return, among which the following three could be attributed to the recession: job loss and return due to financial crisis, expiration of contract (renewal of contract did not take place as expected because of the recession), and compulsory expatriation. The estimates of return migrants due to the crisis are provided in table 5.5.

TABLE 5.5 Estimated Number of Migrants Returning to Kerala Due to Crisis in 2009

Migrants	Sample	Population of Kerala
Total emigrants in 2008 based on 2008 Kerala Migration Survey	3,953	2,193,412
Return emigrants among emigrants of 2008 in Return Migration Survey in 2009	304	168,681
Return emigrants to Kerala due to financial crisis and recession	110	61,036

Source: Zachariah and Rajan 2009.

If we deduce that out of the total of 2.19 million emigrants from Kerala, about 61,036 migrants returned because of the financial crisis, then what could be the number of return emigrants from the Gulf to South Asia? According to the database available from various sources (both formal and informal), we arrived at a figure of 9.5 million South Asian emigrants in the Gulf, and the projected return emigrants from the Gulf region to South Asia at about 263,660.[5] Estimates of return emigrants for each country or region are provided in table 5.6.

TABLE 5.6 Estimates of Emigrants Returning to South Asia from the Gulf Due to Crisis, 2009

Country or region	Number of emigrants	Emigrants returning due to crisis
Bangladesh	900,000	25,044
India	5,050,000	140,526
Kerala	2,193,412	61,036
Nepal	250,000	6,957
Pakistan	2,300,000	64,002
South Asia	9,475,000	263,660
Sri Lanka	975,000	27,131

Source: Estimated by the authors.

One can also estimate the number of return emigrants from the countries of destination in the Gulf to countries in South Asia. For instance, India had 1.7 million migrants settled in the United Arab Emirates, and in the projected number of return emigrants from the United Arab Emirates, there were 47,000 Indians.

Why are the figures so small when compared against predictions? We postulate two important features of Gulf migration from South Asia as potential causes: (1) the cost of migration to the Gulf and (2) the peculiarities of the channels of migration. South Asians incur huge costs to migrate to the Gulf. According to the Kerala Migration Survey 2008, the cost of migration to the Gulf varied between Rs. 53,951 to Kuwait to Rs. 74,606 to Saudi Arabia—between $1,200 and $1,660 at an exchange rate of Rs. 45 to the dollar (table 5.7). This applies to all South Asian countries (see also Rajan and Prakash 2009; United Nations 2009; Zachariah and Rajan 2009). The high cost of migration to the Gulf led many emigrants to borrow from various financial sources. Under such conditions, even if the expatriates lost their jobs in the Gulf, they would prefer not to return home, fearing inability to repay the debt already contracted there. They would rather accept any job at a lower wage and send home remittances to repay their loans even during a crisis in the destination country.

TABLE 5.7 Average Cost of Emigration for Different Migration Corridors from Kerala, 2008

Migration corridor	Average cost (Rs.)
Kerala–Bahrain	57,172
Kerala–Kuwait	53,951
Kerala–Oman	56,840
Kerala–Qatar	66,316
Kerala–Saudi Arabia	74,606
Kerala–United Arab Emirates	61,308
Kerala–United Kingdom	56,589
Kerala–United States	42,080

Source: Zachariah and Rajan 2010.

Another characteristic of South Asian migration to the Gulf is the part played by social networks, which consist of friends and relatives, who perform a major role in the channeling of migration flows by arranging visas and other requirements for the emigration process. For instance, an all-India survey conducted recently revealed that close to 80 percent of Indian emigrants utilized their friends and relatives as an important channel for migration (table 5.8; see also Rajan, Varghese, and Jayakumar 2009). This also ensured that in the event of job loss, migrants could rely on someone to provide them temporary support.

TABLE 5.8 Channels of Migration by Emigrants, 2007

Channel	Number			Percent		
	Male	Female	Total	Male	Female	Total
Friends and relatives	330	185	515	74.2	88.5	78.7
Government agency	3	0	3	0.7	0.0	0.5
Foreign employer	41	7	48	9.2	3.4	7.3
Private recruitment agencies	71	17	88	16.0	8.1	13.5
Total	445	209	654	100.0	100.0	100.0

Source: Rajan, Varghese, and Jayakumar 2009.

Migrants Who Lost Jobs in the Gulf and Have Not Returned to the Country of Origin

One category of migrants is those who "lost jobs in the Gulf and have not returned to the country of origin" and who remain unemployed in the destination country and continue to look for jobs in sectors less affected or unaffected by the crisis, at lower wages and poorer working conditions. The Return Emigrant Survey 2009 conducted in Kerala offered a unique opportunity to estimate the number of those who lost their jobs in the Gulf countries because of the crisis: According to their estimates, of the 2.2 million emigrants from Kerala, about 39,396 persons lost their jobs between 2008 and 2009 but did not return to their country of origin (Zachariah and Rajan 2009). Using the same methodology we estimate the number of South Asian migrants who lost their jobs in the Gulf to be 170,181 (table 5.9).

TABLE 5.9 Estimates of Emigrants Who Lost Job in the Gulf but Did Not Return, 2009

Country or region	Stock of emigrants	Number who lost job but did not return
Bangladesh	900,000	16,165
India	5,050,000	90,703
Kerala	2,193,412	39,396
Nepal	250,000	4,490
Pakistan	2,300,000	41,310
South Asia	9,475,000	170,181
Sri Lanka	975,000	17,512

Source: Estimated by the authors.

Outflow of Workers from South Asia to Gulf, 2009

No official data showed the extent of outflow from South Asia to the Gulf, and so we estimated the possible trends using the data available from South Asian and GCC countries. All the countries in South Asia, except Sri Lanka, have reported some decline in the flow of workers to the Gulf. The projected decline for India is the largest—about 280,000—followed by Pakistan with just 12,000 (table 5.10).

In regard to the destination, the decline was large for the United Arab Emirates, which has been more severely affected by the crisis than the other countries in the Gulf, but this was more than compensated by the increase in the number who left for Saudi Arabia. This pattern holds for India, Nepal, Pakistan, and Sri Lanka. Thus, the crisis has changed the migration and demographic dynamics of South Asian workers in the Gulf region.

TABLE 5.10 Flow of Migrant Workers from South Asia to the Gulf, 2005–09

Year	Bangladesh	India	Nepal	Pakistan	Sri Lanka
2005	207,089	454,628	88,230	127,810	192,004
2006	307,620	618,286	128,306	172,837	170,049
2007	483,757	770,510	182,870	278,631	188,365
2008	643,424	818,315	169,510	419,842	215,793
2009	—	538,090	152,272	407,077	226,299

Source: This table is based on the country papers prepared by the respective country team at the countries of origin for this project.
Note: — = not available.

Inward Remittances to South Asia in 2009

The money that migrants send home is important not only to their families, but also to their country's balance of payments. In many developing countries, remittances represent a significant proportion of GDP as well as foreign exchange receipts. In a 2009 World Bank publication (World Bank 2009a), among the South Asian countries, India was ranked number one in terms of the volume of remittances, with $52 billion in 2008 (4.2 percent of GDP). Bangladesh was ranked eighth, and Pakistan ranked 11th in terms of remittances. On the other hand, Nepal is listed as one of the top 10 countries with the highest share of remittances to GDP at 22 percent. When the crisis hit in 2008, Ratha, Mohapatra, and Xu (2008) stated, "The outlook for remittances for the rest of 2008 and 2009–10 remains as uncertain as the outlook for global growth, oil and non-oil commodity prices, and currency exchange rates." After several years of strong growth, remittance flows to developing countries began to slow significantly in the third quarter of 2008 in response to a deepening global financial crisis.

In late 2008, responding to a request from the government of Kerala, the Centre for Development Studies prepared a report: "Global Financial Crisis and Kerala Economy: Impact and Mitigation Measures" (Centre for Development Studies 2008). The report predicted that remittances to Kerala were expected to increase from Rs. 30.122 in 2007 to Rs. 42.917 in 2008. Both the World Bank and the Centre reports predicted that the inflows of remittances to South Asia and Kerala were likely to continue, when the general expectation was that it would drastically fall.

Our estimates based on a simple average of remittances for the available months from the country reports prepared by the teams suggest that all countries of South Asia are resilient to the crisis in terms of remittances (table 5.11). Our estimates put

TABLE 5.11 Inward Remittances to South Asian Countries, 2000–09

Year	Bangladesh	India	Nepal	Pakistan	Sri Lanka
Millions $					
2000	1,968	12,890	111	1,075	1,166
2001	2,105	14,273	147	1,461	1,185
2002	2,858	15,736	678	3,554	1,309
2003	3,192	20,999	771	3,964	1,438
2004	3,584	18,750	823	3,945	1,590
2005	4,314	22,125	1,212	4,280	1,991
2006	5,428	28,334	1,453	5,121	2,185
2007	6,562	37,217	1,734	5,998	2,527
2008	8,995	51,581	2,727	7,039	2,947
2009[a]	10,431	47,000	3,010	8,619	2,892
2009[b]	10,525	53,227	2,812	8,856	3,308
Percentage change					
2000–01	6.96	10.73	32.43	35.91	1.63
2001–02	35.77	10.25	361.22	143.26	10.46
2002–03	11.69	33.45	13.72	11.54	9.85
2003–04	12.28	−10.71	6.74	−0.48	10.57
2004–05	20.37	18.00	47.27	8.49	25.22
2005–06	25.82	28.06	19.88	19.65	9.74
2006–07	20.89	31.35	19.34	17.13	15.65
2007–08	37.08	38.60	57.27	17.36	16.62
2008–09[a]	15.96	−8.88	10.38	22.45	−1.87
2008–09[b]	17.01	3.19	3.12	25.81	12.25

Source: World Bank and the country reports prepared by the research team for this project from five countries of South Asia.

a. World Bank estimates.

b. Authors' estimates.

the growth in remittances to India at 3 percent, from $52 billion in 2008 to $53 billion in 2009. The World Bank report "Migration and Remittances Trends 2009" (Ratha, Mohapatra, and Silwal 2009a) confirmed our estimates and stated that the outcomes were better than expected but that significant risks lie ahead.

Why did remittances not decline in South Asia? From our study, the following six observations can be made: (1) the debts contracted to meet the high expenses incurred during their migration kept emigrants from returning to their countries of origin despite the layoffs; (2) the predictions of a large exodus of return emigrants from the Gulf did not come true; (3) although the outflow declined in the first half of 2009, it has still not significantly affected the number of South Asian migrants in the Gulf; (4) the value of the dollar has appreciated vis-à-vis South Asian currencies—for instance, the current exchange rate of the Indian rupee to the dollar is the same as in 2001–02; (5) the continuous rise in oil prices has generated more income in the Gulf; and (6) "reverse migration" has been seen of the crisis-instigated return emigrants back to the Gulf.

Conclusions

The unraveling of the impact of the crisis on output and employment in the United States generated an anticipation of large-scale retrenchment of expatriate laborers in the Gulf region. The anticipated misery and the need for rehabilitation led governments in South Asia to think about plans for the returning migrants. We find that the dimensions of the impact were not as large as was feared earlier. Out of approximately 9.5 million South Asian emigrants in the Gulf, the number who returned due to the crisis was about 264,000 (just about 2.78 percent), and the number who lost jobs but were continuing to stay in the Gulf was about 170,000 (1.80 percent). Overall, less than 5 percent of the South Asian emigrants had lost jobs owing to the crisis, but such an impact had not adversely affected the yearly flow of out-migrants from South Asia. Compared with the outflow of about 2.2 million workers in 2008, the number in 2009 is expected to be close to 2.0 million, which is higher than the corresponding figure in 2007.

In regard to remittances (in dollars), the annual percentage increase since 2004–05 has been over 20 percent for the South Asian countries, except for Sri Lanka. The magnitude of the increase has taken a hit across South Asia, except Pakistan, from which the outflow of migrants had been increasing by about 50 percent every year since 2005. Remittances, however, have not fallen following the crisis; either they have remained stagnant or have shown a mild rise, depending on the estimates. As most of the South Asian currencies have depreciated against the dollar (to which the GCC currencies are pegged) since late 2007, remittances in terms of domestic currencies would have shown an increase. A survey of migrant households in South Asia confirmed these estimates, because 94 percent of the households reported regular remittances during the crisis period like those they had made in previous years, and no significant change in the use of remittances was reported by these households.

Overall, less than 5 percent of the stock of South Asian migrants in the Gulf had lost jobs and either have returned there or were struggling to continue in the Gulf. The flow of workers from South Asia to the Gulf had also not been affected to any significant extent, but changes were seen in the origin (in favor of Pakistan) and the destination (in favor of Saudi Arabia) of the flow. The volume of remittances into South Asia had also not fallen to any significant extent.

In sum, the crisis of 2008-09 is a blip on the radar of labor migration to the GCC countries from South Asia. A few thousand workers lost jobs and had to return home, but the number migrating to the Gulf has hardly fallen. With the quick recovery in 2010, the flow of labor is going to increase, and remittances will follow.

Notes

1. See http://cds.edu/download_files/wp436.pdf.

2. This section is based on the six country reports prepared by the research teams at the Centre for Development Studies. Most of the members of the research team have already visited the Gulf and interviewed stake holders.

3. Dubai World, a holding company owned by the government of Dubai that manages about 90 entities, asked to delay for six months payment on $26 billion of debt, which shook the confidence of investors holding the government's debt.

4. The Return Emigrant Survey 2009 was conducted at the Centre for Development Studies and was sponsored by the Department of Non-Resident Keralite Affairs, government of Kerala (for more details on the survey report, see Zachariah and Rajan 2009). The field work was carried out from June 16 to September 7, 2009.

5. These could be underestimates because the composition of migrants from Kerala would have a lower proportion of unskilled workers.

Chapter 6

Gendered Use of Remittances: The United Arab Emirates–Bangladesh Remittance Corridor

MD MIZANUR RAHMAN AND DANIÈLE BÉLANGER

THE OIL CRISIS OF 1973 caused a shift of migration destinations from Europe to the Gulf countries, and eventually the Gulf countries became large recipients of foreign workers, ending the era of guest worker immigration to Europe (Ambrosetti 2009). The Asian financial crisis that started in Thailand in 1997 and spread quickly to other Southeast and East Asian countries affected the labor markets severely, leading to a halt on new hiring of migrant workers and the deportation of existing migrant workers from almost all affected countries in the region. By the end of 1998, it was estimated that 933,000 migrant workers were expelled or laid off in the migrant-receiving countries of East and Southeast Asia (Rahman 1999: 4).

Temporary labor migration forms a large component of intraregional labor migration in Asia. The primary motivation for such migration is often economic. In this type of labor migration, migrants are not allowed to settle in destination countries for the long term; thus families live under "transnationally split" conditions, with the nonmigrating family members "left behind" (Piper 2005; Yeoh, Graham, and Boyle 2002). Men have always moved beyond national borders for work; now women are choosing to do the same. More and more women migrate independently to realize their own aspirations

The authors wish to thank the International Organization for Migration (IOM)–Dhaka, Bangladesh, for financing this study in the United Arab Emirates. Special thanks go to Rabab Fatima, Regional Representative, IOM-Dhaka; Samiha Huda and Disha Sonata Faruque, also of IOM-Dhaka, provided support and were a joy to work with.

and support their families—a phenomenon known as the *feminization of labor migration* in Asia. The feminization of labor migration is particularly pronounced in Indonesia, the Philippines, and Sri Lanka. However, other Asian countries, such as Bangladesh, Cambodia, Myanmar, Nepal, and Vietnam, have also seen female migration on the rise. An increasing number of women from these countries are now migrating for temporary employment in the intra-Asian labor market.

These migrant workers send remittances to their families left behind, often with instructions on how and where the funds should be used. The use of remittances cuts across gender lines. Despite the feminization of labor migration in Asia, little research has been done to date on the gendered use of remittances. As a result, we are not aware of how men and women differ in their use of remittances under conditions of temporary migration. The existing literature also makes little reference to remittance use by female and male migrant workers who leave for the same host country and share a geographical and social origin. This is particularly important because a general analysis of remittance use without reference to the context of sending remittances may mislead us, because motivations and the implications of remittances from migrants in labor-hiring countries in Asia are supposed to differ from those in the West, where migration is predominantly for permanent settlement. This study attempts to contribute to this understudied area by highlighting remittance use behavior of Bangladeshi male and female migrant workers in the United Arab Emirates and their households in Bangladesh.

Studies of remittance use are mostly concerned with whether remittances are used for productive investment or for consumption (for a review see Garcia and Paiewonsky 2006; Morrison, Schiff, and Sjöblom 2007; Papademetriou and Martin 1991). The existing literature often reports that migrant remittances are spent mainly on housing, education, health care, special meals and celebrations, clothes, and electronic devices and other imported consumption goods, whereas investment in productive enterprises is rare (for a review see Hammar and others 1997; Sørensen, van Hear, and Engberg-Pedersen 2002). As a result, the dominant view is that the money remitted by migrants is mainly spent on consumption and nonproductive investments leading to "a passive and dangerous dependency on remittances" (De Haas 2005). However, evidence is increasing that this pessimistic perspective is founded on a rather poor empirical and analytical basis (De Haas 2005; Hugo 2003).

In a broad sense, remittances are used for "physical capital" and "human capital" (Salomone 2006: 14). Uses of physical capital generate market value, such as incomes and profits (such as from bank deposits, housing, or loans). Uses of human capital are those that contribute to intangible capital formation, such as family maintenance, education, health, and quality of life. Using this broader classification of remittance use resolves some of the limitations inherent in the economic approach to investment. The debate over productive (physical capital) and nonproductive (human capital) use of remittances does not capture the gendered dimensions of remittances. As Mahler and Pessar (2006: 27) claim, gender "seeps subtly into a seemingly neutral notion of 'productive' versus 'unproductive' uses of remittances." In the literature some researchers have reported that women are less likely than men to invest in risky assets (Sunden and Surette 1998) and that women tend to channel remittances into better health, education, and nutrition for their family, thereby supporting the development of stronger, more productive communities (Piper 2005; Sørensen 2005a).

Although a substantial literature is found on traditional female labor source countries in Asia (for example, Indonesia, the Philippines, and Sri Lanka), little research is available on emerging female-labor-source countries such as Bangladesh. The Bangladeshi case is, therefore, expected to add new insights to the field. The next section provides an overview of the Bangladeshi labor migration context. The subsequent sections elaborate on data sources and findings on remittance use. The final section concludes with findings on policy and future directions for gender and remittance research.

The Bangladeshi Migration Context

Since the 1970s, one of the largest labor markets for Maghreb (Algeria, Libya, Morocco, and Tunisia), Mashreq (Egypt, Jordan, Lebanon, Syria, West Bank and Gaza, and Yemen), and Asian (South Asia and Southeast Asia) migrant workers has been that of the Gulf States (Esim and Smith 2004; Humphrey 1991; IOM 2004; Khalaf and Alkobaisi 1999). The six states of the Gulf Cooperation Council (GCC), Bahrain, Kuwait, Oman, Qatar, Saudi Arabia, and the United Arab Emirates, host approximately 10 million foreign workers (Manseau 2005: 25). Foreigners constitute a majority of the labor force in all the GCC countries, with the average for 2004 close to 70 percent (Kapiszewski 2006: 4). The GCC states are also the major destination for female migrant workers. According to one estimate, in the late 1990s about 840,000 women migrants were employed, primarily as domestic workers (Shah 2004: 183). Intraregional migration in Asia takes place under specific migration policies designed to ensure that the low-skilled migrant worker returns to their home country, such as not allowing the family to accompany or visit the worker, tying the worker to a single employer, not allowing the worker to marry a citizen of the country where they are working, and enforcing other restrictions on their rights and movements (Hugo 2003).

Along with other South Asian migrants, Bangladeshi migrant workers have joined the Gulf labor markets since the late 1970s. According to one source, about 5 million Bangladeshi migrants were employed in the GCC states between 1976 and 2008.[1] The number of migrants leaving Bangladesh averaged 250,000 a year between 2001 and 2005, rose to almost 400,000 in 2006, and doubled to 832,600 in 2007. The United Arab Emirates is a destination country of significance in terms of the numbers of Bangladeshi migrants and resultant remittance inflows to Bangladesh (figure 6.1). The annual flow of Bangladeshi migrants to the United Arab Emirates has been on the rise, from roughly 55,000 in 1997 to 420,000 in 2008.[2] The amount of annual remittances from the United Arab Emirates has concomitantly increased steadily since 1991. According to the Central Bank of Bangladesh, Bangladeshi migrants remitted $6,382 million from the United Arab Emirates between 1991 and 2008 (figure 6.2).[3]

FIGURE 6.1 Bangladeshi Labor Migration to the United Arab Emirates, 1976–2010

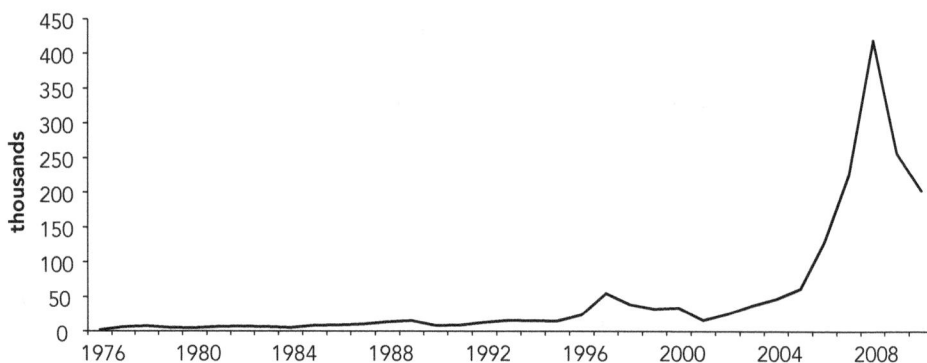

Source: Compiled from data provided in Government Site in Bangladesh, http://probashi.gov.bd accessed in March 2010.

FIGURE 6.2 Inflows of Remittances from the United Arab Emirates to Bangladesh, 1998–2011

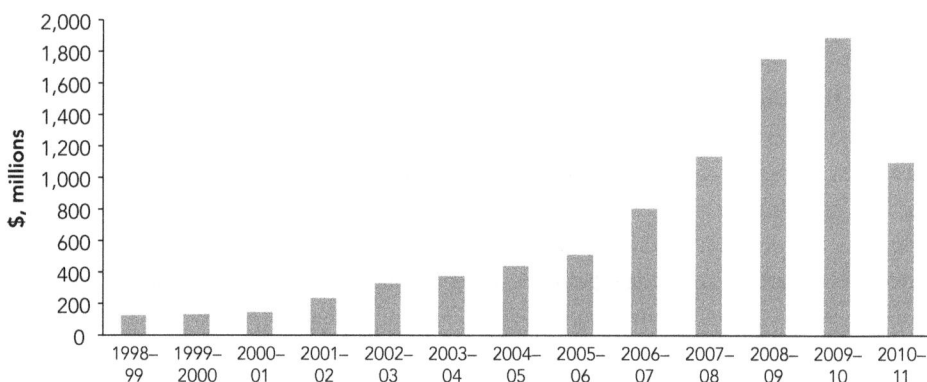

Source: Compiled from data provided in http://www.bmet.org.bd/report.html and http://www.bangladesh-bank.org/econdata/wagermidtl.php.

A significant number of female workers from Bangladesh have also emigrated overseas for work. The data on female migration from Bangladesh are scarce, and the official estimates often belie the reality, mainly because of the undocumented nature of migration. Only 17,784 women migrated officially between 1991 and 2003, less than 1 percent of the total labor migration during that period (Ullah and Panday 2007). In 1997 the government banned the expatriation of all unskilled and semiskilled female labor, following increasing reports of exploitation and abuse of Bangladeshi women overseas. Civil society organizations were against this government move and put pressure on the government to repeal the ban. Facing increasing protests from civil society organizations, the government finally repealed the ban on female migration in 2003. The government now stipulates numerous mandatory protections for female labor, including training courses to educate women about cultural and working conditions abroad and requiring recruiting agencies to compensate female workers in the event of exploitation or lost wages. To go abroad legally as a domestic worker, Bangladeshi women must be at least 25 years of age, submit a "no objection certificate" from their legal guardians (usually a husband), and undergo at least 21 days of training. Despite the introduction of these new measures, the withdrawal of the ban has opened the door for authorized or documented female migration, and more and more women are now migrating overseas for work.

According to recent Bureau of Manpower, Employment and Training statistics, 124,273 female migrants went abroad for work from 1991 to 2009; of this total, 35,630 (29 percent) went to the United Arab Emirates.[4] In 2009, 22,224 female migrants went overseas for work, with 6,095 of them (27 percent) migrating to the United Arab Emirates. Although Bangladeshi female migrants are spread over 21 countries worldwide, their representation is negligible compared with female migrants from other countries in Asia. This is not surprising: Women living in patriarchal societies display lower rates of emigration than their male counterparts, whereas more egalitarian societies have higher rates of female than male migration (Massey and others 1998/2006; Oishi 2005). For example, Massey and his colleagues show that women from patriarchal societies such as Costa Rica and Mexico demonstrate lower rates of emigration, but matrifocal countries such as the Dominican Republic and Nicaragua show higher rates of emigration (Massey and others 1998/2006).

Data Sources

This study is based on two-way surveys: surveys of Bangladeshi male and female migrants and their households in the United Arab Emirates and Bangladesh. Between June and August 2009, 50 female migrant workers and 100 male migrant workers were interviewed face-to-face in the United Arab Emirates. The questionnaire included both structured and unstructured questions. Field work in Bangladesh involved interviewing 50 United Arab Emirates male migrant households and 50 United Arab Emirates female migrant households. The households were selected on the basis of the following criteria: (1) They must have a male migrant working in the United Arab Emirates for the male household survey and a female migrant working in the United Arab Emirates for the female migrant household survey, (2) their migrant members must have been working in the United Arab Emirates for at least one year, and (3) their migrant members must have made remittances to their families during this period. Recipients of remittances were interviewed in the household survey. Both surveyed migrant workers and households hail from rural Bangladesh; therefore, the findings represent predominantly a rural Bangladesh scenario. Placing the remittance process within the household context enables a deeper understanding of the effects of remittances.

In general, household surveys include questions on the amounts and uses of remittances. The data are usually reported in the form of quantitative tables detailing the amounts allocated for different activities. Researchers who collect such data are often confronted with discrepancies between the actual amount of remittances and the amount reported to the interviewers. Naturally, households may be uncomfortable reporting the amounts and uses of remittances to outsiders. Reporting inflated or inaccurate amounts is common because most households do not maintain daily financial records. Given the sensitivity of questions and the potential for biased responses, we have employed an alternative way of collecting information on remittance use. We are primarily interested in pinpointing preferential expenditures so that trends can be captured and used as a baseline, and so we have identified areas of remittance use, especially where expenditures are recurrent and even when the amount is negligible, such as for everyday necessities. We asked respondents to list up to five major areas of remittance use in the "near past" and "near future."[5] This alternative method of collecting information on the use of remittances is expected to generate more accurate information on the use of remittances under conditions of temporary migration (Rahman 2009), because migrants are working on a contract basis, and duration of stay, earnings, savings, and remittances are often fixed in most cases.

Linking Migrants and Their Families

Most female and male migrants surveyed were in their 20s and 30s with about 50 percent between 25 and 30 years of age. All female migrants were less than 40 years old, and a small percentage of male migrants were over 40. In general, more married females tended to migrate relative to their male counterparts. Among the surveyed migrants, 68 percent of females were married compared with 51 percent of males. Given the cultural behavior patterns in Bangladeshi society, this finding is not surprising, because female members of the family usually enjoy freedom of physical mobility after marriage. Bangladesh is a predominantly Muslim country; population by religion in Bangladesh, according to the 2001 census, is Islam, 89.58 percent; Hinduism, 9.34 percent; and Christianity, 0.31 percent.[6] The sample also reflected the national-level data: 96 percent of female and male migrants were Muslims, 4 percent of females were Hindus and Christians, and 3 percent of males were Hindus. On average, the size of female migrant households was 4.97 persons and that of male migrant households was 4.95; the average household size at the national level is 4.8.[7]

Most migrants had some formal education, but male migrants tended to possess higher qualifications than female migrants. Male migrants had also worked in the United Arab Emirates for a longer period relative to their female counterparts. Among surveyed migrants, 59 percent of male migrants and 10 percent of female migrants had been working in the United Arab Emirates for four years or more. Ninety percent of female migrants were working as cleaning staff at educational institutions in the sample. This, however, does not mean that most female migrants working in the United Arab Emirates are cleaners. It was difficult to gain access to domestic workers, and so this study mainly surveyed cleaners. Male migrants worked as construction workers, cleaners, agricultural workers, salesmen, tailors, and drivers and in a wide variety of other occupations (office maintenance, electricians, rental-car washers, painters, carpenters, and others). About half of male migrants interviewed were employed as construction workers and salesmen. Seventy-six percent of female migrants and 52 percent of male migrants were not involved in any income-generating activity in Bangladesh before migration.

The expenses for migration vary along gender lines. Potential female migrants spend a comparatively lesser amount of cash for migration than their male counterparts. The average cost of migration was Tk 106,220 ($1,531) for a female migrant and Tk 141,300 ($2,037) for a male migrant. Lower migration costs are advantageous for female migrants: They have relatively less debt to repay and therefore more money to send home. This gender-differentiated pattern of the financial cost of migration has been cited by some respondents as a factor in the family's decision to send a woman rather than a man to work in the United Arab Emirates. The financial costs of migration for Bangladeshi female and male migrants are higher than those for Sri Lankan female and male migrants. A female domestic worker typically spends $500–$700, and a male migrant spends up to $1,000 to meet the financial cost of Gulf migration in Sri Lanka (Shaw 2007: 162). The Bangladeshi female recruitment procedure is different from that of other countries in the region such as Indonesia, the Philippines, and Sri Lanka. In these countries, female migrants do not need to pay any fee up front; the recruiting fees are usually deducted from their salary once they start work in the destination country. In the case of Bangladesh, female migrants are usually required to pay in full before their departure. Because this amount is beyond the reach of low-income families, they obtain the cash from different sources available to them (Rahman 2009).

In the household survey, the largest group of remittance recipients was the fathers of both female and male migrant workers. Married female and male migrants also preferred sending remittances to fathers than to spouses. Although 42 percent of female migrants and 58 percent of male migrants were married, only 22 percent and 24 percent of their spouses, respectively, were recipients. Female migrants tended to remit to their sisters, and male migrants tended to remit to their brothers. It is interesting that more male migrants than females chose to remit to their mothers. In short, 78 percent and 22 percent of female migrants remitted to male and female members, respectively, and 56 percent and 44 percent of male migrants remitted to male and female members of the family, respectively. A migrant worker survey in the United Arab Emirates revealed similar trends. The largest group receiving remittances was fathers of migrants. Although 68 percent of female migrants were married, only 28 percent of remittance recipients were their husbands. Similarly, 51 percent of male migrants were married, but only 26 percent of the recipients were their wives.

As in the household survey, the migrant worker survey also revealed that more female migrants than male migrants tended to remit to their male family members; 78 percent and 22 percent of the females remitted to male and female members, respectively, whereas 57 percent and 43 percent of the males chose to remit to male and female family members, respectively. Overall trends of receiving remittances are the following: (1) The father as the head of the traditional family tended to enjoy special privileges in receiving remittances, (2) both married female and male migrants tended to prefer remitting to their parents rather than in-laws or even spouses, (3) female migrants preferred remitting to sisters rather than brothers and fathers to mothers, whereas male migrants preferred remitting to their brothers rather than sisters and fathers to mothers, and (4) more female migrants than male migrants tended to remit to male family members.

Use of Remittances: The Migrant Perspective

Both the migrant worker and the migrant household surveys required respondents to list up to five areas in which they had used remittances thus far and up to five areas in which they were planning to use remittances in the "near future."[8] Table 6.1 presents findings from the migrant worker survey in the United Arab Emirates. From the male migrant workers' perspective, the four areas of previous remittance use, ranked in importance, were family maintenance, land purchase, education, and loan repayment, whereas, from the female migrant workers' perspective, the four areas were family maintenance, land purchase, loan repayment, and education. Two major differences are noteworthy in this area: (1) Female migrants did not use remittances for housing, whereas a substantial proportion of male migrants did, and (2) almost half of the female migrants spent remittances on loan repayment, but only a small proportion of male migrants used remittances for this purpose.

TABLE 6.1 "Near Past" and "Near Future" Use of Remittances by Gender: Household and Migrant Worker Surveys, 2009

percent

| | Migrant worker survey, United Arab Emirates[a] | | | | Migrant household survey, Bangladesh[b] | | | |
| | Near past use | | Near future use | | Near past use | | Near future use | |
Area of use	Female	Male	Female	Male	Female	Male	Female	Male
Family maintenance	66	92	0	0	92	90	92	86
Education	24	25	46	11	72	56	74	46
Savings	0	14	66	0	22	10	24	18
Loan repayment	44	16	0	0	48	78	46	70
Medical	0	0	0	0	24	0	36	18
Business	0	0	76	87	0	8	0	0
Housing	0	14	72	30	0	0	0	0
Land purchase	44	50	0	37	0	0	0	0

Source: Authors' data.

a. Survey conducted in 2009; *n* = 150: 50 female, 100 male.

b. Survey conducted in 2009; *n* = 100: 50 female, 50 male.

These trends can be explained by gendered expectations that prevail in Bangladeshi society. Male migrants are more likely to use remittances for homebuilding because Bangladesh is predominantly a patrilineal society, where a woman goes to live in her husband's house after marriage, and not vice versa. As a result, the responsibility for homebuilding falls on the shoulders of male family members. On the other hand, male migrants are less likely to spend remittances on loan repayment because working visas for many male migrants are arranged through their contacts in the United Arab Emirates, and the recruiting fees are paid later while working there. These male migrants were able to use their "migration-specific social capital" in the migration process, whereas female migrants were deprived of this opportunity. From the family perspective, male migrants are considered permanent members of the family, and investment in them, for example, by providing migration expenses, is justified. Sending female migrants abroad is not seen as a future investment for the family, so minimal family resources are available for female migration. Female migration-friendly arrangements found in Indonesia, the Philippines, and Sri Lanka, where female migrants do not have to make up-front payments for recruitment-related services, have yet to develop in Bangladesh. Women migrating from these countries are able to migrate under a "salary deduction program" through which they can repay the recruitment fees from their monthly wages overseas (Ananta and Arifin 2004; Gamburd 2002).

With regard to remittance use in the "near future," most migrants intended to shift from immediate consumption to long-time capital formation. A majority of migrants elected "business" as the future planned use of remittances (87 percent of males and 76 percent of females). For other categories, three gender-differentiated patterns are salient: (1) Female migrants were more likely to plan on investing in savings than male migrants, (2) male migrants were more likely to plan on investing in a land purchase than women, and (3) more female migrants planned on future investments in housing than men. The differences in future intentions to save are striking (no men versus 66 percent of women). In such a patriarchal family context, a woman's earnings are considered the property of male family members, and women may have limited control over the use of remittances they generate. Saving can be a strategy to protect their earnings until their return to Bangladesh. Married women saved for planned investments in their children's future marriages and education. Some unmarried women planned to save to secure a dowry for a future marriage. For those who are married, variations in past and future use also indicate different gendered expectations: Men have more immediate pressure to invest in housing, whereas women postpone these plans. Both men and women invest in land purchases without delay, but only men identify the acquisition of land as a future objective.

Use of Remittances: The Household Perspective

In the household survey, the same questions of "near past" and "near future" use of remittances were given to both male and female migrant households (table 6.1). Savings, education, and medical treatment were the major areas of "near past" use for female migrant households, whereas business and loan repayment were the major areas of "near past" use for male migrant households. Medical treatment was exclusive to female migrant households, whereas business was exclusive to male migrant households. Both male and female migrant households depended on remittances for family maintenance. More female migrant households than male migrant households tended to save remittances. A similar savings trend was also found in the migrant worker survey. For female migrant households, major areas of "future use" of remittances were savings, medical treatment, education, and family maintenance, whereas, for male migrant households, the only major "future use" of remittances was loan repayment. These male migrants in the household survey hailed from areas or villages where migration to the United Arab Emirates was not developed enough to reduce the cost of migration. In other words, they had little or no access to migration-specific social capital, as found in the migrant worker survey in the United Arab Emirates, or family resources to meet the migration expenses, resulting in greater debt. It is important to note that the cost of migration was higher for male migrants than female migrants.

A striking finding in the household survey is that remittances played a crucial role in family maintenance for both female and male migrant workers: On average, 90 percent of migrant households depended on remittances for family maintenance. Given that such a large percentage of migrant households depended on remittances for sustenance, we inquired about the amount of land owned to understand the economic viability of the family, because most migrants came from rural areas where land is considered the main source of family income. Approximately 70 percent of female migrant households and 60 percent of male migrant households reported that they did not possess sufficient land for subsistence living. These results suggest that female migrant households had less land for subsistence, so they had a higher number of female migrants as economic providers.

From the findings on remittance use from both the migrant and household perspectives, it is evident that migrants had dual motivations: investment in physical and human capital. When families invested mainly in physical capital, remittances were used for homebuilding, land purchase, and businesses, whereas, when families invested mainly in human capital, they spent remittances mostly on education, medical treatment, and family maintenance. Because a good portion of remittances is used for recurrent family expenses, some scholars may argue that migrant remittances lead to consumption. Migrant remittances were used for family maintenance because migrants were, regardless of gender, the principal economic providers for the families left behind. On average, 75 percent of the female migrants and 53 percent of the male migrants in both surveys played the role of principal economic providers for their families in Bangladesh, reflecting the dominant status of migration as a survival strategy for Bangladeshi families.

Remittances also make a substantial contribution toward savings, especially for women. In academic and policy circles it is widely assumed that the migrants themselves are all *latent entrepreneurs* and the appropriate agents for undertaking investment from the remittances (Brown and Ahlburg 1999; Connell and Brown 1995). However, Saith (1989) reported a high failure rate of governments' self-employment programs in labor-exporting countries in Asia aimed at converting migrants into small entrepreneurs, and Saith questioned the wisdom of adopting policies to convert *migrant savers* into *migrant investors*. This study finds that the majority of recipients were "savers" and a few were "saver investors." Again, patterns of investment varied along gender lines: Female migrant household recipients of remittances are less likely to invest in material capital, mostly in the absence of their female remitters overseas. However, structural barriers also exist for women investing in business and productive investment in Bangladeshi rural society. In general, a sense of fear and uncertainty among all migrant workers and their families is seen in relation to investing in business ventures, and this is largely attributable to the lack of different markets, such as insurance markets, credit markets, and future markets.

Conclusion

This study has argued that an examination of the gendered use of remittances is needed to understand the dynamics of remittance use and development outcomes. This study introduces an alternative way of reporting by documenting priorities and timelines in remittance use. The study has reported several gendered-differentiated uses in the "near past" use of remittances. First, female migrants did not use remittances for homebuilding, whereas a substantial percentage of male migrants did. Second, male migrants did not spend remittances on loan repayment, whereas almost half of female migrants used remittances for this purpose. Third, and finally, female households spent more on education and medical expenses than did male migrant households. In the "near future" use of remittances, two gender-differentiated patterns are prominent: (1) Female migrants showed more interest in saving remittances than male migrants and (2) land purchase remained mainly a male domain. We find an indication that remittance use is shifting from immediate consumption to long-term capital formation because, in temporary migration, migrants require a few years to recoup the expenses incurred in the migration process, which entails that the positive effects of remittances take longer to be realized. Findings show, however, that these patterns are highly gendered and shaped by gender and power relations in the country of origin. Male and female domains of labor and expenditures that exist before migration largely explain remittance use patterns during migration and on return.

The most frequent use of remittance was family maintenance. Migrant remittances were used for family maintenance because migrants were the principal economic providers for the families left behind. Interestingly, more females than males were principal economic providers for their families, although more males than females were active in the labor market before migration. In this study we found that a greater number of migrants and their households reported saving their remittance earnings. We conclude that it would make better sense for policy to be geared more toward encouraging migrant workers and their families to become more active in domestic capital markets as "investors." The "income security" of migrant households and "development priorities" of government should, wherever possible, be kept separate. Research on the gendered use of remittances under conditions of temporary migration is still in its infancy. For migrants originating from patriarchal societies, gendered patterns of remittance control and use need to be further investigated to thoroughly assess the impact of remittances on development. This study offers insights into gender dimensions of remittance use, but more empirically based research is needed in the field.

The case of Asia shows that patterns in sending remittances are complex and not completely dependent on global economic changes (Skeldon 2010). First, labor markets in receiving countries largely influence whether economic downturns affect remittances. The case of the Philippines has shown that the high demand in the domestic and heath care sectors was maintained in 2008 and 2009, despite massive layoffs in other work sectors (Riester 2009). Likewise, migrants from South Asia working in the Gulf region experienced limited consequences of the economic crisis because oil-producing countries maintained their growth (Skeldon 2010). In this context, migrant workers did not return in large numbers, and recruitment figures were maintained, and so remittances continued to flow. During economic downturns, migrants also use contingency plans. Because of their families' daily dependence on remittances, migrants resort to various strategies to avoid interrupting the flow of remittances, such as sending savings and finding employment in the shadow economy (Ullah 2010). All the above processes are gendered, and a comprehensive gendered analysis of the impact of the 2008 economic crisis on migrants and remittance flows remains to be done.

Notes

1. Bureau of Manpower, Employment and Training, Bangladesh: This agency is responsible for record keeping and granting permission to overseas job seekers at the final stage of migration.

2. http://www.bmet.org.bd/BMET/viewStatReport.action?reportnumber=3.

3. http://www.bangladesh-bank.org/econdata/wagermidtl.php.

4. http://www.bmet.org.bd/BMET/viewStatReport.action?reportnumber=3.

5. In major labor-receiving countries in the Gulf countries, migrant workers are usually issued work permits for two to three years with an option for renewal subject to the availability of the job. In the sample, migrants who were working in the United Arab Emirates for at least one year were interviewed.

6. http://www.bbs.gov.bd/dataindex/census/bang_atg.pdf.

7. http://www.bbs.gov.bd/dataindex/stat_bangladesh.pdf.

8. Because migrant workers were usually issued work permits for two to three years and our respondents were working in the United Arab Emirates for more than one year but less than three years, we refer to "near past" as the first one or two years of a contract and "near future" as the remainder of the contract, which may be one or two years depending on the timing of the interview and the length of the contract.

Chapter 7

Trends and Correlates of Remittances to India

POONAM GUPTA AND KARAN SINGH

RELIANCE ON REMITTANCES IN DEVELOPING countries is great. Even in a relatively large economy such as India's, remittances, along with the exports of services, have been instrumental in turning around the current account and in the accumulation of reserves. The current global economic slowdown had raised the concern that remittances to developing countries would slow. Despite the projected decline, remittances continue to be the most stable type of international flows, as private capital flows and even the export earnings from goods and services have declined more rapidly.

Did all countries experience a decline in remittances in 2009–10, or did some of them beat the odds and see no decline? This chapter examines the remittance flows to India and analyzes their correlates. Remittances to India exhibit strong growth over time averaging about 10 percent a year in constant U.S. dollars since 1991. Remittances in real dollars declined by 7 percent in 2009 but keeping with the global trend rebounded quickly to register a 9 percent growth rate in 2010.

Among the correlates of remittances, the movement of remittances around the trend is limited, and until the early 2000s none of the factors considered in our analyses seemed to have influenced remittance behavior. This pattern has changed somewhat since about 2004, and remittances have responded to movements in the domestic and international interest rates and to price movements in the Indian stock market. In particular, an increase in domestic interest rates, a decline in international interest rates, and an increase in the Indian stock market index are all associated with an increase in remittances. This reflects the fact that in recent years remittances are partly driven by an investment motive that is commensurate with the increasing prosperity of the country, the easing of restrictions on the current and capital account, and the liberalization of the financial sector.

The trend in the growth rate of remittances is not affected by factors such as economic growth in the source and destination countries, interest rate movements, or even potential risk factors such as political uncertainty. As shown elsewhere, growth is likely correlated with the stock of migrants.

In the short run, remittances are susceptible to a domestic or global slowdown if India's attractiveness as an investment destination is reduced—and this is likely to be the case when the interest rates in advanced countries harden, interest rates in India decline, or there is a decline in the Indian stock market. At the same time, however, having weathered the recent developments in the global economic conditions, remittances to India are likely to continue to grow. The only possible case in which the remittances are likely to slow is when global conditions make the pool of migrants from India smaller, but this is unlikely to happen in the near term.

Magnitude, Trends, and Volatility

The sources of data on remittances to India used here are the Reserve Bank of India's (RBI) online interactive database, Database on Indian Economy.[1] The rest of the data are obtained from the Indian Foreign Service, World Economic Outlook, or other sources, as indicated in annex table A.

Remittances to India were quite small up until 1990, and since then remittances have grown rapidly (figure 7.1). In absolute terms, India is the largest recipient of remittances

FIGURE 7.1 Remittances to India

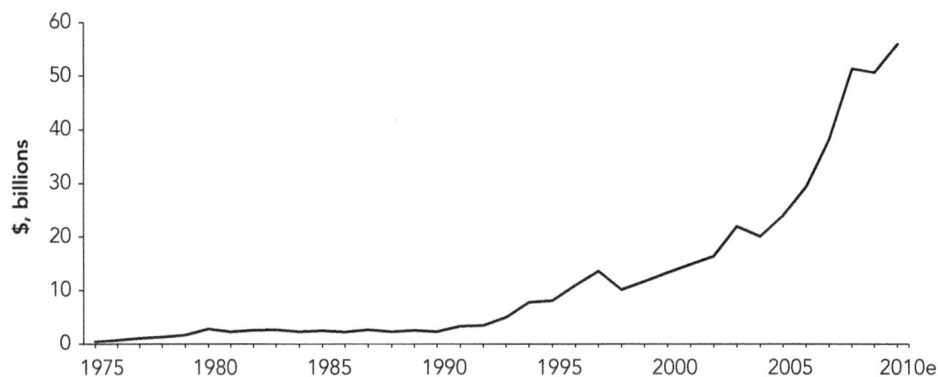

Sources: RBI; World Bank 2011b for 2010.
Note: Data for 2010 are estimated.

globally. The reasons for the low level of remittances in 1975–89 could very well be that a large part of the remittances during this period were sent to India via unofficial and informal channels (*hawala*) because of the heavy restrictions that the central bank imposed on transactions involving foreign currency and fixed exchange rates. Thus the dollar always exchanged at a premium in the unofficial or parallel markets. Another reason why remitters bypassed official channels was that gold attracted high import duties, and, in response, its local price was much higher than the international price. Thus remitters would carry gold with them and sell it for rupees (often to relatives and acquaintances) while traveling to India. Official channels were also cumbersome, and it took longer to remit money though them.

All of this changed with the liberalization in 1991, when the currency was devalued by about 30 percent within a year, the current account transactions were liberalized, the financial sector was liberalized and computerized, and the import duty on gold was gradually brought down and eventually abolished on small amounts of gold that the individuals were allowed to carry with them. All of these developments made the unofficial routes of remitting money broadly redundant, and the remittances as recorded in the RBI database picked up significantly. The buoyancy in remittances since the early 1990s thus probably reflects the fact that the remittances were diverted from unofficial to official channels.

The continued growth of remittances since 1991 cannot be attributed to the diversion of remittances from unofficial channels alone. The pace of growth since then is consistent with the increasing integration of India with the rest of the world and with the advanced economies in particular as well as the greater movement of people and goods and services (figure 7.2).

FIGURE 7.2 Current Account Inflows, 1991–2009

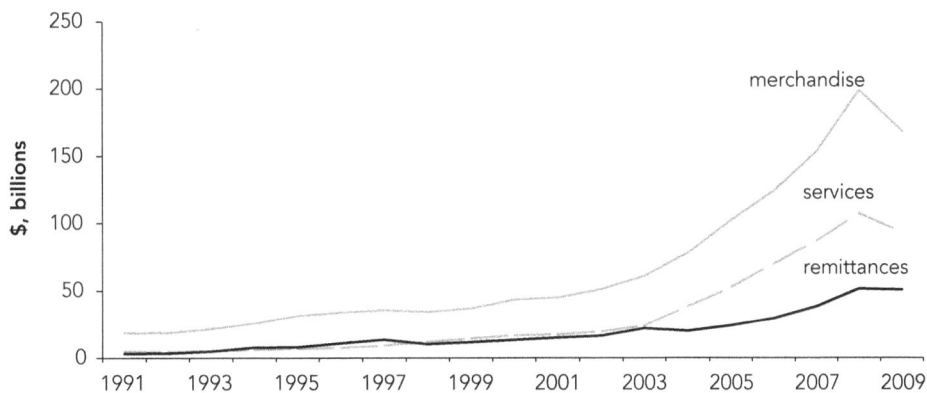

Source: RBI.

Remittances are increasing in tandem with the inflows on account of the gross export earnings from the export of merchandise and services, although they remain smaller in magnitude. However, when compared (figure 7.3) with the net export earnings from merchandise and services exports (that is, exports minus imports), remittances are seen to have contributed a larger amount to the Indian current account balance. Also remittances add more to the Indian balance-of-payments receipts than net portfolio flows (nearly twice as much in 2009) or nonresident Indian (NRI) deposits (several times more).

FIGURE 7.3 Net Remittances versus Net Capital Inflows, 1991–2009

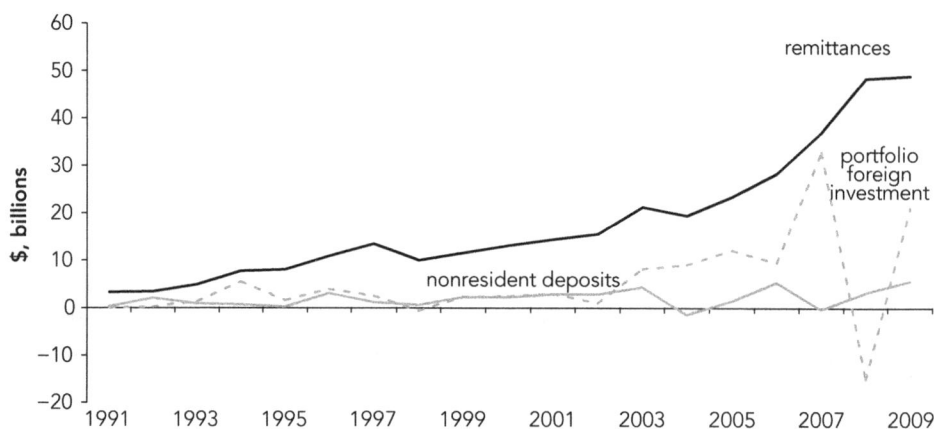

Source: RBI.

An important feature of remittances is that they have proven to be one of the most stable forms of external flows to India, on current as well as on capital accounts. Jadhav (2003) and Gupta (2006) show that the remittances are more stable than NRI deposits or portfolio flows. Remittances are, in fact, seen to be as stable as the export earnings from goods and services. In tables 7.1 and 7.2, we compare the standard volatility measures of remittances and those of various other flows on current and capital accounts. When we look at the volatility of gross flows (table 7.1), we find that remittance inflows are as stable as services and goods exports and more stable than the gross inflows on account of foreign direct investment, portfolio investment, and NRI deposits. In table 7.2 we compare standard volatility of net inflows in current and capital accounts. More remarkably, net remittances are significantly more stable than the net inflows on account of net export earnings from goods and services, portfolio investment, foreign direct investments, or NRI deposits.

TABLE 7.1 Volatility Measure of Current and Capital Inflows

coefficient of variation

Inflow	1990–94	1995–99	2000–04	2005–10
Merchandise exports	0.22	0.08	0.25	0.27
Services exports	0.21	0.31	0.38	0.25
Remittances	0.42	0.20	0.25	0.31
Foreign direct investment	0.95	0.31	0.26	0.52
Portfolio foreign investment	1.23	0.43	0.67	0.50
Nonresident deposits	0.31	0.30	0.42	0.40

Source: Authors' calculations based on RBI.

TABLE 7.2 Volatility Measure of Net Current and Capital Inflows

coefficient of variation

Inflow	1990–94	1995–99	2000–04	2005–10
Merchandise exports	−0.57	−0.23	−0.65	−0.40
Services exports	1.29	1.19	0.83	0.33
Remittances	0.43	0.20	0.25	0.30
Foreign direct investment	0.99	0.31	0.26	0.53
Portfolio foreign investment	1.35	0.88	1.20	1.47
Nonresident deposits	1.76	1.45	1.07	1.02

Source: Authors' calculations based on RBI.

Econometric Analysis

Next we look at the correlates of remittances to India using quarterly data for the first quarter of 1992 through the second quarter of 2010. Since there seems to be little action worth explaining in remittances before the 1990s, and 1991 being a crisis year, we focus only on the period since 1992 in our empirical analysis. We use a simple linear regression model to explore the determinants of remittances to India. The regression framework is given in the following equation:

$$Y_t = \acute{a}\text{Trend} + \Sigma \hat{a}_i \text{Quarterly Dummy}_i + \Sigma \tilde{a}_j \text{Domestic Variable}_j + \ddot{a}_j \text{External Variable}_j + \mathring{a}_t, \qquad (7.1)$$

where Y_t refers to log remittances in constant dollars. The first term on the right-hand side of equation (7.1) refers to the linear annual trend, the second term refers to quarterly dummies, the third term refers to the vector of domestic variables, and the fourth term refers to the vector of external variables. The last term is the error term.

Dickey-Fuller tests indicate that the remittances are trend stationary. We are using quarterly data, so we include quarterly dummies in the regression to deseasonalize the data. Durbin-Watson tests, and the alternative Durbin-Watson tests, show that there is serial correlation of order 1 in the regressions; thus we report our estimates correcting the standard errors for serial correlation and possible heterogeneity using the Newey-West estimates.

Table 7.3 estimates the trend growth rate of remittances and the seasonal patterns. In column I, we include an annual trend, which shows the average pace of growth of remittances in constant dollars to be about 11 percent a year. In column II, we allow the trend to be different from 2004 and find that the pace of growth of remittances has accelerated by 3 percentage points from 2004 (which is marginally significant). In columns III–V we include a quarterly trend and quarterly dummies to detect seasonality. We find the estimate of trends to be similar to the annual one; we also find that there is indeed acceleration in remittances since 2004 and that there is no seasonality in the remittance flows, as shown by the insignificant coefficients of quarterly dummies.

Next, drawing on the existing literature on the regressions, we include a comprehensive set of domestic and external variables as the potential determinants of remittances (Gordon and Gupta 2004; Gupta 2006, 2010). The demand for remittances is likely to be influenced by the economic conditions in the recipient countries, and thus we include gross domestic product (GDP) growth as a measure of the economic strength.[2] The

TABLE 7.3 Trend in Remittances

dependent variable: log remittances in constant dollars

Variable	I	II	III	IV	V
Annual trend from 1992	0.108*** [24.15]	0.098*** [12.64]			
Annual trend from 2004		0.031 [1.62]			
Quarterly trend from 1992			0.024*** [12.95]	0.027*** [23.73]	0.024*** [12.86]
Quarterly trend from 2004			0.009* [1.79]		0.009* [1.72]
Dummy for Quarter 1				0.07 [0.96]	0.06 [0.92]
Dummy for Quarter 2				0.09 [1.28]	0.09 [1.24]
Dummy for Quarter 3				0.06 [0.79]	0.05 [0.73]
Observations	75	75	75	75	75
R^2	0.89	0.89	0.89	0.89	0.89

Source: Authors' calculations.

Note: Standard errors are given in brackets. *, **, *** indicate that the coefficients are significant at the 10, 5, and 1 percent levels, respectively.

remittances would, of course, also be determined by the economic conditions in the source countries.

We account for these forces by including the GDP growth of the United States, the Gulf Cooperation Council (GCC) countries, or the countries in the Middle East—the largest destinations of migrants from India.[3] We also include oil prices as an indicator of the financial health of the GCC countries, from where a substantial proportion of remittances to India originate.

Like any other financial flows, remittances may be driven by an investment motive and thus may be affected by the factors that determine the relative earnings of these investments in the native country and in the host country, such as the interest rates and expected stock market returns. Thus we include the domestic and external interest rates, stock market index, and exchange rate movements as the potential determinants of remittances. Economic or political uncertainties may affect the decision to send remittances, especially if remittances are meant for investment. To account for these factors we include proxies for domestic uncertainties, including the political uncertainty. Finally, to look at the responsiveness of remittances to specific events, we include the dummies for events such as the Asian crisis.

To see which variables might be more susceptible to multicollinearity, we calculate the correlation coefficients between different variables (for this we first regressed each variable on a trend and quarterly dummies and take the residual, and we then calculate the correlation coefficients for these residuals). The correlation coefficients are reported in annex table C. Two things are evident from the correlations. First, even though some of the variables are correlated significantly with each other but the correlations are quantitatively not very large, there seems to be independent variation in each variable. Second, some of the variables are somewhat more highly correlated with each other. These include oil prices, the stock market index in the United States, the Indian stock market index, and the exchange rate.

Another thing that we need to be careful about is the endogeneity. Are the variables that we include as potential determinants likely to be affected by the remittances? For a large economy like India's where remittances are small compared with the size of the economy, it does not seem to be the case, and the remittances are not likely to affect GDP growth, interest rates, stock market variables, political uncertainty, or even the exchange rate.

Using a specification with a linear trend and quarterly dummies, we include all the potential determinants of remittances. The trend and quarterly dummies in the regressions detrend and deseasonalize the dependent and all the independent variables. We start with the kitchen sink specification, including all the potential correlates in the regressions, but as documented elsewhere none of these variables turn out to be significant (Gupta 2010). Thus we find that the price of oil has an insignificant coefficient, which is consistent with the World Bank findings (Ratha and Mohapatra 2009), in which the oil prices do not correlate with remittance outflows from Saudi Arabia since 1980. Instead of oil prices we include the growth rate of GCC countries or the average growth rate of the countries in the Middle East, and their coefficients are found to be insignificant.

We sequentially drop the variables with insignificant coefficients and ones where multicollinearity is likely to be high and estimate parsimonious regression. We present some of these results in tables 7.4, 7.5, and 7.6. When we estimate regressions for the entire period 1992–2010 even in the parsimonious regressions, we still do not find many variables with significant coefficients, as seen in table 7.4.

Thus consistent with the existing empirical studies, we find that none of the variables considered affect the behavior of remittances. Neither the quarterly dummies nor the current or lagged values of other variables such as exchange rates, share prices, or LIBOR (London Interbank Offered Rate) are significant.

One possible reason for the insignificant coefficients could be that the relationship between different variables and remittances has changed over time, and this gets clouded when we force the coefficients to be the same in all periods. It does seem like a valid possibility because the Indian economy has been undergoing drastic changes since the reforms started in the early 1990s. Some of these changes have been gradual, including the financial sector liberalization and the liberalization of transactions on the current and capital accounts. It is reasonable to think that the liberalization of these

TABLE 7.4 Correlates of Remittances between 1992 and 2010

Variable	I	II	III
Annual trend from 1992	0.098*** [4.61]	0.093*** [5.28]	0.108*** [12.40]
Dummy for Quarter 1	−0.011 [0.17]	0.006 [0.09]	−0.011 [0.17]
Dummy for Quarter 2	0.039 [0.50]	0.041 [0.55]	0.039 [0.53]
Dummy for Quarter 3	0.024 [0.38]	0.034 [0.54]	0.031 [0.50]
Share price index in India, log	0.138 [0.88]		
Log exchange rate, period average	0.18 [0.28]		
Lagged share price index in India, log		0.2 [1.61]	0.106 [1.47]
Lagged log exchange rate, period average		0.274 [0.52]	
Lagged LIBOR (three month)			0.021 [1.15]
Observations	74	75	75

Source: Authors' calculations.

Note: Newey-West standard errors are given in brackets. *, **, *** indicate that the coefficients are significant at the 10, 5, and 1 percent levels, respectively.

sectors took hold by the early 2000s. The liberalization of the financial sector has also resulted in the interest rates being determined more by the liquidity conditions in the market rather than being set by the central bank or the public sector banks, and by the remittances reaching India faster and more cheaply.

It seems reasonable to expect that the remittances respond faster to changing macroeconomic conditions in recent years and are able to benefit from the investment opportunities that the country offers. To allow for the effect of variables on remittances to differ over time, we estimate the regressions separately for 1992–2003 and 2004–10.[4] Results are given in tables 7.5 and 7.6, respectively.

None of the variables we considered had a significant coefficient when we included 1992–2003 in the regressions, some of which are shown in table 7.5. Specifically, GDP growth rates in India or the United States, the stock market index in India, or LIBOR did not affect remittances in 1992–2003 but were significant in the post-2004 period. Regression results (table 7.6) show that the way remittances respond to certain macrovariables has changed over time. In particular, remittances have responded significantly differently to changes in LIBOR and the Indian stock market index in more recent years.

Results show that a 10 percent increase in the Indian stock market index was associated with a 5–8 percent increase in remittances. A decrease in LIBOR by 100 basis points increased remittances by 5–8 percent above their trend. One interpretation of

TABLE 7.5 Correlates of Remittances between 1992 and 2003

Variable	I	II	III
Annual trend from 1992	0.117*** [7.62]	0.116*** [7.39]	0.116*** [7.31]
Dummy for Quarter 1	−0.017 [0.21]	−0.015 [0.18]	−0.006 [0.07]
Dummy for Quarter 2	0.026 [0.26]	0.031 [0.32]	0.03 [0.31]
Dummy for Quarter 3	−0.001 [0.01]	0.001 [0.01]	0.001 [0.01]
Lagged share price index in India, log	0.13 [0.63]	0.085 [0.37]	0.085 [0.35]
Lagged LIBOR (three month)	0.045* [1.75]	0.041 [1.58]	0.042* [1.74]
Real GDP growth, United States		0.02 [0.64]	0.017 [0.52]
Real GDP growth, India			0.017 [0.65]
Observations	48	48	48

Source: Authors' calculations.

Note: Newey-West standard errors are given in brackets. *, **, *** indicate that the coefficients are significant at the 10, 5, and 1 percent levels, respectively.

TABLE 7.6 Correlates of Remittances between 2004 and 2010

Variable	II	III	IV
Annual trend from 2004	0.073** [2.15]	0.003 [0.12]	0.011 [0.28]
Dummy for Quarter 1	0.023 [0.24]	0.089 [1.07]	0.083 [0.96]
Dummy for Quarter 2	0.069 [0.73]	0.125 [1.72]	0.123 [1.65]
Dummy for Quarter 3	0.085 [0.91]	0.12 [1.34]	0.119 [1.30]
Lagged share price index in India, log	0.547*** [3.21]	0.820*** [7.02]	0.783*** [4.09]
Lagged LIBOR (three month)	−0.057** [2.49]	−0.084*** [4.90]	−0.073* [1.79]
Real GDP growth, United States		−0.04** [−2.32]	−0.035 [1.22]
Real GDP growth, India			−0.019 [0.33]
Observations	27	26	26

Source: Authors' calculations.

Note: Newey-West standard errors are given in brackets. *, **, *** indicate that the coefficients are significant at the 10, 5, and 1 percent levels, respectively.

these results is that in recent years remittances are being directed to India more for investment purposes than before.

We assess the vulnerabilities of remittances to certain events, such as political uncertainty, possibility of armed conflict, possible loss in confidence in the Asian economies during the Asian crisis, and so on by including dummies for these events in the regressions. When we include these dummies, we do not find the coefficients of these variables to be significant. Thus remittances do not seem to be affected by these events and uncertainties.

Gupta (2006) shows that factors that influence the trend in remittance practice are correlated with the stock of migrants abroad. We do not include this variable here because of the lack of data for the last few years, but as far as the current slowdown is concerned, unless it reduces the stock of migrants abroad, remittances are likely to grow at the same brisk pace as they have in the last two decades. Besides the factors cited by Ratha and Mohapatra (2009), two other factors that probably work in India's favor are (1) it is a large economy and an economy that is proving to be an attractive investment destination for external capital as well as for remittances and (2) migrants from India consist primarily of skilled workers and perhaps work in cyclically insulated services (such as information technology, health, and education) rather than in cyclically volatile sectors such as construction.[5]

Conclusion

We have analyzed the trends in remittances to India and assessed the impact of the current global slowdown on the flow of remittances there. Accordingly, remittances to India are found to have increased at a robust rate of 10 percent a year since 1992. The movement of remittances is limited around the trend and has not traditionally been affected by domestic or external macroeconomic variables. This pattern has changed somewhat since the early 2000s, and remittances have responded to movements of domestic and international interest rates and to price movements in the Indian stock market. Looking ahead, recent developments in the global economic conditions are not likely to slow the flow of remittances to India even if the current global weaknesses persist or deteriorate further.

One possible case in which the remittances are likely to slow is if the global conditions make the pool of migrants from India smaller, which is unlikely to happen in the near term. The risk factors in the short run include an increase in interest rates in advanced countries, a softening of interest rates in India, and a slowdown in the Indian stock market (resulting in fewer investment opportunities in India).

Notes

1. http://dbie.rbi.org.in/InfoViewApp/listing/main.do?appKind=InfoView&service=%2FInfoViewApp%2Fcommon%2FappService.do.

2. Although a priori the effect of growth in the source country on remittances is ambiguous, a high growth rate is likely to increase the remittances, and a low growth rate may lower the remittances; on the other hand, if particularly bad economic conditions force migrants to return to their home countries, then there might be a spurt in remittances as migrants repatriate their accumulated savings.

3. As indicated in the World Bank data on bilateral stock of migrants, the Bilateral Migration Matrix (World Bank 2011b).

4. The choice of 2004 is admittedly arbitrary. Similar results are obtained if we allow for a shift in the relationship starting in other years around 2004.

5. The reasons for the resilience of remittances to India are consistent with Ratha, Mohapatra, and Silwal (2010a): Remittances are sent by the stock of migrants, which is unlikely to be affected in the near term; since these are a small part of the income, remitters even if hit by the global slowdown will be able to send these; the duration of migration has increased as the uncertainties regarding being able to return have increased; returnees are remitting their accumulated savings back home; and the stimulus packages are likely to boost demand in infrastructure and construction, sectors in which the migrants are extensively employed.

Annex

A: Data Sources and Definitions

Variable name	Definition/construction of variable	Source
Remittances in constant dollars		
Private transfers on current account in dollars, CPI for United States for real values		
RBI website		
LIBOR	3-month LIBOR in dollars	IFS
Lending rate	Lending rates minus inflation rate based on CPI for India	IFS
Asian crisis	Dummy takes a value of 1 for the quarters in which crisis occurred in Asia (1997 Q3–4 through 1998 Q1–2); constructed using exchange rate data	IFS
Oil prices	Oil prices in constant dollars	IFS
Stock price index, India	Index in constant Indian rupees: nominal index deflated by CPI for India	IMF, IFS
Stock price index, United States	Index in constant dollars	IMF, IFS
Exchange rate	Exchange rate with respect to dollar	IMF, IFS
Political uncertainty	Dummy = 1 in the quarters during which the central government resigned midterm	Gordon and Gupta (2004), updated
GDP growth rate	Calculated using annual data	Central Statistical Office and IFS, IMF
U.S. growth rate		IMF, IFS

Source: Authors.

Note: CPI = consumer price index; IFS = Indian Foreign Service; IMF = International Monetary Fund; RBI = Reserve Bank of India.

B: Construction of Dummies to Include Nonlinearities

We construct dummies for the periods when different variables assume extreme values. Thus we define a dummy that takes a value equal to 1 when the Indian growth rate is less than 3 percent and 0 otherwise, and another dummy that takes a value of 1 when the Indian growth rate exceeds 7 percent and 0 otherwise. Similarly we define dummies for the quarters when the U.S. growth rate is high or very low. Thus we define a dummy that takes a value of 1 when the U.S. growth rate exceeds 4 percent and 0 otherwise, and another dummy with a value of 1 when the U.S. growth rate is below 1 percent and 0 otherwise.

We also define dummies for large appreciations and large depreciations in the rupee-dollar exchange rate. The dummy for the large appreciation takes a value of 1 when in a quarter the exchange rate appreciates by at least 2 percent and 0 otherwise; the dummy for large depreciation takes a value of 1 when the depreciation exceeds 2.5 percent and 0 otherwise.

As in Gupta (2006) we define a dummy for a year of bad agricultural production. This dummy takes a value of 1 when the agricultural production growth is negative and 0 otherwise.

We also include dummies for large increases or decreases in oil prices. Thus a dummy for large increases in oil prices takes a value of 1 when the oil price increase exceeds 10 percent and 0 otherwise, and another dummy takes a value of 1 when the oil prices decrease by at least 10 percent and 0 otherwise.

C: Correlation Coefficients between Explanatory Variables

Variable	GDP growth India	GDP growth United States	U.S. share price index	Indian share price index	Gas price index	Exchange rate	Lending rate India
GDP growth United States	0.26 (0.03)	1					
U.S. share price index	−0.10 (0.42)	0.60 (0.00)	1				
Indian share price index	0.37 (0.00)	−0.03 (0.82)	−0.45 (0.00)	1			
Gas price index	0.25 (0.03)	0.03 (0.78)	−0.36 (0.00)	0.68 (0.00)	1		
Exchange rate	−0.34 (0.00)	0.12 (0.30)	0.65 (0.00)	−0.85 (0.00)	−0.74 (0.00)	1	
Lending rate India	−0.08 (0.48)	0.04 (0.71)	0.27 (0.02)	−0.17 (0.14)	0.26 (0.02)	0.16 (0.17)	1
LIBOR	0.11 (0.34)	0.10 (0.38)	0.43 (0.00)	0.12 (0.33)	−0.31 (0.01)	0.22 (0.06)	−0.19 (0.10)

Note: Each entry in each cell refers to the correlation coefficient, and the entry below in parentheses is the p value with which the hypothesis that the correlation is equal to zero can be rejected. The correlation has been calculated by first regressing each variable on a trend and quarterly dummies and taking the residuals.

Chapter 8

Shocks Affecting the Flow and Stability of Workers' Remittances to India

BHUPAL SINGH

WORKERS' REMITTANCES ARE GENERALLY KNOWN to be countercyclical and in the Indian context they have provided stability to the current account balance of the balance of payments (BOP).[1] Compared with other forms of cross-border flows, migrant remittances are less likely to be procyclical, which makes them a relatively stable source of external finance. This nature of remittances was evident during 1998–2001, a period characterized by a decline in private capital flows to developing countries in the wake of the Asian financial crisis. Given the stability and resilience of workers' remittances, many developing countries are taking measures to further attract such inflows.

The surge in migrant workers' remittances during the 1980s, responding to the oil boom in the Middle East and during the 1990s to the new wave of the information technology revolution, has placed India among the highest remittance-receiving countries and provided considerable resilience and sustainability to India's BOP. Policies to improve banking access and the technology of money transfers have also helped increase the flow of remittances and promoted their transfer through formal channels (B. Singh 2010). Numerous regulatory measures have also been undertaken in India to facilitate institutional development for wider access to remittance services, enhancing competition by entry of private money transfer agencies in the market and easing of documentary requirements for small-value remittance transactions. Regulatory measures also aim to bring transparency in the operations of entities dealing with the remittance transfer business. In fact, competition and transparency are critical to bringing down the costs at the recipients' end.

This chapter begins with an assessment of the structural shifts in remittance inflows from abroad. Then the stability of workers' remittances is examined. Third, shocks affecting workers' remittances are studied using an error correction model. Finally, conclusions and policy implications are presented.

Structural Shifts in Remittance Inflows

Two clear structural shifts in remittance flows in India can be identified: (1) in the early 1980s following the oil price boom in the Gulf countries and the export of unskilled and semiskilled labor from India and (2) in the mid-1990s, coinciding with the new wave of migration of skilled labor in technology-related sectors. Second, the microstructure of the remittance mechanism shows that in the current decade the share of remittances repatriated through the route of the "local withdrawals" from nonresident Indian (NRI) deposits has risen vis-à-vis the remittances transferred for "family maintenance" (figure 8.1). In the case of the former, the inflows to NRI rupee deposits are subsequently domestically withdrawn by the NRIs or their dependents for local expenditures. Thus, whereas in the "first leg" of inflow, funds remitted form part of NRI deposits, in the "second leg" the funds are withdrawn locally and become unilateral transfers.[2]

FIGURE 8.1 Structure of Workers' Remittances to India, 1975–2010

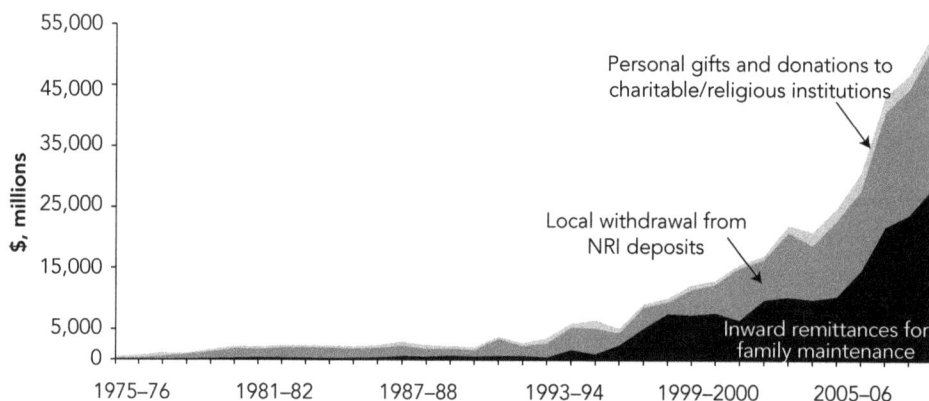

Sources: Invisibles in India's Balance of Payments, Reserve Bank of India Monthly Bulletin, various issues.

This structural change in the channels of remittance transfer seems to suggest that a larger share of remittances could be affected by the motives of domestic investment rather than consumption by the dependent households. Third, unlike capital flows, remittances have emerged as a relatively stable source of financing because these are found to be relatively less sensitive to interest rate changes and have a strong "home bias." Fourth, gold brought home by returning Indians, which used to be an important conduit of remittances by the workers, particularly from the Gulf countries, lost its relevance since the liberalization of gold import policy in the mid-1990s. The government permitted imports of gold by certain nominated agencies for sale to jewelry manufacturers, exporters, NRIs, holders of special import licenses, and domestic users. Nominated agencies and banks were permitted to import gold under different arrangements such as suppliers and buyers credit basis, consignment basis, and outright purchases. Fifth, since the mid-1990s, the source regions of remittances have increasingly shifted from the traditional remitters, the Gulf countries, to the host of the new wave of migration in information technology, the United States.

Historical trends in workers' remittances to India suggest that remittance inflows attained significance in India's BOP in response to the oil boom in the Middle East. The inflows have also been aided by policy measures to foster the use of formal channels for remitting funds with key measures such as the market-determined exchange rate, current account convertibility, liberalization of capital account, speedier processing of remittance transfers through bank branches, and efforts to expand the outreach of remittance services to remote locations. As these factors had considerably reduced incentives for *hawala* transfers, officially recorded inflows rose. The incentives by the banking system to attract remittances from overseas Indians in the form of deposits include numerous deposit schemes. In the 1970s, the two oil shocks shifted substantial resources toward oil-exporting countries, which provided investment and employment opportunities in the oil-rich countries. The Reserve Bank devised specific deposit schemes to tap the savings of NRIs employed in these countries. Special schemes for NRIs were initiated in February 1970 with the introduction of the Non-Resident External Rupee Account. This was followed by foreign currency–denominated schemes.

Since the 1990s, the policy with respect to the nonresident deposit schemes has been to retain the attractiveness of these schemes to maintain capital flows from abroad, while at the same time reducing the effective cost of borrowing in terms of interest outgo and cost to macroeconomic management. In line with these objectives, although the interest rates on these deposits have been gradually deregulated, the reserve requirements and, in the recent period, interest rate ceilings have been fine-tuned in relation to capital flow cycles. The cumulative impact of these factors is reflected in a structural break in the inflows of workers' remittances to India that occurred after 1990–91, broadly mirroring the new wave of migration to technology-related sectors in developed countries.[3]

The economic boom following the oil price shocks of the 1970s and the 1980s created sustained demand for labor in the oil-rich regions of West Asia and North Africa, particularly in the petroleum and construction sectors. Therefore, the major outflow of emigrant workers from India in the last few decades shifted in favor of the Gulf countries. Indian migrant labor in the Gulf countries is estimated to number above 3 million with 70 percent as semiskilled and unskilled workers and 20–30 percent as professionals. Most migrants to the Middle East countries are temporary workers who return to India after the expiration of their contractual employment. The changing pattern of migration from predominantly unskilled and semiskilled to skilled labor is reflected in the structural shift in the regional sources of remittances to India during the 1990s. The share of Asia, representing mainly the Middle East, seems to have moved in tandem with the cyclical changes in the oil economy (table 8.1). The dominance of North America in recent years reflects mainly the pattern of migration to information technology sectors.

TABLE 8.1 Source Regions of Workers' Remittances to India

Year	Asia	North America	Europe	Other	Total ($)
		Percent			
1997–98	31.3	37.1	26.0	5.6	11,875
2000–01	34.3	44.9	19.0	1.8	13,065
2006–07	34.9	32.5	17.0	15.6	30,835
2007–08	34.8	32.7	16.9	15.5	43,508
2008–09	34.9	29.4	19.5	16.1	46,903
2009–10 (April–September)	34.8	29.7	19.5	16.0	27,515

Sources: Report on Currency and Finance, Reserve Bank of India and RBI Monthly Bulletin, April and November 2006.

Are Workers' Remittances Stable Inflows?

The large and volatile movements in capital flows to developing countries since the 1980s have highlighted the risks associated with such flows, that is, asset price volatility, sharp misalignment of the exchange rate, and disruption of the domestic financial sector. Capital flows to developing and emerging economies, specifically short-term private capital, are known to be procyclical. It is in the backdrop of financial crisis in developing countries, particularly in the 1990s, and the pursuit of stability in external financial flows that cross-border remittance flows have gained increasing attention. Workers' remittances are influenced by a different set of factors, including life-cycle savings, family obligations, and implicit loan contracts, therefore such flows are assumed to be less sensitive to factors such as interest rate arbitrage that drive the capital flows. Remittances appear to be a much more stable source of income than private flows, both direct and portfolio, which tend to be more volatile and flow into a limited set of countries (Gammeltoft 2002; Ratha 2003; Sander 2003). The stable nature of workers' remittances is clearly borne out by the measure of volatility, which turns out to be much lower in the case of remittances vis-à-vis components of capital flows to developing countries.

The stable nature of workers' remittances to India is evident in that these inflows have stabilized around 3 percent of gross domestic product (GDP) since the latter half of the 1990s. Workers' remittances appear to be the most stable component among the components of India's balance of payments (table 8.2). This underlines the overall

TABLE 8.2 Relative Volatility of Workers' Remittance Inflows to India

coefficient of variation (%)

Item	1970s	1980s	1990s	2000s
Current account				
Merchandise exports	46.8	24.9	27.9	53.2
Merchandise imports	54.1	17.3	32.9	62.9
Services exports	66.6	14.5	48.5	62.5
Services imports	59.3	28.2	44.6	52.7
Workers' remittances	97.6	7.3	49.3	49.5
Capital account				
Foreign investment	112.6	30.8	69.8	84.7
FDI	—	—	79.6	88.7
Portfolio	—	—	87.4	144.3
External aid	126.3	32.0	48.5	347.2
Overseas commercial borrowings	78.9	61.4	87.9	145.4
Nonresident Indian deposits	120.3	73.4	67.7	67.1

Source: Author's calculations.

Note: FDI = foreign direct investment.

significance of remittances as a source of stable financing for developing countries. Second, unlike the capital inflows, there does not seem to be procyclicality in remittance inflows to India.

It is sometimes believed that the relative stability of workers' remittances may be typically influenced by the predominance of local withdrawal in NRI deposits—an indirect channel of remitting funds by migrant workers, which could be influenced by investment motives. Numerous developing economies mobilize a part of their resources through special deposit schemes designed for nonresidents. Such schemes have been successful in countries with a large expatriate population such as Egypt, Greece, Israel, Lebanon, Pakistan, Spain, Sri Lanka, Thailand, Turkey, and some Eastern European countries. Most of these countries have instituted deposit schemes denominated in foreign currency as well as local currency. These deposit schemes are also designed to attract remittances from overseas workers. As the NRI deposits have been an important route for remittance repatriation to India, the inflows under such deposits are perceived as signaling the pace of future remittances. The empirical evidence, however, is contrary to the perception that a higher share of local withdrawal may have led to higher volatility in remittance inflows to India because of the perceived belief that local withdrawals may be influenced by interest rate movements (table 8.3). The available body of literature on the role of the interest rate and exchange rate differential in causing movement in workers' remittance inflows also seems to be inconclusive.[4]

TABLE 8.3 Volatility in the Components of Workers' Remittances to India

coefficient of variation (%)

Period	Total workers' remittances	Inward remittances for family maintenance	Local withdrawals from NRI deposits
1970s–80s	34.2	56.9	44.7
1990s	49.3	101.9	41.6
2000s	49.5	52.8	49.1

Source: Author's calculations.

Identifying Shocks to Workers' Remittances

The behavior of remittance inflows to India can be captured by various factors, such as activity in the host country, wage differentials, the exchange rate, numbers of migrants, and the like. As far as the sources of remittance inflows are concerned, a significant share of remittances to India continues to be contributed by inflows from the oil-exporting countries of the Middle East. The behavior of remittances to India is likely to be influenced by growth patterns in these countries, best represented in the form of oil prices. Another important source region of remittance inflows to India that has emerged in recent years is the United States. Oil prices of oil-exporting countries are taken as the indicator of economic activity because remittances have predominantly originated from the Middle East. The exchange rate elasticity is found to be significant, which implies that depreciation in the exchange rate enhances the domestic currency value of the funds remitted to the recipient in the home country. Some empirical studies suggest that remittance inflows are a relatively stable source of external finance because these are less sensitive to interest rates (Gupta 2005; Jadhav 2003; Nayyar 1989). The estimates suggest that interest rate differentials may not be significant in determining remittances, which strengthens the argument that remittances are a stable source of developmental finance.

Based on the literature on the behavior of remittance flows, the key determinants of workers' remittances to India can be identified as economic activity in the host country and exchange rate and interest rate differentials.[5] We make an attempt with alternative determinants in capturing the behavior of remittance inflows for the period beginning with the first quarter of 1988 through the third quarter of 2008, taking into account the shadow measures of economic activity in the host country (index of Dubai oil price), real U.S. GDP, exchange rate (rupee-dollar exchange rate), and interest rate differential (differential between the yield on 91-day government of India treasury bills and the six-month London Interbank Offered Rate [LIBOR] interest rate). The data are sourced from the Handbook of Statistics on Indian Economy and the Monograph on India's Balance of Payments, Reserve Bank of India. We use a vector error correction model because the Johansen cointegration test suggests a single cointegrating vector between the variables considered (table 8.4).[6]

TABLE 8.4 Johansen Cointegration Test

Null hypothesis	Alternate hypothesis	Trace statistics	Critical value (0.05)
Model 1			
Unrestricted cointegration rank test (trace)			
$r = 0$	$r = 1$	51.20	47.86
$r \leq 1$	$r = 2$	19.38	29.80
Unrestricted cointegration rank test (maximum eigen value)			
$r = 0$	$r = 1$	31.83	27.58
$r \leq 1$	$r = 2$	13.85	21.13
Model 2			
Unrestricted cointegration rank test (trace)			
$r = 0$	$r = 1$	56.80	47.86
$r \leq 1$	$r = 2$	20.34	29.80
Unrestricted cointegration rank test (maximum eigen value)			
$r = 0$	$r = 1$	36.46	27.58
$r \leq 1$	$r = 2$	12.64	21.13

Source: Author's calculations.

The period from the 1970s to the mid-1990s was dominated by remittance inflows from the Middle East. No single indicator of real activity is available for the Middle East countries, and so we use a proxy, the index of oil prices for the Middle East countries. The benchmark estimates of the long-run determinants of workers' remittances (Model 1) reveal that the oil price ($\log P^{oil}$), capturing the income effect, seems to be a key factor influencing remittance inflows to India (table 8.5). Alternative estimates suggest that a 1 percent increase in oil prices leads to a 0.8–1.1 percent increase in

TABLE 8.5 Long-Run Cointegrating Estimates of Workers' Remittance Inflows to India Based on Vector Error Correction Model

Variable	Model 1	Model 2
$\log P^{oil}_{t-1}$	1.08 (8.02)	0.76 (5.37)
$\log ER^{INR/USD}_{t-}$	0.97 (2.76)	—
$R^{TB91D-LIBOR6M}_{t-1}$	0.15 (4.19)	0.11 (7.13)
$\log Y^{US}_{t-1}$	—	2.50 (5.50)
Constant	0.08	18.37
R^2	0.46	0.46

Source: Author's calculations.

Note: Dependent variable: workers' remittances to India ($\log RMT$). Figures in parentheses are t-statistics.

remittance inflows to India. The responsiveness of remittances to the financial variables, that is, exchange rate (log $ER^{\text{INR/USD}}$) and interest rate differentials ($R^{\text{TB91D-LIBOR6M}}$), is also found to be significant.[7] This implies that a depreciation of the rupee against the dollar enhances the domestic currency value of funds received by the beneficiaries in India and hence provides arbitrage for higher inflows.

The significant response of remittances to the interest rate differential—a measure of arbitrage—could be attributed to the fact that a large part of remittance inflows is in the form of local withdrawals from NRI deposits. It has been argued that the overall behavior of workers' remittances may be influenced by interest rate differentials in the Indian case because the funds locally withdrawn from NRI deposits may be more influenced by interest rate movements (Jadhav and Singh 2006).

Recognizing the United States as an emerging source of remittance inflows to India in recent years, we estimate Model 2 considering both the economic activity in the Middle East (log P^{oil}) and the United States (log Y^{US}). It can be observed that the response of remittances to the level of activity in the United States seems to be higher than that of the Middle East countries, reflecting the altering dynamics of the remittance inflows to India. Although a unit change in oil prices leads to a 0.8 percent change in remittance inflows to India, the impact of a unit change in the real income in the United States leads to a 2.5 percent increase in remittance inflows to India. The relatively high impact of a change in the real incomes in the United States on remittance inflows to India could be attributed to a high level of per capita income of the Indian migrants working in information technology–related areas and financial services and investment motives of the migrants.

Given the above long-run cointegration relation, the short-run response of the variables to the error correction term, that is, the deviation of remittance inflows from long-run trajectory, is presented in table 8.6. The coefficient of the error correction term in the error correction equation of log RMT suggests that there is an adjustment to deviation from the long-run path of remittances in about two and a half to four quarters. This also underlines relative stability in workers' remittances to India.

TABLE 8.6 Error Correction: Short-Run Dynamics

Variable	Model 1	Model 2
$\Delta(\log RMT)$	−0.25 (−4.38)	−0.44 (−4.94)
$\Delta(\log Y^{\text{US}})$	—	0.0 (0.96)
$\Delta(\log P^{\text{oil}})$	0.05 (1.20)	−0.03 (−0.39)
$\Delta(r^{\text{diff}})$	0.62 (1.90)	0.65 (1.30)
$\Delta(\log EXR)$	0.01 (0.59)	—
R^2	0.48	0.46

Source: Author's calculations.

Note: Figures in parentheses are t-statistics. — = not included in the model.

The impulse response analysis reveals that a positive shock to real activity in the host country, that is, the Middle East, causes significant variation in remittance inflows to India for about eight quarters, and in the subsequent quarters the impact is stabilized (figures 8.2 and 8.3). The impact of real activity on remittance inflows is realized with a lag of three quarters. Remittances also respond to a shock to interest rate differentials with a lag of four quarters, and the peak impact is realized by the end of eight quarters. Remittances respond positively to an exchange rate depreciation of domestic currency in the short run as the value of transfers realized in terms of local currency increases. Over the medium to long run, however, the impact of the rupee depreciation on remittance inflows seems to be negative. A significant short-run impact of the residual shocks in the model on remittance inflows is also seen, which could capture the cumulative impact of factors such as economic and financial uncertainties in the host countries, fear of job losses among migrants, precautionary savings by the migrants and planning for contingencies in the recipient countries, and the like.

FIGURE 8.2 Impulse Response of Workers' Remittances to Various Shocks in Model 1

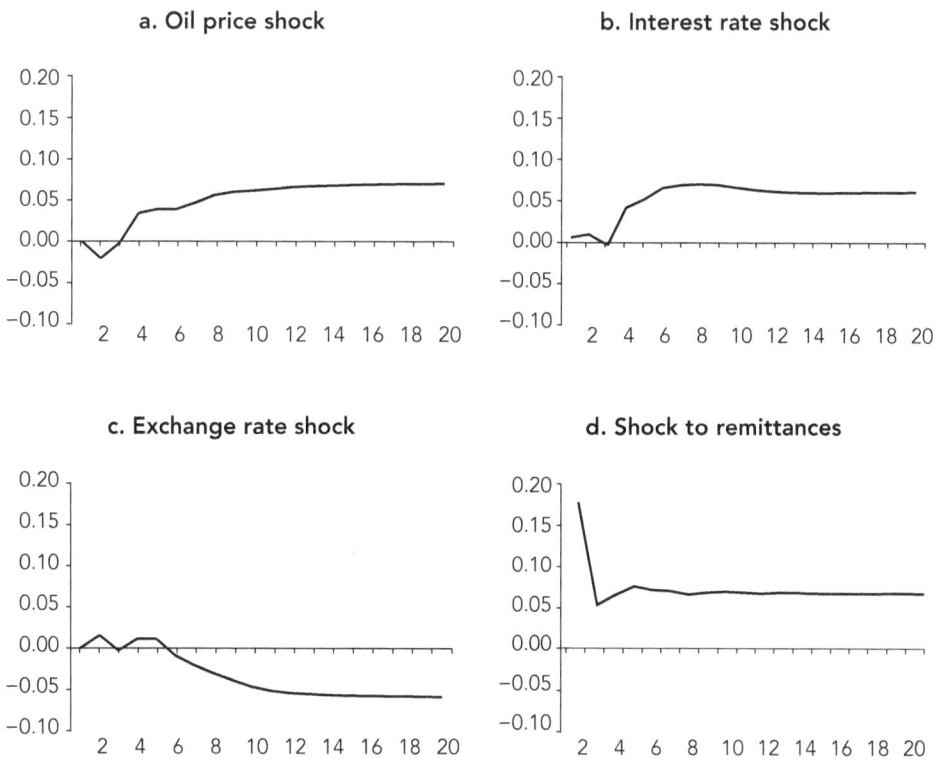

a. Oil price shock

b. Interest rate shock

c. Exchange rate shock

d. Shock to remittances

Source: Author.

FIGURE 8.3 Impulse Response of Workers' Remittances to Various Shocks in Model 2

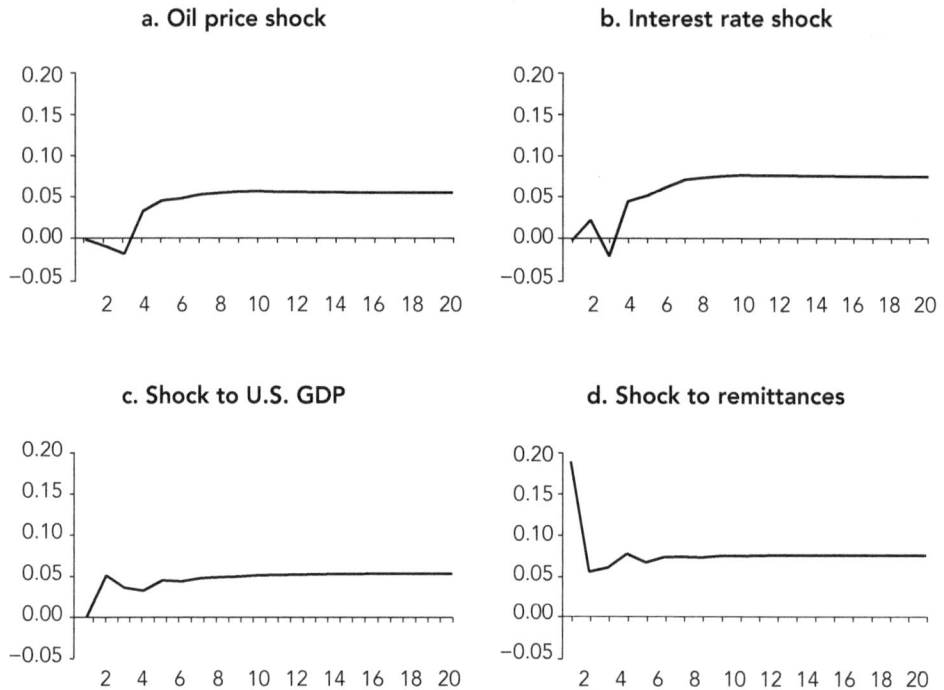

a. Oil price shock

b. Interest rate shock

c. Shock to U.S. GDP

d. Shock to remittances

Source: Author.

Estimates from Model 1 show that shocks to remittances explain the largest share of the fluctuations in remittance inflows to India in the short run; their impact, however, fizzles out over the long run (table 8.7). Shocks to real activity in the Middle East emerge as an important driver of fluctuations in remittance inflows to India in the medium to long run. Interest rate differentials between the remittance-sending and -receiving countries also significantly affect the remittance inflows in the medium to long run.

The variance decomposition analysis based on Model 2 reiterates the results of impulse responses that shocks to remittances explain mainly short-run behavior of remittances. The medium to long-run behavior is, however, explained by the level of real activity in the host countries. Model 2 captures the impact of real activity in another important source region of remittances, the United States. The aggregate impact of real activity in both the Middle East and the United States emerges as the most dominant factor explaining remittance inflows to India. Interest rate differentials also explain a significant part of fluctuations in remittance inflows to India. This could be attributed to the investment motive of migrants sending remittances.

Figure 8.4 reveals that although remittance inflows from overseas migrants to India has witnessed some cyclical slowdown since the third quarter of 2008 because of subdued economic activity in the United States and the Gulf countries, a significant

TABLE 8.7 Variance Decomposition of Workers' Remittances

Quarters	Shocks to real activity in the Middle East	Shocks to real activity in the United States	Exchange rate shocks	Interest rate shocks	Shocks to remittances
Model 1					
1	0.0	—	0.0	0.0	100.0
4	3.1	—	0.8	2.8	93.4
8	10.4	—	2.0	16.2	71.5
12	16.6	—	7.1	19.3	57.1
16	20.2	—	10.9	19.2	49.6
20	22.5	—	13.2	19.1	45.2
Model 2					
1	0.0	0.0	—	0.0	100.0
4	2.6	8.6	—	4.6	84.2
8	10.7	11.9	—	16.0	61.4
12	13.9	13.3	—	21.6	51.2
16	16.3	15.1	—	22.0	46.6
20	17.0	15.7	—	23.3	44.0

Source: Author's calculations.

FIGURE 8.4 Annual Growth Rate in Workers' Remittance Inflows to India, 1992–2010

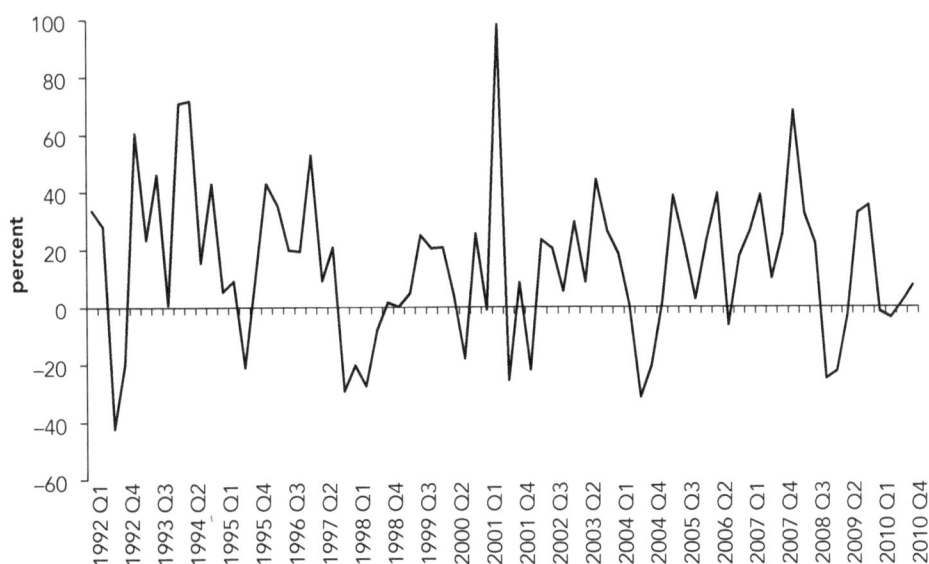

Source: Handbook of Statistics on the Indian Economy, Reserve Bank of India.

deceleration in remittance inflows was witnessed in the fourth quarter of 2008, which continued until the second quarter of 2009. First, oil prices declined from their peak levels, which significantly affected activity in the Middle East region, a significant source of remittances to India. Second, the sharp decline in real activity in the United States along with associated uncertainties seems to have also adversely affected remittance inflows to India. The model estimates suggest a significant impact of real activity shock on remittances, and so it is expected that economic shocks in the host countries could have significantly affected remittance inflows to India. The momentum in remittances, however, was maintained in the subsequent period, though with some stagnation in 2010. Jha and colleagues (2010) suggest that although remittance inflows to developing countries in Asia have slowed in response to the global financial crisis, they have not experienced a sharp drop. They further argue that we are unlikely to see the growth in remittances experienced during the last two decades given that an important share of that growth was due to better recording of remittances and an increased use of wire transfers on the part of migrants.

Empirical evidence suggests that the predominant portion of the cross-border remittances received by Indian households are utilized for family maintenance (61 percent), that is, to meet the requirements of migrant families for food, education, health, and the like (Reserve Bank of India 2010). On average, about 20 percent of the funds received are deposited in bank accounts, and about 4 percent of the funds received are invested in land, property, and equity shares. It might be possible that a slowdown in remittance inflows to India may have affected the consumption of households to the extent they are dependent on remittances for sustenance. As more than half of remittances received are for family maintenance, the possibility exists of a consumption effect.

Conclusion

A structural shift in remittance inflows from migrant Indians occurred in the early 1980s following the oil price boom in the Gulf countries and migration of unskilled and semiskilled labor from India. This was followed by another structural shift in the mid-1990s, coinciding with the new wave of migration of skilled labor in the information technology–related sectors. Empirical estimates suggest inherent stability in remittance inflows to India in the medium to long run, and they emerge as the least volatile component of India's BOP and a stable source of external finance.

Shocks to real activity in the Middle East emerge as an important driver of fluctuations in remittance inflows to India in the medium to long run. Interest rate differentials between the remittance-sending and -receiving countries also significantly affect the remittance inflows in the medium to long run, which could be attributed to the investment motive of migrants sending remittances. Results from alternative models also reveal that shocks to remittances, indicating uncertainties in the host country and precautionary savings, could explain mainly the short-run behavior of remittances, whereas the medium- to long-run dynamics is explained by the level of real activity in the host countries of the Middle East and the United States. The real activity in both the Middle East and the United States together emerges as the most dominant factor explaining remittance inflows to India. A significant part of the remittance inflows to India are utilized for family maintenance, and so the adverse shocks to remittances during the recent global financial crisis may have affected at-home consumption adversely.

Besides the fundamental factors, transfer cost is also an important factor determining inflow of remittances through formal channels. Providers of remittance services in the formal sector typically charge a fee of 10–15 percent of the principal amount to handle the small value transfers typically made by migrants (World Bank 2006a). High fees place a financial burden on the senders and the recipients. The elements of remittance costs typically include an exchange rate, transfer fee, and charges imposed on domestic delivery. A weak competitive environment in the remittance market, lack of access to technology-supporting payment and settlement systems, and burdensome regulatory and compliance requirements all tend to keep fees high. Reducing transaction costs may enhance incentives to remit and significantly increase formal remittance inflows. Cost reduction, however, to a large extent depends on the regulations for small-value transfers and remittance services available in the host country rather than those of the home country because a predominant portion of the cost is determined by the remitting bank or financial entity.

Notes

1. Remittances generally rise when the recipient economy suffers a downturn in activity or macroeconomic shocks due to financial crisis, natural disaster, or political conflict. By compensating for foreign exchange losses due to these shocks, remittances may smooth consumption and thus play a part in maintaining the economic stability of recipient countries.

2. Because the funds remitted by NRIs through the above-mentioned channels are analytically not very different from worker's remittances, such remittances have been categorized with worker's remittances.

3. The statistical results on structural breaks in remittance flows to India for the sample period 1980–81 to 2010–11 indicate the year of regime change as 1991 with log-likelihood ratio = 67.17.

4. Swamy (1981) found that interest rate differentials between the host and the home countries and exchange rates were not significant variables in affecting remittance flows. Straubhaar (1986) also provides empirical support for such observations. Russell (1986), however, argues that these may not be the threshold level of difference that the interest rate and exchange rate differentials have to attain so as to affect remittance flows. In the Indian case, Nayyar (1989) argued that repatriated deposits grew at a faster rate in response to interest rate differentials resulting from declining interest rates in international capital markets. Another study in the Indian case concerning NRI deposit flows concludes that the flow of NRI deposits responds positively to the difference between interest rates for these deposits and LIBOR (Gordon and Gupta 2004).

5. Workers' remittances are recognized to be determined by the migrants' educational level, income, and motivation to transfer the accumulated capital for investment in the home country (Brown 1997). The empirical literature does not seem to be unanimous on the determinants of workers' remittances. The time series data on demographic characteristics of migrants are not available in the Indian context.

6. The robustness of the estimates is calibrated through diagnostic tests such as the Lagrange Multiplier test for serial correlation among the residuals and the Normality test, which indicate that the residuals do not have serial correlation and are multivariate normal.

7. In the Indian context, some empirical studies suggest that remittance inflows are less sensitive to interest rates (Gupta 2005; Jadhav 2003).

Chapter 9

Migrant Remittances in Nepal: Impact of Global Financial Crisis and Policy Options

SANKET MOHAPATRA, DILIP RATHA, AND ANI SILWAL

MIGRATION AND REMITTANCES IN NEPAL have grown in size and importance in recent decades. Given its small size, relative lack of diversification, and rising pressures on domestic labor markets, migration will continue to be a crucial part of Nepal's development strategy. It is therefore important to understand how these flows can be managed better and which policies can improve their development impact. Bringing remittances into formal banking channels and mobilizing remittances for savings and investment remain some of the key challenges for Nepal.

Between 2 and 5 million Nepalese, out of a population of 30 million, are believed to be living abroad, with a large number in India. Nepal has seen a boom in migration since the mid-1990s, primarily to Gulf Cooperation Council (GCC) countries and East Asia. Official data on new deployments show that new migration to destinations outside India fell briefly during the financial crisis before recovering quickly.

Remittances sent by these migrants are the most important source of external finance for Nepal's economy. Officially recorded remittances are estimated to have reached $3.5 billion in 2010. Remittances are larger than other sources of foreign exchange such as exports, official development assistance, and tourism revenues. These flows are an

This chapter—a product of the joint Migration and Remittances Unit of the Development Prospects Group, Development Economics Vice Presidency, and Poverty Reduction and Economic Management Network—was prepared as a background paper for the World Bank's country team for Nepal. We gratefully acknowledge extensive discussions with Hisanobu Shishido.

important source of income for many households and have been associated with a significant reduction in poverty. Remittances have also helped finance Nepal trade deficit over the last decade. With the onset of the financial crisis, remittances to Nepal decelerated in 2009 to 9.5 percent from a staggering growth of 57.3 percent in 2008, but grew by 17.7 percent in 2010 (Mohapatra and Ratha 2010).

Nepal's remittance market appears relatively efficient in the delivery of remittances, with many international and local money transfer operators (MTOs), banks, and other institutions providing remittance services, even in remote regions of Nepal. Although a majority of people do not have accounts with commercial banks, banks typically act as distributors of remittances for MTOs, and very few Nepalese banks actively promote financial products such as savings and deposit accounts, home loans, and health and life insurance to remittance senders or recipients. The lack of valid documentation of migrants in the host countries and consequent lack of access to bank accounts and lack of bank branches near beneficiaries are some of the impediments to the use of formal remittance channels.

This chapter provides an overview of migration and remittance trends in Nepal and suggests policy options to reduce costs, increase competition, and foster use of formal remittance channels. Many of these lessons are drawn from experiences of other migrant origin and destination countries. The chapter is organized as follows. The next section outlines recent trends in migration and remittances and the impact of the financial crisis on these flows. The third section provides an overview of the remittance market in Nepal. The fourth section suggests policy options for improving remittance markets. The fifth section discusses leveraging remittances for improving capital market access through remittance securitization and diaspora bonds. The sixth section discusses measures to improve migration policies and institutions. The final section concludes.

Migration and Remittances in Nepal and the Impact of the Financial Crisis

Migration has historically been important to the Nepalese economy. Most migrants traditionally went to India in search of employment. This has changed in recent years, with migrants going to GCC and East Asian countries. The number of migrants has also increased dramatically. This change in the number and destination of migrants has made remittances to Nepal more linked to the global economy.

Migration Trends

Migration is an important feature of the Nepalese economy. Between 2 and 5 million Nepalese, out of a population of 30 million, are currently believed to be living abroad. This is much higher than official figures. A large share of this migration is to neighboring India with whom Nepal shares an open border; these migrants are largely unrecorded in official statistics. Nepal's 2001 population census estimated that more than 760,000 Nepalese (10 percent of men and 1.2 percent of women) were living abroad in 2000. More than 1 million Nepalese were working abroad in countries other than India in 2004 (World Bank 2006c). Unofficial estimates of the number of Nepalese migrants range from 400,000 in Malaysia, 300,000 in Qatar, and 60,000–70,000 in the Republic of Korea to 1–4 million in India.[1] Some 125,000–275,000 Nepalese migrants are estimated to be working in the United Arab Emirates, of which half are in construction, hospitality, tourism, and security. Although the majority of Nepalese migrants are in India, no official data exist on migration to or remittances from India. A significant number of undocumented Nepalese migrants are found in some countries, with Japan estimated to have 20,000–30,000 such migrants.

Nepal has seen a boom in migration since the mid-1990s. Officially recorded new migration flows to countries outside South Asia increased dramatically during the last decade, from 36,000 in 1999–2000 to 294,000 in 2009–10 (figure 9.1).[2] Almost all new work-related migration is to GCC countries and East Asia.[3] The six GCC countries together accounted for more than three-quarters of new migration from Nepal in fiscal year 2008–09. Of the GCC countries, Qatar was the largest destination with 35 percent of all new deployments, followed by Saudi Arabia (22 percent), and the United Arab Emirates (14 percent). The other major destination was Malaysia, which accounted for 16 percent of new deployments in fiscal year 2008–09. Malaysia was the largest destination of Nepalese migrants, with a share of 40–50 percent of overall deployments between 2001–02 and 2005–06, but its share has fallen substantially as new migration to GCC countries picked up.[4] However, this trend reversed in 2010 after Malaysia increased its hiring of more Nepalese workers.[5]

FIGURE 9.1 Primary Destinations of Nepalese Migrants, Excluding India, 1999–2000 to 2009–10

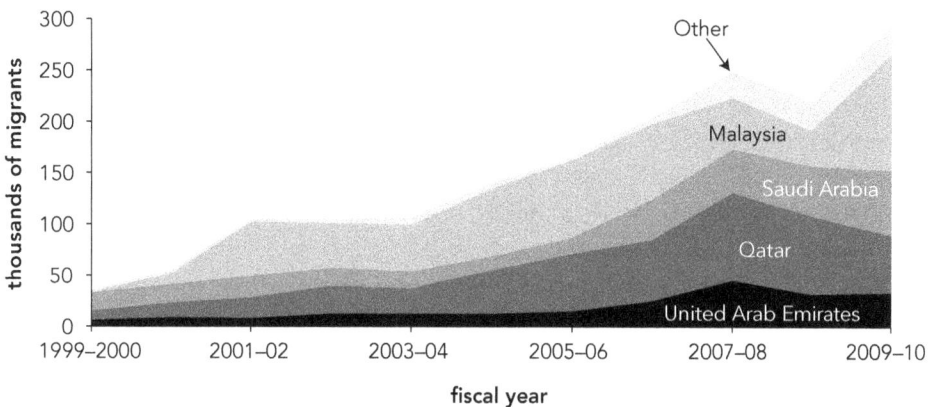

Source: Department of Foreign Employment, Government of Nepal.

Household surveys conducted in 1995–96 and 2003–04 also suggest that the destinations of migrants have changed significantly during this period. India's share in overall migration has declined, with the share of international migrants going to countries other than India increasing from 7 percent in 1995–96 to 31 percent in 2003–04 (World Bank 2006c). The share of officially recorded female emigrants was only 3 percent in fiscal year 2009–10. Many female migrants migrate unofficially through India. They were not allowed to legally migrate for work until 2007. Since most female migrants are undocumented in the Middle East and elsewhere, the capacity of Nepalese embassies to help them is limited.

Official data on new deployments show that new migration to destinations other than India fell since mid-2008 with the onset of the financial crisis. New migrant deployments peaked in August 2008 and fell significantly in subsequent months, likely because of a decline in demand for labor in the destination countries. The deployment of migrants from Nepal declined from 25,000 in August 2008 to 11,000 in April 2009. Deployments fell by 12 percent in fiscal year 2008–09.[6] This was a sharp slowdown in new migration compared with a 22 percent increase between fiscal years 2006–07 and 2007–08. The number of deployments to Malaysia started falling before the onset of the current crisis, but the decline accelerated since August 2008. Malaysia's share of all flows decreased from 20 percent in August 2008 to 7 percent in April 2009 as Malaysia restricted entry of new immigrants.[7] However, this trend reversed in fiscal year 2009–10, which saw an increase of 34 percent in the number of workers leaving for overseas destinations, primarily because of a surge in migrants to Malaysia, increasing to 114,000 from 35,000 in the previous fiscal year.[8]

Migration flows to GCC countries have also slowed since the onset of the financial crisis, with new deployments falling from nearly 19,000 in August 2008 to less than 10,000 in April 2009. Although new migration flows declined, they are still positive. Existing migrants, who usually work overtime, have been forced to work fewer hours because of the crisis, which is reducing their incomes and their ability to send remittances home.[9] Furthermore, no official data on return migration from the Gulf are available. Anecdotal reports suggest that some Nepalese migrants in the Gulf are staying on illegally even after losing their jobs, and working without legal status. The number of returns appears to be small so far.

The destinations of migration will likely change over time. The destinations that could increase in importance are GCC countries and India because these countries are likely to need new workers. GCC countries have abundant financial resources to continue the construction, tourism projects (hotels, resorts, and restaurants), and investments in infrastructure. For example, Abu Dhabi, one of the seven United Arab Emirates, is building Khalifa City, which will need 150,000 new workers from abroad. Qatar's recent winning bid to host the 2022 World Cup will also mean a surge in construction activity, improving employment opportunities for migrant workers in the country. India will remain an important destination, especially for seasonal migration. In the long term,

Poland and Romania and other new members of the European Union as well as possibly the Russian Federation are also likely to need migrant workers from Nepal.

Recent Remittances Trends

Remittances sent by Nepalese migrants abroad are an important source of external finance for Nepal's economy. Officially recorded flows are estimated to have reached $3.5 billion in 2010 (Mohapatra and Ratha 2010). Recorded remittances were 23 percent of gross domestic product (GDP) in 2009, with the true size, including unrecorded flows, likely to be more than a quarter of GDP. Remittances are several times larger than other sources of Nepal's foreign currency earnings, such as exports of goods and services, official development assistance, and tourism receipts (figure 9.2).

FIGURE 9.2 Growth in Remittances and Other Sources of External Finance Sent to Nepal, 1996–2010

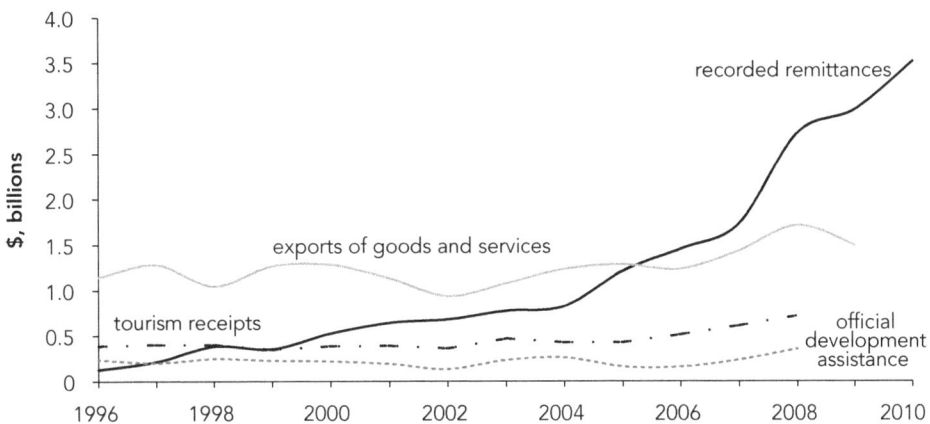

Sources: World Bank; IMF Article IV consultations (remittances data before 2002).
Note: Data for 2010 are estimated.

Remittances have become increasingly important for households in Nepal during the last decade. Thirty-two percent of households received remittances in 2003–04, compared with 23 percent in 1995–96 (World Bank 2006c).[10] Between a fifth and third of the decline in poverty between 1995 and 2004 has been attributed to increased migration during a time of political conflict (World Bank 2006c).[11] Rural households receive a larger share of their remittances from India than do urban households. Remittances were also more important for rural households, comprising 15 percent of household income, than they were for urban households (10 percent of income) in 2003–04.

The share of remittances sent to Nepal from India relative to other countries decreased from about 60 percent in 1995–96 to about 30 percent in 2003–04. Remittances from Qatar, Saudi Arabia, and the United Arab Emirates increased tenfold to 35 percent of foreign remittances during the same period. Remittance flows from GCC countries are important for countries in South Asia, accounting for a fifth of total inflows to the region in 2008.[12] Although oil prices are uncorrelated with remittance outflows, the oil-wealth fueled economic boom in the Gulf resulted in an increase in demand for migrant labor in the Gulf countries. Anecdotal reports suggest that remittances to Nepal from the Gulf, Japan, and Korea are substantially higher than those from India. The average remittance sent from India is about Rs. 10,000 per person per year, whereas those from the Gulf are about Rs. 90,000–100,000 and from Japan and Korea about Rs. 300,000.[13]

With the onset of the financial crisis, remittance flows to developing countries began to slow significantly in the third quarter of 2008 in response to a deepening global financial crisis.[14] Remittance flows to developing countries fell by 5 percent in 2009 (Mohapatra and Ratha 2010). The financial crisis has led to a significant decline in construction, hospitality, and other sectors in GCC countries where many South Asian migrants are employed.[15] Growth has also slowed in other destinations of Nepalese migrants such as India, Korea, and Malaysia. As a result, the growth of remittances to Nepal decelerated significantly in 2009, although flows recovered quickly and grew by 18 percent in 2010 (table 9.1 and figure 9.3).

TABLE 9.1 Remittance Flows to South Asia and to Nepal Grew at a Slower Rate during the Global Financial Crisis but Did Not Decline

Country	2007	2008	2009	2010[a]	2007	2008	2009	2010[a]
	Billions of dollars				Growth rate (%)			
Developing countries	278.0	325.0	307.0	325.0	23	17	−5	6
South Asia	54.0	72.0	75.0	83.0	27	32	5	10
Nepal	1.7	2.7	3.0	3.5	19	57	9	18

Source: Mohapatra and Ratha 2010.
a. Estimate.

Nepal's central bank reports that its data collection methodology does not allow it to identify the source country of remittance inflows (Irving, Mohapatra, and Ratha 2010). The central bank estimates informal remittance flows based on the number of workers who went abroad, workers' average monthly income, and average duration of stay (Irving, Mohapatra, and Ratha 2010). To improve data collection the central bank could require banks and MTOs to provide details on the sources of remittances and collect remittances data from banks as well as MTOs and Internet money transfers. Because remittance flows through informal channels, especially for India, are a significant share

FIGURE 9.3 Remittances to Nepal during the Crisis, April 2007–October 2010

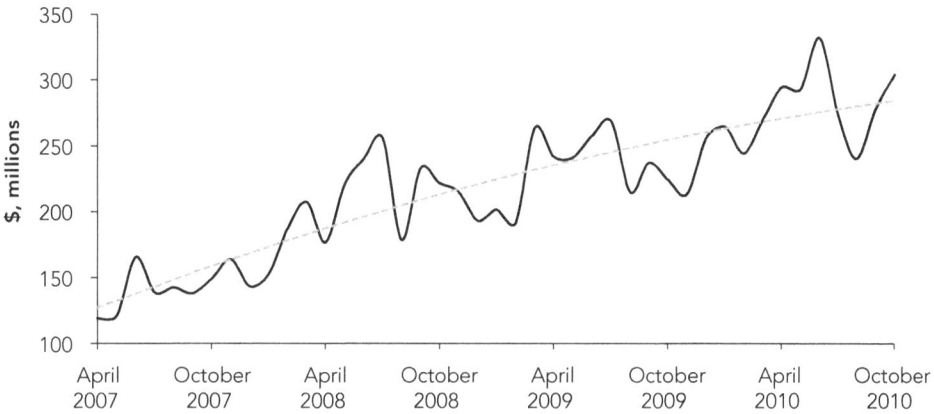

Source: Nepal Rastra Bank.

of total flows to Nepal, collecting data on informal channels is important. In addition to surveys, sources that could be used to estimate informal remittances include foreign exchange bureaus, labor ministries, and embassies in destination countries.

It is important for Nepal to strengthen monitoring of migration and remittance flows (including those to and from India). Improving remittance data collection and dissemination of reliable high-frequency data on remittances and their sources can allow the government to monitor remittances and be a resource for researchers and the media. This would first imply having better data on where people currently live. Although information on migration to GCC countries and to countries other than India is collected, data on return migration and sources of remittances are not available. Nepal and destination countries can cooperate to include migration questions in upcoming censuses and in destination countries to collect better data on stocks of migrants.

The Remittance Market in Nepal

Many providers of remittance services in Nepal and many international and local MTOs, banks, and other institutions provide remittance services even in remote regions of Nepal. Remittances are usually delivered the same day in urban areas, within three days in rural areas, and in less than a week in remote areas. The major money transfer companies and banks have subagents that deliver remittances to recipients in remote areas. However, a majority of people do not have accounts with commercial banks. There were only 1.8 bank branches per 100,000 people in Nepal in 2006, compared with 4.7 in India, whereas ATM access is 0.28 per 100,000 people.

Table 9.2 provides the typical cost of sending remittances to Nepal from different destination countries through the major money transfer companies such as Western

TABLE 9.2 Cost of Sending $200 to Nepal, June 2009

$, billions

Transfer service	Qatar	United Arab Emirates	Saudi Arabia	Malaysia	Korea, Rep.	United States	United Kingdom
Western Union	4.1	6.8	4.8	4.0	22.0	10.0	8.2
MoneyGram	..	5.5	5.3	5.0	15.0	10.0	16.5
UAE Exchange	5.0	5.5	..	..	..	..	8.2
Prabhu Money Transfer	..	..	..	2.8	..	..	..
Muncha Money Transfer	..	..	..	..	..	7.0	9.9
Thamel Money Transfer[a]	10.0	10.0	10.0	10.0	10.0	10.0	10.0

Sources: "Mystery shopping" by World Bank staff; www.money.muncha.com; www.thamelremit.com.

Note: Fees do not include exchange rate commission. Remittance fees were converted to dollars using the respective exchange rates on June 24, 2009. ·· = negligible.

a. Requires international Visa or MasterCard.

Union, MoneyGram, UAE Exchange, Prabhu, and several online remittance providers. These were obtained from the MTO websites and from "mystery shopping" by calling the agents of these MTOs located in the destination countries. These suggest that remittance fees, especially for sending remittances from the Middle East and Malaysia, are in the range of 2–5 percent of the amount, which is significantly lower than the global average of about 9–10 percent.[16] The cost for sending money from Korea is substantially higher.

Online remittance providers such as Muncha.com and Thamel.com provide dedicated money transfer service for Nepalese and are operated by Nepalese diaspora entrepreneurs. These allow direct deposit into recipients' bank accounts and physical delivery of a bank draft to recipients. Thamel even allows migrants to send goods and offers mortgages and vehicle and education loans for nonresident Nepalese residing in the United States in partnership with Kumari Bank. Another provider, International Money Express, offers direct deposits to bank accounts in Nepal, with the money transferred immediately to the partner IME Financial Institution Limited, although it takes longer to reach other banks.

Nepal's remittance market appears relatively efficient in the delivery of remittances, but several issues are found. No legal requirement exists for money transfer companies to operate in partnership with commercial banks to receive inward remittances. However, many Nepalese banks work in de facto or de jure partnerships with major international money transfer companies. Banks typically act as distributors of remittances for MTOs. Very few Nepalese banks actively promote financial products such as savings and deposit accounts, home loans, and health and life insurance to remittance senders or recipients. This may reflect relatively low banking penetration, prevailing high levels of inflation, and the uncertain macroeconomic environment, which might make Nepalese banks unwilling to extend credit to retail borrowers in general, including to non-resident Nepalese. Microfinance institutions cannot send or receive remittances but are allowed only to distribute remittances, acting as subagents of the firms authorized to receive inward remittances. No mobile phone operator in Nepal is authorized to send or receive remittances.

The lack of valid documentation for many Nepalese migrants in the host countries in Europe, North America, and the Gulf and the consequent lack of access to bank accounts and lack of bank branches near beneficiaries are some of the impediments to the use of formal banking channels for remittances. However, several MTOs already operate in the destination countries and facilitate remittance transfers from Nepalese migrants. For example, Prabhu Money Transfer has been allowed to accept deposits in Malaysia and to operate in several locations in India.

As discussed earlier, a large number of Nepalese migrants live in India. In 2008 the Reserve Bank of India and the Nepal Rastra Bank collaborated to launch a cross-border Indo-Nepal remittance service that allows money transfers from any Indian bank to any Nepalese bank and some designated MTOs. However, the take-up of this service has been limited. It requires identification documents and proof of residence, which many Nepalese migrants may not have. Indian banks have very little incentive to offer this service, partly because of a lack of awareness and partly because of the relatively low fee structure mandated by the Reserve Bank of India.[17]

Reducing Remittance Costs and Improving Access to Remittance Services

This section discusses policy options to reduce costs, increase competition, and foster use of formal channels in Nepal, drawing on regional and global experiences. These include improving remittance data collection and awareness of remittance channels, reducing remittance costs, enhancing links between remittances and financial access (by encouraging participation of rural banks, microfinance institutions, and post offices), fostering use of new mobile money transfer technologies, improving retail payment systems, balancing anti–money laundering and countering the financing of terrorism concerns with increasing access to money transfers, and leveraging Nepal's large remittance inflows for improving its access to international capital markets.

Allowing more Nepalese banks and MTOs to operate in destination countries would facilitate remittance flows through formal channels. Providing identification (ID) cards to migrants could facilitate remittance transfers through formal banking channels (World Bank 2006a).[18] These cards would not substitute national passports but would primarily be used by migrants to access financial and other services in both Nepal and destination countries. If Nepal wants to introduce ID cards for migrants, it needs to negotiate with governments of major migrant destination countries to accept these cards. Establishing appropriate infrastructure in embassies abroad to use the new identification documents will also be necessary to build timely data on migrants in destination countries.

Improving national and regional retail payment systems for remittance transmission will reduce transfer costs for businesses and retail customers while fostering new technologies. Improving retail payment systems for facilitating domestic and cross-border remittances requires accelerated efforts to create a national automated clearing and settlement system for real-time fund transfers. Such a system would reduce the time it takes for transferring domestic and international remittances and allow linking banks with point-of-sale devices in retail locations to enable use of debit cards, smart cards, and mobile devices.

Money transfer can act as an entry point for providing remittance senders and recipients without bank accounts in rural areas other financial products and services, such as deposits, savings, and credit facilities. Nepal may need to amend existing regulations to allow these institutions to more fully participate in providing remittance services, instead of simply distributing remittances for money transfer companies. Microfinance institutions may need legal permission to receive foreign exchange. They may also need access to national clearance and settlement systems.

Post offices typically have very strong networks in both urban and rural areas, with significant potential to reach poor populations. To increase involvement of post offices in remittance services, Nepal needs to extend domestic money order facilities to international remittances by linking up with post offices, banks, and MTOs in destination countries. Allowing post offices in rural areas to offer basic checking and savings accounts to remittance recipients and others would promote savings out of remittances received by households. Eliminating exclusive partnerships and encouraging post offices to partner with more money transfer companies or even banks may result in revenue losses in the short term, but these will likely be offset by larger volumes, benefiting the postal networks, migrants, and remittance recipients. Encouraging participation of rural banks and microfinance institutions in providing remittance services will help to improve financial access.

New technologies such as mobile companies and smart cards can also provide fast, convenient, and cheap remittance services within Nepal and help expand financial access. Post offices, microfinance institutions, and rural banks in Nepal can play an important role in providing cheap and convenient remittance services. There could be efforts within Nepal to encourage banks and finance companies to link remittances to consumer loans, housing loans, and small business investments. Mobile and card-based remittances are new technologies that have grown rapidly in recent years.

Although use of mobile phones is at a nascent stage in cross-border transfers, mobile phone and telecom service providers are active in transmitting remittances domestically in countries such as Kenya, the Philippines, and South Africa. Access to mobile phones is a recent phenomenon in Nepal, with the first mobile phones distributed in 1999 when 5,000 lines were issued (Nepal Telecom 2009). By 2008, 15 out of every 100 Nepalese had a mobile phone (figure 9.4).[19]

FIGURE 9.4 Growth in Mobile Phone Subscriptions in Nepal, 2003–08

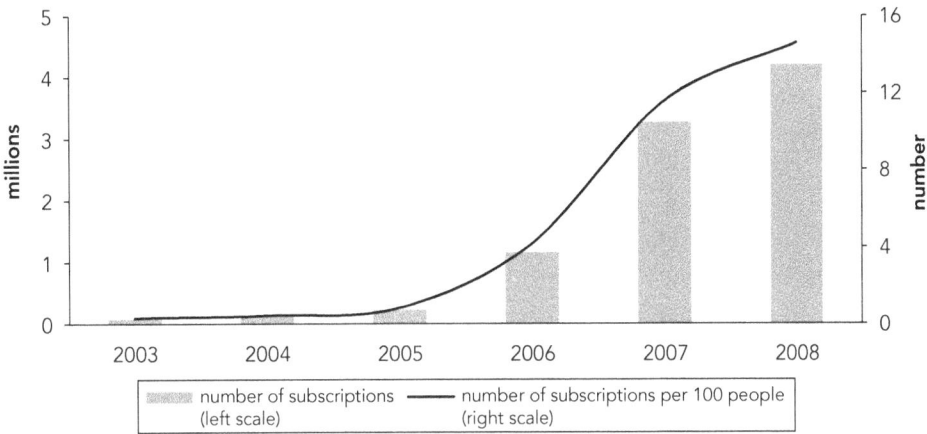

Source: WDI 2009.

Introducing card-based money transfers may be challenging in Nepal given the availability of ATMs outside major cities. To introduce mobile remittances and card-based money transfers, Nepal may need to introduce new telecom and financial services regulations to allow mobile phone operators to provide money transfer services and vice versa. Using mobile and card-based technology for international remittances would require cooperation with destination country banks and governments.

A national price database for available methods to send money and their cost can help remittance senders choose the appropriate channel and improve transparency and competition.[20] If a national price database were established in Nepal, it should be updated frequently (daily or weekly) to capture the latest players, prices, and channels. A website can be used to disseminate the price database. Fliers could be distributed to migrants at the airport before departure, during predeparture orientation, or at embassies in destination countries. This would be a way to reach migrants who do not have easy access to the Internet.

Regulations need to be proportionate with regard to the risk of money laundering and financial crimes, so as not to stifle entry and competition in the remittance marketplace. Many countries have imposed burdensome reporting and compliance requirements for banks and money transfer firms to address concerns of anti–money laundering and countering the financing of terrorism. Balance must be sought between these legitimate concerns and the need to provide incentives for formal transfer. To strike this balance, Nepal needs to recognize remittance transfers as a stand-alone service separate from banking, so that more players can enter the remittances market. Eliminating exclusive partnerships can benefit both migrants and recipients of remittances.

Capital Market Access Leveraging on Remittances: Securitization and Diaspora Bonds

Nepal's large and stable remittance inflows can be used for raising financing from international capital markets at lower cost and at longer maturities for financing infrastructure and other development projects. Banks in Brazil, Egypt, El Salvador, Guatemala, Kazakhstan, Mexico, and Turkey have been able to raise more than $15 billion since 2000 by securitization of future remittance flows (Ketkar and Ratha 2009). The remittance securitization structure mitigates several elements of sovereign risk and makes the remittance-backed bonds attractive to foreign investors but does not affect remittance flows to the ultimate beneficiaries.

Diaspora bonds can be an attractive instrument for governments and the private sector to access the wealth of the diaspora. India and Israel have raised nearly $40 billion by issuing diaspora bonds, often in times of crisis when external sources of finance dry up (Ketkar and Ratha 2009; Ratha 2010a). Nepal recently floated a five-year local currency "Foreign Employment Bond" in June 2010 targeted at its diaspora in Malaysia, Qatar, Saudi Arabia, and the United Arab Emirates. The initial objective was to raise Rs. 7 billion (about $100 million) for infrastructure development. However, the amount floated in the market in mid-2010 was Rs. 1 billion (about $15 million), and the funds that were finally raised were reportedly much lower. This was in part because of limited marketing efforts, a short two-week window of sale, lack of targeting to relatively wealthier members of the diaspora in Europe and North America, and a lower local currency interest rate (9.75 percent) compared with what was being offered by Nepalese commercial banks. The initial launch will provide useful lessons for both Nepal and other developing countries considering issuance of diaspora bonds.

For Nepal to improve its access to capital markets through remittances, it needs to take several measures. Nepal currently does not have a sovereign rating from any of the three major rating agencies: Standard and Poor's, Moody's, and Fitch. Obtaining a sovereign rating, and ensuring that its large and stable remittance inflows are reflected in the sovereign rating, will help to provide a benchmark for both the government and subsovereign entities. Donors and international institutions could provide technical assistance in obtaining credit ratings and in setting up remittance securitization structures and issuing diaspora bonds.[21] Encouraging the flow of remittances through formal banking channels better allows the use of these innovative financing mechanisms for Nepal's development.

Improving Migration Policies and Institutions

Many Nepalese migrant workers face lack of transparency in employment contracts regarding wages, delayed payment of wages, and at times, abuse from employers in destination countries. Bilateral agreements between Nepal and destination countries could help in regulating the recruitment process and protecting rights of migrant workers. Embassies can play a bigger role by having labor attachés in embassies who can verify offer letters and employment contracts, monitor employment conditions through site visits, and monitor recruitment agencies in destination countries.

Countries such as the Philippines have successfully implemented predeparture seminars to disseminate information on travel regulations, immigration procedures, settlement concerns, employment and social security concerns, and rights and obligations of Filipino emigrants (Lueth and Ruiz-Arranz 2007; Mohapatra and Ozden 2009). Often implemented in partnership with the private sector, these programs provide skills related to work at the destination and financial literacy, tools to respond to mistreatment, exploitation, and abuse, and education of workers on remittance channels. Nepal could also utilize predeparture training to migrants to provide information on available remittance channels. Fliers with the latest available options and prices for sending remittances from the destination country can be distributed during these workshops (see the previous section on a remittance price database). Embassies can collaborate with banks to offer seminars on deposit, savings, and credit products at the location of migrants in major destinations.

A migrant welfare fund can improve services to migrants and help in reintegration of returnees by self-employment opportunities and loans for small businesses as well as provide training facilities for skills and languages in demand. The Philippines has successfully implemented a wide range of institutions to protect the rights of their emigrants and made efforts to reintegrate returning migrants. Bangladesh, India, Pakistan, the Philippines, Sri Lanka, and Thailand have also introduced similar funds. Nepal could also greatly benefit from a welfare fund that provides services for overseas workers, helps reintegrate returning migrants, and provides training on sought-after skills in current and potential destination countries.

India will remain a key destination, especially for seasonal migration, due to geographic proximity. India has also been relatively less affected by the current crisis and will remain a driver of regional growth. Although Nepalese migrants are allowed to travel and work in India, they continue to face difficulties in sending remittances through formal channels. Improving opportunities for safe and legal migration and facilitating remittance flows both internationally and within the region can increase their contribution to Nepal's development.

Nepal should continue to explore new labor markets in GCC countries, East Asia, and Europe. This would require implementing training programs in languages and skills to match the changing needs of the global labor market. In the long term, Poland, Romania, Russia, and new members of the European Union are likely to need migrant workers. GCC countries have abundant financial resources to continue investing in infrastructure investments. Nepal could help to equip prospective migrants with skills to match demands of the global labor market. Improving training facilities for sectors such as hospitality, health care, and information technology could allow migrants to move up the skills ladder.

Conclusion

Remittances are the most important source of external finance for Nepal's economy. Officially recorded flows are estimated to have reached $3.5 billion in 2010. Although new migration flows and remittances to Nepal decelerated in 2009 during the global financial crisis, these flows quickly recovered in 2010. Remittances are larger than other sources of foreign exchange such as exports and tourism revenues. This chapter has outlined recent trends in migration and remittances in Nepal and discussed policy options to make remittance services cheaper and more convenient, and to leverage remittances for improving financial access of migrants, their beneficiaries, and financial intermediaries. Some of these measures include increasing information available to migrants on available remittance channels, financial literacy for prospective migrants, working with microfinance institutions and post offices for remittance transactions, increasing trust in the banking system, and improvements in broader payment systems. We have also discussed measures to improve migration policies and institutions.

The remittance market in Nepal is relatively efficient, but market inefficiencies in destination countries ought to be addressed. Major money transfer operators and banks are able to deliver remittances reliably and effectively in Nepal. However, negotiations with authorities in destination countries can improve access to remittance services. Making it easier for migrants to open bank accounts in destination countries will facilitate remittance flows. Increased awareness and better training of prospective Nepalese migrants in languages and skills needed to meet the changing needs of the labor markets in destination countries would also help to improve the development impact of migration.

Notes

1. Based on interviews with money transfer companies, banks, recruitment agencies, embassies, and government officials.

2. The Nepalese fiscal year runs from July 15 to July 14.

3. Nepal Department of Foreign Employment.

4. Malaysia accepted about 75,000 new migrants in fiscal years 2005–06 and 2006–07 and 50,000 new migrants in fiscal year 2007–08.

5. "Malaysia Says 'Yes' to Nepali Housemaids," *Himalayan Times*, January 1, 2011. According to the article, some 400,000 Nepalese are currently working in Malaysia, of which 175,000 are in the manufacturing sector.

6. The figures for fiscal year 2008–09 are from Nepal's Department of Foreign Employment. Media sources have reported employment numbers that are generally consistent with what is presented in this chapter. The *Kathmandu Post*, however, reported on May 18, 2009, that the number of Nepalese migrant workers leaving for foreign destinations during the first 10 months of the current fiscal year decreased by 21 percent to 147,545 compared with 185,817 in the same period of the previous year (see http://www.kantipuronline.com). The article also reported that some 37,000 people left using their personal contacts in the 10 months up to April 2009.

7. "Suspension of New Work Permits Hits Nepal's Economy," *Xinhua,* January 25, 2009 (http://news.xinhuanet.com/english/2009-01/25/content_10716897.htm). In March 2009 Malaysia canceled the work visas of 55,000 Bangladeshi workers but since expressed its intention to restore the visas after the end of the economic crisis (http://www.bdnews24.com/details.php?cid=2&id=88433&hb=3).

8. "Nepal's Labor Export Up 34 Percent," *Republica*, November 20, 2010 (http://www.myrepublica.com/portal/index.php?action=news_details&news_id=25394).

9. Based on interviews with money transfer companies, banks, recruitment agencies, embassies, and government officials.

10. During this period, the average remittances that households received increased from Rs. 3,500 to nearly Rs. 6,000 in 1995 rupees. See table 4.5 of World Bank (2006c). Data are from nationally representative Nepal Living Standard Surveys I and II; 3,373 households were sampled in 1995–96 and 5,072 households in 2004–05.

11. Poverty reduction and development benefits of remittances in the form of improvements in human capital accumulation and health outcomes have been observed in other countries in South Asia. De and Ratha (2007) find that children of Sri Lankan migrant-sending households had higher birth weight and the households spent more on private tuition, a possible contributor to better education outcomes. According to Mansuri (2007), in rural Pakistan, school enrollment rates increased by 54 percent for girls in migrant-sending households. Rupee remittances from India help the Nepalese government finance Nepal's bilateral trade deficit vis-à-vis India and maintain the exchange rate anchor.

12. These are significantly more for Bangladesh and Pakistan, accounting for 63 and 52 percent, respectively, of the remittance inflows in 2007.

13. Interviews with money transfer companies and recruitment agencies. The average official exchange rates for 2009 and 2010 were Rs. 77.5 and Rs. 72.4 per dollar, respectively.

14. Overall remittances to developing countries are estimated to have reached $328 billion in 2008, up 15 percent from the level in 2007.

15. Crude oil prices declined from over $120/barrel in August 2008 to less than $40/barrel in December 2008. They have since risen to nearly $70/barrel in June 2009.

16. See the World Bank's Remittance Prices Worldwide (remittanceprices.worldbank.org).

17. http://rbidocs.rbi.org.in/rdocs/notification/PDFs/CINRS.pdf.

18. Mexican migrants, for example, can obtain *matricula consular* from Mexican consulates in the United States, which can be used to open bank accounts and to apply for a driving license. The Tunisian *carte consulaire* can be used for special customs clearance, reduced airfares, and foreign currency bank accounts in Tunisia. India also issues a Person of Indian Origin card, which allows cardholders access to various facilities in India.

19. WDI (2009).

20. The World Bank's Remittance Price Database (http://remittanceprices.worldbank.org) is another example of a price database. It has data on 134 remittance corridors in the world and is updated every six months.

21. The United Nations Development Program has helped several African countries obtain sovereign ratings in partnership with Standard and Poor's. The International Finance Corporation (part of the World Bank Group) helped Fedecredito, a credit cooperative in El Salvador, to raise $30 million of debt financing by securitizing its future remittance flows. These funds will be used to expand credit to microentrepreneurs and low-income people in El Salvador.

Chapter 10
Nepal: Migration History and Trends

JEEVAN RAJ SHARMA

MIGRANTS IN SEARCH OF WORK are not a new phenomenon in Nepal. Historical and ethnographic evidence suggests that migration has historically been a significant feature of household livelihoods amid fragile socioeconomic and environmental contexts (Hitchcock 1961; MacFarlane 1976; Pfaff-Czarnecka 1995; Whelpton 2005). The *first* wave of migration began in the eighteenth and nineteenth centuries when state policies and agrarian changes forced peasants in the hills to move off their land and seek their livelihoods elsewhere, both within Nepal and across the border into India (Regmi 1978). The opportunities for work in the bordering states of India in sectors such as tea plantation, coal mining, and construction attracted a larger number of Nepalese as laborers.

Labor migration of young men started with recruitment to serve in the army of the Sikh ruler Ranjit Singh and then in the British army in India (Seddon, Adhikari, and Gurung 2002). Although the Nepalese state resisted the recruitment of Nepalese by the British until 1885 out of concern that returning army servicemen would bring revolutionary ideas into the country, the policy changed in 1886 to allow the recruitment of Nepalese into the British Indian Army—a practice that continues to this day. Substantial temporary work migration has been seen from the hills to the plains and across the border into India to make up for the low income of the hill regions and to cover the needs of local rural communities throughout the year. Migrants in search of work in India have become a part of the life experience of a large number of Nepalese and account for just under half of Nepal's migrants. Pushed by difficult economic conditions at home, Nepalese have long relied on the comparatively large economy of their immediate neighbor in the south, where they migrate in search of various work opportunities. The flow of Nepalese migrants has been facilitated and sustained by social networks among the migrants and their households (Thieme 2006).

The unique open border between the two counties, formalized by the treaty of 1950, allows citizens of both countries to cross the border without having to produce official documents, and the treaty offers equal treatment of both citizens.

Over the years the proportion of migration of Nepal workers to India has decreased from 80 percent in 2001 to 41 percent in 2009, mainly because of the emergence of other migrant destinations following the second wave of work migration from Nepal.

The *second* wave of migration started in the mid-1980s, accelerated in the 1990s, and dramatically increased in the mid-2000s, when Nepalese continued to migrate to work in India and began to migrate to new destinations, mainly the Gulf States and Malaysia. The opening of new markets for Nepalese laborers in these destinations and the decentralization of passport issuance policy in Nepal contributed to this new wave of migration, which has become an extremely important part of the Nepalese economy and culture. Excluding India, the latest official data show that Malaysia (32.04 percent), Qatar (28.71 percent), Saudi Arabia (19.81 percent), and the United Arab Emirates (12.68 percent) are popular destinations in the Gulf States (Government of Nepal 2010). About 5–7 percent are estimated to have migrated to Australia, European nations, Japan, the Republic of Korea, the United Kingdom, the United States, and other countries with globally strong economies; these are the desired destinations of Nepalese migrants seeking to earn foreign currency overseas.

Both men and women have been migrating from Nepal for 200 years, although the nature and pattern of migration have changed. In the past, women's migration was largely limited to short-distance mobility and/or was mostly accompanied by family members. Since the 1990s, Nepalese women have begun to migrate on their own to various international destinations albeit now without gender discrimination, risks, and control on their mobility.

These migrations have created new transnational links, connecting very distant countries, cultures, and economies. This is a significant period in the history of work migration because it has led to large-scale migration and remittance flow, making policy makers recognize for the first time the remittance-dependent economy of Nepal. This period also marks the age of rising expectations among young Nepalese to migrate and participate in a world of modernity, consumption of commodities, and global interconnectedness (Sharma 2008). This is also the period when increasing numbers of Nepalese began to use labor recruitment agencies to facilitate their migration out of Nepal, especially beyond the traditional destinations in India.

The establishment and the expansion of migrant recruitment agencies also significantly contributed to the rapid increase in migration to the Gulf States and Malaysia. The number of recruitment agencies increased from 103 in 1998 to 630 in 2009. This period also saw a sharp increase in migration of men and women in search of further educational opportunities along with the growth of international education consultancies (IECs). About 1,000 IECs are operating in Nepal, which provide assistance to potential students who want to study and work abroad. Ideas about and practices of migration for education dominate the aspiration of the young middle class in major cities and towns in Nepal and involve a significant economic investment and capital flight.

With the increase in migration, a wide range of Nepalese migrant associations began to form in countries of destination. In 2004 the worldwide nonresident Nepalese organization was established, with chapters in different countries, to bring together in a single body all Nepalese organizations, whether cultural, religious, social, or political. The establishment of Nepalese diaspora organizations of different natures and in different countries has led to the increased engagement of diaspora Nepalese in Nepal's political and economic development.

Migrant remittances have played a key role in sustaining the rural economy and people's livelihoods during the decade-long Maoist conflict. The official contribution of remittances to Nepal's gross domestic product (GDP) in 2009 was $2.7 billion or 22 percent of GDP. However, with large amounts also being sent outside the official banking system and including remittances from India, the actual contribution of remittances could be as high as 30 percent of Nepal's GDP (World Bank 2009e). Remittances from Nepalese abroad grew by 20 percent a year between 1995–96 and 2003–04, rising from less than 3 percent of GDP in 1995–96 to about 12 percent by the end of 2003–04 (World Bank 2006c).

The Gulf States have become one of the key destinations since the mid-1990s and certainly one of the most dynamic phenomena (Graner and Gurung 2003). The trend over the last two decades shows that about one-third of Nepalese migrants seek travel abroad to the Gulf States to work as contract workers. Unpublished records available at the Department of Labor show that official figures for the early 1990s was only 2,000, which increased to 6,500 in 1997–98 and 20,000 by 1999–2000. In 1997 about 40,000 migrant workers from Nepal went to the Gulf States (Seddon, Adhikari, and Gurung 2002). Official statistics suggest that this number increased to 1,045,655 by 2009–10.

The global recession did have an impact on migration flow from Nepal: Migrant worker outflows have decreased by 13 percent. The official statistics show that 217,164 individuals left the country for employment in 2008–09 compared with 249,051 in 2007–08.

Overall, the pervasiveness of migration both within and outside of Nepal challenges the notion that Nepal is a traditional and agrarian society. Households have transformed into multilocale households with the out-migration of a large number of men and an increasing number of women to various global destinations. Remittance flows have further boosted the incorporation of Nepal into the global economy, as confirmed by the opening of Western Union outlets even in the remotest areas as soon as road and/or telecommunication networks reach these. As migrant remittances, associated commodification, and market expansion become the defining features of the economy, it is the poorer households that are unable to send migrants that will face increased risk of marginalization.

Chapter 11

Resilience of Remittances during the Global Financial Crisis and the Entrenchment of Migration

ANDREA RIESTER

IN PSYCHOLOGY AND SINCE THE 1970s, the term *resilience* has been applied to people who in situations of great stress, trauma, or adversity still retain their emotional stability and sanity. Children who face extremely difficult socioeconomic circumstances, or who suffer from abuse and violence, and who still grow up to be responsible, healthy adults display considerable resilience (Welter-Enderlin and Hildenbrand 2006; Werner, Bierman, and French 1971). The term *social resilience* has been applied to communities' ability to cope with rapid socioeconomic change or external shocks in development studies (Adger 2000; Adger and others 2002). In this chapter the term resilience is applied to individual migrants who also suffer from various impairments to their development and still are able to overcome them: first, they are negatively affected by the working conditions and salaries for migrants in countries of destination because both generally tend to be unsatisfactory (D'Souza 2010). Second, when sending money to their families back home, migrants have to pay exorbitant fees in the not-so-transparent market for international money transfers, which reduces the amount of remittances actually arriving in the families' households in countries of origin (Beck and Martínez Pería 2009). Third, the global economic and financial crisis has drastically reduced the number of formal jobs worldwide, and with this it has also reduced opportunities for migrants to earn their livelihood abroad (IOM 2009). Despite all these difficulties, migrants keep working, and remittances keep flowing back to their countries of origin.

I compare three countries where large parts of the population depend on migrants' contributions to household incomes and ask how the global economic and financial crisis affects the situation. I compare countries in three different regions of the world: Mali in Sub-Saharan Africa, Nepal in South Asia, and Tajikistan in Central Asia. Although Tajikistan largely depends on migration to Russia, migrants from Mali and Nepal are mostly involved in South-South migration and to a lesser degree in South-North migration. The comparison shows that despite large differences between these cases one general tendency becomes evident: Some factors have contributed to the relative stability of remittances during the crisis, particularly because of the resilience of migrants and because migration has become entrenched.

Data and Methods

Empirical evidence for my argument is drawn from a series of country studies on the nexus between the global economic and financial crisis, return migration, and remittances carried out in early 2009 by the German Development Cooperation on behalf of the German Federal Ministry for Economic Cooperation and Development (GTZ 2010). Overall, this research series covered eight different countries, which were selected according to the following criteria: importance of migration from these countries (either South-North or South-South), economic dependency on remittances, and being partner countries of German development cooperation. The goal of the different case studies, carried out by local consultants with various scientific backgrounds (social sciences, political sciences, economics), was to provide first-hand information on the immediate impact of the global and financial crisis while it was still in full swing. Research methods included the analysis of current research and qualitative interviews with representatives of institutions dealing with migration and remittances, as well as with returnees and families of migrants still working abroad. The data collected varied considerably (as was to be expected from this practice-led approach), but they presented us nevertheless with solid interdisciplinary insights into the effects of the crisis on countries of origin.

Overview of the Three Case Studies

Migration plays a major role in all three countries: approximately 1.2 million Malians, 1.6 million Nepalese, and 800,000 Tajiks are working abroad.[1] This means that 6–11 percent of the entire population of these countries has emigrated (Mali, 9 percent; Nepal, 5.9 percent; Tajikistan, 11 percent). The socioeconomic and gender profile of migration varies greatly between these countries. Tajik migration is made up mostly of young men working in the construction sector in the Russian Federation and to a small degree also in Kazakhstan (Olimova 2010). Only 6 percent of Tajik migrants are women, who mostly work in the services industry or in petty trade. Apart from approximately

250,000 Nepalese who, for historical reasons, are employed in the Indian public sector (mainly the army and police), it is generally poorer Nepalese migrants (men and women equally) who move to neighboring India (Kollmair and others 2006; Seddon 2005). They are not registered anywhere because they have no visa requirements; their employment is mostly irregular on plantations, in manufacturing, in construction, or in services. Those Nepalese migrants who can afford to migrate via regular channels usually go to Malaysia (39 percent), Qatar (27 percent), Saudi Arabia (19 percent), or the United Arab Emirates (10 percent). Of those Nepalese migrants going to the Gulf States, most work as semi- or unskilled workers in construction; only 5 percent of them are women, who usually work as domestic helpers.

Of all Malian migrants, 80 percent remain in the West African region, with Côte d'Ivoire being the major destination country (Barajas and others 2010: 18). In the coastal areas, Malians usually work in plantations and the service industry. Malian women are particularly active in regional transnational trade (Sieveking and Fauser 2009). In Europe, France is the main destination country because of colonial ties and linguistics, but only 2.7 percent of Malian migrants live there. In recent years, Spain has become the second most important European destination country because of labor shortages in its agricultural sector.

The fact that migration has become an important livelihood strategy in all three countries is reflected in the enormous amounts of remittances sent annually by citizens abroad. According to World Bank figures from November 2009, $0.3 billion was sent to Mali, $2.7 billion to Nepal, and $2.5 billion to Tajikistan in 2008. This is the equivalent of 3.9 percent of gross domestic product for Mali, 21.6 percent for Nepal, and 49.6 percent for Tajikistan. The figure for Mali seems low in comparison and suggests the country is not dependent on remittances. However, compared with other African countries this figure is relatively high (Barajas and others 2009), and it does not include informal remittances. These are likely to be high, given that the Malian financial sector is weak and banking infrastructure in rural areas largely nonexistent. Additionally, most migration from Mali takes place within the region, proximity being a factor fostering informal transfers as well. It then becomes very likely that Mali is as dependent on remittances as the other two examples.

Crisis and Remittances

Worldwide remittances reached $328 billion in 2008 (Ratha, Mohapatra, and Silwal 2009a) which is nearly three times as high as worldwide official development assistance of $120 billion. Remittances to Asia have more than doubled since 2002. They play an important role in poverty reduction (Adams and Page 2005), but because of migration patterns, remittances primarily contribute to households and families that are already better off and can afford the expenses of migration (Riester 2010a). Via consumption of local goods or investment in education, health, and businesses, possibly resulting in job creation, larger parts of society will benefit from the inflow of remittances (World Bank 2006a).

Remittances are generally reduced by job losses by migrants abroad and the devaluation of currencies in countries of destination (such as the Russian Federation or the United States); on the other hand, incidental evidence suggests that the demand for cheap migrant labor and, subsequently, migrants' employment has remained high. Additionally, the crisis gave an incentive to remit more: Studies have shown that remittances are countercyclical; in times of crisis, family members generally appeal to their relatives abroad, who are then likely to remit more than before, even if that means cutting down on their own (sending members') expenditures (Orozco 2009). Currency devaluations in countries of origin can also increase the value of remittances, which provides a good opportunity to invest. Therefore, global remittances generally remain stable in comparison with other financial flows such as foreign direct investment or portfolio flows.

The pattern of remittance flows roughly follows that of migration. Therefore, the extent of return movement determines the decline in remittances. Central Asian republics experienced a sharp decline in remittance flows from the Russian Federation: remittances to Tajikistan shrank by approximately 30 percent in the first two quarters of 2009, relative to the same period in 2008. Whereas in 2007 the average monthly amount remitted by migrants was as high as $256, in 2009 it had decreased to $181 (both expressed in 2007 dollars) (Danzer and Ivaschenko 2010).

In contrast between January and March 2009, remittances to Nepal even rose by 28 percent relative to the same period in the previous year. This astonishing rise can be linked to migrants' preparation to return home and transferring savings home before their return or to the significant appreciation of the dollar between 2008 and 2009, which led to a larger transfer of savings to Nepal and investment in real estate in Kathmandu by Nepalese abroad. One should also bear in mind that the collection of remittance data has improved considerably since the World Bank brought their importance to public attention (Ratha 2003).

For Mali, data on remittances are not satisfactory. Barajas and colleagues (2009) show the discrepancy between the official International Monetary Fund figure of $0.2 billion remittances in 2006 and International Fund for Aid and Development (IFAD) estimates of $0.7 billion for the same year.

IFAD estimates were derived from home and host country sources and allegedly include informal transfers. The latter are the rule for African countries, and so it is fair to assume that the IFAD estimate might be more realistic.[2] According to chief executive officers of money transfer operators in Bamako, interviewed during the course of the GTZ country study, formal remittances from Europe decreased in the first half of 2009 between 25 and 60 percent.

Anecdotal evidence indicates that informal remittances from migrants in the West African region have remained relatively stable. Thus, overall remittances to Mali might not have decreased as drastically in 2009, which is in line with findings that attribute a shock-absorbing role to remittances in Sub-Saharan Africa (R. J. Singh 2010). If Mali's growth and thus poverty reduction was in danger of being affected by the global financial and economic crisis, it was because it has a high share of foreign-owned banks (Massa and te Velde 2008).

Crisis and Return

The global financial and economic crisis has resulted in job losses, particularly in industrialized countries, and was therefore expected to cause massive return migration to developing countries. However, the analysis of the real extent of return migration in the wake of the crisis is difficult to assess. First, this is because much migration is taking place in an undocumented manner, that is, without a work permit, visa, or other travel documents, or is becoming irregular over time, such as through visa overstaying (Schiff 2004). Second, return is generally not registered; migrants are usually free to go home whenever they want and without telling the administration in the country of destination (the return migrant generally has no incentive to register in their country of origin). Most important, however, it is hard to distinguish between seasonal and permanent return.

In general, international labor migrants do not come from the poorest part of the population (DRC 2009). Migration initially engenders high costs: You need time, money, and information to obtain a visa, travel tickets, accommodation abroad, and so on (and therefore it is not usually feasible for the very poor). Several studies have also shown wealth differentials between migrants moving between countries within their region and those who move intercontinentally: Wealthier people can afford to move farther away. Therefore, as a rule of thumb, the poorer the persons and their families are, the shorter is their migration distance. Thus, when discussing the effects of the crisis on international migrants and their families, we are generally not talking about the poorest part of the population. However, the economic potential of migrants to accumulate human and financial capital abroad to invest back home makes them important actors in poverty reduction.

Return migration due to the crisis is particularly high where migrants work in recession-sensitive industries, for example, construction, financial services, or tourism, and where migrants depend on one or few countries of destination (Martin 2009b). In this case, if immigration and recruitment policies of the respective main destination countries have tightened, migrants face layoffs or will not be able to renew their work permits like they used to.

Although return migration on a large scale seems the logical consequence of the crisis, the situation in countries of origin is by no means clear cut. Although anecdotal evidence of mass return is reported by the media and has influenced our perception, the information we gathered in our study on the effects of the crisis presents a more nuanced picture.

We did find signs of increased return migration to Tajikistan. Because most Tajik migrants were working in the construction sector in the Russian Federation and

Kazakhstan, they were hardest hit by job losses stemming from the crisis (Danzer and Ivaschenko 2010). In the wake of the crisis, these two destination countries halved their immigration quotas by the end of 2008. Against this, convincing anecdotal reports from both countries claim that migrant workers from Tajikistan can still find work, because they are often willing to work for less money than the locals, and they also work without documents (ICG 2010). It is estimated that 65 percent of all Central Asian migrants working in the Russian Federation have no legal status and that in Kazakhstan the proportion might even be higher (UNDP 2008). One study shows that the stock of Tajik migrants abroad has risen from 2007 to 2009 (Danzer and Ivaschenko 2010). Thus, the result of the cut quotas is not necessarily a decrease in overall migration, but a decrease in regular migration, increasing the problems of documentation as described above. This in turn results in decreasing social protection of migrants who, if without official documents, have no access to health services or insurance and cannot claim their workers' rights.

In Nepal, the situation seems mixed: Data on return are particularly hard to obtain, and official data do not adequately represent the full extent of crisis-induced return. According to the Association of Nepal Foreign Employment Agencies, between June 2008 and March 2009 only 3,000 Nepalese migrant workers returned, mainly from Dubai, Macao, Malaysia, and Qatar. This number includes only regular migrants who were eligible to and did claim social benefits. Returning migrants are ineligible for social benefits if they stayed abroad for more than a year, so many of them have been excluded from public support (as will be elaborated on in the following). Foreign recruitment from Nepal clearly dwindled in 2008–09: The number of new placements abroad shrank by 30 percent. Malaysia for example, the second most important destination country for Nepalese migrants after India, has frozen the issuance of work permits to migrant workers in the manufacturing and services sectors and has introduced "nationals first" employment policies (Punzalan 2009; Sharma and Gurung 2009). However, anecdotal evidence strongly suggests that Nepalese migrants from Malaysia and the Gulf States have not returned in large numbers. They prefer to stay on and work irregularly, because they fear they might not be able to return once they leave.

As mentioned above, the vast majority of Malian migrants move within the African continent and have therefore not been directly affected by the current financial and economic crisis. Looking at those who moved to Europe, one finds a serious lack of reliable data on their migration and return. Our study tried to get a glimpse of migration trends by looking at the work of the newly installed Centre for Migration Information and Management (CIGEM) in Bamako. One important insight was that the number of Malians who should have been allowed to move to Spain under a circular migration agreement between the two countries was cut from 800 to 45 according to CIGEM. Additionally, the number of deported Malians has witnessed a sharp increase too, from 794 in 2007 to 1,834 in 2008. This in turn has exponentially increased the number of those seeking advice from CIGEM since the beginning of the crisis toward the end of 2008. However, the GTZ country study has also revealed an impressive solidarity among migrants abroad who support each other in the case of job loss in order to avoid having to return home.

Conclusion

What does this comparison of the situation of remittances and return migration in Mali, Nepal, and Tajikistan in the wake of the global financial and economic crisis tell us? First, stability of remittances is not guaranteed but is usually a function of a particular migration pattern that the citizens of a country have come to adopt. Fears of mass return and sharp decline in remittances have generally not materialized during the global financial crisis. However, the higher a country's dependency on migration of its citizens to few industrialized countries and within those to sectors susceptible to crisis, the more likely that the famous stability of remittances comes at a high price. In this sense, it is probably adequate to speak of migrants' resilience: Despite worsening labor conditions and rising irregularity, they still hold on to their livelihood strategy of searching for jobs abroad and working in increasingly difficult conditions. Entrenchment of migration despite or rather due to the crisis and subsequent policy restriction in countries of destination is the result.

Notes

1. If not specified, statistical data in this text are derived from GTZ (2010). Where necessary, these data have been amended by additional information from other studies.
2. See www.ifad.org/remittances/maps/index.htm.

Chapter 12

Rural-Urban Migration in the Context of Thailand's Ongoing Uneven Development

In 1961 THAILAND'S FIRST NATIONAL Economic Development Plan established a centralized urbanization and development policy that targeted growth within Bangkok and its metropolitan regions. Bangkok had long provided ideological and material foundations from which inequality and uneven national development stemmed (Dixon 1999). As a result of the new development plan Bangkok emerged as the sprawling central hub for finance, industry, and politics throughout the Thai kingdom (Askew 2002; Doner 2009; Krongkaew and Kakwani 2003). These factors in large part created the economic determinants underlying rural to urban migration. Particularly prominent has been the extensive use of labor mobility as a means to mitigate high poverty rates and unstable employment structures within the predominately agrarian Isaan, or northeast, region of Thailand (Guest 1998; Kakwani and Krongkaew 2000; Skeldon 1997; Tacoli, McGranahan, and Satterthwaite 2008).

During the financial boom of 1986–96 economic and social divisions widened between urban and rural locations, increasing migration to Bangkok (Chalamwong 1998; Kim 1998). However, following the 1997 Asian financial crisis, the Thai government reconsidered decentralizing the nation's economic policy (see the passage of the Decentralization Plan and Process Act of 1999). In effect, the Thai government acknowledged the vulnerability of older economic models within new contexts of neoliberalism and globalization, as well as the need to provide wider employment options for those living in provinces outside the Bangkok Metropolitan Region. Despite such government efforts, internal migration rates from the northeast into Bangkok and its semiurban locations continued relatively unchanged.

Although the 1997 Asian crisis caused an initial outflow of laborers from the central region to provinces in the south, north, and northeast (NSO 2000), the rate of rural-urban migration has increased into Bangkok and its environs in the following years. Similarly, the economic crisis experienced in Thailand over the past several years has resulted in a partial loss of migrants in Bangkok. Many have returned to their home provinces outside the central region as work opportunities in the city have diminished. Remaining migrants often discuss pressures received from family in their origin communities to either continue sending money or if possible increase remittances. In the case of both the 1997 East Asian financial crisis and the current global economic downturn, declining poverty rates have halted or been reversed in sections of the Isaan region.

In these historical contexts, researchers, politicians, and scholars continue to argue that rural-urban migration is driven by poverty and is a functional strategizing feature of households attempting to mitigate financial instability (Bhaopichitr and others 2008; see also Hogue 2005; Jacque 1999; Phongpaichit and Baker 2008). Further, such studies advocate that in high-migration situations and within unstable economic structures, migrant remittances may further local development in the origin community. Remittances might improve standards of living, create higher employment, and increase economic growth. In total, these effects will over time decrease widening rural and urban divisions. However, in the Thai context, local structural variables in labor availability also produce situations where short-term migration does not positively affect relative household wealth. Research on Thailand's National Migration Survey finds that lower-income households will most often send long-term migrants to Bangkok, yet received remittances are insufficient to remove these households from poverty (see, for example, Ford, Jampaklay, and Chamratrithirong 2009; Richter and others 1997). In fact, much of the Thai migration literature, as well as this author's research, shows ambivalent relationships between internal Thai migration and positive outcomes. Therefore, although researchers and government officials may argue that remittances have a positive effect on regions and communities affected by various economic crises, collected data illustrate more complex relationships between migration and development. Yet migration continues insofar that most Thais consider it a normalized feature of life in the kingdom, one that is firmly situated in the collective conscious and through this process is transformed into background noise.

Since 2009 I have examined the ways in which "normalized" internal migration is affected by Thailand's pronounced uneven development, the government's decentralization plans, and ongoing political and economic crises that are partially aggravated by regional divisions (see the 2006 political crisis that began with the military-led coup d'état of former prime minister Thaksin Shinawatra, whose political support is traditionally located in northern and northeastern Thailand). Isaan migrants that compose the sample within my research ($n = 42$) came from various backgrounds and experienced wide variations in income, job type, family socioeconomic standing, and remittance usage. I interviewed investment bankers, housekeepers, construction workers, taxi drivers, street vendors, public relations officers, and others. Motives for migration into

Bangkok coalesced around certain identifiable themes: greater employment options, higher pay, education access, modern or *thansamay* lifestyles, and intimate social networks. Within these varied reasons for migration, I more specifically address the way remittance management might vary based on class, identity, gender, and community infrastructure. I will avoid a prolonged discussion of whether remittances will increase development in the community of origin. Similar to other findings on the intersections between migrant remunerations and market proximity or availability, my research illustrates that if a community is relatively isolated from provincial or urban markets, then land investment is more common. On the other hand, substantial industry surrounding the household tends to produce greater remittance investment in family businesses. These and similar patterns have obvious implications for government agencies attempting to capitalize on the flow of remittances into rural locations with an end objective of increasing regional development in the northeast.

Yet, over the course of seven months of ethnographic research in Bangkok among primarily Isaan migrants, my traditional interests in remittances and migration were complicated by emerging patterns of rootedness and identity construction among "rural" migrants in urban locations, which I believe profoundly affect remittance management. Thailand offers unique opportunities to examine the important social dimensions of remittances within unstable, uneven national economic development, particularly as development policies are further complicated by economic downturns.

One of the dominant ideological formations in migration and development studies is the spatial separation of rural and urban activities (for example, Rigg 1998; Vickers 2004; Williams 1973). This duality maintains its durability not from a pure reflection of reality, but from its imaginative power and how it is invoked to separate—in power, class, status, and identity—the people from urban (*khon muang*) and rural (*khon ban nok*) locations. Researchers have established in various fields that through migration, rural and urban link into singular social formations. The performance of labor mobility (Korinek, Entwisle, and Jampaklay 2005), the at times convergence of cultural tastes and consumptive behaviors between those in the city and those in the countryside (Rigg and others 2008), and the fact that meanings and ideas generated in the city "are informed and shaped by images and processes that are not unique to [the] metropolis alone" (Askew 2002: 5) indicate an increasingly complex relationship between rural-urban locations.

Despite the dissolution of strict rural-urban boundaries through migration, the mental separation of rural and urban citizens remains an active cognitive map for many in my research. Within Bangkok's cosmopolitan cultural landscapes, lower-skilled and/or Isaan migrants at various employment levels are at times marked as unsophisticated or other, and occasionally even the derogatory *aye laos*. In these instances, the uneven development that has historically positioned Bangkok as the kingdom's central city is invoked to draw attention to two key points. First, provinces in the northeast exist distantly outside Bangkok's political, cultural, and economic dominance (despite regional connections created through migration). Second, residents in theses provinces are by association imagined as distantly related, where they transgress culturally established psychological, social, and geographic boundaries upon entering Bangkok seeking work. As such, although structural requirements for migrant labor in Bangkok's economy clearly exist (for example, see Kaur 2010 on Bangkok's decreasing population growth rate and the requirement for migrant labor to drive industrial expansion), migrants are at times regarded as the root of serious social problems. The actions and presence of Isaan migrants in the city, for example, are occasionally analogous to the social and economic problems traced to Burmese migrants in anti-immigrant rhetoric. Most recently, the ongoing political crises arising from the 2006 coup d'état has seen further marginalization of migrant communities from the northeast, where some are identified as *kwai daeng*, or red buffalos, indicating their illogical and gullible support for former Prime Minister Thaksin. Therefore, the challenges some Isaan migrants experience are classed, ethnicized, and regionalized in nature. Furthermore, challenges faced by migrants are very much patterned by Thailand's uneven national development and shaped by ongoing economic and political crises that position groups and regions of people against others.

The ethnographic data indicate that the social, political, and economic divisions within the kingdom produce regular sources of discomfort and (dis)identification for some migrating to Bangkok. Isaan migrants are often aware of the social lines drawn between themselves and some Bangkok residents. In such situations, migrants express an anxious longing to return home and often maintain concrete connections with the origin community. Many participate in community-driven donations for the local Buddhist wat (see, for example, the *phaa paa*, which arguably aligns with "functionalist" traditions on the positive impact of migrant remittances within the origin community), and most will frequently return to visit family and friends. These divisions in turn influence the length and duration of the migration experience, which also influence the form of remittance usage and management. In contrast, some migrants, often with higher education and formal training, will embrace Bangkok, referencing it as their home and over time reducing the salient connections with origin communities. These patterns of migration illustrate that identity and social connections—created within new locations or maintained with origin communities—are variables that deserve greater attention when examining the role of remittances in developing rural or agrarian sections of a country. The class, status, and perceived identity of the migrant have a profound effect on whether or when return migration will occur and, importantly, in what shape and to what degree migrant remittances will flow back to origin communities and funnel into productive investment strategies.

Chapter 13

Migration and Remittances in Bangladesh and Pakistan: Evidence from Two Host Countries

GUNTUR SUGIYARTO, CARLOS VARGAS-SILVA, AND SHIKHA JHA

REMITTANCE FLOWS HAVE BEEN THE object of much speculation in recent years. The worldwide nature of the global financial crisis implied that even sturdier capital flows such as remittances might succumb to deteriorating global conditions. Predictions on the level of the decline differed by country and region, but at one point worldwide remittance flows were expected to decrease by as much as 8 percent (Ratha et al. 2009a). Yet migrant remittances have once again proven to be strong and resilient, and the decline in remittances, although important, was short lived. In this context, it is necessary to analyze the impact of the reduction in global output as a result of the global crisis on migration and remittances to learn lessons for the future.

Several studies have taken on the task of reviewing the dynamics of migration and remittances during the crisis (Barajas et al. 2010; Calì and Dell'Erba 2009; Martin 2009a; Naufal and Vargas-Silva 2010; Ruiz and Vargas-Silva 2010, 2011, to mention just a few). Nonetheless, there is a need for additional comparative analysis of the effect of the crisis on migration and remittances. The impact of the crisis on these flows may vary vastly across regions, because of differences in financial systems, migration patterns, and the stage of economic development. Therefore, it is useful to compare the effect of the crisis

This chapter is based on the results of the Asian Development Bank's project Research and Development Technical Assistance (RDTA) 7436: Global Crisis, Remittance and Poverty in Asia. The views expressed in the chapter are those of the authors and do not necessarily reflect the views or policies of ADB.

on remittances in specific corridors. Comparisons across corridors during the crisis and its aftermath will eventually enable the establishment of broad generalizations and facilitate the design of clearer and better policy recommendations and prepare for the future.

This chapter concentrates on two countries in South Asia that are among the top remittance recipients in the world and that report monthly remittance data: Bangladesh and Pakistan. First, we review the data reported by these countries' central banks to analyze the current status of remittances, focusing on flows from two host countries: the United Kingdom and the United States. These are two of the key destination countries for Bangladeshi and Pakistani migrants. In the second section, in addition to exploring the changes in the volume of money flowing in these corridors, we look at the overall change in the importance (that is, relative to the rest of the world) of these corridors during the crisis. In the next two sections, we explore the relationship between remittances to Bangladesh and Pakistan and the economic conditions of migrants from these countries in the United States and United Kingdom during the financial crisis. The emphasis is on labor market indicators (unemployment rates, labor force participation rates, and the like). In the fifth section, we look at other possible factors that could affect remittances such as exchange rate changes between the currencies of the four countries.

Changes in Remittance Flows during Times of Crisis

The Difference between the Current Crisis and Previous Crises

It is important to understand the history of the global crisis, also known as the "Great Recession." Although scholars have not come to a consensus about the reasons for the financial decline, there is agreement that one of the major drivers of the crisis was a liquidity problem in the U.S. banking system that resulted in the collapse of important banking institutions. One of the leading forces in the crisis was a weak housing market that resulted in thousands of foreclosures around the world and in long-lasting vacancies for new homes. In fact, the bursting of the housing bubble in the United States has been attributed a large share of the blame for the crisis. Eventually the crisis led to a reduction in global credit availability and international trade (IMF 2009b).

International trade was not the only international flow affected by the crisis. Many host countries imposed new restrictions on admissions of international migrants, and in other cases unemployed migrants decided to return home. The obvious consequence of the grim picture about international migration was an increasing anxiety about the future of workers' remittances. There was a special cause for concern in countries in Asian developing countries, which have received large flows of remittances from their international migrant workers during the last few decades.

Another reason for the increasing anxiety about the future of international migration and remittances was the nature of this crisis as compared with previous economic downturns. For example, in 1973, oil prices increased dramatically because of the Organization of the Petroleum Exporting Countries embargo and the conflict between Israel and several Arab countries. The consequence of the sharp increase in oil prices was a major economic crisis in oil-importing countries. As a response to the crisis, many European countries terminated their guest-worker programs. Nonetheless, many migrants decided not to return home and used some of the rights that they had acquired over the years to bring their families to the host country (Martin 2001). Hence, instead of a decrease in migration, there was a change in the type of migration from labor-oriented to family reunion migration. Moreover, although an economic downturn was seen in oil-importing countries, economic expansion occurred in oil-exporting countries. Many of these countries started to recruit foreign workers (often from Asian countries), and that caused a change in the direction of labor migrant flows (Martin 2009a). A massive inflow of migrants to the Middle East took place. Yet the recent crisis was different because there was a global reduction in output affecting most migrant host countries, including the United Kingdom and the United States.

The Asian financial crisis was also unique. During the 1990s Asia attracted a large portion of global capital inflows, leading to a bubble in asset prices. After the burst of the bubble in about 1997, a serious economic contraction affected countries such as Indonesia, the Republic of Korea, and Thailand. Nonetheless, the economic downturn was temporary, and no major implications were seen for the long-term trajectory of international migration. Moreover, the impact was mostly regional, quite the opposite of the recent global crisis, which was a worldwide phenomenon.

The Status of Remittances to Bangladesh and Pakistan

Figures 13.1 and 13.2 show the level and growth rate of monthly remittance flows to Bangladesh and Pakistan, respectively, for the period January 2007 to September 2010. As shown in figure 13.1, for Bangladesh a significant decline in the growth rate (year-to-year) of these transfers started about mid-2008. The growth rate remained positive for 2009 and increased toward the end of that year. Since mid-2010 a slight decrease in remittances to Bangladesh has occurred.

In the case of Pakistan (figure 13.2), there was a marked downturn in the growth rate during October 2008, so some evidence of the effect of the crisis may be seen, but this downturn was short lived. However, more worrisome is the current drop in the growth rate of remittances that has been occurring since October 2009, one year after the peak of the crisis. This tendency is somewhat similar to that of Bangladesh. For both countries, flows seem to be slowing or decreasing since October 2009.

FIGURE 13.1 Remittances to Bangladesh

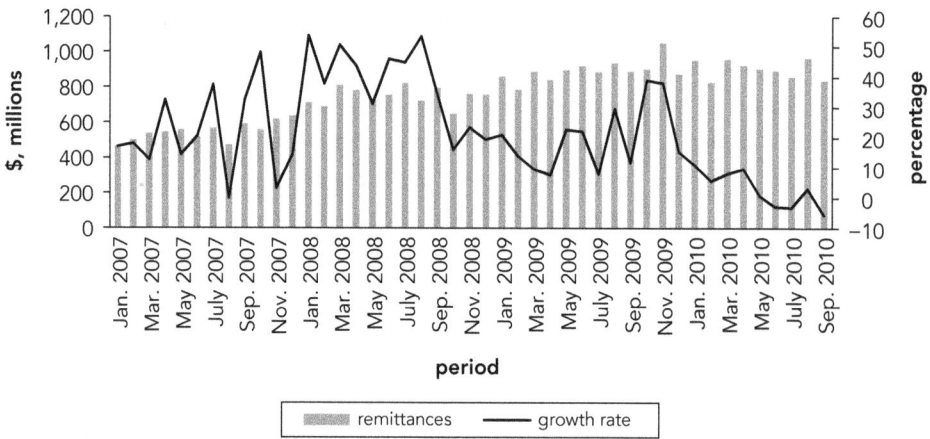

Source: Central Bank of Bangladesh.
Note: The growth rates are taken with respect to the same month of the previous year.

FIGURE 13.2 Remittances to Pakistan

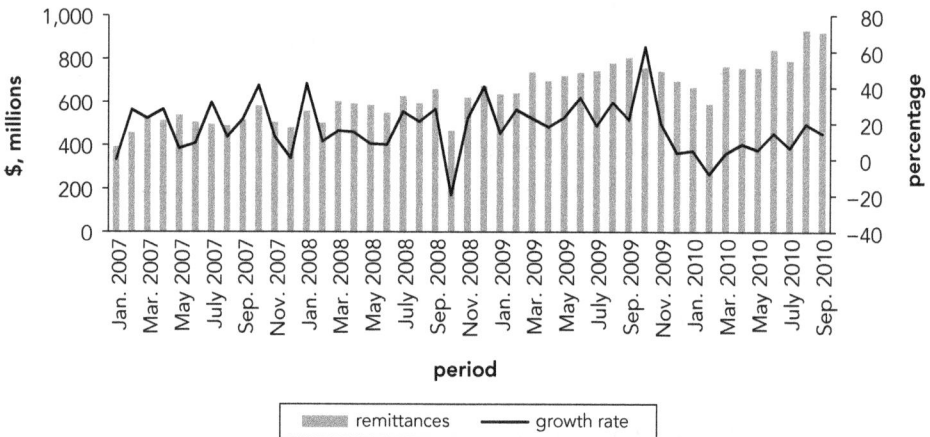

Source: Central Bank of Pakistan.
Note: The growth rates are taken with respect to the same month of the previous year.

Global Financial Crisis, Migration Policy, and Remittances from the United States and United Kingdom to Bangladesh and Pakistan

Changes to Migration Policy

Emigrants from Bangladesh and Pakistan typically migrate to a broad array of countries. Nonetheless, there are some consistently popular destinations among emigrants from these countries including India (the favorite destination), Saudi Arabia, the United Kingdom, and the United States. Given the availability of data regarding labor market conditions for migrants of these countries or from the region (that is, Asia) in the United Kingdom and the United States, these two destination countries are the focus of the current study.

The crisis had a serious impact on migration to the United States. There was a 23 percent decrease in intracompany transfers in 2009 compared with 2007, and the number of low-skilled seasonal workers decreased by half over the same comparison period (Migration Information Source 2010). The recession and criticism of the U.S. H-1B visa program also prevented U.S. employers from obtaining an increase in the program cap.[1] Instead, in January 2010 the U.S. Department of Homeland Security announced a stricter enforcement of H-1B worker rules. In August 2010, the United States also raised H-1B visa fees by $2,000 for employers (with 50 or more employees) who have at least half of their workforce under H-1B visas (Migration News 2010).

In the United Kingdom, the government announced a cap on the number of economic migrants from outside the European Economic Area (EEA) that come under the country's points-based system (PBS).[2] The cap cuts the number of economic migrants from outside the EEA by about 20 percent compared with the number in 2009 and closed, almost entirely, the highly skilled migrant category (tier 1 of the PBS). With the changes, now almost all migrants from outside the EEA coming to the United Kingdom for work purposes must have a job offer and a sponsor. The U.K. government has announced that further cuts in the number of migrants coming to the United Kingdom (such as students) should be expected in the near future (Home Office 2010b).

Remittances from the United States and United Kingdom to Bangladesh and Pakistan

Table 13.1 provides some insights on remittances from the United Kingdom and the United States to Bangladesh and Pakistan. The first four columns provide information on the amount of remittances received by the countries from the United Kingdom and the United States during each year and the share of the total amount received (from all over the world) represented by these flows. For instance, the first number in column 1 (5,484.1) is the total volume of remittances received by Bangladesh from all over the world during 2006. The number in the next row (826.2) is the volume of remittances received by Bangladesh from the United States during 2006. The number in the third row (15.1) is the share of total remittances to Bangladesh for which the United States accounts (that is, (826.2/5,484.1)×100). Columns 5, 6, and 7 compare the years 2010 and 2009 for the period January to September.

In the case of Bangladesh, it seems that the United Kingdom and the United States accounted for about 21–30 percent of the remitted flows. For Pakistan it seems that both countries account for about 29–35 percent of the remitted flows. Hence, in both

TABLE 13.1 Remittances to Bangladesh and Pakistan

Source		2006 (1)	2007 (2)	2008 (3)	2009 (4)	2010 (5)	2009 (6)	Growth (%) (7)
				Bangladesh				
Total	$, mil.	5,484.1	6,557.8	8,979.0	10,717.7	8,113.1	7,892.6	2.8
United States	$, mil.	826.2	1,086.8	1,582.5	1,514.7	1,130.4	1,167.7	−3.2
	Share	15.1	16.6	17.6	14.1	13.9	14.8	−5.8
United Kingdom	$, mil.	802.9	905.4	823.3	858.9	585.8	623.8	−6.1
	Share	14.6	13.8	9.2	8.0	7.2	7.9	−8.6
Combined	Share	29.7	30.4	26.8	22.1	21.2	22.7	−6.8
				Pakistan				
Total	$, mil.	5,109.5	5,989.5	7,023.3	8,700.6	7,022.0	6,502.1	8.0
United States	$, mil.	1,315.7	1,674.6	1,791.3	1,770.8	1,344.7	1,331.1	1.0
	Share	25.8	28.0	25.5	20.4	19.1	20.5	−6.5
United Kingdom	$, mil.	455.6	438.6	471.5	848.6	690.5	600.9	14.9
	Share	8.9	7.3	6.7	9.8	9.8	9.2	6.4
Combined	Share	34.7	35.3	32.2	30.1	29.0	29.7	−2.5

Source: Authors' calculations.

Note: The preliminary comparison in columns 5, 6, and 7 includes data from January to September. Data come from respective countries' central banks. The "share" row is the share of total remittances received from all over the world for which that country's (the United Kingdom or the United States) accounts, and the "combined" row is the sum of the shares for the United Kingdom and the United States.

cases these two countries (the United Kingdom and the United States) account for an important share of the remitted flows.

In the case of Pakistan the total volume of remittances from around the world has increased, but the share represented by the United Kingdom and the United States has decreased. This decrease has been driven by a reduction in the share of remittances accounted for by the United States. In the case of Bangladesh, the total volume of remittances increased in comparison with the previous year, but the amount sent from each of these two host countries and the share that they account for have decreased. The decrease seems to be larger (in percentage terms) for flows from the United Kingdom.

In order to explore this last point further (the decrease in flows from the United Kingdom and the United States to Bangladesh), figures 13.3 and 13.4 display remittances from the United Kingdom and the United States to Bangladesh by month. Notice how in the case of the United Kingdom there is a declining trend in the series since October 2009 (similar to that of the overall flows). In addition, the series is volatile, and the growth rate becomes negative at several points (including the latest observation) but typically becomes positive again.

FIGURE 13.3 Remittances from the United Kingdom to Bangladesh

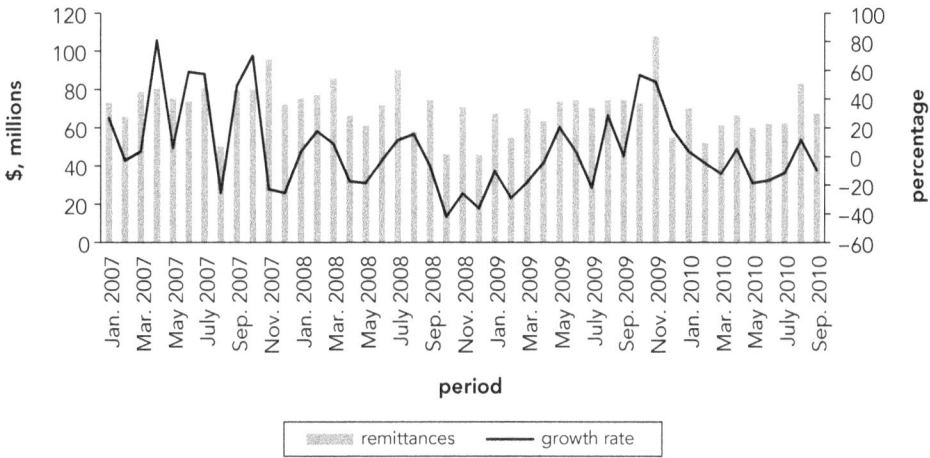

Source: Central Bank of Bangladesh.
Note: The growth rates are taken with respect to the same month of the previous year.

FIGURE 13.4 Remittances from the United States to Bangladesh

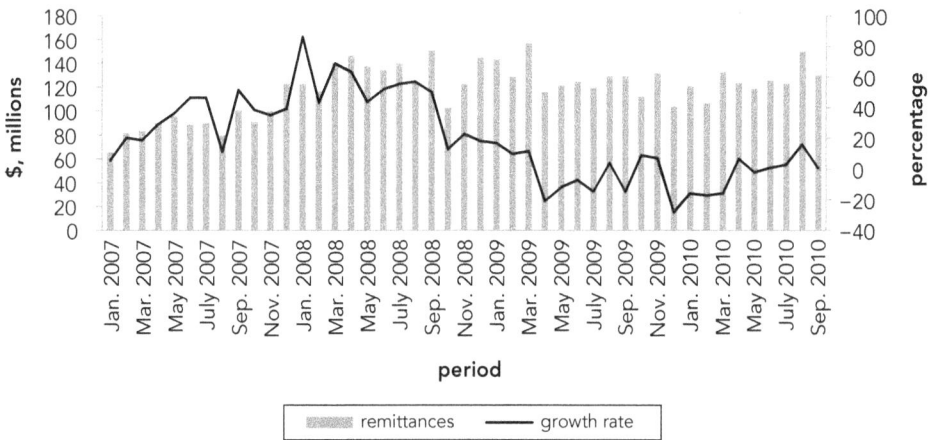

Source: Central Bank of Bangladesh.
Note: The growth rates are taken with respect to the same month of the previous year.

This differs markedly from the case of the United States (figure 13.4), where the growth rate is positive at first and then steadily becomes negative. Hence, in the case of the United Kingdom the volatility of the series may account for some of the recent decrease in remittances, whereas in the case of the United States a steady decrease is seen in the growth rate of these flows.

An implication of figures 13.3 and 13.4, together with table 13.1, is that even if aggregate remittances to these countries (Bangladesh and Pakistan) did not decrease significantly, the sources of these money transfers may have shifted.

Given the short time period that has elapsed since the global crisis surfaced, it is difficult to conduct a meaningful exercise that can robustly pinpoint the determinants of changing remittance flows during this period. Yet the economic situation of migrants from Bangladesh and Pakistan in these countries (the United Kingdom and the United States) during the crisis is likely to have a strong bearing on their remittance flows. This relationship is explored in the next two sections.

Remittances and the Economic Condition of Migrants in the United States

The discussion of the United States concentrates on estimates of labor market indicators of individuals of Asian ethnic origin in the country. All the labor market indicators of Asians in the United States come from the U.S. Bureau of Labor Statistics and are estimates from the U.S. Current Population Survey. It is important to emphasize that the Bangladeshi and Pakistani community in the United States account for a minority of a diverse Asian population (especially when compared with Chinese, Filipinos, Indians, Japanese, Koreans, and Vietnamese, among others). However, there are no a priori reasons to expect the dynamics of labor market characteristics for these groups to differ systematically from the overall Asian population in the United States.

Figure 13.5 reports on the labor force participation rate of individuals of Asian ethnic origin in the United States. As is clear from the figure, a marked downtrend has been seen for the labor force participation rate of this group. In fact, since the peak of the crisis in October 2008, the year-to-year growth rate has been negative. In April 2008 the labor force participation rate for this group was 67.7 percent, but for April 2010 it was 65.5 percent.

This fact becomes more worrisome looking at figure 13.6, which reports unemployment rates for Asians in the United States. There was a steady increase in the unemployment rate for this group starting in October 2008, although the growth rate seems to have decreased in mid-2010. In general, there is a smaller proportion of the U.S. Asian population in the labor force and a higher proportion of those who are active members of the labor force who are unemployed. The unemployment rate of Asians in the United States during the crisis (and before) has been consistently lower than that of the general U.S. population; however, the increase in the unemployment rate during the crisis for Asian workers was higher than that of the overall U.S. population.

To link these indicators related to the labor market conditions of Asians in the United States to remittance transfers, table 13.2 shows correlation coefficients between the growth rate of remittances and the growth rate of several U.S. labor market variables for the Asian population. These variables are the total population, total labor force participants, labor force participation rate, total employed, employment ratio, total

FIGURE 13.5 Labor Force Participation Rate of Asians in the United States

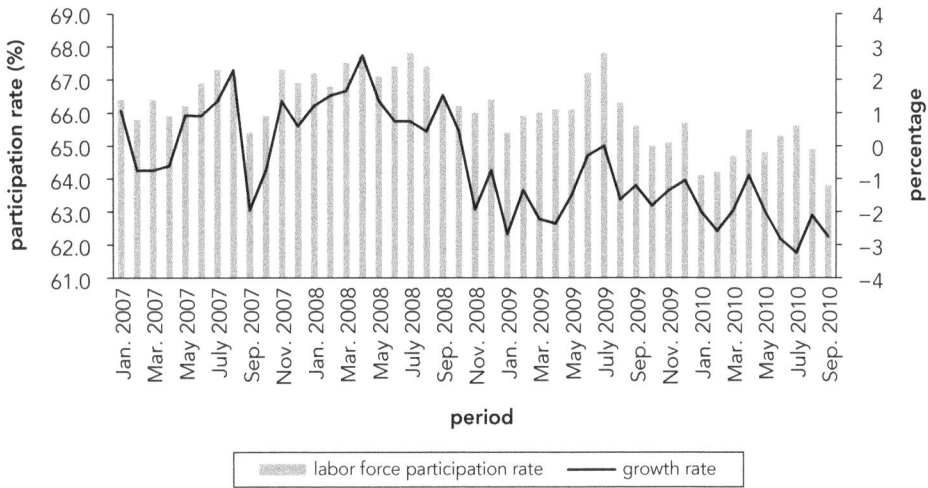

Source: U.S. Bureau of Labor Statistics.
Note: The growth rates are taken with respect to the same month of the previous year.

FIGURE 13.6 Unemployment Rate of Asians in the United States

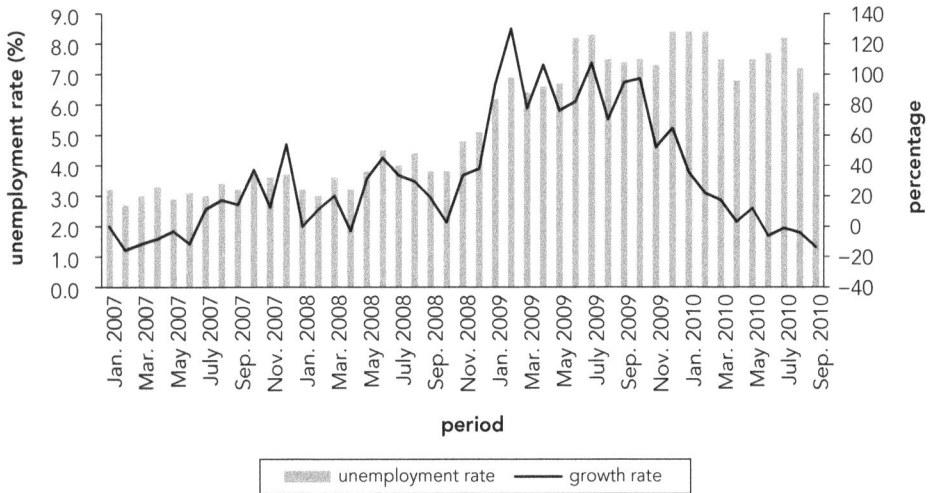

Source: U.S. Bureau of Labor Statistics.
Note: The growth rates are taken with respect to the same month of the previous year.

unemployed, unemployment rate, and total out-of-the-labor-force individuals. The correlations are estimated using the current values of the variables and using up to two leads of the remittance series. The data are by monthly frequency, and the period of estimation is January 2007 to September 2010.

Remittances received from around the world are used in the two countries, as well as remittances from just the United States. For example, the first row for "Bangladesh all" reports the correlation coefficients of remittances received from all over the world and the U.S. labor market indicators, the next row reports similar estimates but with the remittances series shifted forward one period, and the third row reports the coefficients with the remittances series shifted forward two periods. Rows 2 and 3 are meant to capture any lagged effects of changes in labor-market indicators reflecting changes in remittances. The "Bangladesh United States only" estimates present the same analysis but using only remittances from the United States to Bangladesh.

TABLE 13.2 Correlation of Remittances and U.S. Labor Market Indicators

Country/lead remittances	Correlation of growth rate of remittances with growth rate of							
	P	LFP	LFR	E	ER	U	UR	NLF
Bangladesh all								
Remittances *t*	−0.24	0.16	0.49*	0.10	0.31*	0.05	0.03	−0.58*
Remittances *t* +1	−0.13	0.24	0.52*	0.17	0.33*	0.09	0.06	−0.55*
Remittances *t* +2	0.00	0.43*	0.67*	0.34*	0.47*	−0.01	−0.05	−0.64*
Bangladesh United States only								
Remittances *t*	0.17	0.55*	0.66*	0.58*	0.72*	−0.36*	−0.39*	−0.52*
Remittances *t* +1	0.31*	0.65*	0.68*	0.65*	0.72*	−0.34*	−0.38*	−0.48*
Remittances *t* +2	0.43*	0.72*	0.68*	0.75*	0.79*	−0.52*	−0.56*	−0.42*
Pakistan all								
Remittances *t*	−0.09	−0.08	−0.04	−0.16	−0.17	0.31*	0.30*	−0.02
Remittances *t* +1	−0.02	−0.09	−0.11	−0.15	−0.21	0.32*	0.32*	0.10
Remittances *t* +2	0.00	0.10	0.15	0.05	0.07	0.10	0.09	−0.14
Pakistan United States only								
Remittances *t*	0.59*	0.62*	0.31*	0.59*	0.44*	−0.33*	−0.37*	−0.02
Remittances *t* +1	0.66*	0.62*	0.28	0.59*	0.40*	−0.31*	−0.34*	0.06
Remittances *t* +2	0.63*	0.71*	0.43*	0.66*	0.52*	−0.36*	−0.39*	−0.10

Source: Authors' calculations.

Note: An asterisk indicates that the correlation coefficient is different from zero at the 5 percent level. The category "Bangladesh (Pakistan) United States only" includes remittances just from the United States to Bangladesh (Pakistan). Monthly data from January 2007 to September 2010 were used in the estimation. Data on remittances come from respective countries' central banks. E = employed; ER = employment ratio; LFP = labor force participation; LFR = labor force participation rate; NLF = not in labor force; P = population; U = unemployed; UR = unemployment rate.

The estimates in table 13.2 follow the a priori expectations for the case of Bangladesh and to a lesser degree Pakistan, namely, that improved labor-market indicators are associated with higher growth in remittances. In the case of Bangladesh, evidence is available of a positive correlation between remittances and Asian labor force participation in volume and as a rate and with Asian employment in volume and as a ratio. Meanwhile, unemployment (level and rate) and the number of Asians out of the labor force have a negative correlation with remittances, when the focus is on the United States–Bangladesh corridor. In fact, as expected, the relationships are stronger when the focus is on remittances in the United States–Bangladesh corridor.

In the case of Pakistan, overall remittances are not strongly correlated with most U.S. economic indicators. In fact, the few significant coefficients for overall remittances are counterintuitive because remittances seem to relate positively with unemployment. However, once the analysis is limited to remittances from the United States (that is, the United States–Pakistan corridor only) it is possible to obtain many significant coefficients. In this case, remittances seem to relate positively to population levels, labor force participation (level and rate), and employment (level and ratio) and negatively with unemployment (level and rate). It is not possible to make strong conclusions about causality based on simple correlation coefficients, but the data suggest that better economic conditions of migrants in the United States relate to increased transfers to Bangladesh and Pakistan.

Of course, this conclusion is far from being something new. If migrants are altruistic agents and family consumption is a normal good, then it is expected for migrants to remit more if their economic condition improves. Likewise, if migrants are remitting to build a retirement nest egg in the home country, improved economic conditions should encourage more transfers. Nonetheless, the key suggestion from the results is that this relationship is evident even in times of global financial distress (that is, the correlations are estimated using data for the January 2007–September 2010 period). Hence, the crisis does not seem to have had major implications for remitting behavior in regard to deviations from previous expectations.

Remittances and the Economic Condition of Migrants in the United Kingdom

The distinction between place of birth and nationality in the United Kingdom is relevant for migration because (unlike the United States) not all persons born in the United Kingdom have the immediate right to British citizenship. The number of individuals born in Pakistan and Bangladesh who currently reside in the United Kingdom stands at about 428,000 and 194,000, respectively. As figure 13.7 shows, this number has increased over the crisis period for Pakistanis but has decreased for Bangladeshis. The number of individuals who are nationals of Pakistan and Bangladesh residing in the United Kingdom is smaller for this measure, but the dynamics remain the same. There is an increase in nationals of Pakistan and a decrease in nationals of Bangladesh.

Figure 13.8 reports the unemployment rate of individuals born in Bangladesh and Pakistan who currently reside in the United Kingdom, and figure 13.9 reports the unemployment rate of individuals who are nationals of Bangladesh and Pakistan and reside in the United Kingdom.

FIGURE 13.7 Number of Bangladesh and Pakistan Nationals Currently Residing in the United Kingdom

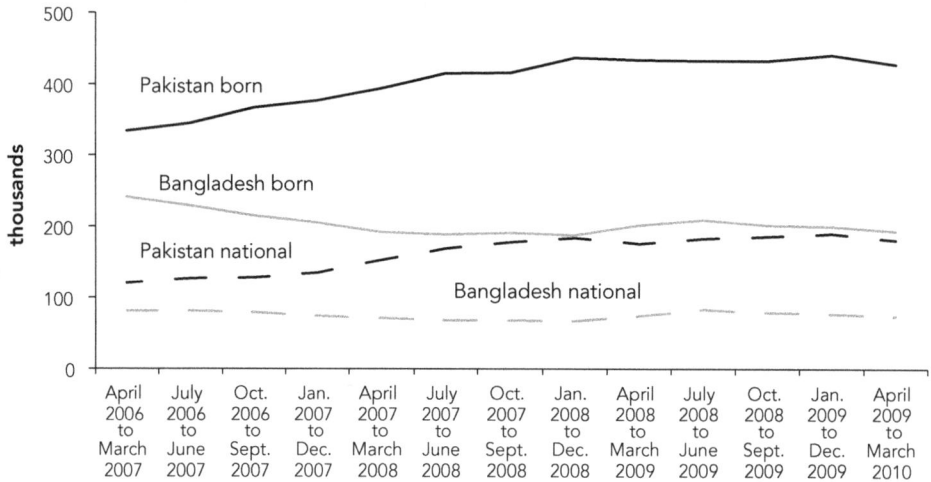

Source: U.K. Office for National Statistics.

FIGURE 13.8 Unemployment Rate of Those Born in Pakistan and Bangladesh Currently Residing in the United Kingdom

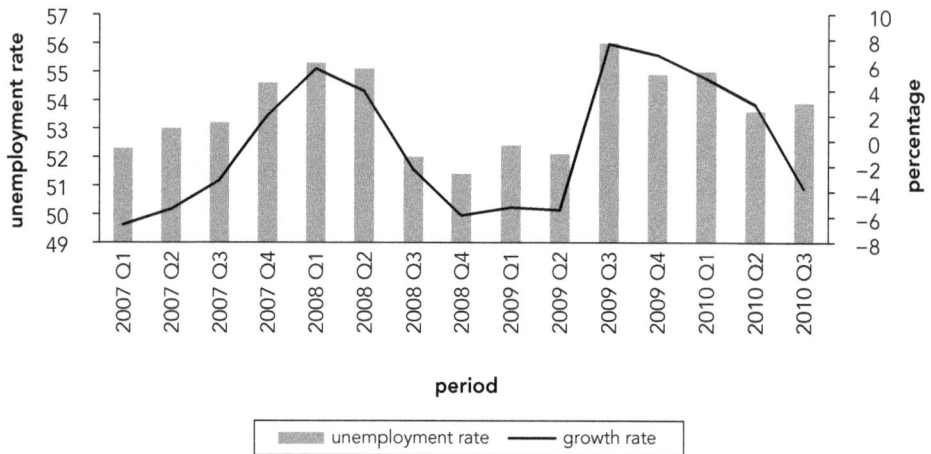

Source: U.K. Office for National Statistics.

Note: Defined as 100 = employment rate. The growth rates are taken with respect to the same quarter (Q) of the previous year.

It is important to highlight that the estimated unemployment rates for both of these groups are large, and the latest numbers suggest an unemployment rate of over 50 percent. It is possible that these figures do not fully capture the labor market characteristics

FIGURE 13.9 Unemployment Rate of Nationals of Pakistan and Bangladesh Currently Residing in the United Kingdom

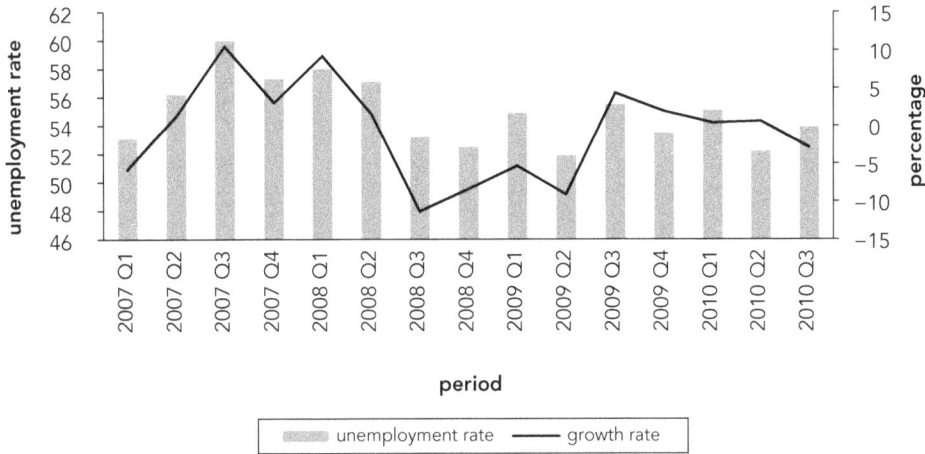

Source: U.K. Office for National Statistics.

Note: Defined as 100 = employment rate. The growth rates are taken with respect to the same quarter (Q) of the previous year.

of these groups given that these groups may have a tendency to find jobs in the informal sector. Nonetheless, the numbers are just too high and point to serious labor market problems for Bangladeshi and Pakistani migrants in the United Kingdom. Furthermore, previous research has shown that gender differences are important and that Pakistani and Bangladeshi women in the United Kingdom generally have lower rates of economic activity and higher rates of unemployment compared with other minority ethnic groups and white women (Dale 2008). In terms of the dynamics, it seems that in both cases no increase in the unemployment rate occurred during the crisis. There was actually a decrease in unemployment that started in early 2008 and lasted until mid-2009.

Table 13.3 gives the correlation coefficients of remittances to Bangladesh and Pakistan, with two measures of labor market conditions of migrants from these countries who reside in the United Kingdom. The first measure is the total employment (level) for individuals born in Bangladesh and Pakistan and for individuals who are nationals of these countries. The second measure is the unemployment rate presented with a similar division. The data for the U.K. labor market indicators come from the U.K. Office for National Statistics and are estimates from the U.K. Labour Force Survey. The data are by quarterly frequency, and the period of estimation is the first quarter of 2007 to the third quarter of 2010.

It is important to note that given that the data are by quarterly frequency, the correlation coefficients are estimated with a limited number of observations. In fact, there is significance for only a few coefficients. For example, evidence shows a negative correlation between the unemployment rate of those born in these countries and remittances to Bangladesh if two leads of the U.K. corridor remittance series are used.

TABLE 13.3 Correlation of Remittances with U.K. Labor Market Indicators

Country/lead remittances	Correlation of growth rate of remittances with growth rate of			
	Employed born	Employed nationality	Unemployment rate born	Unemployment rate nationality
Bangladesh all				
Remittances t	−0.09	−0.26	−0.24	−0.14
Remittances $t+1$	−0.23	−0.22	−0.16	−0.31
Remittances $t+2$	−0.51*	−0.28	0.24	−0.38
Bangladesh United Kingdom only				
Remittances t	0.08	−0.16	0.10	0.35
Remittances $t+1$	0.20	−0.04	0.00	0.18
Remittances $t+2$	0.30	0.14	−0.48*	−0.22
Pakistan all				
Remittances t	−0.20	−0.14	0.07	0.04
Remittances $t+1$	−0.39	−0.34	0.38	0.15
Remittances $t+2$	−0.57*	−0.66*	0.72*	0.38
Pakistan United Kingdom only				
Remittances t	−0.39	−0.50*	0.35	0.03
Remittances $t+1$	−0.23	−0.19	−0.05	−0.30
Remittances $t+2$	0.14	0.31	−0.52*	−0.75*

Source: Authors' calculations.

Note: "Born" refers to statistics about the labor market conditions of individuals born in Bangladesh and Pakistan currently residing in the United Kingdom. "Nationality" refers to statistics about the labor market conditions of individuals who are nationals of Bangladesh and Pakistan currently residing in the United Kingdom. An asterisk indicates that the correlation coefficient is different from zero at the 5 percent level. The category "Bangladesh (Pakistan) United Kingdom only" includes remittances from just the United Kingdom to Bangladesh (Pakistan). Quarterly data from the first quarter of 2007 to the third quarter of 2010 were used in the estimation. Data on remittances come from respective countries' central banks.

For Pakistan, results with overall remittances are mostly counterintuitive. For instance, aggregate remittances seem to be positively correlated with the unemployment rate. Nonetheless, when the focus is exclusively on the remittance flows from the United Kingdom, there is a significant negative correlation between remittances (two leads) and the unemployment rate of Bangladeshi and Pakistani nationals. This relationship between remittances and unemployment also holds for the case of those born in these countries. In general, two explanations are possible for the lack of significance of most coefficients. First, the estimation uses a small number of observations. Second, the official unemployment rates for these migrants in the United Kingdom are very high and may not accurately reflect their labor market conditions.

Exchange Rate Changes

Immigrants typically earn money in the host currency, but their transfers are converted into the home currency for the household to consume or invest the money. Therefore, appreciations of the home currency decrease the purchasing power of remittances in the home country. Ceteris paribus, after an appreciation of the domestic currency, each host currency unit of remittances (for instance, each dollar or each British pound) will buy less for the receiving household. This means that the household needs additional units of host currency to consume a given bundle of goods (again, assuming no changes in prices). If the purpose of the transfer is to make a certain bundle of goods available to the household, then the foreign worker should increase the amount of host currency sent abroad. Furthermore, if the foreign worker is making a long-term investment with remittances or remitting to build a retirement nest egg, then additional host currency is necessary to accomplish a certain investment goal. On the other hand, now each unit of host currency remittances is worth less in the home country. Ceteris paribus, if workers have investments in both countries, it may be wise to reduce remittances and put the money into investments in the host country. Overall, in theory, remittances may increase or decrease after a depreciation of the host currency, depending on which of these two effects dominates. Nonetheless, it is generally agreed that currency value changes may have important effects on remitted flows.

Figures 13.10 and 13.11 show the daily exchange rates of the Bangladeshi taka and the Pakistani rupee with respect to the dollar and the British pound for the period January 1, 2007, to January 31, 2010. It seems that in all cases the dollar remains stable with respect to the home currencies. In the case of the Pakistani rupee evidence suggests a trend toward depreciation of the local currency with respect to the dollar, but changes are not dramatic. Meanwhile, for the pound the story is completely different. In this case for the two currencies it is possible to observe an appreciation of the home currencies vis-à-vis the pound.

This is important because previous evidence suggested that appreciation (depreciation) of the home (host) currency may lead to decreases in remittances. For instance, Yang (2008b) shows that appreciation of an immigrant's host currency against the Philippine peso leads to increases in remittances received from overseas. Therefore, the declining trend in the value of the British pound with respect to these two currencies may result in further decreases in remittances.

Concluding Remarks

Fear was expressed among policy circles about international migration becoming one of the causalities of the global crisis during the months leading up to its peak. There were clear reasons for this fear. The global crisis resulted in many host countries imposing new restrictions on admissions of migrants to counteract rising domestic unemployment.

FIGURE 13.10 U.S. Dollar and U.K. Pound Exchange Rate with Respect to Bangladeshi Taka

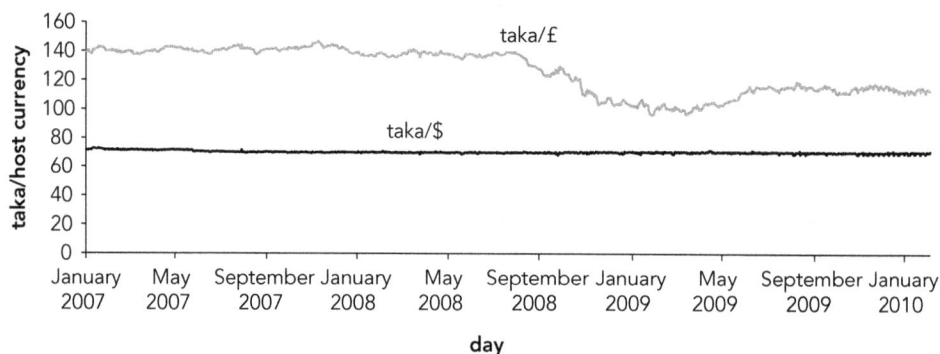

Source: http://www.xe.com/.

Note: Currency values are for the interbank rate and are daily observations.

FIGURE 13.11 U.S. Dollar and U.K. Pound Exchange Rate with Respect to Pakistani Rupee

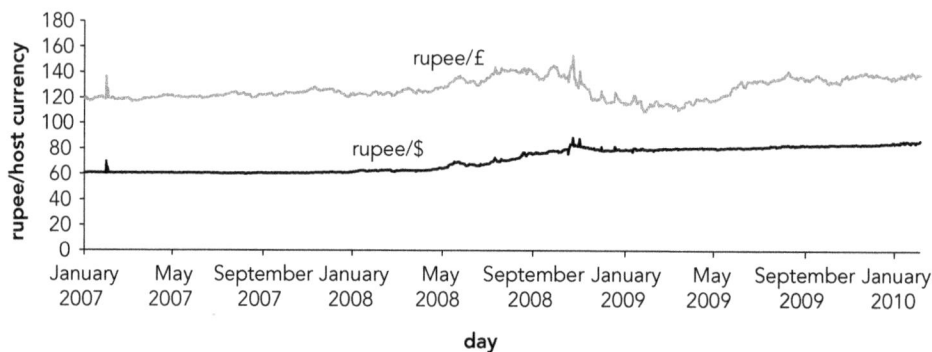

Source: http://www.xe.com/.

Note: Currency values are for the interbank rate and are daily observations.

Moreover, the crisis led to increasing hostility toward migrants because they were seen as illegitimate members of the labor force who were taking away the few jobs available. This in turn led to increased discrimination in the employment sector.

The empirical evidence so far, however, shows that the impact of the recent economic turmoil, although important, was temporary, and migrant flows seem to be growing once again. The results of our simple analysis suggest that remittances were related to better economic conditions for Bangladeshi and Pakistani migrants in the United States during the crisis period. In particular, the evidence is stronger for the volume of remittances sent from the United States only (versus overall remittance flows) to these countries. Less evidence is at hand of migrant economic conditions in the United Kingdom having an impact on the remitted flows to Pakistan and Bangladesh, most likely because of the smaller number of observations available.

In addition, for the case of Bangladesh it seems that the country is receiving fewer remittances from the United Kingdom and the United States, but that increases from other countries more than compensate for the decrease. Finally, it seems that although there have not been dramatic changes in the value of the dollar with respect to the two home currencies (although there was some appreciation with respect to the Pakistani rupee), these currencies have gained ground when compared with the British pound. If this trend continues, it may lead to further decreases in remittances from the United Kingdom to these countries.

In regards to migration, both the United Kingdom and United States have become more restrictive in recent years. In the United States, the Department of Homeland Security announced stricter enforcement of the rules of the H-1B visa program, and the U.S. Congress raised the H-1B visa fee for employers with more than 50 percent H-1B visa holder employees. In the United Kingdom, the Home Office announced a cap on the number of non-EEA economic migrants coming under the country's point-based system and announced further cuts in migration. These measures may have long-term implications for migration from Bangladesh and Pakistan to these countries.

In general, the evidence suggests that the behavior of remittance flows during the crisis was similar to the commonly held expectations about these flows. Further exploration of the impact of the global economic downturn on remittance flows in other countries and different contexts is necessary to facilitate cross-country comparisons and ultimately establish the likely long-term consequences of the crisis for remittances.

Notes

1. The U.S. H-1B visa program allows the employment of foreign workers in specialty occupations. There is a cap of 65,000 workers who may be issued a visa, although the cap has been raised on several occasions. Foreign workers in universities and nonprofit research institutions are excluded from the cap.

2. The PBS is a system for managing migration for those wishing to enter the United Kingdom for work or study from outside the EEA and Switzerland. Tier 1 allows for the entry of highly skilled individuals without a job offer. Tier 2 allows for the entry of skilled workers with a job offer. Tier 3 allows for the entry of low-skilled workers but has been permanently closed. Tier 4 is for students, and tier 5 is for temporary workers.

Chapter 14

Impacts of the Crisis on Migrants and Their Families: A Case Study from Bangladesh

GUNTUR SUGIYARTO, SELIM RAIHAN, CARLOS VARGAS-SILVA, AND SHIKHA JHA

THIS CASE STUDY SUMMARIZES THE results from a household survey in Bangladesh that explores the impact of the global financial crisis on migrants and their families. Bangladesh is one of the top-10 remittance-receiving countries in the world and one of the major labor-exporting countries in Asia (Irving, Mohapatra, and Ratha 2010; Mohapatra and Ozden 2009; Rahman 2009; Ullah and Panday 2007). Other similar countries included in the survey were Indonesia and the Philippines. The survey is part of an effort to examine the impact of the global crisis on migration and remittance in Asia and is conducted at different levels, that is, international, country, sectoral, and migrant household levels.

The survey explored the impact of the global crisis on out-migration and remittances received, migrants' and households' coping mechanisms, and the general knowledge of households about the global crisis. The overall results suggest that although it is possible to observe a significant impact of the global financial crisis on migration and remittances at the macrolevel in Bangladesh, the impact of the crisis differs across different geographical locations and reflects the economic and social background of the migrants and their countries of destination.

This chapter is based on the results of the Asian Development Bank's project Research and Development Technical Assistance (RDTA) 7436: Global Crisis, Remittance and Poverty in Asia. The views expressed in the chapter are those of the authors and do not necessarily reflect the views or policies of ADB.

The Survey

The sample consists of 217 randomly chosen migrant households (defined as a household that had at least one member working abroad during the August 2007 to September 2008 period) from three subdistricts (*upazillas*) of three different districts. The selection of districts was made to obtain samples from divergent backgrounds, and the selection of the migrant households was independent of the status of the migrant (that is, regular or irregular) in the country of destination. The selection of the three *upazillas* facilitates drawing information from migrants located in several destination countries. Table 14.1 provides the distribution of the sample by geographical location. The migrants from Manikganj and Gazipur districts generally go to the Middle East, whereas migrants from Hobiganj district travel to the United Kingdom. Their choice of countries is a reflection of the migrants' education and skills as well as the existing migration network. Given the sample size and distribution, it is clear that the survey is not intended to provide results representative of the whole population in Bangladesh but to provide a quick diagnostic of the impact of the crisis on migrants and their households in the country.

TABLE 14.1 Distribution of Samples

District	Upazilla	Village	Number of households
Manikganj	Singair	Khan Baniara and Hindu Baniara	75
Gazipur	Joydevpur	Bhanua and Pajulia	77
Hobiganj	Hobiganj Sadar	Pailgram, Richi, and Nabiganj	65
Total			217

Source: Authors' calculations.

Key Results

The questions in the survey collect crucial pre- and postcrisis information on selected variables such as the dynamics of migrations and remittances and the migrants' and migrant households' coping mechanism. These variables are linked with the main characteristics of the migrants and their families. The period before the financial crisis corresponds to the period from August 2007 to September 2008, and the period of the financial crisis corresponds to the period from October 2008 to September 2009. It is common to consider October 2008 as the peak of the financial crisis. Lehman Brothers had just filed for bankruptcy in September 2008, representing the largest bankruptcy in U.S. history. At global levels, the financial crisis extended until late 2009 and beyond in some countries. Hence, the period that we denote "during" the financial crisis may not yet represent the total effect of the crisis.

Knowledge and Expectations about the Crisis

On average about half of the migrant households have no knowledge of the global financial crisis, especially less educated and skilled migrants from Manikganj and Gazipur
districts. Households sending migrants to the United Kingdom seem to have much better knowledge of the crisis (49 percent have relatively good knowledge and 17 percent
have very good knowledge; see figures 14.1 and 14.2 for details). Those who have either
"relatively good" or "very good" knowledge about the crisis mostly think that the crisis
will last for one or two years (figure 14.3).

FIGURE 14.1 Knowledge about the Global Financial Crisis

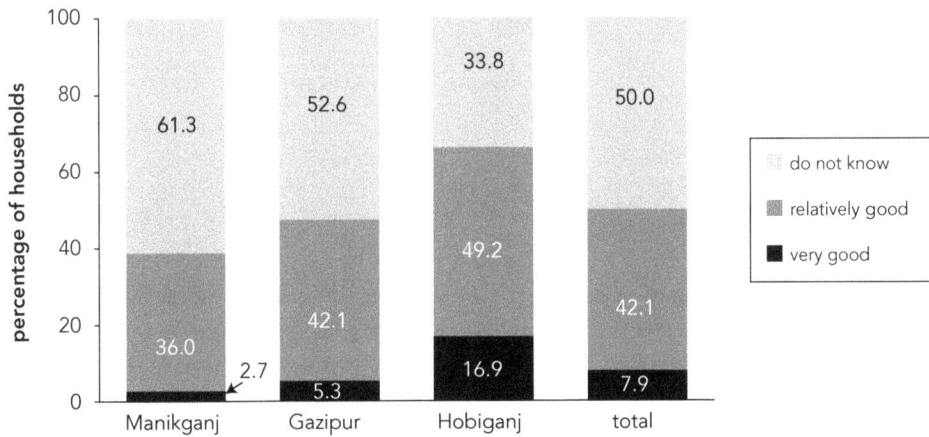

Source: Authors' calculations.

**FIGURE 14.2 Expected Period of Impact of Global Financial Crisis According to
Households Reporting Relatively or Very Good Knowledge**

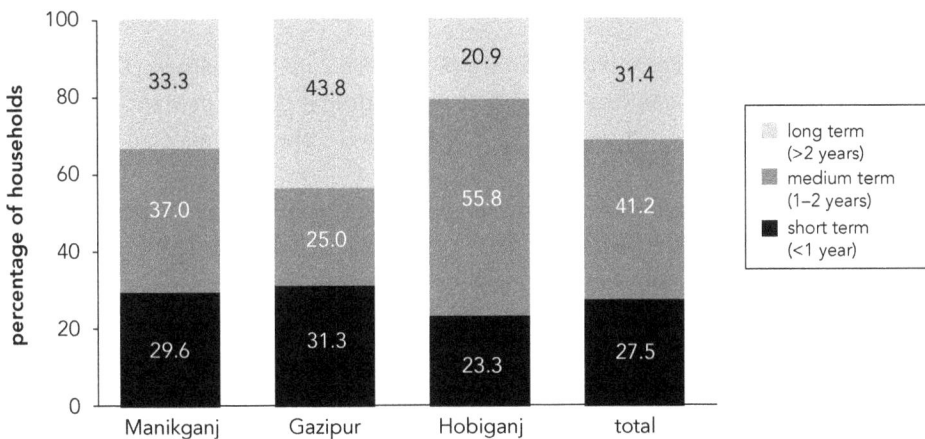

Source: Authors' calculations.

FIGURE 14.3 Average Number of Family Members Working Abroad before and during the Financial Crisis

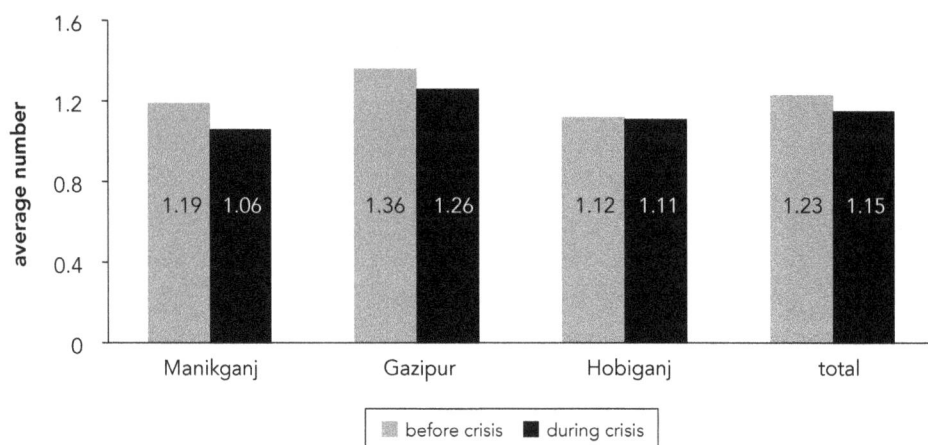

Source: Authors' calculations.

Impacts on Out-Migration

The impact on out-migration can clearly be seen in the number of family members working abroad, which declined during the crisis. For the total sample, the decline is nearly 7 percent (from an average of 1.23–1.15 family members abroad). Households in Manikganj appear to experience the largest drop, followed by Gazipur. On the other hand, there was almost no change in Hobiganj. Therefore, the impact of the crisis decline in out-migration was not universal across districts in Bangladesh, which relates directly to the migrants' education and skills (figure 14.3).

Impact on Remittances

The impact on remittances is evident from the 6.4 percentage point drop in the number of households receiving remittances (table 14.2). The drop is greater in Manikganj (close to 12 percentage points), whereas Gazipur appears to be the least affected (a 1.5 percentage point drop).

In terms of remittance income, migrant households, on average, experienced an 18.8 percent fall in remittance income during the crisis period (table 14.3). In Hobiganj households suffered a 58 percent fall in remittance income. Gazipur was the exception, where the volume of remittances increased by 13 percent.

A majority of households that received remittances on a frequent basis (such as monthly) before the crisis were also receiving transfers at the same frequency during the crisis. Yet many of those that had been receiving remittances less frequently (for example, four times per year) received these flows with even less frequency during the

TABLE 14.2 Receiving Remittances from Migrants

Receiving remittances	Manikganj		Gazipur		Hobiganj		Total	
	Before	During	Before	During	Before	During	Before	During
Percentage of households	98.6	86.5	94.6	93.2	93.8	89.2	95.8	89. 7
Percentage change		−12.1		−1.4		−4.6		−6.1

Source: Authors' calculations.

TABLE 14.3 Average Amount of Remittances Received

Remittances received	Manikganj		Gazipur		Hobiganj		Total	
	Before	During	Before	During	Before	During	Before	During
Average (taka)	137,608	132,403	138,806	157,286	201,593	84,466	156,444	127,077
Percentage change		−3.78		13.31		−58.10		−18.77

Source: Authors' calculations.

crisis. About 87 percent of the households receiving remittances on a monthly basis before the crisis also received remittances on a monthly basis after the crisis (table 14.4). The figure for those receiving remittances every other month is 77 percent, four times a year almost 60 percent, and twice a year 67 percent. All of them received remittances less frequently during or after the crisis.

TABLE 14.4 Frequency of Remittances Received before and during the Crisis

percentage of households

Remittances before the crisis	Remittances during the crisis					
	Monthly	Every other month	Four times a year	Twice a year	Once a year	Other
Monthly	86.96	4.35	0.00	0.00	4.35	4.35
Every other month	0.00	77.42	8.06	6.45	0.00	8.06
Four times a year	0.00	2.47	59.26	25.93	6.17	6.17
Twice a year	0.00	0.00	6.67	66.67	13.33	13.33
Once a year	0.00	0.00	0.00	50.00	33.33	16.67
Other	14.29	14.29	0.00	0.00	0.00	71.43

Source: Authors' calculations.

The crisis seems to have increased the use of formal channels such as bank and money transfer institutions and reduced the use of informal channels such as *hundi* (a formal traditional form of money transfer). This change could be because migrants have become more knowledgeable about the existing formal channel services, and/or those who used to send remittances through informal channels could not do it again for various reasons, including being laid off, having no money, and the like. Table 14.5 also suggests that households receiving remittances from banks before the crisis tend to continue receiving remittances from banks (76.8 percent). On the other hand, about 20 percent of households who used to receive remittances through *hundi* before the crisis now receive remittances through banks. This is a good development, which has resulted from both supply and demand sides in the transfer market, and it is clear that the change from informal to formal channels seems to be independent of the amount of remittances.

TABLE 14.5 Channels of Remitting before and during the Crisis

percentage of households

Channel before the crisis	Channel during the crisis				
	Bank	MTO	Friends/coworkers	Hundi	Other
Bank	76.82	19.21	0.66	2.65	0.66
MTO	10.00	90.00	0.00	0.00	0.00
Friends/coworkers	0.00	0.00	100.00	0.00	0.00
Hundi	20.00	20.00	0.00	60.00	0.00
Other	37.50	50.00	0.00	0.00	12.50

Source: Authors' calculations.

Note: MTO = money transfer operator.

Coping Mechanisms of the Migrant Households

Almost 50 percent of the migrant households experienced a decline in income during the period under consideration. The negative impact is most prominent in Hobiganj, where 64 percent of the migrant households' income fell. The situation is different in Gazipur, where 73.7 percent of the migrant households actually experienced a rise in income (figure 14.4). This dynamic is something that cannot be observed at the macrolevel.

On average, more than half of the households (51.88 percent) that experienced a drop in income during the crisis period reported that it was due to a reduction in remittance income (table 14.6). The share is greater in Gazipur, about 62 percent, where a complicated picture emerges, as the remittance income increased on average, but for those households that experienced a decrease in income during the crisis, a reduction in remittances was the main source of the decrease.

FIGURE 14.4 Change in Household Income between 2008 and 2009

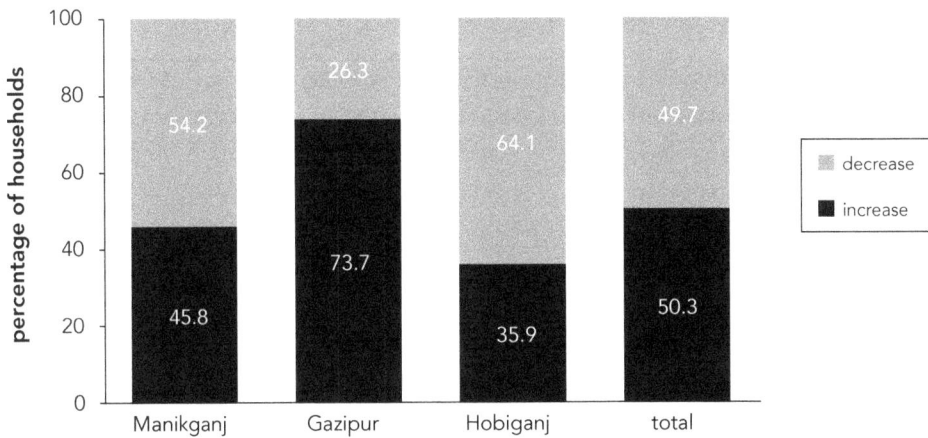

Source: Authors' calculations.

TABLE 14.6 Reasons for the Decrease in Income

percentage of households

Reason	Manikganj	Gazipur	Hobiganj	Total
Reduction in remittance income	47.82	62.50	34.99	51.88
Job loss among family members	43.48	25.00	5.00	9.22
Wage cut among family members	8.70	12.50	37.55	26.62
Other	0.00	0.00	22.46	12.29

Source: Authors' calculations.

More than 45 percent of the households that experienced a reduction in remittances decided to work more to compensate for the decline in income (table 14.7). The main source of compensation for income loss among the households that experienced a wage cut also was working additional hours. About 50 percent of the households that experienced job losses among family members compensated by consuming their savings. Therefore, the use of savings seems to be a last resort, which was used after the loss of a job.

Coping Mechanism of the Migrants

In response to the crisis, migrants can return home when they are laid off or lose their job, or they can work in more jobs and/or for more hours to compensate for any reduction in their income. The percentage of migrants returning home increased during the

TABLE 14.7 Reasons for Income Loss and Ways to Compensate

percentage of households

Reason for decrease in income	Response				
	Working more	Borrowing	Savings	Selling	Other
Reduction in remittance incomes	45.45	18.18	33.33	0.00	3.03
Job loss among family members	0.00	16.67	50.00	16.67	16.67
Wage cut among family members	64.71	23.53	11.76	0.00	0.00
Other	87.50	12.50	0.00	0.00	0.00

Source: Authors' calculations.

crisis period, and the number in Hobiganj is significantly higher (over a 10 percentage point increase) (table 14.8). It seems that in general, migrants adjusted to the adverse situation by lowering their expenses and using their savings (table 14.9). Some of the migrants who experienced a reduction in "working hours" and "overtime without pay" also had to look for new jobs.

TABLE 14.8 Migrants Returning Home in 2008 and 2009

percentage of households

	Manikganj		Gazipur		Hobiganj		Total	
Returning migrant	Before	During	Before	During	Before	During	Before	During
Percentage of migrants	13.6	20.7	22.1	26.7	7.4	17.5	14.5	21.8
Percentage change	7.1		4.6		10.1		7.3	

Source: Authors' calculations.

Most of the migrants faced the problem of a wage cut with the exception of agricultural workers, because there is no change in their employment condition during the period under consideration. A significant portion of service workers, domestic workers, construction workers, administrative workers, technical workers, and other workers had to work overtime without extra pay to keep their job.

Conclusions

This case study provides a quick diagnostic of the impact of the global financial crisis on migrants and migrant households in three *upazillas* in Bangladesh. Overall results suggest that despite the low level of knowledge about the global financial crisis among migrant households, they really felt the dynamics of the impact although the adverse impacts vary considerably. As a result of the crisis, the number of family members working abroad declined by about 7 percent, and a corresponding 6.4 percent drop was

TABLE 14.9 Change in Employment Condition and Responses

percentage of households

Change in employment condition	Lowering expenses	New job	Savings	Borrowing from family	Borrowing from friends	Other	No change
				Response to change			
Wage cut	0.00	0.00	0.00	0.00	0.00	0.00	100.00
Benefit reduction	25.00	0.00	25.00	0.00	0.00	0.00	50.00
Working hour reduction	18.92	3.60	25.23	1.80	1.80	5.41	43.24
Overtime without pay	4.35	21.74	43.48	8.70	0.00	0.00	21.74
Other	10.00	15.00	55.00	5.00	0.00	0.00	15.00
No change	9.35	0.00	3.74	1.87	0.00	4.67	80.37

Source: Authors' calculations.

seen in the number of households receiving remittances and a 19 percent decline in remittance income. There are, however, marked differences across *upazillas* in regard to the impact of the crisis. Therefore, although at the macrolevel one may come up with a certain conclusion about the impact of the crisis on migration and remittances in a country such as Bangladesh, very important differences are still found across regions and local levels that can be strongly linked with the background of migrants, such as their education and skill levels.

Given the strong variation of the impact of the crisis, it seems that a "one size fits all" policy approach fails to address the dynamic impacts on migrants and their family. Policies to address the issue should carefully consider the nature of migration and remittance practices, as well as the factors driving mobility. The policy should also consider the migrants' background carefully. There is a need to protect migrants and their families as they cope with the crisis and emerge as stronger individuals. This means pushing for programs that support training and improving the adverse conditions that have fueled the push factors of migration. An optimal forward-looking migration policy should promote a "win-win-win" solution that benefits the host country, the sending country, and the migrant workers and their families.

PART III

Chapter 15

The Impact of the Financial Crisis on Remittance Flows: The Case of El Salvador

PABLO ACOSTA, JAVIER BAEZ, RODOLFO BEAZLEY, AND EDMUNDO MURRUGARRA

THE 2009 INTERNATIONAL FINANCIAL CRISIS hit El Salvador severely. After almost two decades of economic growth, gross domestic product (GDP) fell by 3.5 percent in 2009 driven by a decline in the manufacturing sector (output that accounts for 23 percent of the Salvadoran GDP). Exports also fell by 16.5 percent during 2009 and by 22.9 percent in the maquila sector (39 percent of the Salvadoran exports), a highly labor-intensive activity. About 46 percent of the Salvadoran exports go to the United States.

The unemployment rate for 2009 increased by 25 percent, from 5.8 percent in 2008 to 7.3 percent in 2009, the highest of the decade. Rural unemployment is still higher than urban unemployment even as the international crisis hit harder those employed in urban areas, where the unemployment rate grew 29 percent (compared with 17 percent in rural regions). Unemployment also rose considerably among young people, by 2.6 percentage points, from 10.7 percent in 2008 to 13.3 percent in 2009. Most of the reduction in employment was registered in the formal sector of the economy. About 22,000 private sector formal jobs (proxied by the number of contributors to the social security system) were lost in 2009 (about 3.4 percent of the total formal employment), 8,000 of them in the manufacturing sector (a 5.2 percent decline in the number of formal manufacturing jobs), which in 2009 accounted for 27 percent of the jobs in the country. The pace of formal job destruction reached its worst level in August 2009, when more than 10,000 formal jobs were lost. Some workers moved to the informal sector, which grew by 1.9 percent between 2008 and 2009.

Salvadorans were not only affected by the employment crisis and lower domestic incomes. The fall in international migrant remittances affected the budget of numerous households that rely on them as the main source of income or as insurance in a context of lower domestic income sources (Halliday 2006; Yang and Choi 2007). A significant proportion of Salvadorans are living abroad, mainly in the United States, where the international financial crisis started in September 2008. Migration has created both a strong dependence on remittances for families left behind and a high exposure to external shocks. Official migrant remittances, which reached $3.5 billion in 2009, fell by 8.5 percent in 2009, the first decline in 20 years. Monthly data show that until March 2010 remittances were still lower than the year before in absolute terms, and that the recovery thereafter has been milder than expected (figures 15.1a and 15.1b). As a consequence, accumulated remittance flows from January to July 2010 were still lower in absolute terms than in the same period in 2008. The crisis in the U.S. economy also

FIGURE 15.1 El Salvador: Main Macroeconomic Indicators

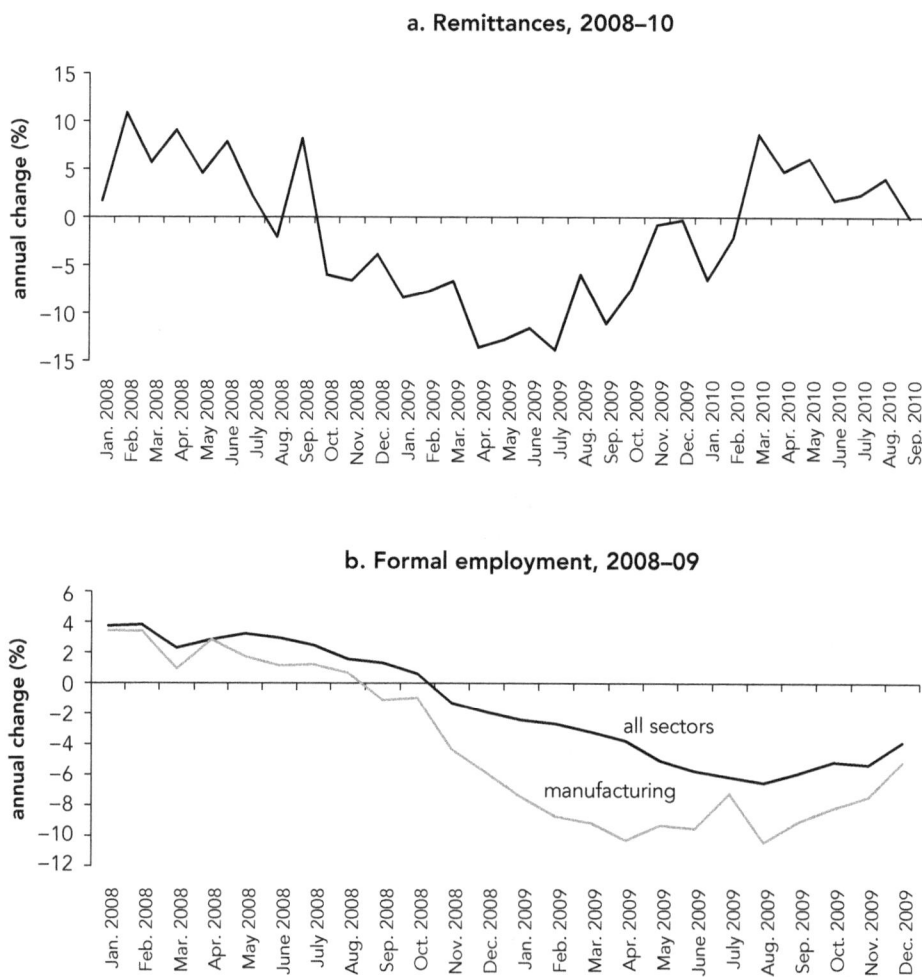

a. Remittances, 2008–10

b. Formal employment, 2008–09

Sources: Central Bank of El Salvador, U.S. Bureau of Economic Analysis, and U.S. Bureau of Labor Statistics.

reduced the prospects of economic opportunities for future migrants in El Salvador, particularly young people, building additional pressure on local labor markets.

The 2009 financial crisis is not the first external shock to uncover the high vulnerability of El Salvador to external forces. In 2007–08, during the international food and fuel crisis, the rise in these commodities prices wiped out almost all the gains in terms of poverty reduction achieved by 2007, bringing the country back to the poverty levels observed in 2001. The poverty head count rate increased from 35.5 percent in 2007 to 42.3 in 2008, reaching the highest ratio since 2002, and showing that the Salvadoran economy is fragile and highly vulnerable to external shocks. Once again, the 2009 international financial crisis has made it clear that El Salvador is quite vulnerable to the evolution of the U.S. economy, not only in terms of exports but also through the migrant remittances channel.

This chapter focuses on the transmission channel of remittances from the United States in a context of crisis in the development prospects of El Salvador, including its ultimate impact on poverty and welfare.

Migration and Remittances in El Salvador

Starting in the 1970s, armed conflicts displaced a large proportion of the Salvadoran population. Approximately 15 percent of the population emigrated between 1979 and 1989 (Funkhouser 1997). Estimates suggest that in 2005 about 1.13 million Salvadorans were living abroad, representing 16 percent of the total Salvadoran population (Ratha and Shaw 2007). Of these migrants, approximately 914,000 Salvadorans (81 percent of migrants) went to the United States.

In 2009 about 16 percent of Salvadoran households had one or more members living abroad, a figure that has been almost stable for the last decade. Despite this stable migration trend, a change in the segment of population that migrates has taken place. In the late 1990s migration was rather equally distributed across area of residence and gender, but since 2000 the majority of migrants are males from urban areas, reflecting the economic slowdown during 2001 (World Bank 2009g). In 2009, of the households with at least one member who had out-migrated, 60 percent were urban, and 40 percent were living in rural areas. During the last 10 years, about 68 percent of the Salvadorans leaving the country were less than 30 years old at the time of migration. Despite an increase in the fraction of low-income households with external migrants in the last years, households at the top of the income distribution are still more than twice as likely to have migrants as the ones at the bottom.

Young people are more likely to migrate because they face lower costs in moving and have higher lifetime returns. About 60 percent of Salvadorans who migrated between 1998 and 2007 were aged 18–30 in the year of migration. This proportion of young migrants is much higher than for other developing countries, where just half of the migrants are between 12 and 30 years old. Nearly 63 percent of them are male, and

75 percent have parents living in El Salvador. About 94 percent of the migrant youth are working in the destination country (as opposed to studying), and 79 percent of the young working migrants send remittances back home at least once a year.

Indeed, Salvadoran migration has led to a strong dependence on remittances. In 2009 total financial inflow of remittances was close to $3.5 billion. In relative terms, they represented around 16.4 percent of GDP. El Salvador ranked 11th among the top world remittance recipients as measured by the ratio of total remittances to GDP in 2007.

About 21.3 percent of the households reported having received money from abroad in 2009 (World Bank 2009c). Rural households and mid-low and middle-income segments of the population are more dependent on remittances. Measured by their share in the total income, the dependency on remittances for people in mid-low and middle quintiles is nearly 45 percent larger compared with the dependency found at the bottom (12.8 percent) and top (8.8 percent) of the income distribution (World Bank 2009c).

Remittances represent a significant share of total domestic budget. Before the crisis, remittances amounted to 11.4 percent of the total household income (data for 2007). This share is much larger when looking only at recipient households: 42 percent of their total incomes. Nevertheless, remarkable differences can be seen in the weight of remittances by area. Indeed, the share of remittances in total incomes is 15.4 percent in rural areas and 9.2 percent in urban areas.

The Effects of the Financial Crisis on Remittances and Migration Prospects

In the case of El Salvador, remittance transfers are sent typically by nationals who reside in the United States. Consequently, the flow of transfers is highly dependent on U.S. economic business cycles. During the 2000s, data indicate that remittances are procyclical, with comovements in fluctuations between real U.S. GDP growth and the real growth in the flow of remittances sent to El Salvador (figure 15.2a).

Between 2000 and 2010, the conditional correlation between remittances and U.S. GDP was 0.926, after accounting for time trends and quarterly effects. That is, on average a decline of 1 percent in the U.S. quarterly real GDP growth rate is associated with a reduction of almost similar magnitude in the quarterly real growth rate of remittances being sent to El Salvador. A similar conclusion can also be derived from the correlation between total unemployment in the United States and remittances sent to El Salvador, which moves in opposite directions (figure 15.2b). An increase of unemployment in the United States by 1 percent would reduce the growth rate of remittances by more than 6 percent.

The evolution of these key U.S. macroeconomic indicators explains the fall in remittances to El Salvador during 2009. GDP in the United States declined by 3.5 percent in 2009, and the unemployment rate in December 2009 in the United States was 10 percent, up from 7.4 percent a year before. Moreover, the U.S. unemployment rate for Hispanics

FIGURE 15.2 Growth in Remittances to El Salvador in Comparison to Growth in U.S. GDP and Unemployment

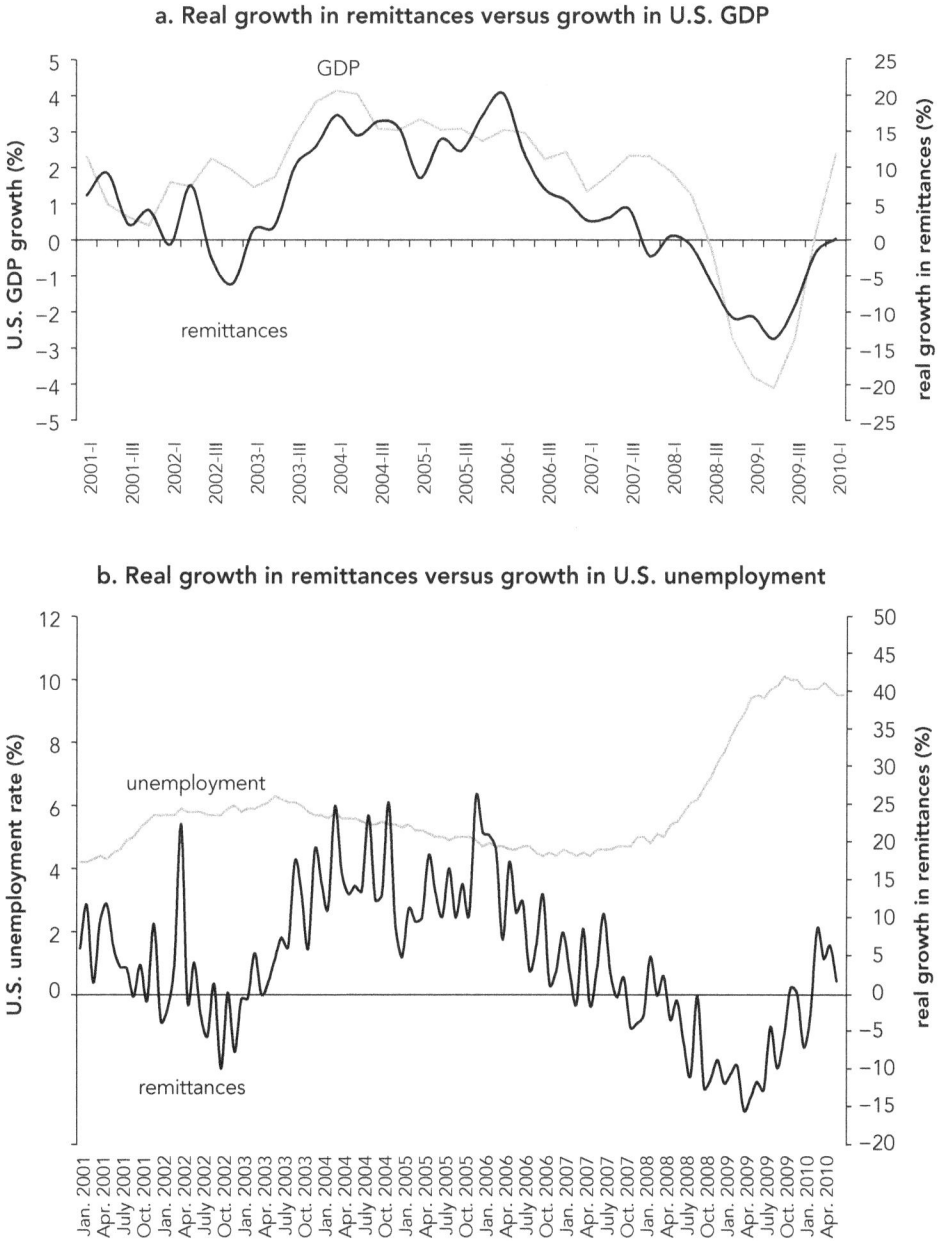

a. Real growth in remittances versus growth in U.S. GDP

b. Real growth in remittances versus growth in U.S. unemployment

Sources: Central Bank of El Salvador, U.S. Bureau of Economic Analysis, and U.S. Bureau of Labor Statistics.

in December 2009 was 12.9 percent, a rate significantly higher than the 9.4 percent of a year before (overall, the Hispanic unemployment rate in the United States is at any time much higher than for the rest of U.S. workers) (figure 15.3).

FIGURE 15.3 U.S. Unemployment Rates for Total Population and for Hispanics, 2005–10

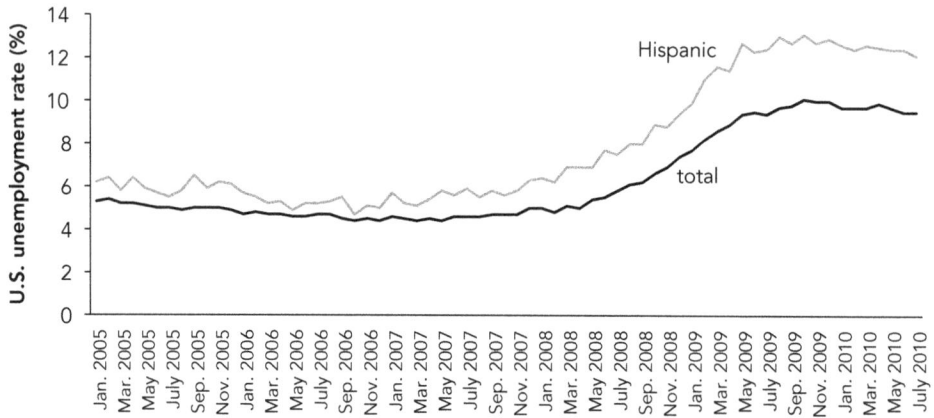

Source: U.S. Bureau of Labor Statistics.

In parallel, recorded remittances to El Salvador fell 8.5 percent in 2009 (in nominal terms), the most dramatic decline in the last two decades. Moreover, according to household survey data (which may also include remittances flowing through informal channels), the drop was even more drastic: around 11.9 percent. According to the elasticities estimated before, this fall in remittances is more in line with the predicted evolution of U.S. unemployment, and higher than the one predicted by the evolution of U.S. GDP.

Although rural households tend to rely more on remittances, the decline in remittance flows was sharper in urban areas (figure 15.4). In 2009 remittance inflows decreased by 12.6 percent in urban households and 11.7 percent in rural households. The metropolitan area of San Salvador was among the most affected regions, with a decline of about 15 percent. The Oriental area (where most of the migrants come from and predominantly rural) was for some reason better off; remittances decreased there by 7.6 percent.

Using 2009 household survey data, we estimate that a 10 percent average decline in remittances in El Salvador in 2009 (the average between the actual declines in macroeconomic and microeconomic figures of 8.5 and 11.9 percent, respectively) would have increased national poverty by 1.6 percentage points, from a counterfactual 41.7 percent to the real value of 43.3 percent in 2009. The poverty-increasing effect of lower remittances would have been stronger in rural regions, given the higher dependency on remittances as a source of income. In urban regions, poverty would increase from 37 (counterfactual) to 38.2 percent (actual) under an average 10 percent decline in remittances for 2009, and in rural regions the change would be from 49.6 to 52 percent.

Unfortunately, a counterfactual scenario is very hard to construct in the absence of information on migrant characteristics to estimate the amount that would have been

FIGURE 15.4 Annual Growth in Remittance Inflows to El Salvador by Region

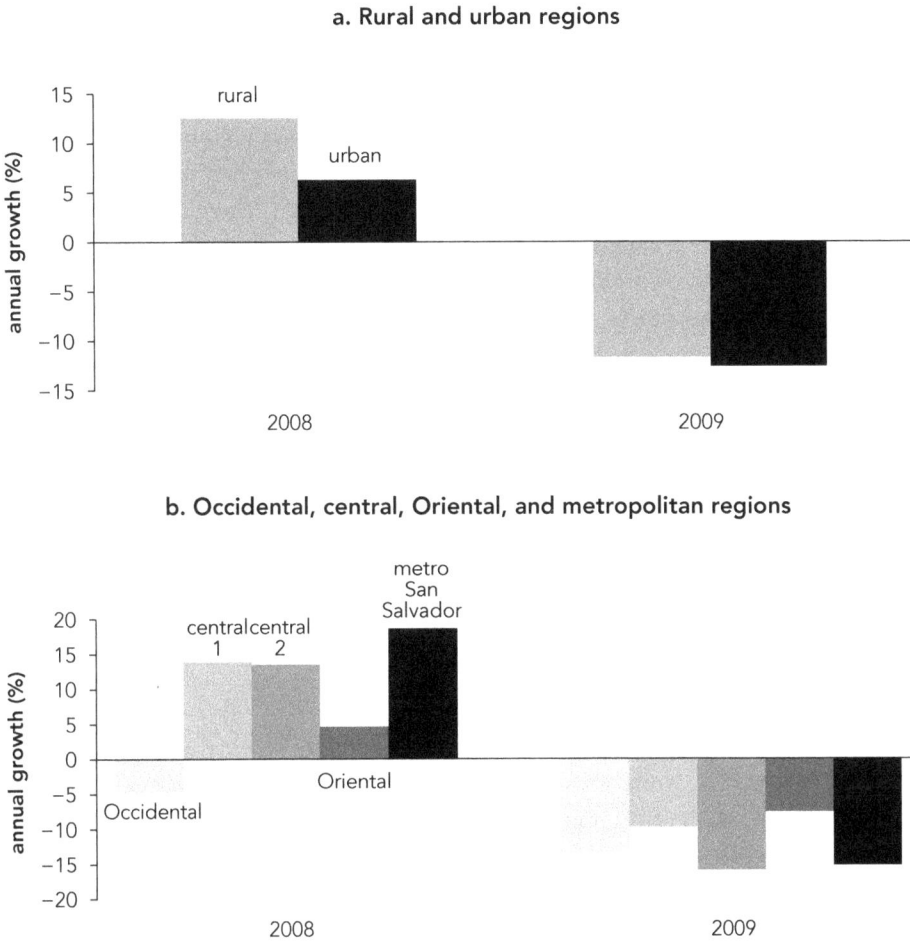

a. Rural and urban regions

b. Occidental, central, Oriental, and metropolitan regions

Source: DGEC 2009.

remitted if the crisis had not taken place (Acosta and others 2008). A much simpler (though imperfect) exercise is to subtract a determined fraction of remittances from the total income of households and recalculate the poverty head count.[1]

An effect associated with the 2009 financial crisis is that, unlike previous crises, migration prospects are now low, exerting higher pressure on local labor markets to absorb those entering the labor force. In the past, young people have sought out-migration as an economic strategy in times of increased youth unemployment (World Bank 2009g). Local conditions at their destination that had worsened may also hamper migration prospects because migrants may not be able to afford to cover the migration costs of family members who stay behind. Evidence among Salvadorans in California shows that 80 percent of recent migrants received help from relatives and friends in the United States to cover trip expenses (Menjivar 2000).

However, the concurrent crisis in the United States may reduce incentives for young people considering migration as an economic opportunity (Mandelman and Zlate 2010). For instance, recent data from the U.S. Department of Homeland Security on Salvadoran immigration rates show that the number of nonimmigrant entries into the United States in 2009 (including visits and legal migration) reached the lowest level in the decade and declined by 14 percent with respect to 2008. There is a clear decline in illegal immigration: Whereas in 2005 and 2006 more than 40,000 Salvadorans were apprehended at the Mexican border, these figures were less than half for the period 2007–09, with a decline of 6 percent in 2009. The reduction in out-migration flows has increased the local labor supply and placed increasing pressure on improving youth employability. Moreover, some migrants in the United States are returning to the country: Although the total number of return migrants is not available yet, data from deportations (forced return migration) from the United States doubled in 2007–09 with respect to 2000–06 to reach more than 20,000 returns and a 2 percent increase in 2009.

As a consequence, we envisage additional difficulties for Salvadoran labor markets to absorb larger cohorts of young people looking for domestic employment opportunities.

Discussion and Policy Options

The 2009 international financial crisis triggered a serious economic downturn in El Salvador, not to mention significant setbacks in social gains. For a recovery to occur, and to protect the incomes of the most vulnerable population, a set of effective policies are being put in place. However, shielding the incomes of Salvadorans from declines in remittances from abroad has traditionally been out of the scope of policy makers in El Salvador. Given the increasing importance of remittances among Salvadoran households, public interventions in the medium run should be designed to mitigate the impact of remittance declines. Furthermore, because forecasts of U.S. GDP and unemployment growth for 2011 are modest at best, remittances are likely to continue along the lower boundary.

Policies should aim to facilitate remittance transfers, as well as to guarantee their safety and transparency. This is a complex issue, but it is also a key element of migration policies. For instance, a well-developed financial sector or entity (public or private) that articulates the inflows of remittances can enhance both the security and the velocity of the process. It might also lower the cost. Evidence from El Salvador already shows that a $1 reduction in fees can lead migrants to send up to $25 more in remittances per month (Aycinena, Martinez, and Yang 2009). Also, savings instruments that allow a greater degree of control of the use of the funds at home by the remitting migrant can also create incentives to send more money back home (as shown in Ashraf and others 2009, for the case of El Salvador).

El Salvador can also tap innovative sources of financing such as securitization of remittances. Some initiatives to induce remittances to contribute to the granting of loans to microentrepreneurs and low-income El Salvadorans are already in place (for instance, by Fedecredito, the largest federation of credit associations and workers' banks in El Salvador, with the support of the International Finance Corporation). Several authors have discussed how remittances can contribute to entrepreneurship in migrant origin countries by relaxing credit constraints to businesses (Woodruff and Zenteno 2007; Yang 2008b).

Besides reducing the complexity of the transactions, policies should also take into account that remittances are highly exposed to external shocks. All the U.S. economic slowdowns will reduce the remittances received by El Salvador, and this is out of Central American governments' reach. However, policies exist that can reduce the impact of the collapse and boost transactions; for instance, programs that subsidize remittance transfers (such as matching funds) can mitigate reductions.

Finally, the policies that regulate the inflows of remittances should be coordinated with other social policies. For example, remittance policies can benefit the same population that social policies aim to help, while reducing the costs on increasing the subsidies to the transfers. Because of the importance that the remittances have in Salvadoran households' economy, a progressive regulation can complement the efforts of the social policy.

Still, during the crisis, the government of El Salvador did not have appropriate fiscal space and policy instruments to address the problem of the urban population. First, the fall in output and remittances has also negatively affected the amount of fiscal revenues collected by the government of El Salvador. Government revenues fell by 13 percent in 2009 with respect to the year before, and as a consequence the fiscal deficit reached 5.4 percent of GDP in 2009, compared with 3.1 percent in 2008. To strengthen public finances, in March 2010 the government reached a standby arrangement with the International Monetary Fund of about $790 million to help the country mitigate the adverse effects of the global crisis. One of the key priorities of this agreement is to increase the reach and efficiency of social programs through the government's general anticrisis program (Programa General Anti-Crisis [PGA]), which will allow for almost 1 percent of GDP (or around $200 million annually) in social spending in 2010–11.

The PGA includes an expansion of the conditional cash transfer program (*Comunidades Solidarias*), the creation of a temporary employment program, and the launch of a special public investment program concentrated on health, education, and infrastructure. Water and electricity subsidies are also being redesigned to protect the most vulnerable. These interventions aim to protect the incomes of the most vulnerable households from current and future global and local economic slowdowns, including declining remittances or massive job cuts. For instance, by taking advantage of the well-targeted existing conditional cash transfers to the poor, rural areas of the country can provide additional short-term benefits to participants and others in need of assistance.

An alternative scheme that the government is setting up as targeted social safety nets for urban areas (since conditional cash transfers target rural areas) includes the development of workfare programs, social funds, entrepreneurship and training programs, and microcredit schemes. In this context the government has set up a comprehensive Temporary Income Support Program (Programa de Ayuda Temporal al Ingreso [PATI]), to offset the impacts of the economic slowdown. PATI is a workfare labor market program that provides a temporary income transfer to targeted individuals in exchange for their participation in community activities and services and their participation in training activities. The government's objective is that PATI become a policy instrument capable of reaching targeted urban areas in a very short time, with interventions that do not require the lengthy procedures of typical infrastructure projects. PATI was initiated as a pilot intervention in two municipalities in 2009 and will expand in 2010 to reach 40,000 participants. PATI will require an effort of $40.5 million, or 0.7 percent of GDP, and is currently financed by the World Bank.

Despite these efforts, the government of El Salvador still needs to coordinate these interventions with proper policies that regulate migration and remittance inflow. As was shown, remittances sent by out-migrant members of households play a key role in the standard of living of recipient families. Well-designed policies and their coordination with social and labor policies can reduce El Salvador's vulnerability to adverse external shocks.

Note

1. These exercises could suffer from biases in two directions. On the one hand, the projections of an artificial decline in remittances and its effect on poverty could overestimate the true effect if households attempt to compensate—at least partially—for the decline in remittances with other sources of income, for example, by increasing their labor supply. On the other hand, the forecast could underestimate the effect of the decline in remittances on poverty if part of these transfers is used—as is very likely—to engage in new economic activities and, thus, generate additional income. In addition, their use for consumption purposes can also have multiplicative effects for the economy. Furthermore, responses such as increases in labor supply can have aggregate equilibrium effects such as a fall in wages, which would also bias the projections downward.

Chapter 16

Remittance Flows to Mexico and Employment and Total Earnings of Mexican Immigrant Workers in the United States

JESÚS A. CERVANTES GONZÁLEZ AND ALEJANDRO BARAJAS DEL PINO

DURING RECENT YEARS, MEXICO HAS become the world's third highest receiver of remittances. In the 2000–06 period, remittance flows to Mexico quadrupled, increasing from $6,573 million in 2000 to $25,567 million in 2006, representing an average annual growth of 25.4 percent (figures 16.1 and 16.2). This behavior responded mainly to two factors: considerable Mexican migration to the United States, legal and illegal, that implied a higher remittance inflow, and the significant progress made by Banco de México in recording remittance transactions.[1] An additional factor contributing to the increase in remittance flows to Mexico in recent years and their shift to the formal market is the considerable reduction in the costs of sending such transfers. From 1999 to the present, the cost of sending remittances to Mexico fell by four-fifths.[2] However, from the second half of 2006, and particularly in 2007, the downturn in the U.S. economy weakened remittance flows to Mexico, which grew just 1.9 percent during the latter year. In 2008 remittance flows contracted 3.5 percent as the United States entered a recession, and in 2009 this source of external revenues weakened even further, falling 15.5 percent.

We examine the factors that contributed to the significant decline in remittance flows to Mexico during 2007–09. The analysis focuses on developments and the impacts of the declines in the U.S. labor market, considering that practically all remittance flows to Mexico originate in that country. We also evaluate the recent impact of several employment indicators on Mexican workers in the United States that have fostered an improvement in annual remittance flows to Mexico since the second quarter of 2010.

FIGURE 16.1 Evolution of Remittance Flows to Mexico, 2000–10

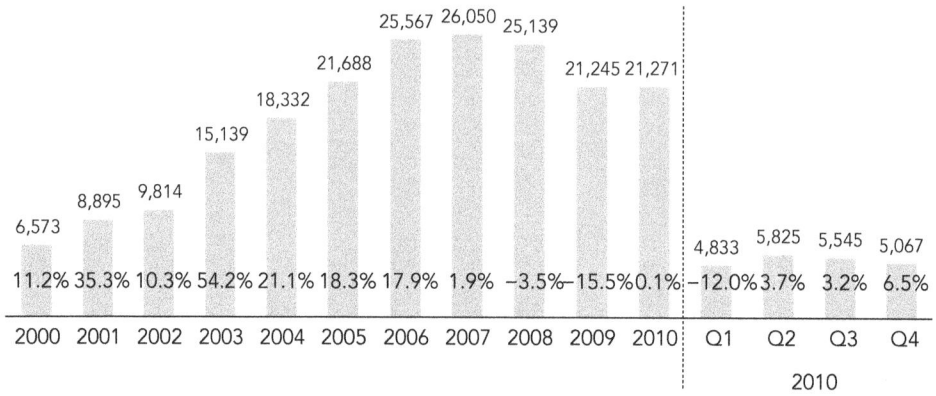

	2000	2001	2002	2003	2004	2005	2006	2007	2008	2009	2010	Q1	Q2	Q3	Q4
Value	6,573	8,895	9,814	15,139	18,332	21,688	25,567	26,050	25,139	21,245	21,271	4,833	5,825	5,545	5,067
%	11.2%	35.3%	10.3%	54.2%	21.1%	18.3%	17.9%	1.9%	−3.5%	−15.5%	0.1%	−12.0%	3.7%	3.2%	6.5%

2010 (Q1–Q4)

Source: Banco de México.

FIGURE 16.2 Remittance Flows to Mexico, 1996–2010

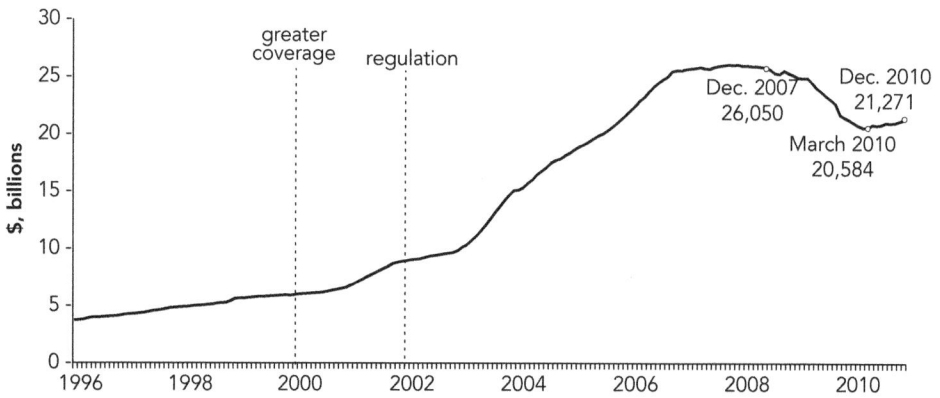

Source: Banco de México.

The main sections of the chapter focus on the following aspects: changes in the number of Mexican immigrants in the United States in the face of the economic downturn during 2008 and 2009, the characteristics of employment and unemployment among these Mexican workers, the change in the industry sector distribution of Mexican immigrant workers resulting from the economic downturn, the significant difference shown by employment indicators for Mexican workers according to their gender, the important shift in the structure of employment between full- and part-time jobs, the changes during the recession of average earnings of wage and salary Mexican immigrant workers, and the size of the decline in 2009 of total earnings of wage and salary Mexican immigrant workers.

It is worth mentioning that the decline of total earnings was larger for Mexicans without citizenship and with lower levels of educational attainment.[3] Most of the indicators shown in this chapter are the authors' own estimates based on information from the Current Population Survey (CPS), conducted by the U.S. Census Bureau.[4]

Mexican Immigrants in the U.S. Population and Labor Force

In 2009 there were 31.7 million Mexicans in the United States (table 16.1).[5] Of these, 11.6 million were immigrants (3.9 percent of the total population) and represented almost one-third (31.1 percent) of the total immigrant population. The labor force participation rate of Mexican immigrants was 66.2 percent, a much larger rate than that observed for the U.S. population as a whole (51.2 percent). The latter reflects the fact that most Mexican immigrants are of working age and have a greater need to work than their American counterparts (given that most of them do not have access to unemployment insurance and social security).

TABLE 16.1 Population and Immigrants in the United States, 2008–09

Population group	Population		Variation	
	2008	2009	Absolute	Relative
Total population	299,083,400	301,364,940	2,281,540	0.76
Native	261,489,638	264,056,021	2,566,383	0.98
Immigrant	37,593,762	37,308,919	−284,843	−0.76
Total Hispanic	46,384,662	47,833,218	1,448,556	3.12
Mexican	30,801,801	31,671,267	869,466	2.82
Native	19,031,027	20,073,834	1,042,807	5.48
Immigrant	11,770,774	11,597,433	−173,341	−1.47
Total labor force	154,286,645	154,142,007	−144,638	−0.09
Total employed	145,362,386	139,877,462	−5,484,924	−3.77
Mexican immigrant labor force	7,674,183	7,677,143	2,960	0.04
Employed Mexican immigrant	7,122,007	6,786,220	−335,787	−4.71

Source: Authors' calculations.

Note: Total population figures take into account only the civilian noninstitutional population; that is, they do not include the population residing in penal institutions, mental institutions, or the military on active service.

In the United States during 2009, the total number of immigrants declined on average by 285,000 individuals (0.76 percent; table 16.1). Of this number, 61 percent (173,000 individuals) were Mexican, implying a 1.47 percent reduction in the Mexican immigrant population. This decline was influenced not only by the weakness of labor demand in the United States, but also by a significant increase in deportations. Thus, the number of Mexican immigrants removed from the United States rose from 169,031 and 186,726 Mexicans in 2005 and 2006, respectively, to 208,996 and 246,851 individuals in 2007 and 2008 and to 282,666 Mexicans in 2009 (Office of Immigration Statistics 2009). Also, the number of Mexican immigrants employed in the United States fell by 336,000 individuals, implying a larger percentage contraction of employment (4.71 percent) than that registered by the labor force as a whole in that country (3.77 percent, at an annual average rate).

Figure 16.3 shows that in 2009 the number of Mexican immigrants in the United States was equivalent to 10.4 percent of the total population of Mexico, but the corresponding percentage was higher among males (11.8 percent) than females (9.1 percent). It also indicates that the labor force of Mexican immigrants in the United States in 2009 was equivalent to 16 percent of the economically active population of Mexico.

FIGURE 16.3 Mexican Immigrants in the United States, 2009

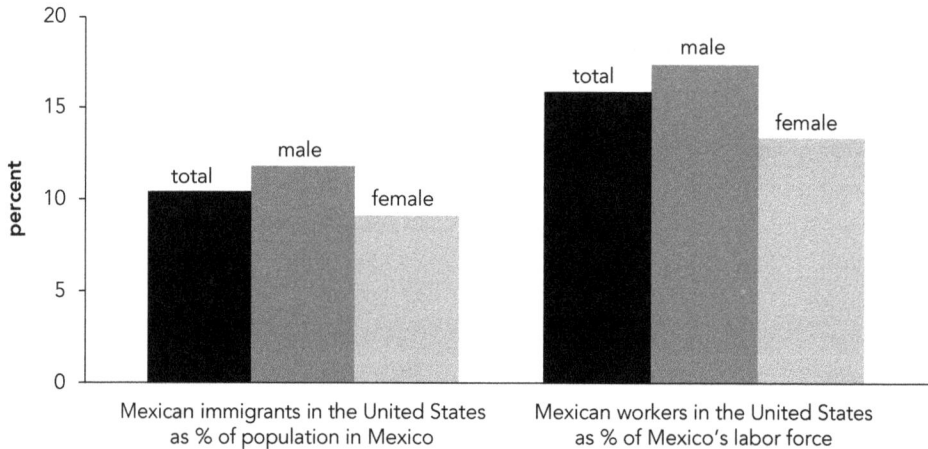

Sources: The Mexican data are from INEGI (National Institute of Statistics) and Encuesta Nacional de Ocupación y Empleo, adjusted to incorporate the Preliminary Results of the Population Census, 2010 (INEGI 2011). The U.S. data are the authors' estimates based on the Current Population Survey, U.S. Census Bureau.

The estimates of Mexican immigrant workers' earnings in the United States include wage and salary workers in full- and part-time jobs.[6] In 2009 the number of wage and salary immigrants of Mexican origin in the U.S. labor force included 6,161,148 individuals (table 16.2), 80.4 percent of the total Mexican immigrant labor force (7,677,143 workers; table 16.1). This number was made up of 4,207,711 men (68.3 percent of the total) and 1,953,437 women (the remaining 31.7 percent). Wage and salary Mexican immigrant workers accounted for 5 percent of the wage and salary U.S. labor force.

TABLE 16.2 Mexican Workers and Immigrants in the United States, 2009

Worker group	Number			Percent		
	Total	Male	Female	Total	Male	Female
Wage and salary Mexican workers	11,606,259	7,082,131	4,524,128	9.3	11.1	7.4
Immigrant	6,161,148	4,207,711	1,953,437	5.0	6.6	3.2
Citizen	1,548,183	906,211	641,972	1.2	1.4	1.1
Noncitizen	4,612,965	3,301,500	1,311,465	3.7	5.2	2.1
Native	5,445,111	2,874,420	2,570,691	4.4	4.5	4.2
Non-Mexican immigrants	12,993,485	6,895,187	6,098,298	10.4	10.9	10.0
Total immigrants	19,154,633	11,102,898	8,051,735	15.4	17.5	13.2
Total natives	105,335,238	52,435,666	52,899,572	84.6	82.5	86.8
Total workers	124,489,871	63,538,564	60,951,307	100.0	100.0	100.0

Source: Authors' estimates with data from U.S. Census Bureau Current Population Survey.

Average Earnings of Wage and Salary Mexican Immigrant Workers

During 2009 monthly average earnings of wage and salary Mexican immigrant workers in the United States were $2,190 (table 16.3). However, the average earnings of those who had U.S. citizenship ($2,758) were 38 percent higher than those without it ($1,999). This partly reflected higher levels of schooling of Mexican immigrants with citizenship than those without it and differences in the industry sector distribution of these two groups of Mexicans.

TABLE 16.3 Average Monthly Earnings of Wage and Salary Mexican Immigrant Workers in the United States, 2008–09

Worker group	2008			2009			Percentage variation		
	Total	Male	Female	Total	Male	Female	Total	Male	Female
Wage and salary Mexican workers	2,528	2,762	2,148	2,490	2,713	2,140	−1.5	−1.8	−0.4
Immigrant	2,247	2,451	1,778	2,190	2,385	1,768	−2.5	−2.7	−0.6
Citizen	2,707	3,039	2,187	2,758	3,139	2,220	1.9	3.3	1.5
Noncitizen	2,106	2,299	1,602	1,999	2,179	1,546	−5.1	−5.2	−3.5
Native	2,857	3,242	2,425	2,829	3,194	2,425	−1.0	−1.5	0.0
Other immigrants	3,614	4,132	3,019	3,590	4,056	3,082	−0.4	−1.8	2.1
Total immigrants	3,174	3,490	2,727	3,146	3,423	2,763	−0.9	−1.9	1.3
Total natives	3,484	4,053	2,907	3,498	4,080	2,920	0.4	0.7	0.4
Total workers	3,438	3,956	2,884	3,441	3,963	2,898	0.1	0.2	0.5

Source: Authors' estimates with data from U.S. Census Bureau Current Population Survey.

Mexican immigrants' monthly earnings ($2,190) were only three-fifths of those obtained by wage and salary workers in that country ($3,441). Also, within the Mexican immigrant labor force, average men's wages and salaries ($2,385) were considerably higher (35 percent) than those of women ($1,768), although a similar figure (40 percent) was also observed within the native U.S. labor force. On average, the monthly earnings of wage and salary Mexican immigrants who have obtained citizenship were practically the same as the earnings of Mexican U.S. natives.

Table 16.3 shows that average monthly nominal earnings of wage and salary Mexican immigrant workers fell 2.5 percent in 2009, mainly in response to a decline in men's earnings (–2.7 percent), whereas those of women decreased only slightly (–0.6 percent). The fall in Mexican immigrants' average monthly earnings mostly stemmed from the decline in earnings of those without citizenship (–5.1 percent); earnings increased for citizens (1.9 percent).

Total Earnings of Wage and Salary Mexican Immigrant Workers in the United States

The total nominal earnings obtained in 2009 by wage and salary Mexican immigrant workers in the United States were $161,885 million (table 16.4). Those earnings do not include income earned by Mexican immigrants who work as nonwage and salary freelance workers or in self-employed or entrepreneurial business activities. These individuals accounted for 19.7 percent of the total employed Mexican immigrant labor force in 2009.

TABLE 16.4 Total Earnings of Wage and Salary Workers and of Mexican Immigrants in the United States, 2009

Worker group	Annual earnings per worker ($)			Annual total earnings of wage and salary workers ($, millions)		
	Total	Male	Female	Total	Male	Female
Wage and salary Mexican workers	29,879	32,561	25,681	346,782	230,598	116,183
Immigrant	26,275	28,625	21,213	161,885	120,447	41,438
Citizen	33,097	37,670	26,641	51,240	34,137	17,103
Noncitizen	23,985	26,142	18,556	110,645	86,310	24,335
Native	33,957	38,321	29,076	184,897	110,152	74,745
Rest of immigrants	43,188	48,675	36,985	561,165	335,622	225,543
Total immigrants	37,748	41,076	33,158	723,049	456,068	266,981
Total natives	41,968	48,950	35,047	4,420,694	2,566,703	1,853,991
Total workers	41,319	47,574	34,798	5,143,743	3,022,771	2,120,972

Source: Authors' estimates with data from U.S. Census Bureau Current Population Survey.

In 2009 the total nominal earnings of wage and salary Mexican immigrant workers in the United States fell by $11,574 million compared with 2008 (table 16.5), a decrease of 6.7 percent that exceeded the decline of 3.6 percent recorded for the total earnings of wage and salary workers in that country. One outstanding feature of such a decline in the total earnings is that it encompassed only those without citizenship, a decline of $13,995 million or 11.2 percent, whereas the earnings of Mexican immigrants with citizenship actually increased 5 percent. The segment of Mexican workers without U.S. citizenship represents an important source of remittances received in Mexico. This segment accounts for 74.9 percent of wage and salary Mexican immigrant workers and generates 68.3 percent of such workers' total earnings.

TABLE 16.5 Variation in the Total Earnings of Wage and Salary Workers and of Mexican Immigrants in the United States, 2009

Worker group	Absolute variation ($, millions)			Relative variation (%)		
	Total	Male	Female	Total	Male	Female
Wage and salary Mexican workers	−15,647	−14,526	−1,121	−4.3	−5.9	−1.0
Immigrant	−11,574	−11,361	−213	−6.7	−8.6	−0.5
Citizen	2,421	729	1,692	5.0	2.2	11.0
Noncitizen	−13,995	−12,090	−1,905	−11.2	−12.3	−7.3
Natives	−4,072	−3,164	−908	−2.2	−2.8	−1.2
Rest of immigrants	−27,497	−23,802	−3,694	−4.7	−6.6	−1.4
Total immigrants	−39,072	−35,164	−3,907	−5.1	−7.2	−1.4
Total natives	−152,410	−113,879	−38,531	−3.3	−4.3	−2.0
Total workers	−193,494	−150,326	−43,169	−3.6	−4.7	−2.0

Source: Authors' estimates with data from U.S. Census Bureau Current Population Survey.

Tables 16.6 and 16.7 show the sources of the decline in the total earnings of wage and salary Mexican immigrant workers in the United States during 2009. It therefore also allows greater knowledge of the factors behind the decline in remittance flows to Mexico. In this regard the following observations are noteworthy:

- The decrease in 2009 in the nominal total earnings of wage and salary Mexican immigrant workers reflected net job losses totaling 272,905 jobs (4.2 percent) and a $685 (2.5 percent) decline in their average annual earnings.

- The decline in the employment of Mexican immigrant workers stemmed from the combination of a significant increase of those in part-time employment amounting to 260,824 individuals (33.5 percent increase) and a severe contraction of wage and salary Mexicans in full-time employment of 533,728 jobs (9.4 percent decline).

TABLE 16.6 Number and Annual Total Earnings of Wage and Salary Mexican Immigrant Workers in the United States with Full- or Part-Time Jobs, 2008–09

Year	Total			Males			Females		
	Total	Full-time	Part-time	Total	Full-time	Part-time	Total	Full-time	Part-time
Number of workers									
2008	6,434,053	5,655,211	778,842	4,482,348	4,206,813	275,536	1,951,705	1,448,398	503,307
2009	6,161,148	5,121,483	1,039,666	4,207,711	3,738,338	469,374	1,953,437	1,383,145	570,292
Absolute variation	−272,905	−533,728	260,824	−274,637	−468,475	193,838	1,732	−65,253	66,985
Relative variation	−4.2%	−9.4%	33.5%	−6.1%	−11.1%	70.4%	0.1%	−4.5%	13.3%
Annual earnings per worker ($)									
2008	26,960	28,786	13,696	29,406	30,253	16,473	21,341	24,526	12,175
2009	26,275	28,758	14,044	28,625	30,185	16,205	21,213	24,902	12,266
Absolute variation	−685	−28	348	−781	−68	−268	−128	376	91
Relative variation	−2.5%	−0.1%	2.5%	−2.7%	−0.2%	−1.6%	−0.6%	1.5%	0.7%
Annual total earnings of wage and salary workers ($, millions)									
2008	173,459	162,792	10,667	131,808	127,268	4,539	41,651	35,524	6,128
2009	161,885	147,284	14,601	120,447	112,841	7,606	41,438	34,443	6,995
Absolute variation	−11,574	−15,508	3,934	−11,361	−14,427	3,067	−213	−1,081	867
Relative variation	−6.7%	−9.5%	36.9%	−8.6%	−11.3%	67.6%	−0.5%	−3.0%	14.1%

Source: Authors' estimates with data from U.S. Census Bureau Current Population Survey.

• Thus, a large number of Mexican immigrants in the United States sought to avoid unemployment by taking part-time jobs, obtaining average earnings equivalent to almost half of what they had earned in full-time jobs.

• The above represent a considerable increase from 2008 to 2009 in the share of part-time employment (from 12 to 16.9 percent), which implied that Mexican immigrant workers' average annual earnings declined 2.5 percent despite the fact that average earnings for full-time employment remained practically unchanged from 2008 to 2009 and even increased 2.5 percent in the case of part-time jobs (table 16.6).

• In 2009 the decline in Mexican immigrant workers employment was totally concentrated in male workers, with 274,637 job losses (6.1 percent). The aforementioned, combined with a reduction in these workers' average annual earnings, meant their total earnings of wages and salaries fell by $11,361 million (8.6 percent).

• The contraction of employment among wage and salary Mexican immigrant workers was totally concentrated in those without citizenship (table 16.7), whereas employment of those with citizenship increased. Thus, during 2009, annual employment of

TABLE 16.7 Number and Annual Total Earnings of Wage and Salary Mexican Immigrant Workers in the United States by Citizenship Status, 2008–09

Year	Citizens			Noncitizens		
	Total	Male	Female	Total	Male	Female
Number of workers						
2008	1,503,128	916,032	587,096	4,930,925	3,566,316	1,364,609
2009	1,548,183	906,211	641,972	4,612,965	3,301,500	1,311,465
Absolute variation	45,055	−9,821	54,876	−317,960	−264,816	−53,144
Relative variation (%)	3.0	−1.1	9.4	−6.5	−7.4	−3.9
Annual earnings per worker ($)						
2008	32,478	36,470	26,250	25,277	27,591	19,229
2009	33,097	37,670	26,641	23,985	26,142	18,556
Absolute variation	619	1,200	391	−1,292	−1,449	−673
Relative variation (%)	1.9	3.3	1.5	−5.1	−5.3	−3.5
Annual total earnings of wage and salary workers ($, millions)						
2008	48,819	33,408	15,411	124,640	98,400	26,240
2009	51,240	34,137	17,103	110,645	86,310	24,335
Absolute variation	2,421	729	1,692	−13,995	−12,090	−1,905
Relative variation (%)	5.0	2.2	11.0	−11.2	−12.3	−7.3

Source: Authors' estimates with data from U.S. Census Bureau Current Population Survey.

the former group fell by 317,960 jobs (6.5 percent), this decline being more noteworthy for men (264,816 individuals or 7.4 percent) than for women. These changes in employment of wage and salary Mexican immigrant workers without citizenship was accompanied by a significant decline in their average annual earnings amounting to $1,292 (5.1 percent), implying a fall of $13,995 million (11.2 percent) in their total earnings. During 2009 the increase in employment for Mexican immigrants holding citizenship might have resulted from the fact that official U.S. figures show that 164,920 Mexican immigrants obtained permanent residence that year. We will see later in more detail the relationship between citizenship, earnings, and remittances.

Industry Distribution of Mexican Immigrant Workers

The industry distribution of Mexican immigrant workers in the United States shows important differences from the rest of the labor force (table 16.8). Thus, in 2009, 81 percent of the U.S. labor force was concentrated in the services sector (without taking into account Mexican immigrants), whereas this figure was 61.6 percent in the case of Mexican immigrant workers. The latter are employed more than the rest of the labor force in the agricultural and industrial sectors (5.1 and 33.3 percent, respectively, as

TABLE 16.8 Total Employed Labor Force and Mexican Immigrant Workers in the United States by Industry Sector, 2009

Industry sector	Number			Percent		
	Total	Mexican immigrant	Other	Total	Mexican immigrant	Other
Labor force						
Primary	2,102,955	345,501	1,757,454	1.5	5.1	1.3
Industrial	25,844,411	2,256,568	23,587,843	18.5	33.3	17.7
Construction	9,701,750	1,193,523	8,508,227	6.9	17.6	6.4
Manufacturing	14,202,161	1,017,170	13,184,991	10.2	15.0	9.9
Mining	707,244	32,279	674,965	0.5	0.5	0.5
Electricity	1,233,257	13,597	1,219,660	0.9	0.2	0.9
Services	111,930,095	4,184,151	107,745,944	80.0	61.6	81.0
Total	139,877,462	6,786,220	133,091,242	100.0	100.0	100.0
Annual variation						
Primary	−64,940	−20,453	−44,487	−3.0	−5.6	−2.5
Industrial	−3,077,577	−406,448	−2,671,129	−10.6	−15.3	−10.2
Construction	−1,272,326	−294,544	−977,782	−11.6	−19.8	−10.3
Manufacturing	−1,701,514	−92,547	−1,608,967	−10.7	−8.3	−10.9
Mining	−111,522	−11,102	−100,420	−13.6	−25.6	−13.0
Electricity	7,785	−8,254	16,039	0.6	−37.8	1.3
Services	−2,342,407	91,113	−2,433,520	−2.0	2.2	−2.2
Total	−5,484,923	−335,787	−5,149,136	−3.8	−4.7	−3.7

Source: Authors' estimates with data from U.S. Census Bureau Current Population Survey.

compared with 1.3 and 17.7 percent for the remaining labor force) and within the latter sector mainly in the construction and manufacturing industries. In 2009 Mexican immigrant workers accounted for 16.4, 12.3, and 7.2 percent of total employment in the primary (raw material extraction industries such as mining and farming), construction, and manufacturing sectors, respectively. The aforementioned was despite the fact that they accounted for 4.9 percent of the total employed labor force.

Production in the construction and manufacturing industries weakened significantly, leading to greater job losses in these sectors in 2008 and 2009. The larger relative concentration of Mexican immigrant workers in these activities meant their unemployment rate was higher than that for the labor force as a whole.

Table 16.8 shows that in 2009 employment of the labor force fell in almost all the main sectors of economic activity (the only exception was electricity, but this activity represented only 0.9 percent of total employment), resulting in a total decline of 3.8 percent. In contrast, during 2009 the employed Mexican immigrant labor force increased 2.2 percent in the services sector, representing an average annual increase of 91,113 jobs. Nevertheless, total employment of Mexican immigrant workers fell 4.7 percent, that is, more than for the labor force as a whole. This was because of their greater concentration in sectors where employment contracted most. The shift of Mexican immigrant workers to the services sector was also a move to less well-paid jobs than those they previously held, and this also contributed to the fall in their total earnings of wage and salary.

Unemployment Rate among Mexican Immigrant Workers

During 2008–09, the unemployment rate among Mexican immigrant workers in the United States was higher than that of most other ethnic groups, both native and immigrant, except African Americans (table 16.9). The increase in the unemployment rate from 2007 to 2009 was also greater among Mexican immigrants (6.67 percent) than for natives (4.49 percent). The level of unemployment among Mexican immigrants with citizenship (9.46 percent) was very close to that observed among native workers as a whole (9.18 percent) in 2009.

TABLE 16.9 Unemployment Rates in the United States, 2006–10

percent

Population group	2006	2007	2008	2009	2010	Change 2007–09	Change 2009–10
Total	4.62	4.62	5.78	9.25	9.63	4.63	0.38
Native	4.74	4.69	5.78	9.18	9.60	4.49	0.42
Male	4.84	4.87	6.18	10.35	10.64	5.48	0.29
Female	4.62	4.48	5.33	7.90	8.46	3.42	0.56
White	3.86	3.86	4.74	7.80	8.04	3.94	0.24
African American	9.43	8.63	10.44	15.27	16.45	6.64	1.18
Asian	3.81	3.74	4.41	8.23	7.91	4.49	−0.32
Mexican	6.11	6.44	8.26	12.88	13.65	6.44	0.77
Nonnative	3.99	4.28	5.83	9.68	9.80	5.40	0.12
Non-Hispanic	3.52	3.71	4.77	7.93	8.28	4.22	0.35
Hispanic	4.45	4.85	6.91	11.43	11.32	6.58	−0.11
Mexican	4.48	4.93	7.20	11.60	11.19	6.67	−0.41
Male	3.68	4.05	6.41	11.09	10.59	7.04	−0.50
Female	6.31	7.03	8.99	12.73	12.46	5.70	−0.27
Citizen	2.81	3.79	5.36	9.46	9.29	5.67	−0.17
Noncitizen	4.91	5.25	7.77	12.33	11.84	7.08	−0.49

Source: Authors' estimates with data from U.S. Census Bureau Current Population Survey.

The higher unemployment rate of Mexican immigrants as compared with that observed among natives and other immigrants is associated with the industry sector distribution of these workers, as well as their disadvantage in terms of educational attainment.[7] Table 16.10 shows that in 2009 the number of years of education of unemployed Mexican immigrant workers was lower than those with employment. One outstanding aspect of the performance of the unemployment rate among Mexican immigrant workers, measured using seasonally adjusted data, is that it is more sensitive to the U.S. economic cycle than that of the labor force as a whole (figure 16.4). Furthermore, both the "spike" and "trough" of the Mexican immigrant unemployment rate seem to anticipate the corresponding "spikes" and "troughs" of the total unemployment rate in the United States.

TABLE 16.10 Years of Education of Mexican Immigrants, 2009

Labor force and citizenship status	Mexican immigrant workers	Total immigrants
Total	9.5	12.1
Employed	9.9	12.7
Unemployed	9.2	11.6
Discouraged[a]	8.8	11.1
Citizens	10.2	13.2
Employed	10.9	13.9
Unemployed	10.4	13.1
Discouraged[a]	9.2	11.8
Noncitizens	9.2	11.3
Employed	9.5	11.8
Unemployed	8.9	10.7
Discouraged[a]	8.8	10.5

Source: Authors' estimates with data from U.S. Census Bureau Current Population Survey.
a. Workers who left the labor force because of their inability to find work.

Educational attainment among wage and salary Mexican immigrant workers in the United States is generally lower in those without citizenship, in males, and in those with part-time jobs (table 16.11).

On the other hand, table 16.12 shows that in 2009 the weakness of economic activity and labor demand in the United States had a greater impact on Mexican immigrants with lower levels of educational attainment who were males, noncitizens, and those with full-time jobs. In contrast, employment of Mexican immigrants with high levels of education, that is, those who had completed a bachelor's or graduate degree, did not decline and actually increased. It is worth mentioning that table 16.12 also shows that for the same level of education, the average earnings of a Mexican immigrant worker who obtained U.S. citizenship are higher than those of a worker without citizenship.

FIGURE 16.4 Unemployment Rate of Mexican Immigrants, Native Population, and Total Population in the United States

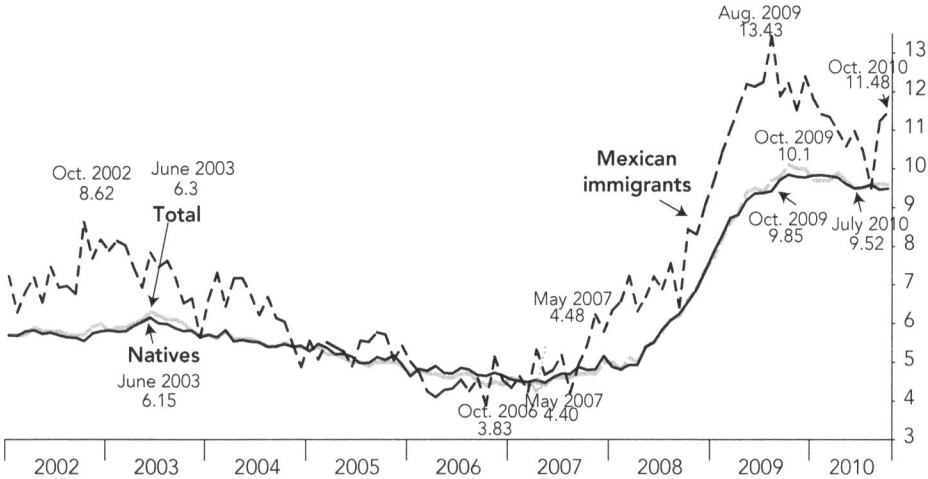

Source: Authors' estimates with data from U.S. Census Bureau Current Population Survey.

Note: Data are seasonally adjusted; two-month moving average up to June 2008.

TABLE 16.11 Educational Attainment among Wage and Salary Mexican Immigrant Workers, 2009

percent

Worker category	I	II	III	IV	V	VI	Total
Male	43.3	12.9	29.3	9.2	3.8	1.5	100.0
Female	39.6	10.7	27.8	14.9	5.3	1.7	100.0
Citizen	28.9	10.4	31.4	19.3	7.2	2.8	100.0
Noncitizen	46.5	12.8	28.0	8.3	3.3	1.1	100.0
Full-time employee	41.9	12.1	29.6	10.4	4.4	1.6	100.0
Part-time employee	43.4	12.5	25.4	14.0	3.6	1.1	100.0
Total	42.1	12.2	28.9	11.0	4.3	1.5	100.0

Source: Authors' estimates with data from U.S. Census Bureau Current Population Survey.

Note: I: up to 9th grade; II: more than 9th and up to 12th grade without high school diploma; III: high school diploma; IV: associate's degree or some college but no bachelor's degree; V: bachelor's degree; VI: graduate or professional degree.

It seems that citizenship allows higher labor mobility and a movement of Mexican immigrant workers toward higher-paying jobs, which originates from higher levels of productivity. The aforementioned suggests that migratory reform would lead to productivity gains for the U.S. economy, and it would enable immigrant workers to move freely toward activities with higher productivity and benefit their job search. In contrast, Mexican immigrant workers without citizenship face more urgency to grab the first job available, resulting in a match between workers and jobs that is inefficient and not optimal.

TABLE 16.12 Variation in Number and Annual Earnings of Wage and Salary Mexican Immigrant Workers by Educational Attainment, 2009

Worker category	I	II	III	IV	V	VI	Total
Absolute variation in number of workers							
Male	−191,633	−61,207	11,287	−31,188	−1,491	−405	−274,637
Female	28,962	−790	−29,696	−9,877	6,220	6,913	1,732
Citizen	15,512	−8,797	15,642	9,121	7,406	6,171	45,055
Noncitizen	−178,183	−53,199	−34,052	−50,186	−2,677	337	−317,960
Full-time employee	−315,540	−85,292	−63,047	−69,455	−4,572	4,179	−533,728
Part-time employee	152,869	23,296	44,637	28,390	9,301	2,330	260,823
Total	−162,671	−61,996	−18,410	−41,065	4,729	6,508	−272,905
Relative variation in number of workers (%)							
Male	−9.5	−10.2	0.9	−7.4	−0.9	−0.7	−6.1
Female	3.9	−0.4	−5.2	−3.3	6.4	26.4	0.1
Citizen	3.6	−5.2	3.3	3.2	7.1	16.8	3.0
Noncitizen	−7.7	−8.3	−2.6	−11.6	−1.8	0.7	−6.5
Full-time employee	−12.8	−12.1	−4.0	−11.5	−2.0	5.3	−9.4
Part-time employee	51.3	21.8	20.3	24.3	32.8	25.9	33.5
Total	−5.9	−7.6	−1.0	−5.7	1.8	7.4	−4.2
Average annual earnings ($)							
Male	24,387	25,465	30,252	34,368	47,528	64,116	28,625
Female	16,178	16,810	21,654	27,244	38,242	53,521	21,213
Citizen	25,719	26,644	32,989	36,271	48,111	74,608	33,097
Noncitizen	21,149	22,066	25,612	27,444	40,731	48,676	23,985
Full-time employee	24,003	25,189	29,885	34,679	48,499	66,108	28,758
Part-time employee	12,123	12,831	14,699	18,972	16,330	18,421	14,044
Total	21,939	23,048	27,628	31,322	43,866	60,418	26,275

Source: Authors' estimates with data from U.S. Census Bureau Current Population Survey.

Note: I: Up to 9th grade; II: More than 9th and up to 12th grade without high school diploma; III: high school diploma; IV: associate's degree or some college but no bachelor's degree; V: bachelor's degree; VI: graduate or professional degree.

During 2009 the total earnings of wage and salary Mexican immigrant workers decreased by $11,574 million or 6.7 percent (in response to declines of 4.2 percent in employment and 2.5 percent in average earnings), falling from $173,459 million in 2008 to $161,885 million in 2009. Nevertheless, the corresponding decline in the total earnings amounted to 11.4 percent in those with up to 9 years of education and 11.6 percent in those with between 9 and 12 years of education but no high school diploma (table 16.13).

TABLE 16.13 Total Earnings of Wage and Salary Mexican Immigrant Workers by Educational Attainment, 2009

Worker category	I	II	III	IV	V	VI	Total
			Total earnings ($, millions)				
Male	44,414	13,801	37,366	13,372	7,534	3,961	120,447
Female	12,522	3,530	11,746	7,918	3,948	1,773	41,438
Citizen	11,530	4,298	16,025	10,832	5,349	3,206	51,240
Noncitizen	45,406	13,033	33,087	10,458	6,133	2,528	110,645
Full-time employee	51,470	15,659	45,228	18,534	10,867	5,526	147,284
Part-time employee	5,466	1,672	3,884	2,756	615	208	14,601
Total	56,936	17,331	49,112	21,290	11,482	5,734	161,885
			Absolute variation in earnings ($, millions)				
Male	−7,085	−2,006	−538	−2,352	817	−174	−11,361
Female	−225	−266	−544	−357	568	610	−213
Citizen	269	−411	452	193	1,022	896	2,421
Noncitizen	−7,579	−1,861	−1,534	−2,902	363	−482	−13,995
Full-time employee	−8,976	−2,698	−1,724	−3,790	1,250	430	−15,508
Part-time employee	1,666	426	642	1,081	136	−16	3,934
Total	−7,310	−2,272	−1,082	−2,709	1,385	414	−11,574
			Relative variation in earnings (%)				
Male	−13.8	−12.7	−1.4	−15.0	12.2	−4.2	−8.6
Female	−1.8	−7.0	−4.4	−4.3	16.8	52.4	−0.5
Citizen	2.4	−8.7	2.9	1.8	23.6	38.8	5.0
Noncitizen	−14.3	−12.5	−4.4	−21.7	6.3	−16.0	−11.2
Full-time employee	−14.8	−14.7	−3.7	−17.0	13.0	8.4	−9.5
Part-time employee	43.8	34.2	19.8	64.6	28.2	−7.2	36.9
Total	−11.4	−11.6	−2.2	−11.3	13.7	7.8	−6.7

Source: Authors' estimates with data from U.S. Census Bureau Current Population Survey.

Note: I: up to 9th grade; II: more than 9th and up to 12th grade without high school diploma; III: high school diploma; IV: associate's degree or some college but no bachelor's degree; V: bachelor's degree; VI: graduate or professional degree.

The significant increase in the total earnings of wage and salary Mexican immigrant workers with citizenship during 2009 was equivalent to $2,421 million or 5.3 percent and responded to both an increase in the number of those with such migratory status (45,055 individuals and 3 percent increase; table 16.12) and in their average earnings (2.2 percent). The latter mainly reflected the fact that most of the Mexican workers who obtained citizenship were those who had completed a bachelor's or graduate degree.

Mexican Immigrant Worker Employment in 2010

During the first half of 2010, demand in the U.S. labor market remained weak (annual decrease of 1.4 percent; see table 16.14). However, employment of Mexican immigrant workers increased slightly (0.6 percent). This performance strengthened even further in the second half of the year as the number of employed Mexican immigrant workers rose by 136,000 individuals or 2 percent.

The weakness of labor demand in the United States during the first semester of 2010 was accompanied at the industry sector level by a decline in employment in the industrial sector. However, in the case of Mexican immigrants, annual increases were observed in employment during the second semester in all three sectors of economic activity: industrial, services, and primary. In fact, the annual growth of Mexican immigrant employment in the second half of 2010 was also driven by an increase in the manufacturing sector (3.5 percent).

Recovery of Remittance Flows in 2010 and the Decline of Unemployment among Mexican Immigrant Workers

During 2010, remittance flows to Mexico increased slightly by 0.12 percent in annual terms, but such a figure must be taken in the context of a 12 percent fall in the first quarter and annual increases of 3.7 percent, 3.2 percent, and 6.5 percent in the second, third, and fourth quarters, respectively. This recent improvement in remittance flows has responded to higher employment of Mexican immigrant workers in the United States (table 16.14), which has also fostered a significant decline in their unemployment rate.

The weakness of labor demand in the United States in 2009 implied a shift in employment structure from full- to part-time jobs (figure 16.5). Under this assumption, one positive indicator is that the 20.3 percent "spike" in the share of part-time wage and salary jobs in total U.S. employment took place during the first half of 2010 (17.6 percent among wage and salary Mexican immigrant workers; figure 16.6) and declined to 19.3 percent in the second semester. The scenario for wage and salary Mexican immigrant workers has improved gradually; in fact, figure 16.5 shows that the number of these workers in full-time employment increased in annual terms during the first and second semesters of 2010. Finally, figure 16.7 shows that the improvement in employment levels among wage and salary Mexican immigrant workers and the increase in the participation of full-time jobs led to a slight rebound in their total earnings of wages and salaries.

Conclusion

This chapter has presented an analysis of the factors that led to an almost $5 billion annual decline in remittance flows to Mexico during 2008 and 2009. Given the fact that

TABLE 16.14 Total Employed and Unemployed Labor Force and Mexican Immigrants, First and Second Semesters, 2009 and 2010

Worker category and year	Employed		Unemployed	
	Semester I	Semester II	Semester I	Semester II
Total labor force				
2009	140,358,203	139,396,720	13,819,860	14,709,230
2010	138,446,156	139,681,781	15,279,901	14,369,642
Annual % change	−1.4	0.2	10.6	−2.3
% change I to II: 2009		−0.7		6.4
% change I to II: 2010		0.9		−6.0
Mexican immigrant workers				
2009	6,697,550	6,874,891	899,883	881,962
2010	6,738,138	7,011,080	919,903	812,455
Annual % change	0.6	2.0	2.2	−7.9
% change I to II: 2009		2.6		−2.0
% change I to II: 2010		4.1		−11.7
Labor force without Mexican immigrant workers				
2009	133,660,654	132,521,830	12,919,977	13,827,268
2010	131,708,018	132,670,701	14,359,998	13,557,186
Annual % change	−1.5	0.1	11.1	−2.0
% change I to II: 2009		−0.9		7.0
% change I to II: 2010		0.7		−5.6

Source: Authors' estimates with data from U.S. Census Bureau Current Population Survey.

FIGURE 16.5 Annual Percentage Variations of Wage and Salary Mexican Immigrant Workers in the United States, 2008–10

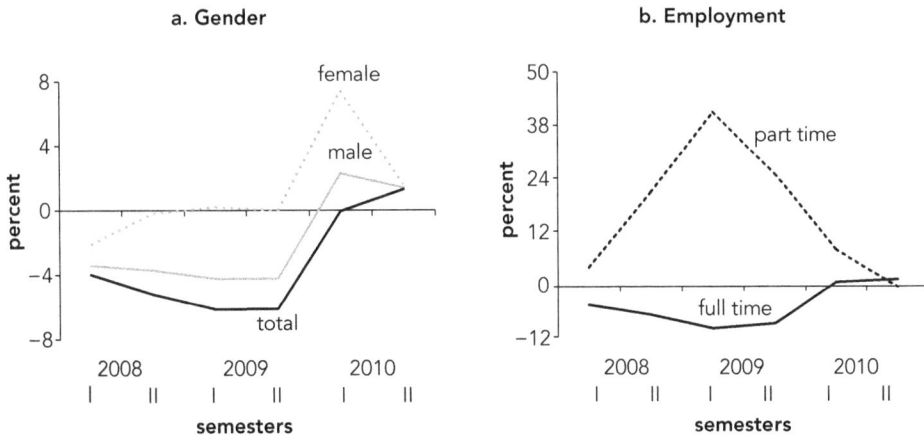

Source: Authors' estimates with data from U.S. Census Bureau Current Population Survey.

FIGURE 16.6 Proportion of Part-Time Employed among Wage and Salary Mexican Immigrant Workers, 2007–10

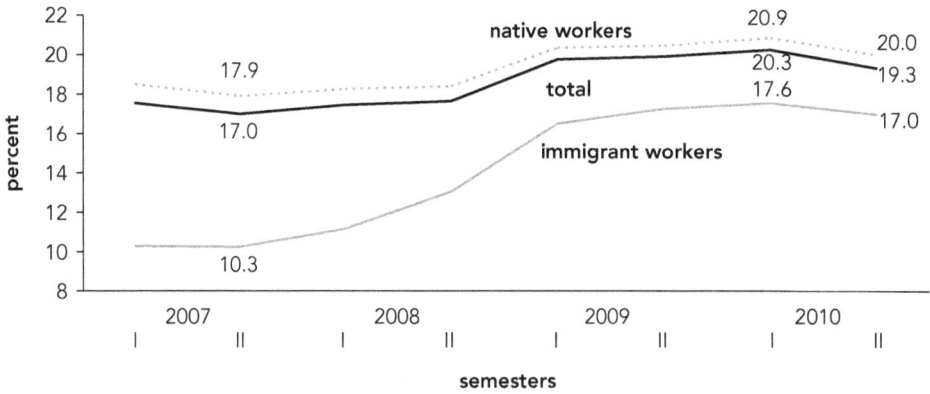

Source: Authors' estimates with data from U.S. Census Bureau Current Population Survey.

FIGURE 16.7 Number of Wage and Salary Mexican Immigrant Workers in the United States and Their Annual Total Earnings, 2007–10

a. Annual earnings   b. Number of workers

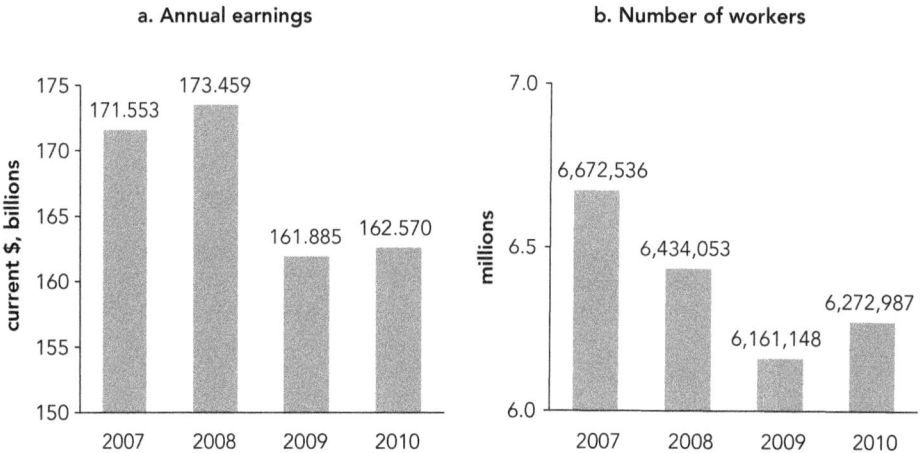

Source: Authors' estimates with data from U.S. Census Bureau Current Population Survey.

almost all remittances to Mexico originate from the United States, we have focused on Mexican immigrant workers there.

Our results show that the total earnings of wage and salary Mexican immigrant workers in the United States fell by almost $11.6 billion (6.7 percent), declining from $173.5 billion in 2008 to $161.9 billion in 2009. This responded to a decline in the employment of these workers (a net fall of 273,000 jobs or 4.2 percent) and in their average earnings (2.5 percent). The weakness of employment was totally concentrated in men (275,000 jobs and 6.1 percent), whereas employment among female Mexican immigrants remained practically unchanged. Meager labor demand in the United States also meant that over half a million wage and salary Mexican immigrant workers lost their full-time job.

Another finding is that the declines in employment, average earnings, and the total earnings of Mexican immigrant workers almost were affecting only those without citizenship. From 2008 to 2009, employment in this segment fell by 318,000 jobs (6.5 percent), and their average earnings declined more than $100 per month (5.1 percent), implying a $14 billion fall in their total earnings of wages and salaries (11.2 percent).

It is also noteworthy that the contraction in the employment of Mexican immigrant workers was relatively larger than that observed among other immigrant workers and the labor force as a whole in the United States. Furthermore, from 2007 to 2009 the deterioration in the unemployment rates of Mexican immigrant workers was higher than others. This is because Mexican immigrants tend to work in sectors of economic activity that are sensitive to the economic cycle. Such sectors are characterized by higher levels of unemployment. During the period studied, employment increased in services at the expense of a decline in the industry jobs. This was also evident in the case of Mexican immigrant workers. Mexican workers' move to service jobs also meant a shift toward lower-paying jobs. This has led to a sharp fall in the total earnings of these workers.

The scenario described for 2008–09 changed in 2010. Despite the persisting weakness of labor demand in the United States, employment of Mexican immigrant workers recorded a small positive annual variation in the first semester of 2010 (0.6 percent) and a larger increase in the second (2 percent). This improvement in the employment of Mexican immigrant workers reflected in the second half of the year showed annual increases in all three sectors of economic activity: agriculture, services, and industry. Within the last sector, annual increases were observed in the manufacturing industry during the second semester. Finally, the recovery of Mexican immigrant worker employment in the United States and the small improvement in the participation of those with full-time jobs began to be reflected in a slight rebound in their total earnings of wages and salaries. This combination of factors explains the annual increase already exhibited by remittance flows to Mexico since the second quarter of 2010.

Notes

1. In recent years Mexico has been the main source of immigrants who obtain permanent residence in the United States. During fiscal years 2000–07, an average of 169,011 Mexicans per year obtained permanent residence, and in fiscal years 2008, 2009, and 2010 the corresponding figures were 189,989, 164,920, and 139,120 Mexicans, respectively (Office of Immigration Statistics 2010). A fiscal year is the 12-month period beginning October 1 and ending September 30.

2. The total cost of a $300 remittance to Mexico sent from different cities in the United States and made via electronic transfer dropped from an average of $28.50 in 1999 to $23.20 in 2000 and to $5.60 in 2009 (Bonilla and Cervantes 2010).

3. A worker who is a nonnative of the United States is considered a citizen once they receive citizenship from that country's immigration service. All nonnative workers in the United States without citizenship are classified as noncitizens. The latter can be either legal or illegal immigrants.

4. The CPS provides the basic information on the labor force, employment, and unemployment in the U.S. economy. The survey is conducted monthly for the Bureau of Labor Statistics by the U.S. Census Bureau.

5. The CPS database considers Mexicans to be those who were born in Mexico and those individuals who declare themselves Mexican, irrespective of whether they were born there.

6. A full-time worker is a worker who usually works 35 or more hours per week at their sole or principal job, whereas a part-time worker usually works fewer than 35 hours per week at their sole or principal job.

7. For a comparison of educational attainment levels of Mexican and other immigrant workers in the United States see Cervantes and Barajas (2009).

PART IV

Chapter 17

The Impact of the Global Economic Downturn on Remittances from the European Union

OSCAR GÓMEZ LACALLE

GLOBAL REMITTANCE FLOWS ARE ESTIMATED to carry over $400 billion per year, of which $300 billion is received by developing countries. In many low-income destinations remittances have become a major source of external financing, providing income to the poor and contributing to growth and poverty reduction. In the past, remittances have been relatively stable compared with other external flows and generally unrelated to business cycles, especially in remittance-source countries (Ratha, Mohapatra and Silwal 2010a). Yet the impact of the recent global downturn on remittance flows suggests that the economic environment in remittance-source countries is relevant for remittance flows. In turn, depending on the degree of dependence on remittances in destination countries, remittances may become a significant transmission channel of the crisis from developed to developing countries.

The objective of this report is to assess the impact of the recent global economic downturn on remittance flows from the European Union (EU). For this purpose, in the next section I give an overview of the main macroeconomic determinants of remittances considered in the literature. Recent developments, magnitudes, and distribution of EU remittances are presented next. Evidence is collected to identify empirically which determinant(s) predominantly drive EU remittance trends in the

The views expressed in this chapter are exclusively those of the author and do not necessarily correspond to those of the European Commission.

short term. On the basis of these findings, I forecast EU remittances in the period 2010–12. An assessment of the vulnerability of EU remittances to recipient regions then is presented. Finally, the last section discusses the limitations of this exercise and briefly presents the main policies implemented in the EU, which may have an impact on remittance flows.

Channels of the Impact of an Economic Slowdown on Remittance Flows

The volume of remittance flows in a given corridor depends on a few factors (Labeaga, Jiménez-Martín, and Jorgensen 2007), and the impact of an economic slowdown on remittance flows can be identified by looking at each of these factors separately:

- The stock of migrant workers in a remittance-source country is unlikely to respond in the short run because the process of migration usually involves high fixed costs, which would be lost on returning home. Higher unemployment rates, especially when coupled with strict immigration policies, can slow new immigration. Then, depending on the depth and length of a recession, long-lasting difficulties for making a living may eventually force more migrant workers to leave.

- Most short-term adjustments are likely to work through migrants' income. Migrants are often employed in sectors sensitive to economic cycles such as construction or low-wage segments of manufacturing, although they are also employed in sectors more resilient to economic downturns (such as health care or personal services). Migrants tend to be less protected by social security systems, and so they are usually more flexible in the labor market and ready to take lower-paying jobs under difficult work conditions to avoid longer spells of unemployment. Lower wages might see counterbalancing effects on purchasing power in the recent downturn, because prices of housing, food, and energy, probably together representing the bulk of migrants' consumption, have decreased considerably.

- The share of income that migrants send home, also referred to as the *propensity to remit*, is reportedly more responsive to economic conditions in remittance-recipient countries than in remittance-source countries. This is often explained by the fact that average remittance transfers account for only one-fifth of migrants' income (Ratha, Mohapatra and Silwal 2010a), which allows migrants to adjust marginally current expenses and keep remittance flows stable.

- The costs of transferring remittances, which have come down, on average, over the last few years but can still be up to 20 percent of the amount sent, should be less affected by the economic slowdown. The only sizeable effect can come from tighter migration policies aiming to expel illegal migrants, which may induce illegal migrants to make more use of unofficial and more expensive transfer channels, in order not to be traceable.

- Changes in exchange rates may also have an effect, depending on whether migrants keep their remittances in the currency of the remittance-source or of the remittance-recipient country. Exchange rate developments will also have an effect on the general attractiveness of countries for migrants because they influence the income differential to their home countries.

- Developments in the above areas may also have statistical effects. Tighter labor markets coupled with stricter immigration rules could push more migrants into jobs in the informal sector and into making more use of unofficial transfer channels, resulting in underestimations of real flows, because unofficial transfers are more difficult to capture and tend to escape statistical systems.

On balance, although remittances overall are less volatile and less sensitive to economic downturns than other financial flows, estimates suggest the recent global downturn has had a negative impact on remittance flows. Depending on the length and depth of the downturn, it is reasonable to expect a slower increase or even a decrease in most remittance corridors, compared with the rather buoyant growth of the years preceding the crisis, when almost all of the determinants of remittances were exerting positive effects.

Remittances from the EU: Volume, Distribution, and Recent Developments

Recent Eurostat estimates (figure 17.1) show that remittances from the EU-27 fell for the first time in 2009 after a long expansion and amounted to €76.5 billion.[1] Intra-EU remittances were the largest flows throughout the period (about €45 billion, 60 percent of total flows), although most of the overall increase was due to extra-EU flows, which recorded double-digit annual growth rates between 2005 and 2008. However, the latter fell more in 2009 (−7.2 percent) than intra-EU flows (−3 percent).

FIGURE 17.1 EU Remittances by Destination, 2004–09

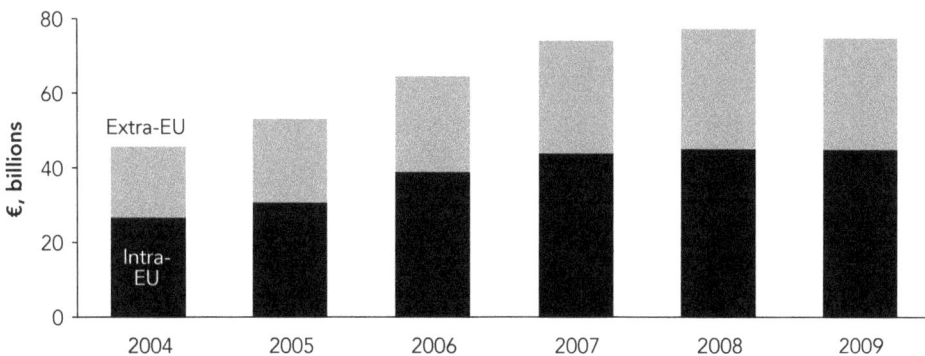

Source: Eurostat.

In 2009 Germany was the most important source of remittances from the EU, recording €11 billion, 14.4 percent of EU remittance outflows (table 17.1), followed by Italy (€9.3 billion), Spain (€8.6 billion), and the Netherlands (€7.3 billion). The top 10 remittance-sending EU member states account for two-thirds of total EU outflows.

TABLE 17.1 Top 10 Remittance-Sending Member States, 2009

Country	€, billions	% of total
Germany	11.0	14.4
Italy	9.3	12.1
Spain	8.6	11.3
Netherlands	7.3	9.6
France	3.7	4.9
Belgium	3.0	3.9
Austria	2.1	2.8
Czech Republic	1.8	2.4
Greece	1.3	1.7
Poland	0.9	1.2

Source: Eurostat.

Estimates of workers' remittances (excluding compensation of employees)[2] amounted to €30.3 billion in 2009 (figure 17.2), after a drop of 7.1 percent from the previous year. As opposed to compensation of employees, most workers' remittances (almost 75 percent) are destined to go to non-EU countries and show a higher degree of concentration at origin (table 17.2). In fact, the top 10 member states together send 80.8 percent of EU workers' remittances, and Italy and Spain each records remarkable shares in excess of 20 percent of total EU workers' remittances.

FIGURE 17.2 Workers' Remittances by Destination, 2004–09

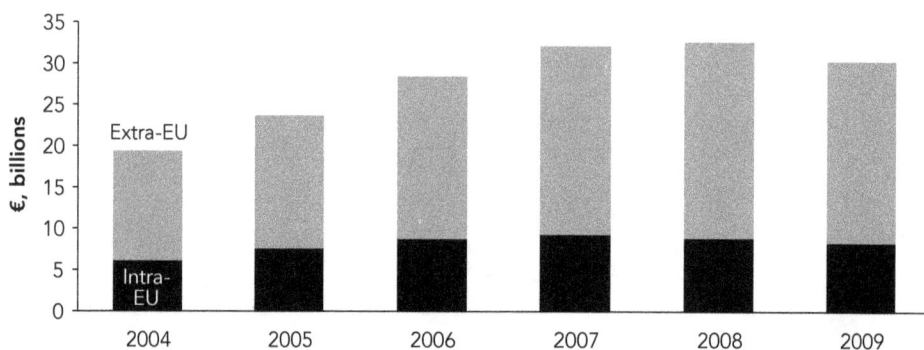

Source: Eurostat.

TABLE 17.2 Top 10 Workers' Remittance-Sending Member States, 2009

Country	€, billions	% of total
Spain	7.1	23.6
Italy	6.8	22.3
Germany	3.0	9.9
France	2.8	9.4
Netherlands	1.5	4.9
Greece	0.9	3.0
Austria	0.8	2.6
Portugal	0.6	1.8
Czech Republic	0.5	1.8
Belgium	0.4	1.5
Total	24.5	80.8

Source: Eurostat.

Note: Details may not sum to totals because of rounding.

Impact of the Crisis on EU Remittance Outflows: Main Transmission Channels

The size and direction of remittance flows are shaped by a variety of factors, whose impacts may be either instantaneous or delayed, incidental or long lasting, cumulating or offsetting, or strengthening or phased out (see discussion above). Such complexity, along with data scarcity, makes it difficult to obtain a general pattern of remittances that is comprehensive for factors and easily able to monitor remittance flows. A solution consists of narrowing the time frame allowed for determinants to influence remittances. Because observations to date may provide evidence of short-term impacts of the crisis on remittance flows, such will be the scope of the present analysis.

Therefore, I will focus on those determinants that are considered to have the most important short-term effect on remittances, notably migrants' income. I shall also look for empirical evidence of another important driver of remittances: migrant stocks.

Migrant Stocks

Remittance aggregates (by country, region, or corridor, for example) sum up the individual migrants' transfers. The number of migrants is, by definition, a direct determinant of remittance flows. This is important when the amounts per transfer within remittance corridors tend to remain rather stable.

However, as reported in the literature, migrant stocks are unlikely to respond rapidly to economic shocks such as the recent economic downturn. First, the process of migration usually involves high fixed costs, which would be lost upon returning home. Second, migrants are a flexible labor force, because they are less reluctant to move geographically and sectorally in seeking a job. Third, evidence of "reverse remittances" (Ratha, Mohapatra, and Silwal 2009b) is reported in some countries where migrants prefer to dip into their savings and assets back home and rely on their families for financial help, rather than return home.

These considerations might imply that migrant stocks and remittances will not necessarily respond equally to an external sock in the short run. Evidence of this can be observed in Spain, which is a relevant example for being (1) one of the largest origins of remittances from the EU, (2) one of the member states hardest hit by the recent downturn (European Commission 2010), and (3) one for which data on remittance outflows and migrants' stocks are available on a quarterly basis.[3]

Figure 17.3 plots year-on-year growth of Spain's migrant active population and remittance outflows for the first quarter of 2006 through the second quarter of 2010. It reveals a strong correlation between these two variables in 2006 and 2007.

FIGURE 17.3 Spain: Migrant Active Population and Remittance Outflows, 2006–10

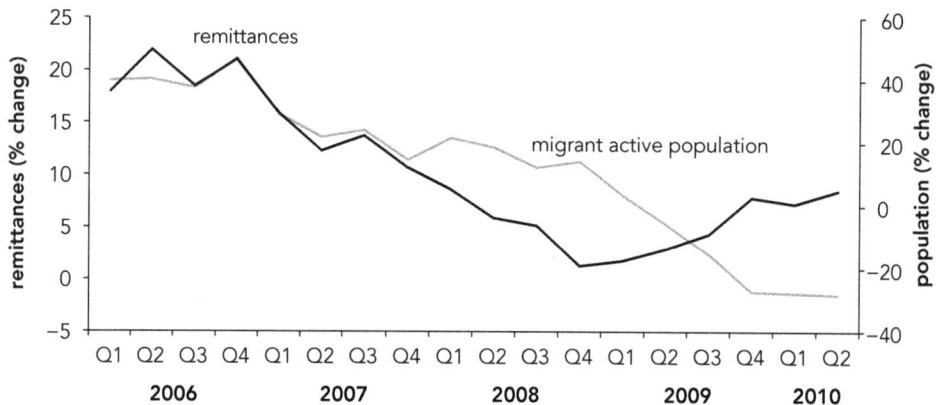

Source: Author.

This correlation is broken in the first quarter of 2008, when the Spanish economy started decelerating markedly. Spanish remittance outflows fell through 2008 and 2009, whereas the stock of active migrants continued increasing, although decelerating, until the fourth quarter of 2009,[4] when the number of active migrants declined for the first time.

Therefore the drop of remittance outflows in Spain was not due to fewer migrants but to migrants sending less money home. This performance seems to confirm the theory above and provides evidence that changes in migrant stocks are not a driving determinant of changes in remittances from Spain in the recent economic slowdown.

Migrants' Income

Direct estimates of migrants' income in the EU are unfortunately unavailable. Yet indirect evidence can be obtained through an indicator that approximates migrants' income. Such an indicator should be (1) observable (data should be available for the period covered by the analysis) and (2) faithful (accurately emulating the performance of the original variable).

In this vein, the economic and statistical literature (ILO 1998) has long recognized estimates of income from employment. Although such estimates assume that employment is the only source of income, this is a reasonable assumption in the case of migrants because most migrants' income-earning activities are either paid employment or self-employment. Another caveat of the employment measure of income is that it disregards unemployment benefits. In the case of migrants, however, such an underestimation may not be of much significance, because migrants' social protection levels are, on average, considerably lower than those of native workers, especially in the case of low-skilled migration. The employment measure of income also assumes unchanged wages, which is an acceptable assumption in the short term for registered employment (workers with legal contracts), given the rather rigid wage formation structures in force in most member states. Finally, changes in total (native + migrant) employment are preferred to foreigners' employment, mainly because considerably higher levels of unregistered active and employed migrants are likely to hinder the reliability of the latter series, whereas total employment should provide a more sound overall picture of labor market performance.

Accordingly, figure 17.4 plots quarter-on-quarter (q-o-q) percentage changes in remittance outflows from the EU (right-hand side) against total EU employment growth (q-o-q) (left-hand side).[5] Employment data sources are member states' Labor Force Surveys, as reported by Eurostat, whose estimation methodology is unrelated to the

FIGURE 17.4 EU: Total Growth in Employment and Remittance Outflows, 2006–10

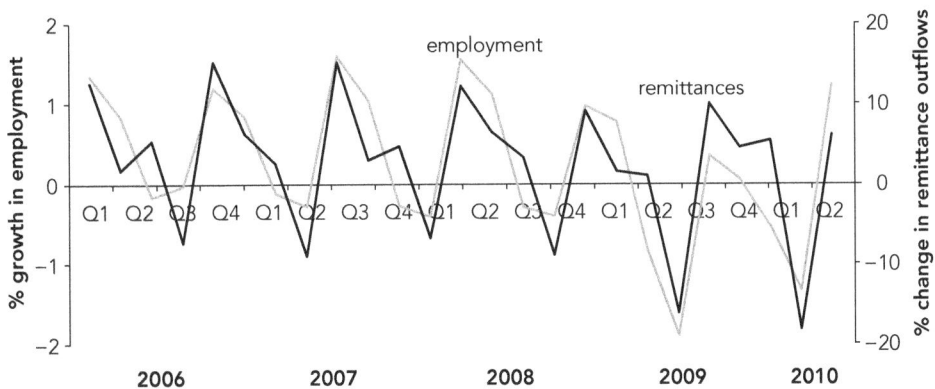

Source: Author.

balance-of-payments accounting methodology, from which remittance figures are collected.

Figure 17.4 reveals a high correlation (>80 percent) between both variables during the period considered. Assuming remittances is the dependent variable, these results suggest that employment growth is driving most of remittances' short-term fluctuations in the EU. Additionally, the subcomponent workers' remittances similarly shows a high degree of correlation with employment in the EU. Higher volatility of remittances compared with employment suggests that EU remittances could be highly sensitive to the economic environment of migrants' host countries.

Projections

In view of these results, accurate flash estimates of quarterly EU remittance flows can be easily derived from quarterly data on employment. Similarly, short-term projections of remittances can be computed when quarterly forecasts on employment are available.[6]

European Commission (2010) projections of annual employment growth in the period 2010–12 may provide an indication of the possible orders of magnitude of the impact of the crisis on EU remittances. For this purpose I apply a statistical projection based on a simple ordinary least squares regression of remittances growth on employment growth. According to the equation derived from observations (2004–09), changes in remittances explained by changes in employment (R^2) are higher than 60 percent. Subsequently, this regression is run to generate remittance growth from employment growth in 2010–12. The estimation returns an increase of EU remittances by 2 percent in 2010, 6 percent in 2011, and 7.5 percent in 2012 (figure 17.5).

FIGURE 17.5 Total Employment and Remittance Outflows in the European Union, 2004–12

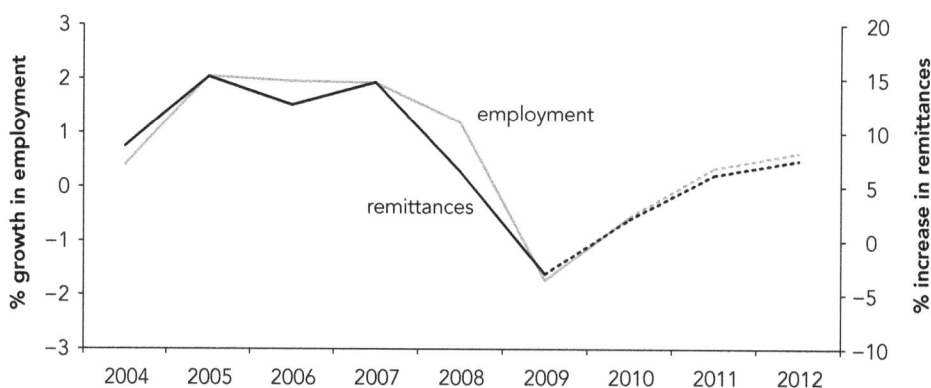

Source: Authors; projections based on OLS estimation.

Note: Dotted lines indicate projections.

These figures should, however, be treated with caution, because this simple model with only one explaining variable and a low number of observations affects the accuracy of the results.

Relative Vulnerability of Destination Regions to the Decline in EU Remittances

The decline in EU remittances is not likely to affect all destination countries or regions equally. Vulnerability to a decline in EU remittances depends on (1) the share of EU flows for total remittances received and (2) the share of EU remittances for other sources of income at destination. In addition, the relative contribution of individual member states to EU remittance aggregates is likely to differ from one corridor to another, which can be relevant should member states' remittance outflows fluctuate unevenly in size and in time.

Table 17.3 reveals divergences in employment prospects (European Commission 2010) for the main member states contributing to remittance flows, ranging from −4.7 percent (Greece) to +0.9 percent (Austria) in 2010, from −0.8 percent (Ireland) to +2.9 percent (Greece) in 2011, and from −0.3 percent (Portugal) to +1.9 percent (Greece). Insofar as employment growth is assumed to explain main short-term adjustments in EU remittances, these divergences should lead to different trends in remittance flows from each member state. The table highlights relatively higher vulnerability of Albania to a decline in remittances from Greece, Ukraine to remittances from the Czech Republic, and Romania to remittances from Italy (table 17.4).

TABLE 17.3 Selected Member States' Employment Forecasts, 2009–12

annual percentage change

Country	2009	2010	2011	2012
Austria	−0.9	0.9	0.7	0.7
Czech Republic	−1.1	−0.5	0.2	0.3
France	−1.2	0.0	0.5	0.7
Germany	0.0	0.3	0.7	0.4
Greece	−9.9	−4.7	2.9	1.9
Ireland	−8.2	−4.0	−0.8	0.6
Italy	−1.7	−0.5	0.1	0.4
Netherlands	−1.1	−1.1	0.2	0.3
Portugal	−2.6	−0.9	−0.7	−0.3
Spain	−6.6	−2.5	−0.2	1.1
EU-27	−1.8	-0.6	0.3	0.6

Source: European Commission.

TABLE 17.4 Main EU Corridors, 2009

remittances as share of total received

Sending member state	Share of total remittances received (%)	Recipient country	Total received as % of GDP
Austria	6.2	Serbia	12.6
Czech Republic	21.6	Ukraine	2.0
France	17.9	Portugal	1.5
	16.1	Morocco	6.6
Germany	—	Turkey	0.2
	14.2	Italy	0.1
Greece	36.4	Albania	10.9
	19	Israel	0.7
Ireland	—	Poland	2.0
Italy	5.7	China	1.0
	5.6	Philippines	11.7
	23.3	Romania	4.4
Netherlands	—	Suriname	0.1
Portugal	11.7	Brazil	0.3
Spain	—	Colombia	1.8
	—	Ecuador	4.5
	—	Bolivia	6.1

Source: Eurostat and World Bank.

Note: — = not available.

Conclusions

This chapter examined the main short-term channel of impact on EU remittance outflows. Evidence was found of a high positive correlation between employment and remittance trends, on the basis of which EU remittance growth was projected. This exercise generally found that remittances from the EU can be expected to recover gradually during the forecast horizon. Such a recovery is expected to be felt unevenly in destination countries, depending on employment performance in member states.

Although this exercise provides estimates of immediate adjustments in remittances, it is unable to inform underlying remittance levels or adjustments from determinants with lagging effects. Some of those determinants are certainly being shaped by the recent downturn and would require special attention to assess their impact on remittances in the medium term. One notable example is the uncertain effect on migration of labor market adjustments currently taking place in member states (European Commission 2010).

In turn, medium-term analysis is relevant to orient development policies that aim to facilitate remittances, to reinforce the link between remittances and development, or to attenuate the negative impact of remittance declines in recipient countries.

EU member states have long agreed on a set of commitments on remittances, which are currently in the process of being implemented. The objective of these commitments is threefold: (1) Improving data on remittances: For this purpose member states are increasingly adopting the recommendations made by the Luxembourg Group regarding the quality and coverage of data on remittances. (2) Favoring cheaper, faster, and more secure remittance flows: Substantial progress has been achieved by the EU through the adoption of the Payment Services Directive in November 2007 and the new E-Money Directive, adopted in October 2009. (3) Enhancing the development impact of remittances: This is achieved through various development cooperation programs in the European Community and member states to support the creation of a business environment more conducive to remittances in developing countries.

Additionally, the EU adopted in 2009 a range of immediate actions to help developing countries mitigate the economic and social consequences of the financial crisis. For this purpose the EU has mobilized about €2 billion in addition to the EU's contributions to international financial institutions' activities. These actions include, notably, an ad hoc "Vulnerability FLEX" instrument for 2009 and 2010, acting countercyclically to allow those developing countries worst hit by the crisis to continue social safety net spending. This is in addition to a "food facility" for 2009–11 adopted to support the agricultural sector in developing countries and respond to the negative effects of volatile food prices on local populations.

Notes

1. Unless mentioned otherwise, remittances include the "compensation of employees" and "workers' remittances" as defined in the balance-of-payments statistics.

2. EU workers' remittances would mainly refer to those from immigrants who come from outside the EU, whereas compensation of employees mainly refers to payments of cross-border and seasonal workers who usually come from neighboring countries.

3. No quarterly data on remittances are available for the EU as a whole.

4. Series in figure 16.3 are plotted on different scales to take account of the different volatility of both series.

5. Series in figure 16.4 are plotted on different scales to take account of the different volatility of both series.

6. The European Commission does not publish quarterly forecasts on employment. However, this issue is currently under consideration, and estimates are likely to be included in future forecast publications.

Chapter 18

Remittances and Evolving Migration Flows from Central and Eastern Europe to the United Kingdom

SIMON PEMBERTON AND LISA SCULLION

In RECENT YEARS, THERE HAS been an increasing focus on the migration of people to the United Kingdom from Central and Eastern European (CEE) countries.[1] A key factor that has influenced CEE labor migration patterns to the United Kingdom has been the European Commission Accession Treaty (2003). This set out that for a maximum of seven years, the EU-15 (pre-2004 countries) would continue to regulate access to their labor markets because of the uncertainty of the impact of CEE migrants on different sectors of employment and access to social benefits (Traser 2006). Of the EU-15, only the United Kingdom (along with Ireland and Sweden) decided to "fully" open their labor markets to CEE workers. This created significant "diversion effects" in the postenlargement flows of CEE migrant workers to the United Kingdom and Ireland (Ruhs 2006).

Indeed, U.K. Worker Registration Scheme (WRS) figures have highlighted that over 1 million registrations for work have been made since 2004 by CEE economic migrants (Home Office 2010a). These figures need to be set against initial U.K. government expectations of around 20,000 CEE economic migrant workers arriving per annum (Stenning and others 2006).

Political and media debate, as well as a growing body of academic studies, have sought to highlight the impact such movements have had on indigenous workers and associated employment opportunities (Green, Jones, and Owen 2007; Syrett and Lyons 2007) as well as the implications for public services within the United Kingdom (Pemberton 2008, 2009). There has also been an interest in the economic contribution of such workers.

In addition, numerous studies have been carried out across the United Kingdom that consider the experiences and needs of CEE migrant workers (for example, see Hunt and Steele 2008; MSIO 2006). Many of these investigations have focused on issues such as employment, accommodation, skills and qualifications, and community cohesion. The majority have adopted a survey approach, and, although they have provided very useful information on a range of issues, more in-depth analysis relating to people's experiences is still lacking—and in particular their migration decisions and remittance practices during a period of increasing economic uncertainty.

Consequently, this chapter seeks to provide a more in-depth understanding on such issues and CEE migrants' remittance patterns in respect to savings and expenditure. It highlights how structural factors and individual agency intersect in different ways for such groups within an era of global financial crisis. In particular, the analysis provides new insights into the near-term impact of such crises on CEE migrants' motivations, aspirations, and expectations for traveling to or remaining within the United Kingdom, and the subsequent nature and resilience of their remittance practices.

Context: CEE Migration and Remittances

Existing studies highlight that other than "accessibility," individuals have migrated to the United Kingdom based on the perception of the availability of employment and higher wages than in their home country, where there may be more limited work opportunities (Bell, Jarman, and Lefebvre 2004). Although employment opportunities are key for CEE migrants, recent research has also highlighted a range of additional factors shaping their decisions to come to and/or remain in the United Kingdom, including access to welfare, as well as education and training opportunities (Scullion and Pemberton 2010).

It has been claimed that many CEE migrants are keeping well informed about the economies in their home countries and are willing to make decisions concerning their movement on fairly short notice (Finch and others 2009). Such decisions have been related to a fall in recent WRS approvals for CEE migrant workers in the United Kingdom, which declined by over a third between March 2008 and March 2009 (Home Office 2009). Indeed, it has recently been estimated that as many as 500,000 CEE migrant workers may now have left the United Kingdom (Finch and others 2009; Pollard, Latorre, and Sriskandarajah 2008).

However, such arguments assume that migrants act as rational economic decision makers, and they do not necessarily account for the variety of individual circumstances and other noneconomic factors that influence motivations to migrate to, from, and within countries such as the United Kingdom (Scullion and Pemberton 2010). In the context of migration flows and remittances, this is important and warrants further attention in the discussion that follows. Indeed, evidence is already available from a recent study in North West England that many CEE migrants have remained *in situ* despite rising unemployment (Scullion and Morris 2009).

Furthermore, if an individualistic approach is taken, research has found that both migration and remittance decisions and practices can vary greatly depending on age, family ties, and profession (McKay and Winkelmann-Gleed 2005). For example, it has been claimed that Polish migrants sent home almost £1 billion in the first quarter of 2007 (Slack 2007), and in a more recent analysis, Smyth (2010) has claimed that Polish workers in Britain and Germany provided the largest amount of remittances to Poland last year, although these had fallen since 2007. Some commentators have argued that the reduction has occurred as a by-product of family reunification or CEE migrants having children while in the United Kingdom. In turn, although sending countries may suffer through such processes, receiving countries (such as the United Kingdom) may benefit given that money that was previously sent home may now be spent or saved in the host country (Cortina and Ochoa-Reza 2008).

What we also need to be aware of is the extent to which remittance practices may be informed by the interplay between the agency of individual migrants and the structural context within which CEE migrants seek to maneuver (Phizacklea 2000: 119). Structure can be viewed in terms of its manifestations in institutional factors, government policy being the most obvious of these. Successive legislation in the United Kingdom has created an immigration system that provides differential access to basic rights and services, depending on a migrant's area of origin, skills level, and so on. These factors influence what resources people are able to draw on and their capacity to act. CEE migrants are not passive recipients of such policies and can seek to elaborate or modify structural conditions (Hunt 2008: 282).

It is important to recognize that the public demands for "managed migration" to the United Kingdom has led to the Points-Based System to restrict migration from outside the European Economic Area (EEA) (initiated in February 2008) and the introduction of a permanent cap on non-EEA workers in April 2011. Additionally, the introduction of the Resident Labour Market test required employers to demonstrate that they have failed to fill vacancies from within the United Kingdom and EEA before they were able to recruit from outside Europe (UKBA 2008). Such changes were driven by the global economic downturn and a greater focus on the local impact of international labor migration (Anderson and Ruhs 2009). However, they were also driven by a belief that the increasing numbers of CEE migrants arriving in the United Kingdom would enable the phasing out of low-skill immigration schemes for individuals from other parts of the world (Home Office 2006).

Many studies have promoted an economic discourse in terms of the contributions made by CEE migrants to the United Kingdom, with arguments that such individuals bring with them numerous positive benefits for employers and the national economy, namely, (1) reducing the average age of the workforce, (2) reliability and a good work ethic helping businesses to expand and diversify, (3) a willingness to work long and/or antisocial hours, and (4) high rates of productivity while minimizing labor costs and the threat of inflation (Green, Jones, and Owen 2007). It has also been estimated that in the

North West region alone each migrant worker will account for more than £7,000 of tax revenue (MSIO 2006).

Given this context, it is not surprising that CEE economic migrants are viewed as a resource to fill occupations with both "skills" and "people" shortages (McClaughlin and Smith 2005; Rennie 2005), although the issue of "brain waste" is also of relevance given their concentration in less skilled occupations, regardless of skills, experience, or linguistic capability. Hence although it may appear that U.K. immigration policy may be privileging CEE migrants above others (non-EEA migrants), the fact that many CEE migrants appear to be underemployed (and yet have remained in the United Kingdom) will also have a significant influence on shaping their patterns of migration and the impact of their remittances. It also provides an interesting parallel to the situation in non-EEA countries where remittances have been a "valuable source of development finance," but with migrant workers finding it increasingly difficult to get access to the U.K. labor market (Datta and others 2006: 11).

Method

The research methodology involved 25 semistructured in-depth interviews conducted during late 2009 and early 2010 with CEE migrant workers who featured prominently in public and political debates in the United Kingdom. The interviews were carried out by a community researcher, with appropriate language skills, and a mix of "purposive" and "snowball" sampling was used.

In particular, Czech, Lithuanian, Polish, and Slovak migrant workers were targeted for both pragmatic reasons (resource and time constraints and language skills and community links of the interviewer), but also because of such communities being relatively prominent within the case study area selected for the research: North West England.

The basis for selecting the North West was threefold: First, the North West region has experienced a population decline of 3 percent over the last 20 years, which, coupled with an aging population (a 12 percent decline in those aged 16–24 has been forecast by 2020), means that there is an increasing reliance on migrant workers to fill both "skills" and "people" shortages (NWDA 2006). Second, the employment rate for the region is currently 2 percent below the average for England and with the highest proportion of individuals reliant on the incapacity benefit in England. The region also has high rates of working age adults with no qualifications (Office for National Statistics 2010). This means that migrant labor has been important in addressing job gaps.

With regard to the profile of the Czech, Lithuanian, Polish, and Slovak individuals who participated in the research, there was both a mix of young and more mature individuals and there was a balance between those who identified themselves as single (and living with friends or on their own) and those who had families. The majority were currently employed in jobs that mirrored national patterns for the employment of CEE workers in the United Kingdom (such as warehouse operatives, food processing, packing, cleaning, and production-line work). A small number were employed in more skilled occupations (such as teaching). Three people indicated that they were currently unemployed. In addition, the interviewees primarily held intermediate-level qualifications in the form of diplomas (or equivalent), but in overall terms such qualifications appeared to have little influence on their current type of employment in the United Kingdom.

Results

The results provide a detailed insight of CEE migrants' motivations, aspirations, and expectations for traveling to or remaining within the United Kingdom. The discussion considers the extent to which these have remained the same or changed over time in an era of global financial crisis, and why this may be the case. This is crucial because without having a detailed insight into such issues, it becomes difficult to understand current practice in respect to the nature and level of CEE remittances and how these may evolve in the future.

CEE Migrants' Motivations and Expectations for Traveling to or Remaining within the United Kingdom and the Influence of the Global Financial Crisis

Consistent with the existing literature on CEE migration, economic motivations—in terms of both high rates of unemployment or a lack of opportunities in the labor market in their country of origin (a "push" factor) and perceived or actual employment opportunities in the United Kingdom (a "pull" factor)—were identified as *the* key reason for moving by virtually all of the interviewees.

But on the other hand, existing studies do not tend to focus on the extent to which the relative importance of push-pull factors have changed over time for CEE migrants. In this respect, the study revealed that for around 60 percent of respondents, the influences on their decision to come to the United Kingdom (and the North West region) had not changed since they had arrived. This was despite, in theory, their "agency" increasing as a result of becoming eligible for certain forms of state benefits (such as income support and housing benefit) once they had been in continuous employment for more than 12 months. As one interviewee summarized: "Work and solid pay is still the main motivation to stay despite the current downturn…this country (the United Kingdom) currently provides much more employment opportunities for people than in Poland."

For most of the remaining respondents, the research revealed that securing employment in the United Kingdom, coupled with a view that conditions in their home country had deteriorated further relative to the U.K. labor market (and a perception of fewer opportunities for their children in the future), had simply served to *reinforce* the importance of the "push" and "pull" factors that had caused them to move before the economic downturn. As another respondent noted: "At the moment I am here because I know that it is easier to support myself than in Poland …If I move back, I would possibly not find a job and would lose lots of money."

With reference to the impact of the financial crisis on relocation within the United Kingdom and/or return to their host country, the availability and type of employment (locally) to CEE migrants was argued to be the key issue on whether they stayed within their local neighborhood, the North West region, or within the United Kingdom. Nevertheless, increasing intramigrant tensions—which it was suggested were increasing as a result of more competition for fewer jobs—were also cited as an additional factor in influencing the movement of CEE migrants from their existing neighborhoods. For example, a Czech migrant complained that he was moving elsewhere in the United Kingdom for work because "most agencies in the region were run by Poles and they just block you off."

Failure to remain in work was therefore regarded as having a substantial impact on the motivation of CEE economic migrants to remain in the United Kingdom. Indeed, one well-qualified individual commented, "We were planning to stay for five years …Now? I will be happy if we survive 'til the end of next year [2011] …I am interested mainly in keeping the job I do now. If I lose it and will not be able to find a similar teaching job, then I would lose my major reason for staying in the United Kingdom."

Only two interviewees highlighted that their experiences of work (in terms of satisfaction with current working conditions and levels of pay) were leading to a reconsideration of whether they wished to remain in the United Kingdom. This overriding economic imperative in the current climate is interesting because other studies have suggested that disillusionment with work or poor wages have been a key factor in shaping return migration (Coats 2008; Finch and others 2009). In contrast, the research in North West England indicated that the effects of the global financial crisis was leading CEE migrants to reassess their relative agency: Many were reluctant to even consider changing jobs, and some almost showed "gratitude" toward having employment.

There was also divergence with certain arguments within the existing literature on the extent to which CEE migrants were making a deliberate and concerted effort (over and above their general perceptions; see above) to be kept informed about the state of the economy in their home country. Moreover, most respondents—regardless of having knowledge of conditions in their home country—indicated that this was not acting as an influence on their motivation to return, which again is contrary to some previous studies (Coats 2008). In contrast, respondents perceived that economic conditions were currently pretty much the same everywhere and that their experiences in the United Kingdom since arrival had reinforced their decision to come in the first place. In the words of another Czech migrant, "I don't follow the situation over there [in the Czech Republic]. The real differences between the countries are minimal now. It's so much linked together and mutually dependent that the local situations are pretty much the same."

The amount of time CEE migrants have been in the United Kingdom and the impact of family reunification and family stability in the current economic climate must also be taken into account. Accordingly, the perceptions that many CEE migrants appear to hold over the "upheaval" of moving (particularly with families and dependents) appears to have reduced their propensity to move, regardless of economic conditions back home. Indeed, a father of four commented that he did not want to drag his family all over Europe now that his children were in British schools.

Very few CEE migrants appeared to have an awareness of where and when labor market restrictions in other EU countries were to be relaxed. Those who did tended to be older and had been in the United Kingdom for a reasonable length of time, and the majority did not think that this would have an impact on their future motivations. Some respondents—particularly those who were more qualified—did suggest, however, that they may be more likely to leave in the first instance, with Belgium, Denmark, Finland, Germany, and Sweden seen as potential destinations. Job availability and a positive local (built) environment (for example, good quality housing) were key reasons for moving to such countries. This was summed up by a young female Polish interviewee who stated,

> If I am single like now, I will go to Germany. And I will try to start there again, from zero. Because I speak German as good as English—at the same level. Berlin...it is clean in the city, the houses are better quality ...Just walk in Berlin or Düsseldorf, you feel like being in Europe there. But here, Kensington, Toxteth, it's the Third World."

At the same time, linguistic capability was viewed as a limiting factor on the "alternatives" available to many CEE migrant workers. In essence, only Ireland was seen as a viable alternative for those who had no knowledge, understanding, or expertise in other languages. This is even less likely to be a suitable alternative given the budgetary problems that have arisen in Ireland during the latter half of 2010.

Thus to summarize, it is apparent that from an economic perspective, the global financial crisis appears to have compounded or reinforced the decisions of CEE migrants who currently remain in the United Kingdom to remain *in situ*. However, it is also clear that other noneconomic factors—such as family stability and linguistic capability, as well as the structural privileging of such individuals in terms of the United Kingdom's immigration policy—have intersected with CEE migrant agency and their lack of motivation to return home. Having said this, if the financial crisis deepens further—increasing competition for even fewer jobs between CEE migrants, non-EEA migrants, and the host population—this may lead to individuals reassessing their options. This could equally be the case for both skilled, well-qualified CEE migrants, as well as those with fewer skills and qualifications given the nature of cuts that are envisaged in the next three to five years in the United Kingdom across the public and private sectors.

The Evolving Nature and Level of CEE Remittances

Having discussed some of the influences that motivate CEE migrants to remain in the United Kingdom in a period of economic uncertainty, it also becomes possible to consider the impact of such influences on the nature, resilience, and future of CEE migrants' remittance practices.

It was clear that the changing economic situation had an effect on the resilience of remittances in several different ways. For example, CEE migrants who remain in the United Kingdom indicated that they were now actually spending the majority of their income in the United Kingdom. The percentage of wages that individuals spent ranged from all of their wages to around 50 percent of their wages (on a weekly or monthly basis). Following the three key expenses (rent, food, and utilities), individuals made reference to spending their income on transport and travel (this included to and from work, as well as for leisure purposes), clothes, mobiles phones, Internet access, as well as leisure activities such as museums, cinemas, and theaters. A number of respondents also made reference to membership at local gyms or sports centers.

Hence very few CEE migrants made reference to sending money back to their home country. In the words of one interviewee, "The people who saved their money are the ones who have now returned home. But we live like [we are] at home here." This, perhaps, is a key finding. The length of time that CEE migrants have been in the United Kingdom appears to relate directly to spending and saving ratios. The general perception of CEE migrants—and this has been supported in other research studies (Pollard, Latorre, and Sriskandarajah 2008)—is that that new CEE arrivals to the United Kingdom were more likely to save in the first instance. After living for some time in the United Kingdom, however, individuals started to spend their savings. In some cases this was due to changing circumstances; for example, CEE migrants no longer wished to live in shared accommodations, possibly because of family reunification issues. However, some respondents simply referred to wanting to buy additional things as time went on.

Of those who have remained and who indicated that they were saving some of their income, this was not generally remittance related. Rather, they were attempting to build a "safety net" to allow them to remain in the United Kingdom while they sought alternative employment if they were made redundant. Interestingly, some CEE migrants also made reference to having accumulated large debts through being employed on an inconsistent basis in the United Kingdom as a result of the global economic downturn and that they now needed to pay off. Once again, this appeared to be impinging on the resilience of their remittances and the extent to which sending countries such as the Czech Republic, Lithuania, Poland, and Slovakia were benefiting, and where unemployment rates have remained generally at a much higher level than in Western Europe (Smyth 2010).

Linking with current spending and saving patterns and the impact on remittances, the study explored possible changes to CEE migrants' future remittance practices. What emerged was a perception that they were likely to *save less* and *spend more* in the future. Generally, this was not because of any desire to spend more money on particular activities or items, but rather because of the financial crisis pushing up the cost of living in the United Kingdom coupled with an emphasis on a reduction in salary costs:

When I arrived in the United Kingdom, my first wage was £5.10 an hour. Now I get minimum wage again and it is £5.73. So the difference after four years of work is only 60p. So how many percent increase is that? And now compare the increase of prices: I think the prices went up almost 50 percent, for example, for food and local transport. So I rather expect shrinking savings and remittances as we move forward. (Polish female interviewee, aged 53)

To conclude, most of the interviewees who participated in the study had been in the United Kingdom for a considerable period of time and had plans to stay in the medium-to-longer term. This appeared to affect their individual agency and decisions over remittances. Indeed, there was very little evidence of CEE migrants (in the current climate) sending remittances home. Most were spending the majority of their income in the United Kingdom. The percentage of wages that migrants currently spent ranged from all of their wages to 50 percent of their wages. Numerous respondents did try to save some money; however, this was often because of a desire for a "safety net" in the United Kingdom over and above that provided by the welfare state. With regard to the latter point, there was little reference made by most CEE migrants to claiming state benefits, nor a desire to do so. Perhaps the one exception in this respect was more mature CEE migrant workers, who noted that they were hoping to remain in work within the United Kingdom to become eligible for some form of future U.K. state pension.

Conclusion

This chapter has highlighted some of the near-term impacts of the global financial crisis on patterns of migration to and from the United Kingdom by CEE labor migrants. It illustrated that the crisis has led to a degree of transience of such individuals who have remained in the United Kingdom, although further job losses may influence significant large-scale return migration for both those filling "skills" and "people" shortage occupations. However, such a movement would also be dependent on the economic conditions in sending (CEE) countries, other EEA countries, and a series of noneconomic factors, such as migrants' propensity to move, based on family, linguistic, and other cultural factors.

From a remittance perspective, the financial crisis has had some impact on the level of remittances sent by CEE migrants remaining within the United Kingdom: In essence, they appear to be at a lower level than was the case for those CEE migrants who migrated temporarily to the United Kingdom during an earlier period of economic growth (2004–07) but who have now returned home. Hence the benefits over time may have shifted toward the receiving country (United Kingdom) compared with the sending (CEE) countries, and this may exacerbate future unevenness in economic performance of EEA countries. Nevertheless, better capitalization of CEE migrants' skills, qualifications, and experiences may be required to generate further benefits for the United Kingdom. Equally, there is a need to ensure that the benefits to the local or regional economy of CEE migrant expenditures in the United Kingdom are better calculated. For example, the New Economics Foundation's Local Multiplier 3 approach (or a suitable equivalent) could be used to assess the local multiplier that emerges from (1) public sector support to CEE migrants and (2) CEE migrants' disposable income spent within the neighborhood or region.

Finally, over the longer term, there is uncertainty over the extent to which the United Kingdom's current policies of "managed migration" and restrictions on non-EEA migration will help to ameliorate or exacerbate economic recovery, especially if CEE migrants are unable or unwilling to address both skills and people shortages. Thus it is perhaps critical that attempts are made to secure and support the existing stock of CEE migrants in the United Kingdom to ensure that they can be drawn upon to fill vacancies as required, but at the same time acknowledging the importance of remittances to the economic well-being of sending countries and that these migrants may require additional support (from host countries) to address their future economic challenges.

Note

1. The Czech Republic, Estonia, Hungary, Latvia, Lithuania, Poland, Slovakia, and Slovenia (commonly referred to as the A8 countries); Bulgaria and Romania (commonly referred to as the A2 countries).

Chapter 19

Effects of the Global Crisis on Migration and Remittances in Albania

ILIR GEDESHI AND NICOLAAS DE ZWAGER

THIS CHAPTER SEEKS TO EXAMINE ways in which the global financial and economic crisis influenced Albanian international migration trends and remittance practices while also discussing the potential repercussions for the future.

Our analysis draws on a study including a questionnaire survey with 2,470 long-term migrants, qualitative interviews, and focus groups with migrants carried out between December 2009 and January 2010. We compare these quantitative data with a baseline survey conducted a year earlier using the same methodology (de Zwager, Gressmann, and Gedeshi 2010). Following the methodology, the chapter is divided into three sections. First, Albanian migration and migrants along with household characteristics are described; then the impact of the global economic crisis on Albanian migrants and migration, based on quantitative and qualitative data, is presented; finally, the impact on remittances and return migration is discussed.

The study is based on the analysis of both primary and secondary data. It includes a review of the existing literature and qualitative and quantitative methods (cross-referenced). The qualitative and quantitative methods include six focus group discussions with migrants, 39 semistructured interviews with migrants, and a quantitative socioeconomic survey with 2,474 migrants. Each of these techniques was used to verify the results of the others.

The survey methodology was adapted from the previous research carried out by CESS and IASCI in 2008–09 (de Zwager, Gressmann, and Gedeshi 2010). This survey of 2,202 migrants provides the baseline data against which the findings from the current survey are measured.

The migrant survey was carried out around late December 2009 and early January 2010. During this period a large number of Albanian migrants, mainly from Greece, Italy, and other European countries, return to Albania to celebrate traditional winter festivities. The survey was carried out at the main ports of entry to Albania. The number of interviews conducted at the border points with Greece and Durres Port reflect the estimated number of Albanian migrants in Greece and Italy, respectively. At Tirana International Airport, the survey targeted migrants residing in other countries of Europe.

The questionnaire contained 54 questions designed to elicit quantitative responses only. We have collected information on sociodemographic characteristics of migrant households, their financial characteristics (that is, incomes, expenditures, savings, investments, and remittances), the impact of the global economic crisis on the households, as well as household strategies for coping with its consequences.

The respondents were selected on the basis of having lived more than a year abroad, being more than 18 years old at the time of the interview, and having migrated for employment purposes.

Teams of trained and experienced CESS interviewers carried out the questionnaire survey. The interviewers surveyed the migrants while they were waiting in the customs area of the ports of entry. This ensured anonymity and a low refusal rate of less than 1 percent. The interview method was face-to-face, and supervisors monitored the process.

The survey has certain limitations of which the reader should be aware. It excludes short-term migrants, irregular migrants, and those who, because of difficult economic or other circumstances, might not have chosen to visit their home country at that time.

We have also conducted qualitative interviews in focus groups using semistructured questionnaires about the impact of the economic crisis on the migrant households as well as their coping mechanisms. Focus group participants were long-term migrants of different ages, education, socioeconomic status, and occupations. Seven to 12 migrants participated in each focus group. Various quotations have been included in this report, all with fictitious names.

All data presented in the following pages were gained under the current survey and compared against the available baseline data stipulated above, unless specifically mentioned and sourced otherwise.

Socioeconomic Characteristics of Albanian Migrants

During the last two decades, mass migration has been at the very core of the political, economic, and social changes occurring in Albania (UNDP 2006). At the end of 2009, about 1.2 million people or more than 25 percent of the Albanian population and more than 35 percent of the labor force were estimated to be living abroad, mainly in Greece and Italy (de Zwager, Gressmann, and Gedeshi 2010). Smaller numbers were spread throughout different European countries as well as Australia, Canada, and the United States. Thus, Albania became a country *on the move,* as claimed by Carletto and others

(2006), or a "sort of laboratory for studying new migratory processes," if we take King's description (2005).

Overall, nearly 65 percent of surveyed migrants migrated in the decade before 2000. After 2000 the flux of migration from Albania has declined. This decline can be attributed, on the one hand, to improvements in the Albanian economy. For instance, from 2000 to 2008, the real average annual gross domestic product (GDP) growth rate was about 6 percent (World Bank 2010b). Another factor was perhaps tighter migration controls, particularly in Greece and Italy.

Studies show that economic factors such as difficult living conditions, unemployment, and low salaries represented more than three-fourths of motives to migrate (ETF 2008). Unemployment in Albania was 26 percent in 1992 and 22.6 percent according to the census of 2001 (INSTAT 2002). Real wages dropped drastically in the early and late 1990s. Almost 26 percent of the population lived below the poverty line, and 4.7 percent lived in extreme poverty (World Bank 2003). At the end of the 1990s, 149,000 households or about 20 percent of the country's households were dependent on "economic aid" provided by the state. Consequently, migration was primarily economic and best defined as a form of "survival migration" (Barjaba 2002). However, along with difficult economic conditions, other factors such as political uncertainty and violence, personal freedom, education, and professional career development played a role too (Vullnetari 2007).

Amnesties and other forms of status regularization efforts in Greece and Italy, mainly during the 1995–2002 period, helped Albanians settle in these countries (Vullnetari 2007). The survey data show that 96 percent of married Albanian migrants in Italy and 90 percent of those in Greece have realized family reunification. Almost 1.8 persons, usually husband and wife, work and secure the household income. Children go to school, and financing their education constitutes one of the main objectives for saving for many migrant families. Most of the migrants interviewed speak "fluent" (42 percent) or "well" (52 percent) the language of their host country, showing a high level of integration. Meanwhile, 36 percent of migrants residing in Germany, Italy, and the United Kingdom have received language courses and/or professional training. Some have enrolled at universities. Thus, Albanians abroad have gradually improved their socioeconomic status (ETF 2008).

According to the migrant survey the main sectors of employment for Albanians abroad are construction (35 percent), services (21 percent), manufacturing and industry (17 percent), domestic help (15 percent), and agriculture (10 percent). Job sector division exists by gender among the migrants. Males mainly work in construction (49 percent), services (19 percent), and manufacturing and industry (18 percent). Females work mainly as domestic help (53 percent), as well as in services (26 percent) and manufacturing and industry (13 percent). Distinctions exist among sectors of employment for those who migrate to Germany, Greece, Italy, and the United Kingdom. Compared with Greece, a larger percentage of migrants in Italy and other European Union (EU) countries work in manufacturing and services (such as in the United Kingdom), and a lower percentage works in agriculture.

A distinctive feature is that 56 percent of the migrants in Italy and 59 percent of those in Germany and the United Kingdom say that they work as qualified workers, against 43 percent in Greece. This can be largely explained by the labor needs of the host country economy. Greece, for instance, has had a higher demand for unqualified work in construction, agriculture, and services (Lyberaki and Lambrianidis 2004). Albanian entrepreneurs in host countries followed the same pattern: We found that about 8 percent of Albanian migrants have created businesses in their host country, and these businesses were mainly in construction (43 percent) and services (29 percent) (figure 19.1).

FIGURE 19.1 Employment Sectors of Albanian Migrants in Host Countries, 2009–10

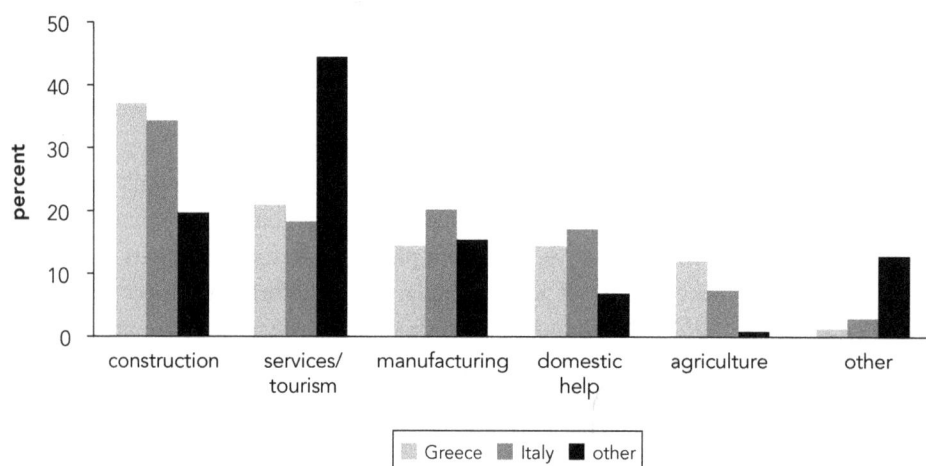

Source: CESS Migrant Questionnaire, 2009–10.

The Impact of the Global Economic Crisis on Albanian Migrant Households

Greece and Italy, the two primary countries of destination for Albanian migration, have been severely affected by the global economic crisis. GDP in Italy dropped by −1.3 percent in 2008 and by −5.0 percent in 2009, and unemployment reached 8.4 percent in December 2009 and 8.6 percent in December 2010 (Eurostat 2011). Greece saw an average annual increase of 4 percent of GDP during the first five years of the new millennium, but this dropped to −2.0 percent in 2009 and a further −4.2 percent in 2010 (Eurostat 2011) (figure 19.2). This signaled Greece's entry into its deepest and most severe recession of the last 30 years (Bastian 2010). Unemployment rose from 8.8 percent in February 2009 to 10.2 percent in December 2009, 12.2 percent in June 2010, and 12.9 percent in September 2010 (Eurostat 2011). Since then the impact of the crisis on Greece has only deepened, in large part because of the sovereign debt

FIGURE 19.2 GDP Growth and Unemployment Rates in Greece and Italy, 1998–2012

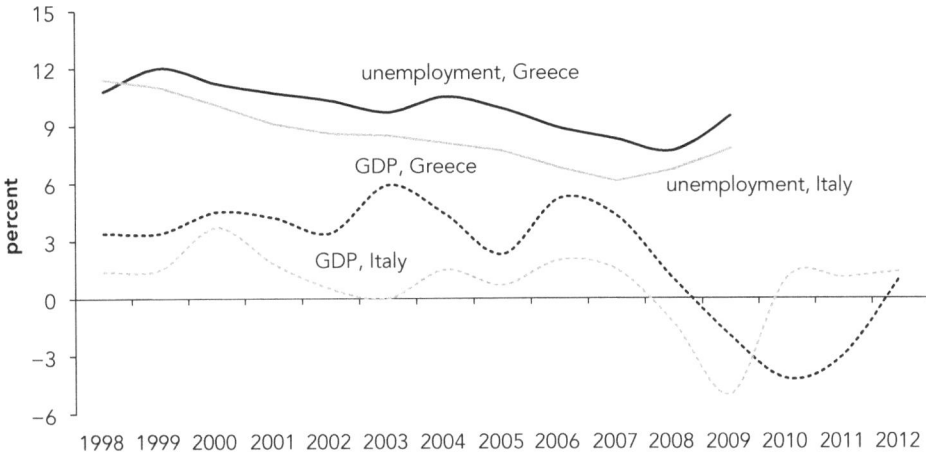

Source: Eurostat 2011.

crisis and commensurate severe cutbacks in public spending (10 percent of the state budget in 2010).

In Albania, official data from the end of 2008 showed GDP growth rates slowing from quarter to quarter. In 2009 official GDP growth for Albania was 2.5 percent versus 7.5 percent for the same period in 2008 (World Bank 2010b).

FIGURE 19.3 Impact of Economic Crisis on Albanian Households in Migration in 2009

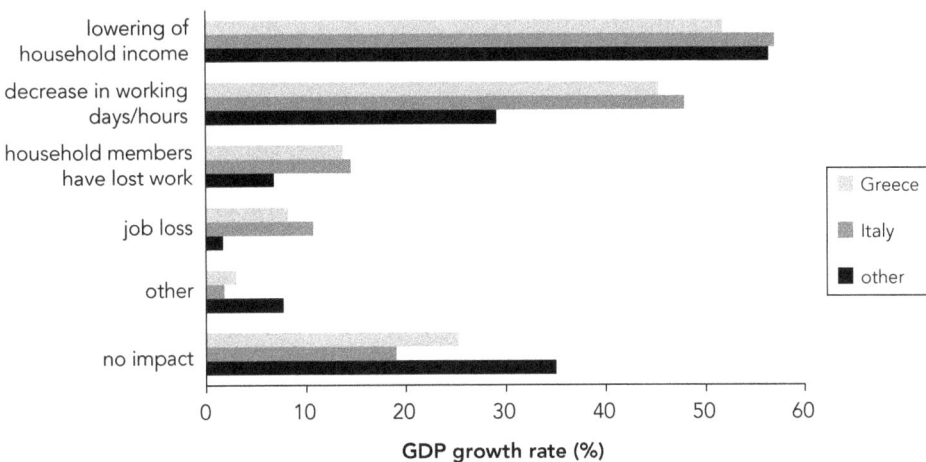

Source: CESS Migrant Questionnaire, 2009–10.

The impact of the global economic crisis on Albania is further seen in the deterioration of other key indicators of economic activity. Foreign debt in 2009 reached 24.3 percent of GDP, from 18.4 percent in 2008 (World Bank 2010b). Exports, three-quarters of which go to the EU area, dropped in 2009 because of reduced demand there. Remittances from migration, which officially dropped for the first time in 2008 by 12 percent, fell a further 6.5 percent in 2009 and 4.6 percent in the first nine months of 2010 (Bank of Albania 2010). In 2009 remittances dropped to 10.8 percent of GDP from 13.5 percent in 2007.

Our respondents reported that the most felt effects of the economic downturn on migrant households were "decrease in working days or working hours" (46 percent), "loss of employment by a member of the family" (14 percent), "personal loss of employment" (9 percent), and "increase in prices and cost of living" (2.2 percent). Taken together, these factors reflect a decrease in household income shared by 54 percent of interviewed migrants. In contrast, only 23 percent of respondents felt that by the time of the interview the effects of the economic crisis had not affected their households.

Unemployment

In most EU countries, especially in those most affected by the current economic crisis, unemployment among migrants is more prevalent than that of the local population (UNDP 2010). Migrants are often "last hired, first fired" and have the socioeconomic profile and demographic characteristic of employees who are most vulnerable to unemployment and underemployment during an economic crisis (Fix and others 2009). They commonly work in cyclical and seasonal sectors of the economy such as construction, manufacturing, hotels, and restaurants. They are often younger, less qualified, and less educated than the local population and are more likely to work in informal sectors or without regular work contracts (IOM 2010).

Empirical data from the present survey show that the average unemployment level of Albanian migrants at the end of 2009 was 9 percent, or slightly higher than the general average within the two primary host countries. The level of unemployment was higher among Albanian migrants in Italy (11 percent) than those in Greece (8 percent). On the other hand, the data also indicate that the unemployment level was rapidly increasing in Greece during the last months of 2009. This reflects the deepening economic crisis in that country. As can be seen in figure 18.4, almost 75 percent of unemployed Albanian migrants in Greece lost their employment during the last four months of 2009, whereas in Italy "only" 30 percent of Albanians lost their jobs in the same period (figure 19.4).

In addition, 14 percent of respondents reported "one or more members of their household in migration" losing their place of employment over the previous year. As a result, and at the end of 2009, it is possible to estimate that about 22.5 percent of Albanian migrant households had at least one unemployed member who had been employed the year before.

FIGURE 19.4 Months of Unemployment for Albanian Migrants in Greece and Italy, 2009

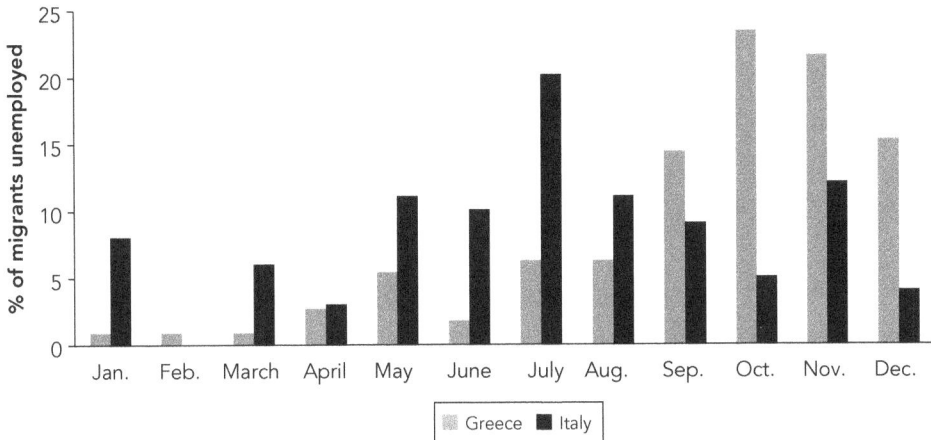

Source: CESS Migrant Questionnaire, 2009–10.

Rising unemployment has been felt more strongly among the young (up to 24 years old) and those over 50, skilled migrants in Greece and unskilled ones in Italy, as well as more recent migrants compared with others. Arben, a young migrant working in Italy explains: "The economic crisis has affected most of the migrants that I know. However, those that have migrated for a long time have more acquaintances and can find work easier. Regarding recent migrants, finding a job is very hard for them."

Almost every sector in which large numbers of Albanian migrants work has seen a rise in unemployment to some degree, but the most affected sectors are domestic help and manufacturing, especially those industries producing for export. Women predominately work in these two sectors, so this partly explains the higher level of unemployment among them (16 percent) compared with men (6 percent).

In domestic help, Albanian female migrants are more likely to be involved in maintaining the houses of middle-class employers and taking care of the elderly (rather than babysitting or au pairing) (Catherine 2007). As a consequence of the economic crisis, many families no longer employ migrants to clean their houses. This is explained by Mimoza, a migrant in Greece, when she says: "The crisis is felt primarily through the availability of work; and at the moment Greeks are not offering employment to the same degree. They themselves have started to save and do not take servants for their houses. ... Due to the economic crisis Greek families have reduced employment of migrant women for cleaning their houses." On the other hand, those Albanian migrant women employed to take care of the elderly seem to be less vulnerable to unemployment, perhaps because they are not easily replaced (King and Vullnetari 2010).

The empirical data show that only 57 percent of unemployed Albanian migrants have received unemployment benefits in Greece and Italy. The numbers on benefit is lower in Greece (53 percent) where the informal sector is relatively larger (Triandafyllidou and Lazarescu 2009) than in Italy (61 percent) (figure 19.5). Further, unemployment benefit coverage is lower for women (50 percent), especially in Greece where they work in housekeeping or part time in services, mainly in hotels and restaurants (figure 19.6).

FIGURE 19.5 Rate of Unemployment of Albanian Migrants in Italy and Greece, by Sector, 2009–10

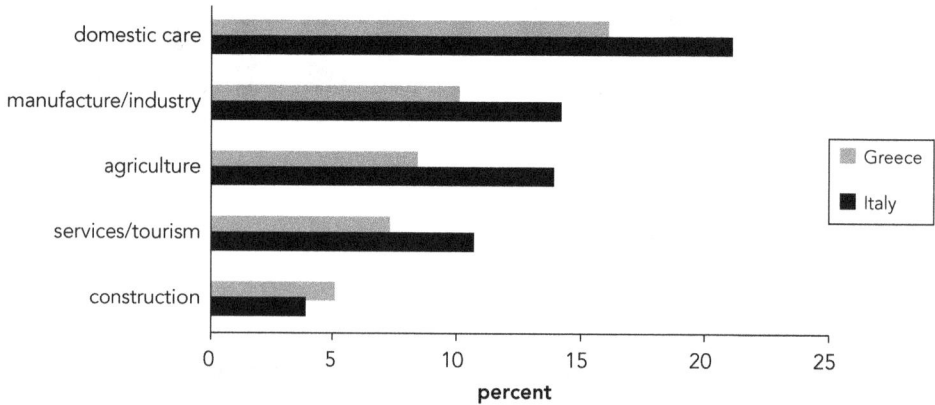

Source: CESS Migrant Questionnaire, 2009–10.

FIGURE 19.6 Unemployment Benefit–Receiving Migrants in Main Host Countries by Gender, 2009–10

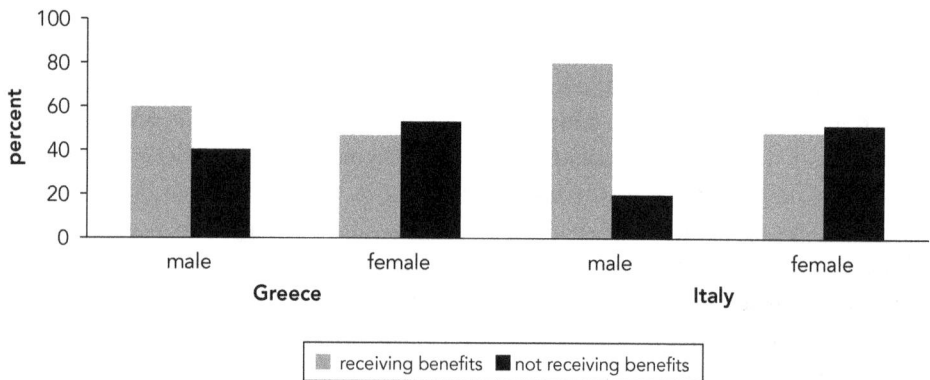

Source: CESS Migrant Questionnaire, 2009–10.

A large majority of unemployed migrants believe that they have "few chances" (63 percent) or that it is "impossible" (17 percent) to secure employment in the place of migration within the first six months of 2010. This percentage is significantly higher among female migrants than among males. This can be explained by the tight labor market and lack of real choices for women in the two primary host countries.

In many cases, an increase in unemployment within a given sector results in the displacement of the migrants to another sector, but with significantly lower incomes. This mobility is observed especially in the construction sector, which is severely affected by the economic crisis, and toward agriculture or other sectors. Official Greek statistics show that in 2007 the average value of a working day for males engaged in construction was €56, and in other sectors this was €36 (Triandafyllidou and Lazarescu 2009). Consequently, when displaced from one employment sector to another, the migrants' income lowers significantly.

Others move from higher to lower skilled jobs. This is the case with Luan, who said: "Until recently I worked in a small factory in Athens and received €1,200 per month. It closed down, and now I have to work as night watch in a trade magazine. The work does not correspond to my education and skills, and the salary is much lower."

Underemployment: In Working Days and Hours

Forty-six percent of migrants stated that one of the consequences of the economic crisis was a "shortage of working days or hours," which resulted in lower household incomes. According to the migrants, this reduction in working days and hours is experienced most in the agriculture sector (52 percent), construction (50 percent), and housekeeping (48 percent). It is somewhat less evident in Italy (48 percent) than in Greece (45 percent). It is worse for irregular migrants, that is, those who work in the informal sector or do casual jobs. Sandri, a migrant who every day goes to "Omonia Square" (the place where migrants find informal and casual work), as he calls it, says: "Before I used to work some days a week. Now, although the daily pay rate has been reduced, I am finding less and less work."

Many others have second jobs, a phenomenon that is widespread among migrants in Greece. Bashkim, a migrant for several years in a tourist area of Greece, tells of his experience:

> In the construction firm where I worked I was employed for six days a week and I was paid €50 a day. On Sunday, I worked only for myself and could earn more than €50 for the day. … However, I also did other jobs during the week such as painting, repairs, and so on. As a result, I could earn about €2,000 per month from all these sources. … Now I see no future and everything seems harder. My income is much lower.

Other migrants report that in conditions brought on by the economic crisis, the price of work per unit of production has been reduced, and thus their income has diminished. This was confirmed by Agim, a migrant who worked for years in the construction sector in Greece, where, he says:

Our incomes have shrunk considerably. Completing one cubic meter of concrete (standard measurement unit in construction) earned €50 before, but now the price has dropped to €30. ... Actually, we work more but earn less. ... There are other migrants that are unemployed and accept the jobs for lower payment.

The crisis has also worsened their economic and social status. The average salary of migrants in Greece—for the same job—is often lower than that of local hires. This difference is smaller in construction, but higher in other sectors. In 2007, for instance, the average salary of Albanian migrants was 85 percent of the average salary of equivalent Greek workers, whereas in other sectors this figure was much lower (Gropas and Triandafyllidou 2008). With the economic crisis, Triandafyllidou and Lazarescu (2009) state that this difference has not only increased, but migrants fearing unemployment can and do accept even lower salaries. Consequently, many entrepreneurs in conditions of increasing competition are more interested in using cheaper and more flexible workers (those who accept work without social insurance and regular contracts), who are often immigrants.

Diminishing Household Income and Savings

Household incomes declined as a result of the increases in unemployment, decreases in pay levels, reductions in working hours and days, and shifts from highly paid sectors to low-paid ones. Thus it contributed to the decline in migrant households' socioeconomic status. Fifty-two percent of migrant families in Greece stated that their household incomes decreased during 2009 because of the economic crisis. At the same time, everyday basic expenditures have increased as the prices of goods and services have gone up. Thus, financial well-being has worsened for 58 percent of migrants compared to a year earlier, and 10 percent say that it is "much worse" (table 19.1).

TABLE 19.1 Estimate of Financial Well-Being of Albanian Migrant Households Comparing 2008 and 2009

Comparison of well-being	Greece		Italy		Other		Average	
	Frequency	%	Frequency	%	Frequency	%	Frequency	%
Much better	9	0.7	2	0.2	0	0	11	0.4
Better	132	9.6	11	1.1	5	4.3	148	6.0
Same	346	25.1	233	23.9	40	34.5	619	25.1
Worse	823	59.7	554	56.9	64	55.2	1,441	58.4
Much worse	69	5.0	173	17.8	7	6.0	249	10.1
Total	1,379	100.0	973	100.0	116	100.0	2,468	100.0

Source: CESS Migrant Questionnaire, 2009–10.

In January 2009, de Zwager, Gressmann, and Gedeshi (2010) carried out a survey with 2,202 migrants visiting Albania for their Christmas and New Year holidays. The survey contained detailed questions on the migrants' income, expenses, savings, and remittances. A comparison of the results of the two surveys[1] shows that the average incomes of households of Albanian migrants in Greece diminished by about 11 percent from 2008 to 2009—or from €2,123 per household to €1,897—while the household budget decreased by an average of 4.1 percent (table 19.2).

TABLE 19.2 Comparison of Incomes, Expenses, and Savings of Migrant Households in Greece in 2008 and 2009

	2008 (euros)	2009 (euros)	Difference (%)
Average monthly household income	2,123	1,897	−10.7
Average monthly household expenditure	1,365	1,310	−4.1
Average monthly household savings	758	587	−22.6
Average yearly household savings	9,096	7,044	−22.6

Source: CESS Migrant Questionnaire, 2009–10; see also de Zwager, Gressmann, and Gedeshi 2010.

This negative trend is reflected in a significant decrease in the financial savings of the Albanian migrant households. When comparing 2009 with 2008, the average annual savings of Albanian migrant households—one of the major objectives of migration—effectively decreased from €10,176 to €8,988 per annum.

The survey data show that savings have reduced more in Italy, where 76 percent of migrant households report that they have saved less than a year ago, compared with Greece (66 percent) and other European countries (61 percent) (table 19.3).

The decline of average incomes and savings of migrant households in host countries has two direct impacts. First, it leads to a lower flow of remittances to Albania, and second, it affects the term of the migration cycle, by either shortening it or extending it.

TABLE 19.3 Savings Levels of Albanian Migrant Households in 2009

Savings level	Greece		Italy		Other		Average	
	Frequency	%	Frequency	%	Frequency	%	Frequency	%
Higher	107	7.7	6	0.6	9	7.7	122	4.9
Same	345	25.0	214	21.9	37	31.6	596	24.1
Lower	914	66.1	740	75.9	71	60.7	1,725	69.7
Do not know	16	1.2	15	1.5	0	0.0	31	1.3
Total	1,382	100.0	975	100.0	117	100.0	2,474	100.0

Source: CESS Migrant Questionnaire, 2009–10.

Remittances Dynamics

The yearly flow of remittances sent to Albania through formal and informal channels has increased since 1990 and parallels the rising number of migrants. According to Central Bank of Albania estimates, remittances by Albanian migrants reached $1,304.5 million by 2007, rising from $150 million in 1992 (increasing by 870 percent over 15 years).

After 1990, the value of remittances ranged between 10 and 22 percent of Albania's GDP (almost the size of an economic sector) and were higher than exports, net foreign direct investments, and official development aid. These effectively covered almost half the trade deficit (World Bank 2010b), representing the main foreign financial source, and one of the main factors determining the *extroversion* of the Albanian economy (Ditter 2008; Samson 1996). At the microlevel, the most important role played by remittances relates to economic survival and poverty alleviation for many Albanian households. They represent one of the main factors in distinguishing between "poor" and "not-poor" households (de Soto and others 2002).

Remittances are used primarily to support basic daily needs (food, clothing, and the like) of receiving households and thereafter to improve living conditions (such as buying furniture or home equipment), and, last, to expand or build a new house. A part of remittances are also used to organize important household and social events (such as weddings, baptisms, or funerals), whereas a small component might be deposited in the bank system or, more likely, saved in cash at home (de Soto and others 2002; de Zwager and others 2005; de Zwager, Gressmann, and Gedeshi 2010; Gedeshi 2002; Vullnetari 2007). Only small parts of remittances are used to invest in economic activities,[2] mainly in microenterprises within the service sector (de Zwager, Gressmann, and Gedeshi 2010). On a larger scale, remittances are mostly used for the import of consumer goods and "nonproductive" investment, such as housing. Consequently, remittances have improved the living conditions of many families in Albania but have had a limited role in sustainable development or job creation.

It is expected that remittance flows to Albania, despite a current steady increase, would decline in the medium term (Civici, Gedeshi, and Shehi 1999; de Zwager and others 2005; Gedeshi 2002; Gedeshi and Mara 2003). This prognosis was based on effects associated with the "maturation of the Albanian migration cycle." Nikas and King (2005) warned that an economic crisis in Greece, one of the main destinations of Albanian migration, would lead to a rapid decrease in remittance volumes and thereby have negative consequences for the Albanian economy.

Central Bank of Albania data indicate that the pace of remitting slowed during the second half of the previous decade, declining sharply in 2008. The Central Bank of Albania (2010) estimated that remittances fell to €833 million in 2008 (or €119 million less than 2007) and to €782 million in 2009, and this tendency continued during 2010.

Remittances in 2009–10

We have found that 61 percent of Albanian remittance-sending migrant households reported remitting less in 2009 compared with 2008. In 2009 this drop was significantly larger among Albanian migrants in Italy, where 73 percent have sent less remittances compared with those in Greece (54 percent; see table 19.4).

TABLE 19.4 Comparison of Estimates of Household Remittance Levels to Albania 2008–09

percent

Country	More	Less	Same	Do not know
Greece	13.3	54.0	22.3	10.3
Italy	2.1	73.0	19.6	5.3
Other	7.2	62.9	22.7	7.2
Average	9.1	61.1	21.4	8.4

Source: CESS Migrant Questionnaire, 2009–10.

Within the context of the structural discussion above, two obvious factors directly influence the volume of remittances sent to Albania: The first is the actual number of households that send remittances, and the second is the amount these households send.

Comparison of the results of the current survey and the previous survey (de Zwager, Gressmann, and Gedeshi 2010) shows that the number of remittance-sending households has decreased by 11 percent and the average value of remittances has decreased by about 4 percent. The decline was much bigger for Albanian immigrants in Italy (table 19.5).

TABLE 19.5 Comparison of Migrant Household Remittances in 2008–09

Country	Percentage of households remitting		Average amount of remittance sent per household (euros)	
	2008	2009	2008	2009
Greece	79.3	72.9	2,089	2,095
Italy	76.6	57.4	2,009	1,710
Other	70.5	62.4	3,548	4,610
Average	77.5	66.3	2,149	2,074

Source: CESS Migrant Questionnaire, 2009–10; de Zwager and others 2010.

Comparison of the data from the two surveys indicates a decline of about €117 million in 2009 compared with 2008.[3] Even when sample differences are corrected between the two household surveys, an estimated €109 million drop in remittance values, or about 16 percent, can be estimated for 2009. Thus the decline in remittances continues.

The Central Bank of Albania estimates that, during the first nine months of 2010, total remittances from Albanian migration shrank by a further 4.6 percent because of the rapidly deepening economic crisis in Greece and the structural reasons introduced above.

As can be seen from table 19.6 many migrants expected such a drop, with 18 percent of the migrants interviewed (but almost 26 percent of those from Greece) forecasting that they would be remitting less in 2010. In addition, about 59 percent of surveyed migrants reported that they "did not know" the future value of their remittances. Nearly 71 percent of migrants in Italy could not predict their remittance intentions in 2010. This can in large part be explained by the high level of insecurity caused by the economic crisis in Italy at the time of the survey.

TABLE 19.6 Migrant Household Remittance Amounts Forecasted for 2009–10

percent

Country	More	Less	Same	Do not know
Greece	7.3	25.8	17.1	49.7
Italy	11.7	9.4	8.0	70.9
Other	25.0	7.8	8.6	58.6
Average	10.0	18.3	13.0	58.7

Source: CESS Migrant Questionnaire, 2009–10.

Albanian Return Migration in Response to the Economic Downturn

During the survey, migrants were specifically asked to select and rate the three most important strategies for coping with the impact of the economic crisis on their households in their host country (table 19.7). A large number of respondents selected either "reducing household expenditures in the host country" or "finding a second job or working overtime" as their primary strategy. Many respondents indicated "finding a second job or working overtime" and "use of savings until they find another job" as their secondary strategies. Finally, a number of respondents stated that they would be "reducing remittances" and returning to Albania as alternative strategies to cope with the crisis.

A smaller number of respondents to the survey favored "bringing a part of their families to Albania" should the crisis continue to have a negative impact on their households. The objective of this strategy is to reduce daily expenditures in the host country (for instance, by living in smaller flats or dividing costs with two or three friends).

TABLE 19.7 Planned Strategies for Managing the Effects of the Economic Crisis, While in the Country of Migration

Possible strategy	Most important	Second most important	Third most important
Reducing household expenditures in host country	49.4	12.4	3.2
Finding a second job or working overtime	17.7	28.3	3.8
Using savings for living expenses until finding a new job	3.2	14.6	14.8
Reducing remittances sent to family, parents, or relatives in Albania	2.0	9.0	13.7
Return to Albania by part of the household (children or parents)	0.9	1.1	4.1
Return to Albania (whole household)	2.8	1.9	11.8
Other	0.2	0.0	0.2

Source: CESS Migrant Questionnaire, 2009–10 ; see also de Zwager, Gressmann, and Gedeshi 2010.

Despite the fact that return of the "complete household" to Albania is not a favored option, anecdotal evidence shows that a low level of return migration might have taken place as a result of the economic crisis. This, of course, merits further research.

Who Will Return to Albania?

Albanian migrants in Greece are more likely to consider return migration compared with those in Italy or other countries. Most migrants considering this option rate their financial positions as "bad" or "very bad." Ana, a migrant in Italy, explains:

> Our family was not affected by the crisis because neither me nor my husband lost our jobs. … However, most of the Albanian families I know are going through a deep economic crisis. … In the family of a friend of mine, the husband and the two sons became unemployed. They survive on the income of my friend (the wife/mother) who works in house cleaning and by the unemployment insurance payment received by one of her sons. … I know of migrants that started to ask their families in Albania for money. For instance, last year, the family of a friend of mine, was in such a difficult economic situation due to unemployment that they started to take debts. … They have still to pay for their house credit to the bank. … The family of her sister in Albania helped them by sending them money.

As shown in figure 19.7, the majority of migrants considering return as an option will postpone this eventuality for as long as possible. About 65 percent of migrants in Greece considered return happening within the year (such as during 2010), and 26 percent say that this can happen within the first six months. This "wait and see" attitude makes it difficult to predict how migrants might act in the future. Clearly it will be dependent on environmental factors that will shape the return migration prospects. The length and depth of the crisis and its impact on sectors in which Albanian migrants are employed

FIGURE 19.7 Projected Time to Return Home of Respondents Who Are Considering This Option, 2009–10

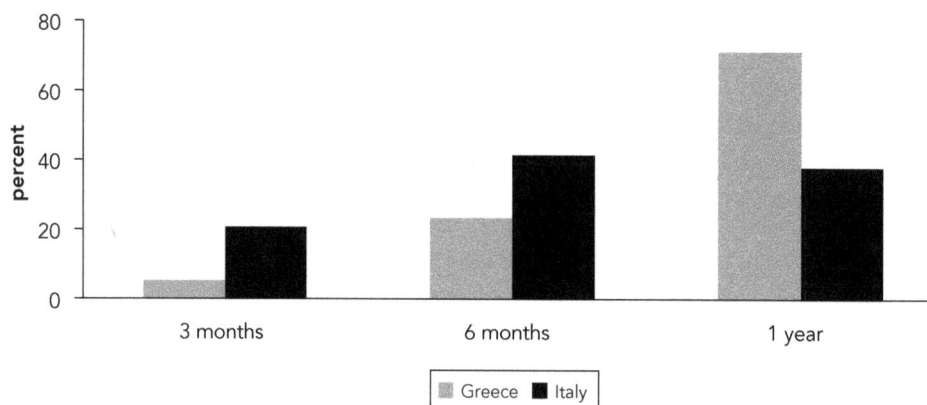

Source: CESS Migrant Questionnaire, 2009–10.
Note: n = 396 respondents.

will be important. The corollary factor is the concurrent economic and social situation in Albania, representing the return environment faced by migrants. Should the socio-economic situation in Albania deteriorate—in part because of the global economic crisis—migrants are less likely to return.

Repeated quantitative and qualitative surveys by the authors, and notwithstanding the impact of the economic crisis discussed above, show that the majority of Albanian migrants have an existing intention of returning to their homeland, but only after they have reached their migration objective (usually a savings goal) and thereby successfully concluding their migration cycle. This group of potential returnees, however, might be influenced to move their return forward because of the effects of the economic crisis on their personal situation. Some members of this group of migrants may choose to hasten their return if the effects of the economic crisis disturb their migration-related savings objectives. Erion, who intends to remain in migration for five more years in order to save to invest in Albania, personifies this common behavior: "However, if the crisis deepens and unemployment rises, we can also return next year ... We cannot stay unemployed and consume our savings."

Consequences for Albanian Migration and Economic Trends

An overall impact has been a decrease in the flow of migration, mainly because of high unemployment rates, a lack of opportunities, and restrictive policies on migrant workers pursued by host countries.

In the midterm an impact is observed in the reaching of migration objectives, particularly savings, which can lead to the restructuring of migration cycles. Saving behaviors of migrants are particularly interesting to study, because they constitute one of the major objectives of the migration experience itself (de Zwager, Gressmann, and Gedeshi 2010). The average annual savings of Albanian migrant households has effectively decreased by 12 percent between 2008 and 2009. This delay in achieving primary savings objectives affects the term of the migration cycle—that is, it extends it.

As noted, it is anticipated that the ongoing economic crisis in Greece will result in both a further reduction in the number of households remitting as well as lowering the average value of transfers of the remaining remitters. Assuming that the response of Albanian migrants in Greece was the same in 2010 as that of the migrants in Italy in 2009, the decrease of remittances will have been significant. For instance, a 25 percent decrease of remitting households, combined with a decrease of 15 percent of the average value of the remittances, would result—with other factors remaining constant—in a drop of about €110–112 million in overall remittance value.

When considering the likelihood of the above remittance scenario, two additional factors need to be taken into account. First, because of a number of migration-related factors, a lower number of migrants in Greece have realized family reunification to date, when compared with Albanian migrants in Italy. Second, a significant number of migrants in Greece originate from the eastern part of the country and from rural areas, that is, where poverty levels are higher. In these conditions, Albanian migrants in Greece presumably have a higher obligation to remit to keep supporting their families, even when their incomes and savings fall. In addition, it is important to note that according to repeated surveys (de Zwager, Gressmann, and Gedeshi 2010), remittances actually represent a relatively small part of the overall migrant household budget in Greece (about 9 percent).

Remittances constitute an important driver of Albania's domestic demand. Further and continued decreases in the flux of remittances would lower the standard of living for many households, cause serious hardship for many, and negatively influence some macroeconomic indicators. Econometric estimates by the World Bank (2010b) suggest that for the overall economy (excluding agriculture), a 10 percent decline in remittances would lead to a 3.6 percent reduction in domestic demand, as measured by the index of sales. Key contributors to Albania's GDP and most affected sectors are construction, services, and food. It is believed that declining inflows from workers abroad has resulted in sharp contractions, evidenced in Albania's construction sector over the previous years.

It is estimated that as much as 4 percent of poverty reduction has been lost because of the effects of the crisis in Albania (World Bank 2011b). This effectively stalled an accelerating decline in poverty experienced over the preceding decade, even though the country was one of the least affected by the crisis. In fact, Albania's GDP growth remained positive throughout the period of the crisis.

According to the survey and following anecdotal experience, no massive return to Albania is likely or evidenced. Nonetheless, we can draw some scenarios regarding the possible consequences of the return of migrants.

The first is that returning migrants can put further pressure on already high and increasing unemployment rates in Albania. At the end of 2010, INSTAT estimated unemployment at about 13 percent, up from 12.7 percent at the end of 2008. According to the survey, 47 percent of those migrants who might decide to return as a direct consequence of the economic crisis would seek employment in Albania. Of these, 28 percent wish to work in their profession within the private sector, 10 percent in the public sector, and 62 percent will "work at whatever job is offered to them."

A second scenario—perhaps more optimistic—is related to the transfer of accumulated savings and to the creation of new working places by the migrants themselves, should they be prepared and wish to invest their financial, human, and social capitals in Albania. Previous experience in Albania shows that returned migrants create small enterprises, mainly in the service sector (ETF 2008; Kilic and others 2007; Lyberaki and Lambrianidis 2004; World Bank 2007a). Confirming this trend, data from the survey show that 53 percent of migrants who wish to invest their savings intend to do so mainly in small commerce (47 percent), agriculture (15 percent), and construction (11 percent).

A third possible scenario is where a part of the family (parents, children, or women) returns to Albania, which might then be accompanied by an increase of inward remittances to support the resulting increase in daily household expenses in Albania.

Conclusions

In this chapter we argue that the economic global crisis and its negative consequences in Albania can be seen as an impetus and opportunity to implement new reforms and policies. In a recent publication (de Zwager, Gressmann, and Gedeshi 2010), it was found that financial remittances are only a small part of the wealth produced during the past two decades of Albanian migration. For instance, the authors conclude that the yearly and accumulating savings of the Albanian migrants are almost five times higher than remittances over the same period. Further, continued high voluntary return intentions (49 percent) among Albanians, and the accompanying financial, human, and social capital they would bring to Albania, can represent an untapped dynamic for economic and social development in Albania. As always, this potential opportunity is founded on the precondition that the social, economic, and institutional environment exists in Albania so that migrants are attracted to return and effectively use their substantial accumulated wealth.

Notes

1. Both surveys use the same methodologies.
2. Twelve percent according to the ALSMS 2002 and 11.8 percent according to 2007 ETF study (see de Zwager, Gressmann, and Gedeshi 2010).
3. This number is much higher than that estimated by the Central Bank of Albania and must be carefully interpreted.

Chapter 20

The Impact of the Global Financial Crisis on Migration to and Remittance Flows from Spain

MARTA ROIG AND JOAQUÍN RECAÑO-VALVERDE

SPAIN, A COUNTRY OF EMIGRATION for decades, has rapidly become one of the world's main destination countries of immigration. In January 2010, there were 6.6 million foreign-born persons in Spain, according to the population register; they represented 14 percent of the total population. Right before the economic crisis hit, in 2007, migrants living in Spain sent nearly €8.5 billion back to their home countries,[1] making Spain the fifth largest remittance-sending country in the world in absolute terms, after the United States, Saudi Arabia, the Russian Federation, and Switzerland (Ratha and Xu 2008).

This chapter describes migration flows to Spain and remittance outflows from Spain during the economic crisis. It also explores the influence of recent migration and labor market trends in the different responses to the crisis observed in remittance flows to the main receiving countries, namely, Bolivia, Colombia, Ecuador, Morocco, and Romania.[2]

Migration Flows and the Economic Crisis

The Spanish economy enjoyed a long period of growth from the early 1990s to 2008. Although some European countries entered recession in early 2008, Spain was able to

This study has been carried out as part of the projects "La movilidad geográfica de la población extranjera en España: factores sociodemográficos y territoriales" (SEJ2007-61662) and "Inflexión del ciclo económico y transformaciones de las migraciones en España" (CSO2010-19177) funded by the Plan Nacional de I+D+i of the Spanish Ministry of Science and Innovation.

maintain positive economic growth until the third quarter of 2008. Unemployment started to grow before that, in early 2008, with the number of persons unemployed increasing from 2.2 million in the first quarter of 2008 to 3.4 million in the fourth quarter of 2008 and peaking at 4.6 million, 21 percent of the labor force, in the second quarter of 2010.

Immigration grew rapidly during the years of prosperity and Spain became the main European destination country for immigration in 2004 (Eurostat 2011). The inflow of migrants reached a peak in 2007, with close to 1 million entries recorded in the population register for the full year, including a record inflow of 200,000 migrants from Romania. Immigration started to decline in the second quarter of 2007 and continued to fall until the end of 2009, stabilizing at some 120,000 entries per quarter in 2010 (INE 2011a). In other words, the observed decline in immigration preceded the economic crisis.

As shown in figure 20.1, such a decline was due mainly to a rapid decline in immigration from Romania, which joined the European Union on January 1, 2007, and in the number of entries from Bolivia. Inflows from the other main origin countries, Colombia, Ecuador, and Morocco, continued growing until early 2008.

FIGURE 20.1 Inflow of Foreign-Born Persons by Country of Birth, 2004–09

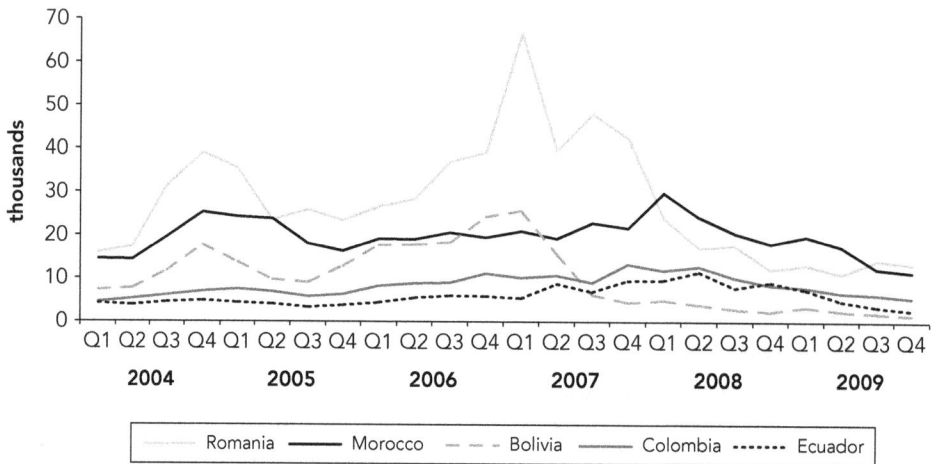

Source: Authors' calculations based on microdata from the population register ("Estadística de Variaciones Residenciales") for 2004–09 (INE Population Register).

As a result of these trends, the total number of foreign-born persons grew rapidly until 2008, passing from 1.5 million in 2000 to 4.4 million in 2005 and reaching more than 6 million in 2008, and it has grown slowly since then. In 2010, Colombia, Ecuador, Morocco, Romania, and the United Kingdom were the main countries of origin among the 6.6 million foreign-born, as shown in figure 20.2. The share of migrants from Latin America increased from 25 percent in 2000 to 41 percent in 2004 and fell to 36 percent

FIGURE 20.2 Foreign-Born Population by Country of Birth (Selected Groups Only), 2000–10

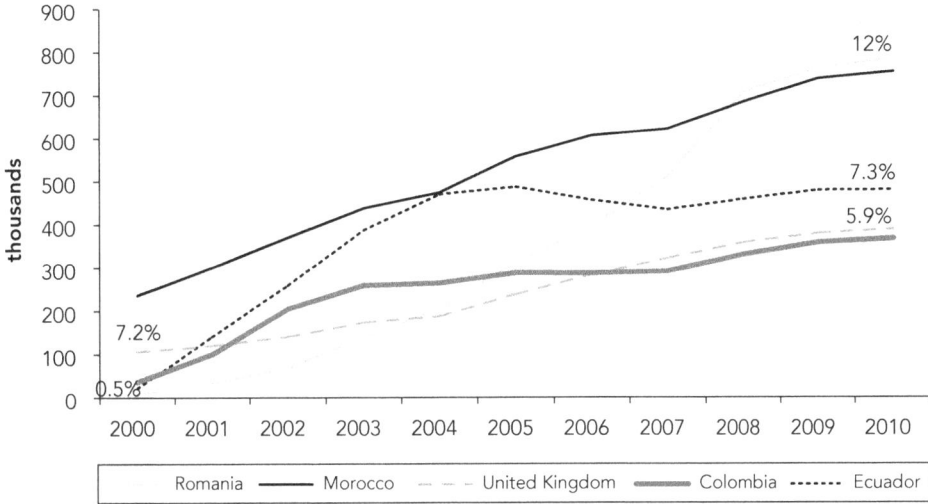

Source: INE Population Register.

Note: The figures displayed for Ecuador, Romania, and the United Kingdom are the percentage of migrants from these countries compared to all migrants in 2000 and 2010.

in 2010, with the number of Ecuadorians even declining from 2005 to 2007. The number of Moroccan and other northern African migrants has increased steadily since the 1990s and up to 2010, whereas the number of Romanians and other Eastern European migrants (mainly from Bulgaria, Poland, and Ukraine) experienced dramatic growth from 2000 to 2008 and has continued growing, although at a slower pace, in 2009 and 2010.

Although a majority of immigrants (52.5 percent) are men, the composition of the foreign-born population by sex differs by group. Although females constitute the majority of immigrants from Bolivia (58 percent in 2010), Colombia (56 percent), and Ecuador (51 percent), they account for only 38 percent of immigrants from Morocco and 47 percent of immigrants from Romania.

Many of these migrants are in an irregular situation: Namely, the number of foreigners with a valid residence permit was 4.7 million in September 2010 (MTIN 2010), more than 1 million below the number of foreigners enumerated by the population register. The number of applications lodged in the latest regularization process, which ended on May 7, 2005, was close to 700,000, or 1.1 million if dependents are included (Sandell 2005).

Recent Changes in International Migration Policies

Migration trends and the composition of migration flows are greatly influenced by the migration policy framework. Based on Spain's first immigration law (*ley de extranjería*), approved in 1985, nationals of Latin America did not require a visa to enter the

Schengen area. However, starting in 1999, the European Union established the need for a Schengen visa for nationals of Cuba, the Dominican Republic, and Peru; later it required a Schengen visa for nationals of Colombia (since January 2002), Ecuador (August 2003), and Bolivia (April 2007) (MNAEC 2009). Each of these changes caused a significant increase in migration flows from the countries affected, in the months before the visa requirement went into effect, and a decline in the number of entries afterward. As shown in figure 20.1, migration from Bolivia peaked in the first quarter of 2007 and declined sharply after that.

Irregular migration has been an issue in Spain since immigration started to grow in the early 1990s. As a result, successive Spanish governments resorted to five exceptional regularization processes from 1991 to 2005. The wave of immigration observed from late 2004 to the first half of 2005 was partly motivated by the 2005 regularization campaign (Proceso de Normalización de Trabajadores Extranjeros 2005), which was the largest campaign carried out in Spain. In 2006 the Spanish government put in place a new procedure that allows undocumented migrants to obtain a temporary residence permit if they meet certain conditions, such as being registered where they live, being well established in their community, and having family members or a job in Spain.[3] With the approval of this new procedure, regularization becomes an individual and permanent process.

In response to the economic crisis, the Spanish government tightened provisions for family reunification in 2009, requiring a higher minimum income and stricter housing conditions from those aiming at bringing family members. The government has also launched a new voluntary return-assistance program. The program, approved in November 2008, offers legal migrants who are eligible for unemployment benefits free transportation to their country of origin. Eligible migrants receive 40 percent of their accumulated unemployment benefits before departure if they agree to surrender their work and residence permits and other Spanish documentation and must not return to Spain within three years of their departure. As of June 2009, the government had approved about 4,000 principal applicants for the return program (McCabe, Lin, and Tanaka 2009).

The Spanish government has strongly backed the European Pact on Immigration and Asylum launched by the government of France and endorsed by all heads of state of the European Union in 2008. The pact argues for a comprehensive, European Union–wide approach to legal immigration and supports the application of a single, simplified procedure to attract highly skilled migrants (the "Blue Card" proposal). It calls on member states to enhance cooperation for the selective repatriation of undocumented migrants, stresses the need for more effective border controls, and underscores the benefits of temporary (and circular) migration (Arango 2010).

Trends in Remittance Flows from Spain

Quarterly outflows of workers' remittances from Spain reached a maximum of €2.3 billion in the fourth quarter of 2007, right before the crisis hit, declined for the first time after a period of growth in 2008, to a low of €1.6 million by the first quarter of 2009, and have experienced a slow, erratic recovery after that, as shown in figure 20.3. The total outflows recorded increased by 4 percent between the first three quarters of 2009 and the first three quarters of 2010. In relative terms, remittances in 2010 were not at an all-time low. Quarterly remittance outflows relative to the migrant population hovered between €250 and €300 per capita until late 2005 (about €1,100 per year) as shown in figure 20.3, experienced a strong increase during 2006 and early 2007, and declined after that, fluctuating once again between €250 and €300, at current prices, from the first quarter of 2009 on.

FIGURE 20.3 Outflows of Remittances per Quarter, Total and per Foreign-Born Person, 2000–10

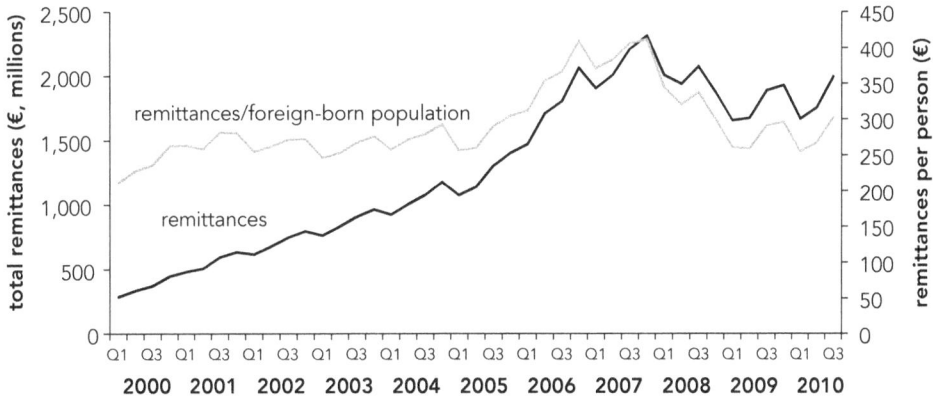

Source: Bank of Spain, Balance of Payments.

Remittance levels and trends differ by country of destination.[4] Bolivia, Colombia, and Ecuador, the three main remittance-receiving countries, saw dramatic increases before the crisis, with total remittances from Spain almost doubling from 2004 to 2007 in the cases of Colombia and Ecuador, and almost tripling in the case of Bolivia, as shown in figure 20.4. Remittances to Morocco and Romania almost multiplied by two as well. In 2007, remittances per migrant to Bolivia and Colombia amounted to over €5,000, to Ecuador were close to €3,000, and to Romania were €1,200, and migrants from Morocco sent just over €900. From 2007 to 2009, total remittance flows from Spain declined by more than 25 percent in all cases but that of Colombia, which saw remittances decline by only 9 percent during the period: from €1.43 billion in 2007 to €1.30 billion in 2009. Remittance flows to Morocco fell by over 40 percent, from €528 million in 2007 to €299 million in 2009.

According to data from the Central Bank of Colombia, remittances to Colombia from the United States, which declined by over 25 percent from 2008 to 2010, have experienced a larger drop than those from Spain, which fell by 13 percent during the

FIGURE 20.4 Outflows of Remittances by Country of Destination, 2004–09

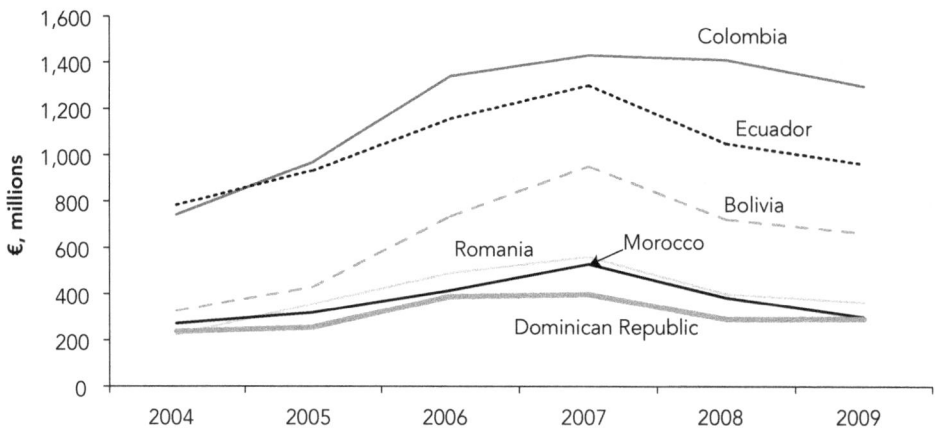

Source: Bank of Spain, Balance of Payments.

same period (BRC 2010). Whereas remittances from Spain increased by 17 percent between the first and third trimesters of 2010, those from the United States increased by 2 percent during the same period.

What Explains Differences in Remittance Flows from Spain by Country of Destination?

Family Reunification

The existing evidence shows that having a spouse and children outside the country of residence strongly influences the amount remitted (for example, Bollard and others 2009; Echazarra 2010). It is possible that, in response to the crisis, some groups of migrants opted to bring their family to Spain and reduce the amount remitted to their countries of origin. There are practically no official data on family reunification, because it is not a formal category among long-term residence permits. However, sudden changes in the composition of migration flows by age and sex, as recorded by the Continuous Population Register, may suggest a wave of family reunification (table 20.1).

Overall, the proportion of women in all migrant flows varies significantly by group. Women constitute 55 percent of all Latin American migrants who arrived during the period 2004–09; on average, although a large majority of Moroccan migrants are men, only 34 percent are women. The proportion of children is larger among Colombian and Ecuadorian migrants than among the other two major migrant groups. However, the crisis has not brought about significant changes in the composition of migration flows by sex or by age among these groups so far (from 2007 to 2009), suggesting that family reunification has not been a major response by migrants to the crisis.

TABLE 20.1 Proportion of Women and Children among Migrants Entering Spain by Country of Origin, 2004–09

Year	Bolivia	Colombia	Ecuador	Morocco	Romania
		Proportion of women			
2004	55.9	53.6	49.6	31.3	46.6
2005	57.8	53.0	48.8	33.8	48.3
2006	55.5	53.4	48.1	36.1	47.9
2007	54.3	51.6	47.9	34.4	43.3
2008	53.8	51.4	47.7	35.6	47.3
2009	51.3	51.9	48.1	37.8	48.9
		Proportion of children (0–14 years old)			
2004	11.5	21.7	13.0	13.1	9.4
2005	15.6	21.2	24.4	13.7	11.7
2006	14.6	18.0	23.9	13.5	13.1
2007	11.1	17.3	25.8	12.4	11.8
2008	9.3	15.2	23.1	11.9	13.9
2009	9.9	16.4	20.0	12.0	11.1

Source: Authors' calculations based on microdata from the population register ("Estadística de Variaciones Residenciales") for 2004–09 (INE Population Register).

It has also been suggested that the crisis actually triggered a return of family members to their countries of origin, as a strategy to reduce household expenditure and diversify risk (Lynch 2010). The reliability of data on migration outflows from Spain is questionable, because migrants often do not de-register before leaving. Data on the migrant stock by age show that, from 2008 to 2010, the number of children aged 0–14 declined significantly among Bolivian, Colombian, and Ecuadorian immigrants (by 21, 12, and 18 percent, respectively), while it continued to grow among Romanian and Moroccan immigrants (by 4 and 7 percent, respectively). The fact that Latin American immigrants sent dependents back home in larger numbers could explain why remittances to these countries remained higher than those sent to Romania or Morocco during the crisis, although it does not make clear why remittances to Colombia remained more stable than those sent to Bolivia or Ecuador.

Proportion of Migrant Women

Research conducted before the crisis indicates that migrant women remit more than migrant men, even though men constitute a majority of migrants as well as a majority of remitters (Moré and others 2008). In 2006 migrant women sent €4.2 million to their countries of origin, whereas migrant men remitted €2.6 million. Women remitted smaller amounts but did so more often than men. Additional research has shown that remittances sent by women from Spain to Colombia are more often delegated to health and education expenses than those sent by men (UN-INSTRAW and IOM 2008). A stronger presence of women among Latin American migrants may explain why Colombians and Ecuadorians remit more than other groups, but it does not make clear why remittances to Colombia have been more resilient to the crisis than those sent by all other major Latin American groups.

The Cost of Sending Remittances

The cost of sending remittances may also have affected how much migrants remitted before and during the crisis. In 2008 the average cost of sending remittances to Morocco (8.4 percent for an average remittance of €135) was higher than that of remitting to Colombia (6.8 percent), Ecuador (6.7 percent), or Romania (6.6 percent) (World Bank 2010d). However, remittance fees to Morocco declined significantly during the crisis, to reach 5.8 percent in the third quarter of 2010, whereas the cost of remitting to Colombia and Ecuador remained close to 6 percent. Yet the amount of remittances sent to Morocco dropped significantly whereas remittances to Colombia proved resilient to the crisis.

Remittance costs are not uniform across the country. Madrid, which is home to 50 of the 61 money-transfer companies registered in Spain, offers the lowest remitting costs in the country and, more generally, in Europe (Remesas 2009). Lower costs and better access to money-transfer agencies make it easier for immigrants in Madrid to remit regularly and more often than those living in other parts of Spain. A survey based on a sample of 1,071 foreign-born persons and 20 money-transfer agencies suggests that remittance flows from Madrid, which declined by 5.4 percent from 2008 to 2009, were more resilient at the onset of the crisis than those sent from the rest of Spain: On average, remittance outflows from Spain declined by 9.5 percent during the same period (Comunidad de Madrid 2010). In January 2010, 33 percent of Ecuadorian immigrants living in Spain resided in Madrid; so did about 25 percent of Bolivian, Colombian, and Romanian immigrants but only 12 percent of Moroccans. Thus, place of residence may have contributed to a lower propensity to remit among Moroccan migrants, but it does not explain why remittances sent by Colombian immigrants have been the most resilient.

The Colombian peso lost less value than other currencies during the first two years of the crisis. According to data by the Bank of Spain and the IMF on monthly exchange rates of the euro to selected currencies, the Colombian peso appreciated by 6 percent, on average, between 2007 and 2009, the Ecuadorian dollar appreciated by 1 percent, whereas the Bolivian boliviano depreciated by 9 percent, and the exchange rate of the Moroccan dirham remained practically constant (Bank of Spain 2011b). In addition, fluctuations in the exchange rate of the Colombian peso against the euro were less significant than those suffered by the boliviano or the dollar. This may have contributed to the stability of remittance flows to Colombia and may also make an eventual return to the home country more attractive. However, the Colombian peso depreciated by 16 percent against the euro from 2009 to 2010. The impact of this shock on remittance flows during 2010 remains to be seen.

Immigrants and the Labor Market

Some groups of migrants fared better than others in the labor market once the crisis hit. Unemployment has generally been higher among foreigners than among nationals, and the crisis has heightened the differences between groups. As shown in figure 20.5, although the unemployment rate increased from 7.6 percent in 2007 to 18.0 percent in 2010 among Spanish workers, it grew from 11.5 percent to 33.9 percent among foreigners during the same period.[5] The record-high unemployment rate observed among Moroccans (close to 50 percent in 2010) may explain why remittances to Morocco have declined faster than those sent by other groups. However, it does not explain why remittances to Colombia have been more stable, because unemployment levels and trends among Colombians are comparable to those observed among other major migrant groups.

FIGURE 20.5 Unemployment by Nationality, 2001–10

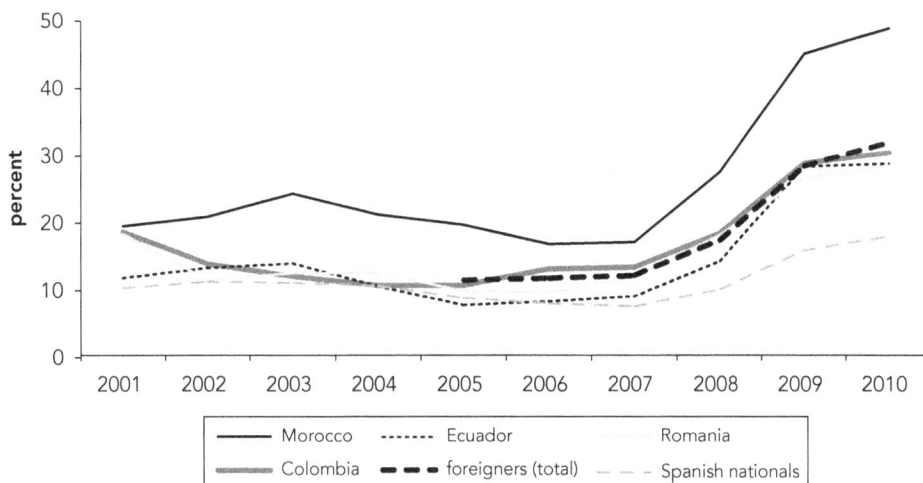

Source: Authors' calculations based on microdata from the Labour Force Surveys ("Encuesta de Población Activa") for 2001–10. Microdata available at http://www.ine.es/prodyser/micro_epa.htm.

It has been suggested that participation in the informal economy is keeping migrants afloat (for example, CCOO 2009). The size of the informal economy was estimated at 23 percent of Spain's gross domestic product in 2008, and migrants are overrepresented in the largest informal sectors, namely, construction and services. Could some groups of migrants have fared better than others in the informal economy during the crisis? Survey data on employment trends in the formal and informal sectors combined show that total employment fell the most in the construction sector (by 24 percent from the fourth quarter of 2008 to mid-2009 alone, and by 14 percent from mid-2009 to mid-2010) and significantly in the industrial sector, while it kept growing in the services sector for most of the period, declining by only 5 percent from late 2008 to mid-2009, and in agriculture.[6] Information on the distribution of foreigners by sector of the economy and occupation indicates that the share of migrants in the services sector is significantly higher among Latin Americans than among all other migrant groups: two-thirds of Latin American migrants, including close to 90 percent of Latin American women, worked in personal services, catering, security, and sales, on average, in 2005–10, with a high percentage of them in domestic services. The proportion of all other non-EU migrants working in services was 40 percent, on average, during the same period.[7]

According to recent labor market trends, migrant employment is recovering. During the second and third trimesters of 2010, immigrants gained more jobs (109,000) than natives (42,000), even though they constitute 17 percent of the labor force. Employment grew by 10 percent in the construction sector among migrants (while it declined for natives) and by 4 percent in services. Based on these trends, remittances should continue growing in the last quarter of 2010 and during 2011, although it is too soon to determine whether the recovery will be long lasting.

Conclusion

In conclusion, the inflow of migrants to Spain started to decline before the onset of the economic crisis. Political and policy changes—the entry of Romania into the European Union in January 2007 and the requirement of an entry visa for Bolivians starting in April 2007—are the main causes of the strong decline in immigration observed in 2007. Migration flows continued to decline, although at a slower pace, during the initial years of the crisis.

The propensity to remit is higher among Latin American migrants from the countries selected than among Moroccans or Romanians. In addition, remittances to Latin America, particularly Colombia, have also been more resilient to the recent economic shock. The impact of the crisis on various currencies and differences in unemployment trends among each group partly explain the different responses to the crisis observed in remittance flows to the countries selected. But other mechanisms may be at play. Although the higher participation of Latin American migrants in services jobs that have been less affected by the crisis may have kept these migrants afloat, even if they have subsisted mainly in the informal economy, we cannot discard the influence of different behaviors in the response of migrants to the crisis. It is possible, for instance, that remittances sent by women, who represent a majority of Latin American migrants, are more resilient than those sent by men. It is also possible that some groups of migrants,

Colombians in particular, may have sent their children back home and continued to send remittances despite increasing economic hardship in preparation for an eventual return. All in all, this initial overview based on aggregate-level data suggests the propensity of migrants to remit is not determined by macroeconomic factors only.

Notes

1. Equivalent to approximately $12.5 billion using end of 2007 nominal exchange rates. The World Bank estimates that outflows of remittances were higher, over $15 billion, in 2007 (see http://www.worldbank.org/prospects/migrationandremittances).

2. Data on remittance flows to the European Union (EU 15) are available only for the period 2005–07. In 2007, remittances to the EU 15 constituted only 9.4 percent of all remittances from Spain. Remittances to the United Kingdom (the main country of origin among the EU 15) were only 1.6 percent of the total.

3. The new procedure is called *arraigo*, which can be translated as being well established or having roots in the place of residence.

4. The Bank of Spain does not provide quarterly data on remittances by country of destination. The overview that follows is based on total annual flows.

5. The information provided by the Economically Active Population Survey (Encuesta de Población Activa) is available only by country of citizenship of workers in the sample.

6. Manpower, "El mercado de trabajo en los trimestres centrales de 2010 y el impacto de la crisis en las CCAA," Indice Laboral Manpower, No. 37, December 2010. The analysis is based on data from the Economically Active Population Survey.

7. Information on the distribution of foreigners by sector of the economy and occupation is available only by major regional group (Latin America and the Caribbean, European Union, other European countries, and rest of the world).

Annex

A: Total Inflow of Foreign-Born Persons, 2004–10

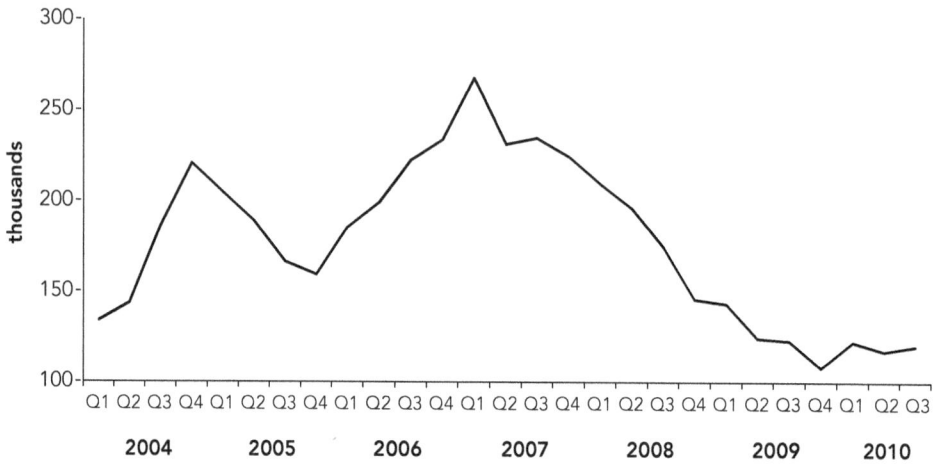

Source: INE, Microdata of Estadística de Variaciones Residenciales (2004–09), data available at http://www.ine.es/prodyser/micro_varires.htm. Authors' calculations. For 2010, flows based on population estimates by the National Statistics Institute, data available at http://www.ine.es/jaxi/menu.do?type=pcaxis&path=%2Ft20%2Fp259&file=ine base&L=.

B: Foreign Population by Country of Birth, Total Population and Percentage of Men, on January 1, 2010

Country of birth	Total	% male
TOTAL	5,747,734	52.50
Europe	2,679,456	52.00
European Union	2,459,180	52.70
Austria	9,450	48.30
Belgium	33,282	51.20
Bulgaria	161,599	53.90
Czech Republic	9,067	43.90
Cyprus	258	59.70
Denmark	12,021	51.40
Estonia	1,409	39.90
Finland	12,255	45.20
France	103,574	50.60
Germany	178,402	49.90
Greece	3,917	64.30
Hungary	8,253	48.40
Ireland	16,180	52.40

Country of birth	Total	% male
Italy	90,337	62.50
Latvia	3,247	42.70
Lithuania	20,855	52.20
Luxembourg	730	54.50
Malta	255	55.30
Netherlands	46,217	52.50
Poland	80,540	52.20
Portugal	125,702	63.50
Romania	781,343	52.70
Slovak Republic	7,826	47.50
Slovenia	1,127	51.80
Spain	364,392	51.60
Sweden	20,563	45.50
United Kingdom	366,379	50.70
Non EU-Europe	220,276	44.80
Albania	1,712	60.00
Andorra	1,033	49.60
Armenia	10,924	52.90
Belarus	3,434	35.00
Bosnia & Herzegovina	1,600	52.00
Croatia	1,553	50.80
Georgia	10,571	55.70
Iceland	1,338	48.40
Liechtenstein	53	54.70
Macedonia, FYR	501	51.50
Moldova	17,317	51.20
Norway	17,832	50.10
Russian Federation	48,910	30.70
Serbia	3,150	52.40
Switzerland	18,424	49.50
Turkey	2,962	64.90
Ukraine	78,706	45.80
Rest of Europe	256	53.10
Africa	928,602	65.40
Algeria	54,146	70.40
Angola	3,562	58.00
Benin	371	71.40
Burkina Faso	1,055	77.30
Cameroon	5,454	64.50

Country of birth	Total	% male
Cape Verde	3,456	44.30
Congo, Dem. Rep.	1,262	62.30
Congo, Rep.	2,059	63.60
Côte d'Ivoire	2,941	77.40
Egypt, Arab Rep.	3,151	73.30
Equatorial Guinea	14,043	34.90
Ethiopia	1,012	52.00
Gambia, The	17,438	82.90
Ghana	14,833	84.60
Guinea	10,937	75.20
Guinea-Bissau	6,595	80.20
Kenya	1,225	32.70
Liberia	626	75.40
Mali	23,011	93.40
Mauritania	10,781	82.20
Morocco	645,156	61.80
Nigeria	37,684	62.10
Senegal	57,852	84.90
Sierra Leone	998	69.30
South Africa	1,662	54.80
Togo	439	72.40
Tunisia	2,140	68.20
Rest of Africa	4,713	56.50
Americas	1,843,720	45.30
Central America	200,252	40.20
Costa Rica	1,950	45.80
Cuba	57,111	45.10
Dominica	546	36.60
Dominican Republic	89,026	41.70
El Salvador	5,926	40.00
Guatemala	4,184	41.70
Honduras	26,209	30.00
Nicaragua	11,975	26.20
Panama	2,424	42.90
Rest of Central America	901	48.90
North America	52,166	45.70
Canada	3,074	44.60
Mexico	26,226	42.10
United States	22,866	49.80

Country of birth	Total	% male
South America	1,591,302	45.90
Argentina	187,104	51.50
Bolivia	206,635	42.40
Brazil	121,287	38.20
Chile	47,316	49.70
Colombia	292,212	44.50
Ecuador	387,367	49.40
Paraguay	84,323	32.70
Peru	141,309	49.20
Uruguay	59,020	50.60
Venezuela, R. B. de	64,443	43.10
Rest of South America	286	43.40
Asia	292,786	61.30
Bangladesh	10,434	81.30
China	137,020	53.80
India	31,692	72.30
Indonesia	1,918	57.40
Iran, Islamic Rep.	3,514	61.30
Iraq	1,195	62.80
Israel	1,983	61.30
Japan	5,120	38.30
Jordan	887	67.60
Kazakhstan	969	39.70
Korea, Rep.	2,781	43.20
Lebanon	1,616	62.00
Nepal	2,454	80.00
Pakistan	54,834	85.80
Philippines	26,402	38.60
Saudi Arabia	369	60.20
Syrian Arab Republic	2,373	63.80
Thailand	1,439	22.40
Vietnam	703	53.30
Rest of Asia	5,083	49.60
Pacific Islands	3,170	53.40
Australia	2,189	51.50
New Zealand	795	57.90

Source: Population register. Data available at http://www.ine.es/jaxi/menu.do?type=pcaxis&path=%2Ft20%2Fe245&file=inebase&L=.

PART V

Chapter 21

Forecasting Turkish Workers' Remittances from Germany during the Financial Crisis

ŞULE AKKOYUNLU

THE 2008 FINANCIAL CRISIS HAS had a noticeable impact on remittance flows to developing countries. Remittances to developing countries fell to $307 billion in 2009, which is a 5.5 percent decline from 2008.[1] However, the impact of the financial crisis on other financial flows was even more noticeable; for example, foreign direct investments (FDIs) and private debt and portfolio equity flows declined by 40 and 80 percent, respectively.[2] The situation for Turkey was not so different from that of other developing countries. Remittances to Turkey decreased from $1.4 billion in 2008 to $0.93 billion in 2009, FDIs in Turkey decreased from $15.7 billion in 2008 to $6.9 billion in 2009, and overseas development aid decreased from $2.02 billion in 2008 to $0.05 billion in 2009. Only portfolio investments increased from −$5.1 billion in 2008 to $0.20 billion in 2009. Turkish workers' remittances have been an important source of foreign exchange flows to Turkey, especially in the early 1970s. Figure 21.1 shows the ratio of total Turkish workers' remittances to current account inflows.[3] Although following the trade liberalization in the early 1980s the role of exports of goods and services has become a more dominant source for foreign exchange flows, Turkish workers' remittances are still a *stable* source of foreign exchange flows to Turkey.

Developing countries depend heavily on foreign capital flows for economic development and infrastructure, because domestic capital in these countries is scarce. Understanding the determinants and future trends of these capital flows to developing countries, especially during and/or after the economic crisis, is essential for economic stability and economic development as well as for economic policy analysis.[4]

FIGURE 21.1 Ratio of Total Turkish Workers' Remittances to Current Account Inflows to Turkey, 1963–2009

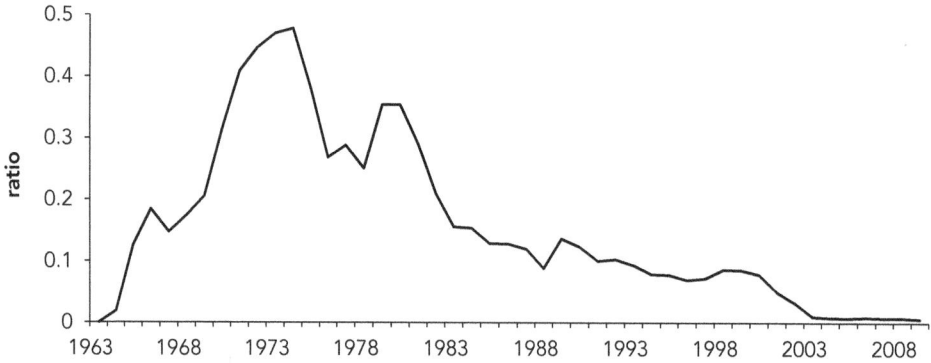

Source: Central Bank of Turkey.

Given that remittances are "unrequited transfers" and therefore are a more desirable and more stable source of foreign exchange flows to developing countries, in this chapter I focus on forecasting the future of remittance trends.[5] The purpose of this study is fourfold. First, it forecasts Turkish workers' remittances from Germany based on a model by Akkoyunlu (2010) for 2010, 2011, and 2012. This model is chosen because it is statistically satisfactory, economically sensible, and able to forecast five years ahead. In addition, the empirical findings are consistent with the altruistic theory of remittances that financial incentives are not important determinants of Turkish workers' remittances. Therefore, the real exchange rate rather than the real interest rate differentials should have a role in explaining and forecasting Turkish workers' remittances. Second, it analyzes the impact of the 2008 global financial crisis on Turkish workers' remittances from Germany. The 2008 crisis started in rich countries and spread to developing countries, so therefore I argue that both host and home country factors are important in determining remittance flows. I focus in this study on Turkish workers' remittances from Germany to untangle the effect of the host country income on remittances, because each host country had a different experience with respect to the economic crisis, and the total remittances include remittances from resource-rich countries. Third, it includes real exchange rates as well as conventional variables such as per capita real gross domestic product (GDP) in the host and home countries and the number of migrants in the host country. Barajas and others (2010) emphasize the importance of the exchange rate in forecasting remittances but exclude it from their calculations. In addition, the economic variables used here are in real terms compared with other studies that use nominal variables; see Mohapatra and Ratha (2010) and Ratha, Mohapatra, and Silwal (2010a). Fourth, it provides guidelines for forecasting workers' remittances.

The next section provides a brief discussion of Turkish workers' remittances. Information on data with respect to the main economic variables that affect remittances is illustrated in the figures. Section 3 discusses the determinants of Turkish workers' remittances from Germany based on Akkoyunlu (2010). Section 4 describes the methodology for forecasting remittances and discusses the results. Section 5 concludes.

Turkish Remittances and the Financial Crisis

Turkish workers' remittances to Turkey constitute important financial flows (figure 21.2a). Although total Turkish workers' remittances saw an increasing trend from the beginning of the sample and were little affected by the economic crises in Turkey in the early 1970s and 1980s and in 1994, the impact of the 2001 Turkish banking crisis on Turkish workers' remittances is very clear.[6] Despite the recovery of the remittances in 2003, it is evident that the remittances decreased in 2008 because of the 2008 global financial crisis. Thus, Turkish workers' remittances were affected by the home country conditions as well as the global economic circumstances or the economic conditions in the host countries.

Remittances by Turkish workers in Germany constitute an important share of the total remitted by Turkish workers abroad (figure 21.2) because of the fact that the largest share (2 million emigrants) of Turks abroad is in Germany, and the majority of them emigrated for employment reasons. In addition, Turkish workers' remittances from Germany, at €1 billion per year, seem to be more stable in the last five years than the total Turkish workers' remittances, including the 2008 financial crisis.

FIGURE 21.2 Turkish Workers' Remittances Total and from Germany, 1963–2009

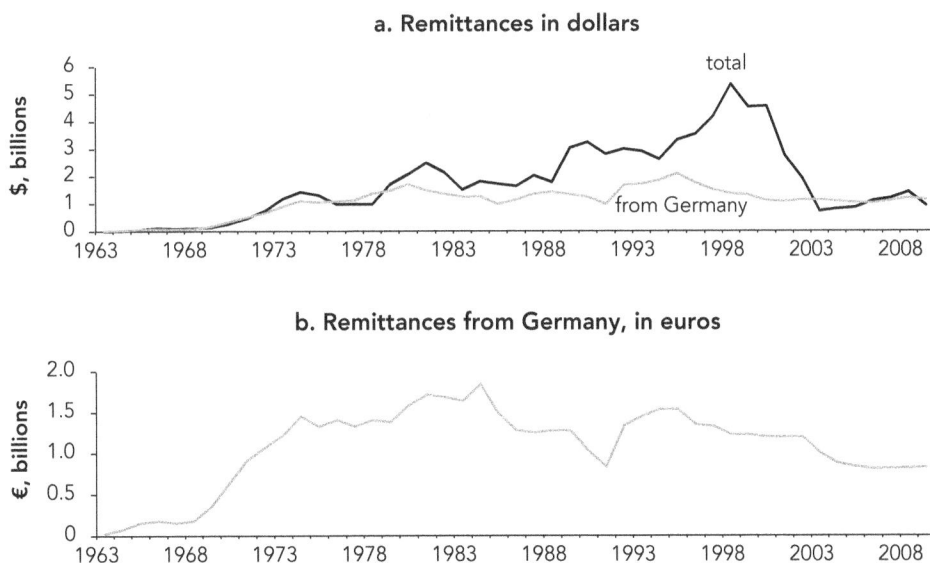

a. Remittances in dollars

b. Remittances from Germany, in euros

Sources: Central Bank of Turkey and Deutsche Bundesbank.

Figure 21.3 shows data on Turkish workers' remittances only from Germany, total FDI, total official aid to Turkey, and portfolio equity in Turkey.[7] Turkish remittances are very stable and an important source of foreign reserves compared with FDI, portfolio equity, and official aid.

FIGURE 21.3 Turkish Workers' Remittances from Germany and Other Financial Flows to Turkey, 1963–2009

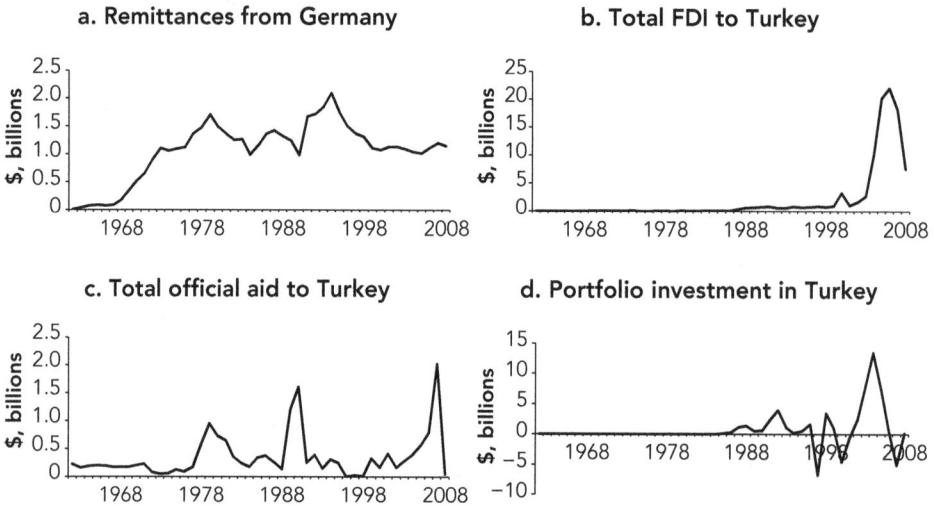

a. Remittances from Germany

b. Total FDI to Turkey

c. Total official aid to Turkey

d. Portfolio investment in Turkey

Sources: Central Bank of Turkey, Deutsche Bundesbank, and World Bank Development Indicators.

Table 21.1 shows the important effects of the 2008 financial crisis on capital flows to Turkey. Indeed, almost all the financial flows to Turkey were affected by the global crisis.

The 2008 crisis started in developed countries and spread to developing countries, and therefore it is important to understand how the developed country, in this case Germany, was affected by the 2008 economic crisis and how this in turn affected remittances by Turkish workers. Figure 21.4 shows the per capita real GDP growth and unemployment rate for Germany, which were negatively affected by the crisis. The per capita real GDP growth was negative, and the German unemployment rate was high in 2009. It is expected that remittances will decrease as the income and employment opportunities decline in the host country.[8]

Turkish real GDP per capita growth was negative in 2008 but recovered in 2009; however, the Turkish unemployment rate continued to increase following the 2008 financial crisis (figure 21.4). If Turkish workers are altruistic, then the increase in Turkish economic growth should decrease remittances, and this was the case in Turkey. However, if they had investment motives, the remittances would have increased. In addition the data on the difference between Turkish and German real short-term interest rates show

TABLE 21.1 Capital Transactions, 2008–10

$, billions

Capital transaction	2008	2009	2010
Current account balance	−41.9	−14.4	−33.6
Capital account (excluding reserves)	35.2	9.9	44.4
Direct investments (net)	15.7	6.9	5.7
Portfolio investments (net)	−5.1	0.2	12.4
Other investments (net)	24.6	2.8	26.3
Capital flows by use	19.5	3.0	38.7
Public	−2.9	−0.2	12.6
Private	22.4	3.2	26.0
Direct investments (net)	15.7	6.9	5.7
Workers' remittances	1.41	0.93	0.96
Overseas development aid	2.02	0.05	—
Reserves	1.1	−0.1	−10.8
Net errors and omissions	5.6	4.6	0.1
Direct investments (net)/current account balance	−37.5	−47.8	−16.9
Net errors and omissions/current account balance	−13.4	−32.2	−0.2

Sources: Turkish Central Bank and World Bank.

Note: 2010 reports data until August 2010. — = not available.

FIGURE 21.4 Growth Rates of Real per Capita GDP and Unemployment for Germany and Turkey

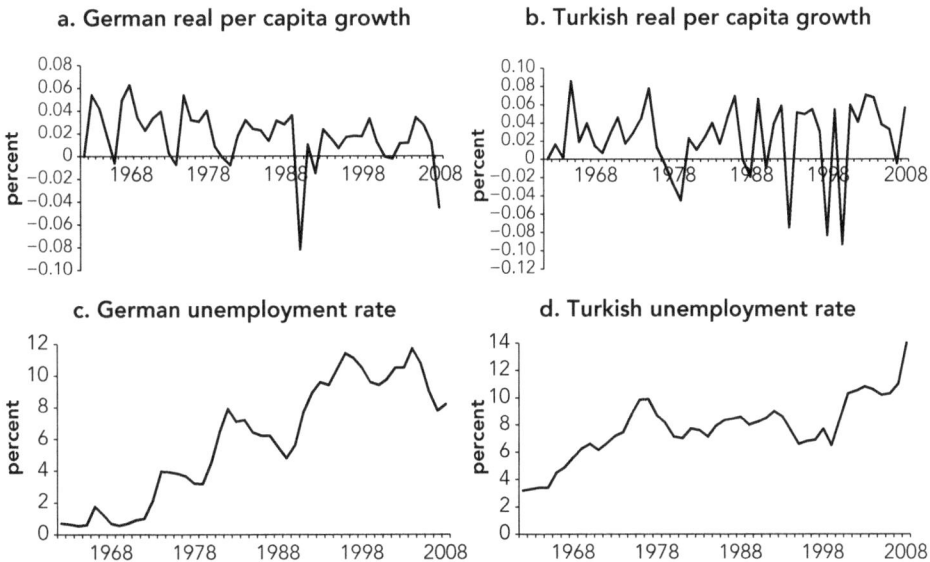

a. German real per capita growth

b. Turkish real per capita growth

c. German unemployment rate

d. Turkish unemployment rate

Source: German Federal Statistical Office and Turkish Statistical Institute.

no correlation between Turkish remittances from Germany (figure 21.5). These data further support the empirical findings of Akkoyunlu (2010) that Turkish workers are driven largely by altruistic motives.

FIGURE 21.5 Turkish and German Real Short-Term Interest Rates, Their Differences, and Turkish Workers' Remittances from Germany, 1963–2009

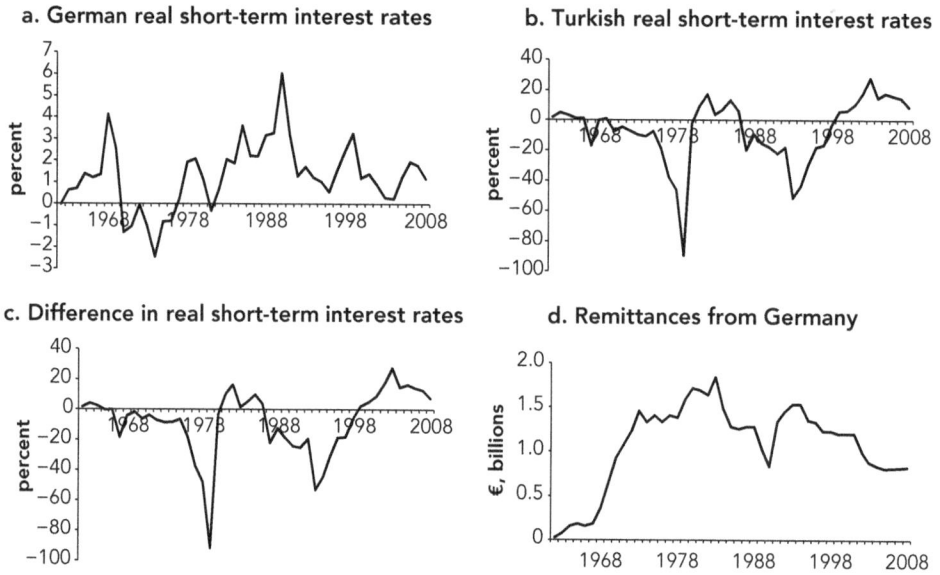

a. German real short-term interest rates

b. Turkish real short-term interest rates

c. Difference in real short-term interest rates

d. Remittances from Germany

Source: Deutsche Bundesbank and Central Bank of Turkey.

Remittances rates are affected when Turkish workers have lost jobs because of the economic crisis. However, the data on the employment of Turkish workers in Germany show that total employment of Turkish workers in Germany and their employment by sectors were not affected by the 2008 financial crisis (figures 21.6 and 21.7).[9] This can be explained by the findings of Akkoyunlu and Vogel (2008) that the transition of industrial employment of Turkish migrants took place before the 2008 financial crisis. In addition, if immigrant households that receive social security or unemployment insurance are more likely to remit than other immigrant households, then the high unemployment rate for Turkish workers should not interrupt remittance rates.[10]

In addition, figure 21.8 shows that the unemployment of Turks in Germany did not change during this period. The most important insight comes from the data on the flow of the Turkish population and from Germany. Figure 21.9 shows that return migration increased as a result of the economic crisis,[11] and the net flows as well as the stock of Turkish population in Germany decreased.

The Turkish population is an important determinant of remittances; even though the economic crisis affected both sending and receiving countries negatively, the constant

FIGURE 21.6 Total and Turkish Employment in Germany, 1991–2009

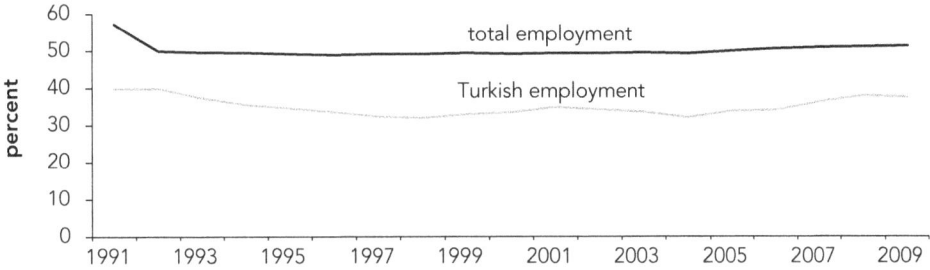

Source: German Employment Agency (Bundesagentur für Arbeit).

FIGURE 21.7 Turkish Employment in Germany by Sector, 1987–2009

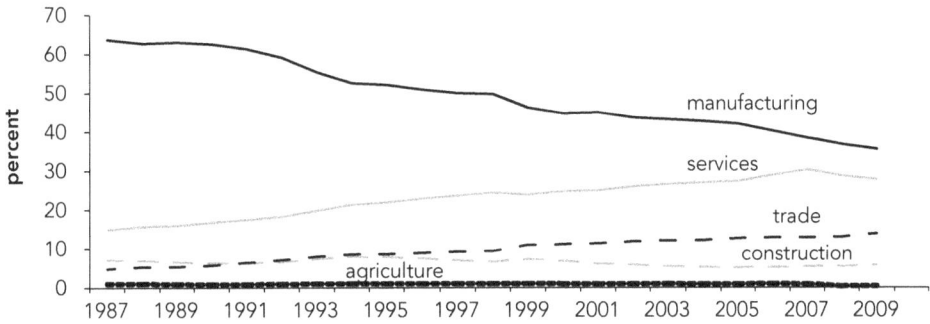

Source: German Employment Agency (Bundesagentur für Arbeit).

Note: Trade data consists of "Trade and repair of motor vehicles, motorcycles, and personal and household goods." Services include "Hotels and restaurants; real estate, renting, and business activities; and health and social work."

FIGURE 21.8 Total and Turkish Unemployment in Germany, 1998–2009

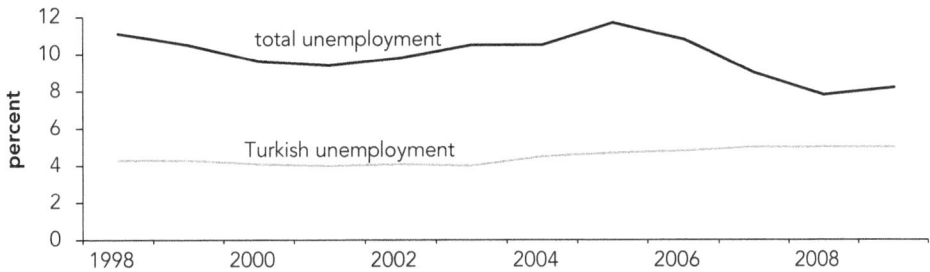

Source: German Employment Agency (Bundesagentur für Arbeit).

FIGURE 21.9 Turkish Population in Germany and Turkish Inflows, Outflows, and Net Flows, 1963–2009

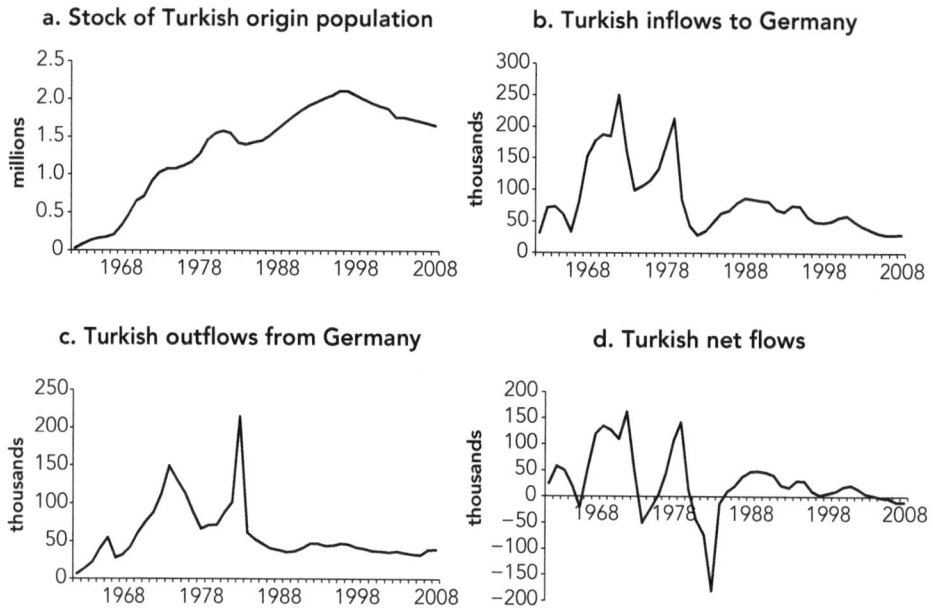

a. Stock of Turkish origin population

b. Turkish inflows to Germany

c. Turkish outflows from Germany

d. Turkish net flows

Source: German Federal Statistical Office.

growth of the Turkish population can keep remittances constant. If remittances are also a small part of the income of these migrant stocks, then the remittances will remain stable even during the economic crisis. The numbers of migrants are the most significant determinant of remittances (Barajas and others 2010; Calì and Dell'Erba 2009; Freund and Spatafora 2008; Lueth and Ruiz-Arranz 2008; Ratha and Shaw 2007; Singh, Haacker, and Lee 2009; Vargas-Silva and Huang 2006).

Determinants of Turkish Workers' Remittances from Germany

Akkoyunlu (2010), who models Turkish workers' remittances to Germany for the period 1963–2005 (see also Akkoyunlu and Kholodilin 2008),[12] finds that in the long run the real Turkish per capita GDP and the real German per capita GDP contribute negatively to Turkish remittances,[13] while the stock of Turkish migrants, the real exchange rates, and the political instability contribute positively to Turkish remittances.[14] The negative coefficient of the real Turkish per capita GDP is consistent with the altruistic theory. The number of Turkish migrants enters with a unitary coefficient in the long-run equation. The result of the long-run relationship is given as (Akkoyunlu 2010: 10)

$$\ln R_t / Y_{ht} = 39.156 - 2.608 \ln pcY_{ht} - 4.046 \ln pcY_{ft} + 1.495 \ln S_t$$

(SE)   (3.595)   (0.521)   (0.765)   (0.094)

$$+ 0.448 \ln e_t + 0.127 P_t$$

(SE)   (0.235)   (0.063).

(21.1)

In the short run German GDP has a positive impact on remittances, and the sum of coefficients on the home and host countries' income is equal to one, which is consistent with the altruistic theory (see equation [21.2]). The altruistic theory implies that an increase in a migrant's income by €1, coupled with a €1 drop in the income of the migrant's family left behind, raises the amount transferred by exactly €1. The unit coefficient of the stock of Turkish migrants is also confirmed by the econometric analysis. The negative coefficient of Turkish income with a positive coefficient of the real exchange rate further supports the altruistic theory.[15] The coefficient of the real exchange rate, which is larger than one, indicates that real depreciation leads to higher remittances even when the remittances are expressed in terms of the host country's good (Faini 1994). Furthermore, consistent with the logic of transnational migration theory, the positive long-run as well as short-run impact of political instability suggests that Turkish migrants are altruistic. Thus, Turkish migrants respond positively to political and economic changes in their home country.

$$\Delta \ln R_t / Y_{ht} = -0.033 - 1.346 \Delta \ln pcY_{ft} + 2.083 \Delta \ln pcY_{ft} + 1.131 \Delta \ln S_t$$

(SE)   (0.031) (0.433)   (0.734)   (0.087)

[t]   [−1.07] [−3.11]   [2.82]   [13.00]

$$+ 1.022 \Delta \ln e_t + 0.076 P_t - 0.569 \, ecm_{t-1}$$

(SE) (0.151)   (0.034)   (0.071)

[t]   [6.75]   [2.21]   [−8.06],

(21.2)

$R^2 = 0.909$, $F(6,36) = 60.08$ [0.00], $\hat{\sigma} = 0.103$, DW = 1.77,

RSS = 0.3849 for 7 variables and 43 observations,

$F_{ar}(2,34) = 0.448$ [0.64], $F_{arch}(1,34) = 2.134$ [0.15],

$\chi^2_{nd}(2) = 0.32$ [0.85], $F_{hetero}(11,24) = 0.22$ [0.99],

$F_{reset}(1,35) = 0.36$ [0.55], $T = 43$ (1963-2005).

The present forecasting exercise of Turkish workers' remittances from Germany for 2010, 2011, and 2012 will be based on this long- and short-run relationship.

Forecasting Turkish Workers' Remittances from Germany

The importance of remittances in poverty reduction, economic development, and economic growth in developing countries has raised serious concerns about the likely effects of the recent financial crisis on future remittance flows to developing countries, and several studies attempt to forecast remittance flows. Calì and Dell'Erba (2009) forecast the total remittance flows to developing countries for 2009 and 2010. These studies adopt the model for remittances reported by Laeven and Valencia (2008), which adds directly the measure of systematic banking crisis to take into account the effects of the current financial crisis on remittances. Calì and Dell'Erba (2009) include only the effects of host country income growth and the direct effects of the crisis (the systematic banking crisis) in their forecasting exercise and exclude the effects of control variables such as inflation, exchange rates, population, real interest rates, and unemployment, even though they include these variables in their baseline model. Similarly, Barajas and others (2010) forecast the remittance growth in 36 Sub-Saharan African countries based on the forecast changes in GDP in the host countries in 2009 and 2010.[16] However, the calculations are based on changes in the host country income. They admit that they omit the most important factor, the exchange rate, which determines remittances during the crisis.

The results of these forecasting exercises deliver different results depending on the chosen econometric models and specifications, data sources, and baseline scenarios, whether the sample consists of the richest host countries and the highest remittance-receiving countries, and most importantly whether the forecast values are based on nominal or real GDP and whether control variables are included in the forecasting exercises.

The exercise on forecasting remittances differs from these previous studies. First, the forecasting exercise relies on a formal econometric model of remittances that includes the long-run as well as the short-run effects of economic variables. Second, it includes forecast values of real variables. Third, it includes forecast values of control variables such as real exchange rates.

This chapter uses data on forecast values of Turkish and German GDP from the Organisation for Economic Co-operation and Development (OECD) and Eurostat, which differ. Therefore, I perform the forecasting exercise using the data from both sources. I explain the forecasting methodology as follows:

- *Step 1:* I calculate the long-run solution (*ecm*) from equation (21.1) for 2009 from the actual values of the log of the share of nominal remittances of Turkish workers in Germany to the Turkish nominal GDP ($\ln R_t/Y_{ht}$), the log of the real per capita Turkish GDP ($\ln pcY_{ht}$), the log of the real per capita German GDP ($\ln pcY_{ft}$), the log of the number of Turkish migrants in Germany ($\ln S_t$), and the log of the real exchange rate ($\ln e_t$) using the sources in the annex.

- *Step 2:* I calculate the change in the log of the share of nominal remittances of Turkish workers in Germany to the Turkish nominal GDP ($\Delta\ln [R_t/Y_{ht}]$) for 2010 from equation (21.2) with the *ecm2009* that I calculated in step 1 and estimated values of the log of the real per capita Turkish GDP ($\ln pcY_{ht}$), the log of the real per capita German ($\ln pcY_{ft}$), the log of the number of Turkish migrants in Germany ($\ln S_t$), and the log of the real exchange rate ($\ln e_t$) for 2010 using the sources in the annex.

- *Step 3:* I calculate $\ln R_t/Y_{ht}$ for 2010 from $\Delta\ln (R_t/Y_{ht})$ for 2010 that I calculated in step 2.

- *Step 4:* I calculate R_t for 2010 from the forecast value for the nominal Turkish GDP for 2010 using the sources in the annex.

- *Step 5:* I repeat the same exercise for 2011 and 2012.

The basic assumptions for the results in table 21.2 are the following:

- The estimated values of Turkish real GDP per capita and German real GDP per capita are obtained from the OECD.

- The stock of the Turkish population in Germany is assumed to be decreasing.

I have tried different estimated values for the Turkish real GDP per capita, German real GDP per capita from the OECD and Eurostat, and the number of Turkish population, which is assumed to be decreasing or constant.

The results are presented in table 21.2.[17] The results give very similar values for the remittances to the Turkish GDP ratio R_t/Y_{ht}, which varies between 0.0027 and 0.0029 for 2010, 0.0023 and 0.0026 for 2011, and 0.0021 and 0.0024 for 2012.

TABLE 21.2 Summary of Steps

Step	For calculating R_t for 2010	For calculating R_t for 2011	For calculating R_t for 2012
1	Calculate *ecm* for 2009 from equation (21.1)	Calculate *ecm* for 2010 from equation (21.1)	Calculate *ecm* for 2011 from equation (21.1)
2	Calculate $\Delta\ln(R_t/Y_{ht})$ for 2010 from equation (21.2)	Calculate $\Delta\ln(R_t/Y_{ht})$ for 2011 from equation (21.2)	Calculate $\Delta\ln(R_t/Y_{ht})$ for 2012 from equation (21.2)
3	Calculate $\ln R_t/Y_{ht}$ for 2010 from $\Delta\ln(R_t/Y_{ht})$ for 2010	Calculate $\ln R_t/Y_{ht}$ for 2011 from $\Delta\ln(R_t/Y_{ht})$ for 2011	Calculate $\ln R_t/Y_{ht}$ for 2012 from $\Delta\ln(R_t/Y_{ht})$ for 2012
4	Calculate R_t for 2010 from R_t/Y_{ht} for 2010	Calculate R_t for 2011 from R_t/Y_{ht} for 2011	Calculate R_t for 2012 from R_t/Y_{ht} for 2012
Result	R_t/Y_{ht} = 0.0028 R_t = €1,127.00 million	R_t/Y_{ht} = 0.0025 R_t = €1,184.22 million	R_t/Y_{ht} = 0.0022 R_t = €1,161.96 million

Source: Author's calculations.

I further forecast remittances in values of liras and euros (tables 21.3 and 21.4). The values are again very close under different assumptions of the Turkish and German real GDP per capita and the stock of Turkish population in Germany.[18] The forecast values vary only between €1,086.77 million and €1,167.27 million for 2010, €1,089.48 million and €1,231.59 million for 2011, and €1,109.14 million and €1,267.59 million for 2012.

The results of the forecasting exercises are consistent with the theory of altruism in the motivation to remit and with the previously estimated underlying model for Turkish workers' remittances from Germany in Akkoyunlu (2010). Thus, if Turkish migrants have altruistic motivations, and they therefore care for the well-being of their relatives and friends, then they keep sending a constant amount of money from their earnings

TABLE 21.3 Forecast Results

Variable	R_t/Y_{ht}[a]	pcY_{ht}	pcY_{ft}	S_t	e_t
Model 1: Per capita real GDP forecast values are from OECD; decreasing stocks are assumed					
2009 (actual)	0.0025	2089.701	26616.51	1658083	0.054849162
2010 (forecast)	0.0028	2139.854	27611.97	1628238	0.049015436
2011 (forecast)	0.0025	2170.240	28371.30	1598929	0.044081796
2012 (forecast)	0.0022	2194.980	29052.21	1570149	0.042010283
Model 2: Per capita real GDP forecast values are from OECD; constant stocks are assumed					
2009 (actual)	0.0025	2089.701	26616.51	1658083	0.054849162
2010 (forecast)	0.0029	2139.854	27611.97	1658083	0.049015436
2011 (forecast)	0.0026	2170.240	28371.30	1658083	0.044081796
2012 (forecast)	0.0024	2194.980	29052.21	1658083	0.042010283
Model 3: Per capita real GDP forecast values are from Eurostat; decreasing stocks are assumed					
2009 (actual)	0.0025	2089.701	26616.51	1658083	0.054849162
2010 (forecast)	0.0027	2225.532	27636.582	1628238	0.049015436
2011 (forecast)	0.0023	2232.295	28304.950	1598929	0.044081796
2012 (forecast)	0.0021	2240.555	28988.236	1570149	0.042010283
Model 4: Per capita real GDP forecast values are from Eurostat; constant stocks are assumed					
2009 (actual)	0.0025	2089.701	26616.51	1658083	0.054849162
2010 (forecast)	0.0028	2225.532	27636.582	1658083	0.049015436
2011 (forecast)	0.0024	2232.295	28304.950	1658083	0.044081796
2012 (forecast)	0.0023	2240.555	28988.236	1658083	0.042010283

Source: Author's calculations.

a. R_t/Y_{ht} values for 2009 are actual data whereas the values for 2010, 2011, and 2012 are calculated by the author from equations (21.1) and (21.2) from the actual values of pcY_{ht}, pcY_{ft}, S_t, and e_t for 2009 and from the estimated values of pcY_{ht}, pcY_{ft}, S_t, and e_t for 2010, 2011, and 2012. The sources of data are in the annex.

TABLE 21.4 Value of Turkish Workers' Remittances from Germany

Model	Currency	2009 actual	2010 forecast	2011 forecast	2012 forecast
1	Million liras	1,788.66	2,348.57	2,344.37	2,300.30
	Million euros	824.00	1,127.02	1,184.22	1,161.96
2	Million liras	1,788.66	2,432.45	2,438.15	2,409.42
	Million euros	824.00	1,167.27	1,231.59	1,267.59
3	Million liras	1,788.66	2,264.69	2,156.82	2,195.74
	Million euros	824.00	1,086.77	1,089.48	1,109.14
4	Million liras	1,788.66	2,348.57	2,250.60	2,404.86
	Million euros	824.00	1,127.02	1,136.85	1,214.77

Source: Author's calculations.

and maintain the consumption patterns of their relatives and friends, especially during the economic crisis or unexpected events.

Conclusions

The importance and benefits of remittances for developing countries and the sudden decline of these flows with the current financial crisis have encouraged researchers to forecast remittance flows. The results of forecasting exercises show that some regions are and will be more affected than others (Ratha, Mohapatra, and Silwal 2010a, b). Indeed, Ruiz and Vargas-Silva (2010) show that remittances to Latin America were affected differently from those to other regions. In addition, each Latin American country had a different experience with respect to remittances; for instance, a significant correlation is found between the volume of remittances in previous years to Mexico and the severity of the housing crisis at the state level in the United States. Therefore, there are certain advantages in analyzing remittances on a single-country level. First, the definitions of remittances as well as the types of migrants vary across countries. Second, remittances to some countries decreased more dramatically during the economic crisis depending on the severity of the economic crisis in the remittance-sending host country. Therefore, it is important to analyze the determinants and the future patterns of remittances on a single-country level to understand the global patterns of remittances. In this study I forecast Turkish workers' remittances from Germany because these flows constitute the largest share of the total remittances to Turkey, and these flows as well as their ratio to GDP have been stable over the last few years. Therefore, it was important to study whether these flows will be stable after the current crisis, based on the medium-term outlook of the variables that influence Turkish workers' remittances from Germany.

The forecasting exercises are based on a previously estimated model of Turkish workers' remittances from Germany by Akkoyunlu (2010). This model found that Turkish workers' remittances are determined by the Turkish real GDP per capita, the German real GDP per capita, the number of Turkish workers in Germany, and the real exchange rate in the long run as well as in the short run. The present forecasting exercises are based on the predicted values of the Turkish real GDP per capita, the German real GDP per capita, the number of Turkish workers in Germany, the real exchange rate for 2010, 2011, and 2012, and forecast remittances for 2010, 2011, and 2012.

The forecasting results show that the ratio of the Turkish workers' remittances from Germany to the Turkish GDP for 2010, 2011, and 2012 will remain almost the same as during the precrisis period. This can be explained by the altruistic motivations for remittances, which are stronger during economic crises or unexpected events.

The most important contributions of my forecasting exercises are as follows. First, I include predicted values of GDP for the host country (Germany) and the home country (Turkey) in real and per capita terms. Second, I include the real exchange rate. The importance of the exchange rate movements for the dollar (or the host country currency) valuation of remittances has also been pointed out by Mohapatra and Ratha (2010), who discuss the fact that in dollar terms, remittance flows to Armenia, the Kyrgyz Republic, and Tajikistan declined by 15, 33, and 34 percent, respectively, in the first half of 2009 compared with the same period in 2008. However, in ruble terms, remittances to the Kyrgyz Republic in fact increased by 17 percent and those to Armenia and Tajikistan decreased by only 8 and 10 percent, respectively. Similarly, they also observed in countries such as Bangladesh, Ethiopia, India, Moldova, Nepal, Pakistan, and the Philippines that a depreciation of these countries' currencies led to a surge in remittance flows to these countries.

The findings in this study have important policy implications and suggest that policy makers should consider the impact of their policy measures such as price stabilization and devaluation of remittances. For instance, real devaluation of the lira with an aim to increase Turkish exports will also have an effect on future remittances.

Notes

1. In fact, Ratha and others (2008, 2009a, b) note that the global decrease in remittances started in the third quarter of 2008.
2. See Ratha, Mohapatra, and Silwal (2010b).
3. The current account inflows are composed of foreign exhange inflows due to exports of goods and services, to incomes, and to unrequited transfers.
4. It is shown that remittances alleviate poverty (Adams, Cuecuecha, and Page 2008; Adams and Page 2003, 2005; Quartey and Blankson 2004; World Bank 2006a) and promote human and physical capital accumulation, economic growth, and development (Adenutsi 2010; Amuedo-Dorantes and Pozo 2011; Edwards and Ureta 2003; Fajnzylber and Lopez 2007; Gupta, Pattillo, and Wagh 2009; Hildebrandt and McKenzie 2005; Phillips 2009; Straubhaar and Vadean 2006; Valero-Gil 2009; Ziesemer 2006). See also, for extensive empirical literature on the impact of remittance, Ghosh (2006).
5. Avendano, Gaillard, and Parra (2009), Bugamelli and Paterno (2009), Chami, Hakura, and Montiel (2009), Giuliano and Ruiz-Arranz (2009), Gupta, Pattillo, and Wagh (2009), Ratha (2003, 2005, 2007, 2010a), and World Bank (2006a) state that remittances contribute to stabilizing the current account position, reduce the volatility of capital flows and output volatility of remittance-receiving countries, improve the debt sustainability and creditworthiness of developing countries, and help facilitate access to international capital markets and to formal financial services.
6. However, several studies (Akkoyunlu and Kholodilin 2008; FEMIP 2006; Galliana 2006; Unan 2009) point out that, in fact, the dramatic decrease of data from the official Turkish sources (Central Bank of Turkey) on total Turkish workers' remittances after the 2001 banking crisis is due to the measurement. The Central Bank of Turkey underwent a major methodological change of this data in 2003: The new definition of remittances does not include transfers from Turkish workers going to Germany with a tourist visa but includes transfers with an objective to earn money. Unan (2009) also argues that during the crisis the official data on remittances show a decrease, but unofficial transfers increase. Therefore, it is very important to have a reliable data source on remittances. The Deutsche Bundesbank provides

consistent and reliable data on Turkish workers' remittances, which enables us to analyze the effects of economic crisis on remittances.

7. Official aid refers to official development assistance.

8. The importance of the host country's conditions is also confirmed by Barajas and others (2010), Calì and Dell'Erba (2009), Chami, Hakura, and Montiel (2005), Elbadawi and Rocha (1992), El Mouhoub, Oudinet, and Unan (2008), El-Sakka and McNabb (1999), Glytsos (1997), Straubhaar (1986), Swamy (1981), and Vargas-Silva and Huang (2006).

9. Turks are mainly concentrated in sectors such as manufacturing and services (such as hotels and restaurants).

10. Taylor (2000) found that public transfer schemes in the United States increased remittances to Mexico.

11. As Ratha (2003) points out, remittances increase with return migration.

12. Akkoyunlu and Kholodilin (2008) adopt the vector autoregressions approach in their study.

13. The negative long-run coefficient on German GDP that I found in these estimations can be explained by an increase in income inequality that took place in recent years in Germany; see Dustmann, Ludsteck, and Schönberg (2009). The vast majority of Turkish workers are unskilled, and therefore the growth rate of their income is very low (almost zero) and is certainly much lower than the overall economic growth in Germany. Hence the negative long-run relationship between remittances and German real GDP may reflect this sharp increase in income dispersion.

14. The theoretical determinants of remittances were provided in a painstaking paper by Lucas and Stark (1985), who studied remittances on a household level. The signs of the coefficients on household income and migrant income help identify the motives for remittances. In macrostudies the host country GDP per capita is used to measure economic conditions in the host country that represent migrants' employment and earnings prospects. Similary, home country economic activity is measured by the home country GDP per capita. Negative economic conditions in the home country encourage migrants to send remittances if they have altruistic motives. In macromodels, economic policies and economic and political stability as well as institutions in the home country matter. Therefore, in macromodels interest rate differentials and exchange rates are added to identify whether migrants have an investment motive or an altruistic motive. The investment motive suggests that devaluation discourages remittances. However, altruistic models predict that a real devaluation positively affects remittances (IMF 2005: ch. 2).

15. The positive response of remittances to an increase in the host country's GDP is reported in Frankel (2010), Glytsos (1997), Ruiz and Vargas-Silva (2010), and Vargas-Silva and Huang (2006). In addition, Clarke and Wallsten (2004), Frankel (2010), Ratha, Mohapatra, and Silwal (2010b), World Bank (2006a), Yang (2008b), and Yang and Choi (2007) find a negative or countercyclical relationship between the remittances and the home country GDP.

16. Singh, Haacker, and Lee (2009) also adopt a similar approach to forecasting remittances to Africa.

17. The annex provides the data sources.

18. I keep the forecast values of real exchange rates the same in all the forecasting exercises because these values do not differ from the Deutsche Bundesbank and the OECD.

Annex: Data Sources

Data	Source of actual data
Turkish workers' remittances from Germany	Deutsche Bundesbank
Nominal and real Turkish GDP	Turkish Statistical Institute
Real German GDP	Deutsche Bundesbank
Turkish population	Turkish Statistical Institute
German population	German Federal Statistical Office
Nominal exchange rate (liras/euros)	Deutsche Bundesbank
Turkish CPI	Turkish Statistical Institute
German CPI	Deutsche Bundesbank
The stock of Turkish population in Germany	German Federal Statistical Office
Data	**Source of estimated values**
Real Turkish GDP	Eurostat and OECD
Real German GDP	Eurostat and OECD
Turkish population	Turkish Statistical Institute
German population	German Federal Statistical Office
Nominal exchange rate (liras/euros)	Deutsche Bundesbank
Turkish CPI	OECD and Eurostat
German CPI	OECD and Eurostat

Source: Author.

Note: CPI = consumer price index.

Chapter 22

Remittances in an Environment of Human Insecurity: The Kurdish Case

IBRAHIM SIRKECI

SEVERAL STUDIES IN THIS BOOK and elsewhere claim that remittances are resilient to crisis. Migrants' responses can be different when faced with other types of crises. This short case study looks at the case of Kurdish immigrants from Turkey and their remittance sending patterns. It adds to our understanding by showing that two major ethnic groups from Turkey report differences in their remittance-sending and usage behavior. The major difference between the two segments is that the Kurds have been under long-term stress because of an ongoing ethnic conflict (Sirkeci 2006).

Remittances can be seen as an indicator of return migration tendencies. However, when there is armed conflict in the country of origin, what motivates migrants to remit? Do their remittance practices differ from the dominant ethnic group (that is Turkish)? As table 22.1 shows, 39 percent of Turkish Kurdish migrant households in Turkey received remittances, whereas the corresponding figure for the Turks is 21 percent.

TABLE 22.1 Percentage of Households in Turkey Receiving Remittances

Type of household	Turkish	Kurdish
Migrant	21	39
Nonmigrant	4.5	2.5

Source: TIMS 1996 household data.

Family members, especially spouses, children, and brothers and sisters, sent most of the remittances identified in the TIMS survey (table 22.2). The lower rate for sending remittances among some individuals is often related to the duration of the stay abroad according to the international migration literature. Remittances from immigrants who have stayed abroad longer often tend to decrease for two basic reasons: Close family members may join them, and relations with other family members and relatives may weaken over time (Martin, Hönekopp, and Ullmann 1990; Massey and others 1998/2006).

The patterns of sending remittances are related to the nature of relations between migrants and their relatives left behind and the economic conditions of the members of the household who stayed in Turkey. If sending remittances and investing at home means stronger ties with the country of origin and an indicator of return intentions, it is clear that a majority of migrants from both ethnic groups are unlikely to return. However, transnational living space allows Turks and Kurds to control their investments in Turkey without actually returning home (Ammassari and Black 2001).

Table 22.1 shows that more Turkish Kurdish households seem reliant on remittances than do Turk households. This can be related to the fact that the Kurdish-populated areas have been known for striking underdevelopment compared with the rest of the country (Sirkeci 2006). However, when the sources of remittances are examined, hardly any difference is observed between Turkish and Kurdish households (table 22.2). Both ethnic groups received remittances from their family members, and particularly from their spouses, brothers, sisters, and children. The only difference is that Turkish Kurds, unlike Turks, also received remittances from friends. One can relate this to the stronger communal ties among the Kurds. Patterns of the use of remittances elaborated below may cast light on this issue (table 22.3). Kurds received more remittances for community purposes than the Turks. These may have come not only from relatives, but also from friends.

TABLE 22.2 Sources of Remittances for Households in Turkey

percent

Sender of remittances	Turkish	Kurdish
Migrant	15.8	13.3
Spouse	28.1	28.9
Children	31.6	15.6
Parents	8.8	11.4
Sibling	24.6	24.4
Relative	3.5	4.4
Friend	0.0	6.6
n	57	45

Source: TIMS 1996 household data.

Remittance-sending spouses represent divided families. This usually refers to a husband working abroad while his wife stays in Turkey. Children sending remittances, on the other hand, often indicate parents are left behind in Turkey.

Many migrant households also received goods from abroad, including 11 percent of Turkish and 15 percent of Turkish Kurdish migrant households. Although these goods consisted of electronic devices, consumer goods, and clothes for the Turks, they were only clothes and jewelry for Turkish Kurds (table 22.3).

TABLE 22.3 Household Goods Received from Migrants

percent

	Turkish	Kurdish	Total
Received goods from abroad	11	15	12
Have not received goods from abroad	89	85	88
Received television and/or music equipment	4	0	3
Received other consumer goods	1	0	1
Received clothes	10	14	11
Received jewelry	0	1	0
n	294	108	402

Source: TIMS 1996 household data.

Cash remittances are often used for paying daily household expenses, including food, clothing, and rent. Most of the households that received money from abroad used it for their daily expenditures (70 percent of Turkish and 80 percent of Turkish Kurdish households; see table 22.4). The rest of the money was used for paying medical bills and financing the marriage of family members in Turkish Kurdish households. Again a very large portion of remittances were used for daily expenses and probably indicate struggling family economies in Turkey. This may also mean a member or members of the family who live abroad are obliged to take care of the finances of their families left behind in Turkey.

A contrast is seen between Turkish and Turkish Kurdish households with regard to remittances received for community purposes. As table 22.4 shows, 17 percent of Turkish Kurdish households received such remittances as opposed to 11 percent of their Turkish counterparts; however, the difference is not statistically significant. Most of these contributions were used for religious purposes including building or repairing mosques, maintaining religious ceremonies, and festivities. Among Turkish Kurds, two-thirds of all community purpose remittances were used for alms in Ramadan. This is important because it can be an indicator of community-level dependency on remittances received from abroad, because alms in Ramadan are the only source of income for poor people in some sending areas.

TABLE 22.4 Use of Most Remittances in Turkey

percent

Type of remittance use	Turkish	Kurdish	Total
Received remittance	19.5	42.1	25.5
Did not receive remittance	80.5	57.9	74.5
Use			
To pay for daily household expenses	13.6	34.6	19.2
To buy consumer goods	0.3	0.0	0.2
To buy land	0.0	0.9	0.2
To buy fertilizer, seeds, food for animals, and so on	0.7	0.0	0.5
To buy, build, or renovate a house	0.7	0.0	0.5
To pay for medical bills	1.4	3.7	2.0
To repay other debts	0.3	0.0	0.2
To finance the marriage of family members	1.0	2.8	1.5
To finance other family or religious celebrations	0.3	0.0	0.2
Other	1.4	0.0	1.0
n	294	108	402
Received remittances for community purposes[a]	10.5	16.7	12.2
Contribution to mosque	5.0	5.0	5.0
For alms in Ramadan	5.0	10.0	7.0
For religious festivities (such as a feast in Ramadan)	1.0	6.0	2.0
Other	2.0	5.0	3.0
n	294	108	402

Source: TIMS 1996 household data.

Note: Community purpose: $\chi^2 = 2.766$; significance = 0.096.

a. Details do not sum to totals because more than one purpose was indicated by some respondents.

Turkish Kurdish immigrants interviewed in Cologne highlighted the dependency of their households left behind in Turkey. They also reported the expectations of their families in Turkey, although they did not say much about the community. These expectations are usually in two forms: (1) cash and in-kind remittances to contribute to the family's economy and (2) help for migration of other members of the family or friends.

Emrah Kuzucu, for example, is under pressure from his family who live in the village of Urfa in southern Turkey. He was just 22 when he arrived in Germany in 1998, and the cost of 8,000 DM (£2,700) for his journey through the Balkans and Austria was paid for by his family: "The 400 DM (£130) I receive from the [German] government is a very small amount. Those I left behind in the village expect money from me. They don't know my situation here. I have to send money to them." At the same time, he was dealing with the expectations of potential migrants in his village in Turkey: "My friends [in Turkey] ask 'Shall we come there?' I say 'No, don't come.' I say 'You should acquire a profession first and then you can come here.' I am insisting that 'If you don't have a profession, there is no job for you here.'"

These expectations could be the results of reciprocity between the migrant and those of his or her family left behind. According to the qualitative research, migrants pay a high (higher in the case of clandestine migration) cost for their migration adventure, and the families left behind have often paid this cost collectively. Thus, in return, the family left behind expects benefits from its investment.

Migrants' future plans are made in relation to their direct investment patterns as well. A very small portion of remittances goes toward investments in Turkey (table 22.4), but the qualitative interviews may shed further light on what immigrants do with their savings. Many of the immigrants interviewed in Cologne reported that they own some property or business interest in Turkey. Immigrants' family members who lived in Turkey ran most of these businesses and properties. These investments can be perceived as an indication of an inclination to return, but again, the interviewees in Cologne did not seem too keen on returning but yet make investments, perhaps for the possibility of returning in the distant future.

The transnational nature of migration and migrant communities enables those individuals and families to pursue lives in more than one country. Remittances invested in Turkey shall be considered as part of such transnational investment portfolios for some Kurdish immigrants in Germany rather than indicating an intention to return. This case study shows us that different ethnic groups from the same country of origin may present different remittance patterns, which are shaped by their cultural traditions, intensity of relations within households and communities, their time spent abroad, as well as the relative deprivation (or socioeconomic development) levels that those left behind have to face in the country of origin. In this case, the Kurds seems to be in need of more support, for which remittances provide.

Chapter 23

Financial Crisis and Remittances from Denmark to Turkey

PINAR YAZGAN AND IBRAHIM SIRKECI

IN THIS SHORT CASE STUDY, we look at a relatively understudied international migration stream, migration from Turkey to Denmark, with a focus on remittance-sending behavior. Our analysis draws on recent fieldwork carried out in Denmark in between 2008 and 2011, thus covering the most recent global financial crisis. Such economic crises are expected to have an adverse effect on the volume of remittance flows. We have examined this effect in the case of Danish Turks, who represent the largest group among Muslim immigrants in Denmark. Our analysis shows that the Turkish immigrants to Denmark over several decades have developed a transnational space based on frequent visits home and have maintained ties with the hometowns and villages in the country of origin, Turkey. We therefore believe that such a transnational space plays a role in the continuation of remitting practices across generations of Turkish immigrants in Denmark and partly explains the resiliency of remitting behavior to the financial crisis. We have limited our analysis to the survey data and qualitative material we collected during the fieldwork. Nevertheless, our study also presents overall statistics about the Turkish immigrant population in Denmark.

Turkish Migration to Denmark

In line with the overall Turkish international migration patterns to Western Europe, Denmark has attracted many Turkish immigrants since the 1960s. These migration flows to Western Europe have also represented a move from the rural countryside to urban centers. Over the years, the composition of Turkish migration to Denmark has evolved from the initial government-led labor migration to include, first, family migrations, then refugee flows, and finally irregular migration responding to changes in admission policies and the overall economic and political environment. Such evolution of migration was evident in the periodization suggested elsewhere (Sirkeci 2005). Hence four distinct chronological periods of the Turkish migration in the twentieth century can be identified: (1) individual migrations motivated by personal reasons, from the late nineteenth century onward, (2) compulsory migrations of the non-Muslim minority populations of Turkey from 1900 until the late 1970s, (3) mass labor migrations and family reunifications, mainly between 1961 and 1980, and (4) irregular migration, including refugees, asylum seekers, and those making clandestine migrations and the like from 1980 until the present time.

Turkey signed bilateral labor exchange agreements with various European countries starting with the Federal Republic of Germany in 1961. According to the Ministry of Labour and Social Security, there were 3,693,121 Turkish citizens living abroad by the end of 2006. There were also 1,480,256 Turkish citizens who were naturalized by other countries. Denmark has its share of Turkish immigrants. Despite the fact that no bilateral agreements were in force between the two countries, Danish firms recruited Turkish workers by individual invitations from the late 1960s until 1973 and continued until 1980. Following the military intervention in Turkey (September 12, 1980), large numbers of Turkish and Kurdish refugees and asylum seekers arrived in Denmark. By 1973, 15,000 Moroccan, Pakistani, and Turkish immigrants were living in Denmark (Jorgensen 2008: 119).

Although only 2,377 Turkish immigrants were in Denmark in 1970–71, by 1980 the number of Turkish immigrants in Denmark had grown to 15,841. According to the Turkish Ministry of Labour and Social Security, the total increased to 21,544 by 2003. The Denmark Statistical Office reports 60,031 Turkish immigrants constituting the largest ethnic group among the 540,000 immigrant population in Denmark, whose overall population was 5,534,730 (Statistics Denmark 2011). By January 2011, there were 30,992 people who were born in Turkey along with 29,039 others who are descendants of the Turkish born (Statistics Denmark 2011). Figure 23.1 shows the growth of the immigrant population who were born in Turkey. Thus the Turkish minority in Denmark is much larger than it seems at first.

Data and Methods

We carried out a mixed-method research including a questionnaire survey and qualitative in-depth interviews with Turkish immigrants in Denmark. Our results are based on 450 completed questionnaires and 31 qualitative interviews. The survey sample included 182 women and 268 men, 64 percent of whom were either self-employed or employees. The question we asked about remittances was as follows: *Do you send money to your relatives, friends, or others in need of support in Turkey?* The analysis presented

FIGURE 23.1 Turkish-Born Immigrants in Denmark, 1990–2011

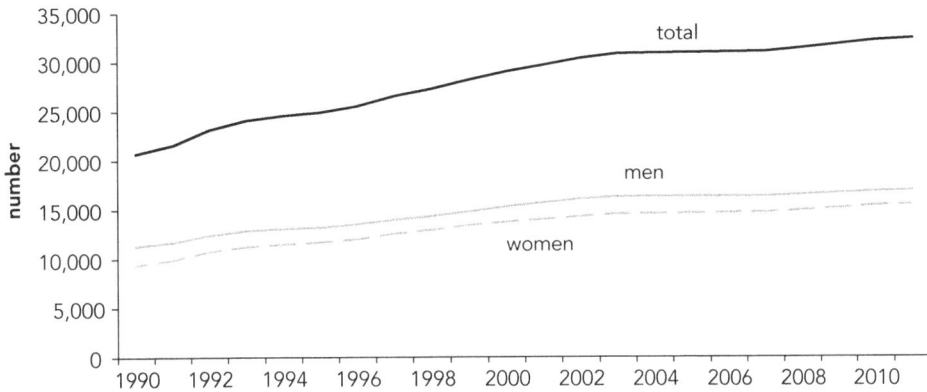

Source: Statistics Denmark 2011.

in this chapter refers to a subsample of these 450, from which we have excluded those whose were not born in Turkey or Denmark.

In-depth interviews were carried out with 31 individuals (17 women and 14 men), half of whom were born in Turkey and the others were born in Denmark. All questionnaires and interviews were conducted in Turkish, and materials used in presentations were translated into English. Participant observation during the fieldwork also helped in interpreting the quantitative findings. Further details of the fieldwork, sampling, and instruments are explained elsewhere (Yazgan 2010).

Transnational Ties and Remittance Practices

Sending remittances and migration are part of a decision-making process that begins with the choice to leave one's household, community, and often nation (Cohen 2005). Families and households are crucial in remittance-sending patterns (Gentry and Mittelstaed 2010: 23). Traditional social relations and networks as well as are maintained through migration. Transnational networks of immigrant groups with common backgrounds living in different countries are an exemplar of this. These networks not only link and ensure cultural and social flows between different countries but also serve for financial flows. The Denmark-Turkey remittance corridor is characterized by family ties and money transfers between extended family members.

In April 2009 interviews that we conducted at the Roskilde Culture Association, respondents stated that at that time a chain migration was in existence between the Sarkisla district of Sivas, Turkey, and Roskilde. They had formed a community as their relatives and friends from Sarkisla arrived. Many were able to create a life between home, cultural association, mosque association, and work. Thus they told us that they felt it was like living at home in Turkey. This transnational living space had kept them in touch with what is happening in Turkey through the ties with relatives and friends in Denmark and Turkey. It was clear to them that they were aware and engaged with what is happening in Turkey. A middle-aged Turkish immigrant (Mehmet, aged 45, born in Turkey) explained this complex web of relations as follows: "At least we are speaking to our relatives over the phone, going there on holidays, financially helping them. Those in Turkey don't follow the news as we do it from here. When we go there, we see they have no clue about what is going on in Turkey."

Those who were left behind live in a relatively deprived environment in their towns and villages in Turkey. This deprivation was among the key reasons for emigration in the first place. Thus it is interesting to understand whether migrants send remittances to and contribute to these communities and individuals back in Turkey. In our survey, about three-quarters of both Turkish-born (73.5 percent) and Danish-born (71.4 percent) Turks in Denmark send remittances to their families, relatives, and friends (*n* = 363, of whom 294 were born in Turkey and 63 were born in Denmark). A high level of remittance sending among Danish-born Turks can be an indication of strong ties by the second and third generations with their parental homeland.

Both men and women were largely remitting home, although the percentage of women sending money to Turkey (67 percent) was lower than that of men (77 percent).

When employment status is analyzed, we found that 74 percent of those who are in temporary employment were sending money. The corresponding figures were 69 percent for the self-employed and 71 percent for employees. The highest rates we observed were among the retired (81 percent), students (80 percent), and unemployed (80 percent). One can speculate on the higher propensity to remit among the retired, students, and unemployed because this can be linked to regulated welfare benefits they may receive as well as potential income from informal economic activities. Nevertheless, this requires further investigation.

FIGURE 23.2 Remittance-Sending Behavior of Danish Turks by Country of Birth, 2010

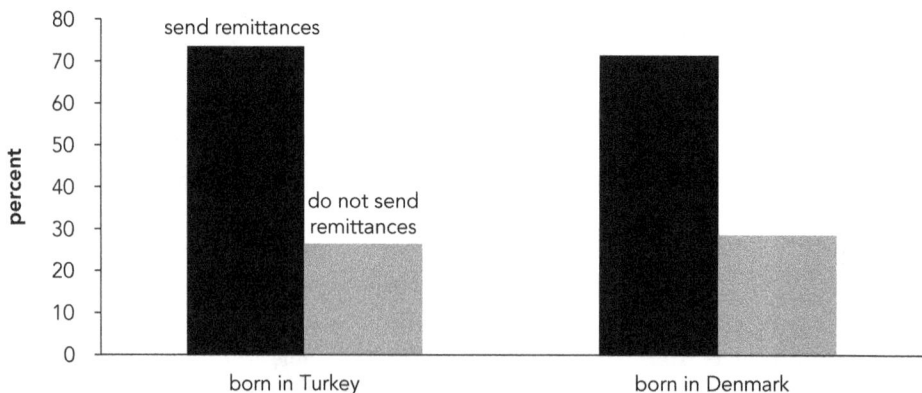

Source: Authors' field data.

Many of our respondents in the qualitative survey also indicated their commitment to send money to their families and relatives in Turkey. It was often put as if sending money is a moral obligation while also assuming there is need for it:

> As a family we are sending money. Usually we send it to our aunt and grandfather to support them. Because they need it. My father and his two brothers send them some money every month. Families are sending money, but we as children, young or grown up, are too contributing as much as we can. Recently, my 15-year-old sister brought her first ever salary and said, shall we send this to my grandfather? (Ayla, aged 23, born in Denmark).

Ayla, born in Denmark, is a postgraduate student. She, like others in her family, is very close with her relatives in Turkey, and she sends money to them. Her siblings are also sending remittances to their grandmother in Turkey. Similarly Eren, another postgraduate student aged 19 and born in Denmark, states that his peers, like himself, have strong ties with their relatives in Turkey and send remittances to them: "Many of those here have strong family ties. For example, we gather as a family and one by one pick [up] the phone and speak to my grandfather and grandmother in Turkey as we miss them so much. Whenever they need we help them financially."

Cihan, aged 32, had come to Denmark from Turkey when he was nine years old. He told us that financial support to his relatives in Turkey is important and the economic crisis did not affect that:

> My uncles and grandmother still live in Turkey. I am on good terms with them. I am always in touch with my grandmother. She rings me, I ring her. Both my mother and myself, we never leave her without money, we send as much as we can possibly do. She lives with my uncle anyway. We have a very large family... Facebook also helped us to be in touch more regularly. [The] economic crisis did not affect us in this regard.

Serpil, aged 48, with her husband came to Denmark from Turkey as a political refugee at the beginning of the 1980s. They financially support their families left behind as much as economic migrants. This money flow continues over many years and is maintained by new generations, too. Danish Turks' marriages with distant relatives in Turkey also contribute to the maintenance of remittance flows. These marriages strengthen the transnational ties. Serpil's son is married to a relative in Turkey:

> I used to send some pocket money to my elder sister. We send [money] even if it's a small amount. My son completed his military service in 2005 and began seeing his aunt's daughter. When his uncle [in Turkey] was not able to pay his insurance, my son had paid it for him. He paid it to support [him]. We have always been supportive to our family; solidarity continues after the crisis... I got my papers as a refugee in November 1982. Since then I send money to Turkey, sometimes documented, sometimes undocumented. Sometimes I give gold [or] send money instead for Eid ul-Fitr... In the past, people were buying or building houses in Turkey; nowadays they see themselves permanent here. So they still send money to Turkey but don't buy houses like it was in the past. They adjust to Denmark. Lifestyles changed but solidarity continues.

Some have mixed networks of friends including people other than Turks who came from the same districts or towns in Turkey. Sadik, aged 34, came to Denmark when he was only two years old because his parents, both teachers, were appointed to positions in Denmark. Therefore, Sadik and his parents are not sending regular remittances to Turkey except some money sent to his uncles occasionally. Nevertheless, despite the fact that he tried to portray himself as different from other Turks in Denmark, he is still in touch with his relatives and friends in Turkey and also sends remittances, albeit very small amounts:

> Since I arrived 32 years ago, I visit my hometown Tokat once every other year when I go to Turkey for holiday. Except one, all my relatives live in Turkey. Annually I call a few relatives at Eid. If there is somebody very ill, then I call them. I talk to some relatives over Facebook monthly... I did not help economically much, but only as a gift I had given €100 to a few relatives who I feel close to—for example when they had their babies. As far as I know, my parents don't send much money either, but they had helped my grandmother and uncle so much... Irregularly they send pocket money to my grandmother who was widowed 10 years ago. [The] economic crisis did not affect us in this regard.

Although we cannot know for sure the size of the volume of remittances sent by Turkish immigrants and their children and grandchildren, the total volume of remittance outflows from Denmark has increased sharply since the late 1990s (figure 23.3).

FIGURE 23.3 Remittance Outflows from Denmark, 1992–2009

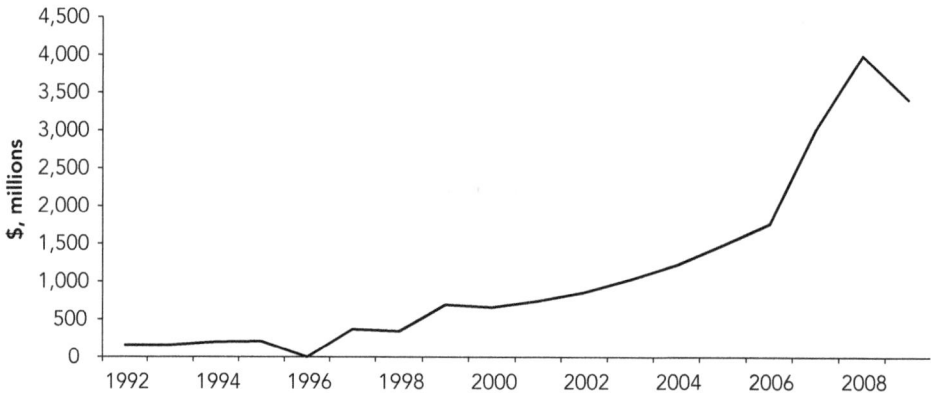

Source: World Bank 2011b.

It seems that the most recent financial crisis has not prevented Danish Turks from sending money home, but some of our interviewees revealed that they have been sending more and more often recently: "Following the crisis, our support continues as it was before. The more we have the more we are trying to send to them; [the] same continues on special dates too" (Ayla, quoted above). Although most of them told us stories reflecting that relations, family ties, and indebtedness are very important and thus the financial crisis appears to be irrelevant, a few of the respondents also underlined the adverse effects of the financial crisis on their lives and earnings in Denmark. This is no surprise to anybody, and hence not surprisingly they also told us that the amounts and frequency of remittances sent to those left behind in Turkey have changed since they cannot afford to send large amounts or as frequently anymore.

Conclusion

Remittances, if we take a broader definition, carry ideas, opinions, attitudes, politics, and culture in general between Denmark and Turkey. The contribution of remittances, thus, to local development in sending areas is evident though difficult to measure. The transnational ties are essential in these flows attached to people flows; as observed by Sørensen (2005a: 36), immigrants act as interpreters between the geographies they are associated with. These flows should not be seen as one-way but mutual.

As we mentioned earlier, financial flows are often based on family and social ties. Despite the expectation that these ties with the country of origin and communities of origin will loosen as time goes by and among new generations, our interviews provided evidence that Turkish and Kurdish migrants in Denmark tend to continue remitting. We believe the strong transnational ties between the origin communities and the diaspora deserve some credit for this trend. Thus remittances continue to be sent in the same amounts and frequency as in the past. The transnational space created by Turkish immigrants in Denmark is characterized by a network of a limited number of locations in Turkey. These networks between the communities strengthened over time as they provided for the individuals and households involved in migration. These strong networks may also explain at least partly why remittances were resilient in the most recent financial crisis.

Chapter 24

Work and Remittance Patterns of Irregular Immigrants in Turkey

OĞUZHAN ÖMER DEMIR AND M. ALPER SOZER

MIGRATION LITERATURE IS DOMINATED BY studies on remittance practices of legal migrants. Because of the unavailability of data and difficulty in conducting studies with undocumented immigrants, remittances by irregular immigrants are understudied. In this chapter, we present results from recent field research to outline the work and remittance patterns of permanent, transit, and semitransit irregular immigrants caught by authorities in Turkey while also relating it to the global financial crisis, which has had a clear impact on remittance flows globally (see *Migration Letters*, special issue on remittances and financial crisis 2010).

Turkey is a historically receiving and sending country for migration (IOM 2008; Kirisci 2002). The trend of migration beginning in the 1990s is considerably different from the trends in the past. Turkey has experienced an increased wave of regular and irregular migration in the last two decades, and the country has since become a popular destination point for migrants (Icduygu 2006; Sirkeci 2009). Turkey has been a place of interest for short-or long-term visitors and immigrants for various reasons, such as tourism, education, and employment. The number of foreign visitors has increased almost four times between 1990 and 2008. Entry numbers of foreigners increased 100 percent between 1990 and 2000, and the increase was almost 260 percent between 2000 and 2008.

Turkey is also a transit place for irregular immigrants who are destined for Europe. Others use Turkey as a semitransit location, and they stay over in Turkey for a period of time (Icduygu 2003; Koç and Onan 2004). Official statistics show that 660,000 irregular immigrants were caught by law enforcement authorities in Turkey between 2000 and 2009 (Sirkeci 2009). Of this number, the nationals of Afghanistan, Bangladesh, the

Islamic Republic of Iran, Iraq, Pakistan, Somalia, and the West Bank and Gaza accounted for the largest irregular immigrant groups. Many of these were apparently transit irregular immigrants: That is, they entered Turkey illegally and tried to leave Turkey illegally to reach a European country. Before leaving Turkey, some of these groups, however, stayed and worked in the country (Icduygu 2003).

This study is designed as an exploratory case study. Qualitative and quantitative data were used to understand irregular transit migrants' work and remittance patterns. The primary data were collected through a questionnaire survey and interviews. The first data set was generated through a nationwide survey that includes irregular migrants' migration experiences to and through Turkey. The survey included 70 questions in seven modules: (1) the decision-making process of migrants, (2) transportation patterns, (3) experiences during the journey, (4) relationships with smugglers, (5) payments, (6) experiences in Turkey (time, work, earnings, police record, remittances, and the like), and (7) demographics. We benefited from Chin's (1999) questions in formulating the questionnaire. A focus group meeting was held with the participation of experts and academics in the field to strengthen measurement validity and reliability. In addition, in January 2010, a set of preliminary interviews were conducted in Ankara to test this data collection method. After doing cross-checks to strengthen the measurement validity and reliability, the questionnaire was finalized and sent to police departments of 33 provinces in Turkey where irregular immigrants are captured. Between January 2010 and November 2010, a total of 1,189 irregular immigrants consented to participate in the survey. Participation in the survey was absolutely voluntary, and none of the irregular immigrants were forced to respond to the questions. A data set was generated based on the participants' responses to the questionnaire. Descriptive and bivariate analyses were carried out on these data.

We are well aware that the setting has a crucial role in fieldwork, and carrying out questionnaires via security forces is particularly problematic in terms of reflexivity issues identified in the methodological studies. We are also aware that respondents may not have freely expressed their opinions or disclosed their practices fully in fear that the information may not work in their favor because their cases were ongoing during the field research. Therefore, we would like to warn readers to be cautious in interpreting the results and findings of the study. Nevertheless, we have tried our best to ensure the survey data are confidential and no identifying personal data were collected.

The qualitative data were collected through in-depth interviews held with 65 irregular immigrants in different settings in the cities of Istanbul, Edirne, Izmir, Mersin, Hatay, Van, and Ankara between January 2010 and November 2010. All interviews were conducted on a voluntary basis. Obviously, we lacked a sampling list of irregular migrants in Turkey; therefore, we used nonprobability sampling techniques. To reach irregular immigrants in their natural setting, we utilized the snowball sampling technique. Moreover, as a convenient sample, we visited immigrant removal centers and conducted interviews with subjects awaiting deportation. We ensured every interviewee that we would keep their personal information confidential. We told them they could stop the interview if they felt uncomfortable. We asked several questions to understand immigrants' experiences, including remittance and work patterns. The interviews took between 30 minutes and 2.5 hours. Interviews were tape recorded when interviewees permitted; otherwise, notes were taken. All interviews were fully transcribed and read by two different researchers. An open coding technique was utilized, which enabled researchers to capture even minor details. Next we formed subthemes and then combined these subthemes into recurrent themes. For this study, we have used only a portion of the data, which covers immigrants' work, stay in Turkey, and remittance patterns.

Findings

The findings are presented in a deductive way. First, brief demographics of our sample are presented. Second, irregular immigrants who sent remittances to their homelands are examined. This section is followed by presentation of variables that include reason for being in Turkey, work experience, duration of stay, links with homeland, and remittances. In addition to these descriptive analyses, we attempt to discover possible patterns of remittance sending by making a bivariate analysis.

Our findings revealed that the majority of irregular immigrants in Turkey are male (88 percent); however, there are female migrants (12 percent) who often travel with their families (husband, children, grandfathers, and others). Although most of the irregular migrants are single (70 percent), a considerable portion are married (28 percent). We observed that most married males were traveling alone and had left their families in their homeland.

The mean age of the irregular immigrants is 26 although 7 percent were girls and boys under the age of 18. The vast majority of immigrants are either uneducated (26 percent) or undereducated (61 percent). Like their education level, their income level is considered low. Almost half of all irregular migrants make $100 or less per month. A third were unemployed in their homeland, another third were self-employed, 13 percent were workers, 5 percent were housewives, and 1 percent were public officials (table 24.1).

Only 8 percent reported any work experiences while in Turkey (table 24.1). The work patterns of irregular immigrants vary according to their nationality. Irregular migrants coming from Afghanistan, the Islamic Republic of Iran, Iraq, and Uzbekistan have ties and networks with at least an individual with a long-standing history in Turkey.

When they enter Turkey migrants are easily integrated and absorbed into their communities and diasporas. They can find jobs and rent houses, and their nationals provide all other logistics in a short time. However, Bangladeshi, Myanmar, and Pakistani nationals show different patterns; their duration of stay in Turkey is considerably shorter.

Surprisingly, 82 percent of irregular migrants reported that they did not have family members in their homeland. Reporting no family ties in their countries may be a preventive strategy to avoid deportation, or a strategy for seeking asylum. However, in our interviews, we observed many irregular immigrants with separated or lost families. This

TABLE 24.1 Characteristics of Irregular Migrants in Turkey

Variable	Mean
Age (years)	26 (7.3)
Gender (%)	
Male	88
Female	12
Marital status (%)	
Single	70
Married	28
Divorced	1
Widowed	1
Education (%)	
Illiterate	26
Secondary school or less	61
High school	11
University or more	2
Occupation in homeland (%)	
Unemployed	33
Worker	13
Public official	1
Self-employed	37
Housewife	5
Other	11
Income ($)	263 (972)
0–50 (%)	21
51–100 (%)	27
101–250 (%)	29
251–5,000 (%)	23
Worked in Turkey (%)	
Yes	8
No	92
Has family members in the country of origin (%)	
Yes	18
No	82

Source: Authors' calculations.

Note: n = 1,189. Standard deviations are in parentheses.

is especially true when we consider Afghan immigrants because most of our subjects did not come from Afghanistan, but from Pakistani refugee camps or from bordering regions of the Islamic Republic of Iran. Many reported that their family members died in conflicts, and many did not know or remember any family members.

Remittance Senders

Our findings about families in their homeland give us a clue about potential remittance patterns. If there are no family members in the countries of origin, then remittances, if they are sent, are sent out of a concern that there is a need beyond the family for money.

Only 3 percent of irregular migrants reported that they send remittances to their countries. They were from Afghanistan, Azerbaijan, the Islamic Republic of Iran, Iraq, Myanmar, Pakistan, Rwanda, Senegal, Sudan, the Syrian Arab Republic, Turkmenistan, and Uzbekistan.

The mean age of remittance senders is 29 (three years older than the general sample), and the gender distribution consists of 73 percent males and 27 percent females. The rate of married people is 5 percent higher in remittance senders (33 percent) compared with the entire sample. The uneducated or undereducated population is also 10 percent higher than the entire sample. Half of remittance senders were making $100 or less in their countries (table 24.2).

To perform further analysis on this issue, we examined variables related to stay, work, and remittances and tried to understand why an irregular migrant sends money, while another one does not.

TABLE 24.2 Characteristics of Irregular Migrants in Turkey Who Send Remittances to Their Country of Origin

Variable	Mean
Age (years)	29 (7.8)
Gender (%)	
Male	73
Female	27
Marital status (%)	
Single	50
Married	33
Divorced	10
Widowed	7
Education (%)	
Illiterate	21
Secondary school or less	37
High school	28
University or more	14
Occupation in homeland (%)	
Unemployed	21
Worker	14
Public official	3
Self-employed	41
Housewife	21
Other	
Income ($)	277 (683)
0–50 (%)	17
51–100 (%)	33
101–250 (%)	39
251–5,000 (%)	11

Source: Authors' calculations.

Note: n = 30. Standard deviations are in parentheses.

An irregular migrant stays in Turkey on average 37 days, whereas the duration of stay for remittance senders is about one year (366 days). Moreover, the majority of remittance senders (63 percent) came to work and stay in Turkey. In addition, 87 percent reported that they work (or worked), which is apparently much higher than the full sample's work experience (8 percent of the total reported any work experience). Their work experiences range from a construction worker to a salesperson, and from babysitting to street peddling. Slightly over half of all remittance senders (54 percent) stayed in an apartment. Only 7 percent reported that they stayed in a temporary place such as a hotel room, which is considered to be a classic accommodation facility for irregular migrants (table 24.3).

Unlike the full sample, the majority of remittance senders (75 percent) reported that they had family members in their homelands. Most of our subjects had a kind of family tie with their countries. A younger Afghan immigrant who has been living in Turkey for almost two years explained why and how he sent remittances to his homeland:

> I had a carpet store in Afghanistan with a good business partner. We were making good money. In the meantime, I got married. Although we had years of successful business, then we could not manage it financially. Our business was bankrupted. I was full of debts. My brothers were in Turkey at that time. I decided to go to Turkey. I am here almost for two years. I knew Pakistani, Afghani, and English languages. I found many jobs here. I sold clothes. I worked as a salesperson in Grand Bazaar, because I was communicating with foreign tourists very well. Then I worked in a fabric store. In short, I worked in many places with my brothers to pay my debt back. I sent money to my family many times. I did not use banks to transfer money. The easiest way was to find a trusted friend who was going to Afghanistan. Until now, I could pay all my debt. I plan to bring my family here to Turkey if I can get a residence permit.

A younger Afghani immigrant, who was deported twice and captured a third time by the police, explained why he has to send money to his country:

> My family lives in Afghanistan. I have seven sisters and brothers. Two of them have jobs and can afford their lives. However, others are students and they are dependent on me. I have to work and send money for their expenses. I worked in a restaurant for a long time in Turkey. I send money through bank transfer. Now I am about to be deported, and I have nothing, barely no money!

A Myanmar immigrant mentioned why he sent remittance to his homeland as follows: "I work for a textile company and I make almost $400 every month in Turkey. My parents were passed away and I have only a sister in my homeland. I send money to her whenever I find a trusted person going back to my country."

One can ask why one-fourth of remittance senders transfer money to their homelands, despite having no family members there. Our interviews indicate that some of those senders have debts or planned investments in their countries. An elderly irregular immigrant from Turkmenistan living in Turkey for over two years explained his remittance experiences:

TABLE 24.3 Work and Remittance Patterns of Irregular Migrants Who Sent Remittances to Their Country of Origin

Variable	Mean
Duration of stay in Turkey (days)	366 (404)
Reason to leave homeland (%)	
To make money	70
To find lost family	7
Other	23
Reason to enter Turkey (%)	
To go directly to Europe	13
To work for some time in Turkey, then go to Europe	17
To work and stay in Turkey	63
Other	7
Ever worked in Turkey? (%)	
Yes	87
No	13
Type of work in Turkey (%)	
Construction worker	24
Industry worker	12
Babysitter/housekeeper	16
Street peddler	4
Other	44
Where lived in Turkey (%)	
Hotel room	7
Apartment	54
Workplace	25
Other	14
Family members in country of origin (%)	
Yes	75
No	25
How remittances were sent to country of origin (%)	
Bank transfer	17
Western Union	37
Cash sent via friends/relatives	37
Other	10

Source: Authors' calculations.

Note: n = 30. Standard deviations are in parentheses.

I had a wife in my homeland. We got divorced two years ago, and I decided to go to Turkey to make some money. I had a lot of debts. When I first came in here, I worked in a car wash company for long years. Then I worked in a construction site. All I was doing was working and making some money. My boss was a smart guy. He was sending my money through bank transfer to bank accounts of people whom I owed. I sent all my earnings to pay my debts. Fortunately, I have no debt anymore, I paid almost $10,000.

Various sending methods were used; however, irregular immigrants usually send money through an official transfer system (banks or Western Union), and a large number reported that they sent money through a trusted friend or a fellow national.

Relationship between Stay, Work, Causes of Migration, and Remittance Patterns of Irregular Migrants in Turkey

To further explore remittance patterns, we examined the relationship between remittance sending and related variables. First, we cross-tabulated the two variables: sending remittances and the reasons for entering Turkey (table 24.4). The results indicate that immigrants who go to Turkey to go directly to a European country are less likely to send remittances to their countries. The likelihood of sending remittances is higher when the immigrant goes to Turkey to work and then goes to Europe, and much higher when the immigrant goes to Turkey to work and stay.

TABLE 24.4 Reasons for Migration and Remittance-Sending Status

Sending remittances	Reason for entering Turkey			X² (degrees of freedom)	Significance
	Go directly to Europe	Work in Turkey, then go to Europe	Work and stay in Turkey		
Yes	1	5	10	59.144 (4)	0.000
No	99	95	90		

Source: Authors' calculations.

Note: n = 1,189.

Moreover, we examined the link between remittance-sending status and duration of stay in Turkey (table 24.5). The findings reveal that when the duration of stay is shorter, it is less likely for an irregular migrant to send remittances to his or her country.

TABLE 24.5 Duration of Stay in Turkey and Remittance-Sending Status

Sending remittances	Duration (days)					X² (degrees of freedom)	Significance
	0–30	31–90	91–180	181–365	365–999		
Yes	1	2	7	29	45	201.280 (5)	0.000
No	99	98	93	71	55		

Source: Authors' calculations.

Note: n = 1,189.

The final bivariate analysis was made as to whether remittance sending and work experience has any relationship (table 24.6). The findings reveal that remittance senders who work in Turkey are more likely to send money to their countries.

TABLE 24.6 Employment and Remittance-Sending Status

Sending remittances	Work in Turkey?		X^2 (degrees of freedom)	Significance
	Yes	No		
Yes	28	6	262.929 (1)	0.000
No	71	94		

Source: Authors' calculations.

Note: n = 1,189.

Discussion and Conclusion

Our findings clearly indicate that some irregular migrants send remittances to their countries of origin. Although they are a small group of people within our total sample, they are clearly distinct in terms of age, having a family member in the homeland, duration of stay, work experience, and reasons for entering Turkey.

For many respondents Turkey was an ideal destination, especially during the financial crisis. This sometimes even attracted back those who transited Turkey to go to Europe. A Rwandan and a Senegalese immigrant, for instance, mentioned that they came back to Turkey from Greece because, as they reported, Athens has become a city of irregular immigrants and you cannot find employment there (see also *Hürriyet* 2011).

Our interviews with some irregular migrants show that they were affected negatively by the financial crisis in 2008 and 2009, and therefore they decided to leave their countries. On the other hand, based on our data, it is difficult to say that the financial crisis affected remittance-sending habits of irregular migrants.

Most male irregular migrants work in industry and the construction sector, whereas female irregular migrants usually find jobs as housekeepers or babysitters. These jobs do not come with high earnings, and thus remittances are sometimes small; nevertheless, many migrants will try to send home as much of their remaining earnings as possible. Their remittance habits are related to whether they work and make money. When they can make money, many send it because they have to take care of people back in their homeland. Remittances usually go to family members (usually to children and wives), while some send money to pay their accumulated debts in their homelands. Only a few irregular migrants send their earnings home to make investments.

As we have mentioned, studies of irregular migration involving interviews and/or surveys need to be treated cautiously. This particular type of human mobility is the most difficult to capture in statistics and equally difficult to capture in qualitative studies because of its nature and the risks and fears of migrants. Financial behavior is in itself a difficult subject to study because in many cultures it is not so common to disclose earnings or any details of monetary affairs. Revealing such information to an outsider or as in our case in the context of an irregular migrant removal center is even more difficult. The results and interpretation might have been completely different if the study had been carried out in another context and by another team of researchers. Thus reflexivity of the context and researchers must be kept in mind in interpreting the findings of this study.

PART VI

Chapter 25

Labor Migration, Overseas Remittances, and Local Outcomes in the Contemporary Philippines

TY MATEJOWSKY

FEW COUNTRIES TODAY ARE MORE closely associated with an entrenched economic dependence on the deployment of contract labor abroad and the infusion of overseas remittances than the Philippines (DeParle 2010). For the state, labor emigration has emerged as an indispensible source of hard foreign currency that, since the 1970s, has done much to keep the national economy afloat and ameliorate socioeconomic conditions by alleviating chronic under- and unemployment problems and contributing to the rise of a consumer-oriented middle class.

This market alignment has, less favorably, impeded the development of a sound domestic economy, leaving the country exposed to global market fluctuations and promoting a trend of "brain drain" whereby highly skilled and educated Filipino workers seek more financially remunerative employment opportunities internationally. Notably, the Philippines is currently experiencing a significant manpower shortage in its education and health care sectors because thousands of teachers and medically trained physicians have left their respective professions to take advantage of in-demand nursing jobs in North America, East Asia, and elsewhere across the global North (Teves 2005).

Notwithstanding these problematic dimensions, policy makers have consistently favored exporting labor overseas above local job creation as a way to generate sustained economic growth. By 2010 nearly one-tenth of the nation's population of nearly 100 million were either living or working abroad. The amount of dollars sent home by overseas Filipino workers (OFWs), which represent approximately 13.5 percent of the country's gross domestic product, has more than doubled from $7.6 billion to $17.3 billion between 2003 and 2009 (Onishi 2010). The Philippines would be unable to maintain recent levels of market expansion without these vital income streams. Theoretically, such financial linkages remain relatively fragile and reversible because they are so closely wedded to the economic performance of OFW host countries.

Beyond its economic implications, the continued outflow of labor overseas also has important social dimensions because it significantly informs Filipinos' sense of national identity (Perlez 2002). Dependence on OFWs reinforces popular stereotypes of Filipinos as not only tenacious and resourceful when it comes to confronting adversity but also remarkably selfless in contributing to the welfare of family and community. Such sentiments are reflected in government public relations efforts that urge Filipinos to view their compatriots abroad as the nation's "new heroes" (Rafael 1997). Less positively, this reliance on OFWs and their remittances highlights the state's profound inability to meet many of its obligations to citizens. This failure to provide adequate domestic employment opportunities, in turn, instills little public confidence in state institutions and leaders (Aguilar 1996).

At the household level, overseas contract work demands considerable sacrifice on the part of workers and their dependents. The emotional anxieties of family separation, spousal fidelity, tenuous social support networks within receiving countries, and possible exploitation by job contractors, travel agents, and foreign employers are just some of the hardships OFWs face. Perhaps more troubling, the absence of a parent, spouse, or other valued household member does much to disrupt traditional patterns of domestic stability and community life (Assis 1995). In fact, the number of Filipinos growing up with at least one parent working abroad reached nearly 6 million in 2008 (Conde 2008). Many of these children, although now better materially provided for, fail to develop deep emotional ties with their absent OFW parent. The sporadic presence of a mother or father in their sons' or daughters' lives not only places the burden of child rearing on the remaining spouses, grandparents, or more extended kin, but also works to complicate existing intrafamilial relations.

I witnessed such complexities first hand while living with a Filipino family during the late 1990s in Dagupan City, Pangasinan. The unmarried and childless household head, then in her early fifties, ended up raising her niece (born out of wedlock) while the girl's mother worked as a hired domestic, first, in Hong Kong and then, years later, in the Middle East. Although such familial arrangements are traditionally rather common in the Philippines, this particular setup complicated issues between the sisters about parental discipline, authority, and allegiance. Such conflictive dimensions placed additional stress on the sisters' relationship that became particularly acute, especially for the niece, when her mother returned to the Philippines for a few weeks' vacation. Over time, the girl's mother assumed only a secondary role in her daughter's life that continued throughout adolescence and young adulthood.

Despite these hardships, most OFWs maintain, if not an emotional presence, then certainly an influence within their respective households as breadwinners despite remaining away for months or years at a time. Workers are able to bridge this distance primarily through income remittances that augment domestic budgets and expand the financial prospects of relatives and dependents. Significantly, the flow of remittances back home contributes to a transformation in the social and material character of many local neighborhoods. Most OFW homes stand in appreciable contrast to those of their neighbors in terms of architectural character and material trappings. In areas where most houses are modest, if not austere, these larger domiciles are typically set behind privacy walls and feature modern amenities such as air conditioning, Internet access, cable television, and floor plans that by local standards are quite luxurious. Similarly, in neighborhoods where residents commonly depend on jeepneys (jeeps converted into minibuses) as their basic mode of transport, it is not uncommon to find one or two private automobiles parked outside these homes.

In essence, this cycle of overseas labor migration and income remittances represents nothing if not a practical response to the state's inability to create adequate employment opportunities at home. Filipinos are willing to take on the risks of working abroad because it remains one of the few avenues available to natives toward generating income and upward mobility. Even as the global economic downturn continues to wreak havoc on world markets, the deployment of laborers from the Philippines carries on unabated. Most OFW households remain largely shielded from the crisis's more adverse effects as the amount of money remitted home trends increasingly upward (DeParle 2010).

Chapter 26

The New Zealand–Pacific Remittance Corridor: Lowering Remittance Costs

DON ABEL AND KIM HAILWOOD

REMITTANCES ARE A KEY FACTOR in Pacific island countries, representing 12 percent of gross domestic product (GDP) on average, yet the Pacific region has some of the highest remittance fees in the world.

To address this issue of remittance fees, in June 2007 the World Bank's Pacific office convened a high-level public-private stakeholder meeting in Sydney, attended by the Central Banks of Australia, Fiji, New Zealand, Samoa, and Tonga as well as executives from the primary remittance service providers in the region. The meeting recorded that although remittance fees were trending downward in other parts of the world, rates being charged in the Pacific were unreasonably high. At that time, remittance providers were routinely charging 15–25 percent of the value of the transaction and sometimes even more.

This meeting marked the beginning of the New Zealand–Pacific Remittance Project, a project that over the next three years would be responsible for reducing the cost of sending money between New Zealand and Pacific island countries. The purpose of this case study is to record how this was achieved—what worked and what did not.

Background

Although individual remittances from New Zealand to Pacific island countries are often relatively small sums—a few hundred dollars sent home each month—the market as a whole is far from "low value." Remittances to the Pacific region (principally from

Australia, New Zealand, and the United States) are estimated by the World Bank to be worth over $470 million annually (World Bank 2010c). This estimate does not capture payments made through informal, unrecorded channels. The World Bank (2006b) notes this could add at least another 50 percent to the official estimate.

Most Pacific island economies are dependent on remittances as an important source of household income and foreign exchange. Samoa and Tonga are among the top 10 global recipients of migrant remittances as a share of GDP (World Bank 2010d). As well as providing income directly to households to improve living standards, remittances are an important source of current account financing, enabling higher levels of imports, which contribute to macroeconomic stability (Browne and Mineshima 2007).

In Samoa and Tonga remittances far surpass official development assistance receipts. In these countries, remittances exceed a fifth of GDP (World Bank 2010c). New Zealand is a key source of remittances for both countries. The simple model of sending money home has enabled a whole industry to grow and prosper on the back of transacting remittances.

According to Gibson, McKenzie, and Rohorua (2006) the high transactional costs of Pacific remittances cannot be justified in terms of scale. They analyzed two non-Pacific countries (Ghana and Mozambique) with scales of remittances similar to the New Zealand–Tonga corridor. Both African countries had substantially lower money transfer fees, and the transaction could be completed at one-third of the cost.

The impact of the fees charged on remittances can be dramatic, particularly in relation to the small amounts sent, the purchasing power in the receiving country, and the typically lower incomes of New Zealand family members sending the money. Any decrease in remittance costs would result in more money remaining in the pockets of Pacific peoples. It is estimated that remitters to the Pacific may face additional charges of up to $90 million in remittance fees each year—equaling 20 percent of the total amount formally remitted in 2008 (Luthria 2009).[1]

The World Bank's 2006 *Global Economic Prospects* highlighted three strategies for lowering the cost of remittances: promoting competition, improving migrants' access to the financial system, and disseminating information.

In 2007 the Reserve Bank of New Zealand established the cross-government New Zealand–Pacific Remittance Project, which included representatives from the New Zealand Ministry of Pacific Island Affairs and the Ministry of Foreign Affairs and Trade (which manages the New Zealand Aid Programme), in cooperation with the World Bank. The project's goals were to reduce the total transaction cost of remittances to between 5 and 7 percent by encouraging competition (including access to banking products and services), by promoting transparency and fee disclosure, and by building financial awareness.

Initially the project was hampered by the lack of remittance data needed to assist policy makers and to inform potential market entrants. By working with the Samoan and Tongan Central Banks, however, and using the seminal paper of Gibson, McKenzie, and Rohorua (2006), sufficient information was gathered to make a start.

Competing Financial Services

Australian banks dominate the financial markets in Pacific island countries. Although these Pacific island–domiciled banks have sustained high levels of profitability over the past decade—30–40 percent return on equity—they have not been significant competitors in the provision of household remittance services.

A key objective of the New Zealand–Pacific Remittance Project was to encourage a New Zealand–based Australian bank to compete effectively in the New Zealand–Pacific remittance corridor through using inexpensive electronic means.

In reviewing the electronic card market it was clear that cross-border transactions could be and were being made using these means without any oversight by authorities. Although the potential money launderer could use this method with impunity, the genuine, hardworking family member was forced to send small amounts of money home through traditional banking channels at considerable cost. The apparent barriers to banks developing electronic cards to remit funds across borders were the regulations for anti–money laundering (AML) and countering the financing of terrorism (CFT).

The product identified by New Zealand–based banks as most easily deployed to achieve low-cost remittances was a card facility using the banking system's international ATM and EFTPOS networks. To encourage such product development required a change to AML/CFT legislation in New Zealand, and, consequently, the Financial Transactions Reporting (Interpretations) Regulation was implemented in 2008.

A New Zealand–domiciled Australian bank was the first financial institution to take advantage of the regulatory change with the launch of a new card facility in 2008. This facility allowed funds to be loaded onto a special remittance card account by a New Zealand–based remitter, while a second card was issued remotely to an overseas resident, which allowed money to be withdrawn in the overseas country through the ATM and EFTPOS networks. The facility had to operate within tightly specified parameters, including monitoring on a daily basis. This meant that the opportunity for abuse was mitigated effectively.

The remittance card was judged by a New Zealand weekly newspaper as the best new banking product of the year in a 2009 business feature article. Simultaneously a website (www.SendMoneyPacific.org) was developed, cofunded by Australian and New Zealand governmental aid agencies, to allow remitters to compare the costs of sending money through various providers from Australia and New Zealand to Pacific island countries. The website was accredited as meeting the World Bank's standards for remittances databases in 2010.

In part, high fees are the result of a lack of competitive pressure, with operators in the marketplace able to "hide" the real costs of remitting money home in complex fee structures. And, in part, high fees have been driven by regulatory costs imposed by customer identification and verification requirements. With the introduction of the Financial Transactions Reporting (Interpretations) Regulation, increased competition from a new remittance product, and transparency in the market from information provided via the SendMoneyPacific website, costs began to fall.

On average, for every country surveyed by the SendMoneyPacific website (table 26.1), it is significantly cheaper to remit money to the Pacific from New Zealand than from Australia.[2]

TABLE 26.1 Cost of Sending $NZ 200/$A 200 from New Zealand/Australia to a Pacific Island Country as Percentage of Total Amount Sent

	Papua New Guinea			Solomon Islands	
Method	New Zealand	Australia	Method	New Zealand	Australia
Banks	22.7	28.1	Banks	19.6	28.9
MTOs	21.9	25.5	MTOs	14.6	23.3
	Tuvalu			Kiribati	
Method	New Zealand	Australia	Method	New Zealand	Australia
Banks	14.0	13.1	Banks	12.3	13.1
MTOs	12.5	13.8	MTOs	13.0	17.5
	Vanuatu			Fiji	
Method	New Zealand	Australia	Method	New Zealand	Australia
Banks	17.7	27.2	Banks	13.0	19.6
MTOs	11.9	15.7	MTOs	9.7	13.7
	Samoa			Tonga	
Method	New Zealand	Australia	Method	New Zealand	Australia
Banks	16.4	27.2	Banks	17.3	27.8
MTOs	6.1	9.0	MTOs	6.9	13.2

Source: SendMoneyPacific.org as of June 2010.

Note: MTO = money transfer operator.

Financial Education

Over the course of a year, the fees paid by one New Zealand–based remitter can equal more than one week's salary. Since remitters do not, as a rule, increase the amount they transmit to take account of these fees, the net result of higher charges is that the recipient simply receives less money. The problem is often compounded by the low level of financial capability among both remitters and beneficiaries.

New low-cost remittance products can be fully successful only when consumers are empowered with the skills, the knowledge, and the motivation to engage effectively with financial services and make informed choices. To effect real change, an understanding of the components of the transfer cost (the fee and the currency exchange rate commission), knowledge about competing products, and how the low-cost products might be used is required. Studies highlight limited take-up internationally of new remittance products if there is not a direct link to financial education (Orozco 2004).

Programs that promote financial capability within the Pacific remain on a passive footing. There is a gap in the provision of relevant, easy-to-access financial information and advice to help Pacific peoples, which is impartial, jargon free, not geared to sell products, and tailored to their personal circumstances.

The second phase of the project, MoneyPACIFIC, began in 2009 with the goal of providing targeted financial education to Pacific peoples in New Zealand and the Pacific region, contributing to a long-term vision of better-informed and more confident citizens, able to take advantage of increased competition and choice in the financial sector.

MoneyPACIFIC is directed at building awareness, engagement, and confidence. The MoneyPACIFIC "brand" consists of a simple logo and a tag line "Financial care is being aware." It has a clear terminology link to the SendMoneyPacific website.

The first MoneyPACIFIC initiative was to produce 35,000 bilingual wall calendars for Pacific households in New Zealand, Samoa, and Tonga, incorporating financial tips and information relating to the cost of remitting money. The 2010 calendars were made available through schools, churches, and community groups. Following the success of the first calendar, the print run for the 2011 calendar was doubled to 70,000. The Central Banks in Samoa and Tonga were key partners in this work.

The original proposal was to distribute an A4-sized information sheet on remittances and other financial issues. However, once a piece of paper has been read, it is easily discarded. It was agreed that with monthly Pacific photo shots, a calendar would be a permanent fixture in the homes of Pacific families. The benefit was that the calendar would be in the household for a year and referenced mainly by mothers, who largely manage the household and family finances.

The financial tips in the calendar are being expanded through a public awareness campaign that focuses on remittances and the teaching of good money skills to children. To date these messages have been transmitted on Pacific radio stations in New Zealand.

Initial outreach work conducted within the New Zealand Tongan community points to this population becoming more aware of different remittance options and the benefits of shopping around since the introduction of the two-card remittance facility, the SendMoneyPacific website, and the MoneyPACIFIC calendar (Developing Markets Associates 2010, as cited in Australia and New Zealand 2010).

What Has Been Achieved, What Did Work, and What Did Not

The introduction of the remittance card increased competition in the New Zealand–Pacific corridor, placing pressure on other operators to protect their market share by reducing costs below the 7 percent targeted by the New Zealand–Pacific Remittance Project. Surprisingly, though, and against expectations, the two-card remittance product was not adopted in Australia nor was it widely publicized in Pacific island countries. Consequently, the costs of remitting funds from Australia and New Zealand have diverged widely with, for example, the average cost for a person remitting from Australia to Samoa currently almost twice that from New Zealand.

This points to the importance of political engagement on the issue of the cost of remittances. Both the Australian and New Zealand governments have a keen wish to see these costs reduced for Pacific island communities, and there is a strong trans-Tasman initiative to meet this objective. In addition, South Pacific economic ministers and Central Bank governors have agreed that they need to play a leading role in advocating the importance of financial education and to drive collective national actions to achieve a strong focus on financial capability within the Pacific region. A set of MoneyPACIFIC goals were agreed on in 2009 by the Pacific Islands Forum economic ministers to strengthen financial capability in the Pacific region over the coming decade. They include goals on financial education, access to basic financial services, and consumer protection. Despite a relatively limited budget, the New Zealand–Pacific Remittance Project worked because it brought together a range of public sector institutions (including the World Bank) and private sector interests that jointly believed the cost of remitting funds to Pacific island countries was unnecessarily high. Their combined effort meant that change became inevitable.

Notes

1. A further impetus to look at remittance costs in New Zealand arose from the temporary worker migration program: the Recognised Seasonal Employer Scheme. This program, which began in 2007, each year draws up to 8,000 workers to New Zealand, predominantly from Pacific island nations, to work in the horticulture and viticulture sectors. Their earnings are often sent home as remittances or repatriated savings.

2. A comparable trans-Tasman cost disparity can also be seen in the World Bank's Remittance Prices Worldwide database.

Chapter 27

Role of Trade Openness, Remittances, Capital Inflows, and Financial Development in Vanuatu

RONALD R. KUMAR

VANUATU, ONE OF THE DEVELOPING Pacific island countries (PICs), has a population of about 240,000, which is growing at a rate of 2.5 percent per year. However, despite the worldwide adverse impact of the global financial crisis, the economy has been relatively less affected. Agriculture is the main driver of the economy; however, in terms of revenue inflows, the tourism sector stands out in addition to remittance inflows in gaining momentum (ADB 2009b, 2009c; Bedford 2010; Bedford, Bedford, and Ho 2010; Economic Intelligence Unit 2009).

In this chapter, a macrolevel investigation is carried out to determine the nexus between remittances, trade openness, financial development, foreign direct investment, foreign aid, and income.

Inward remittances have surpassed official development assistance of developing countries (figure 27.1) and have been growing substantially despite the worldwide economic crisis affecting most of the remittance sending countries (WDI 2009).

Remittances, when spent, among other things, on housing, sanitation, health care, food, and schooling, result in improvements in welfare and human capital, which in turn have the possibility to increase productivity, freedom of choice, and capacity to participate in public debate and reduce poverty (Buch and Kuckulenz 2010; De Haas 2005; Maclellan and Mares 2005; Ratha 2007; Sen 1999), besides providing "buffer cash" during economic crises and natural disasters (Browne and Leeves 2007; UN ESCAP 2007).

FIGURE 27.1 Remittance and Capital Flows to Developing Countries, 1990–2009

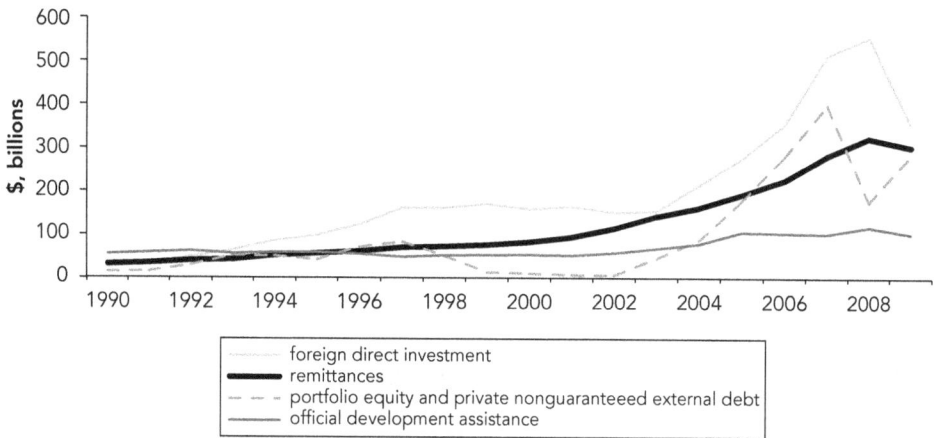

Sources: WDI 2009, World Bank 2006b, 2008, 2009d.

A substantial body of literature exists on how financial sector development (Beck, Levine, and Loayza 2000; King and Levine 1993; Levine, Loayza, and Beck 2000), trade liberalization (Kar, Peker, and Kaplan 2008; Wacziarg and Welch 2008; Winters, McCulloch, and McKay 2004), remittance inflows (Jayaraman, Choong, and Kumar 2009, 2010a, b), and foreign direct investment vis-à-vis developed financial markets (Alfaro and others 2010) promote economic growth. On the other hand, Shleifer (2009) and Bowman and Chand (2007) are skeptical of aid having any significant effect on growth.

Recent Trends in Remittance Inflows

Vanuatu, whose key indicators are given in table 27.1, has a relatively high inflow of remittances in absolute terms, particularly in the early period of 1980–2004. However, the country has since experienced a decline and leveled off to about $7 million in 2009 (table 27.2).[1] On average, before 2005, remittances were at about $14 million. The trend in remittances is also supported by the high amount of out-migration (table 27.3).

Vanuatu's financial sector includes the Reserve Bank of Vanuatu and four main commercial banking institutions (table 27.4).

Findings

The study looks into the nexus between remittances, trade openness, capital flows, and economic activities over a 28-year period (1981–2009). Table 27.5 presents the data used in the study.

TABLE 27.1 Vanuatu: Selected Key Indicators

Indicator	Value
Land area (square kilometers, thousands)	12.2
Population, 2010 (thousands)	239.8
Population growth, 2008 (%)	2.5
Per capita GDP current prices, 2007 ($)	2,712.6
Aid per capita, 2008 ($)	396.1
Aid as percentage of GNI, 2001–08	11.5
Annual average growth rate, 2001–09 (%)	3.3
Annual average inflation (CPI), 2001–08 (%)	2.8
Fiscal balance of central government, 2001–07 (% of GDP)	−0.4
Current account balance, 2001–07 (% of GDP)	−5.7
Rural population as percentage of total population (2008)	75.2

Sources: ADB 2009a, UN ESCAP 2007, WDI 2009.

Note: Interval periods are averages calculated by the author. CPI = consumer price index; GDP = gross domestic product; GNI = gross national income.

TABLE 27.2 Pacific Island Countries: Remittances, 1970–2009

Year	Fiji $, mil.	Fiji % of GDP	Kiribati $, mil.	Kiribati % of GDP	Papua New Guinea $, mil.	Papua New Guinea % of GDP	Samoa $, mil.	Samoa % of GDP	Solomon Islands $, mil.	Solomon Islands % of GDP	Tonga $, mil.	Tonga % of GDP	Vanuatu $, mil.	Vanuatu % of GDP
1970–74	—	—	—	—	—	—	—	—	—	—	2	7.5	—	—
1975–79	4	0.5	2	4.5	10	0.6	10	13.2	—	—	6	16.4	—	—
1980–84	8	0.7	2	6.9	5	0.2	19	19.0	—	—	10	16.5	8	7.0
1985–89	26	2.2	4	15.8	9	0.3	34	33.8	—	—	19	22.5	8	6.0
1990–94	24	1.6	6	19.3	17	0.4	37	28.1	—	—	21	15.4	12	6.4
1995–99	30	1.5	7	15.2	13	0.3	44	19.6	2	0.6	61	37.7	22	8.3
2000–04	73	3.6	7	13.3	11	0.3	54	18.9	4	1.6	61	37.7	22	8.3
2005	184	6.2	7	11.4	13	0.3	110	25.9	7	2.4	66	30.6	5	1.4
2006	165	5.2	7	11.3	13	0.2	108	24.0	20	6.0	72	30.5	5	1.2
2007	165	4.8	7	9.0	13	0.2	120	22.9	20	5.1	100	39.6	6	1.1
2008	175	4.7	9	10.7	13	0.2	135	24.0	20	4.8	100	36.9	7	1.2
2009	119	3.9	9	6.7	13	0.2	131	26.5	2.4	0.4	91	29.1	7	1.1

Source: WDI 2009, World Bank 2009d.

Note: The five-year intervals are averages calculated by the author. — = not available.

TABLE 27.3 Demographic Profile of Vanuatu

Year	Net migration	Population growth rate (%)	Population (10-year average, thousands)	Remittances ($, millions)
1961–70	3,182	3.0	73.5	—
1971–80	3,540	3.1	99.6	—
1981–90	2,455	2.4	130.8	8.2
1991–2000	1,508	2.4	169.9	20.0
2001–05	1,038	2.5	199.8	14.2
2006	—	2.6	216.4	5.0
2007	—	2.6	222.2	5.5
2008	—	2.5	228.0	7.0
2009	—	2.5	233.9	6.9
2010	814[a]	2.5	239.9	—

Source: United Nations, Department of Economic and Social Affairs, Population Division 2009.

Note: — = not available.

a. Indicates the average for 2006–10 from the database. All figures for interval years for other variables are averages calculated by the author.

TABLE 27.4 Commercial Financial Institutions in Vanuatu

Type of institution	Number of institutions	Assets (billions of vatu)	Assets as % of GDP	% of total assets held
Commercial banks (total)	5	43.1	147.2	11.2
State-controlled	1	2.7	8.5	0.7
Offshore banks	36	337.5	1,061.3	87.8
Insurance companies	3	0.5	1.6	0.1
Pension funds	1	3.1	9.7	0.8
Total	45	384.2	1,219.8	100.0

Source: Jayaraman and Choong 2010: 8.

Note: GDP = gross domestic product.

It is hypothesized that the variables used in the study will have a positive effect on income. Using the conventional Cobb-Douglas production function, with the Hicks-neutral technical progress, the per worker output (y_t) is defined as

$$y_t = A_t k_t^\alpha, \ 0 < \alpha < 1, \tag{27.1}$$

where A = stock of technology, k = capital per worker, and α is the profit share.

It is also plausible to assume for our purposes that

$$A_t = f(T, REM, TR, FIN). \tag{27.2}$$

TABLE 27.5 Vanuatu: GDP, Remittances, Trade, and Financial Indicators

Year	Real GDP Growth rate (%)	Remittances REM (% of GDP)	Exports of goods and services XGS (% of GDP)	Trade TR (% of GDP)	Private sector credit FIN (% of GDP)	Net FDI FDI (% of GDP)	Net ODA ODA (% of GNI)
1981–85	7.9	7.3	48.4	105.2	32.3	5.1	26.8
1986–90	1.7	5.8	38.1	103.1	33.2	6.7	30.1
1991–95	3.3	6.5	44.8	99.9	35.9	13.5	23.1
1996–2000	3.6	10.1	42.6	93.2	33.2	8.9	14.4
2001	−3.3	19.7	36.7	84.8	32.3	6.7	12.1
2002	−4.3	1.5	38.2	89.6	35.9	5.2	10.6
2003	3.7	1.2	42.1	88.9	37.3	5.6	10.6
2004	4.4	1.3	42.6	90.0	38.6	5.3	10.8
2005	5.1	1.3	43.6	94.0	42.4	3.3	10.4
2006	7.2	1.1	40.7	87.7	41.4	9.7	11.4
2007	6.7	1.0	39.4	85.5	41.5	6.3	11.0
2008	6.3	1.1	42.6	98.0	52.5	5.1	15.0
2009	4.0	1.1	—	—	—	4.2	—

Source: Data from ADB 2009b and WDI 2009.

Note: The five-year intervals are averages calculated by the author. Real GDP is used instead of growth rate.
FDI = foreign direct investment; GDP = gross domestic product; GNI = gross national income; ODA = overseas direct investment; — = not available.

The effect of *REM* and *FIN* on total factor productivity *(TFP)* can be captured with *TR, REM,* and *FIN* entering as shift variables into the production function. The capital stock utilized for the study has been built up by a perpetual inventory method.[2] Labor is proxied by annual population data because we have no consistent time series data on employment. All data used in the analyses are sourced from *World Development Indicators* (2009).

Because the number of observations is small, the bounds-testing approach under the autoregressive distributed lag (ARDL) procedure developed by Pesaran, Shin, and Smith (2001) is deployed.[3]

The ARDL equations are given as follows:

$$\Delta Ly_t = \beta_{10} + \beta_{11} Ly_{t-1} + \beta_{12} Lk_{t-1} + \beta_{13} LREM_{t-1} + \beta_{14} LTR_{t-1} + \beta_{15} LFIN_{t-1}$$

$$+ \beta_{16} TREND + \sum_{i=1}^{p} \alpha_{11i} \Delta Ly_{t-i} + \sum_{i=0}^{p} \alpha_{12i} \Delta Lk_{t-i} + \sum_{i=0}^{p} \alpha_{13i} \Delta LREM_{t-i} \quad (27.3)$$

$$+ \sum_{i=0}^{p} \alpha_{14i} \Delta LTR_{t-i} + \sum_{i=0}^{p} \alpha_{15i} \Delta LFIN_{t-i} + \varepsilon_{1t},$$

$$\Delta Ly_t = \beta_{10} + \beta_{11}Ly_{t-1} + \beta_{12}Lk_{t-1} + \beta_{13}LREM_{t-1} + \beta_{14}LTR_{t-1} + \beta_{15}LFDI_{t-1}$$

$$+\beta_{26}TREND + \sum_{i=0}^{p}\alpha_{21i}\Delta Ly_{t-i} + \sum_{i=1}^{p}\alpha_{12i}\Delta Lk_{t-i} + \sum_{i=0}^{p}\alpha_{13i}\Delta LREM_{t-i} \qquad (27.4)$$

$$+\sum_{i=0}^{p}\alpha_{14i}\Delta LTR_{t-i} + \sum_{i=0}^{p}\alpha_{15i}\Delta LFDI_{t-i} + \varepsilon_{1t},$$

$$\Delta Ly_t = \beta_{10} + \beta_{11}Ly_{t-1} + \beta_{12}Lk_{t-1} + \beta_{13}LREM_{t-1} + \beta_{14}LTR_{t-1} + \beta_{15}LODA_{t-1}$$

$$+\beta_{26}TREND + \sum_{i=0}^{p}\alpha_{21i}\Delta Ly_{t-i} + \sum_{i=1}^{p}\alpha_{12i}\Delta Lk_{t-i} + \sum_{i=0}^{p}\alpha_{13i}\Delta LREM_{t-i} + \sum_{i=0}^{p}\alpha_{14i}\Delta LTR_{t-i} \qquad (27.5)$$

$$+\sum_{i=0}^{p}\alpha_{15i}\Delta LODA_{t-i} + \varepsilon_{1t}.$$

Two steps are used in examining the relationship between *Ly, Lk, LTR, LREM,* and *LFIN.* First, equations (27.3)–(27.5) are estimated by ordinary least square techniques,[4] and then the existence of a long-run relationship can be traced by imposing a restriction on all estimated coefficients of lagged level variables equating to zero. The results of the bounds test are reported in table 27.6.[5]

Next, the estimation of the long- and short-run equations is carried out. The results are presented in tables 27.7, 27.8, and 27.9. The diagnostic test results indicated that all equations performed well. In addition, the CUSUM and CUSUM of squares plot showed that the parameters of the models are relatively stable over time.[6]

From table 27.7, a 1 percent change in trade liberalization (*TR*) contributes to about 0.8 percent change in income in the long run and about 0.3 percent in the short run. Remittances (*REM*) contribute to about 0.07 percent in the long run and 0.04 percent in the short run. However, financial development (*FIN*), foreign direct investment (*FDI*), and official development assistance (*ODA*) are statistically not significant contributors to income.

The coefficient of the per capita capital stock, on average from tables 27.7–27.9, which denotes the profit share, is about 0.26 and is close to the stylized value of one-third. Similarly, the error correction terms (*ECT*), an indicator for the speed of convergence to long-run equilibrium, are significant with correct negative coefficients for all the results and on average are about –0.68.

TABLE 27.6 Results of Bound Tests

(a)		(b)		(c)	
Dependent variable	Computed F-statistic	Dependent variable	Computed F-statistic	Dependent variable	Computed F-statistic
Ly	6.0288**	Ly	4.7838**	Ly	7.2534**
Lk	1.6965	Lk	2.1623	Lk	2.0691
LREM	3.5616	LREM	0.7158	LREM	1.3667
LTR	1.6704	LTR	1.5971	LTR	2.4055
LFIN	1.7661	LFDI	1.2647	LODA	2.5335

	Pesaran, Shin, and Smith (2001)		Narayan (2005)	
Critical value	Lower bound value	Upper bound value	Lower bound value	Upper bound value
1 percent	3.41	4.68	4.537	6.370
5 percent	2.62	3.79	3.125	4.608

Sources: Narayan (2005: 10); Pesaran, Shin, and Smith (2001: 300).

Note: ** indicates significance at 5 percent level.

TABLE 27.7 Dependent Variable: *RGDP/Labor (Ly)*, ARDL (1,1,1,0,1)

Long-run coefficients			Short-run coefficients		
Regressor	Coefficient	t-ratio	Regressor	Coefficient	t-ratio
Lk	0.28	3.006***	ΔLk	−0.12	−0.8142
LTR	0.80	3.021***	ΔLTR	0.27	2.7422**
LREM	0.07	3.996***	$\Delta LREM$	0.04	3.1983***
LFIN	0.19	1.148	$\Delta LFIN$	−0.02	−0.2926
C	4.04	2.018*	C	2.53	1.3568
T	0.02	4.001***	T	0.01	3.8326***
			ECT(−1)	−0.63	−3.3649***
			$\bar{R}^2$		0.62
			DW statistics		2.538

Diagnostic tests				
	LM version	p-value	F version	p-value
Serial correlation	$\chi^2(1) = 2.8214$	0.093[a]	$F(1,14) = 1.7810$	0.203[a]
Functional form	$\chi^2(1) = 0.6892$	0.406[a]	$F(1,14) = 0.3969$	0.539[a]
Normality	$\chi^2(2) = 0.2898$	0.865[a]	n.a.	
Heteroscedasticity	$\chi^2(1) = 1.4937$	0.222[a]	$F(1,23) = 1.4616$	0.239[a]

See table 27.9 for source and notes.

TABLE 27.8 Dependent Variable: *RGDP/Labor (Ly)*, ARDL (1,0,1,1,0)

Long-run coefficients			Short-run coefficients		
Regressor	Coefficient	t-ratio	Regressor	Coefficient	t-ratio
Lk	0.25	2.454**	ΔLk	−0.13	−0.8443
LTR	0.84	3.460***	ΔLTR	0.29	3.1454***
LREM	0.06	4.411***	ΔLREM	0.04	3.3054***
LFDI	0.01	0.382	ΔLFDI	0.01	0.3879
C	4.90	2.858**	C	3.44	1.8424*
T	0.02	4.885***	T	0.01	5.2822***
			ECT(−1)	−0.70	−3.9360***
			$\bar{R}^2$		0.59
			DW statistics		2.218

Diagnostic tests				
	LM version	p-value	F version	p-value
Serial correlation	$\chi^2(1) = 0.54244$	0.461[a]	$F(1,15) = 0.33268$	0.573[a]
Functional form	$\chi^2(1) = 0.45949$	0.498[a]	$F(1,15) = 0.28086$	0.604[a]
Normality	$\chi^2(2) = 0.68973$	0.708[a]	n.a.	
Heteroscedasticity	$\chi^2(1) = 1.49360$	0.222[a]	$F(1,23) = 1.4614$	0.239[a]

See table 27.9 for source and notes.

TABLE 27.9 Dependent Variable: *RGDP/Labor (Ly)*, ARDL(1,1,1,0,0)

Long-run coefficients			Short-run coefficients		
Regressor	Coefficient	t-ratio	Regressor	Coefficient	t-ratio
Lk	0.26	3.503***	ΔLk	−0.05	−0.356
LTR	0.88	3.787***	ΔLTR	0.29	3.446***
LREM	0.06	4.904***	ΔLREM	0.04	3.768***
LODA	0.05	1.438	ΔLODA	0.03	1.525
C	4.41	2.797**	C	3.13	1.857*
T	0.02	4.952***	T	0.01	5.871***
			ECT(−1)	−0.71	−4.265***
			$\bar{R}^2$		0.63
			DW statistics		2.335

Diagnostic tests				
	LM version	p-value	F version	p-value
Serial correlation	$\chi^2(1) = 1.5799$	0.330[a]	$F(1,15) = 1.0119$	0.330[a]
Functional form	$\chi^2(1) = 1.0066$	0.330[a]	$F(1,15) = 0.6293$	0.440[a]
Normality	$\chi^2(2) = 0.2420$	0.330[a]	n.a.	
Heteroscedasticity	$\chi^2(1) = 1.8140$	0.330[a]	$F(1,23) = 1.7994$	0.193[a]

Source: Author's calculations.

Note: *, **, *** indicate significance at the 1, 5, and 10 percent levels, respectively; n.a. = not applicable.

a. Rejection of null hypothesis at 1 percent level of significance.

Conclusions

While reemphasizing the importance of remittances and trade liberalization in a small and developing economy such as Vanuatu,[7] for policy purposes vis-à-vis growth and development, the following steps are proposed:

Benefits from seasonal employment schemes need to be maximized and thus require that remittances transferred back home be cost effective, appropriate sociocultural policies and trainings should be in place for villages and communities to make the best use of the remittances, and a consistent work-ready pool of migrant labor needs to be available on demand.

Barriers to trade need to be minimized with emphasis on developing tourism and effective negotiation along sectoral lines under mode 4 of the General Agreement on Trade in Services, which covers services provided through temporary movement of natural persons to another country.

Opening up small bank branches in the islands, providing competitive interest rates, facilitating small loans, and investing in microfinance and savings will ensure effective channeling of remittances to productive use. Further, resources committed to improving the economy's infrastructure, options to minimize unnecessary overhead, and ensuring that financial institutions are closely linked with capital investment initiatives are equally important.

Management of and channeling donor (aid) -initiated projects need to be assessed critically while strengthening the institutional framework for long-term sustainability of the key drivers of the economy.

Notes

1. Other PICs have recorded relatively high inflows of remittances as well (table 27.2).
2. Capital stock is computed using the perpetual inventory method, with investment proxied by gross fixed capital formation at constant 1983 prices, initial capital stock two times the 1983 real GDP, and a depreciation rate of 5 percent.
3. The unit root test was also carried out using ADF and Phillips-Perron statistics.
4. Other equations are not provided to save space but were investigated during the analysis.
5. The interaction between FIN and shift variables (ODA, REM, and TR) could not be explored in the study because of the small sample size and multicollinearity problems.
6. The CUSUM and CUSUM of squares plots are not reported to conserve space. However, the results are available on request.
7. The results, however, cannot be generalized for all PICs.

PART VII

Chapter 28

Remittances to Sub-Saharan Africa in the Wake of a Financial Crisis: Source of Resilience or Vulnerability?

WIM NAUDÉ AND HENRI BEZUIDENHOUT

OVER THE LAST 30 YEARS, the stock of migrants worldwide has increased from 84 million in 1970 to over 194 million by 2005, and the value of remittances in dollars rose from $2 billion in 1970 to more than $433 billion in 2008. The growth rate of out-migration from Sub-Saharan Africa (SSA) countries has been the highest in the world in recent years (Naudé 2010). Before, during, and after a financial crisis, remittances can improve resilience in receiving countries by allowing households to diversify income sources, to continue investment in human capital formation, to smooth consumption, and to encourage entrepreneurial activity (Naudé 2009).

The question is how responsive are remittances to, and in which manner are remittances affected by, global financial crises? Do financial crises reduce the potential of remittances to build household resilience? In this study we investigated these questions using data on 23 SSA countries over the period 1980–2008. We look at how remittances have responded to financial crises in the past so as to determine whether they are a source of resilience or perhaps of vulnerability.

During such crises, remittances to SSA can be a source of resilience or of vulnerability. The continent is more dependent than any other region on aid (official development assistance) and the second most on remittances. Taken together—foreign direct investment (FDI), aid, remittances, and portfolio outflows—the amount of financial resources at risk to Africa from a global financial crisis has been estimated at approximately 12–15 percent of Africa's gross domestic product (GDP).

The 2008–09 global economic crisis was not the first external globally synchronized economic shock to Africa. "Synchronized" or "systemic" global economic shocks can be defined as when 10 or more of the world's advanced economies are simultaneously in a recession. Three years before 2009 saw 10 or more of the 21 advanced economies simultaneously in recession: 1975, 1980, and 1992 (IMF 2009a). SSA growth subsequently declined with the exception of the 1980 recession. The 1992 recession was also accompanied by financial crises in advanced economies. The synchronization between contractions in global and African growth appears to be more severe from the 1990s onward.

Remittances can be an important resource to build resilience before, during, and after various crises as well as reduce poverty (Nagarajan 2009). In countries such as Uganda, remittances are said to have taken one in 11 people out of poverty (Ratha, Mohapatra, and Plaza 2008). Remittances have been found to be countercyclical, unlike other capital flows that are largely procyclical. They are also viewed as more beneficial because they are not "tied" (Straubhaar and Vadean 2005), do not require the repayment of interest (Calì and Dell' Erba 2009), and do not decline during crises (Nagarajan 2009).[1] The question is whether remittances to SSA will increase, remain constant, or decline following a financial crisis.

A recent overview of the impact of global financial crises on remittances is provided by Calì and Dell'Erba (2009). Their paper presupposes that the primary impact of a global financial crisis would be to reduce remittances to developing countries. The channels through which remittances would be reduced would be through (1) a reduction in migration from developing to developed countries, in the light of reduced opportunities, (2) a negative income shock suffered by migrants, and (3) a reduction in the amount of money remitted per migrant. The extent of this will be country specific, depending on how that host country has been affected and which sectors have been affected. According to Nagarajan (2009), migrants employed in construction, manufacturing, finance, services, retail, and tourism sectors are most exposed. In contrast, Calì and Dell'Erba (2009: 6) give the example of the Philippines, where many migrants are employed in the health care industry, where expenditures are less likely to decline steeply during an economic downturn.

Calì and Dell'Erba (2009) found that generally the coefficient on the variable denoting a systemic financial crisis for remittances is insignificant. It becomes significant when, in high-income countries, it interacts with unemployment in the host country. This indicates that, although affecting remittances directly, the influence of unemployment on remittances during the times of crisis is also bigger (Calì and Dell'Erba 2009).

Based on the expected impact of the financial crisis on incomes and GDP in host countries, and on their findings of the independent impact of financial crises on remittances, Calì and Dell'Erba (2009) provided forecasts of the impact of the financial crisis on remittances for various regions of the world. They estimate that for developing countries the crisis may result in a decline in remittances of approximately 5–8 percent in 2009, after which remittances will start growing again. For SSA in particular, the decline in remittances is estimated to be between 4.4 and 6.0 percent.

From Calì and Dell'Erba (2009) and the World Bank's estimates, the implication is clear that remittances will decline during a global financial crisis. These declines are, however, relatively modest and set for quick recovery. This is also a finding from previous financial crises, because they report, for instance, that during the 1998 Asian crisis, remittances to East Asia declined by 15 percent in 1998 but recovered to precrisis levels by 1999. Jha, Sugiyarto, and Vargas-Silva (2009) estimate that remittance flows to Asia have slowed and are beginning to recover.

Barajas and others (2010: 10) take the perspective that, in a crisis, having a large share of gross national income (GNI) coming from remittances is not a source of resilience, but a source of exposure. They found that (1) in SSA only a few countries are "remittance dependent" and (2) most African migrants stay within Africa, so they are less affected, and as such they conclude that "the impact of the global decline in remittances on African countries' GDP growth is expected to be fairly mild."

Ratha, Mohapatra, and Plaza (2008) also found that remittances are a more resilient resource flow. They also present evidence to suggest that migrants often maintain their remittances even if their host countries' economic conditions deteriorate. They conclude that remittances are less volatile than other financial flows because (1) they are sent by the migrants, and this tends to be persistent, (2) remittances are often a small part of migrants' incomes, and (3) migrant workers often benefit from fiscal expansion programs during crisis periods in their host countries.

Therefore, we can conclude that SSA's possible lack of extensive and diversified out-migration has left it less exposed to the drop in remittances as a result of a global financial or economic crisis.

Method, Variables, and Data

Based on the literature survey, we will investigate the following hypothesis:

H1: Remittances to SSA will decline during a globally synchronized financial crisis.

Our hypothesis results from the finding in the literature that a host country's income is an important determinant of remittances. Because a significant number of African migrants find themselves in the European Union, a global financial crisis could affect their ability to remit. We have three reasons, however, in addition to that mentioned in the previous section, to suspect that H1 may be rejected. One is that many migrant workers in the European Union may be in jobs that are more recession proof. A second is that there are more SSA migrants in other SSA countries than European Union countries. And third is that a global financial crisis may see SSA countries' exchange rates depreciate, which may lead to increased remittances.

Our strategy is to estimate a regression equation of the determinants of remittance inflows. The estimating equation is informed by the literature on the determinants of remittances as well as data reflecting globally synchronized financial crises (see below). Our panel regression estimating equation, following, for example, Freund and Spatafora (2008) and Lueth and Ruiz-Arranz (2007), is (in log-linear form)

$$R_{it} = \tau_t + X_{it}\beta + c_i + u_{it} \qquad (28.1)$$

For $i = 1, ..., N$, and $t = 2, ..., T$, and where R_{it} = remittances to country i in period t, x_{it} = a $1 \times K$ vector of explanatory variables (see below). Some of these vary over t; c_i = unobserved country characteristics that are constant (fixed) over the time period and influence R_{it}; τ = year-specific fixed effects, and u_{it} = a random error term with the usual properties.

Here x_t is a vector containing the explanatory variables. These include the variables of interest, namely:

- Whether there has been a globally synchronized recession in year t (a dummy variable). If our hypothesis H1 holds, we will find the coefficient on this variable to be negative and significant.

The control variables are also contained in x_{it}. They are the following:

- GNI per capita of the home country. If the coefficient hereon is > 0, then remittances are procyclical, and if <0, then remittances are countercyclical.

- GNI per capita of the host country. It is expected that if the coefficient hereon is > 0, and if it is moreover > 1, then it would indicate that increases in host country incomes are passed on more in proportion to their home countries (see Freund and Spatafora 2008).

- Credit extended to the private sector in country i. This is a proxy for the financial development of country i. The higher it is, the easier it will be to remit, and therefore we expect a positive coefficient.

- The level of the domestic (home country) exchange rate. Remittances are sent as foreign currency. If the coefficient on this variable is found to be larger than zero, it would indicate that in case of depreciation in the domestic (home country) exchange rate, a larger dollar amount of remittances will be sent to make use of the higher, more favorable rate.

- Official development assistance (ODA) to country i. ODA is often claimed to affect remittances. Some observers consider that an increase in ODA to a country will offset remittances. If this is the case, the coefficient on ODA to a country will be negative.

- The population of a country. More populous countries will have larger migrant populations in absolute terms, and therefore a higher absolute level of remittances.

Finally, we will also, where applicable, include dummy variables to capture any time trends between 1980 and 2007 and country dummies to capture country fixed effects (table 28.1).

TABLE 28.1 Summary of Variables and Data Sources

Measure	Description	Source of data
Dependent variable: remittances		
Remittances	Inflows measured in dollars	WDI
Variables: disasters		Online
Globally synchronized recession	A dummy variable = 1 if there was a globally synchronized recession in the particular year. According to the IMF, these were in 1987, 1997, and 2002.	IMF
Variables: controls		
GNI per capita in home country	The gross national product per capita in the home (SSA) country in period t	WDI
GNI per capita in host country	The gross national product per capita in the host country in period t. Here we take the host country income to be that of the SSA average; the main destinations of African migrants are other African countries.	WDI
Credit to the private sector	The credit extended to the private sector in an SSA home country in period i, as a proportion of GDP	WDI
Exchange rate level	The local currency average value for the year in dollars	WDI
Aid received	The amount, in dollars, of aid received from the EU	WDI
Population	The total population in a country in a particular year	WDI

Source: Authors' compilation.

Note: EU = European Union; IMF = International Monetary Fund; WDI = World Development Indicators (World Bank).

Other control variables, such as host country unemployment, interest rates, and inflation, were also investigated, but these were insignificant and did not affect the results.

For the estimator, we estimate equation (28.1) by first using a pooled-data ordinary least squares (OLS), with robust standard errors to account for heteroscedasticity for our benchmark regressions. However, we are aware that using a static OLS estimation method may bias our coefficients because of possible endogeneity and lack of dynamic effects. Remittances may affect the level of the exchange rate, or the volume of aid, or GNI per capita. Also, remittances may be dynamic and depend on past levels (reflecting networks, "family and friends," and a country's migrant stock).

To allow for these considerations and to include lagged values of remittances in equation (28.1), we will therefore also use a "difference" (Arellano and Bond 1991) generalized method of moments (GMM) estimator. The "difference" GMM estimator can be illustrated by taking our basic equation (28.1) and rewriting it in dynamic format as an AR(1) model:

$$\Delta R_{it} = \tau_t + (\alpha + 1)\Delta R_{it-1} + \Delta\chi'_{it}\beta + \Delta u_{it}. \qquad (28.2)$$

In equation (27.2), the regressors will be correlated with the error term (for instance, ΔR_{it-1} depends on u_{it-1}). Consequently, instrumental variables are advisable to be used for the endogenous regressors. Arellano and Bond (1991) proposed the lagged levels of the regressors (such as m_{it-j}) as instruments to avoid endogeneity and derived a "difference" GMM estimator. We used this estimator, and not a "dynamic GMM estimator," given that the number of time periods in our sample is relatively large, so that the lagged levels of the regressors ought to be satisfactory instruments (see, for example, Bond, Hoeffler, and Temple 2001).

Data from 23 SSA countries are used for the period 1980–2007.[2] Because of availability considerations, data are used only from 1980 and because early estimates of remittances were subject to considerable measurement error (Calì and Dell'Erba 2009).

Empirical Findings

Descriptive Statistics

Table 28.2 contains our sample of SSA countries and their respective remittances (on average over the period and as percentages of GDP). Nigeria, Sudan, Kenya, Senegal, and Burkina Faso are the countries receiving the largest volumes of remittances on average, whereas in terms of their contribution to GDP, some countries have a fairly high dependency on remittances, such as Lesotho with 27.7 percent and Cape Verde and Togo with 9 percent.

The table also contains FDI and ODA as a percentage of GDP for comparative purposes. It can be seen that in several countries—Kenya, Lesotho, Nigeria, Senegal, Swaziland, and Togo—remittances exceeded FDI and ODA in 2007. Moreover, remittances are less volatile in terms of percentage change than FDI or ODA. We confirmed this through a test of the equality of means, which rejects the null of equality.[3] This would suggest a rejection of H1.

In terms of our hypothesis, we are interested in the impact of financial crises on remittances. Although remittances may be high in some countries, it does not imply that remittances are more responsive in cases of crises. In fact, the reduced volatility that we found suggests that remittances change less in response to crises than FDI and ODA.

Regression Results

Tables 28.3 and 28.4 contain the pooled OLS regression results. Table 27.3 contains the results when no controls are included. It shows that global financial crises have, as can be expected, a negative and significant impact on remittance inflows.

Table 28.4 contains the results: (1) a basic regression without any of the variables of interest, as a base case, and three further models, introducing (2) global financial crises.

TABLE 28.2 Remittances, Disasters, and FDI and ODA in the Sample Countries

Country	Remittances (annual average, 1980–2007, $)	Remittances, 2007 (% of GDP)	FDI, 2007 (% of GDP)	ODA, 2007 (% of GDP)
Benin	78,652,663	4.13	0.88	8.66
Botswana	25,136,494	1.15	−0.23	0.85
Burkina Faso	125,610,958	0.74	8.87	13.75
Cameroon	28,797,689	0.81	2.09	9.34
Cape Verde	70,061,259	9.68	9.08	11.39
Comoros	7,484,774	2.68	0.18	9.91
Côte d'Ivoire	1,253,193	0.91	2.16	0.83
Ethiopia	88,689,598	1.85	1.15	12.49
Gambia, The	58,153,458	7.36	10.64	11.24
Ghana	28,146,520	0.77	6.41	7.60
Kenya	312,317,929	6.56	3.01	5.27
Lesotho	6,987,569	27.70	8.15	8.09
Madagascar	5,328,739	0.15	13.50	12.08
Mali	92,888,825	3.09	5.25	14.82
Mauritania	7,087,685	0.08	5.78	13.76
Mozambique	22,127,190	1.28	5.49	22.81
Niger	13,311,722	1.87	0.65	12.99
Nigeria	1,351,111,549	5.57	3.68	1.23
Rwanda	5,135,102	1.54	2.01	21.34
Senegal	183,518,466	8.29	0.70	7.55
Sudan	504,477,708	3.83	5.25	4.55
Swaziland	1,300,174	3.47	1.30	2.17
Togo	39,914,031	9.16	2.76	4.84

Source: Authors' compilation based on WDI 2009.

A few comments are in order. The Breusch-Pagan test for heteroscedasticity finds $\chi^2 (1) = 10.9$ and hence rejects the null of constant variances. Therefore, we used the White-Huber procedure (within Stata 10.0) to estimate robust standard errors for the coefficients.

In all regressions, we included time dummies and dummies for country fixed effects.

Table 28.4 shows that global financial crises do not have a statistically significant impact on remittances in the presence of controls. It would suggest that financial crises have a negative effect through their impact on credit extended to the private sector and on income of the host country.

For the control variables it can be seen that the estimates are rather robust across the different models. The single largest determinant of the level of remittances is a country's population, which is indicative of the fact that larger countries can have, in

TABLE 28.3 Pooled OLS Regression Results

dependent variable = log of remittances in dollars, no control variables

Variable	Global financial crises
Constant	18.49 (71.6)*
Global financial crises	−1.25 (−4.37)*
Diagnostics	
R^2	0.77
Time dummies	Yes
Country fixed effects	Yes
N	644
F	67.16

Source: Authors' estimations.

Note: Robust t-ratios are in parentheses. * = significance at 1 percent level.

TABLE 28.4 Pooled OLS Regression Results

dependent variable = log of remittances in dollars, controls included

Variable	Basic model	With global financial crises
Constant	−8.72 (−0.59)	−8.72 (−0.59)
GNI home	−1.92 (−5.86)*	−1.92 (−5.86)*
Income host (SSA GDP per capita)	0.44 (2.10)***	0.44 (2.10)***
Credit private sector	0.61 (5.23)*	0.61 (5.23)*
Exchange rate	0.33 (4.52)*	0.33 (4.52)*
Aid from EU	0.02 (0.17)	0.02 (0.17)
Population	2.30 (2.56)**	2.29 (2.56)***
Global financial crises	—	−0.90 (−1.32)
Diagnostics		
R^2	0.85	0.86
Time dummies	Yes	Yes
Country fixed effects	Yes	Yes
N	300	300
F	75.29*	75.29*

Source: Authors' estimations.

Note: Robust t-ratios are in parentheses. *, **, *** indicate significance at the 1, 5, and 10 percent levels, respectively. EU = European Union; — = not available.

absolute terms, larger migrant populations. To the extent that a country's population is a proxy for its migrant stock, the finding is consistent with the proxy supposition. In a dynamic model, this would mean that lagged remittances ought to have a substantial and significant effect.

Table 28.4 also indicates that a country's home GNI per capita is an important negative determinant of remittances. The negative coefficient suggests that, in the case of SSA, remittances are countercyclical, which could indicate that remittances do function to improve such countries' resilience. In many other studies, however (for example, Freund and Spatafora 2008), home country income is found to be procyclical.

The host country's income per capita, in this case of SSA in general, is significant (when we used income of the second largest destination, the European Union, it was found to be insignificant). A decline in SSA income per capita, such as during a global economic crisis, may therefore have a strong negative impact on remittances to SSA, consistent with H1.

Credit extended to the private sector and the level of the local currency against the dollar have positive signs. Therefore, a better-developed financial system is important for raising the level of remittances, and in the case of SSA, it seems that remittances will increase in response to a nominal exchange rate depreciation. There is no evidence of any significant relationship between remittances and aid (ODA) from the European Union—aid does not seem to displace remittances in the case of SSA.

Table 28.5 contains the "difference" GMM dynamic panel estimation results. Here the dependent variable is the changes in remittances, and all the explanatory variables, except for the dummy variables, are also in first differences. These results therefore

TABLE 28.5 "Difference" GMM Dynamic Panel Estimation Results

dependent variable: first difference of remittances

Variable	Basic model	With global financial crises
Constant	0.06 (0.55)	1.31 (1.31)
ΔRemittances lagged	0.43 (6.73)*	*0.71 (18.8)**
ΔGNI home	0.35 (0.72)	−0.30 (−1.14)
ΔGNI host[a]	0.06 (0.67)	−25.00 (−1.40)
ΔCredit private sector	−0.16 (−1.36)	0.10 (1.58)
ΔExchange rate	0.13 (0.85)	0.14 (3.50)*
ΔAid from EU	−0.02 (−0.44)	0.02 (0.45)
ΔPopulation	2.13 (1.32)	−0.25 (−0.44)
Global financial crises	—	−0.50 (−1.02)
Diagnostics		
Wald χ^2	93.90	666.82
Time dummies	Yes	Yes
Number of observations	213	560
Number of groups	23	23
Sargan test	211.78	340.31

Source: Authors' estimations.

Note: z-ratios are in parentheses. * = significance at 1 percent level. EU = European Union; GMM = generalized method of moments; — = not available.

a. We used GNI per capita of EU because that of SSA was collinear with the dummy for the financial crises.

focus on the short-term impacts on remittances, as opposed to the results in table 28.4, which could be seen as more long term.

Table 28.5 shows that when being able to allow for the dynamic effects of remittances, lagged values of remittances become the single most significant and important determinant of current remittances. There is therefore persistence in remittances—a finding consistent with the earlier finding that remittances tend to be stable and less volatile than other inflows. It suggests the importance of migrant stocks as a determinant of remittances. Given the results, over the short term, that remittances will be influenced only by previous remittances (migration stocks) and incomes, exchange rates and financial sector development have a longer-term impact on the level of remittances, with the response of remittances to crises more long term in the case of SSA.

Concluding Remarks

Africa is particularly susceptible to financial crises. Human migration and corresponding remittance flows have for many decades acted as a potential bulwark against these crises. It is potentially an important source of resilience for households assisting recovery after crises.

What is the remittance response in the wake of a global financial crisis? This is the question we set out to answer in this study. Using panel data on 23 SSA countries over the period 1980–2007, we derived a hypothesis from a review of the literature:

H1: Remittances to SSA will decline during a globally synchronized financial crisis.

We found only qualified support for our hypothesis. Being relatively stable, remittances are less volatile than other forms of financial flows and are therefore a source of resilience during a global financial crisis. Over the longer term, remittances to SSA are mainly determined by incomes in the host and home countries, population (migration growth), the sophistication of the financial system, and the exchange rate. A global financial crisis does not have a significant impact on remittances in the presence of controls. Remittances will decline, albeit slowly, after a global financial crisis to the extent that the crisis affects incomes, migration stocks, exchange rates, and the banking system. If these impacts are brief, then the relative persistence of remittances suggests that they are a good bulwark against global financial crises in SSA. Migration is therefore an important source of resilience in the face of financial crises in SSA.

Notes

1. Nagarajan (2009) and Raja (2009) reported that foreign aid could decline by up to 40 percent during the 2008–09 financial crisis, whereas the World Bank forecast remittances to decline by approximately 8 percent.

2. The countries are Benin, Botswana, Burkina Faso, Cameroon, Cape Verde, Comoros, Côte d'Ivoire, Ethiopia, The Gambia, Ghana, Kenya, Lesotho, Madagascar, Mali, Mauritania, Mozambique, Niger, Nigeria, Rwanda, Senegal, Sudan, Swaziland, and Togo.

3. Results available from the authors on request.

Chapter 29

From Shock Absorber to Shock Transmitter: Determinants of Remittances in Sub-Saharan Africa

RAJU JAN SINGH

REPORTED REMITTANCES HAVE SUBSTANTIALLY INCREASED throughout the developing world (figure 29.1), rising from about $20 billion in 1980 to an estimated $336 billion in 2008. In Sub-Saharan Africa (SSA), an estimated $20 billion in remittances in 2007 corresponded to about 2.5 percent of regional gross domestic product (GDP), an amount similar to the official development assistance the region received. However, on a global scale remittance flows to SSA are quite small; they account for only 5 percent of total remittances to developing countries and in terms of GDP are dwarfed by the amounts received in the Middle East and South Asia.

The general picture hides striking variations by country (figure 29.2). Of the 25 largest recipients of remittances in 2008 in terms of GDP, four were in Africa (Cape Verde, Lesotho, Senegal, and Togo). As a source of foreign exchange, in Benin, Cape Verde, The Gambia, Lesotho, Senegal, Sierra Leone, and Uganda, remittances in 2008 represented more than 25 percent of each country's export earnings. Furthermore, although for the region as a whole the amounts of aid and recorded remittances are similar, in numerous countries remittances were a multiple of official assistance.

The chapter draws on a wider research project including Markus Haacker (London School of Hygiene and Tropical Medicine), Kyung-woo Lee (Columbia University), and Maëlan Le Goff (CERDI–University of Auvergne). This work was carried out when Markus Haacker, Kyung-woo Lee, and the author were at the African Department of the International Monetary Fund. The views expressed in this chapter are those of the author and do not necessarily represent those of the IMF or IMF policy.

FIGURE 29.1 Remittances by Major Region

a. Migrant remittance inflows

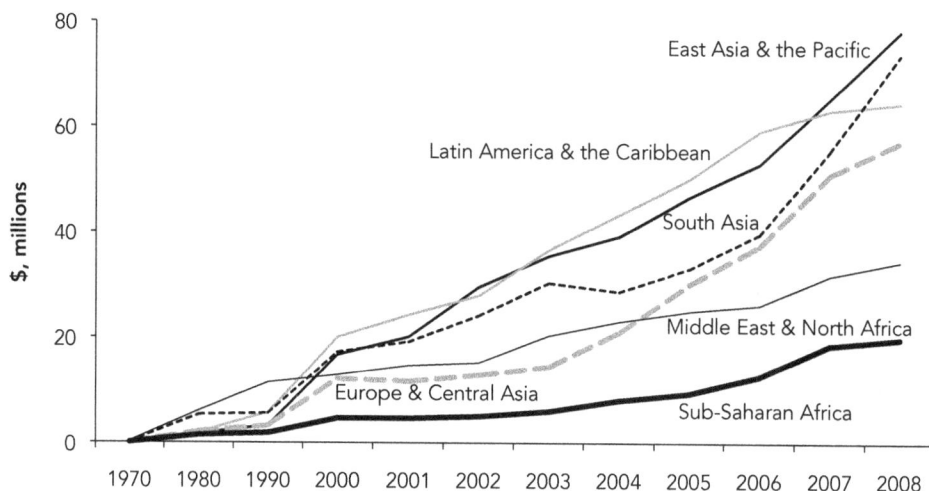

b. Migrant remittances as percentage of GDP, 2008

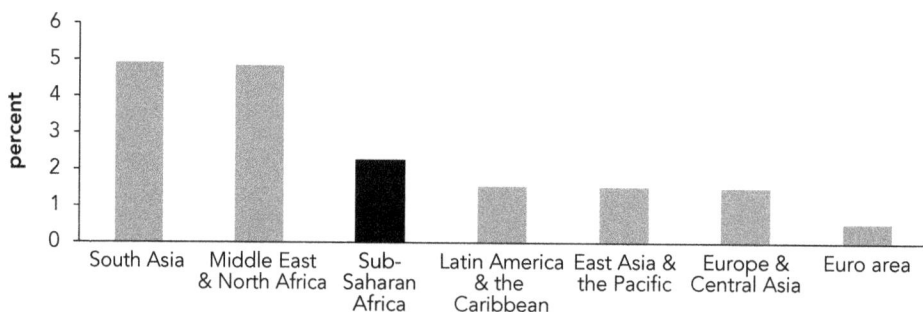

Sources: IMF, World Bank, and author's calculations.

With about 80 percent of their remittances coming from advanced economies, SSA countries are particularly vulnerable to a global economic slowdown. The expected increase in unemployment would be concentrated in countries and sectors where migrant workers are heavily represented (for example, advanced economies and the construction and transport sectors). This would imply reduced job opportunities for migrants and lower remittance flows. According to Ratha, Mohapatra, and Silwal (2009b), remittances are expected to have declined by about 7–10 percent in 2009, putting poverty reduction and employment in home countries at risk.

FIGURE 29.2 Main Recipients of Remittances, 2008

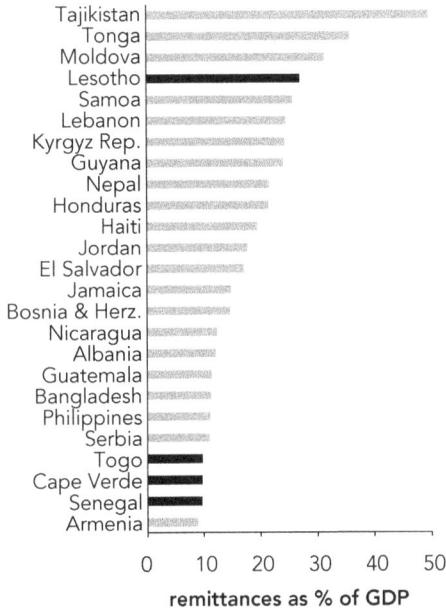

a. Top 25 remittance recipients worldwide   b. Top 15 remittance recipients in SSA

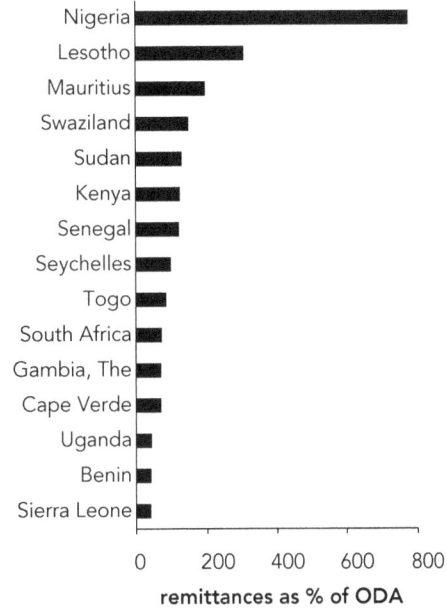

Sources: IMF, World Bank, and author's calculations.

Going forward, concerns have been expressed about a possible rise in discrimination and xenophobia, migrant workers being perceived as taking jobs away from local workers or competing for welfare benefits. Numerous host countries have stopped or imposed restrictions on new admissions of migrants for employment. Home countries are already experiencing inflows of returning migrants, which may result in economic and social instability in poorer countries. Many governments have already adopted more restrictive policies (for example, Australia, the Republic of Korea, the Russian Federation, and the United States), and some have even introduced financial incentives to encourage migrant workers to return home (for example, Japan, Spain, and the United Kingdom). Understanding what drives remittances is therefore crucial. Yet little research has been done on the determinants of remittances to Africa.

Empirical Analysis

The following equation describes the determinants of remittances and includs explanatory and control variables that have been shown to be significant in previous studies (Rapoport and Docquier 2006):

$$\ln{(REM/GDP)}_{it} = \alpha_i + \gamma_t + \beta_1 \ln y_{it} + \beta_2 \ln FinDev_{it} + \beta_3 \ln y_{it}^* +$$
$$\beta_4 \ln(Mig/Pop)_{it} + \beta_5 \ln Ins_{it} + \beta_6 \ln REX_{it} + \beta_7 ID_{it} + \beta_8 Dual_{it} + \varepsilon_{it},$$

(29.1)

where *REM/GDP* denotes the ratio of remittances to GDP, *y* is home income, *FinDev* stands for an index for the financial development, *y** is host income, *Mig/Pop* is the ratio of expatriates to population, *Ins* denotes institutional quality, *REX* is the real exchange rate, *ID* is the interest rate differential, *Dual* is the dual exchange rate dummy variable, and α_i and γ_t are country- and time-specific dummies, respectively. Panel fixed-effect and fixed-effect two-stage least-square estimation methods were used. The dependent variable used here is the ratio of remittances to GDP. Different measures were also tried, such as remittances to population or just the volume of remittances, but the results were robust to the choice of measure for remittances.[1]

The sample comprises 36 countries in SSA for 1990 through 2005.[2] Data on remittances are drawn from the International Monetary Fund's (IMF's) *Balance of Payments Statistics Yearbook* (BOPSY). To estimate the annual stock of expatriates, the study started with the data compiled by Parsons and others (2007) on international bilateral migration. This database provides the number of migrants from each of 226 origin countries to each of 226 destination countries in 2000. From these data were inferred the number of expatriates for these 36 SSA countries during 1990–2005 using the World Development Indicators (see annex for a more detailed discussion). Measures of the differentials in interest rates and income between the home and host countries were constructed as an average of bilateral differentials, weighted by the shares of migrants (from Parsons and others 2007).

Findings

Table 29.1 reports the estimation results. Remittances to SSA do seem to play a shock-absorbing role. The coefficient of real per capita GDP in the home country is negative regardless of the choice of estimation methods. This suggests that when adverse economic shocks decrease incomes in their home country, migrants would remit more to protect their families from those shocks.

The coefficients of host country income and stock of expatriates are, however, positive and robust. Countries with a large diaspora attract more remittances, and the location of expatriate communities matters: The wealthier the country where expatriates are located, the higher the remittances they send back home. This result would suggest that, as the global crisis erodes the incomes and the number of migrants, remittances should be expected to decline, spreading the crisis to home countries rather than sheltering them.

Remittances also reflect portfolio choices about investment opportunities in the home country. The coefficient on institutional quality is significantly positive and robust. This result suggests that countries with better institutions or a more stable

TABLE 29.1 Determinants of Remittances

Variable (log)	M2/GDP	DC/GDP	Financial depth: M2/GDP[a]	Financial depth: DC/GDP[b]
Home income	−3.236* (−6.08)	−2.952* (−4.48)	−3.158* (−5.14)	−3.258* (−3.02)
M2/GDP	0.698* (3.37)		1.232* (3.06)	
Domestic credit/GDP		0.160 (1.15)		0.890* (3.86)
Host income	4.255* (3.64)	4.555* (3.60)	2.567* (2.09)	3.690* (2.66)
Expatriates/population	0.024* (3.59)	0.021* (2.85)	0.027* (3.29)	0.016 (1.59)
Institutions	0.400* (2.72)	0.378* (2.43)	0.491* (3.21)	0.274 (1.60)
Real exchange rate	−0.765* (−3.06)	−0.581** (−2.14)	−0.760** (−2.39)	−0.699** (−1.99)
Interest rate differential	−0.039* (−3.56)	−0.039* (−4.30)	−0.030* (−3.52)	−0.025** (−2.64)
Dual exchange rate	−0.131 (−0.83)	−0.029 (−2.16)	−0.126 (−0.83)	0.113 (0.61)
Observations	352	334	318	296
R^2	0.8171	0.8122	0.8251	0.8129
For weak instruments	n.a.	n.a.	31.289	52.756
p-value[c]	n.a.	n.a.	0.3162	0.2796

Source: Author's calculations.

Note: Standard errors are robust to autocorrelation in errors. t-values are in parentheses. *, **, and *** indicate 1, 5, and 10 percent significance, respectively. Time-specific dummies are included, but estimates are not reported here. DC = domestic credit; M2 = money and quasi-money; n.a. = not applicable.

a. Instrumented: home income, M2/GDP. Instruments: first lag of real GDP per capita and institutions; first and second lags of M2/GDP.

b. Instrumented: home income, DC/GDP. Instruments: first lag of real GDP per capita and institutions; first and second lags of DC/GDP.

c. For overidentification test of all instruments.

political system would receive more remittances relative to GDP. Institutional quality can be viewed as reflecting the business environment, which in turn should influence the amount of remittances driven by the investment motive.

Once migrants have decided how much to remit, they must then decide how to send it. Remittances are estimated to be positively correlated with financial deepening. Countries with more developed financial markets would attract more remittances relative to GDP. Financial development should ease the process of money transfers and may reduce the fees associated with sending remittances through competition, so that it can raise the amount or share of remittances transferred through official channels, which our data on remittances capture.

Conclusions: What Can Be Done?

The findings suggest that remittances vary countercyclically with variations in GDP per capita in the home country, consistent with the hypothesis that remittances can help mitigate economic shocks. However, the size, the location, and the income of the diaspora are also important determinants of remittances. These results would suggest that this time around remittances should not be expected to shelter their home economies from adverse economic shocks, but on the contrary could contribute propagating them. The global scope of the current crisis could turn remittances into shock transmitters.

Against this backdrop, what can home countries do? The results presented in this chapter would suggest several policy options:

- Just as protectionism in trade needs to be avoided, rising protectionism in human mobility in host countries should be resisted, keeping the number of migrants in host countries.

- Efforts should be stepped up in home countries to improve the quality of their institutional environment, particularly their business climate, to encourage migrants to send more remittances.

- In particular, measures should be taken to deepen financial intermediation and facilitate remittance flows through formal channels by lowering transaction costs associated with sending remittances.

Notes

1. The dependent variable used here is the ratio of remittances to GDP. We also tried different measures, such as remittances to population or just the volume of remittances, but the results were robust to the choice of measure for remittances.

2. The countries in the sample are the following: Benin, Botswana, Burkina Faso, Cameroon, Cape Verde, the Comoros, Republic of Congo, Côte d'Ivoire, Eritrea, Ethiopia, Gabon, The Gambia, Ghana, Guinea, Guinea-Bissau, Kenya, Lesotho, Madagascar, Malawi, Mali, Mauritania, Mauritius, Mozambique, Namibia, Niger, Nigeria, Rwanda, São Tomé and Príncipe, Senegal, the Seychelles, Sierra Leone, South Africa, Sudan, Swaziland, Tanzania, and Togo.

Annex

A: Variables and Countries Used for the Analysis

Variable	Description	Source
Remittances	Sum of workers' remittances, compensation of employees, and migrants' transfers in dollars	BOPSY, WDI, IMF African Department
Real GDP per capita	Real GDP per capita in 2000 constant dollars	WDI
Nominal GDP	Nominal GDP in dollars	WEO
Population	Population	WDI
Nominal exchange rate	Nominal exchange rate measured as the amount of dollars for one unit of local currency ($/LCU)	WEO
CPI	Consumer price index (100 in 2000)	WEO
Inflation	CPI inflation	Author's computation
Investment	Gross investment in dollars	WEO
Dual exchange rate regime	Dual exchange dummy, 1 for dual or multiple exchange rate regime	IMF (2010)
M2	Money and quasi-money in dollars	WDI
Terms of trade	Export price index/import price index (100 in 2000)	WEO
Trade openness	(imports + exports)/GDP	WEO
Stock of expatriates	Number of expatriates by origin (see annex B for details)	WDI; Parsons and others (2007)
Private investment	Private investment in dollars	WEO
Public investment	Public investment in dollars	WEO
Institutional quality	ICRG political risk index (0: highest risk, 100: lowest risk)	ICRG, Political Risk Service Group
Deposit rate	Deposit rate	IFS
Real exchange rate	Real exchange rate against dollars ($/LCU$_i$ CPI$_i$/CPI$_\$$)	Author's computation
Government expenditure	General government total expenditure and net lending in dollars	WEO
Host income	Weighted average of real per capita GDP in top four expatriate–receiving countries (in 2000 constant dollars)	WDI; Parsons and others (2007)
Nominal interest rate differential	Deposit rate of home country; deposit rate of country with largest migrants' share from that country	IFS; Parsons and others (2007)
Domestic credit	Domestic credit provided by banks (% of GDP)	WDI

Source: Author.

Note: CPI = consumer price index; ICRG = International Country Risk Guide; IFS = International Financial Statistics; LCU = local currency unit; M2 = money and quasi-money; WDI = World Development Indicators (World Bank 2010c); WEO = World Economic Outlook (IMF).

B: Construction of the Stock of Expatriate Data

The following describes in detail how data are constructed on the number of expatriates from available sources of migration data (figure 29.A1). The data used to compute the stock of expatriates include net migration into each country and the number of migrants within each country (both from the WDI but recorded only every five years as well as the international bilateral migration database compiled by Parsons and others 2007).

Suppose there is a country, which we will call home. We will call the rest of the world foreign. Assume for simplicity that place of birth determines citizenship. Assume further that all available stock data are measured at the end of a given period.

Let us define the following variables (equation 29.A1):

Stocks

H_t = number of people born in home country and living there
H_t^* = number of people born in home country but living in a foreign country
F_t = number of people born in a foreign country but living in home country
F_t^* = number of people born in a foreign country and living there
P_t = population of home country $(H_t + F_t)$

Flows

EH_t = number of home-born people who migrate from home to a foreign country
IH_t = number of home-born people who migrate back home from a foreign country
EF_t = number of foreign-born people who migrate from home to a foreign country
IF_t = number of foreign-born people who migrate from a foreign country to home
E_t = number of out-migration from home $(EH_t + EF_t)$
I_t = number of in-migration to home $(IH_t + IF_t)$
M_t = net migration $(I_t + E_t)$
DH_t^* = number of home-born people who die in a foreign country
DF_t = number of foreign-born people who die in a home country

What we know is this: P_t, F_t (migration stock from the WDI), hence H_t and M_t (net migration from the WDI). But what we want to know is: H_t^* (stock of expatriates). The flow of migration is characterized by the following equations:

$$H_t^* = H_{t-1}^* - DH_t^* + EH_t - IH_t, \qquad (29A.1)$$

$$F_t = F_{t-1} - DF_t + IF_t - EF_t. \qquad (29A.2)$$

Note that births to migrants are counted as increases in the natives for the country where they live on the assumption we made earlier. Turning to net migration we know by definition:

$$M_t = I_t - E_t = (IH_t - EH_t) + (IF_t - EF_t),$$

FIGURE 29.A1 Construction of the Stock of Expatriate Data

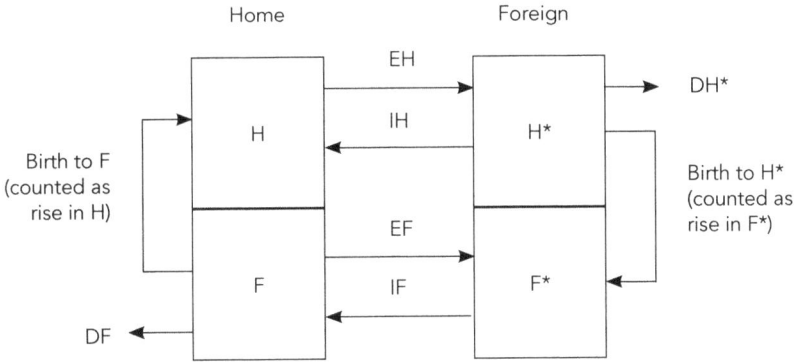

Source: Singh and others 2011.

which implies

$$(EH_t - IH_t) = (IF_t - EF_t) - M_t. \tag{29A.3}$$

Combining (28A.1), (28A.2), and (28A.3), we have

$$H_t^* = H_{t-1}^* - DH_t^* + F_t - F_{t-1} + DF_t - M_t. \tag{29A.4}$$

To construct the stock of expatriates from home, we need a value of H_t^* for some period t as well as the number of deaths of migrants, that is, DH_t^* and DF_t. We address these issues as follows: First, to obtain the stock of expatriates from home at some period, we make use of the international bilateral migration database of Parsons and others (2007). Then, to estimate the number of deaths of migrants, we first assume the death rate depends only on place of birth.

On this assumption, we can compute the death of migrants as follows:

$$DH_t^* = d_t H_{t-1}^*,$$
$$DF_t = d_t^* F_t, \tag{29A.5}$$

where d_t is the death rate of home-born people and d_t^* the death rate of foreign-born people. We use the crude death rate of home, available from the WDI, to measure d_t^* and a simple average of crude death rates for our sample countries to measure d_t^*. Combining equations (28A.4) and (28A.5) yields the equation for computing the stock of expatriates:

$$DH_t^* = H_{t-1}^* (1-d_t) + F_t - F_{t-1} (1-d_t^*) - M_t. \tag{29A.6}$$

One remaining issue in constructing the data as described so far is that data on migration stock within a country, F_t in our term, are available only every five years. Thus we interpolate between two recorded observations linearly to obtain annual data on the stock of expatriates.

Chapter 30

A Comparative Examination of Women's Remittance Practices in Two Somali Communities: Johannesburg, South Africa, and Columbus, Ohio

MARNIE SHAFFER

WOMEN THROUGHOUT THE SOMALI DIASPORA are renowned for their commitment to provide financial support to their families abroad (see, for example, Horst 2007). Although it has only been in recent years that women have been migrating to South Africa, their sense of responsibility to remit is equally as strong as those women's who left Somalia in the early 2000s and before. The author conducted research in Mayfair, a suburb near downtown Johannesburg in Gauteng Province, where the Somali community is most densely populated, and in Columbus, Ohio, where several pockets of Somalis are dispersed around the city. Study results indicate that Somali women living in Mayfair have fewer educational and employment opportunities than those in Columbus, but they nonetheless maintain kinship ties and provide much needed support to family and friends living elsewhere. The Columbus study consists of professional and otherwise employed women, whereas research in Johannesburg is part of a larger ethnographic study that includes employed and unemployed women.

Research in Columbus, Ohio (2008–09), was made possible by the National Science Foundation (REG supplement to NSF Grant No. BCS-0706795), and work in Johannesburg, South Africa (2010), was funded by Ohio State University and supported by the African Centre for Migration & Society at the University of the Witwatersrand in Johannesburg.

The women interviewed in Columbus all hold jobs and in most cases have either completed or are working on university degrees. They work in health care, in retail, or in shops and serve as interpreters. Many of these women provide services to the Somali community, where their language skills and cultural knowledge are marketable and vital to meeting the needs of the growing Somali population. Their length of time living in the United States ranges from 8–28 years, and most have strong English language skills. Women in South Africa tell a different story. Of those interviewed, the earliest one of these women arrived in the country was in 1995, after the end of apartheid. Most women in South Africa have not completed a high school degree or its equivalent, and English proficiency is for the most part limited.

For many women in Johannesburg employment prospects are often confined to low-paying jobs in the Mayfair area. Although a few women run successful businesses selling clothing, shoes, perfume, groceries, and jewelry, others eke out a living dealing *qat*—a plant whose leaves are chewed for its stimulant effects—cooking in restaurants, working in Somali-, Indian-, Ethiopian-, or Pakistani-owned shops, or selling clothing, fruits, and vegetables or homemade food on the street, in shops, or door to door. Employment opportunities for women are limited because it is considered too dangerous for them to work in the townships, where men often earn a living wage selling groceries. The sexual division of labor among Somalis means that men who stay in Mayfair do a variety of jobs, both formal and informal, that generate more income than women's work. Furthermore, unemployment rates in Gauteng, officially recorded at more than 26 percent (Statistics South Africa 2011), reduce women's ability to acquire salaried positions that pay living wages. Many South Africans believe that Somalis rob them of jobs and other financial opportunities, and Somali women have less formal education and speak less English than men; consequently, it is improbable that women will work in the formal sector.

A perception is seen among Somalis in East Africa that anyone living in South Africa or the United States has the financial means to provide critical support to their relatives at home, but this prevailing myth is far from true. Women in the United States receive higher earnings and are engaged in more formal employment than those in South Africa, but remitting responsibilities put a strain on their finances and create stress in their lives. For many women in Johannesburg, life is a daily struggle to collect the money needed to buy food and to pay rent and school fees for their children. Unlike their American counterparts, women's income in South Africa fluctuates according to their success as businesswomen. Given the informality of their jobs, women who work in shops or restaurants receive limited income, and the consequences are that they have just enough money to support themselves and their families in Mayfair. There are also high rates of single mothers who must care for their children and earn an income to support them.

Informants report that the current economic crisis did not disrupt employment levels in Mayfair, but it has affected Somalis who send remittances, which are transferred in dollars. Although the exchange rate is not historically low, the dollar has steadily declined against the South African rand since 2009. Senders who remit $100 a month, for example, must choose between paying more rand to remit the same amount or spending the same amount in rand, which will give recipients less money. The foreign exchange rate can influence remittance amounts, and a weak dollar is especially painful to those who remit regularly.

Despite their limitations, including an unfavorable exchange rate, women in South Africa remit as frequently as they can afford to, and they employ numerous strategies to meet their family commitments. One approach is that when a woman becomes engaged, she and her fiancé may negotiate the terms of the marriage and the financial responsibilities he will assume to his wife and her family. This is particularly important for women who are unable to work because of child-care responsibilities and cultural expectations that confine women to staying in their homes while men provide support. Although some men meet this cultural and religious obligation, others control the family's purse strings and ration the money women receive to run the household. Many Somalis in Mayfair believe that a woman's choice for a husband is made, in large part, by his financial success and ability to support his wife and her family. Failure to assist his wife in this way, particularly when a man has the financial means to do so, may lead to divorce.

Women, whether they work or not, may be part of an *ayuuto*. *Ayuuto* exists throughout the diaspora and comprises a group of people who contribute an equal amount of money to the group every few days, according to the schedule they have created, which is collected and distributed to a designated individual in the group. The recipient rotates so each person receives the pot of money. Women who are not working may save a small amount of money their husbands allocate to them for the weekly shopping. By purchasing cheap items, a woman can set aside money to contribute to her *ayuuto*. For example, Sadia, a business owner in Mayfair, is part of an *ayuuto* with eight people and 15 rounds in each rotation. Each member contributes R 200 every three days. On the third day, one person gets R 3,000. Sadia contributes R 600—she sets aside R 200 each day—so she gets a more frequent distribution. In Sadia's case, she receives *ayuuto* payments on the second, seventh, and ninth distribution days, because those are her numbers in the rotation. Other group members also pay extra, and so they too receive more frequent payments. If Sadia set aside R 200 every day, she would still have R 9,000 at the end of the same period, but she would not save that money without her group; the money would be spent on other things. *Ayuuto* demands discipline while strengthening kinship ties and social networks because other livelihoods are at stake. Sadia has to save because other people are counting on her.

Money acquired through *ayuuto* can be used for remittance purposes. Women who belong to such groups may set aside the money they earn to send to their families abroad. If women are not part of an *ayuuto* and have no job or money when there is a family emergency or relatives are suffering, they can ask friends or extended family members to give them money, called *shaxaad*, which is a gift that will not be repaid. In cases where women do have access to cash but are short in difficult times, they may ask their kin, or even the *xawilaad* businesses that transfer the remittances, for credit so they have something to remit. They borrow money that will be reimbursed, interest free, when they can afford it. Some women resort to cooking and selling food, or selling new clothing or gold jewelry, to raise cash, while others rent rooms in their homes to friends or acquaintances to collect an income. In a few instances, a woman may own shares in a shop and will receive monthly profits from the business even though she is not involved in the daily operations. These cases are uncommon and likely indicate a close familial connection to the primary shop owner.

Research data indicate that the current economic crisis has not disturbed remittance practices among Somalis. Women in Columbus report that they remit to relatives they have never met, or do not know well, primarily because their parents—and mothers in particular—asked them to, and they will continue to do so after their parents are gone. It is too early to test whether this sentiment is echoed in South Africa, but continued research on women's remittance practices will be imperative to understanding how these processes unfold over the next several years. One notable difference between the two communities is that when women in Mayfair have relatives living in the West, they feel less pressure to remit. Although they still consider it their responsibility, they believe their relatives in the West are in a better financial position to support their families in Africa. For women who do not have relatives in Australia, Europe, or North America, the weight of their responsibility is great, and they make many sacrifices to meet the needs of their kin. When they have nothing to give, their relatives do not always believe them and accuse the women of abandonment, something that affects them deeply. For women in Columbus, they are acutely aware of the expectations and implications of the remittances they send, and most of them are happy to help even with the strain it creates. As one woman said, "I am grateful that I can help; I feel good about it. It could be them helping me." For these women, to stop remitting is not an option. The remittances they provide maintain kinship ties and enable the survival of their families around the world.

PART VIII

Chapter 31

The Global Crisis and Expatriates' Remittances to Lebanon

NASSIB GHOBRIL

THE MIDDLE EAST AND NORTH Africa (MENA) region, as with nearly every region of the developing and developed worlds, was not immune from the global financial crisis. But the extent and transmission of the crisis's impact varied from region to region and from country to country. The global financial crisis took its toll on the MENA region through multiple channels, which included terms of trade, capital inflows, tight credit, economic slowdown, higher unemployment, lower hydrocarbon prices, and the bursting of real estate and stock market bubbles. The region's increasing integration in the global economy and capital markets, led by the economies of the Gulf Cooperation Council (GCC), resulted in an unprecedented inflow of capital, both international and intraregional capital, during the high-growth years that preceded the crisis. As such, one of the most visible impacts of the crisis on the region was the decline in capital inflows in general, and of equity and credit flows in particular. The positive trends that encouraged traditional equity and bond flows also helped increase the flow of expatriates' remittances to the region during the boom years.

Based on the World Bank's database of remittance inflows,[1] the nominal volume of remittance flows to the MENA region increased by 5.5 percent in 2006 and rose by 21.5 percent in 2007; before this growth slowed to 12 percent in 2008 and contracted by 6.3 percent in 2009, only to start to recover and grow by 5.3 percent in 2010. In comparison, foreign direct investment to the region contracted by 8.7 percent and tourism revenues declined marginally by 0.4 percent in 2009 (United Nations 2011: 101). Further, remittances increased by a total of $11 billion between 2005 and 2008 for an average of $3.62 billion per year. However, the flows contracted by $2.3 billion in 2009, leading to an aggregate increase of $8.6 billion between 2005 and 2009 for an average rise of $2.2 billion per year. As such, remittances to the MENA region grew by a compound annual growth rate (CAGR) of 12.7 percent during 2005–08, but by 7.6 percent in the 2005–09 period. Further, when comparing various sources of capital and foreign exchange earnings relative to the economy, remittance inflows to the MENA region declined from 3.7 percent of gross domestic product (GDP) in 2008 to 3.5 percent of GDP in 2009, while foreign direct investment declined from 3.7 percent of GDP in 2008 to 3.3 percent of GDP in 2009, and tourism revenues remained stable at 3.5 percent of GDP in each of 2008 and 2009 (World Bank 2011a: 100–01). Therefore, the general trend shows that remittances to the region were clearly affected by the crisis through a slowdown of such inflows, in nominal and percentage terms, in relation to the size of the economy, as well as compared with other sources of foreign capital.

According to the World Bank, migrant remittances are one of the least volatile sources of foreign exchange earnings for developing countries (Ratha 2003). Although capital flows tend to rise during favorable economic cycles and fall in bad times, remittances appear to show remarkable stability over time. The research on the subject has shown that expatriates' remittances tend to be stable or even countercyclical in response to political crisis, economic downturn, or even natural disasters in the recipient country (Mohapatra, Joseph, and Ratha 2009; Ratha 2003; World Bank 2006a). Although several studies have demonstrated the importance of both host and home country factors in determining remittance flows, it was not clear how remittances would behave in response to a significant economic or financial downturn in the host countries (Mohapatra and Ratha 2010).

The MENA region is home to several economies that depend on remittances such as the Arab Republic of Egypt, Jordan, Lebanon, Morocco, and Tunisia, as well as to some of the largest country sources of remittances worldwide, such as Kuwait, Qatar, Saudi Arabia, and the United Arab Emirates. This report will analyze trends in Lebanon, a country that is both one of the smallest Arab economies and one of the largest recipients of remittances in the MENA region, to determine if remittance flows were affected by the crisis and if there was an economic impact as a result. Remittance inflows to Lebanon were equivalent to 21.7 percent of GDP in 2009, the highest such ratio among MENA countries, compared with inflows equivalent to 3.5 percent of GDP for the region during the same year. Further, by the end of 2009, Lebanon became the largest recipient of remittances in the region in nominal terms, relative to its GDP, and on a per capita basis; as such, inflows reached $7.6 billion during the year, and were equivalent to 21.7 percent of GDP and $1,790 per capita.

Remittance Trends during the Crisis

Remittance inflows continued to grow or remained stable during the years of political turbulence in the country. Indeed, inflows to Lebanon grew by 5.6 percent to $5.2 billion in 2006, then increased by 11 percent to $5.8 billion in 2007, and jumped by

24.5 percent to $7.2 billion in 2008. However, the global financial crisis brought a new dimension and raised many questions about the sustainability of such inflows. Indeed, for the first time, the traditional source countries of remittances were threatened by the crisis, thereby potentially affecting the earning power and asset base of Lebanese emigrants, as well as their job security.

A first look at official data on remittance inflows to Lebanon suggest that such inflows were not severely affected by the crisis. Indeed, nominal gross inflows grew by 5.3 percent in 2009 compared with declines in all major remittance-receiving economies in the region: Egypt (–17.8 percent), Morocco (–9 percent), Algeria (–6.5 percent), Mauritania (–6 percent), Jordan (–5.2 percent), the Syrian Arab Republic (–4.8 percent), Sudan (–3.5 percent), the Republic of Yemen (–2.3 percent), and Tunisia (–0.5 percent) during the year, and rose only in the West Bank and Gaza economies (3.4 percent). Also, migrant inflows to Lebanon posted a CAGR of 13.4 percent between 2005 and 2008, but a CAGR of 11.3 percent in the 2005–09 period. This followed the trend in the region, as the growth in 2005–09 slowed compared with growth in 2005–08 in all major remittance-receiving countries. On a region-wide basis, remittance inflows slowed from a CAGR of 12.7 percent in 2005–08 to 7.6 percent in 2005–09. So the slowdown of 2.1 percentage points for Lebanon was much milder than the deceleration of 5.1 percentage points in the MENA region.

Looking at the quarterly fluctuations of inflows at the outset of the crisis gives, however, a different picture. Remittance inflows to Lebanon dropped by 20 percent in the third quarter of 2008, or immediately after the crisis erupted, the highest such drop among remittance-dependent economies in the region. Further, the turnaround from the second quarter of 2008 is even more telling, as the change from growth of 21.8 percent in the second quarter to the drop of 20 percent in the third quarter of 2008 shows a negative "turnaround" of 41.5 percent for Lebanon, constituting the steepest such change in the region when compared with the turnaround of 35.7 percent for Egypt during the same quarters, and to a simple slowdown but continuous growth of inflows to Jordan, Morocco, and Sudan. However, the fourth quarter tells a different story, as inflows to Lebanon grew by a modest 2.4 percent from the previous quarter, compared with drops of 9 percent in Jordan, 36.4 percent in Morocco, and 9.5 percent in Sudan. Still, Lebanon's fourth quarter recovery was mild compared with the 17 percent jump of inflows to Egypt quarter-to-quarter. The picture improved further in the first quarter of 2009 when remittances to Lebanon rose by 8.3 percent from the previous quarter, compared with drops of 24 percent in Egypt, 13 percent in Jordan, and 8 percent in Morocco. However, inflows to Lebanon declined by 5.2 percent in the second quarter of 2009 from the preceding period and by 15.5 percent from the same quarter in 2008, but then recovered by 10 percent in the third quarter from the previous quarter and 16 percent from the same period of the previous year. This recovery continued in the last quarter of the year with growth of 4 percent quarter-to-quarter and of 17 percent from the last quarter of 2008. It appears that Lebanon was affected at the outset of the crisis, but this impact was relatively brief and limited to the third quarter of 2008 and the second quarter of 2009. In contrast, inflows to other remittance-receiving Arab countries had a more delayed reaction to the crisis, as the impact on inflows became more apparent in the fourth quarter of 2008, and became more severe in the first quarter of 2009 and onward through the rest of the year.

In parallel, remittance inflows relative to the economy declined in four Arab countries and rose in four others in 2009 (table 31.1). Lebanon was in the former category, as inflows declined from 24 percent of GDP in 2008 to 21.7 percent of GDP in 2009, a drop of 2.3 percentage points that constituted the most significant drop in the region along with Jordan (−2.4 percentage points). This was caused by a combination of a mild slowdown in economic activity and a more pronounced slowdown of remittance inflows (as detailed above).

TABLE 31.1 Remittance Inflows in MENA as Percentage of GDP, 2008–09

Country	2008	2009	Percentage point change 2008–09
Lebanon	23.9	21.7	−2.3
Jordan	16.7	14.3	−2.4
Morocco	7.8	6.9	−0.9
Yemen, Rep.	5.2	5.5	0.2
Sudan	5.3	5.5	0.1
Tunisia	4.4	4.5	0.1
Egypt, Arab Rep.	5.4	3.8	−1.6
Syrian Arab Republic	2.6	2.5	0.0
Algeria	1.3	1.5	0.2

Sources: Byblos Bank Economic Research and Analysis Department, IMF, Lebanon National Accounts, and World Bank.

Economic Impact

The crisis had a direct impact on economic activity in the MENA region, as real GDP growth slowed down in all major remittance-receiving countries in 2009, with Jordan, Egypt, and Sudan experiencing the largest deceleration in growth. As such, real GDP in Jordan slowed by 5.3 percentage points between 2008 and 2009, followed by Egypt with a deceleration of 2.5 percentage points, and Sudan with a 2.3 percentage-point slowdown. Lebanon posted the second lowest slowdown, with a deceleration of 0.8 percentage point year-on-year, but its real growth rates continued to be the highest among remittance-dependent economies at 9.3 percent in 2008 and 8.5 percent in 2009, which contributed to the decline in the inflows-to-GDP ratio. Indeed, Lebanon's nominal GDP grew by 16.3 percent in 2009, a much faster rate than the 5.3 percent growth in nominal remittance inflows during the year. Further, Lebanon posted the highest growth in nominal GDP among recipient-dependent countries, which led to the steepest regional drop in remittance inflows relative to GDP year-on-year.

Using a different methodology to measure the economic impact of the decline in remittance flows during the crisis on the MENA region, we calculate the impact as the proportion of remittances to GDP in 2008 times the growth rate of remittance inflows in 2009 (United Nations 2011: 22). The result shows that the 6.3 percent drop in remittance inflows in 2009 represents a relatively small shock of 0.23 percent of the region's combined GDP. But the drop in remittances resulted in a negative shock for eight out of nine remittance-dependent countries in the MENA region. Results across countries vary, with Egypt experiencing a shock of –0.95 percent of GDP, the steepest in the region, followed by Jordan (–0.87 percent of GDP), and Morocco (–0.7 percent of GDP) (figure 31.1). In contrast, Lebanon was the only remittance-dependent country in the region where the crisis yielded a positive shock of 1.26 percent of GDP.

FIGURE 31.1 Impact of Crisis on Remittance Inflows as Percentage of GDP

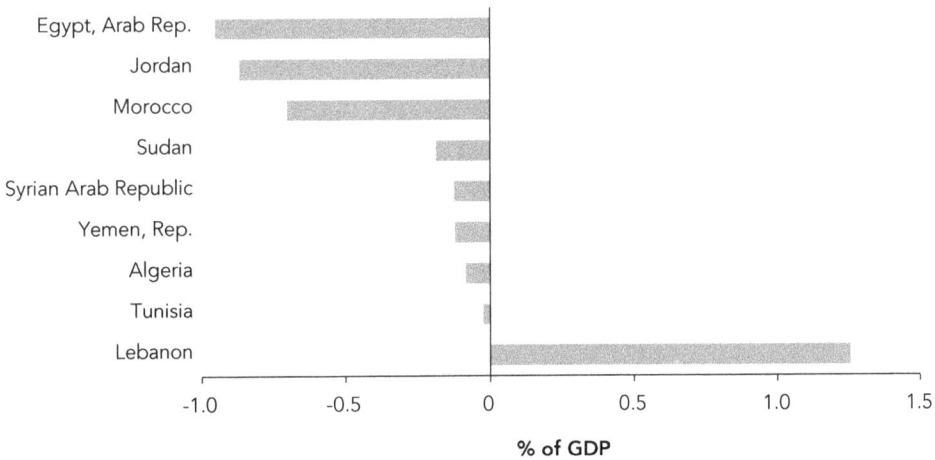

Sources: Byblos Bank Economic Research and Analysis Department, IMF, and World Bank.
Note: Data are calculated as the proportion of remittances to GDP in 2008 times the growth rate of remittances in 2009.

Determinants of Remittance Inflows to Lebanon and Their Stability during the Crisis

Research has shown that remittance flows are mainly affected by the migrant stocks in destination countries and incomes of migrants in the different migrant-destination economies (Mohapatra and Ratha 2010). Further, empirical evidence has revealed that the size of emigrant stocks is probably the most important determinant of the volume of remittances (Lueth and Ruiz-Arranz 2008; Ratha and Shaw 2007; Singh, Haacker, and

Lee 2009). This is because remittances are sent by the cumulated flows of migrants over the years, and not just by recent migrants, a factor that makes remittances persistent over time. But in the case of Lebanon, additional factors such as the lack of exchange rate effects and the absence of mass return migration as well as the increase of economic risks in GCC countries contributed to the resilience of inflows during the crisis.

Continuous Migration

Lebanon is a remarkable case of a remittance-dependent economy, with a steady outflow of emigrants that has ensured a regular inflow of remittances throughout the years. A comprehensive study of emigration trends from Lebanon estimated that the total number of emigrants between 1992 and 2007 was at least 466,000 and that 45 percent of households in Lebanon have at least one family member who has emigrated during the covered period (Kasparian 2009: 7). The number of migrants during the covered period accounts for about 10.3 percent of the Lebanese resident population, reflecting the magnitude of emigration. Further, the distribution of age groups shows that the overwhelming majority of emigrants were at a productive or preproductive stage of their life. Indeed, 15 percent were below 25 years of age at the time of emigrating, 69 percent were between 25 and 44 years old, and 13.5 percent were between 45 and 59 years of age. Moreover, 77 percent of emigrants who left the country during the covered period were between 18 and 35 years of age.

FIGURE 31.2 Main Reasons for Emigration from Lebanon, 1992–2007

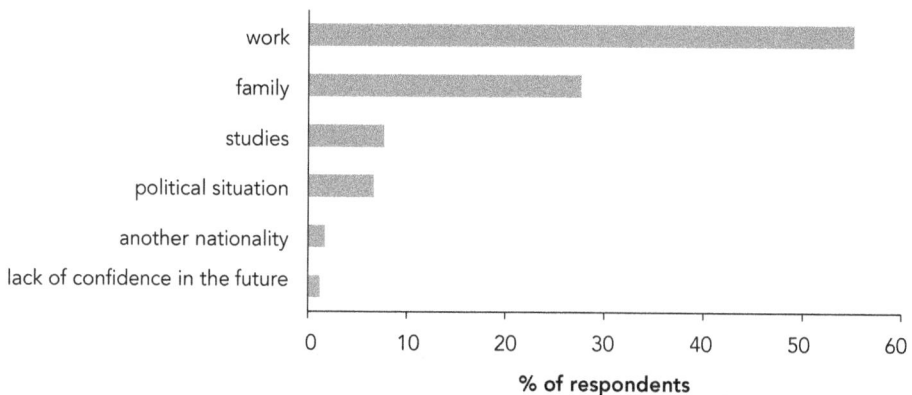

Source: Université Saint-Joseph, Beirut.

Also, emigration accelerated since 2002, as 25 percent of emigrants left the country between 1992 and 1996, 29 percent emigrated during the 1997–2001 period, and

46 percent left Lebanon between 2002 and 2007. At the time of emigration, 53.5 percent considered that emigration is final, 18.7 percent said it was temporary, and the balance of 28 percent did not make a decision at the time (Kasparian 2009: 7). Moreover, emigrants consisted of skilled laborers, as 30 percent had business degrees, 25 percent held engineering diplomas, 13 percent majored in computer sciences, 13 percent were medical doctors, and 12 percent had degrees in social sciences. Further, 45.4 percent of emigrants between 18 and 35 years old had a university diploma compared with 39 percent of those older than 35 years. Even though a clear majority, or 55 percent, of emigrants left the country for work-related reasons, this proportion increased over time, because work was the key driver for emigration of nearly 53 percent of those who left the country between 1992 and 2001, but increased to 58.3 percent during the 2002–07 period (Kasparian 2009: 105). These figures point to the actual and potential earning power of emigrants at the time they left the country.

Financial Support

In parallel, the survey indicated that 49 percent of migrants provide financial support to their families in Lebanon regularly or from time to time. The distribution by emigration bracket shows that earlier migrants tend to be more supportive relative to more recent emigrants. Indeed, 58 percent of those who migrated between 1992 and 1996 financially help their families regularly or from time to time, but this ratio declines to 52.6 percent for those who left the country between 1997 and 2001, and further decreases to 41.6 percent for those who migrated during the 2002–07 period (Kasparian 2009: 126). The smaller share of more recent migrants who send remittances to their families is attributed to the reality that they need time to start generating enough income to allow them to support their family back home. But the proportion of emigrants who help their families is still high, irrespective of the stage of migration. The financial support is reinforced by the fact that 76 percent of migrants who left the country and are between 18 and 35 years old visit Lebanon, including 41.4 percent who visit irregularly and 34.3 percent who visit regularly.

Sources of Remittances

The destination of emigration reflects the sources of remittances to Lebanon. During the 1992–2007 period, 35 percent of emigrants went to Arab countries, 22 percent to North America, 20 percent to Western Europe, 9 percent to Australia, 8 percent to Africa, 3 percent to Latin America, and 2 percent to Eastern Europe. What is noticeable is a trend of rising emigration to Arab countries, mainly GCC countries, over time. In fact, Arab countries were the destination of 20 percent of overall Lebanese emigrants between 1992 and 1996, but this proportion rose to 31 percent between 1997 and 2001 and jumped to 45.5 percent during the 2002–07 period.

The destination of Lebanese migrants has been reflected by the sources of inward electronic cash transfers to Lebanon.[2] The six countries of the GCC accounted for 58 percent of all electronic cash transfers to Lebanon in 2009, and Arab countries overall accounted for about 64.5 percent (figure 31.3). Further, the major advanced economies represented 17 percent of the total, while electronic transfers from Africa and Central and Latin America represented 9.3 percent. The top 10 sources of cash transfers accounted for 80.5 percent of all transfers, and the top 20 sources represented 90.6 percent of the total. The United Arab Emirates were the main source of inward electronic cash transfers with 24 percent of the total in 2009, followed by Saudi Arabia with 13.5 percent, Qatar with 9.3 percent, Kuwait with 8.8 percent, Australia with 6.2 percent, the United States with 6 percent, Iraq with 4.5 percent, Gabon with 3.7 percent, Canada with 2.3 percent, and Jordan with 2.2 percent.[3] The composition of the top 10 countries remained almost unchanged in 2008 and 2009, reflecting consistency, while the rankings of the top 10 sources of e-cash transfers in 2009 saw minor changes from 2008, as Kuwait and Australia switched ranks and Iraq rose to seventh place in 2009, while it was not among the top 20 sources in 2008.

FIGURE 31.3 Main Sources of Electronic Cash Transfers to Lebanon, 2009

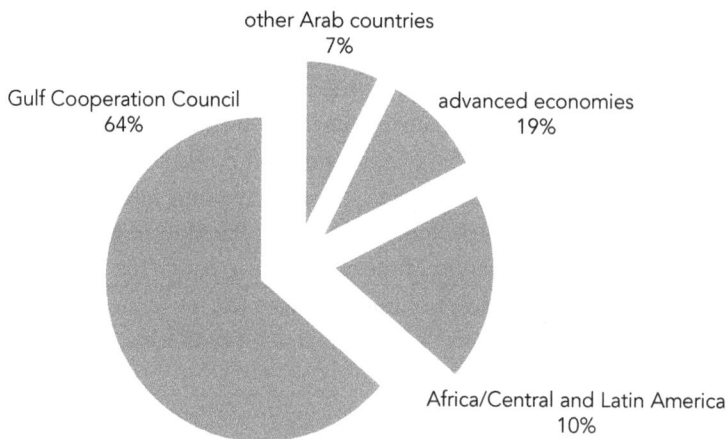

Sources: Byblos Bank Economic Research and Analysis Department and Central Bank of Lebanon.

Exchange Rate Effect

The flow of remittances to several developing economies was severely disrupted by exchange rate effects during the crisis. For instance, the depreciation of the Russian ruble affected remittance flows to Central Asian and Eastern European countries, especially during the first half of 2009 (United Nations 2011: 23). Lebanon did not face exchange rate effects for three main reasons. First, the Lebanese pound has been pegged to the dollar since 1993, and the exchange rate has remained stable despite numerous political, security, and financial shocks in the country since then. Second, as pointed out above, the main sources of remittances to Lebanon had currencies pegged to the dollar and the means to defend any pressure. Indeed, five of the six GCC economies peg their currency to the dollar and the Kuwaiti dinar is pegged to a basket of currencies, and authorities have enormous resources to face any eventuality. Third, other main sources of remittances, such as Australia, Canada, and the United States, did not face currency concerns. Given that Australia, Canada, the GCC, and the United States account for 73 percent of remittance inflows, the general flow of remittances to Lebanon was not affected by any exchange rate effect.

Return Migration

When the global financial crisis erupted and its effects started to spread to emerging markets and developing economies in the last quarter of 2008, speculation in Lebanon was widespread of a mass return of expatriates, particularly from the GCC, given the magnitude of the crisis's early impact on the region and its geographic closeness. Some observers expected the return of between 40,000 and 60,000 migrants overall, and others speculated about the return of 10 percent of Lebanese based in the GCC. Still more considered that the economic downturn in the United States in general, and its financial sector in particular, would entice migrants in the United States to return to Lebanon. But these early expectations did not materialize for several reasons. First, the brunt of the impact in the GCC was on the Emirate of Dubai in the United Arab Emirates. Even though the financial markets of the other countries were affected, the financial and real economic sectors in Dubai were the most severely hit.

Second, the GCC governments responded proactively to the crisis by using their large budget surpluses to create fiscal stimulus that contained the slowdown and propped up economic activity, thereby maintaining consumer and business demand. Third, Lebanese expatriates in the GCC are overwhelmingly white-collar skilled workers, so they were able to shift sectors, move to different cities or countries in the region, or adjust their financial expectations to the new realities and accept lower-paid packages to keep their job or move to other work opportunities. Fourth, Lebanese migrants in the United States found it more practical to shift sectors or even careers, or move to different states within the United States, rather than consider returning to Lebanon.

Fifth, a very important reason return migration did not materialize, and that was somewhat overlooked in Lebanon, is the fact that Lebanese migrants understand the lack of opportunities in the home country on the scale they have been accustomed to. In fact, it constituted the main reason they left the country and was still prevalent at the time of the crisis. Sixth, the still-fresh history of political instability in the country, and its potential recurrence, was a key factor that discouraged migrants from returning to Lebanon. All these reasons combined to disappoint the voices in the country that were already forecasting the multifaceted benefits of returning migrants, from value-added experience and skills, to brain return, to increased demand for goods and services, and the resulting financial windfall. However, there is anecdotal evidence of migrants returning to Lebanon for personal reasons, and of expatriates in the GCC relocating their families to Lebanon to reduce living expenditures. But these represent scattered exceptions rather than a massive trend.

Correlation with Political and Other Risks

Research has shown that expatriates' remittances tend to be stable or even countercyclical in response to a political crisis or economic downturn in the recipient country[4] (Mohapatra, Joseph, and Ratha 2009; Ratha 2003; World Bank 2006a). Lebanon went through severe political turmoil from early 2005 until mid-2008. As a proxy for the level of political risks during this period, we used the PRS Group's Political Risk ratings for Lebanon.[5] The rating value for Lebanon placed the country in the "Moderate Risk"[6] category since June 2000 following the withdrawal of Israeli forces from the country in the previous month. Lebanon was briefly downgraded to the "High Risk" category from January until April 2003, coinciding with the rise in regional tension with the preparations and then the start of war in Iraq. Lebanon remained in the "Moderate Risk" category until February 2005, when it was downgraded to the "High Risk" category following the assassination of Prime Minister Rafiq Hariri and the ensuing political, security, and military instability and uncertainties. Lebanon has remained in the "High Risk" category despite the restoration of political stability and the improvement in security conditions since June 2008. Then, less than four months after political stability was restored in Lebanon, the global financial crisis erupted in mid-September after the collapse of U.S. investment bank Lehman Brothers and started to spread beyond the confines of the U.S. and Western European financial systems.

We conducted a simple correlation analysis that revealed a link between political instability and remittance inflows to Lebanon (table 31.2). We found a 0.3 level of correlation between the level of political risks in the country and the inflow of remittances between 2005 and 2009. We also found a stronger correlation of 0.56 between the level of financial risk in Lebanon and remittance inflows to the country during the same period. In other words, when the level of financial risk increased in Lebanon, the level of remittance inflows grew. The financial risk level is represented by the PRS Group's Financial Risk ratings for Lebanon, which placed the country in the "Moderate Risk" category in August 2004 but downgraded it to the "High Risk" category in August 2008 with the start of the global financial crisis.[7]

We further segregated the timeframe into two periods. The first covers the start of 2005 until May 2008, which is the period of political instability in the country. The second covers the period stretching from the start of June 2008 until the end of 2009, which coincides with the outbreak of the financial crisis and its evolution into a global economic downturn. The results of the analysis for the January 2005 to May 2008 period

TABLE 31.2 Correlation Levels

	Remittance inflows 2005–09	Remittance inflows January 2005– May 2008	Remittance inflows June 2008– December 2009
Lebanon political risk	0.31	0.41	0.11
Lebanon financial risk	0.56	0.18	−0.16
Lebanon economic risk	−0.59	−0.53	0.05
GCC economic risk	0.48	−0.33	0.42

Source: Byblos Bank Economic Research and Analysis Department.

show a stronger correlation of 0.4 between the deterioration of political risks in the country and the inflow of remittances, with a much lower correlation of 0.2 between the level of financial risks and remittance inflows, and a negative correlation with economic risks. In contrast, the results of the June 2008 to the end of 2009 period suggest a decline of the correlation between political risks and remittances to 0.11, as well as a weak correlation level between remittance inflows, on the one hand, and financial and economic risks, on the other. To explain the continuous high level of remittance inflows to Lebanon during the financial crisis, we ran a correlation analysis with the level of economic risks[8] in the six countries of the GCC and discovered a relatively strong correlation of 0.42 between the two variables. In other words, we found that when the level of economic risks increased in the GCC, which is the main source of remittance inflows to the country, the level of remittances to Lebanon increased.

Conclusions

We conclude from this analysis that the high level of remittance inflows to Lebanon was mainly driven by political and resulting financial risks during the period stretching from January 2005 until May 2008, and was carried forward by the increase in economic risks in the GCC from June 2008 until the end of 2009. The latter trend reflects the "safe haven" factor that can cause remittances for investment purposes to return home during economic downturns in the host countries, and that was reflected by an unprecedented level of capital inflows to Lebanon in 2009. As such, we can say preliminarily that the resilience of remittance inflows to Lebanon is determined by both domestic and external factors, as well as by the size of emigrant stock. Further, the global financial crisis had no negative impact on the flow of remittances to Lebanon, contrary to the impact on many developing economies. Indeed, the continuous migration from the country since 1975 has arguably been the single most relevant factor for the continuous inflow of remittances to the country, regardless of domestic political or economic circumstances. In brief, our analysis shows that the first serious external threat to the inflow of remittances to Lebanon in recent history, namely, the global financial crisis, was offset by the large stock of migrants, their income level, the lack of exchange rate effects, and no mass return migration.

Notes

1. Remittances Data, Migration and Remittances Unit, World Bank, http://worldbank.org/ prospects/migrationandremittances.
2. Such transfers provide a reliable proxy for the sources of remittance inflows, because they grew from 8 percent of migrant inflows to Lebanon in 2005 to 14.5 percent of remittances in 2009.
3. Central Bank of Lebanon (2009).
4. Prior to the global financial crisis, the expanding body of research on remittances has shown a trend of stability of such inflows in times of political turmoil and economic downturn in recipient countries. Also, some studies have found that remittances are strongly countercyclical in poor countries, but are procyclical in middle-income countries. But it was not clear how remittances would behave during a deep economic recession in the host countries.
5. The Political Risk Rating includes 12 weighted variables covering both political and social factors. The factors are Government Stability, Socioeconomic Conditions, Investment Profile, Internal Conflict, External Conflict, Corruption, Military in Politics, Religious Tensions, Law and Order, Ethnic Tensions, Democratic Accountability, and Bureaucracy Quality.
6. The PRS Group rates countries in five categories of Political, Financial, and Economic Risks ranging from "Very High Risk" to "High Risk," "Moderate Risk," "Low Risk," and "Very Low Risk."
7. The PRS Group's Financial Risk Rating measures a country's ability to finance its official, commercial, and trade debt obligations. The components that form the rating are Foreign Debt as a Percentage of GDP, Foreign Debt Service as a Percentage of Exports of Goods and Services, Current Account as a Percentage of Exports of Goods and Services, Net International Liquidity as Months of Import Cover, and Exchange Rate Stability.
8. The PRS Group's Economic Risk Rating provides a means of assessing a country's current economic strengths and weaknesses. The components that form the ratings are GDP per Head, Real GDP Growth, Annual Inflation Rate, Budget Balance as a Percentage of GDP, and the Current Account as a Percentage of GDP.

Chapter 32

Migrant Transfers in the MENA Region: A Two-Way Street in Which Traffic Is Changing

GEORGE NAUFAL AND CARLOS VARGAS-SILVA

THIS STUDY EXPLORES REMITTANCES IN the Middle East and North Africa (MENA) region in the face of the current crisis.[1] This is an interesting region given that it hosts some of the top remittance-receiving and remittance-sending countries in the world. For instance, although Saudi Arabia ranks second in the globe in remittance outflows with more than $16 billion, Morocco ranks in the top remittance-receiving countries with $6 billion in inflows (Ratha and Xu 2008). Flows in this region are also remarkable relative to the size of the receiving and sending economies. Bahrain, Lebanon, and Oman rank in the top-10 remittance-sending countries in terms of gross domestic product (GDP), and Jordan and Lebanon rank in the top-10 remittance-receiving countries in terms of GDP. These facts illustrate that remittances in the MENA region should be studied as a two-way flow.

Nonetheless, as a result of the recent financial crisis, remittance flows in both directions might have been affected. Therefore, there is a need for an analysis of the changing patterns of remittances in the region. We attempt this by studying data on remittances received from the MENA region by some of the main labor-exporting countries to the region and data on transfers received by key remittance-receiving countries in the MENA region. We also discuss several labor policy changes that may affect the long-term prospects of migration in the region and, hence, the flow of remittances.

The Response of Migration and Remittances to Crises

A large fraction of the literature on remittances has focused on the determinants of these flows (for example, Brown 1997; Funkhouser 1995; Lucas and Stark 1985). Based on these findings the literature has identified a variety of reasons for migrants' transfers, such as altruism, self-interest, loan repayment, and insurance motives.

In at least three of these motives there are reasons to speculate that remittances would respond to a home country crisis. Altruistic migrants are expected to remit more when the home country gets hit by a crisis to compensate for the decrease in income. Self-interested migrants, especially those who are remitting for investment purposes, may decide to decrease their flows and invest in the host country, where they may obtain more stable returns. Finally, those migrants who have some type of coinsurance agreement with the household are likely to increase their flows to fulfill their part of the deal.

The previous literature does suggest that remittances respond to crises. For instance, Sri Lanka's Central Bank reported an increase in remittances, especially from the Gulf Cooperation Council (GCC) countries, following the 2004 tsunami (Savage and Harvey 2007).[2] Remittances may also respond to ordinary business cycle fluctuations with migrants increasing transfers in reaction to downturns in economic activity back home (Chami, Fullenkamp, and Jahjah 2005). Yet this response of remittances is more likely after local fluctuations in output and in cases in which the majority of the host economies remain stable. In a situation such as the recent financial crisis with a sluggish world economy, migrants are also experiencing economic hardships, and, therefore, it would be challenging for migrants to help households back home.

The distinct nature of this crisis may also lead to long-term consequences for migration and remittances that are different from previous events. For instance, as a response to the 1973 oil crisis, several European countries terminated their guest-worker programs. Nonetheless, many migrants decided not to return home and used some of the rights that they had acquired over the years to bring their families to the host country (Martin 2001). Hence, instead of a decrease in migration, there was a change in the type of migration from labor oriented to family reunion. Moreover, although there was an economic downturn in oil-importing countries, there was an economic expansion in oil-exporting countries. Many of these countries started to recruit foreign workers, and there was a change in the direction of labor migrant flows. To be specific, a massive inflow of migrants to the GCC was seen.

Another relevant episode is the Asian financial crisis. Remittances to Asian countries decreased during the crisis, but the impact was short lived. The evidence also suggests that emigration was part of the coping mechanism of households during that crisis (Hugo 2000).

Migration and Remittances in the MENA Region

In table 32.1 we report the number of times that a country is a top-10 destination for emigrants of one of the MENA countries. There is nothing surprising about the top destinations: Canada, the United States, the United Kingdom, and Germany. Nonetheless, this region also has large numbers of internal migrants, with the GCC countries being the most popular destinations. For instance, for almost half of the countries, Saudi Arabia is a top destination.

TABLE 32.1 Top-10 Destinations of Migrants from MENA Countries, 2005

Destination	Number of times[a]	Percent
Canada	20	100.0
United States	19	95.0
United Kingdom	16	80.0
Germany	16	80.0
France	15	75.0
Australia	14	70.0
Saudi Arabia	9	45.0

Source: Ratha and Xu 2008.

a. Number of times (out of 20) that a destination is listed as a top-10 destination for migrants of one of the MENA countries.

This intraregional migration in the MENA region is usually more common in younger workers given that in this part of the world unemployment is high for first-time job seekers (Kabbani and Kothari 2005). Finally, foreign workers in this region come mainly from Asia, particularly from countries such as Bangladesh, India, Pakistan, and the Philippines (Ratha and Xu 2008).

The top portion of table 32.2 lists several countries in the MENA region along with the mean value of annual remittance inflows for 1970–2008. Five countries recorded an average of remittance inflows that surpassed $1 billion, and three countries reported an average double-digit remittances' share of GDP. In the last two columns of table 32.2, we link the financial crisis with the traditional remittance receivers in the region by reporting the growth in gross national income (GNI) for these countries for 2008 (purchasing power parity per capita). It seems that some of the main remittance receivers in the region such as the Republic of Yemen are among the countries most affected by the crisis in terms of a decrease in GNI. Meanwhile, the Arab Republic of Egypt, the top remittance receiver during the period, seems to be the least affected country.

As seen in the bottom portion of table 32.2, the average remittance outflows surpassed the $1 billion mark in at least seven countries. Interestingly, it seems that the economy of Saudi Arabia, the undisputed remittance-sending champion of the region, has remained relatively strong, with its GNI increasing by 5 percent. The working conditions of foreign workers in Saudi Arabia may change because of recent labor policy changes. For instance, many Asian workers in Saudi Arabia are "domestic helpers" (about 1.5 million) and have recently benefited from new laws that improve their legal protections (Human Rights Watch 2009a). Although the legal improvements are a step forward in terms of human rights, there may also be a negative effect on migrant earnings given that the law limits these workers to nine hours of work per day. These changes in labor policy may affect migrants' incomes and thus their capacity to remit money back home.

TABLE 32.2 Remittance Inflows and Outflows in Selected MENA Countries, 1970–2008

	Value ($, millions)		Percentage of GDP		GNI growth 2008	
	Rank	Mean	Rank	Mean	Rank	Percent
Remittances to						
Egypt, Arab Rep.	1	3,721	4	7.79	1	7.5
Lebanon	2	2,889	1	21.73	2	6.6
Morocco	3	2,184	5	6.68	4	6.1
Jordan	4	1,285	2	18.50	3	6.5
Yemen, Rep.	5	1,218	3	16.44	11	-9.4
Algeria	6	819	9	1.81	8	3.1
Tunisia	7	690	6	4.12	6	4.3
Israel	8	540	10	1.17	9	2.7
Syrian Arab Republic	9	461	8	2.98	5	4.4
Oman	10	38	11	0.38	—	—
Djibouti	11	22	7	3.39	7	3.6
Libya	12	11	12	0.03	10	0.6
Remittances from						
Saudi Arabia	1	9,232	5	6.04	4	5.1
United Arab Emirates	2	4,145	6	5.45	—	—
Lebanon	3	3,484	1	15.85	2	6.6
Qatar	4	2,008	4	7.71	—	—
Kuwait	5	1,388	7	4.19	—	—
Oman	6	1,247	3	8.75	—	—
Israel	7	1,175	10	1.35	8	2.7
Libya	8	707	9	1.54	9	0.6
Bahrain	9	683	2	11.88	6	3.5
Jordan	10	183	8	2.58	3	6.5
Egypt, Arab Rep.	11	115	14	0.17	1	7.5
Yemen, Rep.	12	102	11	1.12	10	−9.4
Algeria	13	101	12	0.23	7	3.1
Syrian Arab Republic	14	66	13	0.22	5	4.4

Sources: Arab Monetary Fund, Ratha and Xu 2008, and World Development Indicators.

Note: GDP = gross domestic product; GNI = gross national income; — = not available.

One of the lowest increases in GNI for 2008 is that of Israel. This combines with some recent policy changes to reduce migration to Israel. For example, the Israeli government agreed with local farmers to a gradual reduction of permits for foreign workers during the next half-decade in exchange for subsidizes for the adoption of capital-intensive technology (Thai Labour 2009). The ultimate goal is a reduction in the dependency on foreign labor, and this may have important implications for the future volume of labor inflows to the country, potentially resulting in a decrease in remittances.

Figure 32.1 displays remittance inflows and outflows for countries in the region. Remittance outflows followed the inflows closely until 1992, which may be a sign of the high-level intraregional migration. However, this connection vanished between 1992 and 2006. Although remittance outflows continued on the same growth trend, inflows deviated from this path and declined in 1993. A possible explanation for these facts is that GCC countries have progressively substituted regional workers with workers from Asian countries.

FIGURE 32.1 Mean Remittance Flows in the MENA Region, 1970–2008

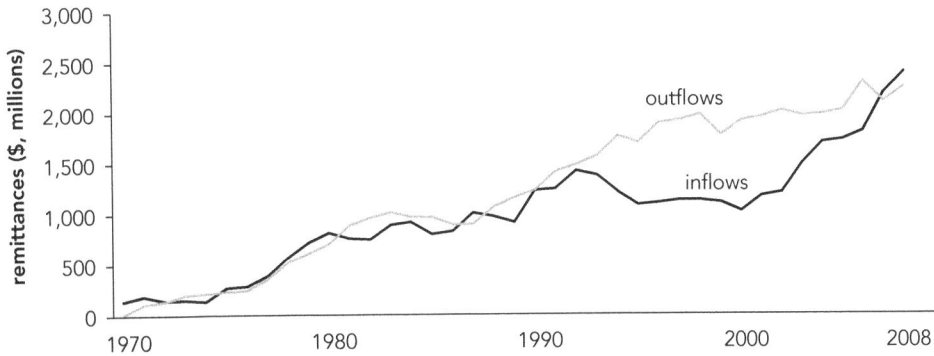

Source: Ratha and Xu 2008.

Remittances during the Crisis

The economic crisis has taken a toll on large segments of the population in MENA countries including foreign workers. These workers took pay cuts and lost jobs, and some had to return home. Therefore, their remitting power is expected to be affected.

This section examines recent data on both remittance outflows and inflows from selected MENA countries to shed more light on the dynamics of these flows during the crisis. Note that we do not control for other factors that could explain some of the changes in remittances. Furthermore, the dynamics presented here do not necessarily reflect the totality of the impact of the crisis because the economic crisis affected countries at different stages, and its ultimate consequences are still not clear.

Outflows

One of the major impediments for migration research in the MENA region is the lack of adequate data. For many countries in the region the data do not exist, and when data are at hand, the data are not accessible. Moreover, a variety reasons are found for expressing concerns about the existing remittance data in the MENA region, which range from inconsistencies in reporting formats by Central Banks to difficulties in measuring informal flows.

Hence, to explore the impact of the crisis on remittances from the MENA region, in table 32.3 we resort to data published by the Central Banks of Bangladesh, Pakistan, and the Philippines. Together with India, these countries represent some of the most important sources of foreign workers for the GCC. We focus first on Bangladesh, Pakistan, and the Philippines because these countries' Central Banks report monthly data on remittances from the GCC. Then we discuss the case of India, for which the data are not readily available.

Columns (1) to (3) provide information on migrant transfers from the GCC countries to Bangladesh. The figures indicate that the leader in remittances from the region is Saudi Arabia with more than $3 billion in remittances during 2009. This sum combines with almost $2 billion from the United Arab Emirates. The growth rate of remittances from the GCC to Bangladesh remains strong for all countries except Bahrain. Columns (4) to (6) provide similar information for Pakistan. As can be appreciated from the last column, a comparison of flows for 2008 and 2009 indicates that flows from all the GCC countries to Pakistan have increased.

Columns (7) and (8) report remittances from the GCC countries to the Philippines for 2008 and 2009. Filipino workers in Saudi Arabia remit over $1 billion per year. Notice also that five countries sent more than $100 million to the Philippines during 2009. Only in one instance have remittances declined in 2009 in comparison with 2008 (Kuwait). Hence, remittances in the GCC-Philippines corridor have remained stable, and, in fact, there is a rise in volume for most countries.

TABLE 32.3 Remittances from GCC to Bangladesh, Pakistan, and the Philippines, 2008 and 2009

Sending country	Bangladesh			Pakistan			Philippines		
	2008 ($, mil.)	2009 ($, mil.)	Growth rate (%)	2008 ($, mil.)	2009 ($, mil.)	Growth rate (%)	2008 ($, mil.)	2009 ($, mil.)	Growth rate (%)
	(1)	(2)	(3)	(4)	(5)	(6)	(7)	(8)	(9)
Bahrain	167.4	154.2	-8	147.8	157.0	6	159.5	166.2	4
Kuwait	949.5	993.9	5	426.9	437.7	3	125.1	104.6	-16
Oman	243.0	337.4	39	264.4	278.5	5	27.8	34.4	24
Qatar	324.8	366.3	13	283.6	375.4	32	122.9	184.6	50
Saudi Arabia	2,733.6	3,194.3	17	1,403.2	1,690.6	20	1,387.1	1,470.6	6
United Arab Emirates	1,379.5	1,958.1	42	1,289.4	2,011.1	56	621.2	644.8	4

Sources: http://www.bsp.gov.ph/statistics/keystat/ofw.htm; http://www.bangladesh-bank.org; and http://www.sbp.org.pk/ecodata/index2.asp.

The discussion of table 32.3 suggests that the reduction of remittances from the GCC to these three countries during the crisis period was only mild. Yet, as shown in figure 32.2, if we look at the remittance growth rates for the period January–May 2010 in comparison with the period January–May 2009, we can detect a further reduction on the flow of remittances from the GCC to some of these countries. In the case of Pakistan, there is a reduction of inflows from Bahrain, Qatar, and the United Arab Emirates; in the case of Bangladesh, there is a reduction in flows from Qatar and the United Arab Emirates.

FIGURE 32.2 Annual Growth Rate of Remittances from GCC Countries to Bangladesh, Pakistan, and the Philippines, January 2009–May 2010

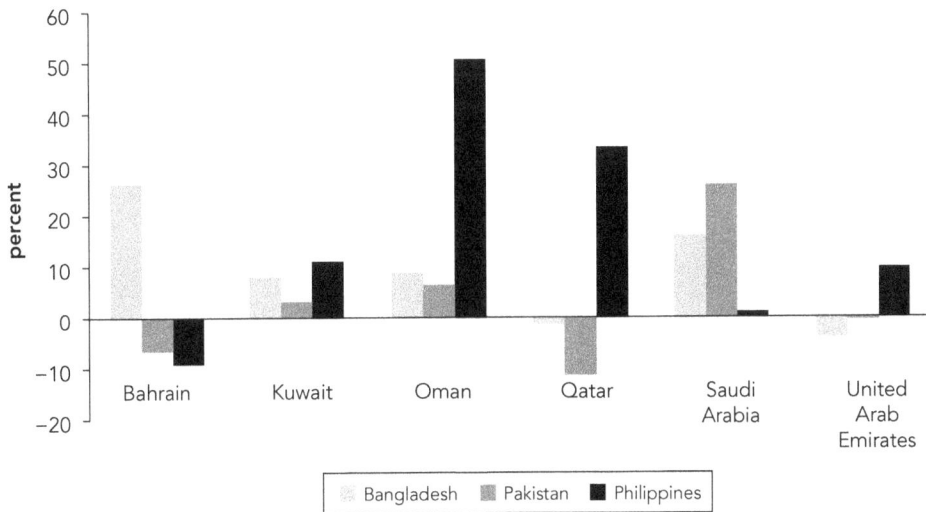

Sources: http://www.bsp.gov.ph/statistics/keystat/ofw.htm; http://www.bangladesh-bank.org; and http://www.sbp.org.pk/ecodata/index2.asp.

Table 32.3 supports our possible explanation for the drift in the growth of remittance inflows and outflows in the MENA region. A large share of remittance flows from the GCC is not directed toward other MENA countries but rather to Asian countries. Two facts may explain this pattern. First, Asian migrants typically do not settle in these countries and do not bring family members with them and, therefore, may have more responsibilities back home (Kapiszewski 2006). Second, it is argued that in the GCC countries, Asians are preferred to Arabs because they are not seen as a political threat. An influx of Arab workers may encourage the idea of a pan-Arab union in which actual national borders in the region are challenged (Kapiszewski 2006).

Notice that in all three cases flows from Kuwait are among the most affected. Yet the situation of foreign workers in Kuwait may improve in the future because of a new law that grants over 2 million foreigners more rights (Human Rights Watch 2009a). However, the law continues to maintain the *kafala* system by which each foreign worker needs a local sponsor, *kafeel*. Other countries in the region have modified their sponsorship system. In Bahrain, for example, the Labour Market Regulatory Authority, and not employers, is now in charge of sponsoring migrants' visas (Human Rights Watch 2009b). Foreign workers in the GCC countries need a sponsor, and their rights vary greatly and mainly depend on their occupation. Therefore, any significant change in these rights will ultimately affect their working conditions and their remitting patterns.

In addition to Bangladesh, Pakistan, and the Philippines, India is one of the main labor-exporting countries to the GCC countries. The United Arab Emirates is the main destination for Indian migrants in the region. About 1.5 million Indian migrants reside in the United Arab Emirates, and Indian migrants are believed to account for about 30 percent of the population of Dubai (Rajamony 2009). These migrants are typically employed in the construction or the service sector. This can be worrisome given that Dubai is experiencing a tough economic downturn with particular prominence of a weak construction sector. Dubai World, the investment company that manages the portfolio of the Dubai government, announced in 2009 that it was suspending the repayment of its debt (Bloomberg 2009). The recent data suggest that migration from India to the GCC countries is actually slowing (Rajamony 2009).

Inflows

As mentioned above, the MENA region is also an important receiver of remittances, and as such it is important to evaluate the impact of the crisis on remittances to some of the main receiving countries.

In table 32.4 we list the quarterly volume of transfers received by Egypt, Jordan, and Morocco since 2008, along with the growth rates with respect to the same quarter of the previous year. Egypt and Morocco are probably the two most important labor exporters in the MENA region; Jordan is another important regional labor exporter, and its Central Bank reports remittances received on a frequent basis. In all cases there is a clear pattern of increasing remittances at the beginning of the period, then decreasing transfers, that is again followed by increasing transfers toward the end of the period. Hence, there is support for the notion that some of the countries in the region suffered a decrease in remittances around the peak of the crisis. In the case of Egypt it seems that the decline in transfers in 2009 was dramatic, with remittances declining by about 24 percent during the second quarter and 25 percent during the fourth quarter. Yet remittances increased significantly during the first quarter of 2010. For Jordan we do not have data after the second quarter of 2009, but the Central Bank of Jordan announced that remittances to Jordan decreased by 4 percent in the first seven months of 2009 relative to the same period of 2008 (Badih 2010). This decrease seems to have been temporary given that the Central Bank of Jordan now reports that remittances have increased by 2.4 percent during the first four months of 2010.[3]

TABLE 32.4 Quarterly Remittances Received for 2008, 2009, and 2010

millions of dollars

Period	Egypt, Arab Rep.		Jordan		Morocco	
	Volume ($, millions)	Growth rate (%)	Volume ($, millions)	Growth rate (%)	Volume ($, millions)	Growth rate (%)
2008: Q1	2,064.8	—	830.9	8.51	1,628.8	17.00
2008: Q2	2,393.2	24.28	985.6	13.88	1,816.4	18.00
2008: Q3	1,950.7	−1.21	1,035.6	13.49	2,120.0	3.00
2008: Q4	2,285.3	7.46	944.0	6.02	1,347.6	−23.00
2009: Q1	1,738.0	−15.83	823.2	−0.93	1,243.7	−24.00
2009: Q2	1,831.7	−23.46	917.7	−6.89	1,446.6	−20.00
2009: Q3	1,855.7	−4.9.0	—	—	1,942.1	−8.00
2009: Q4	1,724.2	−24.6.0	—	—	1,647.0	22.00
2010: Q1	2,877.4	65.6.0	—	—	1,628.8	17.00

Sources: www.cbe.org.eg and www.worldbank.org/prospects/migrationandremittances.

Note: Growth rates are estimated with respect to the same period during the previous year. Q = quarter; — = not available.

Finally, for Morocco there was a significant reduction in transfers starting in the fourth quarter of 2008, but since late 2009 these flows seem to be increasing. Some European countries with large numbers of Moroccan migrants, such as Spain, started voluntary return programs in which they provide incentives to encourage migrants to return home. Although a considerable number of Latin American migrants have signed up for this program in Spain, the program has not been successful with regard to Moroccan migrants (McCabe, Lin, and Tanaka 2009). Hence, it seems that many Moroccan migrants have decided to weather the storm in the host countries instead of returning home.

Conclusion

Remittances from countries in the MENA region followed the remittance inflows into countries in the region closely until 1992, which we take as a manifestation of the high levels of intraregional migration. Interestingly, this connection vanished after 1992. One potential explanation for this fact is the growing dependence of this region on workers from Asia. During the 1970s the thriving GCC countries demanded a large pool of unskilled workers that was largely filled with workers from other MENA countries. However, workers from the MENA region have faced increased competition from Asian workers.

With regard to the financial crisis, it seems that remittances from the MENA region to some popular destinations did not decline in 2009, but some evidence suggests that we may see a slowdown in remittances for 2010. On the other hand, inflows to Egypt,

Jordan, and Morocco decreased significantly during 2009. This was bad news for these countries given that their revenues from tourism and exports were also affected by the crisis. Oil exporters in the MENA region also face challenging conditions (Ellaboudy 2010) given the noteworthy drop in investment that has, in the end, affected the number of jobs available for migrants. However, remittances to the MENA countries seem to have been on an upward trend for 2010; hence, it is possible that the impact of the crisis on remittances was only short term. In general, the short-term prospects of remittance outflows and inflows in this region remain uncertain.

In regard to recent labor policies adopted in the region, most of these policies have been directed toward improving the working conditions of foreigners. Although the majority of these policies fall short of granting full human rights to foreign workers, these policies are a step forward. Only in a few cases such as Israel is there a formal government policy to reduce the number of foreign workers. The new policies that are in place in several countries in the region suggest that there is still considerable demand for foreign labor. As such, the future may bring extra competition between Asian workers and workers from other MENA countries for jobs in the GCC countries.

Notes

1. MENA countries in this study refer to Algeria, Bahrain, Djibouti, the Arab Republic of Egypt, the Islamic Republic of Iran, Iraq, Israel, Jordan, Kuwait, Lebanon, Libya, Morocco, Oman, Palestine, Qatar, Saudi Arabia, the Syrian Arab Republic, Tunisia, the United Arab Emirates, and the Republic of Yemen.

2. GCC countries: Bahrain, Kuwait, Oman, Qatar, Saudi Arabia, and the United Arab Emirates.

3. Source: Central Bank of Jordan Monthly Report. The data for Jordan are available at the Central Bank of Jordan website, www.cbj.gov.jo. but provided in Jordanian dinars. The data suggest that remittances decreased (increased) by 8 and 4 percent during the third and fourth quarters, respectively, of 2009 and increased by 3 percent during the first quarter of 2010.

Bibliography

Acosta, P., C. Calderon, P. Fajnzylber, and H. Lopez. 2008. "What Is the Impact of International Migrant Remittances on Poverty and Inequality in Latin America?" *World Development* 36: 89–114.

Adams, R. 2009. "The Determinants of International Remittances in Developing Countries." *World Development* 37(1): 93–103.

Adams, R. H., Jr. 1991. "The Economic Uses and Impact of International Remittances in Rural Egypt." *Economic Development and Cultural Change* 39: 695–722.

———. 2003. "International Migration, Remittances, and the Brain Drain: A Study of 24 Labor Exporting Countries." Policy Research Working Paper 3069. World Bank, Washington, DC.

———. 2006. "International Remittances and the Household: Analysis and Review of Global Evidence." *Journal of African Economies* 15(Supp.): 396–425.

Adams, R. H., Jr., A. Cuecuecha, and J. Page. 2008. "The Impact of Remittances on Poverty and Inequality in Ghana." Policy Research Working Paper 4732. World Bank, Washington, DC.

Adams, R. H., Jr., and J. Page. 2003. "Poverty, Inequality and Growth in Selected Middle East and North Africa Countries, 1980–2000." *World Development* 31(6): 1047–63.

———. 2005. "Do International Migration and Remittances Reduce Poverty in Developing Countries?" *World Development* 33(10): 1645–69.

ADB (Asian Development Bank). 2009a. "Asian Development Outlook 2009: Rebalancing Asia's Growth." Asian Development Bank, Manila. http://www.adb.org/Documents/Books/ADO/2009/default.asp.

———. 2009b. *Fact Sheet.* December. Asian Development Bank, Manila.

———. 2009c. "Statistical Database System Online." Asian Development Bank, Manila. https://sdbs.adb.org.

Adenutsi, D. E. 2010. "Do International Remittances Promote Human Development in Poor Countries? Empirical Evidence from Sub-Saharan Africa." *International Journal of Applied Economics and Finance* 4(1): 31–45.

Adger, W. N. 2000. "Social and Ecological Resilience: Are They Related?" *Progress in Human Geography* 24(3): 347–64.

Adger, W. N., P. M. Kelly, A. Winkels, L. Q. Huy, and C. Locke. 2002. "Migration, Remittances, Livelihood Trajectories, and Social Resilience." *Ambio* 31(4): 358–66.

Aghion P., G. M. Angelatos, A. Banerjee, and K. Manova. 2005. "Volatility and Growth: Credit Constraints and Productivity-Enhancing Investment." NBER Working Paper 11349. Cambridge, MA.

Aguilar, F. V. J. 1996. "The Dialectics of Transnational Shame and National Identity." *Philippine Sociological Review* 44: 101–36.

Åkesson, L. 2009. "Remittances and Inequality in Cape Verde: The Impact of Changing Family Organization." *Global Networks* 9(3): 381–98.

Akkoyunlu, S. 2010. "Are Turkish Migrants Altruistic? Evidence from the Macro Data." KOF Working Paper 246.

Akkoyunlu, S., and K. A. Kholodilin. 2008. "A Link between Workers' Remittances and the Business Cycles in Germany and Turkey." *Emerging Markets Trade and Finance* 44(5): 23–41.

Akkoyunlu, S., and T. Vogel. 2008. "Self-employment of Immigrants in the UK, the U.S. and Germany." Paper presented at the 22nd ESPE Conference, University College London.

Alfaro, L., A. Chanda, S. Ozcan-Kalemli, and S. Sayek. 2010. "Does Foreign Direct Investment Promote Growth? Exploring the Role of Financial Markets on Linkages." *Journal of Development Economics* 91: 242–56.

Allen, F., and D. Gale. 1998. "Optimal Financial Crises." *Journal of Finance* 53: 1245–83.

Al-Sharmani, M. 2006. "Living Transnationally: Somali Diasporic Women in Cairo." *International Migration* 44(1): 55–77.

Ambrosetti, E. 2009. "The Impact of the Economic Crisis on Migrations Flows between Italy and North Africa." CARIM Analytic and Synthetic Notes 36, European University Institute.

Ammassari, S., and R. Black. 2001. "Harnessing the Potential of Migration and Return to Promote Development: Applying Concepts to West Africa." Sussex Migration Working Papers. Sussex: Sussex Center for Migration Research.

Amuedo-Dorantes, C., and S. Pozo. 2010. "Accounting for Remittance and Migration Effects on Children's Schooling." *World Development* 38(12): 1747–59.

———. 2011. "New Evidence on the Role of Remittances on Health Care Expenditures by Mexican Households." *Review of Economics of the Household* 9(1): 69–98.

Ananta, A., and E. N. Arifin, eds. 2004. *International Migration in Southeast Asia.* Singapore: Institute of Southeast Asian Studies.

Anderson, B., and M. Ruhs. 2009. "Who Needs Migrant Workers? Introduction to the Analysis of Staff Shortages, Immigration and Public Policy." Centre on Migration, Policy and Society (COMPAS), University of Oxford. http://www.compas.ox.ac.uk/research/labourmarket/a-need-for-migrant-labour/#c228.

Andreoni, J. 1989. "Giving with Impure Altruism: Applications to Charity and Ricardian Equivalence." *Journal of Political Economy* 97(6): 1447–58.

Arai, M., and R. Vilhelmsson. 2004. "Unemployment-Risk Differentials between Immigrant and Native Workers in Sweden." *Industrial Relations* 43: 690–98.

Arango, J. 2010. "Después del Gran Boom. La inmigración en bisagra del cambio." In *La inmigración en tiempos de crisis: Anuario de la Inmigración en España*. Barcelona: CIDOB.

Arellano, M., and S. Bond. 1991. "Some Tests of Specification for Panel Data: Monte Carlo Evidence and an Application to Employment Equations." *Review of Economic Studies* 58(2): 277–97.

Ashraf, N., D. Aycinena, C. Martinez, and D. Yang. 2009. "Remittances and the Problem of Control: A Field Experiment among Migrants from El Salvador." Mimeo. University of Michigan.

Askew, M. 2002. *Bangkok: Place, Practice, and Representation*. London: Routledge.

Assis, M. M. B. 1995. "Overseas Employment and Social Transformation in Source Communities: Findings from the Philippines." *Asian and Pacific Migration Journal* 4(2–3): 327–46.

Australia and New Zealand. 2010. "Australia & New Zealand Governments' Joint Report to the Pacific Islands Forum Economic Ministers' Meeting: Trends in Remittance Fees and Charges." http://forumsec.org.fj.

Avendano, R., N. Gaillard, and S. N. Parra. 2009. "Are Working Remittances Relevant for Credit Rating Agencies?" OECD Working Paper 282. Organization for Economic Co-Operation and Development, Paris.

Aycinena, D., C. Martinez, and D. Yang. 2009. "The Impact of Remittance Fees on Remittance Flows: Evidence from a Field Experiment among Salvadoran Migrants." Mimeo. University of Michigan.

Badih, Samia. 2010. "Remittance Flow Remains Strong." *Gulfnews.com*, September 12. http://gulfnews.com/business/features/remittance-flow-remains-strong-1.680688.

Bank of Albania. 2010. "Raporti Vjetor 2009." Tirana.

Bank of Spain. 2011a. "Balance of Payments." http://www.bde.es/webbde/es/estadis/estadis.html.

———. 2011b. "Eurosistema, Estadísticas Complementarias." http://www.bde.es/webbde/es/estadis/infoest/tc_1_3e.pdf.

Barajas, A., R. Chami, C. Fullenkamp, M. Gapen, and P. Montiel. 2009. "Do Workers' Remittances Promote Economic Growth?" Working Paper 09/153. IMF, Washington, DC.

Barajas, A., R. Chami, C. Fullenkamp, and A. Garg. 2010. "The Global Financial Crisis and Workers' Remittances to Africa: What's the Damage?" Working Paper 10/24. International Monetary Fund, Washington, DC.

Barjaba, K. 2002. "Albanian State Emigration Policy." Paper presented at the "International Conference on Albanian Migration and New Transnationalism," Centre for Migration Research, Sussex University, September 6–7.

Bastian, J. 2010. "Economic Fact Sheet Greece 2009/10." February. Eliamep.

Beck, T., R. Levine, and N. Loayza. 2000. "Finance and the Sources of Growth." *Journal of Financial Economics* 58: 261–300.

Beck, T., and M. S. Martínez Pería. 2009. "What Explains the Cost of Remittances? An Examination across 119 Country Corridors." Policy Research Working Paper 5072. World Bank, Washington, DC.

Bedford, C. 2010. "What Can We Learn from the Past about Managing the Future in the Pacific." Keynote address presented at the University of the South Pacific's International Conference, "Future Challenges, Ancient Solutions," November 29–December 3.

Bedford C., R. Bedford, and E. Ho. 2010. "Engaging with New Zealand's Recognized Seasonal Employer Work Policy: The Case of Tuvalu." *Asian and Pacific Migration Journal* 19: 421–45.

Bell, K., N. Jarman, and T. Lefebvre. 2004. *Migrant Workers in Northern Ireland*. Belfast: Institute for Conflict Research.

Bencivenga, V., and B. Smith. 1991. "Financial Intermediation and Endogenous Growth." *Review of Economic Studies* 58(2): 195–209.

Bencivenga, V., B. Smith, and R. Starr. 1995. "Transaction Costs, Technological Choice, and Endogenous Growth." *Journal of Economic Theory* 67(1): 53–177.

Bhaopichitr, K., V. Sirimaneetham, A. Luangpenthong, and R. Thongampai. 2008. *Thailand Economic Monitor*. April. Bangkok: World Bank Office, Bangkok.

Binford, L. 2003. "Migrant Remittances and (Under)Development in Mexico." *Critique of Anthropology* 23(3): 305–36.

Bloomberg. 2009. "Dubai World Seeks to Delay Debt Payments as Default Risk Soars." November 25. http://www.bloomberg.com.

BMZ (Bundesministerium für wirtschaftliche Zusammenarbeit und Entwicklung). 2009. "Studies on the Impact of the Downturn on Migration and Development in the Philippines, Nepal, and Uzbekistan." German Federal Ministry for Economic Cooperation and Development.

Bollard, A., D. McKenzie, M. Morten, and H. Rapoport. 2009. "Remittances and the Brain Drain Revisited: The Microdata Show That More Educated Migrants Remit More." Discussion Paper 26/09. Center for Research and Analysis of Migration.

Bond, S., A. Hoeffler, and J. Temple. 2001. "GMM Estimation of Empirical Growth Models." Working Paper. Nuffield College, University of Oxford.

Bonilla, S. A., and J. A. Cervantes. 2010. "Remesas Familiares; Temas Económicos y Sociales de Actualidad." In *México*, ed. E. Sepúlveda. México, D.F: Banco de México.

Bourdieu, P. 1977. *Outline of a Theory of Practice.* Cambridge: Cambridge University Press.

Bowman, C., and S. Chand. 2007. "Size Matters: The Impact of Aid on Institutions." Research Paper 2007/25. UNU-WIDER. http://www.wider.unu.edu/stc/repec/pdfs/rp2007/rp2007-25.pdf.

BRC (Banco de la República de Colombia). 2010. *Banco de la República de Colombia, Encuesta Trimestral de Remesas.* http://www.banrep.gov.co/estad/dsbb/remesas_paises.xls.

Brettell, C. B. 2007. "Adjustment of Status, Remittances, and Return: Some Observations on the 21st Century Migration Processes." *City and Society* 19(1): 47–59.

Brown, R. P. C. 1997. "Estimating Remittance Functions for Pacific Island Migrants." *World Development* 25(4): 613–26.

———. 1998. "Do Migrants' Remittances Decline over Time? Evidence from Tongans and Western Samoans in Australia." *Contemporary Pacific* 10(1): 107–51.

Brown, R. P. C., and D. A. Ahlburg. 1999. "Remittances in the South Pacific." *International Journal of Social Economics* 26 (1–3): 325–44.

Brown, R. P. C., and J. Connell. 1994. "The Global Flea Market: Migration, Remittances and the Informal Economy in Tonga." *Development and Change* 24(4): 611–47.

Brown, R. P. C., and B. Poirine. 2005. "A Model of Migrants' Remittances with Human Capital Investment and Intrafamilial Transfers." *International Migration Review* 39(2): 407–38.

Browne, C., and A. Mineshima. 2007. "Remittances in the Pacific Region." IMF Working Paper 07/35. International Monetary Fund, Washington, DC.

Browne, R., and G. Leeves. 2007. "Impacts of International Migration and Remittances on Source Country Household Incomes in Small Island States: Fiji and Tonga." Discussion Paper 347. School of Economics, University of Queensland, Australia.

Brumer, A. 2008. "Gender Relations in Family-Farm Agriculture and Rural-Urban Migration in Brazil." *Latin American Perspectives* 35(6): 11–28.

Buch, C. M., and A. Kuckulenz. 2010. "Worker Remittances and Capital Flows to Developing Countries." *International Migration* 48(5): 89–117.

Bugamelli, M., and F. Paterno. 2009. "Do Workers' Remittances Reduce the Probability of Current Account Reversals?" *World Development* 37(12): 1821–38.

Calì, M., and S. Dell'Erba. 2009. "The Global Financial Crisis and Remittances: What Past Evidence Suggests." Working Paper 303. Overseas Development Institute, London.

Cameron, R. 1967. *Banking in the Early Stages of Industrialization.* New York: Oxford University Press.

Carletto, G., B. Davis, M. Stampini, and A. Zezza. 2006. "A Country on the Move: International Migration in Post-Communist Albania." *International Migration Review* 40(4): 767–85.

Carling, J. 2005. "Migrant Remittances and Development Cooperation." PRIO Report 1/2005. PRIO, Oslo.

———. 2008. "The Determinants of Migrant Remittances." *Oxford Review of Economic Policy* 24(3): 581–98.

Catherine, V. 2007. "Femmes immigrées en Grèce. Double vulnérabilité et précarité." *Revue Interrogations* 4(June): 164–82.

CCOO (Centro de Información para Trabajadores Extranjeros). 2009. "Memoria 2009." http://www.ccoo.cat/cite/documentacio/memoria2009/index.htm.

Central Bank of Lebanon. 2009. "Financial Markets Handbook 2009." Bank du Liban Financial Markets Department, December 31, vol. 12, no. 2. http://www.bdl.gov.lb/fm.

Centre for Development Studies. 2008. "Global Financial Crisis and Kerala Economy: Impact and Mitigation Measures." Report submitted to the government of Kerala.

Cervantes, J. A., and A. Barajas. 2009. "Remuneraciones de los trabajadores mexicanos en Estados Unidos." *Revista de Comercio Exterior* 59(9): 735–45.

Chalamwong, Y. 1998. "Economic Crisis, International Migration, and the Labor Market in Thailand." *TDRI Quarterly Review* 13(1): 12–21.

Chami, R., C. Fullenkamp, and S. Jahjah. 2005. "Are Immigrant Remittance Flows a Source of Capital for Development?" *IMF Staff Papers* 52: 55–81.

Chami, R., D. Hakura, and P. Montiel. 2009. "Remittances: An Automatic Stabilizer?" IMF Working Paper 09/91. International Monetary Fund, Washington, DC.

Chin, K. 1999. *Smuggled Chinese: Clandestine Immigration to the United States.* Philadelphia: Temple University Press.

Christiansen, C. C. 2008. "Hometown Associations and Solidarities in Kurdish Transnational Villages: The Migration-Development Nexus in a European Context." *European Journal of Development Research* 20(1): 88–103.

Civici, A., I. Gedeshi, and D. Shehi. 1999. "Migration, Agriculture and Rural Development in Albania, Bulgaria and FYR of Macedonia: The Case of Albania." ACE-Phare Programme, P-96-6070R.

Clarke, G., and S. Wallsten. 2004. "Do Remittances Protect Households in Developing Countries against Shocks? Evidence from a Natural Disaster in Jamaica." Mimeo. World Bank, Washington, DC.

Clemens, M. A. 2009. "Skill Flow: A Fundamental Reconsideration of Skilled-Worker Mobility and Development United Nations Development Programme." Human Development Research Paper 2009/08.

Cliggett, L. 2005. "Remitting the Gift: Zambian Mobility and Anthropological Insights for Migration Studies." *Population, Space and Place* 11(1): 35–48.

Coats, D. 2008. *Migration Myths: Employment, Wages and Labour Market Performance.* London: Work Foundation.

COE (Council of Europe). 2006. *Social Remittances of the African Diasporas in Europe.* Lisbon: North-South Centre of the Council of Europe.

Cohen, J. H. 2005. "Remittance Outcomes and Migration: Theoretical Contests, Real Opportunities." *Studies in Comparative International Development* 40(1): 88–112.

———. 2010. "Oaxacan Migration and Remittances as They Relate to Mexican Migration Patterns." *Journal of Ethnic and Migration Studies* 36(1): 149–61.

Cohen, J. H., and L. Rodriguez. 2005. "Remittance Outcomes in Rural Oaxaca, Mexico: Challenges, Options and Opportunities for Migrant Households." *Population, Space and Place* 11(1): 49–63.

Cohen, J. H., L. Rodriguez, and M. Fox. 2008. "Gender and Migration in the Central Valleys of Oaxaca, Mexico." *International Migration* 46(1): 79–101.

Cohen, J., and I. Sirkeci. 2011. *Cultures of Migration: Global Nature of Contemporary Human Mobility.* Austin: University of Texas Press.

Comunidad de Madrid. 2010. "Cuantificación de las remesas de emigrantes enviadas desde la Comunidad de Madrid en 2009." Madrid, February–March 2010. http://www.remesas.org/files/Informe2010_d.pdf.

Conde, C. 2008. "Generation Left behind by Filipino Migrant Workers." *New York Times,* December 23.

Connell, J., and R. P. C. Brown. 1995. *Remittances in the Pacific: An Overview.* Manila: Asian Development Bank.

Conway, D. 2007. "The Importance of Remittances for the Caribbean's Future Transcends Their Macroeconomic Influences." *Global Development Studies* 4(3–4): 41–76.

Cornelius, W. A., T. J. Espenshade, and I. Salehyan, eds. 2001. *The International Migration of the Highly Skilled: Demand, Supply, and Development Consequences in Sending and Receiving Countries.* La Jolla: Center for Comparative Immigration Studies, University of California, San Diego.

Cortina, J., and E. Ochoa-Reza. 2008. "More Migration and Less Remittances? An Analysis of Turkish, Polish and Mexican Migration as They Evolve from Remitters to Savers." Paper for Migration Task Force Meeting Initiative for Policy Dialogue, Columbia University, New York, April. http://policydialogue.org.

Cox, D. 1987. "Motives for Private Transfers." *Journal of Political Economy* 95(3): 508–46.

Cox, D., Z. Eser, and E. Jimenez. 1998. "Motives for Private Transfers over the Life Cycle: An Analytical Framework and Evidence for Peru." *Journal of Development Economics* 55(1): 57–80.

Curran, S. R., F. Garip, C. Y. Chung, and K. Tangchonlatip. 2005. "Gendered Migrant Social Capital: Evidence from Thailand." *Social Forces* 84(1): 225–55.

Dale, A. 2008. "Pakistani and Bangladeshi Women's Labour Market Participation." Working Paper 2008-02. Catie Marsh Centre for Census and Survey Research, University of Manchester.

Danzer, A., and O. Ivaschenko. 2010. "Migration Patterns in a Remittances Dependent Economy: Evidence from Tajikistan during the Global Financial Crisis." *Migration Letters* 7(2): 190–202.

Datta, K., C. McIlwaine, J. Willis, Y. Evans, J. Herbert, and J. May. 2006. *Challenging Remittances as the New Development Mantra: Perspectives from Low-Paid Migrant Workers in London.* London: University of London.

Davies, S. 2007. "Remittances as Insurance for Idiosyncratic and Covariate Shocks in Malawi: The Importance of Distance and Relationship." MPRA Paper 4463. University Library, Munich, Germany.

De, P. K., and D. Ratha. 2007. "Does the One Who Leaves Provide Better? Impacts of International Remittances on Human Capital in Sri Lanka." Manuscript, New York University.

De Haas, H. 2005. "International Migration, Remittances and Development: Myths and Facts." *Third World Quarterly* 26(8): 1269–84.

DeParle, J. 2010. "Downturn Does Little to Slow Migration." *New York Times*, May 27.

De Soto, H., P. Gordon, I. Gedeshi, and Z. Sinoimeri. 2002. *Poverty in Albania: A Qualitative Assessment.* Washington, DC: World Bank.

De Zwager, N., I. Gedeshi, E. Germenji, and C. Nikas. 2005. *Competing for Remittances.* Tirana: IOM.

De Zwager, N., W. Gressmann, and I. Gedeshi. 2010. "Market Analysis: Albania—Maximising the Development-Impact of Migration-Related Financial Flows and Investment to Albania." Vienna, August.

DGEC. 2009. *Encuesta de Hogares de Propósitos Múltiples (EPHM).* San Salvador: General Directorate of Statistics and Census. http://www.digestyc.gob.sv/MainFrame/EstadisticasSociales.htm.

Diamond, D., and P. Dybvig. 1983. "Bank Runs, Deposit Insurance and Liquidity." *Journal of Political Economy* 91: 401–19.

Ditter, J.-G. 2008. "L'Albanie, de l'autarcie à la mondialisation." *Revue EurOrient* 27(spring): 149–66.

Dixon, C. 1999. *The Thai Economy: Uneven Development and Internationalisation.* New York: Routledge.

Djajić, S. 1986. "International Migration, Remittances and Welfare in a Dependent Economy." *Journal of Development Economics* 21: 229–34.

Doner, R. F. 2009. *The Politics of Uneven Development: Thailand's Economic Growth in Comparative Perspective.* Cambridge: Cambridge University Press.

DRC (Development Research Centre). 2009. *Making Migration Work for Development.* Brighton: University of Sussex and Department for International Development.

D'Souza, A. 2010. *Moving towards Decent Work for Domestic Workers: An Overview of the ILO's Work.* Geneva: International Labour Organization.

Durand, J., William Kandel, Emilio A. Parrado, and Douglas S. Massey. 1996. "International Migration and Development in Mexican Communities." *Demography* 33(2): 249–64.

Dustmann, C., J. Ludsteck, and U. Schönberg. 2009. "Revisiting the German Wage Structure." *Quarterly Journal of Economics* 124(2): 843–81.

Echazarra, A. 2010. "Accounting for the Time Pattern of Remittances in the Spanish Context." Working Paper 5-2010. January. http://www.remesas.org.

Eckstein, Susan. 2010. "Remittances and Their Unintended Consequences in Cuba." *World Development* 38(7): 1047–55.

Economic Intelligence Unit. 2009. "Vanuatu Country Report." July 2009. Economic Intelligence Unit Limited.

Edwards, A. C., and M. Ureta. 2003. "International Migration, Remittances, and Schooling: Evidence from El Salvador." NBER Working Paper W9766. Cambridge, MA.

Elbadawi, I. A., and R. Rocha. 1992. "Determinants of Expatriate Workers' Remittances in North Africa and Europe." Working Paper WPS 1038. Country Economics Department, World Bank, Washington, DC.

Ellaboudy, S. 2010. "The Global Financial Crisis: Economic Impact on GCC Countries and Policy Implications." *International Research Journal of Finance and Economics* 21: 180–93.

El Mouhoub, M., J. Oudinet, and E. Unan. 2008. "Macroeconomic Determinants of Migrants' Remittances in the Southern and Eastern Mediterranean Countries." Working Paper 7115. CEPN, Paris.

El Qorchi, M., S. M. Maimbo, and J. F. Wilson. 2003. "Informal Funds Transfer Systems: An Analysis of the Informal Hawala System." Joint International Monetary Fund and World Bank paper. Occasional Paper 222. International Monetary Fund, Washington, DC.

El-Sakka, M., and R. McNabb. 1999. "The Macroeconomic Determinants of Migrant Remittances." *World Development* 27(8): 1493–1502.

ESCWA (Economic and Social Commission for Western Asia). 2009. "Economic and Social Commission for Western Asia Annual Report: United Annual Report 2008." United Nations, New York.

Esim, S., and M. Smith. 2004. *Gender and Migration in Arab States: The Case of Domestic Workers.* Geneva: International Labour Organization.

ETF (European Training Foundation). 2008. "The Contribution of Human Resources Development to Migration Policy in Albania." Eurostat.

European Commission. 2010. "European Economic Forecast Autumn 2010." *European Economy* 10. Brussels.

Eurostat. 2011. "Statistics Database." http://epp.eurostat.ec.europa.eu/portal/page/portal/eurostat/home.

Eversole, R. 2005. "Direct to the Poor Revisted: Migrant Remittances and Development Assistance." In *Migration and Economy*, ed. L. Trager. Walnut Creek: AltaMira Press.

Fagen, Patricia Weiss, and Micah N. Bump. 2006. "Remittances in Conflict and Crises: How Remittances Sustain Livelihoods in War, Crises and Transitions to Peace." International Peace Academy Policy Paper.

Faini, R. 1994. "Workers' Remittances and the Real Exchange Rate. A Quantitative Framework." *Journal of Population Economics* 7(2): 235–45.

———. 2007. "Remittances and the Brain Drain: Do More Skilled Migrants Remit More?" *World Bank Economic Review* 21: 177–91.

Fajnzylber, P., and H. Lopez. 2007. *Close to Home: The Development Impact of Remittances in Latin America*. Washington, DC: World Bank.

Feinerman, E., and E. J. Seiler. 2002. "Private Transfers with Incomplete Information: A Contribution to the Altruism-Exchange Motivation for Transfers Debate." *Journal of Population Economics* 15: 715–36.

FEMIP (Facility for Euro-Mediterranean Investment and Partnership). 2006. "Study on Improving the Efficiency of Workers' Remittances in Mediterranean Countries." February. European Investment Bank, Rotterdam.

Ferenczi, L., and W. F. Wilcox. 1929. *International Migrations*. Vols. 1 and 2. New York: National Bureau of Economic Research.

Finch, T., M. Latorre, N. Pollard, and J. Rutter. 2009. *Shall We Stay or Shall We Go? Re-Migration Trends of Britain's Immigrants*. London: Institute for Public Policy Research.

Fix, M., D. G. Papademetriou, J. Batalova, A. Terrazas, S. Y. Lin, and M. Mittelstadt. 2009. "Migration and the Global Recession." Report Commissioned by the BBC World Service. September. Migration Policy Institute, Washington, DC.

Ford, K., A. Jampaklay, and A. Chamratrithirong. 2009. "The Impact of Circular Migration and Remittances on Relative Household Wealth in Kanchanaburi Province, Thailand." *Asian and Pacific Migration Journal* 18(2): 283–301.

Foster, A. D., and M. R. Rosenzweig. 2001. "Imperfect Commitment, Altruism, and the Family: Evidence from Transfer Behavior in Low-Income Rural Areas." *Review of Economics and Statistics* 83: 389–407.

Frankel, J. A. 2009. "Are Bilateral Remittances Countercyclical?" NBER Working Paper 15419. Cambridge, MA.

———. 2010. "Are Bilateral Remittances Countercyclical?" *Open Economies Review* 22(1): 1–16.

Freund, C., and N. Spatafora. 2008. "Remittances, Transaction Costs, and Informality." *Journal of Development Economics* 86(2): 356–66.

Funkhouser, E. 1995. "Remittances from International Migration: A Comparison of El Salvador and Nicaragua." *Review of Economics and Statistics* 77: 137–46.

———. 1997. "Labor Market Adjustment to Political Conflict: Changes in the Labor Market in El Salvador during the 1980s." *Journal of Development Economics* 52: 31–64.

Galliana, A. 2006. "The Impact of International Migration on the Economic Development of Countries in the Mediterranean Basin." UN/POP/EGM/2006: 4.

Gamburd, M. R. 2002. *Transnationalism and Sri Lanka's Migrant Households: The Kitchen Spoon's Handle.* New Delhi: Vistaar Publications.

———. 2008. "Milk Teeth and Jet Planes: Kin Relations in Families of Sri Lanka's Transnational Domestic Servants." *City & Society* 20(1): 5–31.

Gammage, S. 2006. "Exporting People and Recruiting Remittances: A Development Strategy for El Salvador?" *Latin American Perspectives* 33(6): 75–100.

Gammeltoft, P. 2002. "Remittances and Other Financial Flows to Developing Countries." Centre for Development Research Working Paper 02.11. August. Copenhagen.

Garcia, M., and D. Paiewonsky. 2006. "Gender, Remittances and Development: The Case of Women Migrants from Vicente Noble, Dominican Republic." INSTRAW, United Nations Population Fund (UNFPA), Santo Domingo.

Gedeshi, I. 2002. "Role of Remittances from Albanian Emigrants and Their Influence in the Country's Economy." *Eastern European Economics* 40(5): 49–72.

Gedeshi, I., and H. Mara. 2003. *The Encouragement of Social-Economic Development in Relation to the Growth of the Role of Remittances.* United Nations Development Programme, Tirana.

Gentry, J. W., and R. A. Mittelstaedt. 2010. "Remittances as Social Exchange: The Critical, Changing Role of Family as the Social Network." *Journal of Macromarketing* 30(1): 23–32.

Ghosh, B. 2006. "Migrants' Remittances and Development: Myths, Rhetoric and Realities." International Organization for Migration (IOM), Geneva, and The Hague Process on Refugees and Migration.

Gibb, H. 2009. "Impacts of the Economic Crisis: Women Migrant Workers in Asia." North-South Institute, IWG-GEM Conference 2009: "Gender and Global Economic Crisis," July 13–14, 2008.

Gibson, J., D. McKenzie, and H. Rohorua 2006. "How Cost Elastic Are Remittances? Evidence from Tongan Migrants in New Zealand." *Pacific Economic Bulletin* 21(1): 112–28.

Gilbertson, G. A. 1995. "Women's Labor and Enclave Employment: The Case of Dominican and Colombian Women in New York City." *International Migration Review* 29(3): 657–70.

Giuliano, P., and M. Ruiz-Arranz. 2009. "Remittances, Financial Development and Growth." *Journal of Development Economics* 90(1): 144–52.

Glytsos, N. 1997. "Remitting Behavior of 'Temporary' and 'Permanent' Migrants: The Case of Greeks in Germany and Australia." *Labour* 11(3): 409–35.

Glytsos, Nicholas P. 2002. "The Role of Migrant Remittances in Development: Evidence from Mediterranean Countries." *International Migration* 40(1): 5–26.

Goldsmith, R. W. 1969. *Financial Structure and Development.* New Haven: Yale University Press.

Gordon, J., and P. Gupta. 2004. "Nonresident Deposits in India: In Search of Return?" *Economic and Political Weekly* 39(37): 4165–74.

Government of Nepal. 2010. *Economic Survey for Fiscal Year 2009–10.* Kathmandu: Ministry of Finance.

Graner, E., and G. Gurung. 2003. "Arab Ko Lahure: Looking at Nepali Labour Migrants to Arabian Countries." *Contributions to Nepalese Studies* 30(2): 295–325.

Green, A. E., P. Jones, and D. Owen. 2007. "Migrant Workers in the East Midlands Labour Market." Report prepared for East Midlands Development Agency. Institute for Employment and Management, Nottingham.

Green, T., and L. A. Winters. 2010. "Economic Crises and Migration: Learning from the Past and the Present." *World Economy* 33: 1053–72.

Greenwood, J., and B. Jovanovic. 1989. "Financial Development, Growth, and the Distribution of Income." *Journal of Political Economy* 98: 1076–1107.

Gropas, R., and A. Triandafyllidou. 2008. "Discrimination in the Greek Workplace and the Challenge of Migration." September. Elliamep.

GTZ (Deutsche Gesellschaft für Internationale Zusammenarbeit), ed. 2010. "Auswirkungen der Wirtschafts- und Finanzkrise auf Migranten, Migration und Remittances. Übergreifende Zusammenhänge und Fallstudien." Diskussionspapier. GTZ, Eschborn. http://www.gtz.de/de/themen/wirtschaft-beschaeftigung/23881.htm.

Guarnizo, L. E. 2003. "The Economics of Transnational Living." *International Migration Review* 37(3): 666–99.

Guest, P. 1998. "Assessing the Consequences of Internal Migration: Methodological Issues and a Case Study on Thailand Based on Longitudinal Household Survey Data." In *Migration, Urbanization, and Development: New Directions and Issues*, ed. R. E. Bilsborrow. New York: United Nations Population Fund.

Gulfnews. 2009. "Remittances from Jordanian Workers Drop." September 12. https://gulfnews.com.

Gupta, P. 2005. "Macroeconomic Determinants of Remittances: Evidence from India." IMF Working Paper 05/224. International Monetary Fund, Washington, DC.

———. 2006. "Macroeconomic Determinants of Remittances: Evidence from India." *Economic and Political Weekly.*

———. 2010. "The Determinants of Remittances to India." *Migration Letters* 7(2): 214–23.

Gupta, S., C. A. Pattillo, and S. Wagh. 2009. "Impact of Remittances on Poverty and Financial Development in Sub-Saharan Africa." *World Development* 37(1): 104–15.

Halliday, T. 2006. "Migration, Risk and Liquidity Constraints in El Salvador." *Economic Development and Cultural Change* 54: 893–925.

Hammar, T., G. Brochmann, K. Tamas, and T. Faist, eds. 1997. *International Migration, Immobility and Development: Multidisciplinary Perspective.* Oxford: Berg.

Harrison, A., T. Britton, and A. Swanson. 2004. "Working Abroad: The Benefits Flowing from Nationals Working in Other Economies." Paper prepared for the Meeting of the Technical Subgroup for the Task Force on International Trade in Services, Movement of Natural Persons—Mode 4, Paris, September. Statistics Division, United Nations Department of Economic and Social Affairs.

Hatton, T. J., and J. G. Williamson. 2005. *Global Migration and the World Economy: Two Centuries of Policy and Performance.* Cambridge, MA: MIT Press.

———. 2009. "Global Economic Slumps and Migration." April 29. www.voxeu.org.

Hicks, J. 1969. *A Theory of Economic History.* Oxford: Clarendon Press.

Hildebrandt, N., and D. McKenzie. 2005. "The Effects of Migration on Child Health in Mexico." *Economia* 6(1): 257–89.

Hitchcock, J. T. 1961. "A Nepalese Hill Village and Indian Employment." *Asian Survey* 1(9): 15–20.

Hogue, C., ed. 2005. *Thailand's Economic Recovery.* Singapore: Institute of Southeast Asian Studies.

Home Office. 2006. *A Points Based System—Making Migration Work for Britain.* London: Home Office.

———. 2009. *Accession Monitoring Report: May 2004–March 2009.* London: Home Office.

———. 2010a. *Control of Immigration: Quarterly Statistical Summary (January–March 2010).* London: Home Office.

———. 2010b. "Government Sets the First Annual Limit for Non-European Workers." Press release, November 23.

Horst, C. 2007. "Connected Lives: Somalis in Minneapolis Dealing with Family Responsibilities and Migration Dreams of Relatives." In *Somalia: Diaspora and State Reconstruction in the Horn of Africa*, ed. A. O. Farah, M. Muchie, and J. Gundel. London: Adonis and Abbey.

Hugo, G. 2000. "The Crisis and International Population Movements in Indonesia." *Asian and Pacific Migration Journal* 9: 93–129.

———. 2003. "Migration and Development: A Perspective from Asia." IOM Migration Research Series 14. International Organization for Migration.

Human Rights Watch. 2009a. "Bahrain: Labor Reforms a Major Advance." May 13. https://www.hrw.org.

———. 2009b. "Saudi Arabia: Shura Council Passes Domestic Worker Protections." July 10. https://www.hrw.org.

Humphrey, M. 1991. "The Changing Role of Asian Labour Migration in the Middle East." *Des Migrations Internationales* 7(1): 45–63.

Hunt, L. 2008. "Women Asylum Seekers and Refugees: Opportunities, Constraints and the Role of Agency." *Social Policy and Society* 7(3): 281–92.

Hunt, L., and A. Steele. 2008. *Migrant Workers in Rochdale and Oldham*. Salford: University of Salford.

Hunte, C. K. 2004. "Worker's Remittances, Remittance Decay and Financial Deepening in Developing Countries." *American Economist* 48(2): 82.

Hürriyet. 2011. "Kathimerini: The Crisis Made Scholars Escape from Greece to Turkey." January 10. http://hurarsiv.hurriyet.com.tr/goster/ShowNew.aspx?id=16722621.

Icduygu, A. 2003. *Irregular Migration in Turkey*. Geneva: IOM Press.

———. 2006. *International Migration Discussions in the Context of Turkey-European Union Relations*. Istanbul: TUSIAD Publications.

ICG (International Crisis Group). 2010. "Central Asia: Migrants and the Economic Crisis." *Asia Report* 183(5).

ILO (International Labour Organization). 1998. "Measurement of Income from Employment. Report II." Sixteenth International Conference of Labour Statisticians. International Labour Organization, Geneva.

———. 2008. *Yearbook of Labour Statistics: Time Series 2008*. Geneva: ILO.

IMF (International Monetary Fund). 2005. *World Economic Outlook 2005*. Washington, DC: IMF.

———. 2008. *Balance of Payments Statistics Yearbook*. Washington, DC: IMF.

———. 2009a. *Regional Economic Outlook: Middle East and Central Asia*. Washington, DC: IMF.

———. 2009b. *World Economic Outlook: Crisis and Recovery*. Washington, DC: IMF.

———. 2010. *World Economic Outlook: Recovery, Risk, and Rebalancing*. Washington, DC: IMF.

INE (Instituto Nacional de Estadística). 2011a. "Population Estimates." National Statistics Institute, Spain. http://www.ine.es/jaxi/menu.do?type=pcaxis&path=%2Ft20%2Fp259&file=inebase&L=.

———. 2011b. "Population Register." National Statistics Institute, Spain. http://www.ine.es.

INEGI. 2011. "'Resultados Preliminares' del Censo de Población y Vivienda 2010." INEGI, Mexico City. http://www.inegi.org.mx/sistemas/TabuladosBasicos/preliminares2010.aspx.

INSTAT. 2002. *Albanian Population in 2001*. REPOBA.

IOM (International Organization for Migration). 2004. *Arab Migration in a Globalized World*. Geneva: IOM.

———. 2008. *Migration in Turkey: A Country Profile*. Geneva: IOM.

———. 2009. "The Impact of the Global Economic Crisis on Migrants and Migration." IOM Policy Brief. March. IOM, Geneva.

———. 2010. *Migration and the Economic Crisis in the European Union: Implications for Policy.* Brussels: IOM.

IPPR (Institute for Public Policy Research). 2009a. "Social Networks and Polish Immigration to the UK." Economics of Migration Working Paper 5, May. IPPR, London.

———. 2009b. "The Impact of the Global Economic Downturn on Migration." Monitoring Report 2. Department for International Development, London.

Irving, J., S. Mohapatra, and D. Ratha. 2010. "Global Survey of Central Banks on Remittances." Mimeo. Development Prospects Group, World Bank, Washington, DC.

Jacque, L. L. 1999. "The Asian Financial Crisis: Lessons from Thailand." *Fletcher Forum of World Affairs* 23(1): 87–99.

Jadhav, N. 2003. "Maximising Development Benefits of Migrant Remittances: The Indian Experience." Paper presented at the "International Conference on Migrant Remittances," Department for International Development and World Bank, London, October 9–10.

Jadhav, N., and B. Singh. 2006. "Worker's Remittances as Stable Financial Flows: Some Evidence from India." *Labour and Development* 11–12(1/2): 23–47.

Jayaraman, T. K., and C. K. Choong. 2010. "Role of Offshore Financial Center Institutions in Vanuatu." Working Paper WP2010/05. School of Business and Economics, University of the South Pacific, Suva, Fiji. http://www.econ.fbe.usp.ac.fj/fileadmin/files/schools/ssed/economics/working_papers/2010/WP5.pdf.

Jayaraman, T. K., C. K. Choong, and R. Kumar. 2009. "Role of Remittances in Economic Growth in Pacific Island Countries: A Study of Samoa." *Perpectives on Global Development and Technology* 8: 611–27.

———. 2010a. "Role of Remittances in Tongan Economy." *Migration Letters* 7: 224–30.

———. 2010b. "A Study on the Role of Remittances in Fiji's Economic Growth: An Augmented Solow Model Approach." Working Paper 2010/06. University of the South Pacific, Suva, Fiji. http://www.econ.fbe.usp.ac.fj/fileadmin/files/schools/ssed/economics/working_papers/2010/WP_6.pdf.

Jha, S., G. Sugiyarto, and C. Vargas-Silva. 2009. "The Global Crisis and the Impact on Remittances to Developing Asia." Asian Development Bank Working Paper Series 185. Asian Development Bank.

———. 2010. "The Global Crisis and the Impact on Remittances to Developing Asia." *Global Economic Review* 39(1): 59–82.

Jorgensen, M. B. 2008. "National and Transnational Identities: Turkish Organising Processes and Identity Construction in Denmark, Sweden and Germany." PhD thesis, Aalborg University SPIRIT, Aalborg University AMID, Academy for Migration Studies in Denmark.

Justino, P., and O. Shemyakina. 2010. "Remittances and Labor Supply in Post-Conflict Tajikistan." Research Working Paper 35. MICROCON.

Kabbani, N., and E. Kothari. 2005. "Youth Employment in the MENA Region: A Situational Assessment." Social Protection Discussion Paper 534. World Bank, Washington, DC.

Kakwani, N., and M. Krongkaew. 2000. "Analysing Poverty in Thailand." *Journal of the Asia Pacific Economy* 5(1/2): 141–60.

Kapiszewski, A. 2006. "Arab versus Asian Migrant Workers in the GCC Countries." Paper presented at the United Nations Expert Group Meeting on International Migration and Development in the Arab Region, Department of Economic and Social Affairs. United Nations Secretariat, Beirut, May 15–17.

Kar, M., O. Peker, and M. Kaplan. 2008. "Trade Liberalization, Financial Development and Economic Growth in the Long Term: The Case of Turkey." *South East European Journal of Economics and Business* 3: 25–38.

Kasparian, C. 2009. "L'émigration des jeunes Libanais et leurs projects d'avenir." Observatoire Universitaire de la Réalité Socio-Economique, Univeristé Saint-Joseph, Presses de l'Univeristé Saint-Joseph, Beirut.

Katz, E., and O. Stark. 1986. "Labor Migration and Risk Aversion in Less Developed Countries." *Journal of Labor Economics* 4(1): 134–49.

Kaur, A. 2010. "Labour Migration in Southeast Asia: Migration Policies, Labour Exploitation and Regulation." *Journal of the Asia Pacific Economy* 15(1): 6–19.

Ketkar, S., and D. Ratha. 2009. *Innovative Financing for Development.* Washington, DC: World Bank.

Khalaf, S., and S. Alkobaisi. 1999. "Migrants' Strategies of Coping and Patterns of Accommodation in the Oil-Rich Gulf Societies: Evidence from the UAE." *British Journal of Middle Eastern Studies* 26(2): 271–98.

Kilic, T., G. Carletto, B. Davis, and A. Zezza. 2007. "Investing Back Home: Return Migration and Business Ownership in Albania." Working Paper 4366. World Bank Policy Research, Washington, DC.

Kim, E. M., ed. 1998. *The Four Asian Tigers: Economic Development and the Global Political Economy.* San Diego: Academic Press.

King, R. 2005. "Albania as a Laboratory for the Study of Migration and Development." *Journal of Southern Europe and the Balkans* 7(2): 133–56.

King, R., M. Dalipaj, and N. Mai. 2006. "Gendering Migration and Remittances: Evidence from London and Northern Albania." *Population, Space and Place* 12(6): 409–34.

King, R., and R. Levine. 1993. "Finance and Growth: Schumpeter Might Be Right." *Quarterly Journal of Economics* 108: 717–37.

King, R., and J. Vullnetari. 2010. "Gender and Remittances in Albania: Or Why 'Are Women Better Remitters Than Men?' Is Not the Right Question." Working Paper 58. University of Sussex, Sussex Centre for Migration Research, Brighton.

Kirisci, K. 2002. *Justice and Home Affairs Issues in Turkish-EU Relations: Assessing Turkish Asylum and Immigration Policy and Practice.* Ankara: Turkish Economic and Social Studies Foundation.

Koç, I., and I. Onan. 2004. "International Migrants' Remittances and Welfare Status of the Left-Behind Families in Turkey." *International Migration* 38(1): 78–112.

Kollmair, M., S. Manandhar, B. Subedi, and S. Thieme. 2006. "New Figures for Old Stories: Migration and Remittances in Nepal." *Migration Letters* 3(2): 151–60.

Korinek, K., B. Entwisle, and A. Jampaklay. 2005. "Through Thick and Thin: Layers of Social Ties and Urban Settlement among Thai Migrants." *American Sociological Review* 70: 779–800.

Krongkaew, M., and N. Kakwani. 2003. "The Growth-Equity Trade-off in Modern Economic Development: The Case of Thailand." *Journal of Asian Economics* 14(5): 735–57.

Labeaga, J. M., S. Jiménez-Martín, and N. Jorgensen. 2007. *The Volume and Geography of Remittances from the EU.* Madrid: FEDEA.

Laeven, L., and F. Valencia. 2008. "Systemic Banking Crises: A New Database." Working Paper 08/224. International Monetary Fund, Washington, DC.

Landolt, P. 2001. "Salvadoran Economic Transnationalism: Embedded Strategies for Household Maintenance, Immigrant Incorporation, and Entrepreneurial Expansion." *Global Networks* 1: 217–42.

Levine, R., N. Loayza, and T. Beck. 2000. "Financial Intermediation and Growth: Causality and Causes." *Journal of Monetary Economics* 46: 31–77.

Levitt, Peggy. 2000. "Migrant Participation across Borders: Towards an Understanding of Forms and Consequences." In *Immigration Research for a New Century: Multidisciplinary Perspectives,* ed. N. Foner, R.G. Rumbaut, and S. J. Gold. New York: Russell Sage Foundation.

Lianos, T. P., and J. Cavounidis. 2010. "Immigrant Remittances, Stability of Employment and Relative Deprivation." *International Migration* 48(5): 118–41.

Livingston, G. 2006. "Gender, Job Searching, and Employment Outcomes among Mexican Immigrants." *Population Research and Policy Review* 25(1): 43–66.

Lopez, J. R., and M. A. Seligson. 1991. "Small Business Development in El Salvador: The Impact of Remittances." In *Migration, Remittances, and Small Business Development: Mexico and Caribbean Basin Countries,* ed. S. Diaz-Briquets and S. Weintraub. Boulder: Westview.

Lowell, B. L., and R. O. de la Garza. 2002. "The Development Role of Remittances in U.S. Latino Communities and Latin America." In *Sending Money Home: Hispanic Remittances and Community Development,* ed. R. O. de la Garza and B. L. Lowell. Lanham, MD: Rowman and Littlefield.

Lozano Ascencio, F. 1998. "Las remesas de los migrantes mexicanos en Estados Unidos: Estimaciones para 1995." In *Migration between Mexico and the United States.* Austin: Mexican Ministry of Foreign Affairs and the United States Commission on Immigration Reform.

Lubkemann, S. 2005. "The Moral Economy of Nonreturn among Socially Diverted Labor Migrants from Portugal and Mozambique. In *Society for Economic Anthropology Monographs* 22, ed. L. Trager. Walnut Creek: AltaMira Press.

Lucas, R., Jr. 1988. "On the Mechanics of Economic Development." *Journal of Monetary Economics* 22(1): 3–42.

———. 2005. *International Migration and Economic Development, Lessons from Low-Income Countries.* Northampton, MA: Edward Elgar.

Lucas, R. E. B., and O. Stark. 1985. "Motivations to Remit: Evidence from Botswana." *Journal of Political Economy* 93(5): 901–17.

Lueth, E., and M. Ruiz-Arranz. 2007. "Determinants of Bilateral Remittance Flows." *B.E. Journal of Macroeconomics* 8(1): article 26.

———. 2008. "Determinants of Bilateral Remittance Flows." *B.E. Journal of Macroeconomics* October.

———. 2009. "A Gravity Model of Workers' Remittances." IMF Working Paper 06/290.

Luthria, M. 2009. "Money Transfers into the Pacific (Transfer Fees Could Stand a Cut-Back)." *Australian Financial Review,* November 10.

Lyberaki, A., and L. Lambrianidis. 2004. "Back and Forth and In-Between: Albanian Return-Migrants from Greece and Italy." *Journal of International Migration and Integration* 5(1): 77–106.

Lynch, A. 2010. "Estrategias de remesas de los emigrantes frente a la crisis." Working Paper 2-2010. January. http://www.remesas.org.

MacFarlane, A. 1976. *Resources and Population: A Study of Gurungs of Nepal.* London: Cambridge University Press.

Maclellan, N., and P. Mares. 2005. "Remittances and Labour Mobility in the Pacific—A Working Paper on Seasonal Work Programs in Australia for Pacific Islanders." Melbourne: Swinburne Institute for Social Research. http://researchbank.swinburne.edu.au/vital/access/manager/Repository/swin:5609.

Maddison, A. 2003. *The World Economy: Historical Statistics.* Paris: Organisation for Economic Co-operation and Development.

Mahler, S. J., and P. R. Pessar. 2006. "Gender Matters: Ethnographers Bring Gender from the Periphery toward the Core of Migration Studies." *International Migration Review* 40(1): 27–63.

Maimbo, S. M., and D. Ratha. 2005. "Remittances: An Overview." In *Remittances: Development Impact and Future Prospects,* ed. S. M. Maimbo and D. Ratha. Washington, DC: World Bank.

Mandelman, F., and A. Zlate. 2010. "Immigration, Remittances and Business Cycles." Mimeo. Federal Reserve Bank of Atlanta.

Manseau, G. S. 2005. "Contractual Solutions for Migrant Laborers: The Case of Domestic Workers in the Middle East." http://www.nottingham.ac.uk/shared/shared_hrlcpub/HRLC_Commentary_2006/manseau.pdf.

Mansuri, G. 2007. "Temporary Migration and Rural Development." In *International Migration, Economic Development, and Policy*, ed. Çaglar Özden and Maurice Schiff. Basingstoke: Palgrave Macmillan.

Martin, P. 2001. "There Is Nothing More Permanent than Temporary Foreign Workers." Backgrounder. April. Center for Immigration Studies.

———. 2009a. "The Recession and Migration: Alternative Scenarios." International Migration Institute Working Paper 13. *International Migration Institute*, University of Oxford.

———. 2009b. "Recession and Migration: A New Era for Labor Migration?" *International Migration Review* 43(3): 671–91.

Martin, P. L., E. Hönekopp, and H. Ullmann. 1990. "Europe 1992: Effects on Labor Migration." *International Migration Review* 24(3): 591–603.

Massa, I., and D. W. te Velde. 2008. "The Global Financial Crisis: Will Successful African Countries Be Affected?" Background paper published by ODI. http://www.odi.org.uk/resources/details.asp?id=2612&title=global-financial-crisis-will-successful-african-countries-be-affected.

Massey, D. S. 1990. "Social Structure, Household Strategies, and the Cumulative Causation of Migration." *Population Index* 56(1): 3–26.

Massey, D. S., J. Arango, G. Hugo, A. Kouaouci, A. Pellegrino, and J. E. Taylor. 1994. "An Evaluation of International Migration Theory: The North American Case." *Population and Development Review* 20(4): 699–751.

———. 1998/2006. *Worlds in Motion: Understanding International Migration at the End of the Millennium.* New York: Oxford University Press.

Massey, D. S., and J. E. Taylor. 2004. *International Migration: Prospects and Policies in a Global Market.* New York: Oxford University Press.

Mazzucato, V., B. van den Boom, and N. N. N. Nsowah-Nuamah. 2008. "Remittances in Ghana: Origin, Destination and Issues of Measurement." *International Migration* 46(1): 103–22.

McCabe, K., S. Y.-Y. Lin, and H. Tanaka. 2009. "Pay to Go: Countries Offer Cash to Immigrants Willing to Go." Migration Information Source, feature story, November. http://www.migrationinformation.org/Feature/display.cfm?ID=749.

McClaughlin, D., and D. Smith. 2005. "Doctors Go West in Polish Brain Drain." *The Observer*, May 15. http://observer.guardian.co.uk.

McCormick, B., and J. Wahba. 2000. "Overseas Employment and Remittances to a Dual Economy." *Economic Journal* 110(463): 509–34.

McKay, S., and A. Winkelmann-Gleed. 2005. "Migrant Workers in the East of England." Project report for the East of England Development Agency, Cambridge. London Metropolitan University, London.

McKinnon, R. 1973. *Money and Capital in Economic Development.* Washington, DC: Brookings Institution.

Menjivar, C. 2000. *Fragmented Ties: Salvadoran Immigrant Networks in America.* Berkeley: University of California Press.

Merkle, L., and K. Zimmermann. 1992. Savings, Remittances, and Return Migration. *Economic Letters* 38: 77–81.

Miera, F. 2008. "Long Term Residents and Commuters: Change of Patterns in Migration from Poland to Germany." *Journal of Immigrant & Refugee Studies* 6(3): 297–311.

Migration DRC. 2009. "Migration and the Financial Crisis: How Will the Economic Downturn Affect Migrants?" Development Research Centre on Migration, G.P. Briefing, Sussex Centre for Migration Research, Brighton, UK. http://www.migrationdrc.org/publications/briefing_papers/BP17.pdf.

Migration Information Source. 2010. "Evidence from the Great Recession Is In: Migration Flows Dropped, Unemployment among Certain Immigrants Rose." December 1.

Migration Letters. 2010. Special Issue on Remittances and Financial Crisis. *Migration Letters* 7(2).

Migration News. 2010. "Unemployment, Projections, H-1B." *Migration News* 17(2).

Ministry of Overseas Indian Affairs. 2009. "Annual Report 2008–09." Government of India, New Delhi.

MNAEC (Ministerio Nacional de Asuntos Exteriores y Cooperación). 2009. "Ministerio Nacional de Asuntos Exteriores y Cooperación." http://www.maec.es.

Mohan, G. 2002. "Diaspora and Development." In *Development and Displacement*, ed. J. Robinson. Oxford: Milton Keynes, Open University and Oxford University Press.

Mohapatra, S., G. Joseph, and D. Ratha. Forthcoming. "Remittances and Natural Disasters: Ex-Post Response and Contribution to Ex-Ante Preparedness." *Environment, Development and Sustainability.*

Mohapatra, S., and C. Ozden. 2009. "Migration and Remittances in South Asia." In *Trade in Services and Investments in South Asia,* ed. Ejaz Ghani. Washington, DC: World Bank.

Mohapatra, S., and D. Ratha. 2010. "Forecasting Migrant Remittances during the Global Financial Crisis." *Migration Letters* 7(2): 203–13.

Moran-Taylor, M. J. 2008. "When Mothers and Fathers Migrate North: Caretakers, Children, and Child Rearing in Guatemala." *Latin American Perspectives* 35(4): 79–95.

Moré, I., A. Echazarra, B. Halloufi, and R. Petru. 2008. "Cuantificación de las Remesas Enviadas por las Mujeres Migrantes desde España." Resúmen, Madrid. June. http://www.remesas.org.

Morrison, A. R., M. Schiff, and M. Sjöblom. 2007. *The International Migration of Women.* Washington, DC: World Bank.

MPI (Migration Policy Institute). 2008. "Top 10 Migration Issues of 2008: Issue #6—Return Migration: Changing Directions?" MPI, Washington, DC. http://www.migrationinformation.org/Feature/display.cfm?ID=707.

———. 2010. "Mexico: A Crucial Crossroads." MPI Country Profiles, Migration Information Source. www.migrationinformation.org.

MSIO (Merseyside Social Inclusion Observatory). 2006. "Supporting Migrant Workers in the North West of England." Briefing Paper 8. MSIO, Liverpool.

MTIN (Ministerio de Trabajo e Inmigracíon). 2010. "Extranjeros con certificado de registro o tarjeta de residencia en vigor y Extranjeros con autorización de estancia por estudios en vigor a 30 de septiembre de 2010." http://extranjeros.mtin.es.

Mundaca, B. G. 2009. "Remittances, Financial Market Development, and Economic Growth: The Case of Latin America and the Caribbean." *Review of Development Economics* 13(2): 288–303.

Nagarajan, S. 2009. "Impact of Global Financial Crisis on Remittance Flows to Africa." November 17. African Development Bank Group, Subha.

Narayan, P. K. 2005. "The Saving and Investment Nexus for China: Evidence from Co-Integration Tests." *Applied Economics* 37: 1979–90.

Naudé, W. A. 2009. "Fallacies about the Global Financial Crisis Harms Recovery in the Poorest Countries." December. CESifo Forum, Munich.

———. 2010. "The Determinants of Migration from Sub-Saharan African Countries." *Journal of African Economies* 19(3): 330–56.

Naufal, G., and C. Vargas-Silva. 2010. "Migrant Transfers in the MENA Region: A Two Way Street in Which Traffic Is Changing." *Migration Letters* 7(2): 168–78.

Nayyar, D. 1989. "International Labour Migration from India: A Macro-Economic Analysis." In *To the Gulf and Back Migration: Studies on the Economic Impact of Asian Labour Migration*, ed. R. Amjad. Geneva: International Labour Office.

Nepal Telecom. 2009. "Annual Report of Nepal Telecom 2009." http://www.ntc.net.np/utilities/annualreport_060-61_to_064-65.pdf.

Newell, S. 2005. "Migratory Modernity and the Cosmology of Consumption in Côte d'Ivoire." In *Society for Economic Anthropology Monographs* 22, ed. L. Trager. Walnut Creek: AltaMira Press.

Niimi, Y., and C. Ozden. 2006. "Migration and Remittances: Causes and Linkages." Policy Research Working Paper Series 4087. World Bank, Washington, DC.

Nikas, C., and R. King. 2005. "Economic Growth through Remittances: Lessons from the Greek Experience of the 1960s Applicable to the Albanian Case." *Journal of Southern Europe and the Balkans* 7(2): 235–57.

NSO (National Statistical Office of Thailand). 2000. *Population and Housing Census 2000.* Bangkok: NSO.

NWDA (North West Development Agency). 2006. *Northwest Regional Economic Strategy 2006.* Warrington: NWDA.

OECD (Organisation for Economic Co-operation and Development). 2000. "The Employment of Foreigners: Outlook and Issues in OECD Countries." In *OECD Employment Outlook.* Paris: OECD.

———. 2005. *Migration, Remittances and Development.* Paris: OECD Publications.

———. 2009a. "International Migration: Charting a Course through the Crisis." OECD Policy Brief, June. OECD, Paris.

———. 2009b. "International Migration and the Economic Crisis: Understanding the Links and Shaping Policy Responses." International Migration Outlook 2009. OECD, Paris.

———. 2010. *International Migration Outlook.* Paris: OECD.

Office for National Statistics. 2010. "Regional Profile—North West: Selected Key Statistics." https://www.ons.gov.uk.

Office of Immigration Statistics. 2009. *Yearbook of Immigration Statistics: 2009.* Washington, DC: U.S. Department of Homeland Security.

Oishi, N. 2005. *Women in Motion: Globalization, State Policies, and Labor Migration in Asia.* Stanford, CA: Stanford University Press.

Olimova, S. 2010. "Global Crisis and Labour Migration: The Case of Tajikistan." http://www.ceri-sciencespo.com/cerifr/transversal/06112009/s_olimova.pdf.

Onishi, N. 2010. "Toiling Far from Home for Philippine Dream." *New York Times,* September 18.

O'Rourke, K. 1995. "Emigration and Living Standards in Ireland since the Famine." *Journal of Population Economics* 8(4): 1432–75.

Orozco, M. 2002. "Globalization and Migration: The Impact of Family Remittances in Latin America." *Latin American Politics and Society* 44(2): 41–66.

———. 2004. *Remittances to Latin America and the Caribbean: Issues and Perspectives on Development.* Washington, DC: Organization of American States.

———. 2006. "International Flows of Remittances: Cost, Competition and Financial Access in Latin America and the Caribbean—Toward an Industry Scorecard." Report prepared for the Inter-American Development Bank, Washington, DC.

———. 2009. "The Global Economic Crisis and Intersecting Variables Determining Remittance Trends." Paper given at the "Conference on the Impact of the Global Economic Crisis on Migrants' Remittances and Its Implications for Development," March 21, Utrecht.

Orrenius, P., and M. Zavodny. 2009. "Tied to the Business Cycle: How Immigrants Fare in Good and Bad Economic Times." Migration Policy Institute, November. www.migrationpolicy.org.

Osili, U. O. 2004. "Migrants and Housing Investments: Theory and Evidence from Nigeria." *Economic Development and Cultural Change* 52(4): 821–49.

———. 2007. "Remittances and Savings from International Migration: Theory and Evidence Using a Matched Sample." *Journal of Development Economics* 83(2): 446–65.

Pantoja, A. D. 2005. "Transnational Ties and Immigrant Political Incorporation: The Case of Dominicans in Washington Heights, New York." *International Migration* 43(4): 123–46.

Papademetriou, D. G., and P. L. Martin, eds. 1991. *The Unsettled Relationship: Labor Migration and Economic Development*. London: Greenwood Press.

Parreñas, R. 2005. "Long Distance Intimacy: Class, Gender and Intergenerational Relations between Mothers and Children in Filipino Transnational Families." *Global Networks* 5(4): 317–36.

Parsons, C. R., R. Skeldon, T. L. Walmsey, and L. A. Winters. 2007. "Quantifying International Migration: A Database of Bilateral Migration Stocks." In *International Migration, Economic Development and Policy*, ed. Ç. Özden and M. Schiff. London and Washington, DC: Palgrave Macmillan and World Bank.

Pemberton, S. 2008. "Supporting Economic Migrants in the North West of England." *Public Policy and Administration* 23(1): 80–99.

———. 2009. "Economic Migration from the EU 'A8' Accession Countries and the Impact on Low Demand Housing Areas: Opportunity or Threat for Housing Market Renewal Pathfinder Programmes in England?" *Urban Studies* 46(7): 1363–84.

Perlez, J. 2002. "Educated Filipinos, Disillusioned at Home, Look Abroad for a Better Life." *New York Times*, April 3.

Pesaran, M. H., Y. Shin, and R. Smith. 2001. "Bounds Testing Approaches to the Analysis of Level Relationships." *Journal of Applied Econometrics* 16: 289–326.

Pfaff-Czarnecka, J. 1995. "Migration under Marginality Conditions: The Case of Bajhang." In *Rural-Urban Interlinkages: A Challenge for Swiss Development Cooperation*. Zurich and Kathmandu: IDA and INFRAS.

Phillips, N. 2009. "Migration as Development Strategy? The New Political Economy of Dispossession and Inequality in the Americas." *Review of International Political Economy* 16(2): 231–59.

Phizacklea, A. 2000. "Ruptures: Migration and Globalisation: Looking Back and Looking Forward." In *Trans-Nationalism and the Politics of Belonging*, ed. S. Westwood and A. Phizacklea. London: Routledge.

Phongpaichit, P., and C. Baker, eds. 2008. *Thai Capital: After the 1997 Crisis*. Chiang Mai: Silkworm Books.

Piper, N. 2005. "Gender and Migration." Paper prepared for the policy analysis and research programme of the Global Commission on International Migration.

Pollard, N., M. Latorre, and D. Sriskandarajah. 2008. *Floodgates or Turnstiles? Post-EU Enlargement Migration Flows to (and from) the UK*. London: Institute for Public Policy Research.

Prescott, E., and J. Boyd. 1987. "Dynamic Coalitions, Growth, and the Firm." In *Contractual Arrangements for Intertemporal Trade*, ed. E. Prescott and N. Wallace. Minneapolis: University of Minnesota Press.

Punzalan, K. 2009. "The Economic Crisis and Labour Migrants: A Test for Human Security?" *NTS Insight* 1 (June). Singapore.

Qatar: Statistical Appendix. 2009. "International Monetary Fund Country Report." 09/32. January. Qatar.

Quartey, P., and T. Blankson. 2004. "Do Migrant Remittances Minimize the Impact of Macro-Volatility on the Poor in Ghana?" Report submitted to the Global Development Network.

Rafael, V. L. 1997. "Your Grief Is Our Gossip: Overseas Filipinos and Other Spectral Presences." *Public Culture* 9: 267–91.

Rahman, M. M. 1999. "The Asian Economic Crisis and Bangladeshi Workers in Singapore." Working Paper 147. Department of Sociology, National University of Singapore, Singapore.

———. 2009. *In Quest of Golden Deer: Bangladeshi Transient Migrants Overseas*. Saarbrücken: VDM Verlag.

Raja, K. 2009. "Financial Crisis Will Put a Damper on ODA Flows." UNCTAD Policy Brief 7. March.

Rajamony, V. 2009. *Impact of the Financial Crisis on Indian Workers in the UAE*. Presentation at the conference "Financial Crisis in the Gulf and Its Impact on South and South East Asian Migrants," Centre for Development Studies, India. July 22.

Rajan, I. S., and B. A. Prakash. 2009. "Migration and Development Linkages Re-Examined in the Context of the Global Economic Crisis." Invited paper for the Civil Society Days of the 3rd Global Forum on Migration and Development, November 2–3, Athens.

Rajan, I. S., V. J. Varghese, and M. S. Jayakumar. 2009. "Overseas Recruitment Practices in India: A Critical Assessment." Report submitted to the International Labour Organization, Thailand, and Ministry of Overseas Indian Affairs, Government of India, New Delhi.

Ramirez, M., Z. Skrbis, and M. Emmison. 2007. Transnational Family Reunions as Lived Experience: Narrating a Salvadoran Autoethnography. *Identities* 14(4): 411–31.

Rapoport, H., and F. Docquier. 2000. "Strategic and Altruistic Remittances." In *The Economics of Reciprocity, Giving and Altruism*, eds. L.-A. Gerard-Varet, S.-C. Kolm, and J. Mercier Ythier. New York: MacMillan and St. Martin Press, chapter 16, pp. 285–97.

———. 2006. "The Economics of Migrants' Remittances." In *Handbook of the Economics of Giving, Altruism, and Reciprocity*, ed. S. Kolm and J. M. Ythier. New York: Elsevier.

Ratha, D. 2003. "Workers' Remittances: An Important and Stable Source of External Finance." *Global Development Finance* 157–75.

———. 2005. "Workers' Remittances: An Important and Stable Source of External Development Finance." In *Remittances: Development Impact and Future Prospects*, ed. S. M. Maimbo and D. Ratha. Washington, DC: World Bank.

———. 2007. "Leveraging Remittances for Development." Policy Brief. Migration Policy Institute, Washington, DC.

———. 2010a. "Diaspora Bonds for Development Financing during the Crisis." People Move blog, October 26. World Bank, Washington, DC. http://blogs.worldbank.org/peoplemove/diaspora-bonds-for-development-financing-during-a-crisis.

———. 2010b. "Mobilize the Diaspora for the Reconstruction of Haiti." In *Haiti: Now and Next.* Social Science Research Council (SSRC), New York. http://www.ssrc.org.

Ratha, D., P. De, and S. Mohapatra. 2007. "Shadow Sovereign Ratings for Unrated Developing Countries." Policy Research Working Paper 4269. World Bank, Washington, DC.

———. 2010. "Shadow Sovereign Ratings for Unrated Developing Countries." *World Development* 39(3): 295–307.

Ratha, D., and S. Mohapatra. 2009. "Revised Outlook for Remittance Flows 2009–2011." Migration and Development Brief 9. World Bank, Washington, DC.

———. 2010. "Revised Outlook for Remittance Flows 2011–2012." Migration and Development Brief. World Bank, Washington, DC.

Ratha, D., S. Mohapatra, and S. Plaza. 2008. "Beyond Aid: New Sources and Innovative Mechanisms for Financing Development in Sub-Saharan Africa." Policy Research Working Paper WPS 4609. World Bank, Washington, DC.

Ratha, D., S. Mohapatra, and A. Silwal. 2009a. "Migration and Remittance Trends 2009: A Better-than-Expected Outcome So Far, but Significant Risks Ahead." Migration and Development Brief 11. World Bank, Washington, DC.

———. 2009b. "Outlook for Remittance Flows 2009–2011: Remittances Expected to Fall by 7–10 Percent in 2009." Migration and Development Brief 10. World Bank, Washington, DC.

———. 2010a. "Outlook for Remittance Flows 2010–11: Remittance Flows to Developing Countries Remained Resilient in 2009, Expected to Recover during 2010–11." Migration and Development Brief 12. World Bank, Washington, DC.

———. 2010b. "Outlook for Remittance Flows 2011–2012: Recovery after the Crisis, but Risks Lie Ahead." Migration and Development Brief 13. World Bank, Washington, DC.

Ratha, D., S. Mohapatra, and Z. Xu. 2008. "Outlook for Remittance Flows 2008–10: Growth Expected to Moderate Significantly, but Flows to Remain Resilient." Migration and Development Brief 8. World Bank, Washington, DC.

Ratha, D., and W. Shaw. 2007. "South-South Migration and Remittance." Working Paper 102. World Bank, Washington, DC.

Ratha, D., and I. Sirkeci. 2010. "Remittances and the Global Financial Crisis." *Migration Letters* 7(2): 125–31.

Ratha, D., and Z. Xu 2008. *Migration and Remittances Factbook.* Washington, DC: World Bank.

Regmi, M. C. 1978. *Thatched Huts and Stucco Palaces: Peasants and Landlords in 19th Century Nepal.* New Delhi: Vikas.

Reichert, Joshua. 1981. "The Migrant Syndrome: Seasonal U.S. Wage Labor and Rural Development in Central Mexico." *Human Organization* 40(1): 56–66.

Remesas. 2009. "¿Cuanto cuesta enviar una remesa desde Europa?" February. http://www.remesas.org.

Remple, H., and R. A. Lobdell. 1978. "The Role of Urban-to-Rural Remittances in Rural Development." *Journal of Development Studies* 14: 324–41.

Rennie, D. 2005. "EU Urged to Give British Welcome to Polish Plumbers." *Daily Telegraph*, September 7. http://www.telegraph.co.uk.

Reserve Bank of India. 2006. "Remittances from Overseas Indians: A Study of Methods of Transmission, Costs and Time." *RBI Monthly Bulletin*, November.

———. 2010. "Remittances from Overseas Indians: Modes of Transfer, Transaction Cost and Time Taken." *RBI Monthly Bulletin*, April.

Richter, K., P. Guest, W. Boonchalaski, N. Piriyathamwong, and N. B. Ogena. 1997. "Migration and the Rural Family: Report of the Northeastern Follow-up to the National Migration Survey." Institute for Population and Social Research, Mahidol University.

Riester, A. 2009. "Impact of the Global Recession on International Labour Migration and Remittances." Background paper. Asian Development Bank, Manila. http://www.adb.org/documents/events/2009/poverty-social-development/WG1C-impact-on-migration-Riester-paper.pdf.

———. 2010a. "The Impact of the Global Recession on Labour Migration and Remittances. Implications for Poverty Reduction and Development in Nepal, Philippines, Tajikistan, and Uzbekistan." In *The Social Impact of the Global Recession in Asia and Pacific*. Manila: Asian Development Bank.

———. 2010b. "Migration and Conflict: The Integration of Burkinabe Migrants Returning from Côte d'Ivoire." PhD thesis, Martin-Luther Universität Halle/Wittenberg.

Rigg, J. 1998. "Rural-Urban Interactions, Agriculture and Wealth: A Southeast Asian Perspective." *Progress in Human Geography* 22: 497–522.

Rigg, J., S. Veeravongs, L. Veeravongs, and P. Rohitarachoon. 2008. "Reconfiguring Rural Spaces and Remaking Rural Lives in Central Thailand." *Journal of Southeast Asian Studies* 39(3): 355–81.

Romer, P. M. 1986. "Increasing Returns and Long-Run Growth." *Journal of Political Economy* 94(5): 1002–37

Rose, S., and R. Shaw. 2008. "The Gamble: Circular Mexican Migration and the Return on Remittances." *Mexican Studies/Estudios Mexicanos* 24(1): 79–111.

Ruhs, M. 2006. "The Potential of Temporary Migration Programmes in Future International Migration Policy." *International Labour Review* 146(1–2): 7–36.

Ruiz, I., and C. Vargas-Silva. 2010. "Another Consequence of the Economic Crisis: A Decrease in Migrants' Remittances." *Applied Financial Economics* 20(1): 171–82.

———. 2011. "Exploring the Causes of the Slowdown in Remittances to Mexico." *Empirical Economics*.

Russell, S. S. 1986. "Remittances from International Migration: A Review in Perspective." *World Development* 14(6): 677–96.

Ryan, L., R. A. Sales, M. Tilki, and B. Siara. 2009. "Family Strategies and Transnational Migration: Recent Polish Migrants in London." *Journal of Ethnic & Migration Studies* 35(1): 61–77.

Saith, A. 1989. "Macroeconomic Issues in International Labour Migration—A Review." In *To the Gulf and Back*, ed. R. Amjad. Geneva: International Labour Organization.

Salomone, S. 2006. "Remittances: Overview of the Existing Literature." European University Institute. http://www.iue.it.

Salt, J. J. Dobson, and A. Latham. 2009. "On the Move? Labour Migration in Times of Recession." Policy Network Paper. www.policy-network.net.

Samson, I. 1996. "Albania Experience among Transition Trajectories." Working paper, Grenoble.

Sanchez, P. 2007. Cultural Authenticity and Transnational Latina Youth: Constructing a Meta-Narrative across Borders. *Linguistics and Education* 18(3–4): 258–82.

Sandell, R. 2005. "Spain's Quest for Regular Immigration." ARI 64/2005. May 18. Real Instituto Elcano de Estudios Internacionales y Estratégicos.

Sander, C. 2003. "Migrant Remittances to Developing Countries: A Scoping Study." Paper prepared for DFID, Bannock Consulting. June.

Savage, K., and P. Harvey. 2007. "Remittances during Crises: Implications for Humanitarian Response." Report Briefing Paper 26. Humanitarian Policy Group, London.

Sayan, S. 2006. "Business Cycles and Workers' Remittances: How Do Migrant Workers Respond to Cyclical Movements of GDP at Home?" IMF Working Paper No. 06/52, International Monetary Fund, Washington, DC.

Schiff, M. 2004. "When Migrants Overstay Their Legal Welcome: A Proposed Solution to the Guest-Worker Program." IZA Discussion Paper 1401.

Schmalzbauer, L. 2008. "Family Divided: The Class Formation of Honduran Transnational Families." *Global Networks* 8(3): 329–46.

Scullion, L., and G. Morris. 2009. *Central and Eastern European Migrants in Tameside*. Salford: University of Salford.

Scullion, L., and S. Pemberton. 2010. *Exploring Migrant Workers Motivations for Migration and Their Perceived Contributions to the UK: A Case Study of Liverpool*. Salford: Migrant Workers North West.

Seddon, D. 2005. "Nepal's Dependence on Exporting Labour." www.migrationinformation.org.

Seddon, D., J. Adhikari, and G. Gurung. 2002. "Foreign Labour Migration and the Remittance Economy of Nepal." *Critical Asian Studies* 34(1): 19–40.

Semyonov, M., and A. Gorodzeisky. 2005. "Labor Migration, Remittances and Household Income: A Comparison between Filipino and Filipina Overseas Workers." *International Migration Review* 39(1): 45–68.

Sen, A. 1999. *Development as Freedom.* New York: Anchor Books.

Shah, N. M. 2004. "Arab Migration Patterns in the Gulf." In *Arab Migration in a Globalizing World.* Geneva: IOM.

Sharma, J., and G. Gurung. 2009. "Impact of Global Economic Slowdown on Remittance Inflows and Poverty Reduction in Nepal." Conference paper for ASEAN/ADB conference, "The Impact of the Global Economic Slowdown on Poverty and Sustainable Development in Asia and the Pacific." http://www.adb.org/documents/events/2009/poverty-social-development/papers.asp.

Sharma, J. R. 2008. "Practices of Male Labor Migration from the Hills of Nepal to India in Development Discourses: Which Pathology?" *Gender, Technology and Development* 12(3): 303–23.

Shauman, K. A., and M. C. Noonan. 2007. "Family Migration and Labor Force Outcomes: Sex Differences in Occupational Context." *Social Forces* 85(4): 1735–64.

Shaw, E. S. 1973. *Financial Deepening in Economic Development.* Oxford: Oxford University Press.

Shaw, J. 2007. "Sri Lanka Country Study." Monash Asia Institute, Institute for Regional Development, University of Tasmania, and Foundation for Development Cooperation.

Shehu, A. Y. 2004. "The Asian Alternative Remittance Systems and Money Laundering." *Journal of Money Laundering Control* 7(2): 175–85.

Shleifer, A. 2009. "Peter Bauer and the Failure of Foreign Aid." *Cato Journal,* 29: 379–90.

Sieveking, N., and M. Fauser. 2009. "Migrationsdynamiken und Entwicklung in Westafrika: Untersuchungen zur entwicklungspolitischen Bedeutung von Migration in und aus Ghana und Mali." Working Paper 68. Center on Migration, Citizenship and Development, Bielefeld. http://www.uni-bielefeld.de/tdrc/ag_comcad/downloads/workingpaper_68_sieveking+fauser.pdf.

Singh, B. 2010. "Workers' Remittances to India: An Examination of Transfer Cost and Efficiency." *International Migration* 48(5): 63–88.

Singh, R. J. 2010. "From Shock Absorber to Shock Transmitter: Determinants of Remittances in Sub-Saharan Africa." *Migration Letters* 7(2): 231–40.

Singh, R. J., M. Haacker, and K.-W. Lee. 2009. "Determinants and Macroeconomic Impact of Remittances to Sub-Saharan Africa." IMF Working Paper 09/216. International Monetary Fund, Washington, DC.

Singh, R. J., M. Haacker, K.-W. Lee, and M. LeGoff. 2011. "Determinants and Macroeconomic Impact of Remittances in Sub-Saharan Africa." *Journal of African Economies* 20(March): 312–40.

Sirkeci, I. 2005. "Diaspora: Turkish." In *Immigration and Asylum from 1900 to the Present,* ed. M. Gibney and R. Hansen. Santa Barbara, CA: ABC-Clio.

———. 2006. *The Environment of Insecurity in Turkey and the Emigration of Turkish Kurds to Germany.* New York: Edwin Mellen Press.

———. 2009. *Improving the Immigration and Asylum Statistics in Turkey [Türkiye'de Uluslararası Göç ve Sığınma İstatistiklerinin Geliştirilmesi].* Ankara: Turkish Statistical Institute.

Skeldon, R. 1997. "Rural-to-Urban Migration and Its Implications for Poverty Alleviation." *Asia-Pacific Population Journal* 12(1): 3–16

———. 2004. "Migration, the Asian Financial Crisis, and Its Aftermath." In *International Migration in the New Millennium*, ed. D. Joly. Aldershot: Ashgate.

———. 2008. "International Migration as a Tool in Development Policy: A Passing Phase?" *Population and Development Review* 34(1): 1–18.

———. 2010. "The Overseas Chinese of South East Asia: History, Culture, Business." *Journal of Ethnic and Migration Studies* 36(7): 1193–94.

Slack, J. 2007. "Polish Immigrants Take £1bn Out of the UK Economy." *Mail Online*, June 28. http://www.dailymail.co.uk/news/article-464759/Polish-immigrants-1bn-UK-economy.html#.

Smyth, J. 2010. "Poles Based in Ireland Repatriate €841m." *Irish Times*, October 26.

Sørensen, N. N. 2005a. "Diaspora, Development and Conflict: The Role of Expatriate Communities in Development." In *FAU Conference 2005: Reconstructing Post-Conflict Societies—Challenge and Possibilities.* Copenhagen: FAU.

———. 2005b. "Migrant Remittances, Development and Gender." Danish Institute for International Studies, Copenhagen. www.diss.dk.

Sørensen, N. N., N. van Hear, and P. Engberg-Pedersen. 2002. "The Migration-Development Nexus: Evidence and Policy Options State-of-the-Art Overview." *International Migration* 40(5).

Stahl, C. W., and F. Arnold. 1986. "Overseas Workers' Remittances in Asian Development." *International Migration Review* 20(4): 899–925.

Stark, O. 1978. "Economic-Demographic Interaction in the Course of Agricultural Development: The Case of Rural-to-Urban Migration." Research Report 2/78. David Horowitz Institute for Research of Developing Countries, Tel Aviv.

———. 1991a. "Migration in LDCs: Risk, Remittances, and the Family." *Finance and Development* 28(4): 39–41.

———. 1991b. *The Migration of Labour.* Oxford: Blackwell.

———. 1992. *Migration in Developing Countries: Risk, Remittances, and the Family.* Tel Aviv: Tel Aviv University.

Statistics Denmark. 2011. "Migration Statistics." http://www.dst.dk/homeuk.aspx.

Statistics South Africa. 2011. http://www.statssa.gov.za/census2011/index.asp.

Stenning, A., T. Champion, C. Conway, M. Coombes, S. Dawley, L. Dixon, S. Raybould, and R. Richardson. 2006. *Assessing the Local and Regional Impacts of International Migration.* Newcastle-upon-Tyne: Centre for Urban and Regional Development Studies.

Stodolska, M., and C. A. Santos. 2006. "'You Must Think of Familia': The Everyday Lives of Mexican Migrants in Destination Communities." *Social & Cultural Geography* 7(4): 627–47.

Straubhaar, T. 1986. "The Determinants of Workers' Remittances: The Case of Turkey." *Weltwirtschafliches Archiv* 122(4): 728–40.

Straubhaar, T., and F. Valdean. 2006. *International Migrant Remittances and Their Role in Development.* Paris: OECD.

Sunden, A. E., and B. J. Surette. 1998. "Gender Differences in the Allocation of Assets in Retirement Saving Plans." *American Economic Review* 88(2): 207–11.

Suro, R., S. Bendixen, B. L. Lowell, and D. C. Benavides. 2002. "Billions in Motion: Latino Immigrants, Remittances and Banking." Report produced in cooperation between the Pew Hispanic Center and the Multilateral Investment Fund. Pew Hispanic Center, MIF Fomin, Washington, DC.

Swamy, Gurushri. 1981. "International Migrant Worker's Remittances: Issues and Prospects." World Bank Staff Working Paper 481. World Bank, Washington, DC.

Syrett, S., and M. Lyons. 2007. "Migration, New Arrivals and Local Economies." *Local Economy* 22(4): 325–34.

Tacoli, C., G. McGranahan, and D. Satterthwaite. 2008. "Urbanization, Poverty, and Inequity: Is Rural-Urban Migration a Poverty Problem, or Part of the Solution?" In *The New Global Frontier: Urbanization, Poverty and Environment in the 21st Century*, ed. G. Marine, G. McGranahan, M. Montgomery, and R. Fernández-Castilla. London: Earthscan Publications.

Tanner, A. 2005. *Emigration, Brain Drain and Development: The Case of Sub-Saharan Africa.* Helsinki and Washington, DC: East-West Books and Migration Policy Institute.

Tatla, D. S. 2002. "A Passage to England: Oral Tradition and Popular Culture among Early Punjabi Settlers in Britain." *Oral History* 30(2): 61–72.

Taylor, J. E. 2000. *Do Government Programs "Crowd-In" Remittances?* Washington, DC: Inter-American Dialogue and the Tomas Rivera Policy Institute.

Taylor, J. E., J. Arango, G. Hugo, A. Kouaouci, D. S. Massey, and A. Pellegrino. 1996a. "International Migration and Community Development." *Population Index* 62(3): 397–418.

———. 1996b. "International Migration and National Development." *Population Index* 62(2): 181–212.

Teves, O. 2005. "Remittances Can't Replace Good Economic Policies, RP Told." Associated Press. http://www.inq7.net.

Thai Labour. 2009. *Farmers Protest in J'lem against Lack of Harvesters.* December 9. https://www.thailabour.org.

Thieme, S. 2006. *Social Networks and Migration: Far West Nepalese Labour Migrants in Delhi.* Munster: LIT Publishing.

Thomas, B. 1954. *Migration and Economic Growth: A Study of Great Britain and the Atlantic Economy.* Cambridge: Cambridge University Press for National Institute of Economic and Social Research.

Trager, L. 1984. "Migration and Remittances: Urban Income and Rural Households in the Philippines." *Journal of Developing Areas* 18: 317–40.

———. 2005. "Women Migrants and Hometown Linakges in Nigeria: Status, Economic Roles and Contributions to Community Development." In *Society for Economic Anthropology Monographs* 22, ed. L. Trager. Walnut Creek: AltaMira Press.

Traser, J. 2006. *European Citizen Advice Service (ECAS): Who's Still Afraid of EU Enlargement?* Brussels: ECAS.

Triandafyllidou, A., and D. Lazarescu. 2009. "The Impact of the Recent Global Economic Crisis on Migration. Preliminary Insights from the South Eastern Borders of the EU (Greece)." CARIM Analytic and Synthetic Notes 2009/40, Series on the Impact of Economic Crisis.

UAE Business Forecast Report. 2009. Business Monitor International Ltd.

UKBA (U.K. Border Agency). 2008. "Sponsorship under the Points-Based System." http://www.bia.homeoffice.gov.uk/employers/points/.

Ullah, A. A. 2010. *Rationalizing Migration Decisions: Labour Migrants in East and Southeast Asia.* London: Ashgate.

Ullah, A. A., and P. K. Panday. 2007. "Remitting Money to Bangladesh: What Do Migrants Prefer? Research Note." *Asian and Pacific Migration Journal* 16(1): 121–36.

Unan, E. 2009. "Microeconomic Determinants of Turkish Workers' Remittances: Survey Results for France-Turkey." Paper presented at the "International Conference on Inequalities and Development in the Mediterranean Countries," May 21–23, Galatasaray University, Istanbul, Turkey.

UNCTAD (United Nations Conference on Trade and Development). 2009. *World Investment Report 2009.* New York and Geneva: United Nations.

———. 2010. *World Investment Report 2010.* New York and Geneva: United Nations.

UN ESCAP (United Nations Economic and Social Commission for Asia and the Pacific). 2007. *Economic and Social Survey, 2007.* Bangkok: UN ESCAP.

UN-INSTRAW (United Nations Entity for Gender Equality and the Empowerment of Women) and IOM (International Organization for Migration). 2008. *Gender and Remittances: Colombian Migration from the Central Western Metropolitan Area (AMCO) to Spain.*

United Nations. 2009. "International Migration." Department of Economic and Social Affairs, Population Division, New York.

———. 2011. *World Economic Situation and Prospects 2011.* New York: United Nations Publications.

United Nations, Department of Economic and Social Affairs, Population Division. 2009. "Trends in International Migrant Stock: The 2008 Revision." United Nations database, POP/DB/MIG/Stock/Rev.2008.

UNDP (United Nations Development Programme). 2006. *From Brain Drain to Brain Gain: Mobilising Albania's Skilled Diaspora.* Tirana.

———. 2008. *National Human Development Report: Russian Federation 2008: Russia Facing Demographic Challenges.* New York: UNDP. http://hdr.undp.org/en/reports/ nationalreports/europethecis/russia/NHDR_Russia_2008_Eng.pdf.

———. 2010. "Overcoming Barriers: Human Mobility and Development." *Human Development Report 2009.* New York: UNDP.

Valero-Gil, J. N. 2009. "Remittances and the Household's Expenditures on Health." *Journal of Business Strategies* 29(spring).

Van Doorn, J. 2004. *Migration, Remittances and Small Enterprise Development.* Geneva: International Labour Organization.

Vargas-Silva, C., and P. Huang. 2006. "Macroeconomic Determinants of Workers' Remittances: Host versus Home Country's Economic Conditions." *Journal of International Trade and Economic Development* 15(1): 81–99.

Vertovec, S. 2009. *Transnationalism.* London: Routledge.

Vickers, A. 2004. "The Country and the Cities." *Journal of Contemporary Asia* 34(3): 304–17.

Vullnetari, J. 2007. "Albanian Migration and Development: State of the Art Review." IMISCOE Working Paper 18. September.

Wacziarg, R., and K. H. Welch. 2008. "Trade Liberalization and Growth: New Evidence." *World Bank Economic Review* 22: 187–231.

WDI. 2009. *World Development Indicators 2010.* Washington, DC: World Bank.

Welter-Enderlin, R., and B. Hildenbrand, eds. 2006. *Resilienz—Gedeihen trotz widriger Umstände.* Heidelberg: Carl Auer Verlag.

Werner, E. E., J. M. Bierman, and F. E. French. 1971. *The Children of Kauai. A Longitudinal Study from the Prenatal Period to Age Ten.* Honolulu: University of Hawaii Press.

Whelpton, J. 2005. *A History of Nepal.* Cambridge: Cambridge University Press.

Williams, R. 1973. *The Country and the City.* London: Chatto and Windus.

Winters, L. A. 1989. "The 'So-Called Non-Economic Objectives' of Agricultural Policy." *OECD Economic Studies* 13(winter): 237–66.

Winters, L. A., N. McCulloch, and A. McKay. 2004. "Trade Liberalization and Poverty: The Evidence So Far." *Journal of Economic Literature* 42: 72–115.

Wong, M. 2006. "The Gendered Politics of Remittances in Ghanaian Transnational Families." *Economic Geography* 82(4): 355–81.

Woodruff, C., and R. Zenteno. 2007. "Migration Networks and Microenterprises in Mexico." *Journal of Development Economics* 82: 509–28.

World Bank. 2003. "Albania—Poverty Assessment." Report 26213-AL. November 5. World Bank, Washington, DC.

———. 2005. *Global Development Finance, Mobilizing Finance and Managing Vulnerability.* Washington, DC: World Bank.

———. 2006a. *Global Economic Prospects 2006: Economic Implications of Remittances and Migration.* Washington, DC: World Bank.

———. 2006b. *Home and Away: Expanding Job Opportunities for Pacific Islanders through Labor Mobility.* Washington, DC: World Bank.

———. 2006c. "Nepal Resilience amidst Conflict: An Assessment of Poverty in Nepal 1995–96 and 2003–04." Report 34834 NP. Poverty Reduction and Economic Management Sector Unit, South Asia Region, World Bank, Washington, DC.

———. 2007a. "Albania: Urban Growth, Rural Stagnation and Migration: A Poverty Assessment." July 24. World Bank, Washington, DC.

———. 2007b. *World Development Indicators.* Washington, DC: World Bank.

———. 2008. *Global Development Finance 2008, The Role of International Banking.* Washington, DC: World Bank.

———. 2009a. *Doing Business 2010—Overview.* Washington, DC: World Bank.

———. 2009b. *Global Development Finance 2009: Charting a Global Recovery.* Washington, DC: World Bank.

———. 2009c. "Income Vulnerabilities and Poverty in El Salvador." Social Protection Policy Note. World Bank, Washington, DC.

———. 2009d. *Migration and Remittance Data.* Washington, DC: World Bank. http://econ.worldbank.org.

———. 2009e. "Nepal Economic Update." Economic Policy and Poverty Team, South Asia Region, World Bank, Washington, DC.

———. 2009f. *Swimming against the Tide: How Developing Countries Are Coping with the Global Crisis.* Washington, DC: World Bank.

———. 2009g. "Youth Employability and Economic Opportunities in El Salvador." Social Protection Policy Note. World Bank, Washington, DC.

———. 2010a. "Accessing Good Quality Jobs: Priorities for Education, Social Protection, Science and Technology in El Salvador." Human Development Policy Note. World Bank, Washington, DC.

———. 2010b. "Albania: The New Growth Agenda." Country Economic Memorandum, Report 53599-AL. November. World Bank, Washington, DC.

———. 2010c. "World Bank Development Indicators Database." https://data.worldbank.org.

———. 2010d. "World Bank Remittances Prices Worldwide Database." remittanceprices.worldbank.org.

———. 2011a. *Global Economic Prospects: Navigating Strong Currents*. Washington, DC: World Bank.

———. 2011b. *Migration and Remittances Factbook 2011*. Washington, DC: World Bank.

Yang, D. 2008a. "Coping with Disaster: The Impact of Hurricanes on International Financial Flows, 1970–2002." *B.E. Journal of Economic Analysis & Policy* 8(1).

———. 2008b. "International Migration, Remittances, and Household Investment: Evidence from Philippine Migrants' Exchange Rate Shocks." *Economic Journal* 118: 1–40.

———. 2008c. "International Migration, Human Capital, and Entrepreneurship: Evidence from Philippine Migrants' Exchange Rate Shocks." *Economic Journal* 118: 591–630.

Yang, D., and H. Choi. 2007. "Are Remittances Insurance? Evidence from Rainfall Shocks in the Philippines." *World Bank Economic Review* 21(2): 219–48.

Yang, D., and C. M. Martínez. 2006. "Remittances and Poverty in Migrants' Home Areas: Evidence from the Philippines." In *International Migration, Remittances, and the Brain Drain*, ed. Ç. Özden and M. W. Schiff. Washington, DC, and London: World Bank and Palgrave Macmillan.

Yazgan, P. 2010. "Belonging and Identity among Migrants from Turkey in Denmark." PhD thesis, Social Science Institute, Sakarya University, Turkey.

Yeoh, B., E. Graham, and P. Boyle. 2002. "Migration and Family Relations in the Asia Pacific." *Asia and Pacific Migration Journal* 11(1): 1–11.

Zachariah, K. C., and S. I. Rajan. 2009. *Migration and Development: The Kerala Experience*. New Delhi: Daanish Publishers.

———. 2010. "Impact of the Global Recession on Migration and Remittances in Kerala: New Evidences from the Return Migration Survey (RMS) 2009." Working Paper 432. Centre for Development Studies, Kerala, India.

Ziesemer, T. 2006. "Worker Remittances and Growth: The Physical and Human Capital Channels." UNU-MERIT Working Paper 2006-020.

Index

Figures, notes, and tables are indicated by f, n, and t following the page number.

www.ingramcontent.com/pod-product-compliance
Lightning Source LLC
Chambersburg PA
CBHW080409270326
41929CB00018B/2959